Table Design Quick Reference

Setting and Manipulating Fields

To	Do This:
Set the Primary Key	In 📇▾ view, select the field; Click 🔑
Tips for smart data type selection	Select a data type from the drop-down box; Check its description in the General tab; alter field size as needed to save memory
Move a column in the datasheet	In ▥▾ view, click the top row (Down-arrow cursor) and select column; Click again and drag to the right of the column where desired and release
Change sort order	In ▥▾ view, select column for sort; select ⬆Z↓ or ⬇Z↓; OR select multiple columns for secondary sorting; left-most column sorts first
View Relationships	With either the Database window or a table window open, click ⬚ or **Relationships** from the **Tools** menu
Create a New	In the Relationships Window, use 🗄 to place tables. Click the Primary key; Drag to foreign key; Set relationship type.

Input Mask Code Characters

Character	Purpose
0	Forces a digit character
9	Allows only a digit, but doesn't require an entry
#	Allows a digit, + or - sign, or space character, but doesn't require an entry
L	Forces an alpha character
?	Allows only an alpha character, but doesn't require an entry
A	Forces an alpha character or digit
a	Allows only an alpha character or digit, but doesn't require an entry
&	Forces an entry, but accepts any character
C	Doesn't force an entry and accepts any character
<	Displays characters to the right as lowercase
>	Displays characters to the right as uppercase
!	Fills the mask from right to left
\	Allows you to include a literal character by displaying the character that follows

Form/Report Design Quick Reference

Selecting Fields

To Select	Use
Single, hard to grasp control	The drop-down Object list box on the toolbar
Multiple, scattered controls	Shift+Left Mouse Click
A line of controls	Click a point on the ruler that crosses all desired controls
A contiguous range	Click the Mouse and drag a loop around the range OR Click and drag across a ruler
All controls	Ctrl+A or Double-click the Selector button in the upper-left corner
The form or report itself	Click anywhere on the background
Deselect all controls	Click a blank space on the background

Manipulating Controls

To	Do
Move a control	Select the control; Use the Hand cursor; click and drag
Move both a label and its control	Select both controls; Place the cursor on the handles between the controls; use the Hand cursor to click and drag
Align controls	Select the controls; Select **Format, Align** and the desired option
Copy format or style	Select the "from" or model control; Click ⟨⟩; Click the recipient control
Bind a control, section, form, or report	Double-click the object; Select **Record** (or **Control**) **Source** property; Click the field to raise the drop-down arrow; select the data source from the drop-down list
Toggle Snap to Grid	Use the **Format** menu, **Snap to Grid** option
Suspend Snap to Grid	Hold down Ctrl while placing controls
Change the grid dots	Double-click the Form or Report Selector; Change the Grid X and Grid Y property values

Query Design Quick Reference

Creating a New Query

To	Do This
View available sources	Click ⟨⟩
Add tables to the pane	Select one or more tables in the Show Table dialog and click **Add**
Add fields to the grid	Click the field and drag from the table/query pane to the desired grid column
Move a column in in the grid	Click the top of the column (Down arrow cursor); Click again on the top spacebar and drag where desired and release
Change sort order	Click **Sort** under the column/field; Select multiple columns for secondary sorting; Left-most column sorts first
Add a criteria	Type one or more valid field values under the column OR Click **Criteria** under the appropriate column; Click ⟨⟩; Create an expression; Click **OK**

Coding Quick Reference

To	Do This
Create a new macro for an event	Double-click the control or object; Select the **Event** tab in Properties; Click in the event's space and click the Builder button; Choose the Macro builder; Create the macro
Attach an existing macro	In the Properties sheet for the object, select the event; Select the macro name from the drop-down list
Create new VBA code for an event	In the Properties sheet for the object, select the event; Select **Event Procedure** from the drop-down list; Click Build
Create new VBA code	With the object open click ⟨⟩; Use the Object drop-down list box to find the object; Use the Procedure drop-down to start the code; Type the new lines

Using
Microsoft
Access®
Second Edition 97

Susan Sales Harkins, et al.

que®

A Division of Macmillan Computer Publishing, USA
201 W. 103rd Street
Indianapolis, Indiana 46290

Contents at a Glance

Using Microsoft Access 97, Second Edition

Copyright © 1999 by Que

International Standard Book Number: 0-7897-1634-8

Library of Congress Catalog Card Number: 98-84139

Printed in the United States of America

First Printing: October, 1998

00 99 98   4 3 2 1

Trademarks

All terms mentioned in this book that are known to be trademarks or service marks have been appropriately capitalized. Que cannot attest to the accuracy of this information. Use of a term in this book should not be regarded as affecting the validity of any trademark or service mark.

Access is registered trademark of Microsoft Corporation.

Warning and Disclaimer

Every effort has been made to make this book as complete and as accurate as possible, but no warranty or fitness is implied. The information provided is on an "as is" basis. The authors and the publisher shall have neither liability or responsibility to any person or entity with respect to any loss or damages arising from the information contained in this book.

Credits

Executive Editor
Rosemarie Graham

Acquisitions Editors
Corrine Wire
Rosemarie Graham

Development Editor
Marla Reece-Hall

Managing Editor
Patrick Kanouse

Project Editor
Andrew Cupp

Copy Editors
Sean Medlock
Kate Givens
Tonya Maddox

Indexer
Kelly Talbot

Proofreader
Kim Cofer

Technical Editors
Damon Darling
Dallas Releford

Software Development Specialist
Michael Hunter

Interior Design
Nathan Clement
Ruth Lewis

Cover Design
Dan Armstrong
Ruth Lewis

Layout Technicians
Michael Dietsch
Ayanna Lacey
Heather Hiatt Miller

Contents

About the Author

Susan Sales Harkins is a private consultant, specializing in Access and VBA development. She also runs an online technical support company named RabbitTracks. Before turning to private consulting, Susan worked for The Cobb Group (ZD Journals) for seven years. During that time, she wrote about Access, VBA, Visual Basic, Excel, and 1-2-3.

James T. Blanchard is the Senior Information Specialist for the Customer Quality Assurance Group at United States Surgical Corporation in North Haven, CT. He is also the Contributing Editor for the Cobb Group's Inside Microsoft Access, and the Co-Host of an Office Chat sponsored by Cobb and ZDNet. Jim specializes in developing information systems using Visual Basic and the Microsoft Office Suite.

Craig Eddy is currently a Senior Developer/Program Manager at Pipestream Technologies, Inc. Pipestream is a leading developer of salesforce automation and customer information management software. He is an author or co-author on several books, including *Sams Teach Yourself Access 97 in 21 Days* and *Sams Teach Yourself Access 97 in 24 Hours*.

Joel Goodling is a Software Engineer working for ABB in their Internet Technologies Group. Joel is currently building Internet and intranet applications for ABB and its customers, most of which are tied to a database backend including several that use Access 97. Joel is obsessed with the creating easy access to data through a Web interface. He has worked as both an author and technical editor for several database related books.

Jon Price has designed and developed Access databases since Access 2.0. Projects that Jon has completed include a salesforce automation database for a communications company, a customer courtesy desk database for a small grocery chain, an ordering and cataloguing database for a small computer firm, a project and clientele tracking database for an engineering firm, a loan history and forecasting database for a major banking company, a production reporting database for a major insurance company and an insurance policy generator, tracker and growth forecasting database for a major insurance company. Jon is currently employed under contract with United Services Automobile Association (USAA) in San Antonio, TX. At USAA, Jon is part of the Office Support Tools Team Project, which is involved in converting all legacy office applications, used by more than the 12,000 employees onsite, over to the Microsoft

Office suite of tools. Jon is currently pursuing the Microsoft Certified Solutions Developer (MCSD) certification. Jon can be reached at jon-price@stic.net

Heath White is a Computer Support Technician for a nationally recognized law firm specializing in product liability defense. He developed his knowledge in Access by creating and maintaining databases for client tracking, case administration, billing, and developing programs for use in the legal field.

Tell Us What You Think!

As the reader of this book, *you* are our most important critic and commentator. We value your opinion and want to know what we're doing right, what we could do better, what areas you'd like to see us publish in, and any other words of wisdom you're willing to pass our way.

As the Executive Editor for the Database Team at Macmillan Computer Publishing, I welcome your comments. You can fax, email, or write me directly to let me know what you did or didn't like about this book—as well as what we can do to make our books stronger.

Please note that I cannot help you with technical problems related to the topic of this book, and that due to the high volume of mail I receive, I might not be able to reply to every message.

When you write, please be sure to include this book's title and author as well as your name and phone or fax number. I will carefully review your comments and share them with the author and editors who worked on the book.

Fax: 317-817-7070

Email: databases@mcp.com

Mail: Executive Editor
          Database Team
          Macmillan Computer Publishing
          201 West 103rd Street
          Indianapolis, IN 46290 USA

Dedication

To my parents, for never telling me who or what I had to be when I grew up.
—Susan

Acknowledgments

To my family for fending for themselves for two months, and to Mark Kimbell
for forcing me take the Access journal five years ago.—Susan

INTRODUCTION

Microsoft Access 97 is the desktop database choice of thousands of users for many reasons. Access is "at home" with the home user who wants to store and retrieve personal data easily, *and* Access works very well in business environments with multiple users, too.

One of the most commonly praised attributes of this data storage and retrieval system is its easy-to-understand graphic interface for creating queries, forms, and reports—something that many larger, more complicated database systems lack. In other words, even inexperienced programmers can use Access to turn a stack of invoices, a card file of customer names, a ledger, and an inventory list into a relational database that makes entering, updating, and reporting information as easy as clicking a button.

Because of its ease of use and quick learning curve, learning your way around Access has another appeal. Creating applications with Access has become a popular inroad for people who want to move into the field of computer development and programming. Many successful data management consultants can tell you that they started out creating simple Access applications, eventually learned VBA and other programming skills, and moved on to professional development. Many of these experts still use Access for their clients' database needs and have pushed this flexible and powerful member of Microsoft Office to its limits.

Access 97 offers more than just a "pretty face" for learning how to manage data. You'll find these benefits and more from using Access:

- Sample databases—Microsoft includes sample databases to help you learn about real-world tables, forms, queries, and reports, and how they are interconnected to form a data management system. The Northwind database (a fictional trading company with data of its own) offers several sample forms and reports that you can alter, and also includes code modules that you can adapt. You can even copy table structures from this database to create your own tables.

- Wizards—Microsoft makes creating an Access database very easy. You can choose from several examples of databases in the Database Wizard for such storage uses as contact information, inventory control, a ledger, and so on. You can create and then modify these databases to meet your own needs.

- Keys to understanding the structure—After you decide how to create and relate your tables, you can easily view all the relationships in your database with the graphical interface in the Relationships window. This makes one of the toughest parts of relational database design much easier and more manageable.

- Microsoft Office integration—You can use Access with Word, Excel, and other Microsoft Office applications to create mail merges, charts, and other helpful uses for your data.

- Easier programming—You can use relatively simple code with macros to automate repeated tasks, or you can try more complex and flexible code with Visual Basic for Applications. Access provides graphical shortcuts and hints to help make writing code easier.

- Common standards—When you're ready for the big time, you can rest assured that Access uses standards that help its applications scale up to work within larger environments. Access uses objects and SQL (Standard Query Language) to make its code, and your learning, adaptable to other applications.

Why This Book?

The *Using* series of books from Que is designed with a variety of needs in mind, but all of them aim to make using your computer application easier and more efficient. *Using Microsoft Access 97, Second Edition* works well in a variety of ways for those who are relatively new to Access, but who use it on a regular basis. New features in this edition include the following:

- An improved index to help you find information under the terms you're used to using. We've tried to anticipate alternate terms for key concepts. Finding the task you want to perform is quicker, and you can resolve your problem without extended searches for help.

- The information is presented more clearly so you can quickly spot the answers to your problems. This information includes figures with expanded callouts, notes in the margins, and easy-to-follow steps in the text. Whether you spot a figure you want to duplicate, a note that provides helpful information, or a task heading that suits your needs, you'll be able to find the answers to solve your problems in easy and clear ways.

- This volume is designed with a dual purpose in mind: reference and tutorial. If you're new to Access or still don't understand certain concepts or procedures, you can follow the book from beginning to end to learn how to use the product. If you're already somewhat familiar with Access but want a resource for how-to solutions or information to expand your knowledge, you can look up a wide variety of tasks for concise answers or instructions.

- With *Using Microsoft Access 97, Second Edition*, you get what you need for long-term use at an affordable price. You won't have to figure out what you want to know from the middle of a long course project or wade through pages of theory and high-end material. You'll be able to pick out any task now or at some point in the future to understand what you want to know.

Who Should Use This Book?

This book is for anyone who uses Access and needs to accomplish a specific task, solve a problem, or learn a technique to make data management more manageable. This book is right for you if any of the following applies:

- You have a basic understanding of Windows, such as menu and mouse operations, but Microsoft Access has been gathering dust on your system and you're ready to put it to good use.

- You have tentatively explored Microsoft Access, playing with the wizards and maybe creating a database from the samples, but you have no idea how it all works or how to modify the database to meet your specific needs.

- You own or work for a business and want to find an easy way to manage all the information you currently have on paper or in clumsy apps: invoices, records, accounting information, customer contacts, vendors, and so on. You print letters and reports that are never quite what you want or that have to be calculated and addressed by hand.

- You are ready to put up-to-date, in-depth information about your business on the World Wide Web.

- Or perhaps you are fascinated by a product that can be used for a simple home business or for a large corporation's presence on the Web. You want to improve your skills and eventually create sophisticated database applications via the most direct route possible. You want a book that starts at the beginning and has an easy learning curve, but that moves you into programming concepts that more advanced books assume you already know.

This book is designed with this variety of goals in mind and will serve as an excellent desktop reference and an easy-to-follow guide.

How This Book Is Organized

Using Microsoft Access 97, Second Edition has task-oriented, easy-to-navigate tutorials and reference information that's presented in a logical progression from simple to complex tasks. It covers features of the program you'll use in your daily work.

Throughout the book, you'll find examples in the figures that you can re-create by using the Northwind sample database or, where indicated, the database the author has created (which can be downloaded from our Web site). However, the tasks are also flexible because when you're ready to perform them on your own database, you can insert your own options, file or control names, or properties. You can work through the book lesson by lesson, or you can find specific information when you need to perform a job quickly.

Using Microsoft Access 97, Second Edition is divided into seven parts:

Part I: Learning the Access Essentials

Two of the most helpful elements in learning Access are getting started quickly and doing so with a solid foundation. If you try to get started too quickly, you will almost certainly end up with errors, confusion, or unreliable data later on. By contrast, if you get bogged down with too much theory and don't see the benefits of using Access quickly, you might think it's too difficult to learn. This section shows you some of the essentials of solid database design and how to lay a blueprint for the database you want to create. Then you'll see just how easy it is to create Access elements by using the wizards.

Part II: Storing and Controlling Data in Tables and Fields

Another essential of database management is ensuring data integrity. This section shows how relationships and certain types of fields work to control data input. In this section, you'll see how to create tables and assign fields on your own without the wizards.

Part III: Manipulating Data for Practical Results

Having a large storehouse of data in your computer's memory does you very little good—unless you know how to retrieve the answers you're looking for. This section starts by showing you how to create simple queries on a single table to retrieve just the data you want to select. You'll also see how to collect specific data from various tables to create a resultset ready for generating a report or viewing onscreen. Access makes creating queries easier by using a graphical interface that writes the code for you. Then you'll find more flexible querying methods with an introduction to querying with SQL (Standard Query Language).

Part IV: Creating the User Interface, Input, and Output

Even if you understand all the workings of your database behind the scenes, an end user who's responsible for inputting and changing data might not. Access makes it easy for you to create a front end where your user can input data on forms. This section shows you how to create these forms and control the user's actions in navigating or changing data.

The other part of the front end that users care about is generating a legible, concise report. You'll see how to create reports with a variety of controls that print the results of queries or other data sources, based on the needs of your business.

Part V: Automating the Database

Beyond creating the basics of a database application, you'll want to refine what you've created for the most efficient use. You might want to automate tasks that you perform frequently, or you might want to create reusable dialog boxes for your user interface. This section shows you how to use macros for simple coding, and then gives you a solid foundation in VBA for customizing the uses of your application.

Part VI: Beyond Desktop Application

If you're working in a multiuser environment, you have to consider such things as security and the number of simultaneous users. You might also want to present information about your company on the World Wide Web. This section shows you how to secure and deploy your database in different ways to make it accessible on a larger scale.

Part VII: Appendix

The first appendix in this section provides you with ready-to-use VBA code snippets that you can employ in your application. Once you've learned the importance and the uses of VBA in Part V, you'll want real-world examples that you can use on your own.

You'll also find a glossary of terms to refresh your memory or explain the details as you read.

Be sure to use the book's tearout card inside the cover. Tear it out and take it with you wherever you use Access. It contains some of the most common information you'll need but might not always remember. Keep it next to your computer as a quick reference.

Web Site

Downloads for this book are available at www.mcp.com/info. At the prompt, type in the book's ISBN: 0-7897-1634-8.

Conventions Used in This Book

The commands, directions, and explanations in this book are presented in the clearest format possible. The following are some of the features that will make this book easy for you to use:

- *Menu and dialog box commands and options.* You can easily find the onscreen menu and dialog box commands by looking for bold text such as this: "Open the **File** menu and click **Save**."

- *Hotkeys for commands.* The characters that are underlined onscreen, indicating that they activate commands and options, are also underlined in this book (as shown in the preceding example).

- *Combination and shortcut keystrokes.* Instructions to hold down several keys simultaneously use a plus sign (+), such as Ctrl+P.

- *Graphical icons, with the commands they execute.* Look for icons like this—⬛ ▾—in text and in numbered steps. These indicate buttons onscreen that you can click to accomplish the procedure.

- *Cross-references.* If there's a topic that is a prerequisite to the current section or that builds further on your task, you'll find the cross-reference after the numbered steps or at the end of the section, like this:

SEE ALSO

➤ *To learn how to place controls on a form or report, see page 323.*

- *Glossary terms.* All items that appear in italic in the text, along with a definition, are found in the glossary in the back of the book.

- *Sidebars.* Information related to the task at hand, including shortcuts, alternatives, warnings, and additional explanations from the author, appears in sidebars next to the related material.

- *Figures and callouts.* The figures in this book often include helpful callouts and more descriptive captions than in other books. These also appear in the margin area so that you can easily spot a figure similar to your current screen. You'll be able to find a quick explanation of a certain control or element related to your problem or task.

What you see on your screen may be slightly different than some of the figures in this book. This is due to various options during installation, as well as hardware setup or Windows size and resolution options.

PART

I

Learning the Access Essentials

What Is Relational Database Theory?

Learn to do your homework—design the database before you build it

Examine the rules of normalization

Review primary keys, foreign keys, and referential integrity

The Importance of a Good Design

Relational Database Theory is based on complex mathematical principles that are beyond the scope of this book. However, the results of these principles—normalization rules—are easy to apply, and that's what we'll discuss in this chapter. *Normalization* is the process of creating and relating tables according to a fixed set of rules. If a database is well designed—normalized—even a non-developer can discern the gist of the database by reviewing its tables and their relationships to one another.

But before we tackle normalization, let's review a few common database terms:

- *Database*—A collection or related data that pertains to a particular purpose or topic and the tools used to manipulate that data. For instance, an Access database may maintain current stock and order information for a company.
- *Table*—A collection of related data that is stored in rows and columns, such as a table of customer addresses.
- *Field*—A column within a table and the smallest unit of data in the entire database. A field might contain a customer's name, phone number, ZIP code, and so on.
- *Record*—A row within a table. This row contains related data for one complete data unit. For instance, a record would contain all the field data for the same customer.
- *Object*—Access components: tables, forms, queries, and reports.
- *Form*—An Access object that displays information stored in a table in non-table (rows and columns) format.
- *Query*—An Access object that stores questions about the stored data.
- *Report*—An Access object that stores the design of a printed report.
- *Recordset*—A group of records that meet specific criteria.

Engaging the Rules of Normalization

The normalizing process consists of several rules, but we're only going to review the three most important ones. For the most part, you won't need to delve any further into the process. After reviewing the rules, you'll design a database from scratch. Here are the three rules:

- All fields should be *atomic*, meaning that the data can't be divided any further.

- All fields in a table must refer to a *primary key*. (A primary key field contains a unique value for each record.)

- All fields must be mutually independent, meaning there are no hidden relationships to other fields in the same table.

SEE ALSO

➤ *For an in-depth look at primary key fields, see page 199.*

Along with these rules for normalizing a database, you'll also want to establish a naming convention standard that you use consistently.

SEE ALSO

➤ *See page 22 later in this chapter for a guideline to naming standards.*

Planning the Database Structure

The first step to designing a database is to consider its purpose. What information will you store? Who will use it? What kind of output will you need? You can answer these questions by examining the data you'll be storing in the database and reviewing the current process for storing that data. If others will use the application, talk to them as well. Ask them how they're accomplishing the task right now, and what they expect from the application.

Dividing the Data into Tables

Once you've got a clear picture of the job your database will do, you're ready to tackle the second step. Simply make a list of each piece of data you plan to store. For instance, let's suppose you want to store product information for a bookstore. Your first list might resemble the one shown in Figure 1.1. It's easy to see that

Planning for size

Remember that Access has a limit of 255 concurrent users. You must also consider the size of the data storage and use areas. These two aspects are more along the lines of physical factors. You will need to explore the size and scale of your eventual application. This chapter concentrates on the theoretical design of a database, regardless of its size.

you have two types of information: book information and publisher information. At this point, your database will require at least two tables. The next step is to design each table.

FIGURE 1.1

A list of the data you might collect in a bookstore database.

Rabbit's Bookhutch #1

Book Title
Book ISBN #
Book Price
Book Author
Book Publisher
Book Category
Publisher Address

Subdividing the Tables into Fields

You now have a good idea which tables you need and the information you'll store in each. The next list, shown in Figure 1.2, is more specific than the first. As you can see, it breaks your data into tables and fields.

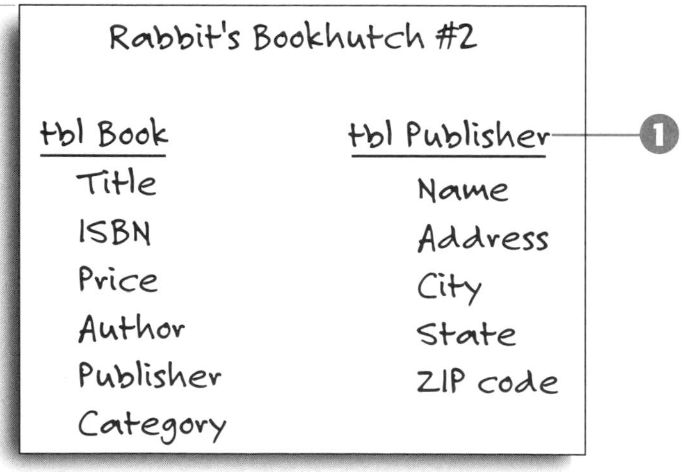

FIGURE 1.2

After breaking the data into tables, it's time to define the fields in each table.

1 You translate regular business object names, such as "Book ISBN #," into succinct table and field names that comply with established standards

Rabbit's Bookhutch #2

tbl Book
  Title
  ISBN
  Price
  Author
  Publisher
  Category

tbl Publisher ──────① 1
  Name
  Address
  City
  State
  ZIP code

The First Rule

Here's where the normalization rules come into play. Remember, the first rule states that each field must be atomic. If you're wondering why, let's consider the Author field in `tblBook`. Currently, you just show one field. You could and should break this data down further into two fields, one for last names and one for first names. Why does it matter? Consider how difficult it would be to sort the table by last name or to query the table for authors by their last names. You'd have to physically scan the database or write a special expression to handle this type of sort or query. On the other hard, atomic fields are easy to work with.

Another concern is repetitive data in a single field. Currently, you have one field to list a book's categories. Although all books will have at least one category, many books may have more than one. For instance, *Jane Eyre* is considered a classic, but it also fits into the gothic and romance categories. Similarly, *Treasure Island* fits into the adventure and children's categories, with adventure being its primary category. You could enter all appropriate categories into one field, but how would you search for a particular category? This setup repeats the same problem discussed earlier with the Author field.

A second solution would be to have several category fields, Category1, Category2, and so on, where Category1 is the book's main category. Although this is a better arrangement, it still has problems. For instance, to search for all books in a particular category, you'd have to search all the category fields, which would be awkward. Another problem is the limit imposed on the number of categories a book can have. You can only have as many categories as you have category fields.

The best solution is to create a third table, outlined in Figure 1.3. This table has no limit on the number of categories a book can have, and searching for those categories will be easy because all the categories are in one field.

At this point, you should be able to see the advantages of having atomic fields in your tables. The table `tblPublisher` appears to be atomic without any further division.

Multiple options

In a table like this one, you can repeatedly use a value that must be unique in another table. For example, the ISBN must be unique in the `tblBook` table, but in `tblCategory` you can repeat the ISBN for each record to list the book in multiple categories. The most important point is that the ISBN in `tblCategory` must match an existing book, which is taken care of in relating fields later in this chapter.

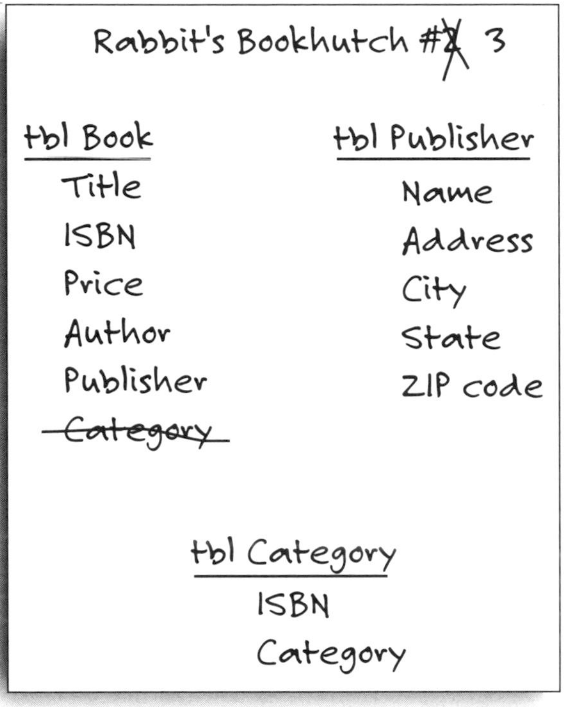

FIGURE 1.3

A third table identifies each book's categories.

Rabbit's Bookhutch #2̶ 3

tbl Book
   Title
   ISBN
   Price
   Author
   Publisher
   ~~Category~~

tbl Publisher
   Name
   Address
   City
   State
   ZIP code

tbl Category
   ISBN
   Category

The Second Rule

The second normalization rule requires each table to have a primary key. We'll discuss keys in more detail later, but a normalized table should have at least one field that contains a unique entry for each record. Such a field is known as a primary key field.

SEE ALSO

➤ *For more information on primary key fields, see page 199.*

One of your tables, tblBook, has a natural primary key—the ISBN number. In contrast, tblPublisher doesn't have a field that you can guarantee will also contain a unique value. You might think the publisher's name is a good candidate, but two publishing firms could have the same name. The easiest solution is to add an AutoNumber field to tblPublisher. It isn't the only solution, but for now, it's the simplest.

Primary key versus index

A primary key isn't an index. Access always indexes a primary key, but they aren't the same thing. An index refers to an internal Jet operation that speeds sorting. A primary key identifies a unique value field.

Having a primary key isn't enough. Each field in the table must refer to the primary key. That means each piece of data must be related to the primary key in some way. The table lists in Figure 1.4. are updated so you can review this rule further. At this point, all three tables appear to fulfill this requirement. The fields in tblBook all relate to the book's ISBN number. Likewise with tblPublisher—all the fields describe PublisherID. It doesn't matter that the value in PublisherID isn't publisher data. It only matters that you can identify the publisher and its pertinent information by an identification number. At this point tblCategory doesn't have a primary key, so don't consider it just yet.

AutoNumber

AutoNumber is just what the name implies. It is a data type you can select for a field, and Access will automatically generate subsequent unique numbers for all records you enter. Using this data type is the easiest way to create a primary field for a unique value such as an ID or invoice number.

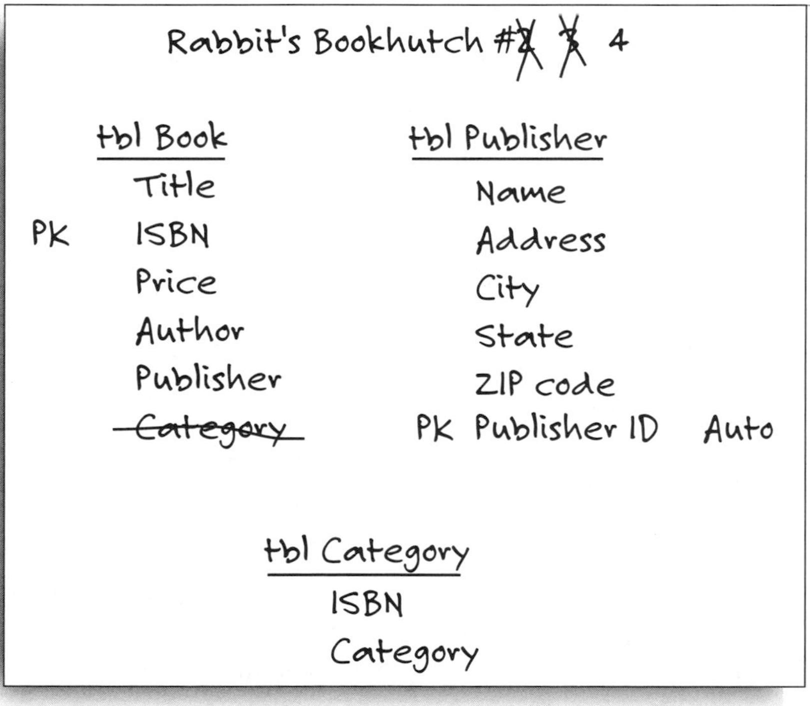

Rabbit's Bookhutch #~~2~~ ~~3~~ 4

tbl Book
- Title
- PK ISBN
- Price
- Author
- Publisher
- ~~Category~~

tbl Publisher
- Name
- Address
- City
- State
- ZIP code
- PK Publisher ID   Auto

tbl Category
- ISBN
- Category

FIGURE 1.4
You've identified or added primary key fields to your tables where appropriate.

The Third Rule

The third rule is that all fields must be mutually independent. Sometimes, this rule can be difficult to discern. Simply put, it means that no field depends on the information in any other field in the same table. All three of your tables fulfill this requirement.

However, that won't always be the case. The trick to finding dependent fields is to consider changing the data. If that change affects any other data in the same table, you have a problem. For instance, if an order table contains a price per unit, the quantity ordered, and a total, you have a dependent field. If you change the value in the quantity field, you must remember to update the value in the total field. You must omit dependent fields to have a normalized table.

Is There a Relationship Between the Tables?

Now that you've successfully divided your data into normalized tables, you can now turn your focus to how that data is related. The first thing you might notice is that every book has a publisher. This means every record in tblBook should refer to a record in tblPublisher. However, not every publisher will have a current listing in tblBook. This arrangement is called a *one-to-many relationship*. In other words, one table contains only one record that contains a unique value for any number of records in a related table, where the unique value can be repeated if necessary. Each record (book) in tblBook refers to only one publisher; each record (publisher) in tblPublisher may refer to many books.

Now let's take a look at tblCategory. Each book will have at least one category record in tblCategory. Unlike your publisher table, each record in tblCategory will relate to a book in tblBook. You won't have a record in tblCategory that doesn't relate to a book. This type of table doesn't fit the requirements of a one-to-many relationship. For now, we'll refer to this table as having an associate relationship because there is an association between the two tables, but no set rules.

SEE ALSO

➤ *Relationships are explained on page 221.*

Linking the Tables

You've done a good job of dividing and subdividing your data into tables and determining the relationships between those tables:

- `tblBook` and `tblPublisher` are related by the publisher.

- `tblBook` and `tblCategory` are related by the ISBN number.

- There is no relationship between `tblCategory` and `tblPublisher`.

Figure 1.5 shows the relationships between your three tables.

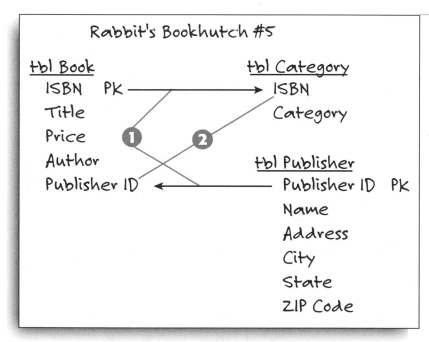

Relationships and Data Protection

You can use these relationships to protect your data. You see, you can't just add and delete records as you like in a properly normalized database. Just as you followed rules to create your tables, you must also follow rules to update them. For instance, you wouldn't want to delete a record from `tblPublisher` while a book from that publisher still resided in `tblBook`. Likewise, you wouldn't want to delete a record from tblBook and leave the category records for that book in tblCategory. Furthermore, you shouldn't add a new book to tblBook if there's no publisher in tblPublisher to relate that book to. As you can see, there's a great deal to be considered before you actually start adding records to your new database.

The Evolving Foreign Keys

When you relate two normalized tables, they produce an off-spring known as the *foreign key*. Specifically, you have a parent table that contains a primary key field. The related child table inherits the primary key as a foreign key. For instance, the ISBN number is the primary key in tblBook. Because you linked tblBook and tblCategory by this field, the ISBN number field becomes tblCategory's foreign key. Similarly, the publisher table's primary key is PublisherID, which becomes the foreign key in tblBook. The relationship between primary and foreign keys has a higher purpose. You can force referential integrity, which will place constraints on the data.

Forcing Referential Integrity

Referential integrity is another set of rules that Access uses to protect the relationships between related tables. Specifically, referential integrity ensures that the relationship is valid and that you don't accidentally corrupt your data by adding or deleting records inappropriately. Here are the conditions that referential integrity checks for:

- Primary key fields must contain unique entries.

- Related fields must be the same data type, with one exception: an AutoNumber field can relate to a Number field.

- Tables must be in the same database or be linked. Linked tables must be Access tables.

- You can't enter a value in a foreign key before entering it in the primary key field.

- You can't delete a record from a parent table if a matching record exists in a related (child) table.

- You can't change the primary key value in the parent table if that record has related records.

Refining the Design

Believe it or not, most of your work is done. You have a good first draft of your database design to evaluate. The final step is easy but crucial, so don't omit it—even if you're in a hurry to get your application up and running. This is the last chance you'll have to catch design errors before actually including them in your database:

- Check each table for a primary or foreign key.
- Make sure each field relates to its key field.
- Review each table's referential constraints for logical restrictions.

The checklist in Table 1.1 shows that each of the tables in your bookstore database does have a key field. Remember, a table doesn't have to have both a primary and foreign key, but it must have one or the other.

TABLE 1.1   Checking Key Fields

Table	Primary	Foreign
tblBook	ISBN	PublisherID
tblPublisher	PublisherID	
tblCategory		ISBN

A quick review of your table design in Figure 1.5 seems to confirm that each field relates to its key. The last step is to review your referential restraints as shown in Table 1.2, and all seems to be fine.

TABLE 1.2   Reviewing Referential Constraints

Primary	Foreign	Restriction
tblPublisher. PublisherID	tblBook.PublisherID	Don't add a record to tblBook if there's no relating PublisherID entry in tblPublisher.

continues...

TABLE 1.2   Continued

Primary	Foreign	Restriction
		Don't delete a record from tblPublisher if there's a related record in tblBook.
tblBook.ISBN	tblCategory.ISBN	Don't add a record to tblCategory if there's no related ISBN entry in tblBook.
		Don't delete a record from tblBook if there's a related record in tblCategory.

Putting the Design to Work

The final step may seem like the easiest one to take. Refer to your final sketch to build the database, and then enter some test data and make sure everything works as expected. You'll find that a well-designed database quickly lends itself to reliable results. Don't expect the database to be perfect, because you may still find a few problems. But because of the work you've put into the design, any problems that crop up should be easy to resolve.

Naming Conventions

The examples in this chapter have used a style of naming tables and fields designed to make identifying objects quicker and more consistent. Naming conventions are the rules you apply when you're naming your application's objects. You can choose an existing convention, or you can develop your own. The key is to adopt one and to consistently apply it. A good name will indicate an object's purpose and class.

Syntax for Naming Objects

For the most part, you'll find that most developers use the following form:

classObjectname

where *class* identifies the type of object and *Objectname* states the object's purpose or task. The *class* argument is lowercase, and *Objectname* is always proper case.

History and Logic of Naming Conventions

This method evolved from a standard convention named the Hungarian convention, pioneered by Charles Simonyi. To discuss the entire breadth of the Hungarian convention would be overkill, so we'll deal specifically with the object-level naming conventions employed in this book.

To apply this method, you need to know an object's class and purpose. The first is pretty obvious—you're naming a table, form, report, control, and so on. The object's purpose can be a little more complicated because you have creative and practical control over this component's name. In other words, you could name a sales report rptRabbit, but no one would know what it was. The one clue would be the rpt component, indicating it's a report. Beyond that, however, they'd just be guessing. A better name might be rptSales.

Now, let's take a look at Table 1.3. It lists several objects by purpose and class and lists the Hungarian method's result. In contrast, it also includes a name with no convention at all. As you can see, you can quickly run into problems. The main problem is determining which object is which. Which donor is the table, and which donor is the report? (Access will allow you to use identical names as long as the classes are different. However, the results are still confusing.) Nor does the name in the third column define the object. In contrast, the Hungarian method names are quite descriptive, identifying the object's class and task.

Advantages of consistency

Following an accepted, widely used convention will make your application more universally understood, not to mention helping out the other developers who might work with you.

TABLE 1.3   **Example of Convention Styles**

Object	Hungarian	No Convention
Donor information	tblDonors	Donors
Donor report	rptDonors	Donors
Donations to date	tblDonations	Donations
Donations report	rptDonations	Donations

Table 1.4 lists the class prefixes used throughout this book. As you can see, this method has been extended to include controls and data types.

TABLE 1.4   **Prefixes for Various Objects**

Access Object	Prefix
Table	tbl
Query	qry
Form	frm
Report	rpt
Macro	mcr
Module	bas
Class module	cls
Byte	byt
Integer	int
Single	sng
Long Integer	lng
Double	dbl
Text	str
AutoNumber	lng
Currency	cur
Date/Time	dtm
Memo	mem
Yes/No	ysn

Access Object	Prefix
Check box	chk
Combo box	cbo
Command button	cmd
Label	lbl
List box	lst
Option button	opt
Subform/subreport	sub
Text box	txt

Creating a Database
with a Wizard

Create a working application with little effort

Reuse wizard-generated database objects

What's a Wizard?

Computers are supposed to make our lives simpler by making our work more efficient and less prone to errors. Access sometimes seems to have gone astray where this reasoning is concerned because it's a complex tool. Fortunately, Microsoft understands that most people simply won't get the full benefit of the program until they're well-schooled in the package. In an effort to reduce the learning curve and make the product easier to use, Microsoft added wizards.

A *wizard* is a specific program that creates an object or performs a task. More specifically, a wizard presents a series of dialog boxes that present the task step by step—each dialog box presents a group of options from which you can choose before continuing to the next step. Using one wizard is pretty much the same as using another. They all follow the same pattern, they just have different functions.

We encourage you to use these wizards; they speed up your work and reduce errors. However, the sooner you learn about Access objects and tasks, the sooner you'll be comfortable using the program. In fact, you must have a little knowledge of Access and its terminology to use even the wizards, so don't hesitate to try your hand at creating objects from scratch. The objects you create this way are generally more flexible. However, wizard and scratch objects can both be modified.

What's an object?

Access is an object-oriented program. That means that you communicate with Access and vice versa through visual objects—tables, forms, reports, and modules. These objects contain the data and code that run your application.

Prototypes

The Database Wizard is the easiest way we know of to create a quick prototype. Doing so can help you introduce your ideas for an application to the users. The users can then respond about what they like and don't like before you've actually spent much time on the design.

About the Database Wizard

The Database Wizard creates an application, producing all the tables, forms, and reports necessary to complete a particular function. The wizard offers 22 databases to choose from, for both personal and business uses. For a complete list, pull down **New Database** from the **File** menu and then click the **Databases** tab.

Using the Database Wizard

1. The program displays the dialog box shown in Figure 2.1 to launch Access. At this point, you can choose between opening an existing database, opening a blank database, or launching the Database Wizard.

FIGURE 2.1

Access allows you to open an existing database or create a new one.

① Click **More Files** to browse through your directories or the network

② Keep in mind that some files you've deleted might still show in this window

2. Select the **Database Wizard** option and click **OK**. The wizard displays the window shown in Figure 2.2. As you can see, this window displays a variety of databases. The options to the right of the Databases window allow you to change the way the wizard displays the list. The **Large Icons** option is the default. The middle option, **List**, displays the files as a list rather than icons. The last option, **Details**, displays the list of database filenames, size, and file type, as well as the date each file was last modified.

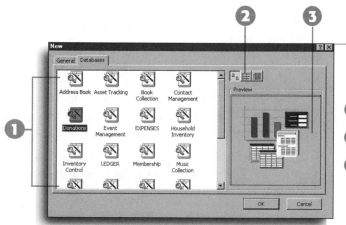

FIGURE 2.2

The first wizard window shows all the available databases.

① These are the available databases

② These are the display options

③ The Preview window graphically identifies the type of application

As you select each database, the wizard updates the Preview window. The graphic in this window helps you identify each file as a business or personal database. We selected Donations.mdb, which is a business application. To choose a database, double-click it or select it and click **OK**.

3. Figure 2.3 shows the wizard's second window. This is a simple File Name dialog box. The wizard gives the new database you're creating a default name, but you can change it. For instance, the wizard named our database Donations1. We're going to keep that name for now. The options along the top are the same ones in the File Open and File Save dialog boxes.

SEE ALSO

➤ *For more details on the benefits and restrictions of using the .MDE file type, see pages 632 and 634.*

Save as file type

The Save as Type option allows you to change the file type. Most users will never use this option. However, when you're ready to secure your database, you can learn more about this option in Chapter 35, "Saving Your Database as an MDE File."

FIGURE 2.3

The wizard gives your new database a default name, which you can change.

4. If you change your mind, click **Cancel** to stop the process. When you're ready to continue, click the **Create** button.

5. The wizard first displays a blank Database window and then displays the window shown in Figure 2.4; the Donations database stores contributor, pledge, and campaign data. If you click **Finish**, the wizard accepts all of Donations' defaults and opens the new application. If you click Cancel, the wizard deletes what you've done up to this point and closes. When you're ready to continue, click **Next**.

6. By default, each table in the new application contains certain fields. The window shown in Figure 2.5 allows you to add to or delete from the defaults.

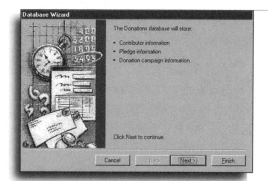

FIGURE 2.4

This window identifies the type of data the new application will store.

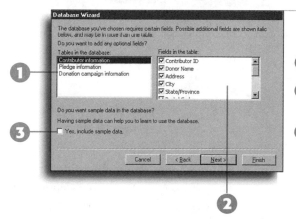

FIGURE 2.5

You can add or delete fields.

① These are the application's tables

② These are the fields in the selected table

③ You can include sample data

The wizard includes any selected fields in the selected table. Deselect any particular field you don't want. Some fields are in italics; these are optional fields that you must select to include. If you don't manually select them, the wizard won't include that field in your table.

If selected, the **Yes, Include Sample Data** option adds actual records to your application. This is a good idea—you can use this data to test your application. When you're ready to add your own, simply delete the sample data from your tables.

We're not going to change any of the field selections, but you can make any changes you like. Click **Next** when you're ready to continue.

Deleting sample data

You have a couple of options when you're through with the sample data but want to keep the table structure. You can open the tables in Design view and use Select All from the Edit menu (or press Ctrl+A); then click the Delete Records icon [×]. You could also copy or export the tables or database and choose to do this without the data.

Moving through the wizard

Keep in mind that any time the wizard still displays a Back button, you can return to your previous screens to change your choices. This is helpful when you're not sure which option, fields, or appearance you want, or if you move fields in the wrong order.

7. The next window, shown in Figure 2.6, allows you to choose the display style from the listed predefined options. We're going to accept the **Clouds** style default. Click **Next** to continue.

SEE ALSO

➤ *Chapter 15, "Designing and Using Queries," gives you some examples of exporting part or all of a database, page 237.*

➤ *Later in this chapter, you'll see how to copy a table structure, page 37.*

FIGURE 2.6

Choose a predefined style.

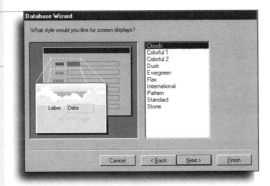

8. Figure 2.7 shows the following window, which asks you to choose from the predefined report styles. We're accepting the default, **Corporate**. When you're ready to continue, click **Next**.

FIGURE 2.7

Choose a report style.

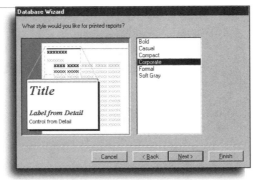

9. In the next window you can change the database's title and identify a default picture to display in your reports; the window is shown in Figure 2.8. This is a good way to include a company logo in your report titles. We're going to retain the title Donations.

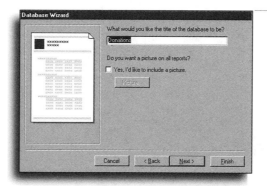

If you want to identify a picture, select the **Yes, I'd Like to Include a Picture** option and then click the enabled Picture button. Doing so displays the Insert Picture dialog box, which is shown in Figure 2.9. Use this dialog box as you would any File Open dialog box. Specifically, use the **Look In** control to browse your folders until you find the appropriate file. You may need to adjust the **Files of Type** option—the default is Graphic Files—to find the appropriate file. We're not going to include a picture in our reports, so we clicked **Cancel** to return to the wizard. If you selected the **Yes, I'd Like to Include a Picture** option earlier, but you're not inserting a picture, be sure to deselect that option now. To continue, click **Next**.

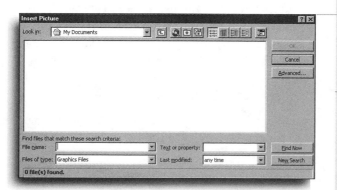

Adding a sample graphic

To get a picture for this example, look in the Microsoft Office\Clipart\Popular directory. Click anything you want to see in the wizard dialog. Click the **Picture** button again to change it.

10. The final wizard window, shown in Figure 2.10, opens the new database if you don't deselect the **Yes, Start the Database** option. You want to open the database, so leave the option as is. If you do deselect it, Access will exit the wizard without opening the application. The Display Help on Using a Database dialog box opens the Help section. Click **Finish** and the wizard displays a meter that shows its progress while it creates your database.

FIGURE 2.10

The final window lets you decide whether to open the database.

If you used the Donations database, as we did, the wizard will ask you to enter your own campaign information. We won't bother with this at this point, so simply close the window. When you do, the wizard displays the Switchboard form; it's shown in Figure 2.11.

At this point, feel free to explore the database by clicking the **Switchboard** options and by reviewing the application's tables, forms, reports, and modules. For instance, clicking the **Enter/View Contributors** option opens the form/subform shown in Figure 2.12, where you enter donation information. Keep in mind that we created this application in just a few minutes. To re-create the same from scratch could take hours or days, depending upon your skill level.

The wizard results will seldom be exactly what you need. You can expect to spend a little time modifying the application.

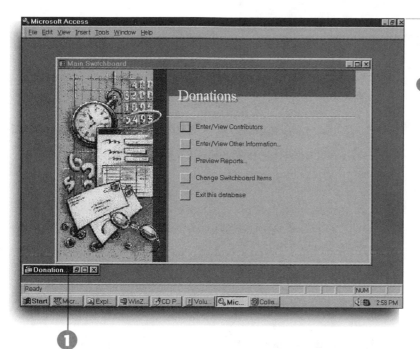

FIGURE 2.11

The wizard displays the new database's Switchboard form.

① The Database window is minimized automatically.

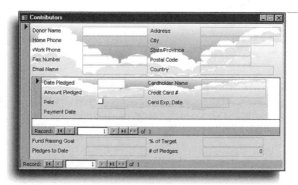

FIGURE 2.12

The Database Wizard created this form/subform in just a few minutes.

To see the structure underneath the Switchboard form, double-click the minimized title bar next to it. This opens the database in the Database window. You can view the objects on the various tabs for tables, forms, queries, macros, and modules. You'll become more familiar with this window throughout this book.

SEE ALSO

➤ *To learn about modifying tables, see page 189.*

➤ *Turn to page 341 to create a form.*

➤ *See page 313 for details about adding controls to forms.*

➤ *Chapter 25, "Creating Effective Reports," shows you how to customize reports, page 439.*

Changing the Database to Accommodate Your Needs

You should print documentation for a database before making changes to it. This begins with the Tools menu's Analyze option paired with the use of the Documenter, but you'll want to specify certain options for this to conserve space. Doing so gives you a record of what you're starting with and helps you discern the existing relationships.

SEE ALSO

➤ *To learn more about documenting a database, refer to "Documenting the Database," page 108.*

Modifying Objects in the Wizard's Database

After examining all the parts of the database you created with a wizard, you can modify any of the forms or reports.

Suppose that after reviewing the Donations1 database, you find some of the data-processing operations inadequate. The following list examines some of these objects and how you might modify them:

- Suppose the main Switchboard form doesn't contain a function or task you want to get to quickly. You can modify the options for quicker access. The wizard even generates a button, **Change Switchboard Items**, on the Switchboard to speed this modification.

- You can modify forms and reports by opening them in the Design view ![icon] for example, you can replace or modify labels next to the fields on a form.

- You can also make any of the fields on the form inaccessible to change by modifying the field control's properties.

- If you want to insert donor addresses into a Word

Using the databases without running the wizard

You don't have to use the Database Wizard to use one of Access' 22 existing databases. The wizard simply offers you the opportunity to tweak these databases a bit. To open one of these databases, choose **New Database** from the **File** menu and then click the **Databases** tab. Double-click the database to open it. After reviewing it, if you want to use it as is, simply make a copy of the database using a new name. You should not make changes to the original databases.

document, you can integrate the database and Word to make addressing letters more efficient.

SEE ALSO

➤ *You can learn how to create and modify switchboards on page 178.*

➤ *You can practice modifying form labels and properties beginning on page 346. For examples of creating tables via a wizard, turn to page 41.*

➤ *For examples of merging Access data with Word documents, turn to page 164.*

Making the Most of the Wizard's Objects

In short, creating a database from one of the wizards puts a lot of usable objects at your disposal in a very short time. If you've found a table or form you want to reuse in another Access database, you can simply copy and build it into another database.

The first step is to explore the objects in the wizard (or another) database to find the structure you're looking to copy. For example, you could run any of the wizards and double-click the minimized database's title bar. Refer again to Figure 2.12, where the Donations database is minimized next to the switchboard. Figure 2.13 shows a table with addresses from a similar wizard because the address structure might be reused in a variety of applications. This table is open in Datasheet view.

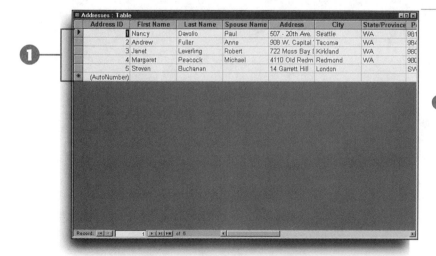

FIGURE 2.13

Find a table with the structure you want to copy. To see a table in this view, double-click the table in the Database window.

1 Copy the entire structure, even if you might not need all the fields in your destination database

Reusing a useful object

1. Open the database that contains your original object and select the object you want to copy (such as the **Addresses** table) in the Database window.

2. Either select **Copy** from the **Edit** menu or press Ctrl+C. The methods are shown in Figure 2.14.

FIGURE 2.14

Select the original item from the Database window and copy it.

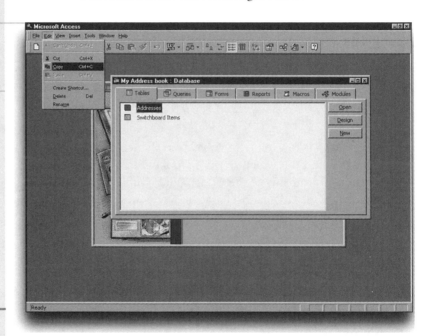

Copying database objects

This process works especially well for tables for several reasons:

You can reuse the table's structure with any of the fields' lengths, captions, and data types determined without having to re-create them.

Regardless of the type of business, many applications use some table structures because they have similar business objects. Customer names and addresses, invoicing, and accounts payable all store similar types of data.

When copying tables, you can also copy data—if it's applicable to the destination's use.

3. To select the destination you have two options:

   - Open a new, blank database—Click the New Database icon ⬜, select the **General** tab and double-click the Blank Database icon. That icon is shown in Figure 2.15.

   - Click **OK**, type in a unique filename, and save the new database. Click **OK**.

   - You can select an existing database from the Open dialog window by clicking 🎚 and double-clicking the filename. You can also select a recently used database from the bottom of the **File** menu.

FIGURE 2.15
Create a new, blank database to
hold your copied object.

4. In the destination database, select the same tab type as the copied object. (That is, if you copied a table, select the **Table** tab.)

5. Choose **Paste** from the **Edit** menu or press Ctrl+V. This brings up the Paste Table As window, shown in Figure 2.16. Type the name of the object as you want it to appear (you might use the same name again). Select one of these options:

- **Structure Only**   Copies only the field and data type information.

- **Structure and Data**   Copies both field information and the values stored in them.

- **Append Data to Existing Table**   If all the field structures match an existing table, you can add data from a copied table to and existing table. This is a much trickier operation than the simple cut-and-paste because Access checks to see if relationships match as well. This is typically used for merging tables that are exactly alike, such as when data collected remotely is added to a master system. Type the name that matches the table you're appending to.

Click **OK** after you type the appropriate object name.

6. The object should now appear in the destination database's tab. Double-click the object to see the results.

Figure 2.17 shows that the destination database now contains a table with the same structure as the original table, minus the data. A form must be *bound* to the data in an underlying table or query before it will show any data.

Working with multiple databases

Don't be surprised if the original database disappears as the new database opens. Access will have just one database open at a time. If you want two databases open at once, you can open two copies of Access for work on your desktop, provided you have the memory and speed to make this practical.

Pasting other objects

Objects such as forms have a simpler Paste As, which requires only the name of the new form.

FIGURE 2.16

Pasting a table works easily if it's a new table. Appending requires identically matched structures and relationships.

1 Using the **Structure Only** option is an alternative way to get rid of sample data

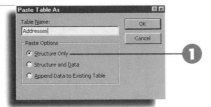

FIGURE 2.17

The destination database now contains a copy of the Addresses table ready for new data.

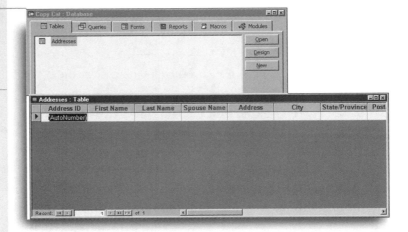

SEE ALSO

➤ *Bound controls are explained on page 338.*

Creating Tables with a Wizard

Create tables quickly and easily

Set primary keys and define relationships with a wizard

Select field options and rename fields with the wizard

What Are Tables?

A *database* is a software application that stores data. We then use specific features to query, analyze, and report that data. To store this data, we entered it into what's known as a table. A table is an Access object that stores data. Specifically, a *table* is a collection of related data stored in rows and columns. Each row contains a *record*—one complete unit of data. Each record consists of *fields*—the smallest unit of data. For instance, if you create a table to store address information, you might have a field for name, street address, city address, state, and zip code. A record would consist of all these fields of information for one person. In other words, a record contains all the data that's related to one person. Your table would consist of many records for all your contacts—all the address information.

SEE ALSO

➤ *For more information on tables, turn to page 13.*

➤ *If you'd like to read more about designing tables, see page 190.*

Whether you use a wizard to build your tables or you build them from scratch, you need a solid understanding of *normalization*—the process of creating and relating tables according to a fixed set of rules. Beyond that, you need to know the database's purpose and each table's purpose. Once you determine what type of information you'll store in your tables, you must break that data down into the smallest possible units or fields. As you consider your field data, you must keep two things in mind:

- The data in each field must be the smallest unit possible, meaning you can't divide the data any further. Remember the earlier example of address data? The proper way to store address data is in separate fields—one each for the street address, the city, the state, and the ZIP code.

- All data should be mutually independent, which means that deleting or changing in one field won't affect another.

SEE ALSO

➤ *For an in-depth review of normalization, see page 13.*

About the Table Wizard

The Table Wizard is one of Access' many wizards, and it will create tables for you after you supply the wizard certain information. You can modify wizard tables if the wizard choices aren't adequate. The wizards do a good job for the most part and they're quick and easy to use. The Table Wizard does several things:

- It offers 25 sample tables on which to base your table.
- It offers helps you set a primary key for the table.
- It helps you define relationships between the table you're creating and any other existing tables.
- It even fills your table with sample data for you to experiment with.

Launching the Table Wizard

There are three ways to launch the Table Wizard and it really makes no difference which one you choose.

Launching the Table Wizard

1. Choose **Table** from the New Object button's [icon] drop-down list.

2. Double-click **Table Wizard** in the New Table dialog box. Alternatively, you can select **Table Wizard** and click **OK**.

   or

1. Click the **Tables** tab and then click the **New** button in the Database window.

2. Double-click **Table Wizard** in the New Table dialog box. Instead, you can select **Table Wizard** and click **OK**.
   or

1. Select **Table** from the **Insert** menu.

2. Double-click **Table Wizard** in the New Table dialog box. You can also select **Table Wizard** and click **OK** instead.

Using the Table Wizard

Once you've launched the Table Wizard, the wizard displays a series of dialog boxes, each one soliciting clues from you regarding the type of data you'll be storing in your table. For instance, you'll need specific fields if you're storing address information, which we've already touched on. You might also require a primary key for your table, and this table will more than likely be related to at least one other table in your database. The wizard helps you create the appropriate table and do so in a matter of minutes.

Creating a table

1. Launch the Table Wizard using any of the methods discussed in the previous section.

2. The wizard's first window, shown in Figure 3.1, offers several tables in the **Sample Tables** control. You select a table from this control. Be sure to select the table that most appropriately represents your table's purpose. The names of these tables are self-explanatory.

Our example

During the accompanying exercise, the wizard helps you define a relationship between the table we're building and an existing table. We'll be using the Northwind database in our example. (Northwind comes with Access, but you must install it.)

FIGURE 3.1

Choose the table that most closely matches your intentions.

1 Choose a table here

2 Select fields here to add them to your table

3 Change this option to view a different list of tables

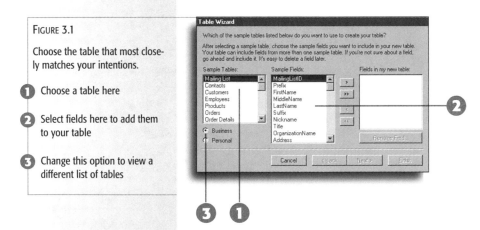

3. The **Business** and **Personal** options are below the **Sample Tables** control. The option you choose determines the list of tables displayed in the **Sample Tables** control. If you don't find what you're looking for under one category, try the other—you may find it there.

4. When you choose a table from the **Sample Tables** control, the wizard updates the list of fields in the **Sample Fields** control accordingly. You have to select each field you want to include in your table and copy it to the **Fields in My New Table** control. Only those fields in that control are included in the table you're creating.

5. Select the table and fields you want to include in your table. We selected the **Addresses** table under the Personal option. We added the following fields to that table:

AddressID	**City**
FirstName	**StateOrProvince**
LastName	**PostalCode**
Address	**Country**

6. If you prefer, you can change a field's name after you move in to the **Fields in My New Table** control. We want to change the **PostalCode** field to **ZIPCode**. To do so, select **PostalCode** in the **Fields in My New Table** control and click the **Rename Field** button.

7. When the wizard displays the Rename Field dialog box, enter the name ZIPCode, as shown in Figure 3.2; click **OK**.

Shortcut for moving fields in a wizard

To move a field from one control to the next, either double-click it or select it and click the appropriate button (**>**, **>>**, **<**, or **<<**); the button is found between the two controls. The single signs move one field at a time, the double signs move all the fields at once.

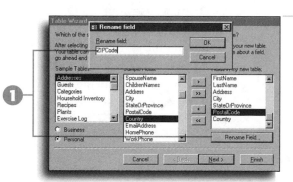

FIGURE 3.2

Enter the field's new name in the Rename Field dialog box.

❶ Rename fields here to comply with normalization and naming standards for related field names

8. Click **Next** once you've added all the fields to the **Fields in My New Table** control and have changed fields names as needed.

9. The second window, shown in Figure 3.3, allows you to
rename the table and set a primary key field. We're going to
retain the name Addresses. In addition, we're going to let
the wizard set the primary key for us; we will retain the Yes,
Set a Primary Key for Me option.

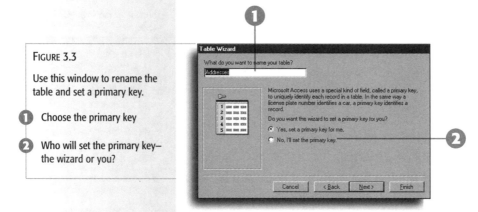

FIGURE 3.3

Use this window to rename the
table and set a primary key.

1 Choose the primary key

2 Who will set the primary key—
the wizard or you?

SEE ALSO

➤ *To learn more about primary keys, turn to page 199.*

➤ *To see the advantages of titling related fields with the same name, see page 14.*

If you want to set the key yourself, choose the **No, I'll Set
the Primary Key** option. Doing so displays the window
shown in Figure 3.4. At this point, you should choose the
field you want as the primary key from the **What Field will
Hold Data That is Unique for Each Record** option's
drop-down list. Define the type of data this field will contain: consecutive values Access adds, values you add, or values and letters you add. Click **Next** after making the
appropriate selections.

SEE ALSO

➤ *Data types for fields are described on page 196.*

10. If you actually displayed the previous window, click **Back** to
return to the window shown in Figure 3.3; then choose the
Yes, Set a Primary Key for Me option. Click **Next** to
continue.

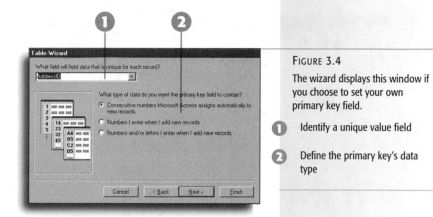

FIGURE 3.4

The wizard displays this window if you choose to set your own primary key field.

1 Identify a unique value field

2 Define the primary key's data type

11. The window shown in Figure 3.5 is where you define any relationships your new table has to existing tables. The **My New 'Addresses' Table Is** control shows the current relationships. Our table isn't currently related to any existing tables.

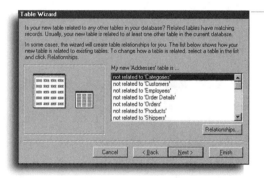

FIGURE 3.5

You can determine whether to define relationships in this window.

To set a relationship, select the appropriate table in the **My New 'Addresses' Table Is** option and then click the **Relationships** button. That displays the window shown in Figure 3.6. You have three choices—the tables aren't related, create a one-to-many relationship between Addresses and your selection (with Addresses being the one side), or create a one-to-many relationship between the two tables (with Addresses as the many side). **The Tables Aren't Related** is the option we're going to retain. If you displayed the Relationships window, click **Cancel** to return to the previous window and then click **Next**.

FIGURE 3.6

Use this window to actually
define relationships.

FIGURE 3.6

Use this window to actually
define relationships.

SEE ALSO

➤ *For more information on relationships, read page 18 and page 219.*

12. At this point the wizard is just about done. The final window, shown in Figure 3.7, has a few more options:

- The **Modify the Table Design** option opens the table
  in Design view.

- The **Enter Data Directly into Table** option opens the
  table in Datasheet view, so you can enter data into the
  table.

- The last option, **Enter Data into the Table Using a
  Form the Wizard Creates for Me** option actually
  creates a data-entry form for you.

- In addition, the **Display Help on Working with the
  Table** option opens the Help section for you. We're
  going to open the table in Datasheet view.

When you're ready, click **Finish**. The completed table is
shown in Figure 3.8.

FIGURE 3.7

The final window allows you to
decide how you want to open the
completed table.

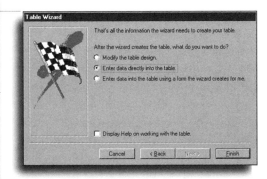

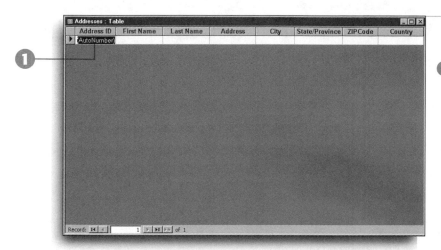

FIGURE 3.8
This is our new Addresses table.
1 The table's primary key field

The AddressID field is the primary key field; you can tell because it's an AutoNumber field. The rest of the fields are those we included in that first window. Notice that the ZIPCode field is just that—not PostalCode—because we changed it.

SEE ALSO

➤ *For instructions on modifying a table, see page 189.*

Using the Query Wizards

Learn how to retrieve records

Create a Crosstab query quickly

Find duplicate entries

Find unmatched records

What Is a Query?

Storing data is only part of most database applications. We generally like to analyze our stored data to find trends; doing so helps us make better business decisions. One of the ways we analyze data in Access is through queries. In addition, queries are often the underlying object for many forms and reports. Queries allow us to view and analyze our data in different ways:

- We can update, change, and even delete data.
- We can sort records by fields or by groups.
- We can view records that meet specific criteria.
- We can perform calculations on groups of records.
- We can combine tables and even other queries.

SEE ALSO

➤ *This chapter reviews queries only as they pertain to the different query wizards. For more information on creating various queries, see page 237.*

➤ *Explore the Design View (also called the QBE grid) on page 257.*

➤ *See how to use the Expression builder to create more complex queries, page 273.*

The Query Wizards

Creating the query you need doesn't have to be a complex task. You can begin by using one of Access' four query wizards:

- Simple Query Wizard—This wizard retrieves data from specific fields. You can include expressions that perform calculations. You can't limit the records it retrieves by setting criteria.
- Crosstab Query Wizard—This wizard summarizes data using expressions on groups of data. Generally, a Crosstab works with more than one set of facts or groups, categorizing the data by all factors.
- Find Duplicates Query Wizard—This wizard locates duplicate field data. You can expand this to find duplicate records.
- Find Unmatched Query Wizard—You might find this wizard the one you use the least. This query finds unrelated records.

SEE ALSO

➤ *A pivot table is a good alternative to a Crosstab. For more information on pivot tables, see page 83.*

What Is a Simple Query?

A *simple query* retrieves data from specific fields—those you indicate in the QBE grid. You can use aggregate functions to return totals, averages, or count records. You can calculate the minimum or maximum value in a field. You can't, however, limit the records the query retrieves by specifying criteria. For instance, you could calculate the total number of customers you have via a simple query, but you couldn't retrieve customers from a specific zip code area. Once you've used the Simple Query Wizard to create the basic query, you can then modify it by adding a criteria expression if needed.

SEE ALSO

➤ *If you'd like to learn how to create a criteria expression, turn to page 265.*

Launching the Query Wizards

Like most of the Access wizards, there are several ways to launch a query wizard.

Launching the query wizards

1. Select **Query** from the New Object button's [icon] drop-down list.

2. Either double-click one of the wizard options or select the appropriate wizard and click **OK**.

   or

1. Click the **Queries** tab in the Database window and then click **New**.

2. Either double-click one of the wizard options or select the appropriate wizard and click **OK**.

   or

1. Choose **Q**uery from the **I**nsert menu.
2. Either double-click one of the wizard options or select the appropriate wizard and click **OK**.

Using the Simple Query Wizard

The Simple Query Wizard retrieves records so that you can include expressions that perform calculations on your records. For instance, you might run this wizard to return a list of customers and their phone numbers or to calculate the total number of customers you have.

Creating a simple query

1. After opening the Northwind database, click the **Queries** tab; then click **N**ew in the Database window.
2. In the New Query dialog box, click **Simple Query Wizard** and then click **OK**.
3. You see the wizard's first window—select the table or query you want to base your query on in the Tables/Queries control. If you select the table or query in the Database window before executing the wizard, Access assumes that the selected table or query is the one you want to base your report on.

   Double-click the fields in the **Available Fields** control that you want to include in your query. Doing so copies the clicked field to the **Selected Fields** control. As you can see in Figure 4.1, I selected the Customers table and want to include only the CompanyName and Phone fields in our query.

   You can include more than one table or query in your query. To do so, simply change the table or query in the **Tables/Queries** control and continue to add fields to the **Selected Fields** control. The order in which you add these fields to the **Selected Fields** control determines how they appear in your query. Once you've added all the fields you need, click **N**ext to continue.

The Design View option

The New Query dialog box has five options: Design View and four query wizards. The Design View option opens a blank QBE grid so you can create a query without benefit of a wizard. You don't have to use a wizard to create a query.

Our example

We'll be using Northwind, the database that comes with Access, in our examples throughout this chapter.

FIGURE 4.1
Select the table or query you're basing your query on.

4. The next (and final) window, shown in Figure 4.2, offers you the option of changing the query's name and opening the query in Datasheet view or Design view. The default is **Open the Query to View Information** and opens the query in Datasheet view, so you can see the query's results. If you want to open the query in Design view, choose the **Modify the Query Design** option. The **Display Help on Working with Queries** option opens the Help section. I changed the query's name to Phone Numbers and retained the other defaults. Once you've made the appropriate choice, click **Finish**. Our query returns each company and its phone number, as shown in Datasheet view in Figure 4.3.

FIGURE 4.2
Choose whether the wizard opens the query in Datasheet view or Design view.

FIGURE 4.3

Our query returns company
names and phone numbers.

Summarizing Your Records

Earlier I told you that the wizard helps you perform calculations
on your records, but our previous query returned just data.
That's because there were no value fields in the query; both
fields were text fields. When the QBE grid includes a Number
or Currency field, the wizard displays a window with summary
options.

Including summary options

1. Chose a table or query in the Database window, select
   Query from the New Object button's drop-down list,
   and then double-click the **Simple Query Wizard**. We're
   basing our query on the Order Details table.

2. Add the appropriate fields to the **Selected Fields** control in
   the wizard's first window. We added the OrderID and
   UnitPrice fields, as shown in Figure 4.4. When you've
   selected the fields you want, click **Next** to continue.

3. This time the wizard displays the summary window shown
   in Figure 4.5. The **Detail (Shows Every Field of Every
   Record)** option displays all the fields for every record, just
   as it claims. Click the **Summary** option to display the
   Summary Options dialog box.

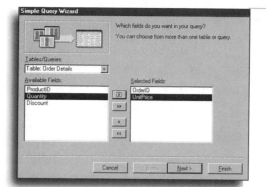

FIGURE 4.4

We're basing our summary query on the Order Details table and displaying two of that table's fields.

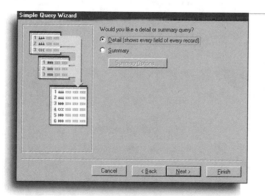

FIGURE 4.5

The wizard allows you to summarize Number and Currency fields.

4. The Summary Options dialog box displays each Number or Currency field you selected earlier. To return a total for each order, select the **Sum** option for the UnitPrice field, as shown in Figure 4.6.

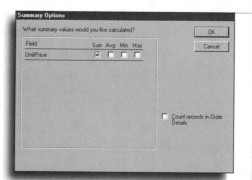

FIGURE 4.6

We want to return a total for each order.

The Count Records in Order Details option return the number of records that make up each total. To do so, the query automatically adds a new field to the query, showing the result of the count. After selecting your calculation options, click **OK** to return to the previous window. Click **Next** to continue.

5. The final window gives the same options as before. You can change the query's default name, determine whether to open the query in Datasheet or Design view, and display Help if needed. We're retaining all the defaults. When you finish making your selections, click **Finish**. Our example query displays the query shown in Figure 4.7.

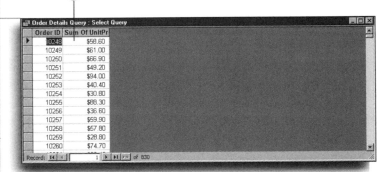

FIGURE 4.7

The wizard displays the query results.

 This field contains the total for all the UnitPrice values for the corresponding OrderID value

If you remember, the table contained multiple records for each OrderID value. The OrderID field in our query contains unique OrderID values. That's because the query combined the UnitPrice values for each OrderID value and returned the total of all those values in the Sum of UnitPrice field.

Figure 4.8 shows the same query with the **Count Records in Order Details** selected. The query in Figure 4.7 did not include a count.

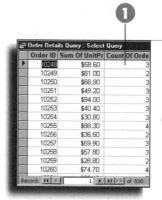

❶

FIGURE 4.8

This query counts the number of records summed for each OrderID value.

❶ This field totals the number of records that correspond to the OrderID value

What's a Crosstab Query?

The previous query, which shows the record count, is actually a Totals query. A *Totals* query performs calculations on groups of records. For instance, you can return a subtotal for a group or the average value for a group.

A Crosstab query is just a more complex Totals query. In a nutshell, a *Crosstab* query summarizes data in rows and columns (similar to a spreadsheet). A Crosstab query must contain three elements:

- A column heading
- A summary field
- A row heading

The Crosstab shown in Figure 4.9 contains all three elements.

SEE ALSO

➤ *The PivotTable feature returns the same result as a Crosstab query. For more information on this feature, turn to page 83.*

The Total of Freight fields lists the total freight cost per day. The remaining columns break down the total freight cost by country. For instance, the freight totals for August 8, 1994 is $107.17; $65.83 of that was used to ship an order (or orders) to Brazil on that date. (We can't see the rest of the query in Figure 4.9, but the remaining costs is for a shipment to France for $41.34.) The first row is a subtotal for each country—that's why there's no date in the Shipped Date field for that record.

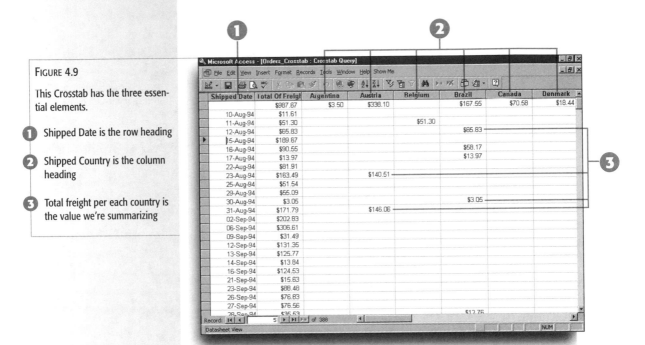

FIGURE 4.9

This Crosstab has the three essential elements.

1 Shipped Date is the row heading

2 Shipped Country is the column heading

3 Total freight per each country is the value we're summarizing

Using the Crosstab Query Wizard

Creating a Crosstab query can be a complex task if you don't know what you're doing. Fortunately, the Crosstab Query Wizard makes the job considerably easier than building the query by scratch.

Creating a Crosstab query

1. Select **Q uery** from the New Object button's drop-down list and double-click **Crosstab Query Wizard** in the New Query dialog box.

2. The wizard's first window, shown in Figure 4.10, prompts you to select the table or query that contains the data you want to include in the query. Specify whether you're querying a table, query, or both in the View options. The control approves updates according to the View option of your choice.

Unlike some queries, you can't include more than one table or query. If you want to include fields from more than one table or query in your Crosstab query, you must create the appropriate query and then base your Crosstab query on the respective query.

The **Sample** control at the bottom of the window shows examples of how your selections during the wizard process look as a Crosstab query. You won't see anything in this control in this first window. We selected the Orders table as the basis of our Crosstab query. Once you've selected your table or query, click **Next**.

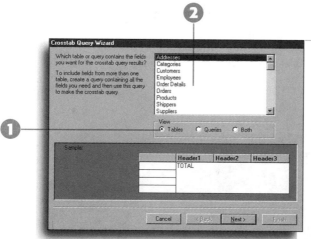

FIGURE 4.10
Here's where you specify the table or query that contains the data you want to query.

❶ Select which objects you want to see

❷ Choose the appropriate table or query

3. Now the wizard wants you to select a field from the **Orders** table to represent the Crosstab's row heading. We selected **ShippedDate**, as shown in Figure 4.11. Notice that the **Sample** control now displays that field in the Crosstab's row heading cells. Click **Next** once you've selected your row heading field.

4. The next window asks you to select the column heading field. As you can see in Figure 4.12, we selected **ShipCountry**. Also notice that the **Sample** control updates to reflect this addition. Once you've made your selection, click **Next**.

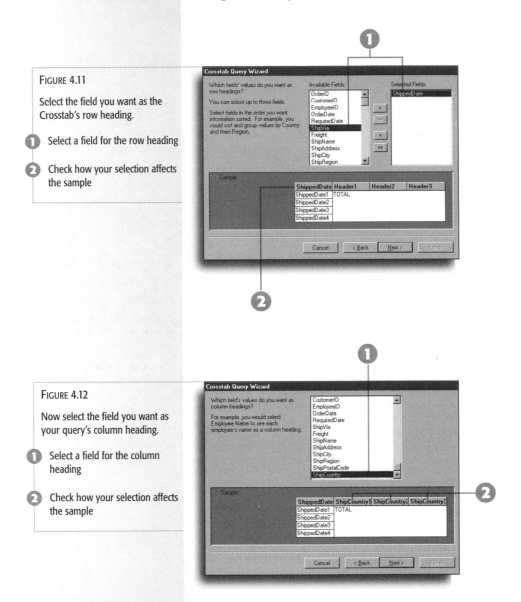

FIGURE 4.11

Select the field you want as the Crosstab's row heading.

① Select a field for the row heading

② Check how your selection affects the sample

FIGURE 4.12

Now select the field you want as your query's column heading.

① Select a field for the column heading

② Check how your selection affects the sample

5. Now the wizard is ready for you to select the field you want summarized in the query and how you want those values calculated. Figure 4.13 shows that we selected the **Freight** field and the **Sum** function. Again, the **Sample** control shows an updated generic version of your selections. As you can see, this control shows a Sum function that adds the values in the Freight field, based on the ShippedDate and the ShipCountry. At this point, if you want to omit the summary row at the top of the query (see Figure 4.9) deselect the **Yes, Include Row Sums** option. Once you've specified the appropriate field and function, click **Next**.

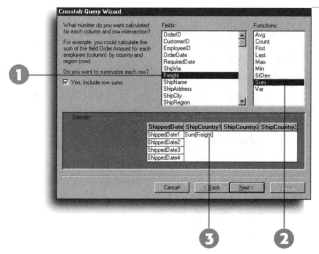

FIGURE 4.13

This window allows you to choose the field you're summarizing and a summarizing function.

1 Select a field for the column heading

2 Choose the calculating function

3 Check how your selection affects the sample

6. The final window gives you the opportunity to change the query's default name, which we won't change for our example. You can also specify whether the wizard opens the query in Datasheet view—choose the **View the Query** option—or in Design view—choose the **Modify the Design** option. If you want to see Help information on Crosstab queries, select the **Display Help on Working with the Crosstab Query** option. When you're ready, click **Finish** to display the query. The wizard opened ours in Datasheet view, as shown earlier in Figure 4.9.

SEE ALSO

➤ *For more information on creating Crosstab queries without a wizard, turn to page 241.*

No criteria expressions in the value field

You can't specify criteria in a Crosstab query. For instance, we specified the Freight field in the current exercise. You couldn't, for example, enter an expression to select only those freight values that are greater than $10. If you require criteria, you must first create a query that retrieves the required data and then base the Crosstab query on that query.

Multiple row headings

You can include more than one row heading in a Crosstab query. However, you need to modify the QBE grid yourself because you can't specify more than one when using the wizard.

Using the Find Duplicates Query Wizard

The data you enter doesn't have to be unique. In fact, you often repeat an entry. Later, however, when you want to locate data, these duplicates can cause a little trouble. For instance, if you want to query a table for a specific entry, you might use that entry in the form of a criteria expression in the query's QBE grid. If, however, you want to query for only those entries that occur more than once, you need the Find Duplicates Query Wizard. You can use that wizard to locate records that share a field entry (duplicate entries). For instance, suppose you want to see if any employees have the same hire date. The easiest method is to simply check the HireDate field in the Employees table for duplicate entries.

Creating a Find Duplicates query

1. Choose **Q uery** from the New Object button's 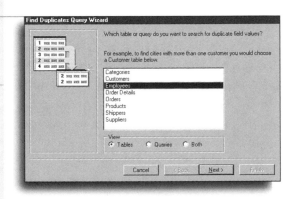 drop-down list and double-click **Find Duplicates Query Wizard**.

2. In the wizard's first window, shown in Figure 4.14, specify the table or query in which you're searching for duplicates. The View options, found just below the list of table or queries, update said list accordingly. We selected the Employees table. Click **Next** after choosing a table or query.

FIGURE 4.14

We want to search for duplicates in the Employees table.

3. In the next window, shown in Figure 4.15, select the field(s) you're searching for duplicates. In this example we're

searching for employees hired on the same date; we double-clicked only the HireDate field to copy that field to the Duplicate Value Fields control.

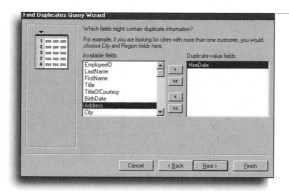

FIGURE 4.15

We want to search for duplicates in the Employees table.

4. At the next window, you can display the contents of other fields along with any duplicate entry. If the query finds any duplicate hire dates, we want to know the employees that share that same hire date. We added the LastName and FirstName fields to the Additional Query Fields control. When you're ready, click **Next**.

5. The final window is typical of most wizards' last window. You can change the query's default name and decide how Access will display the query.

If you choose **View the Results**, the wizard displays the query in Datasheet view.

If you select the **Modify the Design** option, the wizard opens the query in Design view.

If you need more help, you can select the **Display Help on Working with the Query** option.

Click **Finish** to display the results shown in Figure 4.16.

FIGURE 4.16

Two employees share the same hire date.

As you can see, two employees, Michael Suyama and Steven Buchanan, were hired on the same date: October 17, 1993.

Using the Find Unmatched Query Wizard

We have one final query wizard to review—Find Unmatched Query Wizard. This query helps you find records that aren't related to another table in the same database. For instance, you might want to know which of your customers have no orders. To do so, you'd simply compare the related field between the Customers and Orders tables. Any missing CustomerID value in the Orders table indicates customers with no orders.

Creating a Find Unmatched query

1. Select **Query** from the New Object button's [icon] drop-down list.

2. Double-click the **Find Unmatched Query Wizard** option.

3. The wizard's windows are pretty self-explanatory. In its first window, specify the appropriate View option and then select the appropriate table or query. We selected the **Customers** table since we want to find customers that don't have orders. Make your selections and then click **Next**.

4. The second window prompts you to identify the related table or query. As in the first window, specify a View option and then choose the appropriate table or query. We chose **Orders** since this table contains order information. When you're ready, click **Next**.

5. The next window, shown in Figure 4.17, is a little more complex. In it you must identify the related field in both tables. Fortunately, the wizard does a good job of identifying that field for you. In this example, the wizard compares the contents of the CustomerID fields in both tables for missing values in the Orders table. You can change the field in either control if necessary. You must, however, choose fields that have the same data type. Click **Next** to continue.

SEE ALSO

➤ *Data types for fields are described on page 196.*

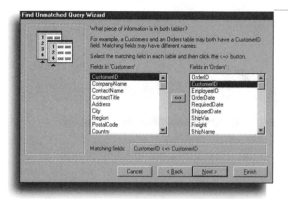

FIGURE 4.17

The wizard selects the related field from both tables to compare.

6. Now you can specify fields you want to display in the query. For instance, we want to see the company's name, its contact, and the phone number for any customer that doesn't have an order—that way we can make a follow-up call to the customer. We added the **CompanyName**, **ContactName**, and **Phone** fields to the **Selected Fields** control. This is shown in Figure 4.18. If you don't specify any fields, the wizard displays all the fields in the first table (Customers). Once you've specified the fields you want in your query, click **Next**.

The missing Archive Query Wizard

Version 2.0 has a wizard that copied records from an existing table to a new table and then deleted those records from the original table. This wizard was named the Archive Query Wizard. If you're used to working with this wizard, you won't find it in Access 95 or Access 97. Instead, run a Make Table query to complete the same task.

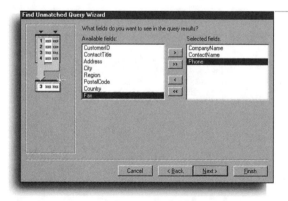

FIGURE 4.18

We want to view the company's name, contact, and phone number.

7. In the final window, you can change the query's name and decide how you want to view the wizard's results. You can choose **View the Results** to see the query in Datasheet view, or you can select **Modify the Design** to open the query in Design view.

We retained the defaults and then clicked **Finish** to display the query shown in Figure 4.19. As you can see, we have two customers with no orders.

Company Name	Contact Name	Phone
FISSA Fabrica Inter. Salchichas S.A.	Diego Roel	(91) 555 94 44
Paris spécialités	Marie Bertrand	(1) 42.34.22.66

FIGURE 4.19

Our query shows two customers without orders.

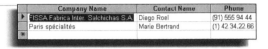

SEE ALSO

➤ *To learn about Make Table queries, turn to page 243.*

Form Creation Using a Wizard

Learn about the four types of forms

Let the wizards do your work

Display charts in your forms

Create pivot tables quickly

A Short Form Orientation

Forms are the objects you use to interact with your data, so you'll probably find yourself working with them more than any other object. Forms make viewing, entering, and modifying your data easier. You can think of a form as a screen representation of the paper forms you're already using.

Forms aren't limited to data-related tasks. Utility forms make searching and sorting data easier. You can also use forms as part of your application's *interface*—the application elements that tell Access what you want to do, such as menus and toolbars. A *switchboard* form, like the one shown in Figure 5.1, presents a menu of options. All in all, you'll find Access forms flexible and versatile—a jack-of-all-trades.

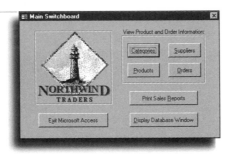

FIGURE 5.1

The Northwind switchboard guides you to several tasks.

About the Form Wizards

The form wizard terms

Throughout this chapter similar terms are used: form wizard, Form Wizard, and AutoForms. When "form wizard" is in lowercase letters, it refers to *all* of the form wizards. "Form Wizard" in uppercase is one of the many form wizards Access offers. "AutoForm" is a type of wizard that generates a specific type of form automatically. Make sure you're clear on these terms to avoid any confusion.

Access' form wizards use different defaults to generate forms based on tables and queries. There are two types of form wizards: the AutoForms and the Form Wizard. The AutoForms automatically generate a specific type of form, using all the fields in the underlying table or query. In contrast, the Form Wizard allows you to specify the fields you want to include in your form. The wizards offer four types of forms:

- Columnar—You can create a form that displays data in one column, with each field on a separate line. Typically, this form displays one record at a time.

- Tabular—This form displays all the data from one record in the same row, in a column format. Each field is a new column. This is a good format for displaying multiple records.

- Datasheet—You can display data in table format, in a form. It's an easy way to display your data in this format without actually opening a table.

- Justified—This form distributes controls evenly between the right and left margins and the top and bottom margins. This type of form is available only with the Form Wizard.

We'll take a closer look at each of these form types later in this chapter. For now, let's take a look at how to launch a form wizard.

Launching the Form Wizard

1. Select the table or query you want to base your form on in the Database window.

2. Choose **Form** from the New Object button's  drop-down list.

3. Double-click **Form Wizard** in the New Form dialog box, shown in Figure 5.2.

FIGURE 5.2
Access offers several form wizards.

Launching an AutoForm

1. Select the table or query you want to base your form on in the Database window.

2. Select **AutoForm** from the New Object button's drop-down list to generate a columnar form. Or you can select **Form** from the drop-down list and choose one of the AutoForms in the New Form dialog box, shown in Figure 5.2.

We've looked at the typical methods you'll use to launch form wizards, but there is one last way to access them.

An alternate way to launch a wizard

1. Click **Forms** and then **New** in the Database window.
2. Select a wizard option in the New Form dialog box.
3. From the drop-down control below the list of wizards, select the table or query on which you want to base your form.
4. Click **OK**. Access will launch the appropriate wizard.

Using AutoForms

Perhaps the easiest way to create a form is to use one of the many AutoForm wizards. The default AutoForm is first on the New Object button's drop-down list, and this is the only way to launch it.

The example for this task

To demonstrate the task of creating a form using AutoForm, the figures show the **Products** table of the Northwind database, which comes with Access if you installed it. However, you can use these steps for any form.

Creating a form with AutoForm

1. Open an existing database.
2. In the Database window, select the table you want to use as the basis for your form.
3. Choose **AutoForm** from the New Object button's drop-down list, and Access will create a form similar to the one shown in Figure 5.3.

FIGURE 5.3

The AutoForm uses the columnar style as its default.

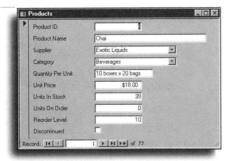

An alternate way to create the same form

1. Open the database.
2. In the Database window, select the desired table.

3. Select **Form** from the New Object button's drop-down list.

4. Double-click **AutoForm: Columnar** in the New Form dialog box, or select **AutoForm: Columnar** and click **OK**.

Both of the forms you just created are *columnar* forms—AutoForm creates a columnar form by default. The wizard arranges all the fields in the underlying table in a single column, and displays one record at a time. This style tends to resemble typical paper forms, so it's good for viewing or entering data.

The *tabular* form is similar to Datasheet view—displaying all the fields in the same row. Generally, there isn't much resemblance between a tabular form and a corresponding paper form. However, the style works well when you display multiple records. We created the tabular form, shown in Figure 5.4, using the AutoForm: Tabular wizard.

Creating a tabular form with AutoForm: Tabular

1. Select the table you want from the Database window.

2. Choose **Form** from the New Object button's drop-down list.

3. Double-click **AutoForm: Tabular** in the New Form dialog box, or select **AutoForm: Tabular** and click **OK**.

AutoForm defaults

If the second form isn't exactly the same as the first, don't worry. The columnar, tabular, and datasheet AutoForms use the settings from the last Form Wizard session as their defaults, or they will use the last format you choose from the **AutoFormat** command on the **Format** menu in Design view. In contrast, the AutoForm you select from the New Object button relies on the form template to produce a columnar form.

Adjusting the wizard forms

Although AutoForm provides a sound start, it rarely produces exactly the form you need. You can expect to alter a few of the settings, such as label contents, text alignment, or color.

The example for this task

The figures in this task use the Order Details table from Northwind.

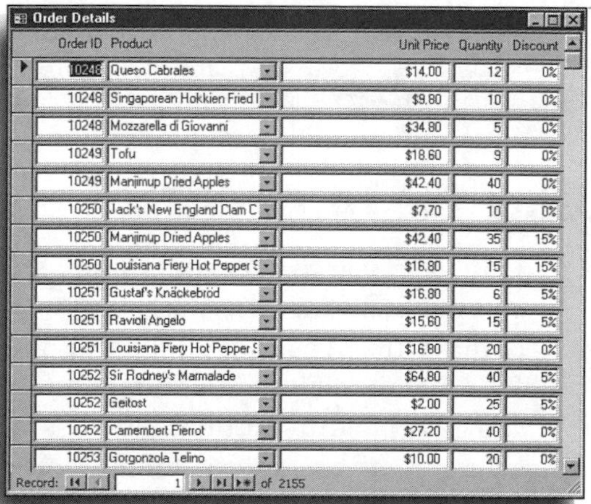

FIGURE 5.4

This tabular form displays all of a record's fields in the same row.

Datasheet forms also resemble Datasheet view, as shown in Figure 5.5. However, they're a closer match to the table format than the tabular style. This style is good for viewing lots of data at the same time or displaying your data in table fashion, without actually opening your table.

Creating a datasheet form with AutoForm: Datasheet

1. Select a table in the Database window.

2. Choose **Form** from the New Object button's drop-down list.

3. Double-click **AutoForm: Datasheet** in the New Form dialog box, or select **AutoForm: Datasheet** and click **OK**.

FIGURE 5.5

A datasheet form resembles a table.

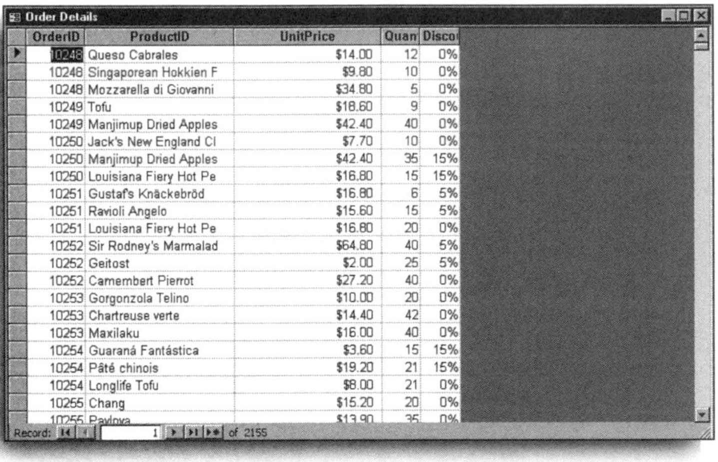

Using the Form Wizard

Until now, you've dealt with wizards that automatically generate a form—including all the fields in the underlying table or query in that form. When an AutoForm isn't adequate, you can use the Form Wizard. This wizard offers the three previous form styles, and adds a fourth—justified. You've already seen the first three styles, so let's create a justified form using the Form Wizard.

You may be wondering what a justified form is. The best way to describe it is to just show you one. The following example creates a justified form like the one shown in Figure 5.6. As you can see, Access has distributed the controls equally between the left and right margins and the top and bottom margins.

FIGURE 5.6

You can create this justified form using the Form Wizard.

Creating a justified form with AutoForm: Justified

1. Select the appropriate table in the Database window.

2. Choose **Form** from the New Object button's drop-down list.

3. Double-click **Form Wizard** in the New Form dialog box, or select **Form Wizard** and click **OK**. Access will display the wizard's first window, shown in Figure 5.7. Notice that the **Tables/Queries** control displays the same table on which you're basing this form.

The example in this task

Use the Northwind Customer table if you want to re-create the screen shown in Figure 5.6.

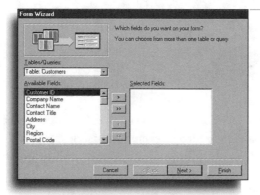

FIGURE 5.7

The wizard's first window allows you to pick and choose the fields you want to include in your form.

4. Select the fields you want to include, as shown in Figure 5.8. Then, click **Next** to continue.

5. The next window prompts you to select one of the four form types, with Columnar being the default. Select **Justified**, the last option, as shown in Figure 5.9. Then click the **Next** button.

Shortcut for moving numerous fields

The easiest way to move all but one or two fields is to click the **>>** button, moving all the fields to the Selected Fields list box. Then, select the exceptions (**Fax** in this example) and click the **<** button to return them to the Available Fields list box.

FIGURE 5.8

All the fields are selected except Fax.

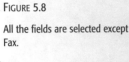 You want to include all the fields except one

2 Use these buttons to move all or a few fields quickly

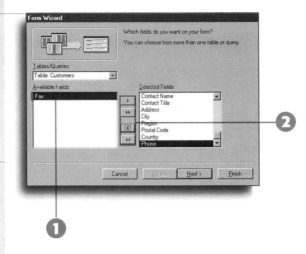

FIGURE 5.9

In the second window, you specify the form type—in this case, Justified.

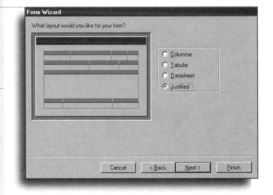

Automatic retention of format

The format you select now will affect the AutoForms because they rely on the last Form Wizard format for their own defaults. That means the next form you create using an AutoForm will default to the same style you just selected.

6. The following window gives you the opportunity to select from several form styles. Select the style of your choice, as shown in Figure 5.10. Click **Next** to continue.

7. Figure 5.11 shows the final window, where you'll give the form a name and specify the way you want to view the completed form. If you want to modify the wizard's design, you should choose the **Open the Form to Enter or View Information** option. In this case you've retained the default design by clicking **Finish**. As a result, Access displays the form in Figure 5.6.

SEE ALSO

➤ *If you're curious about how to modify the form once you create it, see page 341.*

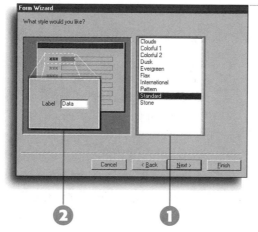

FIGURE 5.10

You chose the Standard style in this window.

1 When you select a style in the right pane...

2 ...a preview of the style appears in the left pane

FIGURE 5.11

The last window prompts you for a form name.

SEE ALSO

➤ *For more specific information on standardizing your forms, see page 349.*

Using the Chart Wizard

Let's finish up this introduction to form wizards by reviewing two rather unusual form wizards: the Chart Wizard and the PivotTable Wizard. As you might expect, you'll use the Chart Wizard to embed a chart in a form by basing a form chart on a table or query. Or you can add a chart to an existing form or report. The PivotTable Wizard is an interactive table that performs calculations. It gets its name from its behavior—it can dynamically modify its layout to match different analysis needs.

Selecting fields in a wizard

When you move a field from the Available Fields list box to the Selected Fields list box, Access keeps track of the order. When the wizard creates your form, the fields are shown in the left-right/top-bottom order they appear in the Selected Fields list. A quick way to reorder the appearance of your form is to click the fields in the left pane in the order you want them to appear in the form.

Adopting a form style

We recommend that you adopt one style for your forms and reports to create a consistent look and feel for your users. The continuity will make your applications easier to learn and use.

Using pivot tables and Excel

You must have Excel installed to create a pivot table in Access. So technically, anytime you're working with a chart or pivot table, you're actually working with an ActiveX control.

The example for this task

The figures in creating a chart form are based on the Category Sales for 1995 query in the Northwinds database.

SEE ALSO

➤ *If the term* pivot table *rings a bell, that's because you can also create a query to make a pivot table, as shown on page 60.*

Access doesn't actually have charting capabilities; instead, the Chart Wizard launches Microsoft Graph 97. After you've embedded the chart in a form or report, you can launch Microsoft Graph to edit the chart. Nor does Access create pivot tables on its own—the PivotTable Wizard actually relies on the same feature in Excel.

Creating a chart form

1. Click the **Queries** tab in the Database window and then select the query you want to use.

2. Select **Form** from the New Object button's drop-down list and then double-click **Chart Wizard,** or select **Chart Wizard** and click **OK**.

3. The first window prompts you to select the fields that contain the data you want to chart. (Figure 5.12 shows **CategoryName** and **CategorySales**.) Click **Next** to continue.

FIGURE 5.12

You want to chart the category name and sales fields.

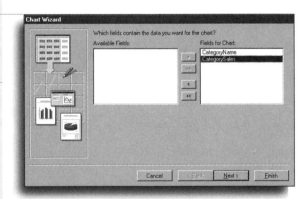

4. In the next window, you can choose from 20 different chart formats. The default is shown in Figure 5.13. Click **Next**.

5. The next window, shown in Figure 5.14, gives you the opportunity to rearrange the chart somewhat. Specifically,

you can drag and drop the field controls to change the wizard's orientation. Or you can simply preview the chart by clicking the Preview Chart button 📊 in the top-left corner of the window.

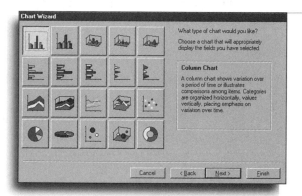

FIGURE 5.13
There are 20 charts to choose from.

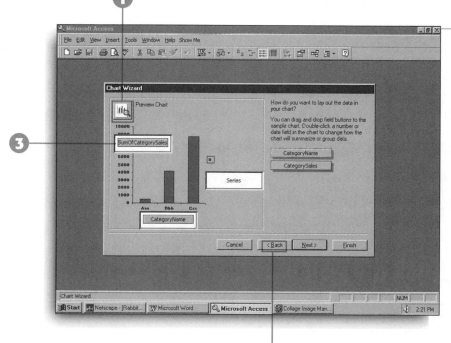

FIGURE 5.14
This window allows you to rearrange the charted data and preview the current settings.

1 Preview the style and appearance of the chart

2 If you don't like the preview, click here to pick a different chart style

3 Click here to call up the Summarize dialog box

To change the calculation from this screen, double-click the control that represents the calculation or measurement in your graph. This displays the Summarize dialog box. (In other words, if your graph shows sales for three years click the control for the sales side of the graph; the example shows the **SumOfCategorySales** control.)

The options available in the Summarize dialog window allow you to change the default calculation—**Sum** is the default. You can choose a **Sum**, **Average**, **Min**, **Max,** or **Count** function.

Choose the calculation you want, as shown in Figure 5.15, and click **OK**. Click **Next** to continue.

Changing the example's calculation

At this point, you can see that Access is charting the sum of each category's sales. This example changes the **SumOfCategorySales** to **Average**.

FIGURE 5.15

The Chart Wizard allows you to change the defaults.

6. The last window is where you'll name the chart and specify a legend. You can also determine how Access displays the completed chart. You retain the default settings for everything else, as shown in Figure 5.16. Click **Finish** and Access will display the chart shown in Figure 5.17.

FIGURE 5.16

The last window allows you to give the chart a title.

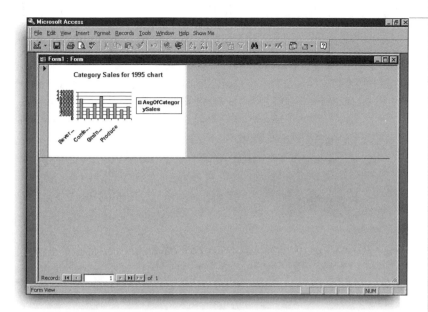

FIGURE 5.17
This chart form displays the average sale for each category.

Adding a Chart to an Existing Form

As mentioned earlier, instead of creating a new form, you can insert a chart into an existing form. The process of creating the form is basically the same, so we won't repeat those steps. The process is simple: you open the form in which you want to insert the chart, and then you create the chart.

SEE ALSO

➤ *To learn how to move a form's controls in Design view, see page 323.*

Embedding a chart in an existing form

1. Open your form in Design view by selecting it in the Database window and then clicking **Design**. Before you create the form, you should consider where you're going to place it because they tend to be rather large. You're going to place your chart to the right of the data controls, which means you have to delete the Picture control to make room. Click the **Picture** control and then press the Delete key.

2. Choose **Chart** from the **Insert** menu.

3. Click inside the form where you want to position your chart. In this example, it's to the right of the company name.

The example for adding a chart

Because this process requires that a form already exist, you'll need a ready form with space available for the graph. If your form doesn't have space for the graph, you can move the controls in Design view first or simply use the Categories form from the Northwind database, used in this example's figures.

4. This calls up the Chart Wizard window. The list box shows all the tables or queries in the database based on which check box you click in the View section.

5. Choose **Queries** from the **View** options at the bottom of the window. Then select the query or table on which you're basing the chart and click **Next**. At this point, repeat steps 3 through 5 from the previous exercise.

6. Since you're dealing with an existing form, Access gives you the opportunity to link your chart to the existing form data in the window that follows, shown in Figure 5.18.

This should be correct, so click **Next**.

FIGURE 5.18

Access attempts to link the chart to a field in the existing form.

 Linking fields makes the chart change dynamically with each record

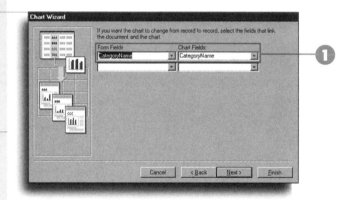

Automatic linking

Access wants to link the chart to the CategoryName field in the existing form. This is precisely the field intended.

7. In the final window, select whether or not you want to display a legend option, and then click **Finish**.

To see the results, similar to those shown in Figure 5.18, choose **No** for the legend option and click View 📧▾ on the Form Design toolbar. The chart displays data for the current record's category.

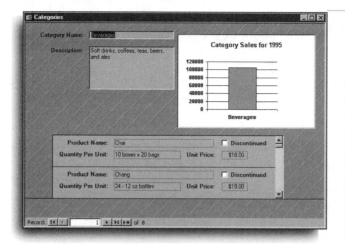

FIGURE 5.19
Access will synchronize the chart data to the current record.

Working with the PivotTable Wizard

A pivot table is very powerful because it lets you produce different viewpoints of the same data. The PivotTable Wizard is flexible—you can easily change the default calculations and format the fields. In addition, a pivot table can display field values horizontally or vertically, calculating the total of the row or column. You can then *pivot* the existing layout to dynamically analyze the data in different ways. The Northwind database has a pivot table in the Sales Analysis form if you'd like to review it. Next you'll create one of your own.

Creating a pivot table

1. Select the query in the Database window, choose **Form** from the New Object button's drop-down list, and then double-click **PivotTable Chart** in the New Form dialog box.

2. To learn more about the pivot table feature, read the resulting window and then click **Next**.

3. Include the fields in the pivot table by clicking **>>** and then clicking **Next**.

4. At this point, the PivotTable Wizard will open the Excel feature and prompt you to create your table. Using the

> **Knowing what to use for a pivot table**
>
> After you've made a few pivot tables, you'll know how they work and which queries you'll want to examine. If you need more experience, use all the fields in the Quarterly Orders by Product query from Northwind, like the example here. Generally, pivot tables work best when categories have multiple subheadings. For instance, the pivot table you create in the following example displays quarterly totals for 1995 by customer. However, you could easily add quarterly totals for other years to this arrangement.

drag-and-drop method, add the fields you want as columns to the **COLUMN** section. Then add the field(s) to the **ROW** section.

Next, add the fields (periods of time or segments of measure) for your data to the **DATA** section, as shown in Figure 5.20.

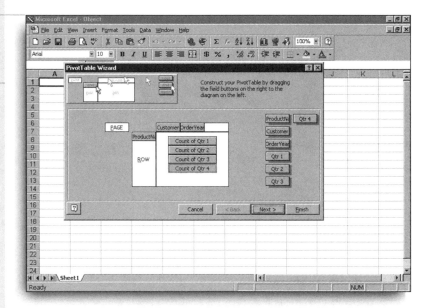

5. At this point, you can double-click any of the DATA fields (**Count of Qtr 1**) to modify them. In the resulting PivotTable Field dialog box, choose one of the operations (**Sum**) from the **Summarize by** list box. Then click the datatype (**Number**), choose any formatting options (**Currency**) from the datatype (**Number**) options, and then click **OK**. Then click **OK** in the PivotTable Field dialog box to return to the PivotTable Wizard window.

7. Repeat this process for each of the remaining DATA (quarter) fields, and then click **Next** to continue.

8. At this point, you can click the **Options** button to see all the wizard has to offer in the way of customizing your form.

These customization options include formats, data source selection, layout, and password protection. We won't review these, but you should know they're available.

9. Click **OK** and then **Finish** to display the pivot table form shown in Figure 5.21. You can edit the form by clicking the **Edit PivotTable** button at the bottom of the form.

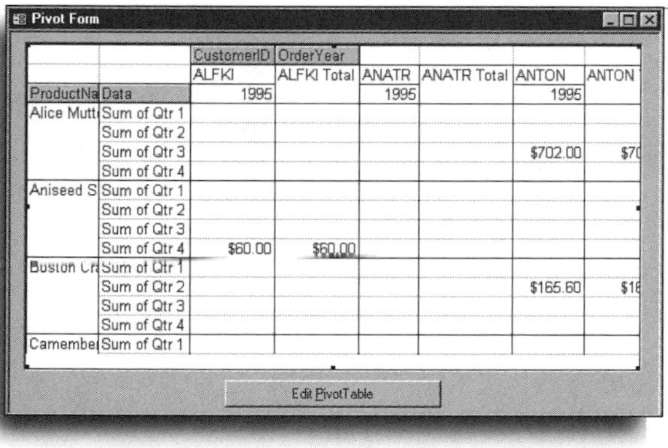

		CustomerID	OrderYear					
		ALFKI		ALFKI Total	ANATR	ANATR Total	ANTON	ANTON
ProductNa	Data	1995			1995		1995	
Alice Mutt	Sum of Qtr 1							
	Sum of Qtr 2							
	Sum of Qtr 3						$702.00	$70
	Sum of Qtr 4							
Aniseed S	Sum of Qtr 1							
	Sum of Qtr 2							
	Sum of Qtr 3							
	Sum of Qtr 4	$60.00		$60.00				
Boston Cr	Sum of Qtr 1							
	Sum of Qtr 2						$165.60	$16
	Sum of Qtr 3							
	Sum of Qtr 4							
Camembe	Sum of Qtr 1							

Edit PivotTable

FIGURE 5.21

The resulting form is a dynamic tool for analyzing your data.

Creating Reports with the Report Wizard

Generate reports quickly and with ease

Add charts to reports

A Short Report Orientation

Many of us can relate to the phrase "I'll need that report first thing tomorrow." If you're using the wrong database, you could cnd up spending the night at the office. If you're using Access, you can print out the report by quitting time and go home—and accept the praise in the morning instead of clearing sleep crust from your eyes.

A report is a printed hard copy of your data presented in a particular format. For instance, you might group your records by date, or you might print a list of customers by region. The only thing that really limits the power of the Access reporting feature is your imagination. Furthermore, you don't have to report on all your data. You can base a report on a table or a query that restricts the report data to certain criteria. If the data exists, you can report it in just about any fashion you could possibly need.

SEE ALSO

➤ *To learn more about restricting data in a query, see page 265.*

The report wizard terms

Throughout this chapter we'll use similar terms: report wizard, Report Wizard, and AutoReports. The term "report wizard" (lower case) is a generic reference to all the report wizards. When we use proper case— "Report Wizard"–we're referring to just one of the many report wizards. The last term, "AutoReports," is also a specific report wizard.

The Report Wizards and Their Capabilities

The report wizards don't do everything, but they're efficient and easy to use. Furthermore, they create a good solid base for most of your report needs. In a nutshell, the report wizards depend on different defaults to generate reports based on your data.

The report wizards are similar to the form wizards in that there are two types: the AutoReports and the Report Wizard. The AutoReports Wizard automatically generates a specific type of report, using all the fields in the underlying table or query. On the other hard, the Report Wizard allows you to specify the fields you want to report on.

There are three types of reports to choose from:

- Columnar—You can create a report that displays data in one column, with each field on a separate line.

- Tabular—This report displays all the data from one record in the same row—each field forms a column.

- Justified—A justified report distributes data evenly between the right and left margins and the top and bottom margins.

Now that you know the types of reports you can generate, let's take a look at how to launch the wizards.

Launching the Report Wizard

1. Select the table or query you want to base your report on in the Database window.

2. Choose **Report** from the New Object button's drop-down list.

3. Double-click **Report Wizard** in the New Report dialog box, shown in Figure 6.1. Or select **Report Wizard** and click **OK**.

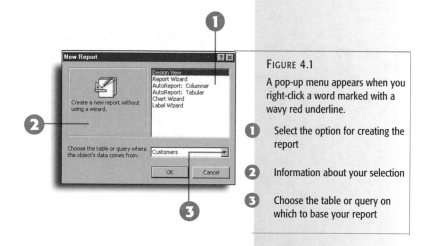

FIGURE 4.1

A pop-up menu appears when you right-click a word marked with a wavy red underline.

1 Select the option for creating the report

2 Information about your selection

3 Choose the table or query on which to base your report

Using the New Object button

When you use the New Object button ⊞▾, be sure to click the drop-down arrow rather than clicking on the object that appears on the toolbar. This icon may change to the object last selected. Then, if you're creating several reports in a row, you will see the Report icon ⊞▾ automatically appear on the toolbar. Access changes the toolbar intuitively to save you an extra mouse click.

The example for this task

The example in this section uses the Product Sales for 1995 query in Northwind, the database that comes with Access, to demonstrate the AutoReport Wizard. You can follow along with almost any table or query.

Launching an AutoReport

1. Select the table or query you want to base your report on in the Database window.

2. Select **AutoReport** from the drop-down list of the New Object button ⊞▾ to generate a columnar report. Or select **Report** from the drop-down list and choose one of the AutoReports in the New Report dialog box.

An alternate launching method

1. Click **Reports** and then **New** in the Database window.

2. Select a wizard option in the New Report dialog box.

3. From the drop-down list below the list of wizards, select the table or query on which you want to base your report.

4. Click **OK**, and Access will launch the appropriate wizard.

Using AutoReports

When you have few requirements, you should consider using the AutoReport wizards. All of them are available from the New Object button's drop-down list.

Using AutoReport to create a report

1. In the Database window, select the table or query that you're basing your report on.

2. Choose **AutoReport** from the drop-down list of the New Object button ⊞▾, and Access will generate a columnar report similar to the one shown in Figure 6.2.

Another way to create the same columnar report

1. In the Database window, select the table or query on which you're basing your report.

2. Choose **Report** from the drop-down list of the New Object button ⊞▾.

3. Double-click **AutoReport: Columnar** in the New Report dialog box, or select **AutoReport: Columnar** and click **OK**.

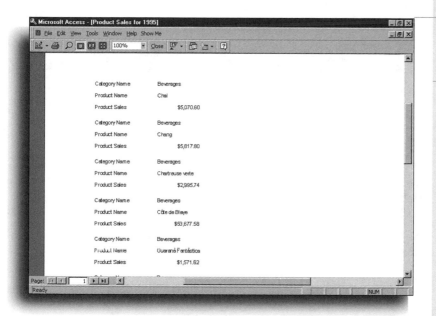

FIGURE 6.2
The AutoReport Wizard was used to create this columnar report.

A *tabular report*, like a tabular form, is similar to Datasheet view because it displays all the fields for one record in the same row. Let's move on to the AutoReport: Tabular Wizard and create a report similar to the one shown in Figure 6.3.

Using the AutoReport: Tabular Wizard to create a report

1. Select the table you want to base your report on in the Database window.

2. Choose **Report** from the drop-down list of the New Object button 🖩▾.

3. Double-click **AutoReport: Tabular** in the New Report dialog box, or select **AutoReport: Tabular** and click **OK**. The wizard will generate a report similar to the one shown in Figure 6.3.

Access doesn't provide an AutoReport: Datasheet or AutoReport: Justified Wizard, as it does for forms.

AutoReport defaults

In Chapter 5, "Form Creation Using a Wizard," you learned that the AutoForm wizards use the settings from the last Form Wizard session as their defaults. The AutoReport wizards are the same. Therefore, you may find some subtle differences between the reports in this chapter and yours.

The example for this task

This example continues to use the Product Sales for 1995 query.

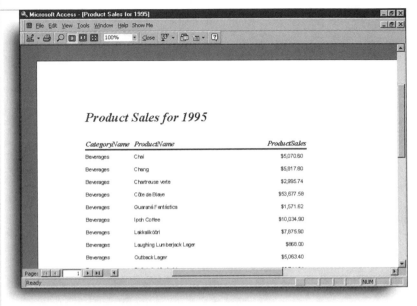

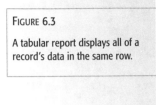

The example in this task

Continue to work with the Product Sales for 1995 query if you want to re-create this example.

Using the Report Wizard

All of the wizards you've explored so far have automatically generated a report and included all of the bound fields in that report. In contrast, the Report Wizard is a little more flexible. It offers a third style—justified—and you can choose the fields you want to include in your report.

We've already reviewed columnar and tabular reports, so let's use the Report Wizard to create a justified report, which is similar in style to a justified form. The wizard will distribute the data equally between the left and right margins and the top and bottom margins of the report's Detail section.

SEE ALSO

➤ *If you'd like more information about bound controls, see page 338.*

Creating a justified report

1. Select the appropriate table or query in the Database window.

2. Choose **Report** from the drop-down list of the New Object button 📄▾.

3. Double-click **Report Wizard** in the New Report dialog box, or select **Report Wizard** and click **OK**. Access will launch the Report Wizard.

4. Select the fields you want to include, as shown in Figure 6.4, and click **Next**.

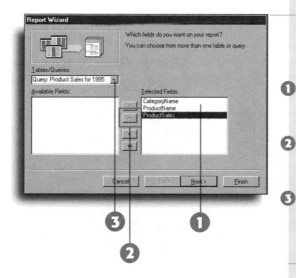

FIGURE 6.4

Choose the fields you want to include in your report from the wizard's first window.

❶ You want to include all the fields in the bound query in your report

❷ Click here to quickly move all the fields to the Selected Fields list box

❸ As with forms, you can add fields from more than one table to a single report by selecting additional tables or queries here

5. In the next window, specify a grouping field. In this example **CategoryName** is selected, as you can see in Figure 6.5. Click **Next** to continue. (You don't have to choose a group field.)

For example, you could select both CustomerID and PostalCode to sort customers in a Customers table. Sorting first by PostalCode and then by each CustomerID in that postal area would show regions and the customers in them.

FIGURE 6.5

You want to group your records by their categories.

1 Use the priority buttons to gauge which criteria will be the first used to sort data

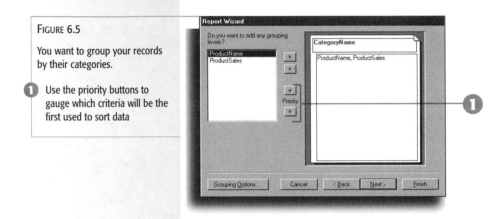

6. You can also sort your records. In this case they're sorted by the contents of the ProductName field, as shown in Figure 6.6. You can sort your records by up to four fields or by no fields at all.

FIGURE 6.6

You want the wizard to sort your records by their product name.

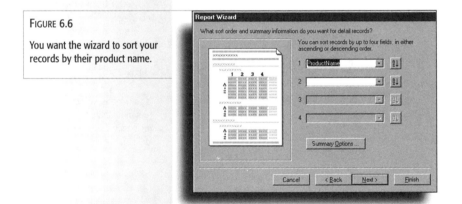

7. At this point, click the **Summary Options** button to display the Summary Options dialog box, shown in Figure 6.7. Using these options, you can include calculations in your reports. Specifically, you can display a field's total, its average, and its minimum or maximum value. The Show options allow you to show only the summary calculations, or the records (details) and the summary calculations. Make your selection if you're adding this component to your report, and click **OK** to return to the previous wizard window.

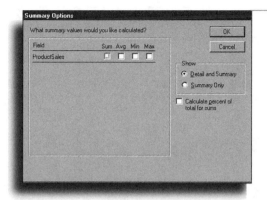

8. The next window, shown in Figure 6.8, allows you to substantially alter the report's layout.

The Layout options offer six different formats. As you click each setting, the wizard will update the sample report data in the picture control to the left. Select each one now so you can see the available settings. In this example, **Block** has been chosen.

The Orientation settings are **Portrait** and **Landscape**, which you're probably familiar with already. **Portrait** prints the report using the paper's length measurement as the top and bottom margins. If you choose **Landscape**, Access will use the paper's width measurement as the top and bottom margins.

The final option, **Adjust the field width so all fields fit on a page**, is self explanatory. The wizard will make the report fit, width-wise, on one sheet of paper. After making the appropriate choices, click **Next** to continue.

9. The next window, shown in Figure 6.9, offers several predefined report formats to choose from. As before, when you click each setting, the wizard will update the view in the picture control to the left. In this case it's the **Corporate** setting. Click **Next** to continue.

Adjusting fields to fit a report

If you click the last option, **Adjust the field width so all fields fit on a page**, and you have selected numerous fields for your reports, this will cause some values to be truncated in order to fit the whole record on the same page. Use this option wisely, or change the direction of your page layout to accommodate numerous fields.

FIGURE 6.8

The **Block** setting has been chosen.

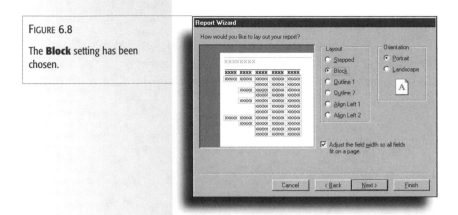

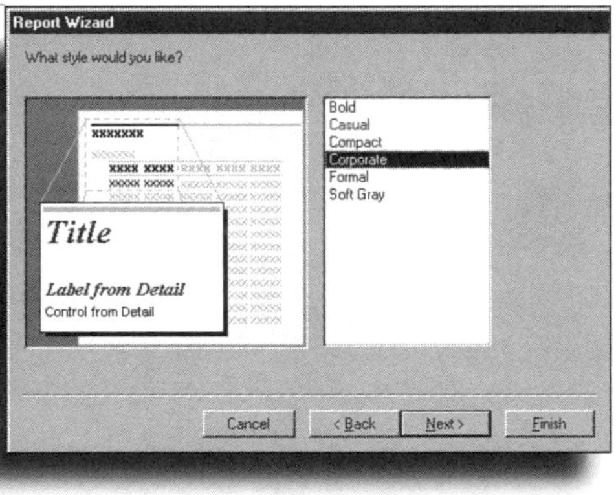

FIGURE 6.9

The Report Wizard offers several predefined formats.

10. The final window prompts you to name the report (you can accept the default if you like). At this point, you can choose between viewing the completed report in Print preview or opening the report in Design view for further modifications. Name the sample report rptSalesfor1995, click the **Preview the report** option, as shown in Figure 6.10, and click **Finish**.

11. The Report Wizard generates the report shown in Figure 6.11.

SEE ALSO

➤ *To learn more about modifying the report, see page 439.*

FIGURE 6.10

To complete the report, give it a name and select a display option.

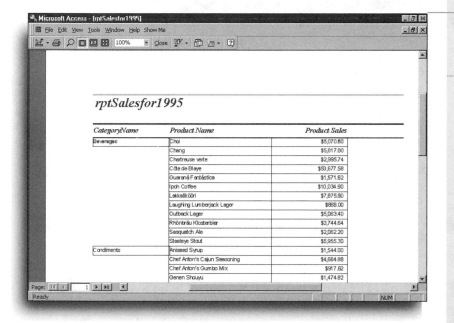

FIGURE 6.11

The wizard displays your finished report in Print Preview.

Using the Chart Wizard

In Chapter 5, you learned how to insert a chart into a form. You can use the same basic routine to insert a chart into a report. You're actually embedding an ActiveX control, because Access doesn't generate charts. Instead, Access relies on Microsoft Graph 97 to create charts based on your Access data.

The example for this task

We're using the Category Sales for 1995 query in the Northwinds database to create the sample chart report.

Creating a chart report

1. Select the table or query you want to chart in the Database window.

2. Choose **Report** from the drop-down list of the New Object button ▣▾ and then double-click **Chart Wizard,** or select **Chart Wizard** and click **OK** in the New Report dialog box.

3. The first window allows you to select the fields you want to chart. As you can see in Figure 6.12, both available fields are included. Click **Next** to continue.

FIGURE 6.12

You're charting the category name and sales data.

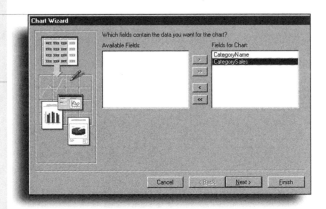

Charting limitations

Unlike the form and report wizards, which allow you to select fields from more than one table or query, the Chart Wizard eliminates the drop-down list box (like the one shown earlier in Figure 6.4, callout 3) for multiple tables and queries. If you want to base a chart on multiple table sources, create a query that pulls all these tables together and base your chart on that query.

4. The next window, shown in Figure 6.13, offers 20 different chart formats. Retain the default, and click **Next** to continue.

5. The third window, shown in Figure 6.14, offers the opportunity to change the default series structure. Or you can simply preview the chart by clicking the Preview Chart button ▥ in the top-left corner of the window.

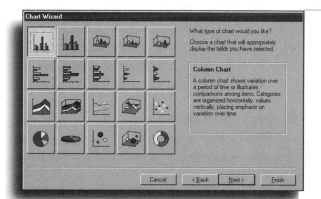

FIGURE 6.13

You can choose from 20 different chart formats. An explanation of each appears in the text control on the right side of the dialog box.

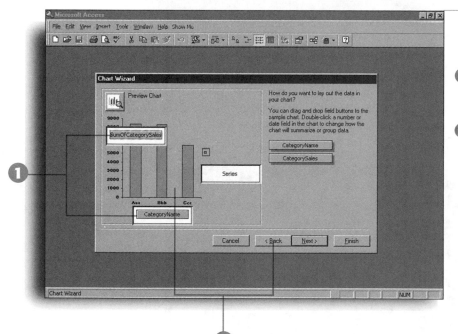

FIGURE 6.14

You can rearrange the default series structure.

1. Click here to bring up the Summarize dialog box and change the calculation options

2. If the style of chart you chose doesn't work for the data (the area for the graph might be blank), click here to select a different style

To change the default calculation, double-click the appropriate field control to open the Summarize dialog box. Then choose a different calculation solution, as shown in Figure 6.15. Once you've made your selection, click **OK** and then **Next** to continue.

FIGURE 6.15

You want to chart the average sale.

6. In the final window, shown in Figure 6.16, you can name the chart and specify whether or not it will contain a legend. If you want to display the report in Print Preview, choose the **Open the report with the chart displayed on it** option. To open the report in Design view, choose **Modify the design of the chart or the report**. Click **Finish** to display the report, shown in Figure 6.17.

FIGURE 6.16

In the wizard's last window, give the report a name.

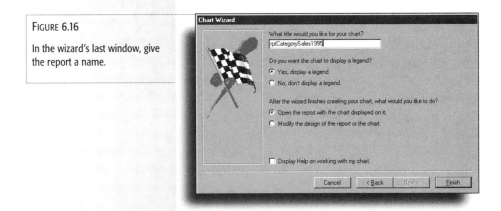

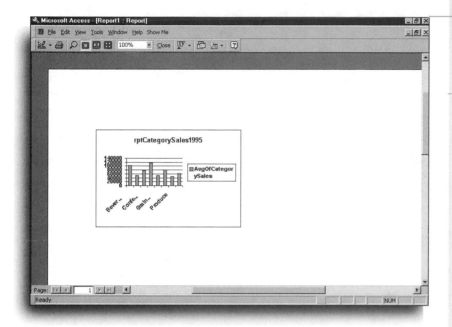

FIGURE 6.17
You used the Chart Wizard to create this chart and display it in a
report.

Adding a Chart to an Existing Report

You don't have to create a new report when displaying a chart.
You can add a chart to an existing report by using the **Insert**
command.

Embedding a chart in an existing report

1. Open the report to which you're adding the chart in Design
view ⬛ ▾.

In this example, you're adding a chart to the Sales by
Category report. This report already contains a chart that
displays all the products by category. You're going to add a
new chart that links to the current record, so first you must
delete the existing chart. To do so, simply select the chart
object to the right of the Sales by Category subreport and
press **Delete**.

2. Select **Chart** from the **Insert** menu.

3. Click inside the report in the area you want to display the
chart, as shown in Figure 6.18. As you can see, a chart was
added at approximately the 3 1/2-inch horizontal mark and
the 1/2-inch vertical mark.

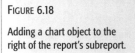
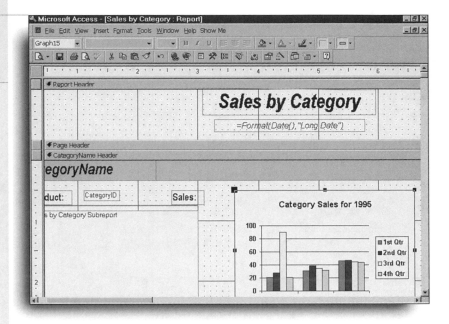

4. Choose the appropriate data object (table or query) and click **Next**. In this case it's the query **Category Sales for 1995**.

5. Repeat steps 3, 4, and 5 from the previous chart exercise.

6. At this point, the wizard will allow you to dynamically link the chart to the current record. In this case the chart and report are linked on the CategoryName field, as shown in Figure 6.19. You can also choose **<No Field>** from the Report Fields and Chart Fields drop-down lists if you don't care to link the chart to the current record. After choosing the appropriate linking fields or choosing **<No Field>**, click **Next**.

7. In the final window, give the report a name, select a legend option, and click **Finish**. As you can see in Figure 6.20, the new chart graphs information for only the current record. You also chose not to display a legend.

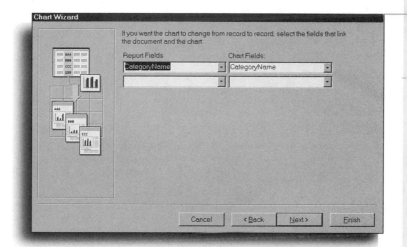

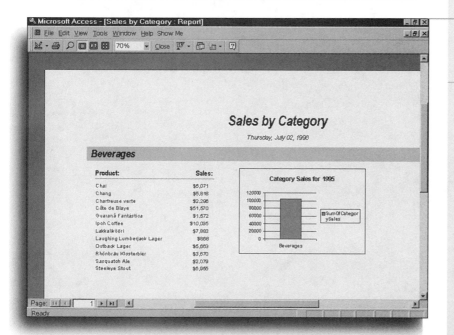

Analyzing and Documenting the Database

Improving performance with the Database Performance Analyzer

Documenting the database

Installation warning

The Database Performance Analyzer Wizard must be installed before you can use it. It is not installed if you chose the **Typical installation** option when you installed Access 97. It is installed under the Advanced Wizards component in the Access 97 Setup application. If you cannot locate the Database Performance Analyzer Wizard, run the Add/Remove Programs applet from the Control Panel folder, select **Microsoft Office**, and click on **Add/Remove**. Then follow the steps to add the Advanced Wizards component.

The Database Performance Analyzer Wizard

Although this book will provide you with all of the information you need to create efficient, usable databases, there's usually room for improvement. The database experts at Microsoft know all the ins and outs of designing well-tuned databases. Some of this knowledge has been provided to you, the Access database developer, in the form of the Database Performance Analyzer Wizard.

Running the Database Performance Analyzer Wizard

1. Using Access 97, open the database whose performance you want to analyze.

2. Click on the **Tools** menu, select the **Analyze** flyout menu, and then click **Performance**. The Performance Analyzer dialog appears (see Figure 7.1).

FIGURE 7.1

The Performance Analyzer's starting dialog, where you select which objects to analyze.

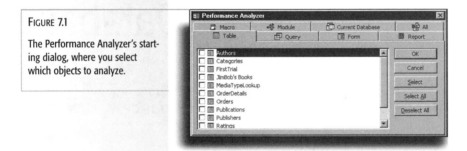

Getting to the analyzer

The wizard will let you choose which objects to analyze, so it doesn't matter what you have selected in the Database window.

3. Using the tabs provided, you can elect to have the wizard analyze specific pieces of the database. In every database, you'll find an entry on the **Current Database** tab for **Relationships** and one for **VBA Project**.

- Select the **Relationships** entry to have the wizard analyze the relationships that exist between the tables in your database.

- Use the **VBA Project** entry to have the wizard analyze the code within the database as a whole.

For most cases, you'll want to click on the **All** tab and click **Select All**. This will cause the wizard to analyze every object in the database. You select an object by clicking its check box.

4. When you've selected the objects that you want to analyze, click the **OK** button to start the process. The wizard will display a dialog that indicates which object is currently being analyzed. When the analysis is complete, you'll see one of two dialogs.

The easiest dialog to deal with is the one that's displayed when there are no recommendations to be made. This indicates that all is well with your database. Click **OK** to acknowledge the message box and return to Access.

The other possible dialog will resemble Figure 7.2. This dialog lists the results compiled by the wizard as it analyzed your database. There are three types of results: **Recommendation**, **Suggestion**, and **Idea**. Click an item in the list.

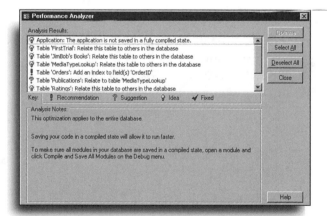

Figure 7.2
The Performance Analyzer's results dialog displays recommendations, suggestions, and ideas.

5. When you select an item, the Analysis Notes frame changes to display information about the selected result. For a recommendation or a suggestion, the wizard can actually perform the optimization for you. To have the wizard perform one of these types of optimizations, select it in the list and click the button. To perform all of the suggestions, click the **Select All** button and then click **Optimize**. After the Wizard performs an optimization for you, its entry in the list will be marked as **Fixed**, as seen in Figure 7.3.

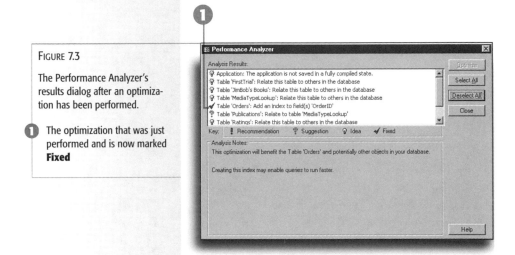

FIGURE 7.3

The Performance Analyzer's results dialog after an optimization has been performed.

① The optimization that was just performed and is now marked **Fixed**

6. Repeat step 5 for each recommendation or suggestion that you would like the wizard to perform for you (you'll have to handle the idea entries yourself). When you've finished, click the **Close** button to end the wizard.

SEE ALSO

➤ *For the details on primary keys and indexes for tables, see page 199.*

➤ *For details on using the Table Analyzer Wizard, see page 124.*

➤ *For more information on working with relationships, see page 221.*

Documenting the Database

Often you'll need to have a hard-copy printout of a database's design. This is not the data that's stored in the database's tables, but rather the design characteristics of the tables, queries, reports, macros, and modules contained within the database.

Using the Documenter Wizard, you can easily create a report that shows the important characteristics of any of the objects within a database. You can even specify which characteristics should be included in the report, making it easy to customize the information provided to various parties. The report that is produced can be printed, saved as a new table within the database, or output to an external file format, such as a Microsoft Excel spreadsheet or an HTML file.

Using the Documenter Wizard

1. Open the database that you want to document. Click the **Tools** menu, select the **Analyze** flyout, and then click **Documenter**. The Documenter dialog appears (see Figure 7.4).

FIGURE 7.4

The Documenter Wizard's main dialog.

2. Using the tabs across the top of the dialog, you can select specific object types to document.

   On the **Current Database** tab, you'll find the same entries for every database: **Properties** and **Relationships**.

   - The **Properties** entry will output the properties of the database file itself (which you can view and modify using the **File, Database Properties** menu).

   - The **Relationships** entry will output the relationships that exist between tables and the properties of those relationships.

   On the **All** tab, you'll find entries for all of the objects in the database, including the two entries from the **Current Database** tab.

   Select each object that you want to document by clicking the check box for its entry. Alternatively, you can use the **Select** and **Select All** buttons to select the item(s) for you.

3. To specify which characteristics of an object are included in the output, click on the object's tab. Or, if you're on the **All** tab, select an object of that type (a table, for example) and then click the **Options** button. A Print *object* Definition dialog appears. The Print Table Definition dialog is shown in Figure 7.5. In this dialog, you can specify exactly which information will be output for that object type. Change the options as appropriate, and click the **OK** button to return to the wizard's main dialog.

FIGURE 7.5

The Print Table Definition dialog, where you specify which characteristics of an object are documented.

Warning

The Print *object* Definition dialog sets documentation properties for *all* objects of the selected type. You cannot set different properties for a specific table, for example. Rather, the properties will apply to all tables.

4. After you've selected all of the objects that you want to document, click the **OK** button. The Object Definition report is created and displayed in a print preview window (see Figure 7.6).

5. Now that you have the Object Definition report, you can print it, save it to a table, or save it to an external file.

6. To print the definition, click the Print toolbar button ⏷. Note that some objects (particularly forms and reports) can produce rather lengthy output, so you may want to scroll through the preview window before clicking the Print button.

7. To save the definition to an external file, click the **Output To** menu item on the **File** menu. A dialog appears where you specify the type of file to create (HTML, Microsoft Excel, MS-DOS Text, or Rich Text Format). Make your choice here and click **OK**. A File Save dialog appears, allowing you to choose the folder and name for the external file.

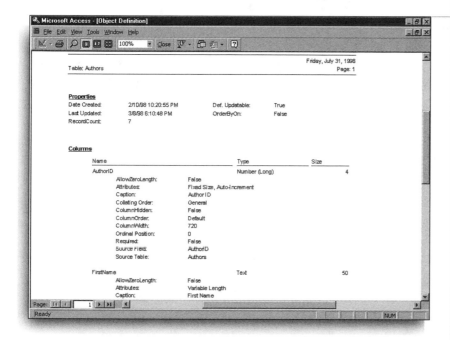

8. To save the definition to a table in the current database, click the **Save As Table** item on the **File** menu. The definition will be saved to a table named Object Definition.

9. When you've finished working with the output, close the Object Definition window.

SEE ALSO

➤ *To learn about creating data reports with a Wizard, see page 92.*

Using Wizards to Manage Data Imports and Input

Import and link data with ease using the import and link wizards

Restrict data entry with input masks

Importing and Linking

At one time or another, you may need to access external data stored in a foreign format (application). The Microsoft Jet database engine includes a number of drivers that you can use to access foreign data. Access can use data from any of the following external data sources:

- Other Access databases (but there's no wizard for this)
- Databases that use the Microsoft Jet Engine, which might include a custom application in Visual Basic or Visual C++
- Excel
- FoxPro, versions 2.0, 2.5, 2.6, 3.0 (read-only)
- dBASE III, dBASE IV, and dBASE V
- Paradox, versions 3.x, 4.x, and 5.x
- Lotus 1-2-3 WK1, WK3, and WKS spreadsheets
- Delimited and fixed-width text files in tabular format
- Tabular data in Hypertext Markup Language (HTML) files
- Open Database Connectivity (ODBC) databases, such as Microsoft SQL Server versions 4.2 and later

What's a Driver?

A *driver* is simply a set of instructions for a specific task. In this case, the drivers help Access copy the external data from its format to the .mdb format. To access external data, the Jet uses one of several drivers, which must be installed first.

Installing data drivers

1. Insert your Office 97 CD. Then, from the **Start** menu, choose **Settings**, **Control Pancl**. Double-click the Add/Remove Programs icon. Select Microsoft Office 97, Professional Edition and click **Add/Remove**.

2. Select **Data Access**, and then click **Change Option**.

3. Select **Database Drivers**, and then click **Change Option**.

4. Select the drivers you want to install, and then click **OK** twice. Then, click **Continue**. If you're searching for additional ODBC drivers, use the ODBC Manager. To do so, double-click **32bit ODBC** in the Windows Control Panel.

To uninstall a driver, return to Dataacc.exe in the ValuPack folder and rerun it. The next time you run this application, it will open a maintenance window similar to the Add/Remove Program window. You simply choose one of the options—**Add/Remove**, **Reinstall**, or **Remove All**, and proceed. The **Add/Remove** option will enable you to add or delete a driver, and **Remove All** will remove them all.

There are three ways to access external data:

- Link your application to the external table
- Open the external table from your application
- Import the external table into your application

Linked tables are just like any other table in your database—you can base queries, forms, and reports on these tables. Just remember, you must have permission to use the foreign application, and you must know any required passwords. However, Access will use a different icon to distinguish between a linked table and your native table. This means the table is available until you delete it, which you can easily do by deleting the icon in the Database window.

Using the Import Spreadsheet Wizard

Importing a spreadsheet is fairly easy because the data is already in tabular style—you don't have to worry about delimiters. A *delimiter* is a character that separates fields of data. For instance, tab or comma characters are often used as delimiters. When Access imports the data, it knows where one field starts and the next begins by noting where the delimiters are.

Finding the Lotus driver

The Paradox and Microsoft Exchange/Outlook drivers aren't installed with Access, but you can find them in the ValuPack. Insert your Office 97 CD and double-click the ValuPack folder after your system displays the CD's contents. Next, double-click the Dataacc folder. At this point, double-click the Dataacc.exe file and then click **Yes** if you want to install the Microsoft Data Access Pack. Choosing **No** will clear the message without installing the application. If you choose **Yes**, the application will run a short installation wizard. Simply follow instructions as you would any wizard. The Lotus driver is in the Data Access Drivers option.

Using the ValuPack

The ValuPack contains all kinds of helpful files besides the drivers. You'll find additional software, more Help files, books, and more. If you don't have the ValuPack, you can visit Microsoft's Web site at www.microsoft.com, and then click the Free Stuff link.

Our example

You'll be working with the Microsoft Excel spreadsheet named Common.xls that comes with Office 97. You'll find this file in the Microsoft Office\Office\Library folder. You can use an Excel or a Lotus 1-2-3 spreadsheet.

Importing selections of data

Access will import an entire spreadsheet or areas known as named ranges. A *named range* in a spreadsheet is a section of the spreadsheet that you've given a specific name to. The spreadsheet recognizes this named range and enables you to work with it in specific ways. You can use a named range to import partial data from a spreadsheet, instead of the entire worksheet. Simply open the spreadsheet in its native application, apply the name to the range of your data that you want to import, and then save and close the spreadsheet. When you import the data, Access enables you to specify whether you're importing the entire spreadsheet or a named range.

Importing a spreadsheet

1. From the Access **File** menu, choose **Get External Data**, and then choose **Import**. Access will open the Import dialog box, which is very similar to the Open dialog box. Navigate through your system's folders until you locate the spreadsheet file that contains the data you want to import. Be sure to choose the correct application from the **Files of Type** drop-down list. Highlight the file and click **Import**, or double-click the file to launch the Import Spreadsheet Wizard.

2. This wizard's first window asks you to choose the worksheet or named range you want to import. Notice that Common.xls has two worksheets and when you select a worksheet in the control to the right of the two selection options, the wizard updates the sample data at the bottom of the wizard window. I selected **Show Worksheets**, and then chose the Employee Info worksheet, as shown in Figure 8.1. After making the appropriate selections, click **Next** to continue.

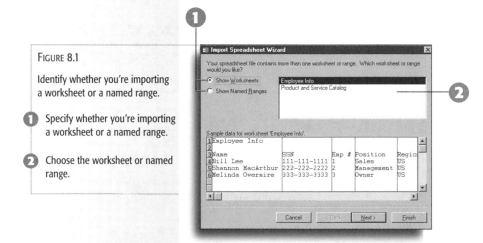

FIGURE 8.1

Identify whether you're importing a worksheet or a named range.

1 Specify whether you're importing a worksheet or a named range.

2 Choose the worksheet or named range.

3. If you want Access to use the worksheet's column headings as field names, click the **First Row Contains Column Headings** option. If you don't, select nothing and click **Next**. When you select the option, Access displays the

message shown in Figure 8.2. This message warns you that
Access can't use some of the headings so the wizard will
name these fields. You'll want to check the field names later
and modify them if necessary. Click **Next** to continue.

FIGURE 8.2

The wizard can't use all the column headings as field names.

4. Now the wizard asks you to decide where you're storing the
data you import from the spreadsheet. You can store it in a
new table or an existing table. When you choose the **In a
New Table** option, the wizard will create a new table for
the data. If you select the **In an Existing Table** option, you
need to identify the table from the list of tables in that control's drop-down list. You're saving the data to a new table,
as shown in Figure 8.3. Once you've made your choices,
click **Next**.

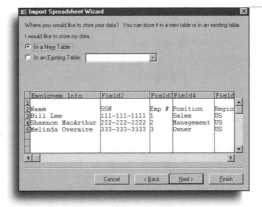

FIGURE 8.3

Specify the table for storing the
imported data

5. This next window will focus on each field in the worksheet
or named range, one at a time. You can specify a new field
name, change the data type (sometimes), create an index,
and even exclude a field from the import process. To change
a particular field, click anywhere within that field, make your

change(s), and select the next field. You're not going to make any changes to the wizard settings, shown in Figure 8.4. You can also see where the wizard created some of the field names—several of them in fact. These fields are named Field*x*, where x represents the field order. Click **Next** to continue.

FIGURE 8.4

The wizard gives you the opportunity to change its default settings.

1 Change wizard-generated column names for clarity.

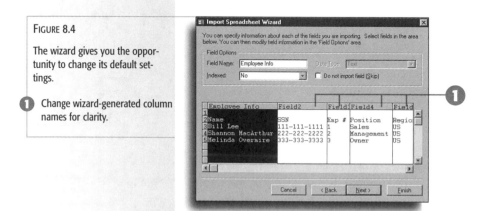

6. At this point, the wizard will help you choose a primary key field for the new table. The default option, **Let Access Add Primary Key**, has added the ID field shown in Figure 8.5. That's because the table didn't have a good candidate for a primary key field. You can select your own by choosing the **Choose My Own Primary Key** option. When you do, you'll need to select a field from that option's drop-down list. You can also select the **No Primary Key** option if you don't want to apply a primary key. Click **Next** when you're ready to continue.

7. This final window enables you to change the wizard's default table now—you're retaining the default. In addition, you can choose to run the Table Analyzer or display Help information after the wizard is finished importing the data. You won't select either of these options. Click **Finish** when you're ready to import the spreadsheet data. Access will notify you when it's finished. Simply click **OK** to clear the message.

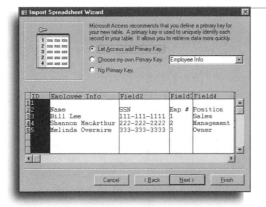

FIGURE 8.5
You're allowing Access to select
the table's primary key.

Figure 8.6 shows the new table. The first row in the Excel worksheet contains only one column heading string—Employee Info.
The wizard didn't import this row because you said to use its
contents as field names. The second row in the worksheet is
blank. The third contains the real column headings, which the
wizard imported as data—you can see them in the new table's
second row. The real data starts at row 3.

ID	Employee Info	Field2	Field3	Field4	Field5	Field6	Field7
1							
2	Name	SSN	Emp #	Position	Region	Department	Manager
3	Bill Lee	111-111-1111	1	Sales	US	Sales	Shannon MacAr
4	Shannon MacA	222-222-2222	2	Management	US	Management	Melinda Overmi
5	Melinda Overmi	333-333-3333	3	Owner	US	Management	
*	(AutoNumber)						

FIGURE 8.6
The table shows the wizard's
choice for column names and primary key.

SEE ALSO

➤ *Microsoft provides other means by which you can integrate Access with other members of
Office, such as Excel. See page 164 or page 672 for examples of using Office Links for
other types of integration examples.*

Linking Spreadsheets

You don't have to import the data. In fact, in certain situations
linking to the spreadsheet is preferable. For instance, you may
need to work with this most recent data. You should know that

working with a linked object is generally slower than working with a native table. Linking a table is considerably quicker and easier than importing that object's data.

Linking spreadsheets

1. Choose **Get External Data** from the **File** menu, and then select **Link Tables**.

2. The Link dialog box is basically the same as the Import dialog box. Locate the spreadsheet you want to link and then double-click it or select it and click **Link**.

3. Identify the worksheet or named range you want to import and click **Next**.

4. Now, decide whether to use the column headings as field names and click **Next** or **Finish**. If you click **Next**, you can change the linked table's default name. If you click **Finish**, the wizard will create the link using the default name. Click the **Tables** tab in the Database window. As you can see, a linked table has a different icon, usually representative of its native application, such as Excel.

Using the Import Text Wizard

There's not much difference between importing spreadsheet data and text. The fact is, the import and linking wizards make the task extremely easy. This doesn't mean you won't run into problems. It just means that the process for importing and linking data is basically the same using a wizard, regardless of the data's format.

There are two types of text files: delimited and fixed-width. A *delimited* file uses a defined character to separate fields of data. The fields in our sample text file are all separated with a tab character. You can use almost any character, but the tab, comma, semicolon, and space are the established delimiters. In a *fixed-width* file, the fields are aligned in columns, and space characters—not tabs—are used to arrange the data.

Before you attempt to import a text file, make sure the fields contain similar data and that the delimiters are a consistent number. The wizard will interpret each delimiter as a new field. If your first row has five tabs, that row will have five fields. If the second one has an additional tab somewhere, you'll end up with six fields and you'll have to fix that manually once you've imported. If your original text file is delimited correctly, you won't have this problem.

Importing a text file

1. From the **File** menu, choose **Get External Data**, and select **Import** from the resulting shortcut menu.

2. Navigate your system's structure until you locate the file you're importing. Remember to select the appropriate file type in the **Files of Type** control. I selected .txt, as you can see in Figure 8.7. When you've found your file, select it and click **Import**, or double-click the filename to import it.

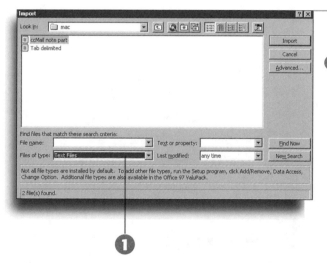

FIGURE 8.7

You will be importing a .txt file.

1 Choose the file type you're importing.

3. Access will launch the Import Text Wizard. The first window, shown in Figure 8.8, will attempt to identify the type of text file—delimited or fixed-width. You can change the wizard's selection if you like, although I didn't. The lower window gives you a reasonable view of the data in the text file. After you've made the appropriate choices for your text file, click **Next** to continue.

FIGURE 8.8

The Import Text Wizard shows a portion of the file you're importing.

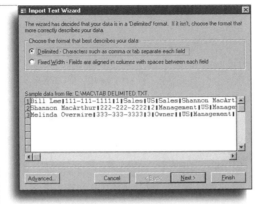

4. This next window prompts you to identify the delimiting character—the wizard attempts a guess, but you can change it. In our case, the wizard has correctly chosen the **Tab** option. The **First Row Contains Field Names** option isn't selected, which is correct because the first row in my text file is data, not field names. You can change this option if your file does contain field names. The **Text Qualifier** option allows the wizard to distinguish between text files and other types of data. You'll need to know ahead of time what character the text file is using, if any. I'm not using a qualifier in the example, as the wizard has shown in Figure 8.9. The control in the bottom of the wizard window shows the wizard's attempt to separate data into fields. The wizard has done a great job with this example. Click **Next** when you're ready to continue.

FIGURE 8.9

The wizard attempts to separate data into fields.

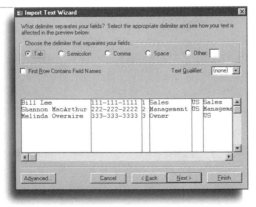

5. At this point, you need to choose between importing the data into a new table or an existing table. The wizard chooses the **In a New Table** option by default. I won't change the selection. However, if you select **In an Existing Table**, you must also choose which table you want from that control's drop-down list. When you're ready to continue, click **Next**.

6. The next window gives you the opportunity to give each field a meaningful field name, assign a specific data type, and even exclude the field from the import process. I renamed my fields accordingly. Unfortunately, I noticed while changing field names that the third record in the newly named Residency field is out of sequence, as shown in Figure 8.10. Remember what I said earlier about making sure each record has the same number of delimiting characters. This is the result of having an extra tab character in that text file's third row. Fortunately, it will be easy to fix later. If you had a large file and you found a number of these discrepancies, it would be easier to return to the text file, fix it, and then start the import process over. Click **Next** when you're ready to continue.

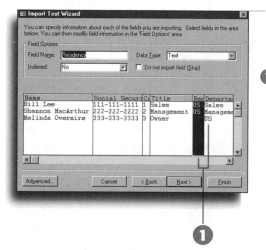

FIGURE 8.10

While naming the fields, I found an error.

① The third row of the text file contained an extra Tab character.

7. At this point, the wizard wants you to assign a primary key field. Because the data doesn't have a natural candidate, the wizard suggests adding the ID field. You can accept the wizard's choice, create your own primary key, or not add a primary key at this time. I'm accepting the wizard's additional ID field as the primary key field. After you make your choice, click **Next** to continue.

8. In the final window, the wizard gives the new table a name. You can retain this name or enter your own. In addition, you can run the Analyze Table Wizard on the new table, and you can display Help. I'm going to run the Analyze Table Wizard to make sure I have a normalized table. To that end, I selected that I would like a wizard to analyze the table after importing the data option, and then clicked **Finish**. The Import Wizard will let you know when it's finished importing the data. Click **OK** to clear the message. Because you clicked the analyzing wizard option, the next message asks if you're ready to proceed with that process. Click **Yes** to continue, or **No** if you don't want to analyze the table. You're going to continue this process in the next section.

SEE ALSO

➤ *See page 22 for tips on naming fields according to an established convention.*

➤ *See page 16 or page 190 for help in determining the Primary key.*

Running the Analyze Table Wizard

Whether you're importing foreign data or creating your own tables from scratch, the Analyze Table Wizard can help you normalize those tables. Specifically, this wizard will split your data into two tables if it encounters duplicate data. Analyzing your tables will ensure that your tables are in optimum condition: Your application will update and retrieve data faster.

Running the Analyze Table Wizard

1. To launch the Analyze Table Wizard, select the table you want to analyze in the Database window and click the Analyze button ⊞ ▾ on the Database toolbar. I selected the tab delimited table (the text file you imported during the last session).

2. The first window shown in Figure 8.11 displays examples
that may help you make decisions as you run through the
wizard. The first example points out the duplicate data in
the sample table. The second example shows you how easy it
is to make mistakes in duplicate data. After you've reviewed
both sample options, click **Next** to continue.

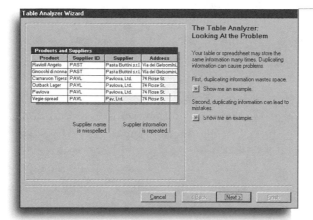

FIGURE 8.11

First the wizard shows you examples of duplicate data and easy-to-make errors.

3. Next, the wizard shows you examples of how it can split
non-normalized tables to avoid duplicate data, as shown in
Figure 8.12. The first sample option explains how splitting
the data can help you avoid unnecessary data entry. The second example then explains how the wizard links the two
resulting tables. When you're ready, click **Next** to continue.

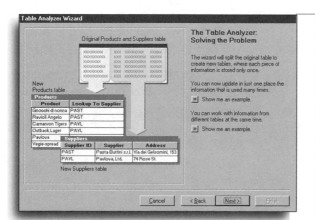

FIGURE 8.12

The wizard continues by splitting a non-normalized table into two tables.

4. Now the wizard wants you to select the table you want to split. The wizard selected tab delimited because you selected that table before you started. You can also deselect the **Show Introductory Pages?** option if you don't want Access to display these windows the next time you run the wizard. Select an appropriate table and click **Next**.

5. The wizard will give you two options—you can decide how to split the tables or you can let the wizard decide. For this example, click **Yes**. You will still have the final say over the arrangement, so don't worry about choosing this option. After you've decided and selected the appropriate option, click **Next**.

6. At this point, the wizard doesn't have any suggestions for splitting the table and displays the message shown in Figure 8.13. However, you can use the wizard to split the table yourself, which is what you're going to do, so click **OK** and continue. If you want to discontinue the wizard, click **OK**, and then click the **Cancel** button in the wizard window.

FIGURE **8.13**

The wizard doesn't want to split the table.

7. The next window, shown in Figure 8.14, displays just one list of fields. If the wizard had decided to split the table, it would have displayed its attempt. But you already know the wizard didn't attempt to split the table. To split data from the original table and create a new one, select the fields you want to remove from the original table and simply drag them out of the **Field** list box. Doing so will prompt the wizard to create a second table consisting of the selected fields, as shown in Figure 8.15. You dragged the Category and Title fields from the **Field** list box and dropped them outside the box (but still within the wizard's window).

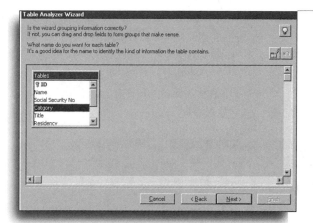

FIGURE 8.14

In this window you can drag fields from the original table's list box to create a new table.

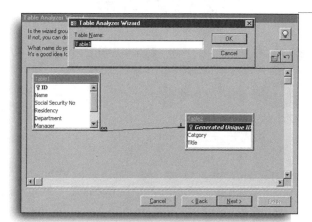

FIGURE 8.15

The wizard creates the new table with the fields you select and lets you name the table.

8. At this point, the wizard asks you to name the first table. The wizard won't modify your original table. Instead, it creates two entirely new tables—that's why you need to provide two new table names. In the text box shown in Figure 8.15, you entered a name for the first table—tblEmployees. Then, you clicked the Rename Table button (in the upper-right corner of the window) and the wizard displayed the same text box. This time, the wizard lets us rename the second table—the one you created. You named this table tblCategory. The results are shown in Figure 8.16.

Furthermore, the wizard has created two new fields and created a relationship between the two tables on this field. In tblEmployees the field is named Lookup to tblCategory; in tblCategory the field is named Generated Unique ID.

When you've split your table and you're ready to continue, click **Next**.

FIGURE 8.16

Split the original table into two and name them `tblEmployees` and `tblCategory`.

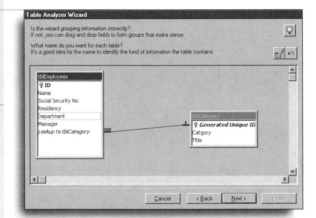

Why split this table?

At this point, you may be wondering why we did this. Typically, the duplicated data is in the same field. For instance, you might repeat the same address for the same supplier over and over again. However, in this table, you seem to be repeating job functions—the contents of the Title and Department fields. This may not be how the data started out, but at this point, that's how you're interpreting it. So, you're creating a table that generates a unique identification value for each category and title. Whether these two fields belong together is debatable, but it really isn't the issue. Rather, I just want you to see how easy it is to split one table into two and have the wizard automatically create a primary key field and link the two tables.

9. This next window enables you to set the primary key fields the way you want them. If you don't like the wizard's choices, simply change them. To do so, highlight a field and click the Set Unique Key button . The wizard will delete the existing primary key and assign the primary key to the highlighted field. If you want the wizard to generate unique identification values for one of the tables, you can do that too by selecting the table and clicking the Add Generated Unique Key button.

In our example, tblCategory already has a Generated Unique ID field—the wizard added it in the previous step. The tblEmployees table also has an ID field. So, you're not going to add a new field or change the primary key for either field. But you can if you need to. If you want to delete an action, simply click the Undo button. When you're ready to continue, click **Next**.

10. At this point the wizard warns you that the fields in tblCategory don't appear to be related, as shown in Figure 8.17. If you receive a warning like this, you should review your table, but don't assume the wizard is correct. If you know the fields are related, proceed by clicking **Yes**. If you decide not to split the table, click **No**. I clicked **Yes**.

FIGURE 8.17

Our tables don't appear to be related to the wizard.

11. The final window considers the fact that you may already have objects bound to the original table. If this is the case, you can still work with them—the query can create a query that will make this possible and then bind the appropriate objects to the new query. I chose **No, Don't Create the Query Option** because I'm working with data that was just imported. You know there are no bound objects to the tab delimited table (the original table). However, if you choose **Yes, Create the Query Option**, the wizard will display an explanation window and then open the Select query in Datasheet view. The wizard names the query based on the original table. In this case, the wizard would have named the query Tab delimited. Click **Finish** when you're ready to continue.

12. You can see the result of the wizard in the Database window, shown in Figure 8.18. The wizard named the original table Tab delimited_OLD and added two new tables— tblEmployees and tblCategory.

If you open the two new tables, you can see that tblEmployees no longer contains the Category and Title fields. In addition, this field has a lookup field—Lookup to tblCategory. From this field, you can choose the appropriate category for the record. Furthermore, the tblCategory field now contains the Category and Title field and an AutoNumber field. Granted, this may not be the structure you want to keep—but using the Analyze Table Wizard is a good place to start.

FIGURE 8.18

You have two new tables now.

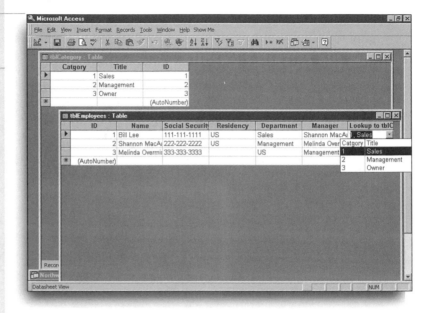

SEE ALSO

➤ *The purpose of the Table Analyzer Wizard is to help ensure you have good table design. See pages 12, 13, and 190 for the ground rules and hints for good design.*

Linking Text Files

In the first part of this chapter you created a link from Northwind to an Excel spreadsheet. You can do the same thing with the tab delimited text file.

Linking a delimited text file

1. From the **File** menu, choose **Get External Data** and then choose **Link Tables** from the resulting shortcut menu.

2. In the Link dialog box, locate the text file you're linking to, select it, and then click **Link**. Or, double-click the filename. Be sure to change the **Files of Type** option to .txt so Access can find your file.

Text files and spreadsheets are tables?

Because Access stores its data in tables, it considers all linked objects as tables. Furthermore, Access works with these objects as though they were tables.

3. The Link Wizard will repeat steps 3, 4, and 5 from our earlier example, Importing a Text File. To repeat, you'll specify
whether you're linking to a delimited or a fixed-width field.
If you choose delimited, you'll identify the type of delimiter,
and then modify the field names or omit a field. When you
finish, the wizard will create the link. Access displays a different icon next to the linked table, as shown in Figure 8.19.
This icon indicates that the linked object is a text file.

FIGURE 8.19

The wizard doesn't want to split
our table.

1 This linked table is an Excel
spreadsheet

2 This linked table is a text file

Importing a Fixed-Width Text File

Until now, you've worked exclusively with Tab-delimited fields.
However, you can also import fixed-width text files. The process
is very similar after you define the fields. Linking a fixed-width
text file is the same as linking a delimited text file.

Importing a fixed-width text file

1. From the **File** menu, choose **Get External Data**, and then
select the **Import** option.

2. This time the Import Wizard chooses the fixed width option
as shown in Figure 8.20. That's because space characters,
and not a delimiting character, separate the data. Click **Next**
to continue.

3. The second window, shown in Figure 8.21, enables you to
redraw the fields. Specifically, the wizard displays a ruler and
adjustable break lines between each field. Simply click the
break line and move it to the left or right to adjust the field
size. To add a new break line, simply click at the desired
position; to delete a delete link, double-click it.

Our example

I'm working with the data
from the Common.xls spreadsheet. Simply copy it to a
Word file and enter spaces
between the fields instead of
tabs as you did to create the
tab-delimited sample file. You
can use any fixed-width text
file.

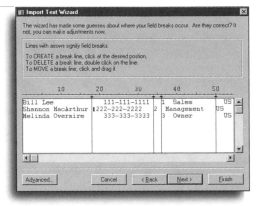

As you can see, our fields aren't exactly straight. The key to successfully importing a fixed-width file is making sure each field contains the same number of spaces. If you run into this problem when importing, you can return to the text file and try to fix it—which can be difficult. Or, you can import the data as is, and then use the Trim() function in a query to delete those extra spaces.

FIGURE 8.21

You can adjust the field sizes.

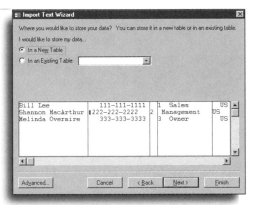

If you click the **Advanced** button, the wizard displays the dialog box shown in Figure 8.22. You've already discussed the File Format options. The **File Origin** option enables you to specify a DOS or OS file. The **Dates, Times, and Numbers** option enables you to specify the different delimiters for each data type. The **Field Information** option enables you to actually change the field's data type, size, and index. You can even omit the field from the import if you like. The **Sa̲ve As** option enables you to save the import setup so you can use it again. This is helpful when you import the same file a lot. Finally, the **Specs** option simply recalls a specific import specification—the settings you save. The **Advanced** settings are available with every window. Click **OK** to return to the previous window and then click **N̲ext** when you're ready to continue.

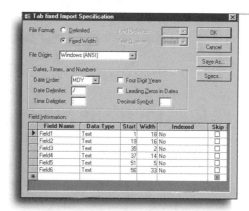

FIGURE 8.22
Advanced features are available.

4. The next three windows are similar to the ones you've seen in each exercise. First, specify whether you're saving the imported data to a new table or an existing table.

5. In the following window, modify the wizard's default settings. Specifically, you can modify the field name and data type, set an index, or even omit the field from the import process.

6. Next, you'll set a primary key. You'll choose between the wizard's choice, choosing your own, or not adding a primary key field.

7. In the final window, name the new table and click **Finish**. The resulting table, shown in Figure 8.23, has a few problems, but nothing you can't easily fix. As you can see, the category numbers for the first and third fields are in the next field. Simply enter the appropriate values where they belong and delete the inappropriate ones. The last field contains the data for the last two fields. You can add a field and copy and paste the data from Field6 to the new field. However, in a larger field this would be very time-consuming. It's easier to work with a consistent text file.

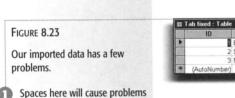

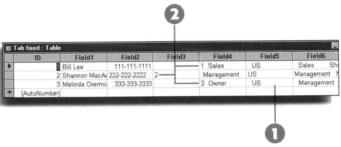

FIGURE 8.23

Our imported data has a few problems.

1 Spaces here will cause problems in querying for the value in this field

2 Digit values are misplaced and leave fields empty

Using the Input Data Mask Wizard

Not all wizards are about creating objects. The Input Mask Wizard helps ensure the integrity of the data you enter by allowing only certain entries. An *input mask* is simply a pattern that you define and Access applies to limit a field's entry, and the Input Mask Wizard will help you create this pattern. The mask character codes determine which characters you can enter and how many.

To create a mask, you can you enter mask characters as a field's Input Mask property or you can choose from one of the wizard's masks—in the beginning, it might be easier to start with the wizard. (You can also enter a mask for a control at the form level.)

Using the Input Mask Wizard to create an input mask

1. Open the table you want to change in Design view, and select the field (for example, the Orders table and the ShippedDate field).

2. Next, select the Input Mask property in the **Field Properties** section and click the Builder button to launch the Input Mask Wizard.

3. Select the mask you want to apply to the active field in the Input Mask Wizard's first wizard, as shown in Figure 8.24. I

chose Short Date. These are not the only masks available—
the wizard is displaying on those masks that are appropriate
for a Date/Time field. Besides these formats, the wizard
offers a mask for zip codes, social security numbers, phone
numbers, phone extensions, and passwords. The wizard only
works with Text and Date/Time fields.

You can try the pre-defined mask on data before you go any
further by typing an entry into the Try It control at the bottom of the window. You can determine at that point whether
the selected mask gives you the limitations you require. If it
does, simply click **Next** to continue to the next window. If it
doesn't, select another mask and try it.

The **Edit List** button will display the dialog box shown in
Figure 8.25. As you can see, this box displays the selected
mask's properties. You can change one or more if you like to
create a custom mask. However, all of the pre-defined masks
are available by simply clicking the **Next** button on the
Customize Input Mask Wizard dialog box's navigational
toolbar. If you click the New button, the wizard will display
a blank form. At that point, you can create a custom mask
that the wizard will apply and remember. You're not going
to alter any of the Short Date mask's properties; nor will you
add a custom mask. To return to the wizard's first window,
click **Close**.

To continue with the process, click the **Next** button. If you
click **Finish** at this point, Access will assign the mask and
close the wizard.

4. The next window, shown in Figure 8.26, enables you to
   modify the mask and specify the placeholder character. The
   default is the underscore character. Choose the placeholder
   you want the user to see in the field. After you have modified the mask, you can use the Try It control to see the
   result. You don't have to change a thing though, and you
   didn't. Click **Next** when you're ready to continue. Then,
   click **Finish** in the last window. The wizard will enter the
   mask you chose, as shown in Figure 8.27.

FIGURE 8.24

You chose a pre-defined mask from the Input Mask Wizard.

 ❶ Use the Input mask wizard builder ![icon], which appears at the right edge of the cell

❷ Select the type of input mask you want

❸ Use the **Try It:** box

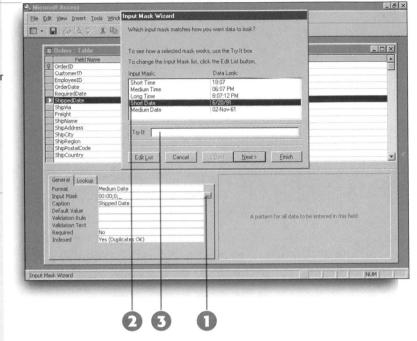

❷ ❸ ❶

FIGURE 8.25

The Input Mask Wizard lets you customize the mask options.

FIGURE 8.26

You can assign a placeholder in this wizard window.

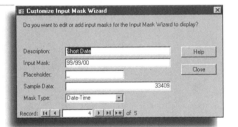

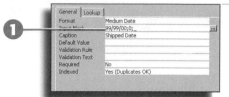

6. Click the View button ⊞ ▾ on the Form Design toolbar, go to the first blank, or New Record ▶✳, and then click the field you modified. I chose Shipped Date. Access displays the mask— _/_/_ —for us. This is a visual guideline to help you enter the appropriate characters.

If you enter an incorrect entry, such as "rabbit," Access just beeps at you because a text string isn't appropriate for a Date/Time field. However, in Figure 8.28, you entered a value— 06898—which represents June 8, 1998. However, the error message tells you that your entry doesn't conform to the field's input mask. You can determine by looking at the result of your attempt to enter this value that something is missing from the month component, because Access doesn't separate the values properly—06/8/98—as you might have expected.

Differences in input and display

It's perfectly legal to enter data in one format and then display it in another—it doesn't create a conflict. In fact, it's a good arrangement because you can define an input mask that limits the data while assigning a completely different format to display the data.

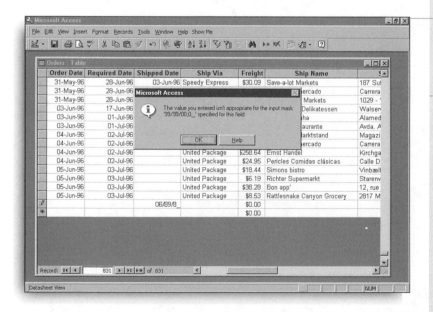

FIGURE 8.28

You tried to enter an invalid date string, but the input mask won't accept it.

To clear the error message, click **OK**. Then, press Esc to delete your entry, and try entering "060898." This time, Access accepts the entry, and displays the entry in Medium Date Format: **06-Jun-98**.

SEE ALSO

➤ *For a complete list of mask codes, turn to page 385.*

➤ *For a list of mask characters and a complete explanation of placeholders, go to page 385.*

➤ *For more information about input masks, see page 385.*

Using Control Wizards and Setting Control Properties

Offer choices with list and combo boxes

Complete tasks with the click of a button

Use option groups to limit choices

About the Control Wizards

The Form and Report Wizards do a good job of producing useable forms and reports. However, you may find that a wizard's final product often needs a tweak or two before you're able to use it. You may change the formatting or even give the form a unique task. Often, you may need to add controls that the wizard just can't anticipate. Fortunately, Access includes several wizards for adding controls to your forms and reports.

The list box and combo box examples

For the most part, the list box and combo box properties are the same. Instead of repeating ourselves in the combo box section, the examples are varied in order to discuss several display possibilities. Just remember that the example is appropriate for a list box or a combo box, unless otherwise noted.

About bound controls

A *bound control* is a control that is attached to a data source–specifically a field. That field can be in a table or a query. For instance, if you bind a list box to a table or query, that list box will display that field's contents as its items (or list).

You can read more about bound and unbound controls beginning in Chapter 19, "Adding Controls to Forms and Reports."

The List Box Control

The Form and Report Wizards' control of choice is the text box, so you're probably very familiar with one. Although they're extremely functional, they're not always adequate. For instance, to display a list of items you might use a list box control. Why would you want to display a list of items? First, it makes things simpler and easier for the user. Instead of remembering all the possible responses and then typing one, the user simply selects the appropriate choice in the list box. From a development standpoint, offering a list of items reduces the chances for errors—the user can't enter an inappropriate response. (The user can, however, choose the wrong item from the list—nothing is totally foolproof.) A list also eliminates typos.

Most list boxes consist of a simple column of choices, as shown in Figure 9.1. Technically, these columns can be just one of several—up to and including an entire record (if you're working with a bound list box). You just might not see the rest of the data.

SEE ALSO

➤ *For more information on the list box control, see page 205.*

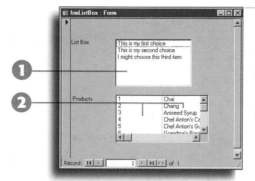

Using the List Box Wizard

After you've decided to add a list box to your form or report, you can create the control yourself or use the List Box Wizard. The wizard walks you through the process of defining an unbound or bound control's list of choices.

Using the List Box Wizard to create an unbound list box

1. Click **Forms** and then **New** in the Database window. (I'm using a form in this example, but you can use a report.) Then, double-click **Design View** in the New Forms dialog box.

2. If Access doesn't open the Toolbox, click the Toolbox button 🛠 on the Form (or Report) Design toolbar.

3. To turn on the Control Wizards, click the Control Wizards icon 🪄 on the Toolbox. At this point, you can click any control that has a wizard—list box, combo box, command button, and option group—to launch that respective wizard.

4. Now, click the List Box tool 🔲 on the Toolbox and then click inside the blank form. In response, Access will launch the wizard and display the first window, shown in Figure 9.2.

5. At this point, you must choose between creating your own list of items or tying your list to the data in a table or query.

   If you're creating your own list, choose **I Will Type in the Values That I Want**.

Report controls

I mentioned that you can place most controls on a report. However, just because you can, doesn't mean you'll want to. For instance, how would you use a list box in a report? That's why I've concentrated on placing controls in forms instead of reports. I don't want to discourage you from experimenting, but I think the average user will find little use for report controls.

FIGURE 9.2

You can create your own list or use the data from a table or query.

If you're relying on a table or query, choose the default setting, **I Want the List Box to Look Up the Values in a Table or Query**.

(I chose the **I Will Type in the Values That I Want** option for this example.) Click **Next** to continue.

6. The next window prompts you for the list box values (or items) as shown in Figure 9.3.

This is where you'll do most of your work. First, you can alter the default number of columns, 1, by simply changing the value in the **Number of Columns** text box to the number of columns you want to display in the list box.

Then, enter the appropriate values in the provided columns.

Next, enter one item in each column cell, in the order you want the control to display them.

Don't press Enter after typing each item; that will take you to the next wizard window. Instead, type the item, and then press Tab. When you've finished, click **Next** to continue.

7. The final window prompts you for a descriptive label. I entered the label "Animals." If you need more help, you can select the **Display Help on Customizing the List Box** option. Click **Finish** to display the completed list box in Design view. After adding your text, you may need to increase the width of the label in order to display the complete string. Do so now if this is the case.

Sizing columns to see text

If a column isn't wide enough to completely display all the items, drag out the column's right edge until the column is wide enough. Or, you can double-click the column's heading cell to apply the Best Fit property.

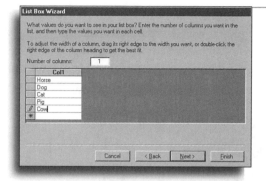

FIGURE 9.3
You entered five values in your list box.

8. In Design view, you may need to increase the size of the label control.

9. To see the list box shown in Figure 9.4, click the View button  on the Form Design toolbar.

As you can see, the list box offers five choices: Horse, Dog, Cat, Pig, and Cow. To choose one, simply select it.

FIGURE 9.4
This list box displays all the options for the user to select. You can stretch the size of the text area in Design view.

SEE ALSO
➤ *For more details on the Toolbox, see page 314.*
➤ *If you need instructions for resizing the label control in this example, go to page 324.*
➤ *If you'd like to know how to use a list box's selected value, go to page 205.*

Modifying the Wizard's Results

You don't have to use a wizard to create this list box (or any other control); you can set the appropriate properties yourself. Figure 9.5 shows the list box from the previous example and its property sheet. The Row Source Type property is set to Value

List, which is a list you provide by entering each item, as you did earlier. To create this list without the wizard, you'd simply choose **Value List** from the **Row Source Type** drop-down list. Then, you'd enter the appropriate values in the Row Source property, separating each with a semicolon.

FIGURE 9.5

This property sheet shows the list box properties you must modify to display a list of values.

Modifying a list box

1. Click **Forms** and then **New** in the Database window. (I'm using a form in this example, but you can use a report.) Then double-click **Design View** in the New Forms dialog box.

2. If Access doesn't open the Toolbox, click the Toolbox button on the Form (or Report) Design toolbar.

3. Deselect the Control Wizard tool on the Toolbox if it's selected.

4. Click the List Box tool on the Toolbox and then click inside the blank form.

5. Now, click the Properties tool on the Form Design toolbar.

6. Select the **Row Source Type** property and choose **Value List** from that field's drop-down list.

7. Next, select the **Row Source** property and enter the string `"Horse;Dog;Cat;Pig;Cow"`. Your property sheet should resemble the one shown in Figure 9.5, although the control's name may be different.

8. Click the View button ⊞▾ to see the results. This list box will behave just the same as the one you created earlier with the wizard.

Creating a Multiple-Column List Box

Now, let's suppose you want to display a set of items, but you don't want to store the displayed items. Instead, you want to store the corresponding value in another field. Or, perhaps you want to return a corresponding value in some other control. Either situation is easily handled by binding your list box to more than one column—use a multiple-column list box.

Creating a multiple-column bound list box using the List Box Wizard

1. Open a blank form, or open the form from the last example in Design view.

2. Open the Toolbox 🛠 if necessary and make sure the Control Wizards 🪄 tool is selected.

3. Click the List Box tool ⊞ on the Toolbox and then click inside the form.

4. Access will launch the List Box Wizard and display the first window. This time, select the **I Want the List Box to Look Up the Values in a Table or Query** option because you're creating a bound list box. Then click **Next** to continue.

5. In the next window, you'll need to choose between a table or query by selecting an option from the **View** section at the bottom of the window shown in Figure 9.6.

The default option is **Tables** and the wizard displays the tables in your application in the list box above.

If you select **Queries**, Access will update the list box with all the queries in your application.

As you might expect, the **Both** option will display all the tables and queries. You're going to display a column from

> **The example for this task**
>
> You'll be working with the Northwinds Categories table throughout this example. However, you can bind a list box to most any table or query.

the Categories table. After making the appropriate selections, click **Next** to continue.

6. At this point, the wizard displays the bound table or query's fields. Simply move the field that contains the values you want to display to the **Selected Fields** list box, as shown in Figure 9.7. As you can see, you've chosen to display the values from both fields in this list box. After you've made your selections, click **Next** to continue.

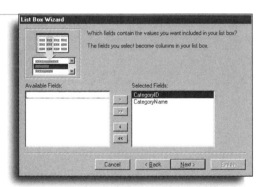

Displaying fields in the list box

The default displays only one field—CategoryName—because it's a Text field. If both fields had contained text values, the wizard would've displayed the first field. (A Text field is more likely to display descriptive choices than a Number or AutoNumber field.)

7. Now the wizard gives you the opportunity to modify the default control's display settings. If you retain the defaults, the wizard will display only the contents of the CategoryName field. However, you will have access to the contents of the CategoryID field. To display all the bound columns in the list box, deselect the **Hide Key Column (Recommended)** option, as shown in Figure 9.8.

At this point, you can resize the width of either column. When you're ready, click **Next** to continue.

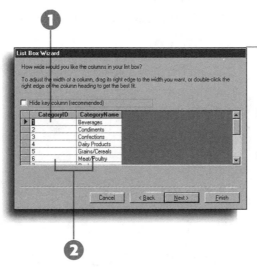

FIGURE 9.8

You want the wizard to display the values in both bound fields.

1 Access will store the value in this column

2 Access will display the values in both columns

8. The following window, shown in Figure 9.9, allows you to specify which value the list box stores when you select an item. You can choose either bound field, CategoryID, or CategoryName. There's no right or wrong in this decision. As a result of our choice, when you select Beverages from the control's list, that control actually stores the value 1, not the string "Beverages." Click **Next** to continue.

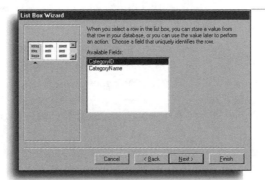

FIGURE 9.9

The default setting will store the contents of CategoryID.

9. This last window prompts us to enter a descriptive label for our list box. You entered "Categories." Click **Finish**, and then click the View button ⊞▼ on the Form Design toolbar to display the form in Form view, as shown in Figure 9.10.

FIGURE 9.10

This list box is bound to the Categories table and displays the contents of two fields.

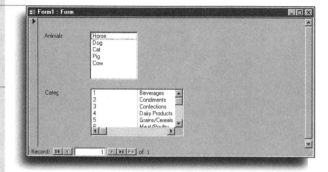

Choosing the right data to store

In this example, you display data from one field while displaying the data in another. Why? If your table contains an AutoNumber field or a primary key, that value is really the best choice for storing because of its uniqueness. You automatically eliminate the possibility of duplicates. Furthermore, most AutoNumber and primary key fields are almost always values, and values are easier to work with in VBA code because they don't require any special treatment. If you store a string, you'll have to enclose it in delimiters when you're ready to actually use it. That's easily done, but you might as well avoid the extra step if you can.

Exploring the Wizard-Generated Properties

This list box is a little different from the one in the first example. You see, although you're selecting what seems like two items, you're storing only the value in the first field—the CategoryID value. Now, let's take a look at the properties shown in Figure 9.11 to see how the second list box works.

What's a Table/Query List Box?

The wizard selected a Table/Query Row Source Type. (Our first control was a Value List box.) A *Table/Query* list box refers to a table or query for its list. You simply specify the appropriate table or query in the Row Source property. If you add or delete an item in the bound table or query, Access will update the contents of the list box accordingly.

What About That Row Source Property?

Instead of specifying the name of a table or query, the wizard entered the SQL statement

```
SELECT DISTINCTROW [Categories].[CategoryID], [Categories].
[CategoryName] FROM [Categories];
```

as the Row Source property. Used in this way, a SQL statement performs similar to a Select query. Our list box displays the contents of both the CategoryName and the CategoryID field from the Categories table. If you remember, your first list box displayed just one column.

FIGURE 9.11

The property sheet shows the combo box settings.

~~combo~~ *List*

SEE ALSO

➤ *You can read more about Select queries on page 237.*

Modifying the Wizard's SQL Statement

When you start to feel a little more comfortable with SQL or you want to experiment on the results you can generate by using SQL, you can modify the code that the wizard creates. Using the wizard to generate the code is both a good way to learn SQL and a good shortcut that can reduce syntax errors. You also can cut and paste the code elsewhere if you need a similar query.

Changing the SQL query

1. To change a SQL query, click the Builder button ![icon] next to the Row Source property field to launch the SQL Statement Builder. This builder displays the current settings in a QBE grid, as shown in Figure 9.12, which you can

easily modify. For instance, you might want to change the field's sort order.

   2. To do so, simply choose one of the options—**Ascending**, **Descending**, and **[not sorted]**—from that field's **Sort** drop-down list.

   3. Now, let's suppose the field you bound to the list box contains duplicate data. Most likely, you'll not want to display an item more than one. You can make this change by displaying the statement in SQL view. First, choose **SQL View** from the View button 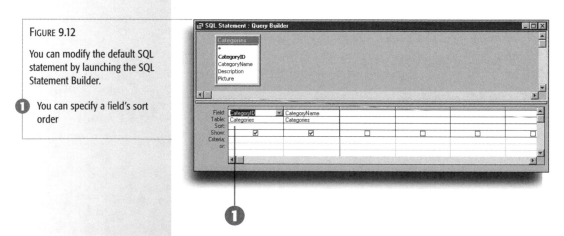 on the Query Design toolbar to display the query's SQL statement. In the case of our example, that statement is

```
SELECT DISTINCTROW Categories.CategoryID, Categories.
CategoryName FROM Categories;
```

The DISTINCTROW predicate determines that the result of the query will contain all entries, including duplicates. This example doesn't contain duplicates, but if it did, you'd simply substitute the DISTINCTROW predicate with the DISTINCT predicate in the form

```
SELECT DISTINCT Categories.CategoryID, Categories.
CategoryName FROM Categories;
```

This query would then display each field entry only once in the bound list box.

   4. To close the QBE grid, simply click the Close button on the window's title bar.

FIGURE 9.12

You can modify the default SQL statement by launching the SQL Statement Builder.

❶ You can specify a field's sort order

SEE ALSO
➤ *For more information on working in the QBE grid, go to page 257.*

What's the Column Count Property?

The next property you want to review is the Column Count property. Our wizard entered the value 2. This means the list box will display two columns. This property must contain an integer between 1 and the maximum number of fields in the bound table, query, or as is the case with our example, the Row Source property's SQL statement.

The Column Heads Property

The Column Heads property, when set to **Yes**, will display a single row of column headings in your list box. Specifically, the property displays the bound field's Caption text. If the field has no Caption text, the property will default to the field name. The default is No, which displays no headings.

The Bound Column Property

Remember earlier when I said I'd discuss which value the list box stores? That's determined by the Bound Column property. The default value is 1, which means the list box will store the value in the first column—in the case of our example, that's CategoryID. If you change that setting to the value 2, the list box would store the value in the CategoryName column. This setting has nothing to do with the columns you choose to display.

So, where does the list box store the selected value? In the case of our example, which is an unbound control, nowhere. However, you can assign the selected value to a variable using VBA. If your list box has a Control Source, the list box will store the selected value in the specified field.

If you set the Bound Column property to 0, the list box won't store the selected item. Instead, the list box will store the selected item's position, as an integer, within the list. This value is

Avoid a common Column Count error

If you're tempted to use the Column Count property to hide a column, don't; you can't control the columns that the list box displays. To hide a column, set that column's width to 0 in the Column Widths property box. For instance, our sample list box displays two columns and the default width for both columns is 1". To hide the first column, CategoryID, you'd change the control's Column Widths property to 0"; 1". To hide the second column, CategoryName, you'd use the setting 1"; 0".

Hiding a column doesn't mean it's off limits. To the contrary, hiding a column in this manner is similar to selecting the wizard's **Hide Key Column** option. Except you can hide any column, and the wizard enables you to hide just the primary key column. Regardless of how you hide the column, you can still store that column's value.

known as the *List Index* value. Furthermore, the List Index values begin with 0, not 1. For instance, in our first example where the list box displayed the items Horse, Dog, Cat, Pig, and Cow in that order, selecting Horse will store the value 0, selecting Dog will store 1, Cat will store 2, Pig will store 3, and Cow will store 4.

About the Combo Box Control

The combo box control is similar to the list box in most respects. Both controls display a list of items and have the capability to store your choice. However, there are a few differences. A combo box is a combination of a list box and a text box. You can select an item in the list, or enter a value in the text box component. Either way, the contents of the combo box is the value of the combo box. The combo box control also has a property that the list box control doesn't. That property, *Limit to List*, can limit the combo box text to only those items in the list.

Using the Combo Box Wizard

Our previous examples apply to both list boxes and combo boxes, so I won't repeat that information. Instead, let's create a combo box using the Combo Box Wizard and explore that control's Limit to List property.

Creating a combo box using the Combo Box Wizard

1. Click **Forms** and then **New** in the Database window.

2. If Access doesn't open the Toolbox, click the Toolbox button ⚒ on the Form Design toolbar.

3. To turn on the Control Wizards, click the Control Wizards icon 🔨 on the Toolbox. At this point, you can click any control that has a wizard—list box, combo box, command button, and option group—to launch that respective wizard.

4. Now, click the Combo Box tool 📑 on the Toolbox and then click inside the blank form. Choose the **I Want the Combo Box to Look Up the Values in a Table or Query** option and click **Next**.

5. In the second window, select the table and click **Next**.

6. Move both fields to the **Selected Fields** list box and click **Next** twice.

7. In the final window, enter the label text, and then click **Finish**.

8. Click the View button ⊞▾ on the Form Design toolbar to display the finished control. Click the control's arrow to display the list of categories shown in Figure 9.13. To return an item, simply select it from the list and Access will copy it to the text box component.

FIGURE 9.13

This combo box displays a list of categories from the Categories table.

Automatically Opening the Drop-Down List

You can save yourself a keystroke by having Access automatically open a combo box's drop-down list when that control gets the focus. To accomplish this, you'll attach a VBA procedure to the control's GotFocus event.

Automatically opening the drop-down list

1. First, open the form that contains your combo box in Design view.

2. Next, click the Code button 🖳 on the Form Design toolbar.

3. In the resulting module, select the combo box from the Objects control and the **GotFocus** event from the Procedures control. Be sure to use the combo box's correct name—I used Combo0 in my listing.

4. Then, enter the procedure shown in Listing 9.1. At this point your module should resemble the one shown in Figure 9.14.

LISTING 9.1 **The Dropdown Method**

```
1 Private Sub Combo0_GotFocus()
2    Me![Combo0].Dropdown
3 End Sub
```

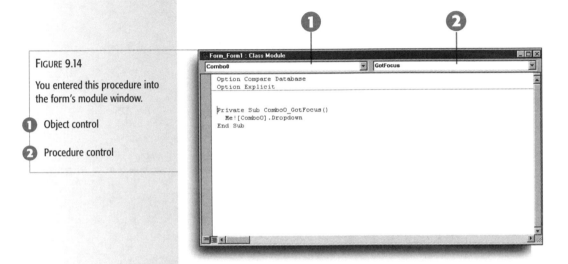

FIGURE 9.14

You entered this procedure into the form's module window.

1 Object control

2 Procedure control

5. Now, return to the form and click the View button [🔳▾] on the Form Design toolbar.

6. Tab to the combo box. As soon as that control receives the focus, VBA will open the drop-down list for you.

SEE ALSO

➤ *If you're not familiar with VBA and its terms, turn to page 596.*

The Limit to List Property

By default, the Limit to List property is Yes, which means you can't enter an item in the text box component of your combo box unless that entry exists in the value list. If you attempt to enter an item that isn't in the list, Access will display the error message shown in Figure 9.15. If you receive this message, click **OK** to clear the message box and then press Esc to delete the invalid entry.

FIGURE 9.15

Access won't let you enter an item that isn't in the value list when the Limit to List property is set to Yes.

Suppressing the Error

You don't have to contend with this error message if you don't want to. You can easily suppress it using the control's Not in List event.

Suppressing the Limit to List error message

1. Open into Design view any form that contains a combo box control—I'm using the form I created in the last example.

2. Open the form's module by clicking the Code button 🐿 on the Form Design toolbar.

3. Select the appropriate combo box from the Object control—I'm working with **Combo2**. Then, select **NotInList** from the Procedures control.

4. Enter the procedure shown in Listing 9.2 and close the module.

LISTING 9.2 **The NotinList Event**

```
1   Private Sub Combo2_NotInList(NewData As String, Response As
    Integer)
2     Response = acDataErrContinue
3   End Sub
```

---

5. Return to Form view by clicking the View button ▥ ▾ on the Form Design toolbar.

6. Enter test into the text box and press Enter. This time, Access doesn't display the error message. Nor does it accept your value because you haven't supplied any further instruction. However, you can add code that will display a more descriptive message, delete the inappropriate entry, or even accept it and add it to the value list.

Displaying constants

A *constant* represents a value that doesn't change. You use symbolic constants in code when you want to refer to a variable that doesn't change. Although you can change a symbolic constant anytime you like, you probably won't change them too often. To declare a symbolic constant, use the **Const** keyword instead of **Dim**.

Access offers a number of constants, known as *intrinsic constants*. These are reserved words and for the most part, ensure compatibility with other VBA-enabled applications. VBA intrinsic constants always start with the letters **ac**. In earlier versions, these constants started with **A_**. These constants always represent a value that doesn't change. For instance, the acDataErrContinue constant you used in this example is an example of an intrinsic constant.

The last kind of constant is a system-defined constant. These are values such as **True**, **False**, and **Null**.

If there's a NotInList event, the Response argument equals 1. To override that constant in the procedure shown in Listing 9.2, you applied the acDataErrContinue constant to the Response argument. To display a list of constants, open any module in Design view and click Object Browser on the current toolbar. You can also press Ctrl+J or F2. After you've displayed the browser, select the appropriate library.

SEE ALSO
➤ For more information on the Object Browser, go to page 557.

The Field List Setting

There's one final type of list and combo box control that the wizards can't create—a Field List control. This type of control lists the bound object's field names rather than the contents of the bound field. If you change a field name, or add or delete a field name, Access will automatically update the bound control accordingly.

About the Command Button Control

A command button simply executes a task. For example, you can open a form by clicking a command button. Or, you can print a report. Most any task you can define with a macro or event procedure can be executed with the click of a command button.

Using the Command Button Wizard

Command buttons can be used for a number of different tasks and the wizard anticipates quite of few of the possibilities—30 of them, in fact.

Creating a command button using the Command Button Wizard

1. Open a blank form, display the Toolbox ⚒, and make sure the Control Wizards button ⬩ is selected.
2. Click the Command Button tool ▭ on the Toolbox and then click inside the blank form.

3. Access will launch the Command Button Wizard and display its first window, shown in Figure 9.16.

The **Categories** list box displays a number of tasks the wizard can automate for you.

The **Actions** list box displays the different choices for the selected **Categories** item.

As you click items in the **Categories** list box, the wizard updates the list in the **Actions** list box accordingly.

Try selecting each item in the **Categories** list box now, so you can familiarize yourself with all the wizard has to offer. When you've finished browsing, select **Report** in the **Categories** list box and **Print Report** in the **Action** list box. Click **Next** to continue.

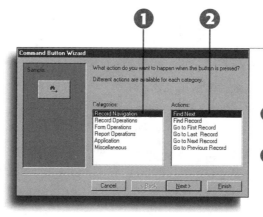

FIGURE 9.16

The Command Button Wizard offers a variety of task possibilities.

1 The Categories list box displays a variety of tasks

2 The Actions list box displays the appropriate choices for the selected task in the Categories list box

4. The next window, shown in Figure 9.17, lists all the reports in the current application. The left pane will be specific to the item you select in the **Categories** list box. I chose the **Invoice** report, and then clicked **Next**.

5. The following window enables you to define the button's caption. Specifically, you can display descriptive text, or you can display an icon. The default option displays a Printer icon. However, you want to display a text, so choose the **Text** option, and then enter the text Print Invoice, as shown in Figure 9.18. When you're finished with this window, click **Next** to continue.

FIGURE 9.17

The wizard lets you choose from
the application's current reports.

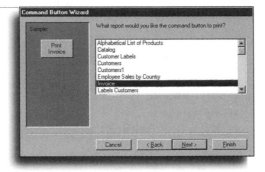

FIGURE 9.18

This window enables you to
define the button's caption.

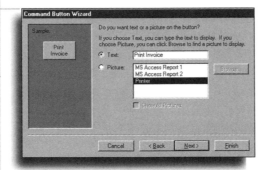

6. The final window prompts you to give the button a meaningful name. I named mine cmdPrintInvoice. Click **Finish** when you're done with this window.

7. At this point, you have a new command button on your blank form in Design view. If you open the form's module by clicking the Code button 🐾 , you will see the code the wizard entered.

   Figure 9.19 shows our example form's module. This code will print the Invoice report when you click cmdPrintInvoice in Form view.

8. To see the button in Form view, as shown in Figure 9.20 click the View button 🖽 ▾ on the Form Design toolbar.

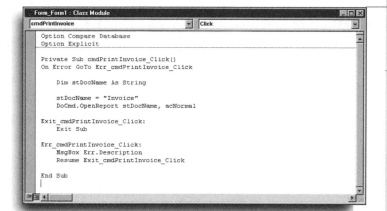

The Option Group Control

The option group control is the last control that offers a wizard.
An option group displays a set of choices, but it's different from
a list or combo box because you can select only one option from
the group. It's also a bit easier to use because you simply click
the appropriate choice. The group returns the value of the
selected item.

An option group consists of a group frame and a set of check
boxes, option buttons, or toggle buttons. When an option group
is bound to a field, only the group frame is bound to the field.
The Option Value property for each check box, toggle button,
or option button equals a unique value. When you select an
option in an option group, the option group returns the Option
Value setting of the selected item.

Using the Option Group Wizard

You can create a bound or unbound option group. If the group is bound, the control will return the group's value to the field specified in the Control Source property. When it isn't bound, you'll want to store the group's value in a variable. In the following example, you'll use an unbound option group control to change the mouse pointer. Specifically, you'll use an option group to offer a set of mouse pointer icons. When you choose one of the options, the control will return that choice's value as the control's value. Then, an event procedure uses that value to change the mouse pointer. You don't store the group's value in a table.

Creating an option group using the Option Group Wizard

1. Open a blank form, display the Toolbox ![toolbox icon], and make sure the Control Wizards tool ![control wizards icon] is selected.

2. Click the Option Group tool ![option group icon] on the Toolbox, click inside the blank form, and Access will display the wizard's first window.

3. Enter a descriptive caption for each option. I entered the labels Select Arrow, I-Beam, NS Size, WE Size, and Hourglass, as shown in Figure 9.21. After you've entered all the necessary labels, click **Next** to continue.

The Option Group represents only one value

Remember, the different options aren't bound to a particular field—only the completed control can be bound. For this reason, you'll need to enter descriptive labels for each option. Remember to press Tab and not Enter between each entry.

FIGURE 9.21

Enter the descriptive labels for each option in the option group control.

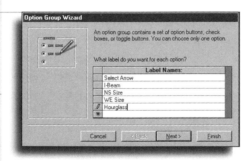

4. In the next window, choose a default value, as shown in Figure 9.22. I selected a default in the **Yes, the Default Choice Is** drop-down list.

If you choose **No, I Don't Want a Default**, Access will select none of the options by default. Click **Next** to continue.

FIGURE 9.22
You can specify a default option for the group.

5. The following window displays default values for each option which the wizard then applies to each option's Option Value property. Each value must be unique to the set. As you can see in Figure 9.23, I've entered my own defaults instead of accepting the wizard's, using the appropriate MousePointer settings for each option. These settings are predefined; I didn't make them up. For more information on the MousePointer property and its settings, you can search on MousePointer in Help. When you're done with these settings, click **Next** to continue.

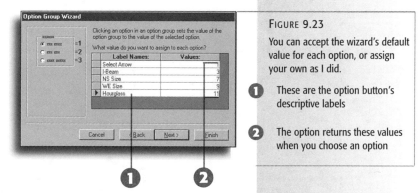

FIGURE 9.23

You can accept the wizard's default value for each option, or assign your own as I did.

1 These are the option button's descriptive labels

2 The option returns these values when you choose an option

6. The following window gives you several display options. The sample control shown in the left side of the window will update accordingly as you select different options in each category. I selected **Option** buttons and the **Raised Style** setting, as shown in Figure 9.24. After you've made your selections, click **Next** to continue.

FIGURE 9.24

Selecting display options.

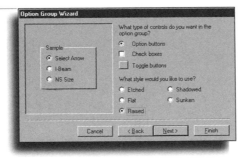

7. In the final window, enter a descriptive label, click **Finish**, and return to Design view.

8. Open the frame group's property sheet and enter the name grpMouseSettings. (Make sure the property sheet title bar reads Option Group.)

9. Next, click the Code button 📖 on the Form Design toolbar. Choose **grpMouseSettings** from the **Object** control and **AfterUpdate** from the **Procedure** control. Then, enter the procedure shown in Listing 9.3.

LISTING 9.3 **Changing the Mouse Pointer**

```
1    Private Sub grpMouseSettings_AfterUpdate()
2        Screen.MousePointer = Me!grpMouseSettings
3    End Sub
```

10. Close the module and click the View button 🖼️ ▾ on the Form Design toolbar to open the form in Form view.

11. When you click one of the options, VBA will update the mouse pointer accordingly, as shown in Figure 9.25—I've selected the Hourglass option. To return the mouse pointer to it's default state, click the **Select Arrow** option.

FIGURE 9.25

Selecting the Hourglass option.

Using the Mail Merge Wizard

Merge Access data with Word documents on the fly

Link Access data to Word documents

Merging Access Data with Word Documents

Access doesn't have a word processor, but you can use the report generator as one if you like. If you have Word, you'll probably prefer to type form letters and such in Word and then merge your Access data into the Word document. An added bonus to this arrangement is the menagerie of formatting tools that Word offers.

The merge process is fairly simple and straightforward. First you store data, such as address information, in an Access database. Second, you use Word to create a mail-merge document. This document will contain the information you want to share, plus special field codes that will refer to fields in your Access tables. When you merge your Access data with the Word mail-merge document, Word will rely on your Access database to fill the field codes in the Word document.

To successfully complete the process, you need two things:

- An Access table or query
- A mail-merge Word document

You can merge with an existing Word document, or you can create a new one on-the-fly. If you're sending the same letter over and over, you'll want to use the first method. But the first time you run the merge, you'll create the Word document as part of the merge process. Let's look at both ways, first creating the document as part of the merge process, and then running a second merge with the existing document.

Creating a mail-merge document

1. In Access, choose the table or query that contains the data you need to merge into Word (in this example, the **Employees** table), and choose the **Merge It with MS Word** option from the OfficeLinks button ▦ on the **Database** toolbar. If you want, you can click the **OfficeLinks** button instead of opening the drop-down list. Doing so will default to the Mail Merge Wizard.

What you need to merge

This section on merging assumes you're using Office 97 or have a standalone copy of both Access and Word. You must have a copy of Word installed to take advantage of the merge feature.

This example

You'll rely on the Employees table in Northwind for your Access table. Because part of the mail-merge process involves adding the field codes to the Word document, you'll create a document as part of this example.

2. The Mail Merge Wizard will display the window shown in Figure 10.1. The **Link your data to an existing Microsoft Word document** option will allow you to merge with an existing document. You don't have a document yet, so select the **Create a new document and then link the data to it** option before clicking **OK**. In response, Word will launch and open a new document. (If not, you can click the New button 🗋 on the **Standard** toolbar to open a new document once Word launches.)

FIGURE 10.1

The wizard wants to know if you're merging with an existing document or creating a new one.

3. The first thing you need in your mail-merge document is the date. Choose **Date and Time** from the **Insert** menu, select the fourth option (month, date, year format) from the resulting dialog box, click the **Update Automatically** option, and click **OK**. The next time you use this merge document, Word will use the current date.

4. Press Enter four times.

5. Now you're ready to insert the merge fields. In this case, you want to add seven fields: **LastName**, **FirstName**, **Address**, **City**, **Region**, **PostalCode**, and **Country**. Because you selected the Employees table in Access before you started the wizard, Word links to that table, and all of the Employees' fields are available in the Insert Merge Field button's drop-down list, as shown in Figure 10.2. Simply insert them in the appropriate order. First, open the Insert Merge Field button's Insert Merge Field ▾ drop-down list and select **FirstName**. Press the spacebar to enter a space between the addressee's first and last name. Then, select **LastName** from the **Insert Merge Field** button's drop-down list.

FIGURE 10.2

All of the Employee table fields are available in Word.

6. Press Enter to move the cursor to the next line.

7. Choose **Address** from the drop-down list and press Enter.

8. Choose **City**, enter a comma, and then press the spacebar. Next, select **Region**. Then press the spacebar and select **PostalCode**. Press Enter to go to the next line.

9. Select **Country**, the final field. At this point, your document should resemble the one shown in Figure 10.3.

10. Press Enter twice and enter the word Dear followed by a space.

11. Choose **FirstName** from the **Insert Merge Field** button's drop-down list, enter a space, and then select **LastName** from the drop-down field. Follow the **LastName** field code with a semicolon, and then press Enter twice.

12. Enter the body of your letter, as shown in Figure 10.4. Remember, you can add field codes to the body of your letter. Simply insert the fields in the appropriate spot in your letter.

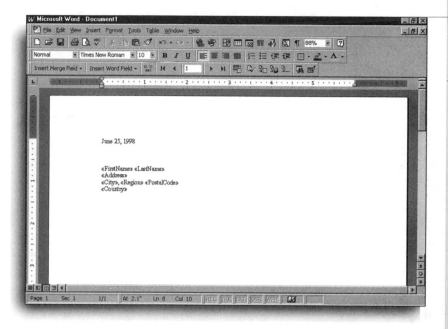

FIGURE 10.3
Address fields have been added to this Word document.

13. Once you've finished your letter, add several blank lines to the top margin to better center it. At this time, you should also apply any special formatting you want.

14. If you want to save the document, do so now by choosing the **Save As** option from the **File** menu. This mail-merge document is named meeting.doc.

When your document is exactly the way you want it and you're ready to merge your Access data, you have two choices:

- Merge to a new document.
- Merge directly to the printer.

SEE ALSO

➤ *See page 672 for more tips on integrating Access with other Office applications.*

If you merge to a new document, you can view and then save the results of the merge. If you merge directly to the printer, you bypass this step and print all the merged letters.

To merge to a new document, click the Merge to New Document button 🔲 on the **Mail Merge** toolbar. If you do, Word creates one document with the default name Form

Letter1, as shown in Figure 10.4. Each page of this document contains one of your merged letters. You can view them, print them, or even modify them. If you want to return to the mail-merge document (the document with your field codes), choose that document from the **Window** menu.

FIGURE 10.4

Your data has been merged to a new document.

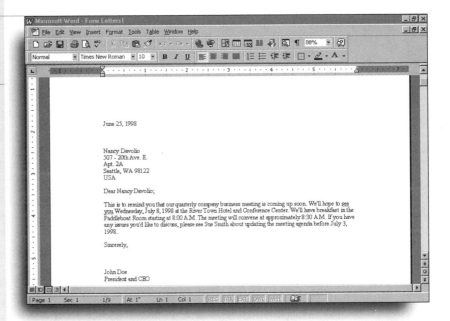

To merge to the printer, click the Merge to Printer button on the **Mail Merge** toolbar. This will print all the merged letters automatically without creating a new document.

Now close Word, return to Access, and repeat the merge using the meeting.doc document you created in the last exercise.

Merging to a linked document

1. Select the **Employees** table in the Database window, and choose **Merge It with MS Word** from the OfficeLinks button .

2. Select **Link your data to an existing Microsoft Word document** and click **OK**.

3. Locate your mail-merge document in the Select Microsoft Word Document dialog box, select it, and then click **OK** to launch Word and open your document.

4. Once Word launches and opens `meeting.doc`, click one of the merge options—merge to a new document or merge to the printer—as you did in the preceding example.

Word's mail-merge feature

Word's mail-merge feature is very flexible and powerful, and we haven't attempted to show you all of its features. We've concentrated on linking Access data with the mail-merge feature.

Using Add-Ins and Builders to Increase Efficiency

Managing add-ins

Installing a new add-in

Creating front-end and back-end databases

Using the Linked Table Manager

Creating and editing Switchboards

Printing your table relationships

Installing and Using Add-Ins

Add-ins are utilities that were not part of the original core functionality of Access. They add to the functionality of the database. Some of the add-ins in previous versions of Access have been added to the core functionality of Access 97. An add-in is a library with its code and database objects stored in a database file that usually has a *.mda extension. Even thought this is not always the case, the add-ins that can be added are usually from a third party other than Microsoft.

The ideas for add-ins don't necessarily originate with Microsoft. In fact, there are companies that make the majority of their profit from the add-in that they have created. One add-in that we will look at later in the chapter, the Print Relationships Wizard, is the product of many users not wanting to use Print Screen to capture the relationships window. Before the Print Relationships Wizard was created, the only recourse was to do a screen print to the Clipboard, paste the screen print into a paint program, and then print it from there.

With the Print Relationships Wizard, the output is very similar to what is shown in the Relationships window. The output is actually what you are used to working with. Because you are used to working with database objects, specifically reports, modifying the look of the output will be much easier than trying to re-create it in a paint program.

Add-In Manager: Managing Add-Ins

The Add-In Manager presents a user interface to install or uninstall any add-in written for Access. If you write an add-in, the Add-In Manager is where you would install and uninstall it.

The Add-In Manager can be started by navigating to **Tools**, **Add-Ins**, **Add-In Manager**. If you look at Figure 11.1, you will notice the list of add-ins available through the menu. If you haven't installed any add-ins yourself, there will be only three listed besides the Add-In Manager. These add-ins will be discussed later in this chapter.

When you start the Add-In Manager, a dialog box is presented with a list of available add-ins. These can be add-ins that you installed at an earlier date; in some cases there will be nothing in the list.

If you look at Figure 11.2, you will see that I have an add-in that I installed at one time. Access maintains a list even if the add-in was uninstalled.

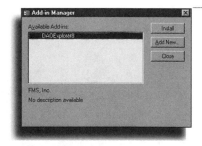

FIGURE 11.2
The Add-In Manager keeps track of what is installed or uninstalled.

If an add-in is installed, there will be an X on the same line as the add-in name. By the same token, if an add-in is not installed, there will not be an X next to the name.

Adding a new add-in

1. Open the Add-In Manager dialog box by clicking **Add-In Manager** on the **Tools**, **Add-Ins** menu.

2. In the Add-In Manager, click on the **Add New** button. An Open dialog box will pop up, prompting you for the location of your add-in that you want to add to the list of available add-ins. Be sure to set the file type as shown in Figure 11.3.

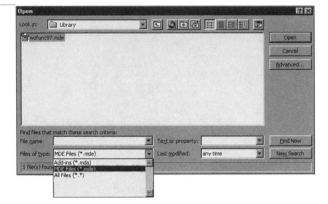

3. Find the file that you want to add. If your add-in is not a *.mda file, but a *.mde, select the correct file extension in the **Files of Type** drop-down list.

4. The new add-in will be installed and put in the list of available add-ins.

When you install an add-in, it generally inserts a menu item underneath Tools, Add-Ins. This is how you start the add-in. The add-in list will show all available add-ins as mentioned before. As you select an add-in from the list, you will notice that a small description of the add-in and the company it came from is displayed. See Figure 11.4 for the description of the add-in.

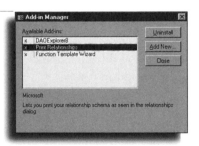

There are multiple add-ins available from Microsoft, third parties, and even from other individuals who have made little utilities that make developing and designing in Access a little easier.

Database Splitter: Front-End/Back-End

The Database Splitter creates a front-end and a back-end database configuration for you. Most Access professionals agree that a front-end/back-end database is the best route to go on any serious database. There are several obvious advantages to a front-end/back-end. Because the data is stored in one database (the back-end) and the user interface is stored in another (the front-end), you can update the user interface database without having to touch the back-end. Another advantage to the front-end/back-end configuration is when the database is multiuser. In a multiuser environment, you can have a copy of the front-end stored locally on each computer, with the tables from the back-end linked into the front-end. This configuration reduces network traffic because user interface traffic is local and not sent down through the network to a computer.

Creating a front-end/back-end structure with the Database Splitter on your database

1. Click **Tools**, **Add-Ins**, **Database Splitter**.
2. The wizard will start, bringing up the first form. The first form explains what the splitter does, warns that it may take awhile, and enables you to continue or cancel the Database Splitter. See Figure 11.5.

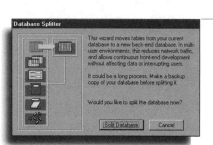

3. Select the **Split Database** button.
4. The Create Back-End Database dialog box will pop up, prompting for a new name for your database. You can choose any legal Access name. I usually make up a name that I know is the back-end for that database. For example, if I

Close all objects first

For this example, I'm going to use the Address Book database as generated by the Address Book Wizard when I created a new database.

Make sure that before you run the Database Splitter, all other database objects are closed. The only exception to this is you have to open the database window.

FIGURE 11.5
The explanation of the Database Splitter Wizard.

have a database named Address.mdb, I'll name my back-end database AddressData.mdb or Address_be.mdb.

5. After you have entered a name for your back-end, click the **Split** button on the Create Back-End Database dialog box. See Figure 11.6.

FIGURE 11.6

Create the back-end database.

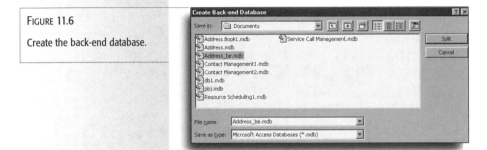

The Database Splitter Wizard will execute, removing all your tables and placing them in a back-end database, and then linking the back-end to the front-end. The Database Splitter will inform you when it is done. Click **OK** to finish.

Linked Table Manager: Managing Attachments

The Linked Table Manager was created out of the need to make managing linked tables a little easier on the end user. Before the Linked Table Manager, when a back-end database or an attached table was moved the user or developer had to delete the link, and then re-attach every table. Using the Linked Table Manager makes it much easier if a database moves or is renamed.

Managing linked tables

1. To get to the Linked Table Manager, navigate to **Tools**, **Add-Ins**, **Linked Table Manager**.

2. The Linked Table Manager shows a list of linked tables for the database, as is the one shown in Figure 11.7.

3. The list shows all the linked tables in the database. Next to the name of the linked table is the last known good path to the back-end tables.

Caution: switchboard placement in a split

If your database is using Switchboards, the Database Splitter puts the Switchboard table in the back-end. If you don't remove the link and then Import the Switchboard table from the newly created back-end database into the front-end database, you will not be able to use the Switchboard Manager.

The example for this exercise

For this example, I'm again using the Address Book database that is created by the Address Book Wizard after the database has been split, as shown in the preceding exercise.

FIGURE 11.7
The form for the Linked Table
Manager.

4. Select all the tables for which you want to check the link
   between the back-end and the front-end. If the Linked
   Table Manager checks the link and finds that the last known
   good path is not correct, the Linked Table Manager
   prompts you for a new location.

5. If you have checked the **Always Prompt for New
   Location** check box, no matter whether the link between
   the back-end and the front-end is a good link, the Linked
   Table Manager will prompt for a new location for you to
   specify in a dialog similar to the Open file or Save As file
   dialog boxes.

6. After you select the new location or name of the back-end
   database, and the tables are found correctly, Access acknowl-
   edges with a dialog. Click **OK**.

7. If you aren't successful you will be presented with the dialog
   box shown in Figure 11.8 for each table that the Linked
   Table Manager can't refresh the link for.

FIGURE 11.8
The Linked Table Manager could
not find the back-end database
that the table was linked to.

SEE ALSO

➤ *For more information and examples of linking tables, see page 114.*

Switchboards: Creating and Managing Switchboards

The Switchboard Manager creates and manages forms for your database application that contain buttons to open forms, reports, run macros or code, go to other switchboards, and exit Access. When you create a database using the database wizards, Access makes switchboards similar to the ones you can create in the Switchboard Manager.

Create a new switchboard

1. Choose **T**ools, **Add-I**ns, **S**witchboard **Manager**.

2. If you have never run the Switchboard Manager on your database, a message box will pop up, telling you that it can't find a valid switchboard (see Figure 11.9).

FIGURE 11.9

If you see this message box, you haven't run the Switchboard Manager on this database.

3. Select **Yes** to create a switchboard for your database.

After a switchboard is created, when you run the switchboard again on subsequent tries, you will add to or edit the switchboard in the Switchboard Manager dialog box (see Figure 11.10).

FIGURE 11.10

The Switchboard Manager dialog box is where you will add new switchboards or edit existing ones.

1 The **Make Default** button selects the form to open when an Access database is opened

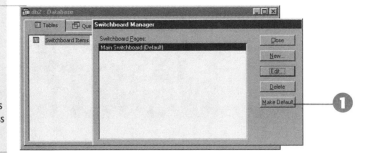

The **New** button is where you create more pages of your switchboard.

Creating new pages for a Switchboard

1. If you don't already have it open, open the Switchboard Manager dialog (see Figure 11.10) by selecting **Tools**, **Add-Ins**, **Switchboard Manager**.

2. Click on the **New** button.

3. The Create New dialog box will pop up, prompting you for the name of the switchboard that you will create (see Figure 11.11).

FIGURE 11.11

Create a new switchboard. This doesn't actually create another form if you already have a switchboard; it creates another page on the form.

4. The suggested name in the **Edit** box of the Create New dialog box needs to be changed to something that you can remember. Choose a name that describes the actions that you will take on the switchboard.

5. After you have entered a name that you are satisfied with, click **OK**.

   Your new page will show up in the Switchboard Manager dialog box (see Figure 11.12).

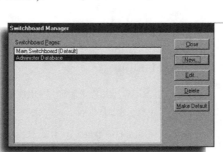

FIGURE 11.12

The new page of your switchboard in the Switchboard Manager dialog box.

The **Edit** button is where you edit the items on your switchboard pages. You can open other forms, switchboards, or reports; run macros or VBA functions; exit Access; and even call the Switchboard Manager.

Add items to your switchboard

1. If you don't already have it open, open the Switchboard Manager dialog (see Figure 11.10) by selecting **Tools**, **Add-Ins**, **Switchboard Manager**.

2. Click the **Edit** button. The Edit Switchboard Page dialog box will pop up (see Figure 11.13).

FIGURE 11.13

Edit your Switchboard page from here.

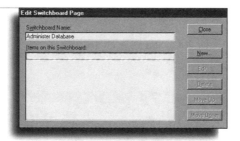

3. Click the **New** button. The Edit Switchboard Item dialog box, shown in Figure 11.14, will pop up, prompting you to name the item and the action that you will be taking with that item.

FIGURE 11.14

Edit your switchboard item in the Edit Switchboard Item dialog box.

If you want to change the item at a later date, you would come back in to the Edit Switchboard Page dialog box and click on the **Edit** button.

1. Follow steps 1 and 2 of the previous Add Items to Switchboard set of steps.

2. Select the item in the **Items on This Switchboard** list box that you want to edit. See Figure 11.15.

3. Click on the **Edit** button. The Edit Switchboard Item dialog box will pop up, enabling you to change any of the items on the switchboard. See Figure 11.16.

   You can also move the item up or down or delete it by using the buttons in this dialog box.

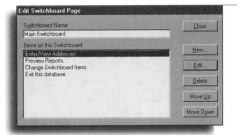

FIGURE 11.15

Select the item that you want to edit.

FIGURE 11.16

Edit, move, or delete the item.

4. Make your changes and then select the **OK** button.

You can also delete items from the switchboard you are editing. Be careful deleting items. To delete a switchboard item, click **Delete**. As usual, Access will let you confirm the delete action.

Using the Switchboard Manager can give your application a common look-and-feel. See Figure 11.17 for a completed switchboard.

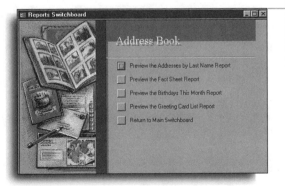

FIGURE 11.17

A completed switchboard.

Caution: deleting Switchboard pages

The **Delete** button on the Switchboard Manager enables you to delete switchboard pages. Be careful of this because you could delete a page that you put a lot of work into. To delete a switchboard page, select the page that you want to delete in the **Switchboard Pages** list box, and click the **Delete** button. Click the **OK** button on the confirmation message box. After you delete a switchboard page, you can't get it back.

Caution: editing Switchboard design

Although you can edit the form that is created by the Switchboard Manager in Design view, be careful not to edit the properties of the buttons or the labels to the right of the buttons. Your switchboard form will no longer work if you change the names of the labels or buttons.

Print Relationships: Putting Your Database Design on Paper

One of the complaints that many have had in the past with Access is the inability to print out table relationships. Microsoft created an add-in to fill that gap. The add-in can be obtained by pointing your browser to the following ftp site:

```
ftp://ftp.microsoft.com/softlib/mslfiles/prels80.EXE
```

or

```
http://www.microsoft.com/accessdev/Articles/printwiz/.
```

After you have downloaded the Print Relationships add-in, you will need to install it.

Installing the Print Relationships add-in

1. In Windows Explorer, double-click the add-in file, prels80.exe, from the location that you downloaded it to from the site. This will start the Print Relationships Wizard setup (refer to Figure 11.18).

2. The next dialog box you will see is the introduction and a copyright notice to the Print Relationships Wizard. You can **Continue** or **Exit Setup** from this dialog box.

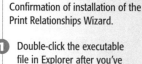

FIGURE 11.18

Confirmation of installation of the Print Relationships Wizard.

1 Double-click the executable file in Explorer after you've downloaded it

3. Read the end-user license agreement (EULA) for using the Print Relationship's Wizard and proceed with the wizard's steps. Select the **Complete Installation** button.

4. The Print Relationship Wizard installation will finish and present you with a completion dialog box. Click the **OK** button.

5. After the installation is complete, start up Access and navigate the menu to **Tools, Add-Ins, Print Relationships**.

6. Depending on the size of your database and the relationships defined, the Print Relationships Wizard will spend anywhere from half a minute to a couple of minutes creating a report. The report will have all your tables and relational links as defined in the Relationship view. For an example, see Figure 11.19.

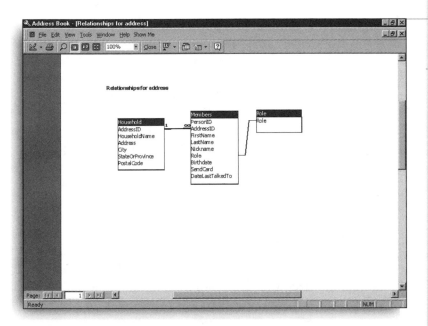

FIGURE **11.19**
The finished report.

7. After you are finished printing or viewing the newly created report, you can either discard it or save it in your database. See Figure 11.20. Click **No** to discard changes, or **Yes** to save the changes.

FIGURE 11.20

Discard or save your report.

8. If you clicked **Yes**, the Save As dialog appears. Enter a legal filename for your report.

After you have saved your report, you can come back to it later to edit or modify it as you see fit. Sometimes in a bigger database, the Print Relationships Wizard will stack the "tables" closer together and may cause them to overlap.

Builders

Builders are similar to add-ins. Usually builders are used for designing the database. For example, the Field Builder works in the Table Design view to present you with a list of predefined, commonly used fields that you can use in your table definition. The Expression Builder can be used in a variety of places, like the Conditions column in the Macro Design window. It also reduces code errors. This sections shows you how to use two other types of builders.

SEE ALSO

➤ *Expression Builder is covered in detail on page 273.*

Picture Builder

The Picture Builder enables you to select a graphics file. This add-in doesn't actually create pictures. It is a picture selector. The picture builder assigns a picture that has been stored on disk to an object that you are working with in Design view. You can also set the picture property of the form to have a background image.

Place an image or picture on the form

1. Open your form in Design view.

2. Go to the Properties window 🖽 and select the property called **Picture**. When you select in the box, the Builder button 🖽 will pop-up. Click it.

3. You will be presented with a dialog box that prompts for a graphics file. Select the file and your background of the form will now be that picture.

Color Builder

The Color Builder is actually a color selector that enables you to pick a color from the current palette and set the ForeColor, BackColor, and BorderColor properties of forms, reports, and controls.

Change the background color of a control

1. Open a form or a report in Design view ![icon].

2. Open the Properties window for the control that you want to change.

3. Click the **Back Color** property.

4. Click the Builder button ![icon]. See Figure 11.21 for the Color dialog box.

FIGURE 11.21
The Color Builder.

5. Select the color that you want by clicking the colored square.

6. Click **OK** to return.

If the colors presented in the Basic Colors section of the form is not what you want, you can create a custom color.

Create a custom color

1. Follow steps 1–4 in the previous step-by-step.

Continuity in your application's appearance

Both the Color and Picture Builders can help you create a unique and common look and feel to your application. You can create, purchase, or download graphics or customized colors and use these throughout the objects of your application.

2. In the Color dialog box, click **D**efine Custom Colors button.

The Color dialog box will expand (see Figure 11.22).

FIGURE 11.22

The custom color picker.

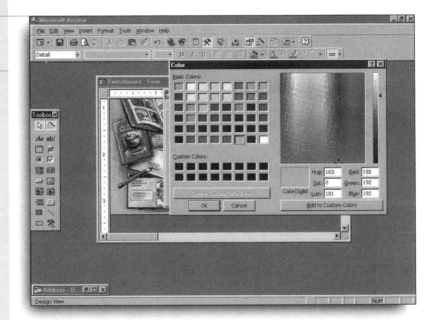

3. Select the approximate color that you want in the large colored rectangle. This is called the *color matrix*.

The thin, tall rectangle is a slider control that adjusts how much white or black is in the color.

You can also type in the actual amount of **R**ed, **G**reen or **Blue** color that makes up the whole color. You can also specify the hue, saturation and luminosity of that color, by typing in the **Hue**, **S**at, and **Lum** boxes respectively.

4. Click the **A**dd to Custom Colors button. You will now be able to use that color anywhere you need it in your application.

Storing and Controlling Data in Tables and Fields

Creating Tables in the Design View

Create and modify tables in Design View

Assign appropriate field and table names

What's an appropriate primary key?

How and when to use indexes

Designing Tables

Much has been said so far about good database design, and tables are the cornerstone of a good design. Before you start working with tables in Design view, let's discuss a few things to watch for.

- Scrutinize large tables carefully. Remember, you want fields that relate to a table's purpose, and sometimes that can be confusing. Before you know it, you may have a hodgepodge of fields in one or two tables, instead of spread out over the seven or eight tables that you really need.

- Sound the alarm if you find yourself repeating data in multiple tables. This is a sure sign that the design may be less than it could be.

- Watch for blank fields—any time you find lots of empty fields, you're looking at a potential design problem. The most likely reason for leaving a field blank is that the data simply doesn't pertain to that record. In a well-normalized table, this will seldom be the case.

Duplicate information

Remember that you might intentionally have duplicate values for foreign keys.

SEE ALSO

➤ *For more information about normalizing tables, see page 13.*

In the end, remember one rule and you'll be well ahead of the game: All fields should relate to the primary key field. In addition, you might want to consider using the Database Wizard to get started. Then, you can modify the tables in Design view as needed, which is what you're going to learn in this chapter.

SEE ALSO

➤ *For more information on primary key fields, see page 19 and page 199.*
➤ *To learn how to use the Database Wizard, see page 27.*

The Table in Design View

At this point, you're probably familiar with tables in Datasheet view. Figure 12.1 shows a typical table—the Customers table from the Northwind database.

FIGURE 12.1

This is a table in Datasheet View.

❶ The columns are fields, each containing a single unit of data

❷ A row constitutes a record and contains all the data that relates to the primary key

Figure 12.2 shows the same table in Design view. This view contains a unique toolbar with tools you'll use only in this environment, which is typical. Table 12.1 gives a short description of these buttons.

TABLE 12.1 **Table Design Toolbar Buttons**

Name	Icon	Task
View		Display table in Datasheet view
Primary Key		Assign a primary key to a field
Indexes		Define indexes
Insert Rows		Insert a field row
Delete Rows		Delete a field row

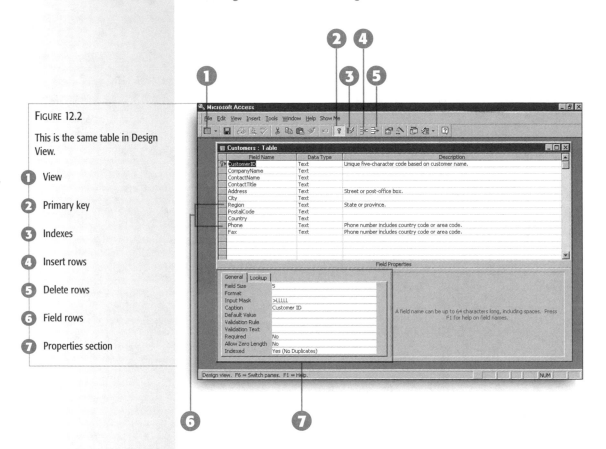

FIGURE 12.2

This is the same table in Design View.

1 View

2 Primary key

3 Indexes

4 Insert rows

5 Delete rows

6 Field rows

7 Properties section

Table Properties

The lower section of the window pane contains all the table's properties. Several properties have drop-down lists, and you simply choose the appropriate option from that list. The Caption and Validation Text require that you select the field and type your setting. As you select each property field, Access updates the information in the panel to the right. Table 12.2 gives a brief review of each property.

TABLE 12.2   **Table Properties**

Property	Explanation	Builder
Field Size	Determines the maximum number of characters you can store in this field	N/A
Format	Determines how Access displays the entry	N/A
Input Mask	Controls how you enter data	Input Mask Wizard
Caption	Access will display this text in a bound field's label control	N/A
Default Value	Enters this value automatically for a new record/field if user doesn't input another value	Expression Builder
Validation Rule	An expression that determines the values Access will accept	Expression Builder
Validation Text	The custom error message Access displays when an entry doesn't conform to the Validation Rule	N/A
Required	Determines whether you can enter a Null value	N/A
Allow Zero	Allows a zero-length string length	N/A
Indexed	Sets an index for the field and determines whether the field can contain duplicate values	N/A

SEE ALSO

➤ *For additional reading on table properties, see pages 380, 385, 374, and 378.*

Establishing Field Names

To add a field to a table, select a field row in Design view, enter the field's name, and choose an appropriate data type. The field name is really up to you, but it should indicate the field's purpose. Perhaps the easiest way to add a new field is to use the Field Builder.

Zero-length strings

A *zero-length string* is an actual string that contains no characters—the equivalent of the " " string. A zero-length string isn't the same as a Null value, which indicates there is no entry or result.

SEE ALSO

➤ *To see examples of table names that follow standard conventions, see page 22.*

Using the Field Builder

1. Open a table in Design view by selecting that table in the Database window and clicking **Design**. Or create a new table by clicking the **Tables** tab in the Database window, clicking **New**, and then double-clicking **Design View**. You're going to create a new table for this exercise.

2. Select a blank field row and click the Builder button 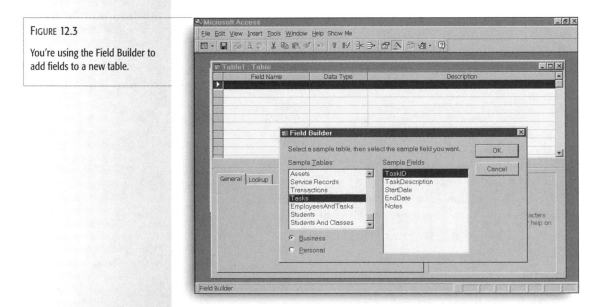 on the Table Design toolbar.

3. The builder's first window displays a list of sample tables. As you highlight the table options in the **Sample Tables** list box, Access will update its contents. The **Sample Fields** list box contains appropriate fields for each table. The **Business** and **Personal** options at the bottom of the window will update the list of tables in the **Sample Tables** list box accordingly. As you can see in Figure 12.3, the **Tasks** table and the first field—**TaskID**—have been chosen. You'll select a table from the **Sample Tables** list box and then choose the appropriate field name from the **Sample Fields** list box. Click **OK** to continue.

FIGURE 12.3

You're using the Field Builder to add fields to a new table.

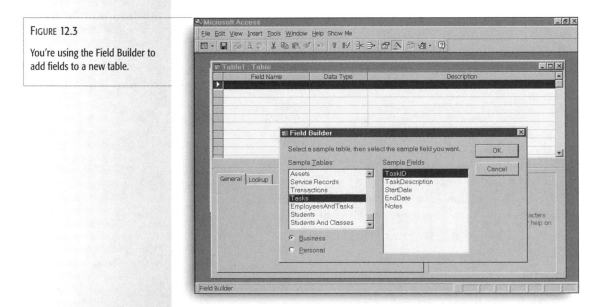

4. Access returns you to the new table in Design view, having added the chosen field for you. Figure 12.4 shows the result of choosing the TaskID field. The Builder has made a lot of default choices for you, which you can modify if need be. For instance, the Builder assigned the Number data type to your field. To change it to an AutoNumber, simply open the TaskID field's **Data Type** drop-down list and choose **AutoNumber**. If you do, Access will automatically update the field's properties accordingly. A field's properties are very dependent on the data type.

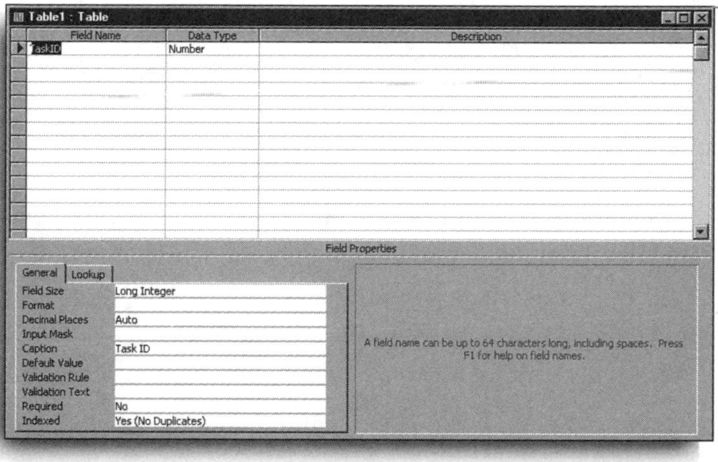

FIGURE 12.4
The Field Builder added the TaskID field to your new table.

5. The Builder doesn't attempt to enter a description for the field, so select the TaskID field's Description field and enter an appropriate explanation.

6. You have one more modification to make—you want to make the field the table's primary key field. With the field row still selected, click the **Primary Key** button [🔑] on the Table Design toolbar and Access will display a small primary key symbol in the field's row cell. Figure 12.5 shows your table up to this point.

SEE ALSO

➤ *For more information on data types, see page 571.*

➤ *If you'd like to know more about choosing primary key fields, see page 19 or 199.*

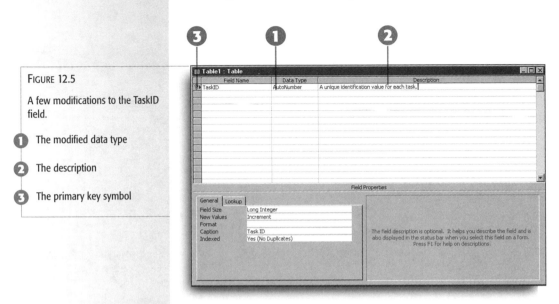

The Field Builder makes many decisions for you, and you are free to change any of them. If you add fields yourself, there are a few things to remember:

- A field name can consist of up to 64 characters—letters, numbers, and spaces.

- Give your fields names that describe their data. For instance, you might name a field that stores a person's last name LastName or Lname.

Setting Data Types Relevant to the Data Being Stored

In the previous example, you changed the TaskID field's data type from Number to AutoNumber. When choosing a data type, you must consider the following:

- The type of data you want to accept and the type of data you want to reject.

- How much memory the data type requires.

- The limits that Access places on each data type.

Spaces in field names

You can include a space in a field name, and at first you might like the idea. However, spaces are difficult to work with sometimes, specifically in SQL statements and VBA code. We recommend you don't use spaces in field names and then enter appropriate text in the field's Caption property. For instance, you might name a field LastName and use the Caption property Last Name. That way the text you see contains a space, but you don't have to deal with that space later.

For instance, if you're entering values, you most certainly don't want to accept alphabetical characters. The Number, Date/Time, and Currency data types will accept only numerical characters. Now, the Date/Time and Currency data types both require eight bytes of memory per field. The Number data type can require as few as one or as many as eight, so you'll want to use the Date/Time and Currency data types only when it is appropriate. Always use the most appropriate data type, but don't waste memory unnecessarily.

Finally, keep in mind that Access won't react the same way to every data type. For instance, if you apply a Text data type to a column of values, such as phone numbers or social security numbers, Access won't sort these values as you might expect. Specifically, Access will sort them alphanumerically. This means that the values 1, 2, 8, 10, and 18 will sort as 1, 10, 18, 2, and 8. Also, you can't sort on a Memo or OLE Object field.

Assigning Table Names That Describe Their Function

Once you've created all the fields your table requires, you need to save the table and give it a name. Simply click the Save button 🖫 or choose **Save As** from the **File** menu. After you save the table, Access will display its name in the **Tables** title bar. A table name can have up to 64 characters—letters, numbers, and spaces. In addition, you'll want to give your table a name that describes its purpose. For instance, you might name a customer table Customers or tblCustomers.

SEE ALSO
➤ *You can read about naming conventions on page 22.*

Tips for Making Tables Efficient Objects within the Database

There are many table design features that can save you time down the line. You assign them at the table level, and other objects inherit them. This means you don't have to apply the feature more than once.

When is a number not a value?

If you're storing numbers that you won't be using in calculations, consider assigning the Text data type instead of the Number data type. For instance, part numbers, addresses, phone numbers, and so on aren't used in calculations. Therefore, you can assign the Text data type and save memory. If you need to sort these values numerically, you can wrap the field in a Val() function in the form

`=Val([field])`

as a query expression. This function does have one limitation when used in this manner—the values you want to sort numerically must be at the beginning of the entry. The Val() function stops reading characters when it encounters any character other than a number. For instance, the Val() function works fine with the string 145XL—it returns the value 145. However, the Val() function won't find the numbers if the part number is XL145.

Reserved words

When naming any Access object, you need to remember that Access has a huge list of reserved words you can't use. For a complete list of these words, run a search in the Help section on reserved words. Also, don't use an object type, such as a field, table, form, module, macro, or report, as an object name.

Many table properties, Format, Caption, Input Mask, Default Value, and Description, are all inheritable at the form and report level. However, you can override these properties at form or report level by simply applying a new property setting for the form or report.

The Caption and Description properties are both unique in this area because they have no real purpose at the table level. Access will display a field's Caption text in a bound control's label control. For instance, Figure 12.6 shows the Caption text—Product Name—for the ProductID field in the Order Details table.

FIGURE 12.6

The Caption property for the ProductID field is Product Name.

1 The ProductID field's Caption property

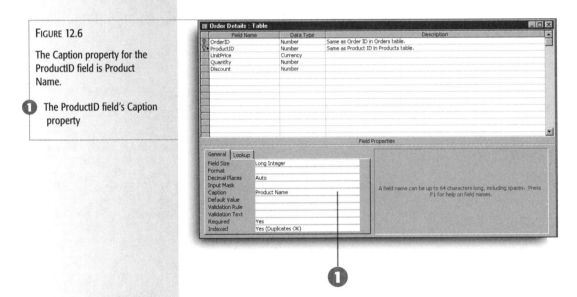

As a general rule, Access displays a field's name in a bound control's label control. However, when you use the AutoForm to base the form shown in Figure 12.7 on the Order Details table, Access displays Product Name instead of ProductID. That's because the Caption property overrides the default label text.

Another useful shortcut is the table's Description property. You supply text that describes the field's purpose. For instance, you might use the text "Enter customer's street address" for an address field. When you give focus to that field, in Datasheet view and in Form view, Access displays this text in the status bar, as shown in Figure 12.8. Even though you set the Description property at the table level, Access displays it in Form view.

FIGURE 12.7

Access displays the Caption property text instead of the field name in the label control.

① The ProductID field's Caption property appears instead of the default text

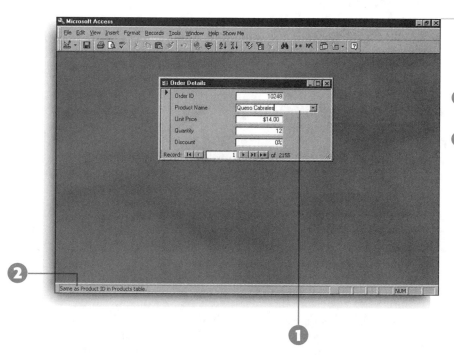

FIGURE 12.8

You set the Description property at the table level, but Access displays it in Form View.

① The ProductID control has the focus.

② Access displays the bound field's Caption property

Primary Keys

Primary keys are an essential component of a relational database. They're discussed throughout this book in various chapters because they're used to find data quickly and to combine data in separate tables. We recommend that each table have a primary key. If your table doesn't have a natural primary key candidate, you can add an AutoNumber field to the table and use it as that table's primary key. A *natural primary key* is a data field (not an AutoNumber) that provides a unique entry for each record.

When choosing a primary key field, there are a few things you should keep in mind:

- A primary key field must contain unique data.
- Access won't allow duplicate entries or a Null value in a primary key field.

Field size and primary keys

The size of your primary key field can slow down your application. Choose the data type that consumes the least memory but is still adequate. In addition, assign the smallest field size possible.

Once you've decided which field is the primary key field, you can set it by opening the table in Design view, choosing the appropriate field row, and clicking the Primary Key button 🔑 on the Table Design toolbar. This button acts as a toggle button, so to delete the primary key, select the primary key field row and click the Primary Key button again.

Multiple-Field Primary Keys

Until now we've discussed primary keys as though they consisted of just one field. The fact is, you can assign a primary key to as many fields as appropriate. A multiple-field primary key will perform the same as a single-field primary key. Access will view the primary key—all the fields involved—as a single entity. This means that when checking for duplicate entries, Access will consider all the fields.

For instance, if you include two fields in your primary key, RabbitID and RabbitName, Access will check the contents of both fields against all the existing records. If you enter the data "593" and "Maggie Rabbit" into the RabbitID and RabbitName fields, respectively, Access will reject the record only if another record contains both of those entries. If the RabbitID "593" already exists but the RabbitName entry isn't "Maggie Rabbit," Access will accept the record, and vice versa. An existing record must contain both "593" and "Maggie Rabbit" before Access will reject the new record.

To set a multiple-field primary key, simply select all the appropriate field rows in Design view and click the Primary Key button on the Table Design toolbar.

SEE ALSO
➤ *You can learn more about primary keys on page 19.*

Indexes

Access indexes are a mysterious lot, and we won't attempt to explain what goes on behind the scenes between the Access objects and the Jet Engine. However, there are some things you should know to create a quick-responding application.

Access uses an index to sort data in logical order, which is determined by the field's data type. This makes perfect sense because text and numbers are sorted differently. Unfortunately, having more than one indexed field in a table can actually slow things down. That's because Access updates the index each time you add or change a record—if you have more than one field indexed.

Access automatically indexes a primary key field. Beyond that, you should consider indexing a second field only if that field meets all of the following conditions:

- The data type is Text, Number, Currency, or Date/Time.
- You will search for data or sort by this data often.
- The field will mostly contain different values.

Additionally, with the speed of today's systems, indexing probably won't significantly improve your search or sort tasks unless you have thousands of records, or your tables have many fields.

Having said all that, if you do decide to assign an index, there are a few rules you must follow:

- Name the index.
- A primary key field is a table's primary index.
- Access won't sort records as you enter them, even if you set an index.
- Access doesn't always sort the way you expect, so don't use an index to control sort order.

The best advice is to set an index only if you're working with large amounts of data and one or more of your fields uniquely identify each record. If you set an index for these fields, you may increase your application's speed. Dabble with indexes any further, and you may slow things down.

To set an index, open the table in Design view and open the Indexes window, or choose **Indexes** from the **View** menu. If your table contains a primary key field, the window will display that field's index. To set an index for a field other than your primary key, enter a name in the Index Name field, identify the field you're indexing, and then select a sort order.

Figure 12.9 shows the Products table's indexes. As you can see, this table has four indexes. Let's see if these indexes conform to the specified rules. It isn't likely that that you'll duplicate the product's name, but you will probably repeat the CategoryID and SupplierID values often. What you won't see is a record that will duplicate all four fields, so this table meets the test. These four fields create a unique identifier for each record.

FIGURE 12.9

The Products table has four indexes.

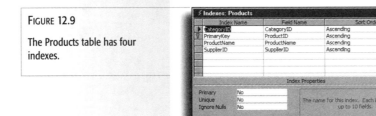

An index has properties just like fields and controls do. The **Primary** property refers to a field that uniquely identifies each record, similar to a primary key field. However, a primary property does not have to be a primary key. On the other hand, if your record contains a primary key field, it will also be the primary index. You can't modify this arrangement. The **Unique** property determines whether the field must contain unique data. The final property, **Ignore Nulls**, allows Access to ignore null values when sorting the table.

Like the primary key field, an index can apply to more than one field. You'll want to use this option when a sort is dependent on more than one field. For instance, if you separate names into first and last name fields, you'll want to consider both fields in a sort task.

Setting a single-field and multiple-field index

1. Create a new table by clicking the **Tables** tab, clicking **New** in the Database window, and then double-clicking **Design View** in the New Table dialog box.

2. Add an AutoNumber field named ID and two Text fields named **LastName** and **FirstName**.

3. Click the Indexes button  on the Table Design toolbar to display the Indexes window. At this point, you have one single-field index on the ID field, as shown in Figure 12.10. This is a natural choice because it's an AutoNumber field—a unique identifier.

FIGURE 12.10
Access automatically sets an index to the **ID** field because it's an **AutoNumber** field.

4. To create the multiple-field index, enter an appropriate name into the Index Name field—in this case, Full Name.

5. Next, identify the first field in your multiple-field index. In this example, that's LastName.

6. Then, select a sort order for the specified field—**Ascending**.

7. Don't enter a new index name in the next row. Instead, select the Field Name column in the next row and enter the name of the second field in your multiple-field index. Then, specify a sort order for that field. This example has the FirstName field and an ascending sort. The completed index is shown in Figure 12.11.

FIGURE 12.11

You added a multiple-field index to this table.

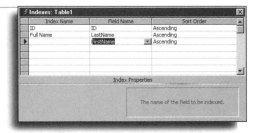

FIGURE 12.11

You added a multiple-field index to this table.

To delete an index, select the appropriate field row in the Indexes window and press the Delete key.

Creating Fields That Look Up Lists or Values in Tables

Lookup fields store one thing and display another

Using *DLookUp( )* to return a value from a specific set of records

What's a Lookup?

The nature of a database—in which storage is done in rows and columns—lends itself to lookup tasks. A *lookup task* is one that returns a value or list by referring to coordinates. Those coordinates can be index values or matching criteria. For instance, if I fill a combo box with three columns from a table or query, I can then use the Column property to return data from any of the three columns. Or, I can use a DLookUp() function to find the first record that matches specific criteria and then return data from another field in that same record.

SEE ALSO

➤ *You'll find an interesting use of the Column property on page 431.*

What's a Lookup Field?

One drawback of a normalized table is that you sometimes get stuck viewing identifying values rather than a customer's name or a product's name. For instance, if you're tracking orders, it makes more sense to list the product's identifying value—perhaps a product number—than to list the product's name. That's because the value field is more likely to be the primary or foreign key than the field that contains the product's name. However, seeing the product's identification number probably isn't all that helpful, because most of us won't readily relate a field of numbers to the product.

Figure 13.1 shows the Northwind Order Details table without the Product field's lookup capability. Instead of displaying the product's name, the Product field displays the ProductID number. Unfortunately, these values aren't all that helpful in identifying the actual product. To remedy that, you can make the Product field a lookup field by running the Lookup Wizard.

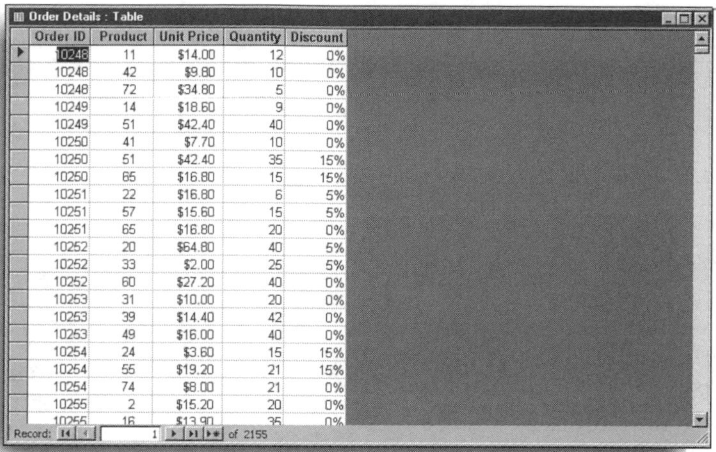

Order Details : Table

Order ID	Product	Unit Price	Quantity	Discount
10248	11	$14.00	12	0%
10248	42	$9.80	10	0%
10248	72	$34.80	5	0%
10249	14	$18.60	9	0%
10249	51	$42.40	40	0%
10250	41	$7.70	10	0%
10250	51	$42.40	35	15%
10250	65	$16.80	15	15%
10251	22	$16.80	6	5%
10251	57	$15.60	15	5%
10251	65	$16.80	20	0%
10252	20	$64.80	40	5%
10252	33	$2.00	25	5%
10252	60	$27.20	40	0%
10253	31	$10.00	20	0%
10253	39	$14.40	42	0%
10253	49	$16.00	40	0%
10254	24	$3.60	15	15%
10254	55	$19.20	21	15%
10254	74	$8.00	21	0%
10255	2	$15.20	20	0%
10255	16	$13.90	35	0%

Record: 1 of 2155

FIGURE 13.1
The Product field displays a value, which doesn't readily identify the product for you.

Exploring the Lookup Wizard

The Lookup Wizard will create a field that displays one of two types of lists:

- Lookup list—An updateable list based on the contents of a particular field in another table or query.
- Value list—A fixed list of items that you enter.

Now, it would be much more informative if the Product field displayed the appropriate product's name. However, you need to maintain the value field because it is a foreign key from the Products table, shown in Figure 13.2. In this table, `ProductID` is an AutoNumber data type and a primary key. There seems to be a conflict: you need to store each product's corresponding ProductID value from the Product table, but you want to see the product's name. Fortunately, by using the Lookup Wizard, you can tell Access to do just that.

Deleting a lookup field

Initially, the Product field in the Order Details table is a lookup field. The underlying data stored in this field is a value, but the table displays the number for that corresponding product instead of the value. In this example, the lookup field was deleted so you could see the real contents of the field.

Creating a lookup field in Datasheet View

1. Open the table to which you're adding the lookup field in Datasheet view by double-clicking that table in the Database window. Or, select that table in the Database window and then click **Open**. In this example it's the Order Details table.

This example

You'll re-create the lookup field for the Product field in the Order Details table by referring to the ProductID field in the Products table. You can use similar tables. Just make sure the field to which you're adding the lookup feature is a foreign key field for the table that contains the related data you're going to display.

2. Select the field to which you're adding the lookup capability by clicking that column's header cell (the gray cell that contains the field's name). In this case it's the Product field.

3. Choose **Lookup Column** from the **Insert** menu to display the Lookup Wizard's first window, shown in Figure 13.3. When you choose this option, the resulting lookup list is dynamic. This means that if you add new items to or delete existing items from the associated table, the list will reflect those changes. In this case you want the lookup column to look up the values in a table or query option. Click **Next** when you're ready to continue.

4. The second window will then prompt you for the table that contains the items you want to display. The **View** options at the bottom of the window update the list box with the appropriate objects: tables, queries, or both. Remember, this table or query must have the primary key field to match the current table's foreign key. Select the **Products** table, as shown in Figure 13.4. Once you've chosen a table, a query, or both, click **Next**.

5. In the following window, you'll identify the field that contains the items you want to display in your lookup fields list. The **Available Fields** list box displays the fields in the table or query you selected in the previous table. Simply

double-click the appropriate field in the **Available Fields** list box to move it to the **Selected Fields** list box. In Figure 13.5, this list box displays the Products table's field names, and the ProductName field is selected. Click **Next** to continue.

FIGURE 13.3

The Lookup Wizard allows you to choose between displaying a list of existing items from a table or query and a list of items you will type.

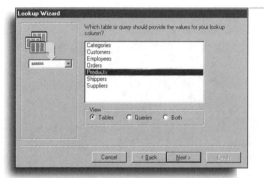

FIGURE 13.4

You want to display the contents of a field in the Products table.

FIGURE 13.5

Select the field that contains the items you want to display in your lookup field's list.

6. The next window gives you the opportunity to change the column's width and to display the primary key field. You can apply the Best Fit property (which will increase the width of the field to accommodate the longest item) by double-clicking the heading field's right border. The heading field is the gray cell that contains the field name. Or, you can simply pull out that border until you're satisfied with the column's width.

The **Hide Key Column (recommended)** option allows you to hide or display the primary key field that matches your current table's foreign key. You'll probably want to hide the primary key field, which is why the option is selected by default. If you want to display it, simply deselect this option. You don't want to display the primary key field, as shown in Figure 13.6. Click **Next** to continue.

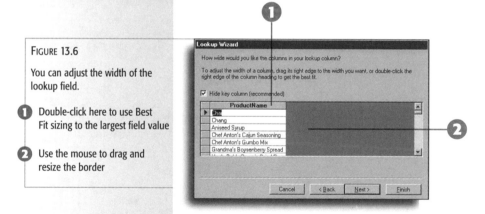

FIGURE 13.6

You can adjust the width of the lookup field.

1 Double-click here to use Best Fit sizing to the largest field value

2 Use the mouse to drag and resize the border

7. The final window allows you to enter descriptive text for your lookup field, such as the string "Product Name." You can also display more information on customizing the lookup field by selecting the **Display Help on Customizing the Lookup Column** option. Bypass this option and click **Finish**.

Figure 13.7 displays the results. The Product field now displays the corresponding product name from the Products table instead of a value. The table still remembers that value, but it doesn't display it.

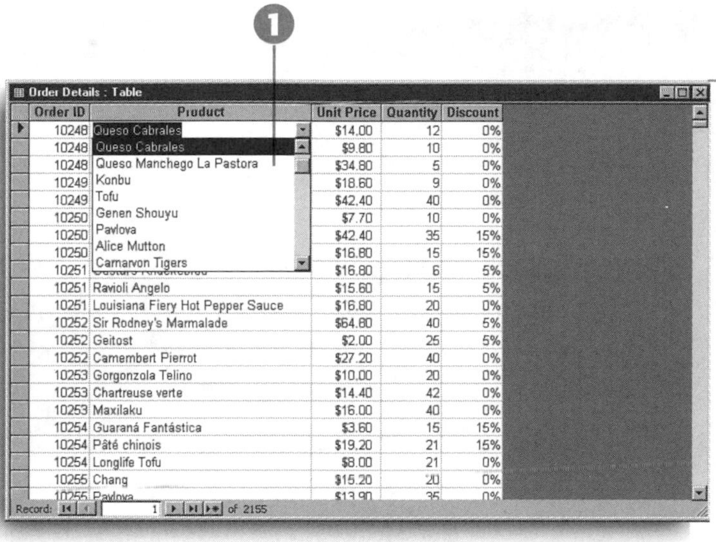

FIGURE 13.7

The new lookup field displays a list of product names.

1 Click the drop-down arrow to see all options for the field

Now, when you add a new record, you can simply choose an item from the Product field's lookup list instead of trying to remember that product's identification number. When you do, Access stores the product's identification number (the value from the ProductID field), not the product's name. Access simply displays the product name because it's more convenient.

You can also create a lookup field in Design view. The resulting lookup field is the same as the field you create in Datasheet view. In this next example, you'll create a lookup field in Design view and type in our own list items instead of displaying a list from a table or query.

Creating a lookup field in Design View

1. Open the table to which you want to add the lookup field in Design view by selecting that table in the Database window—this example uses **Order Details**—and then clicking **Design**.

2. Next, open the appropriate field's **Data Type** drop-down list. The ProductID field's drop-down list is shown in Figure 13.8. Select the **Lookup Wizard** option.

3. Once you've launched the Lookup Wizard, Access displays
   the first window, shown earlier in Figure 13.3. This time,
   choose the **I Will Type in the Values That I Want** option
   and click **Next**.

4. The second window is different from the second window in
   our previous example. This time, the wizard wants you to
   enter the lookup field's items. In addition, you can change
   the number of columns the lookup field will display. Retain
   the default, which is 1. Figure 13.9 shows the items you've
   entered for your lookup list. Once you've made the appropriate entries, click **Next**.

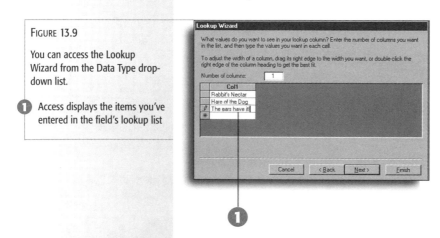

5. In the final window, enter descriptive text for your lookup field and click **Finish**.

6. Now, display the table in Datasheet View by clicking the View button ▓▣▾ on the Table Design toolbar. When Access asks you if you want to save the table, click **Yes**.

7. This time, there's a big difference. Access didn't write over the existing values with a corresponding item from the lookup list, which makes sense because there's no way for Access to relate an item to a value. You can choose an item from the lookup list, as shown in Figure 13.10, or you can leave them as they are and use the list for new records you enter.

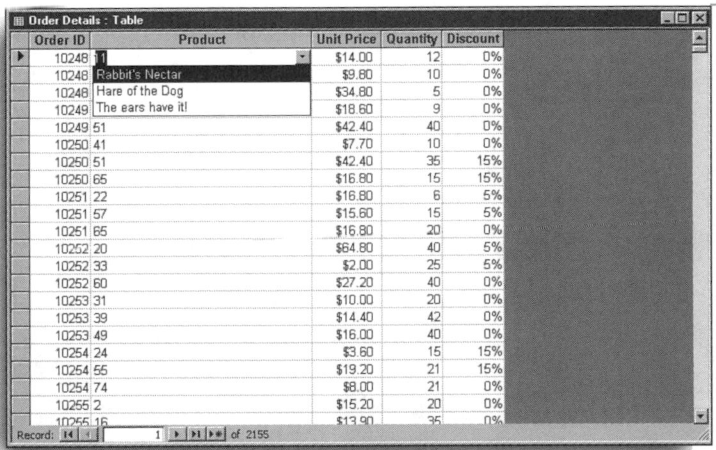

FIGURE 13.10
The new lookup field's drop-down list displays the items you've entered.

Using the *DLookUp()* Function

The DLookUp() function is one of Access' built-in functions and has long been a staple in many applications. You'll use this function to return a value from a specific field in a set domain. (A *domain* is a defined set of records.) This function is versatile and can be used most anywhere—in a macro, a procedure, a query expression, or even a calculated control.

You'll use DLookUp() to return (or display) data that's out of the current scope. In this sense, *scope* refers to the active source.

A lookup field is an inherited property

Access treats a lookup field as any other table property. If you base a form on a table that contains a lookup field, Access will pass on the lookup field's behavior and properties to the field's corresponding bound control.

That source can be a bound field. For instance, in a bound combo box, you might use DLookUp() to return a corresponding field entry from the current record. On the other hand, you can use DLookUp() to look up data in another table or query. Let's suppose the current recordset contains identification numbers that relate to a specific company name in another table. Instead of working with identification values that mean nothing, you could use DLookUp() to return the corresponding company's name.

SEE ALSO

➤ *For a broader definition of scope, see page 582.*

You'll use this function with this syntax:

```
DLookUp(expression, domain[, criteria])
```

expression identifies the field that contains the value you want to return. This argument is pretty versatile. It can be a simple reference to a field, or it can perform a calculation. However, this argument can't include another domain aggregate or SQL aggregate function.

What's a Domain or SQL Aggregate?

Aggregate functions return information about a set of records. DLookUp() is a domain aggregate because it considers a specific set of records in its search (the *domain* argument). There are two types of aggregate functions: domain and SQL. Both do the same thing, but you use them in different ways. Domain aggregates can be used in a VBA module, but not a SQL statement. SQL aggregates are used within a SQL statement, but can't be called in a VBA module. However, you can use both in a calculated control. The aggregate functions are as follows:

- Davg—Returns the average from a specific field within a specific set of records.

- Dcount—Counts the number of records within a specific set.

- DLookUp—Returns a value from a specific field in a set of records.

- DMin and Dmax—These two functions return the minimum or maximum value in a specific field within a specific set of records.

- DStDev, DStDevP—These estimate the standard deviation in a specific field of values within a specific set of records. You'll use DStDevP to evaluate a population and DStDev to evaluate a population sample.

- Dsum—Returns the total of the values in a specific field within in a specific set of records.

- Dvar, DVarP—These estimate variance across a specific field in a specific set of records. You'll use DVarP to evaluate population and Dvar to evaluate a population sample.

The second argument, *domain*, is a string expression that identifies the set of records, and *criteria* is an optional string expression that restricts the range of data. If you're familiar with SQL, you can compare the *criteria* argument to a SQL WHERE clause. However, you don't include the word WHERE. If you omit this argument, DLookUp() will consider all the records specified in *domain*. When you refer to a field using *criteria*, that field must be within *domain*.

Now, let's suppose you have a form based on the Order Details table, similar to the one shown in Figure 13.11. (The lookup field from the Order Details table was deleted before this example was created with the AutoForm Wizard.)

SEE ALSO

➤ *If you need help creating the form in this example, see page 72.*

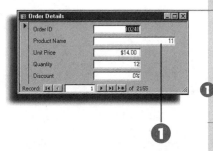

> **DLookUp()** results

If **DLookUp()** finds an appropriate value, it returns that value. If the function finds more than one possible value, **DLookUp()** returns the first value it encounters. If the function finds nothing, it returns null. Therefore, it's a good idea to check the results of a **DLookUp()** for a Null value in the form

    IsNull(DLookUp
    (expression,
    domain, criteria))

before preceding with the results.

FIGURE 13.11
The form displays the real contents of the ProductID field—a value, not the corresponding product's name.

❶ The ProductID value isn't particularly helpful

In the previous example, you created a lookup field to display the record's product name. You can also use the DLookUp() function to do this. Although the lookup field might seem easier to create, the DLookUp() function affects only the form. As is usually the case with Access, there's more than one way to get the job done.

You'll need to decide which solution best fits the situation at hand.

Using *DLookUp()*

1. Open the object to which you're adding the function—form, report, or query—in Design view. You're going to add a function to the Orders form to return the customer's phone number.

2. Add a text box below the City field in the upper-left corner.

SEE ALSO

➤ *To learn how to add a control to a form, see page 318.*

3. Open the text box's property sheet by double-clicking the control or by selecting the control and clicking the Properties button ![icon] on the **Form Design** toolbar. Select the **Control Source** property and enter the expression

   ```
   =DLookUp("[Phone]","Customers","[CustomerID]='" &
   [Forms]![Orders]![CustomerID] & "'")
   ```

   You want to return the phone number, [Phone], from the Customers table, where the table's CustomerID equals the current record's CustomerID value.

4. To see the results, shown in Figure 13.12, click the View button ![icon] on the **Form Design** toolbar. As you can see, the additional text box displays the current customer's phone number.

FIGURE 13.12

The text box you added displays the result of a DLookUp( ) function—the customer's phone number.

1 A DLookUp( ) function has been added to this text box

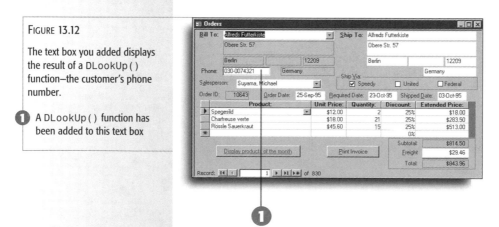

About Those Delimiters

You may have noticed that the DLookUp() function contained some extra delimiters. A *delimiter* is a predefined character that separates one component from another. Specifically, you included a pair of single quotes (') within the criteria argument to separate the actual criteria from the field that contains the data you're searching. This was necessary because you included a reference in the argument and Access sees this reference as a string, even though the control in question—CustomerID—contains a value. You must delimit a string in a WHERE clause in the form

```
"[control you're matching]=' " & reference & " ' "
```

Don't include the spaces between the different delimiters—double and single quotes. They've been added so it's easier to discern which characters you've used and in what order.

SEE ALSO

➤ *If you're not familiar with the concatenation operator (&), read about it on page 395.*

Delimiting Variables

The same is true when you use a string variable in a WHERE clause. Simply substitute the *reference* argument with the variable. However, if the variable contains a value, it requires no delimiters.

If your variable contains a date or time value, use the # delimiter in the form

```
"[control you're matching]=# " & variable & " # "
```

SEE ALSO

➤ *For an example of this technique, see page 430.*

➤ *Both the list box and combo box controls display lookup lists. To learn more about the list box, see page 141 and page 152.*

Replacing delimiters with the Chr() function

Working with delimiters, especially the string delimiters, can be difficult. You can easily avoid problems by replacing delimiters with a Chr() function. The Chr(34) function returns double quotes, so you can concatenate double quotes in the form

```
"[control you're matching]=" &
Chr(34) & variable & Chr(34)
```

Defining and Working with Relationships

Why you need relationships

How to create, modify, and delete relationships

The three joins

Bringing the Information Together

Once you normalize your tables, you can begin entering data and then manipulating, analyzing, and reporting that data. To interact with your database, you'll base forms and reports on your tables (you can also base forms and reports on queries). However, all the data you want to work with won't always reside in one table.

This is where relationships come into play. For your purposes, a *relationship* is an association (link) between two related fields in different tables. In this sense, *related* means *the same*. In other words, a relationship can exist between two tables that share the same data. For instance, if you assign a product number to each of your products, you'd also use that number to identify each product in an order table, an invoice table, a shipping table, and so on. Therefore, the data type would be the same, and that's the critical issue. The field name doesn't have to match, but the data type does, except when the primary key is an AutoNumber. Then Access will relate the AutoNumber field to a Number field.

Benefits of Using Relationships

Access will automatically join related fields between tables if you create a relationship between them. As a result, you can easily base queries, forms, and reports on more than one table. Using multi-table queries for forms or reports will increase your application's flexibility by allowing you to work with one recordset that's based on more than one table.

Subforms and subreports also benefit from relationships. If a relationship exists between the main form and the subform, Access will automatically display records in the subform that relate to the main form's data.

Another benefit is the ability to enforce referential integrity—a set of rules that determine when you can add, modify, and delete records. If there's no relationship, you can't enforce these rules.

SEE ALSO

➤ *If you'd like to know more about the normalizing process, see page 13.*

What's a recordset?

A *recordset* is the collection of records that's attached to an object at any given time. A query's recordset will depend on the tables you add to the query. A form's recordset is determined by its Record Source setting. Same with a report. In addition, you can use VBA to create or modify an object's recordset.

How Relationships Between Objects Work

At this point, you may be wondering just what a relationship does. It pulls associated (related) data together. For instance, if you try to run a query on two unrelated tables, you'll get a mish-mash of data that means absolutely nothing to anybody. If you create a relationship between those tables, however, the query will be more discriminating about which records are included in the results. The same is true with subforms and subreports. Without a relationship, a subform or a subreport displays all its attached records, not just those that pertain to the main form or the current group, respectively. The great part is that Access accomplishes all of this with very little help from you.

Now let's take a look at the three different types of relationships.

One-to-One Relationships

Let's suppose you have two tables, each table has the same number of records, and each record in one table is related to only one record in the other table. That's a one-to-one relationship, probably the least common type. In addition, a subform based on this arrangement would probably be overkill—you might as well display the matching records from both tables together in the main form.

One-to-Many Relationships

A one-to-many relationship is probably the most common relationship between two tables. With this arrangement, the *many* table can contain more than one record for each record in the *one* table, but doesn't have to have a related record for each record in the one table. However, every record in the many table must relate to only one record in the one table.

For instance, your supplier table will contain only one record for each supplier. Furthermore, each record in your product table relates to a particular supplier. However, you can have many records in the product table for each supplier, or you can have no records in the product table for a supplier. You can't have a record in the products table from a supplier that doesn't exist in the supplier table.

Many-to-Many Relationships

The many-to-many relationship is the "problem child" of the group. That's because this relationship requires a third table. In a many-to-many relationship, one table can contain many records for each record in the other table. For example, a specific order in an orders table can relate to many products in a products table. In addition, a product in the products table can appear in any number of orders in the orders table.

Ordinarily, you'd have only one record for each product in the products table, and only one record in the orders table for each order. However, to maintain the relationship, you'd actually end up with several records for each order—a record for each product in each order instead of one record for each order.

Primary Keys and Relationships

The easiest way to define a relationship is to make the related field a primary key. You won't just pick a table at random. Rather, a primary key contains unique values—many developers use the AutoNumber data type to ensure a field of unique entries. For instance, in the previous example, you noted a table for product numbers, orders, invoices, and shipping data. Often your data, such as a product or employee number, will provide a natural primary key. Beyond containing a unique value, each field in your table must be related to the primary key field. In other words, all other data must describe or enhance the primary key field.

In this example, the product number table would be the parent table because it contains the primary key field. Once you make the product number field a primary key, Access will automatically relate any other tables that contain the same field. These related tables will be *child* tables, and the matching field is

Resolving many-to-many duplications

If you end up with a many-to-many relationship, you should create a third table whose primary key is based on the original tables' primary key fields to create a multiple-field primary key. This table will have a one-to-many relationship with both tables. Each record in the first table can have many related records in the new table, but each record in the new table will relate to only one record in the first table. Likewise with the second table.

known as a *foreign key*. Access doesn't mark a foreign key as it does a primary key, so don't look for foreign keys in Design view.

In addition, there are a few other things you should know about relationships:

- Access won't automatically relate tables that don't have a primary key.
- Even if a primary key and foreign key exist, Access won't create a relationship if the field names don't match.
- You can manually relate fields when a primary key doesn't exist or the field names don't match.
- You can't create a relationship between two fields of differing data types or field size.

SEE ALSO

➤ *You can learn more about primary and foreign keys on page 19 and page 199.*

➤ *For a definition of the* AutoNumber *data type, see page 196.*

Using the Relationships Window

You can view the relationships between tables and queries in the Relationships window, shown in Figure 14.1. You'll also see the main toolbar buttons you need to use for this window. Initially, this window is empty. You must add objects to it and then view exiting relationships, create new ones, and even delete them.

Exploring the Relationships window

1. Open the Northwind database.

2. Choose the **Relationships** command from the **Tools** menu, or press Alt+T+R. Access will display this database's Relationships window, as shown in Figure 14.2. This database already has several established relationships. (Until you add objects to the window, Access will open the Show Table dialog box along with the window.)

Don't want an automatic relationship?

Access automatically creates a relationship between two tables when both tables contain the same field data type and field size, and one of those fields is a primary key. If you don't want Access to create these relationships automatically, you can turn off this feature by selecting **Options** from the **Tools** menu. Then, select the **Tables/Queries** tab and deselect the **Enable AutoJoin** option.

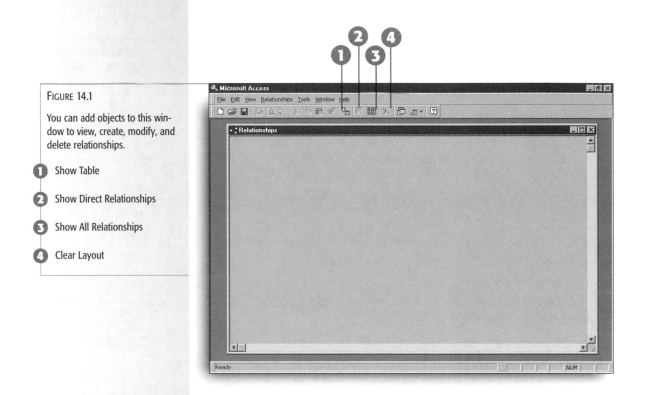

FIGURE 14.1

You can add objects to this window to view, create, modify, and delete relationships.

1. Show Table

2. Show Direct Relationships

3. Show All Relationships

4. Clear Layout

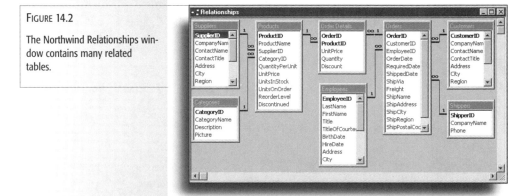

FIGURE 14.2

The Northwind Relationships window contains many related tables.

3. To clear the current layout, click the Clear Layout button
⊠ on the Relationship toolbar. You'll need to confirm your
request by clicking **Yes** on the resulting warning
message.

3. Now add a few tables. First, click the Show Table button
or press Alt+R+T. Access will display the Show Table dialog
box, shown in Figure 14.3. As you can see, this box contains
three tabs—**Tables**, **Queries**, and **Both**. As you click each
tab, Access will update the contents of that tab's control
accordingly. For instance, if you click the **Tables** tab, Access
will display all the tables in the database. The **Queries** tab
will display all the queries, and the **Both** tab will display all
the tables and queries.

FIGURE 14.3

The Show Table dialog box gives
you access to the database's tables
and queries.

4. Select the **Tables** tab, and then double-click **Categories** to
add that table to the window. Then double-click **Products**
to add it as well. Click the **Close** button in the Show Table
dialog box to close that box. At this point, your Relationship
window should resemble the one shown in Figure 14.4.

As you can see, Access has inserted a join line to indicate that
these two tables already have a relationship. You can tell a lot
from this line. First, the relationship is based on an *inner join*.
That means Access selects only those records from both tables
that have a matching value in the related field. In other words, if
the Category table has a value in the CategoryID field that does-
n't exist in the Products table (and vice versa), that record isn't
included in any query results.

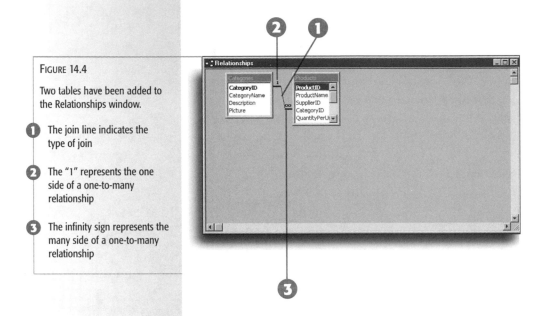

FIGURE 14.4

Two tables have been added to the Relationships window.

1 The join line indicates the type of join

2 The "1" represents the one side of a one-to-many relationship

3 The infinity sign represents the many side of a one-to-many relationship

The "1" and the infinity sign tell you that the relationship is a one-to-many relationship. More specifically, the **Categories** table is the one side, and the **Products** table is the many side. That means the **Products** table can have many records related to any one record in the **Categories** table. The presence of the "1" and the infinity sign also tells us that the relationship forces *referential integrity*—rules that protect your data by restricting when you can add and delete records. If the relationship doesn't force referential integrity, Access displays the join line but no symbols.

There are several ways to select objects in the Show Table dialog box and then add them to the Relationships window.

- Select an object and click the **Add** button.
- Double-click an object.
- Select an object and press Enter.
- Use the arrow keys to highlight an object, and then press Alt+A.

SEE ALSO

➤ *For another look at relationships, see page 18.*

Deleting Relationships

You can delete a relationship at any time. Just select the join line and press the Delete key. If you delete a table from the Relationships window, Access will delete both the table and the join line from the window. However, Access doesn't delete the table from the database or delete the relationship.

Deleting and adding objects and relationships

1. Open the Northwind database, or any database that has related objects. From the **Tools** menu, choose the **Relationships** command. (You can also click the Relationships icon 🔲 or press Alt+T+R.

2. If the window is empty, click the Show Table button 🔲 on the Relationship toolbar and add two or more related objects to the window. Use the Products and Categories tables from the previous exercise.

3. Click one of the field list boxes (it doesn't matter which one) and press the Delete key. This removes the field list box from the workspace.

4. Remember, you didn't delete the table or the relationship; you just deleted those objects from the window. To prove this, add the Categories table back to the window by clicking the Show Tables button and double-clicking the Categories table in the Show Table dialog box. Then click the **Close** button to return to the Relationships window. The window is the same as it was before you deleted the field list box.

5. To delete the relationship, select the join line between the two field list boxes and press the Delete key. When Access asks you to confirm the choice, click **Yes**. Access will delete the join line but leave the field list boxes, as shown in Figure 14.5.

Resizing the field lists

Access displays the Products table with a scrollbar. If you like, you can increase the depth of this field table in order to see all the fields at once, eliminating the scrollbar. Position the mouse on the lower border of the field list, left-click it—but don't release it—and then pull that border down until you can see all the field names. The scrollbar disappears.

An alternate method of adding an object to the Relationships window

In the current exercise, you've deleted a table from the Relationships window and then used the Show Tables dialog box to display it again. You can also use the Show Direct Relationships button 🔲 or the Show All Relationships button 🔲 on the Relationships toolbar. The Show Direct Relationships button will display all the objects related to the current object; the Show All Relationships button will show all the related objects in the database. However, using either button will display not only the table you deleted, but any that are related to it.

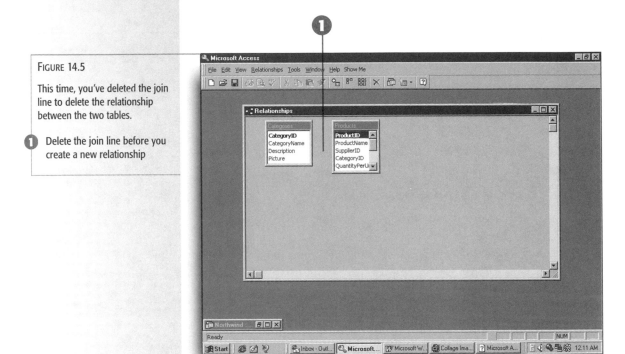

Creating relationships in the QBE grid

If a relationship doesn't exist between two tables and you create one in a query's QBE grid by dragging a primary key field from one table to another, you create a temporary relationship for that object. This relationship affects only that query. Similarly, if a permanent relationship does exist and you delete a join line between two tables or queries in a QBE grid, you don't delete the relationship. You delete the relationship for that query only. To create a permanent and global relationship, you must use the Relationships window.

Creating a Relationship

Adding a primary key is only one way to create a relationship. In the Relationships window, you can create a relationship by dragging the related field from one field list to the same field in another table.

An alternative way to create a relationship

1. Use the last window from the previous exercise, or open the Relationships window and delete a join line.

2. To join (or rejoin) the two tables, click the related field in one field list—but don't relcase the mouse button. Then, drag that field to the other table and drop it on top of the same field in the second list box. In this case, the CategoryID field is dragged from the Products table to the Categories table.

3. When you release the mouse button to drop the field, Access displays the dialog box shown in Figure 14.6. The Table/Query and Related Table/Query controls display the two objects you're relating (joining). You can change the related field by selecting another field from the **Categories** table's drop-down list. You won't use this option very often.

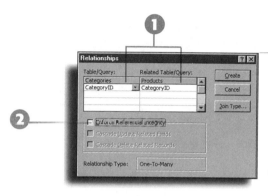

FIGURE 14.6

Use this dialog box to define the relationship you're creating between the Products table and the Categories table.

① The related tables and fields

② This protects the integrity of your data

The **Enforce Referential Integrity** option allows you to turn on this feature. Doing so will keep you from adding or deleting records inappropriately:

- You can't add to the many table if there's no related record in the one table.

- You can't delete a record from the one table if related records exist in the many table.

If you choose this option, you can then choose from the Cascade options, but it isn't necessary to do so. The **Cascade Update Related Fields** option affects your updates:

- If you select this option and then update a primary key field in the one table, Access will update any corresponding foreign key values in the many table.

- If you leave this feature turned off, Access won't allow you to change a primary key value in the one table if the many table contains related records.

The **Cascade <u>D</u>elete Related Records** option is similar to **Cascade <u>U</u>pdate Related Fields**, except it affects the way you delete records:

- When selected, Access will delete related records from the many table if you delete the corresponding primary key record in the one table.
- If you don't select this option, Access won't allow you to delete a primary key record in the one table if the many table contains related records.

4. Now click the **Join Type** button to display the dialog box shown in Figure 14.7. This feature allows you to define the type of join the relationship will produce. A *join* determines how the relationship between two tables affects the result of a query that's bound to those tables. Specifically, the join decides which records are selected or acted on. There are two types of joins:

- Inner join—The default join type, which selects only those records from both tables that have a matching value in the related field.
- Outer join—Includes all the records from one table and only those records in the second that match the value in the related field.

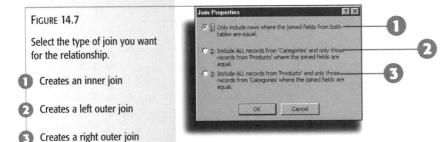

FIGURE 14.7

Select the type of join you want for the relationship.

1 Creates an inner join

2 Creates a left outer join

3 Creates a right outer join

5. You don't want to change the default join type, so click **OK** to return to the Relationships dialog box. Select the **E<u>n</u>force Referential Integrity** option, and then click the **<u>C</u>reate** button. The resulting join line appears just like the original one in Figure 14.4. It displays the "1" beside the Categories table and the infinity sign beside the Products table.

Understanding Joins

Try not to let joins frustrate you—they are really simple. For instance, Figure 14.8 displays the logic behind a simple inner join. Viewed this way, the concept is easy to grasp. If an inner join relationship exists between the Categories and Products tables, a bound query will return only those records from both tables that have a matching value, CategoryID, in the related field. Most queries rely on an inner join relationship.

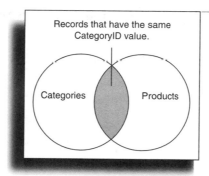

Records that have the same CategoryID value.

Categories   Products

FIGURE 14.8

An inner join is easy to understand if you think of the result as the intersection of two circles.

An outer join is a bit more complex because it includes all the records from one table and only those records from the second table that match the related field's value. You're probably wondering which table is which, right? Either table is correct. You see, there are two types of outer joins: a *left outer join* and a *right outer join*. A left outer join includes all the records from the one table and only the matching records from the many table, as shown in Figure 14.9. A right outer join includes all the records from the many table and only the matching records from the one table, as shown in Figure 14.10.

To modify the join, right-click the join line and click the **Edit Relationship** option to display the Relationships dialog box. If you select a left outer join, the join line points a small arrow at the many table, as shown in Figure 14.11. A right outer join points to the one table, as shown in Figure 14.12.

Why left and right?

The terms "left" and "right" in an outer join come from traditional database design, in which the one table is always drawn to the left of the many table.

FIGURE 14.9

A left outer join includes the entire one table, but only records from the many table that match the primary key value.

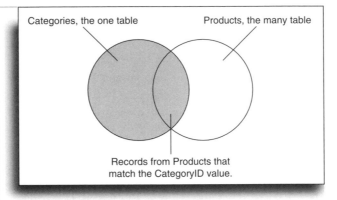

Categories, the one table

Products, the many table

Records from Products that match the CategoryID value.

FIGURE 14.10

A right outer join includes the entire many table but only records from the one table that match the primary key value.

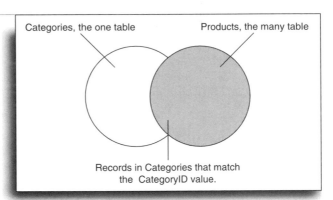

Categories, the one table

Products, the many table

Records in Categories that match the CategoryID value.

FIGURE 14.11

A left join points to the many table.

1 The many table

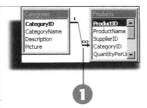

FIGURE 14.12

A left join points to the many table.

1 The one table

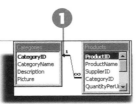

A right outer join points to the one table

Printing the Relationships Window

Access doesn't have a built-in method for printing the Relationships window or a database's relationships. You have two options for doing so.

You can use the Print Scrn key to capture a copy of the screen to the Windows Clipboard, open a graphics application such as Paintbrush, and copy the contents to a new document there. However, this doesn't work for large databases or for showing all the fields in a number of tables.

The second method requires downloading and installing an add-in. You can download a free add-in named Print Wizard from the Microsoft Web site at www.microsoft.com/accessdev/ articles/printwiz/default.htm. Just follow the instructions you find at the site, but be sure to note which directory you download the file to. Once you've downloaded, find the add-in file, Prels80.exe, and double-click it to install it.

When you're ready to print a Relationships window, choose **Add-Ins** from the **Tools** menu and then select **Print Relationships** from the resulting submenu. The wizard will create a report that displays a graphical representation of the current and permanent relationships.

SEE ALSO

➤ *For detailed instructions on downloading this and other add-ins, see page 172.*

Manipulating Data for Practical Results

Designing and Using Queries

Retrieve data from one or more tables using a Select query

Group data and perform calculations with a Crosstab query

Create a new table with selected data using a Make-Table query

Update fields within a table using an Update query

Add records to an existing table using an Append query

Delete selected records from a table using a Delete query

Retrieving Data with Select Queries

In Chapter 4, "Using the Query Wizards," you learned how to create simple Select queries using the wizard. This chapter expands on that information, showing you how to create and modify a number of different queries by using the Design View grid.

Exporting Tables to Create a Sample Database

For the examples in this chapter, you need a database with data and relationships. You can create a database from one of the wizards, or you can create a new database based on an existing database. The examples in this chapter use a database called chap15.mdb. This Access 97 database consists of the Customers and Orders tables exported from the Northwind sample database that comes with Access 97. Because you'll often want to export some or all of a database into another database, let's start with exporting tables into a database that you can use for this chapter's exercises.

To create your own chap15.mdb database by exporting tables from the Northwind sample database, follow these steps:

Exporting existing tables to create a new database

1. Create a new database and name it chap15.mdb. This should be a blank database.

2. Close your new database and open the Northwind sample database that is included with Access 97.

3. Select the Tables tab in the Database Window and right-click the **Customers** table.

4. Select **Save As/Export** from the pop-up menu, as shown in Figure 15.1.

5. A dialog box appears, asking if you want to save the table to an external database or within the current database. Save the file to an external database.

6. Another dialog box appears that allows you to locate the blank database that you created in Step 1. Click on this database and then click the **Export** button.

FIGURE 15.1

Exporting the Customers table from the Northwind sample database.

You can either export just the structure of the table or export both the structure and the data. Export both the structure and the data.

7. The Customers table is duplicated in the blank database that you created in Step 1. Repeat these steps to duplicate the Orders table in your new database.

You should now have a clean database with just two tables, which you can use to practice the art of querying your database.

> **Using this sample database in other chapters**
>
> You might want to copy this database renamed for the next few chapters now so that you have the basic sample database without any queries. That way you don't have to go through the export process to make a "clean" copy if you save the queries you make here.

Creating a Select Query without Using a Wizard

The Select query is the query you are likely to use most often. It is used to retrieve rows of data from one or more tables or queries in your database and display the results in a datasheet. In this section, you'll learn how to create a Select query without using the wizard.

Access 97 makes it very simple to create a query without using a wizard. To create a Select query without using the Simple Select Query Wizard, follow these steps:

Using the Design View Grid to create a simple query

1. Open a sample database, or `chap15.mdb`, or your own sample database. Click the **Queries** tab in the Database window.

2. Click the **New** button, select **Design View**, and click **OK**.

3. The query that you are creating will open up in Design view, as shown in Figure 15.2. The Show Table dialog box will be positioned in front of the Design view. Select one or more tables from this dialog box and click the **Add** button. For this example, you will only select the Customers table.

FIGURE 15.2

Adding tables to your query in Design view.

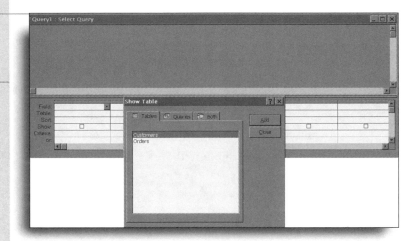

Selecting more than one table at a time

You can select more than one table or query at a time by holding down the Ctrl key while clicking on the items in the dialog box. You can also select a range of items by clicking the first item in the range and then holding down the Shift key while clicking the last item.

4. Once you have added the Customers table, click **Close** to close the Show Table dialog box.

5. To add fields to your query in Design view, drag the field name from the field list down to the design grid. You can add all the fields from a table or query to your query by dragging the asterisk from the field list to the design grid. For this example, drag the CompanyName and ContactName fields down to the design grid. Your query should look like the example shown in Figure 15.3.

6. You can save this query as-is and generate a simple select query, or you can enter criteria for the query or add a sort order to further refine your query. For this example, you will add a sort order so that the result set will be returned to you sorted alphabetically in the CompanyName field.

7. To add the sort order to the CompanyName field, click in the Sort row of the design grid under the CompanyName field. You can sort the query by ascending or descending order.

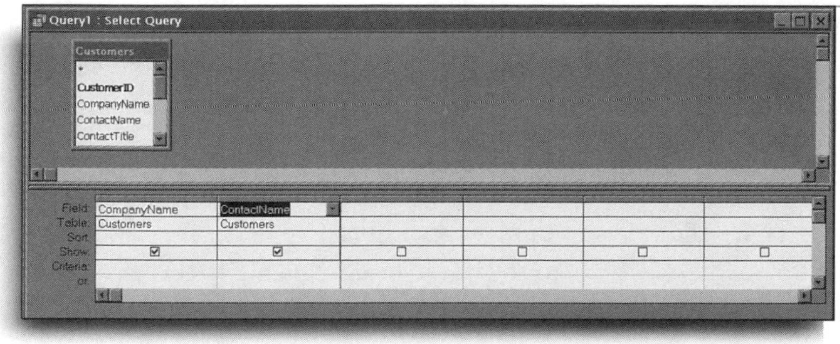

FIGURE 15.3
Adding fields to your query in Design view.

8. Click the Save icon ▣ on the toolbar to save the query. A dialog box will prompt you to name the query before saving it.

Grouping Data and Performing Calculations with a Crosstab Query

Crosstab queries are used to calculate a total for a set of data that is arranged into two groups of information. One group is arranged down the left side of the datasheet as a set of rows, and the other group is arranged across the top as a set of columns. The types of totals that can be calculated using a Crosstab query include sums, averages, and counts.

You saw in Chapter 4 how to use the wizard to create the Crosstab query. In this section you will create a Crosstab query from scratch using the Query Design Grid.

SEE ALSO

➤ *If you want to see how to create a Crosstab query with the wizard, see page 60.*

Creating a Crosstab Query Using the Design View Grid

To create a Crosstab query without using the Crosstab Wizard, follow these steps:

Using the Design View Grid to create a Crosstab query

1. Open your sample database or chap15.mdb. Click the **Queries** tab in the Database window.

2. Click the **New** button, select **Design View**, and click **OK**.

3. Now that your query is open in Design view, double-click the Orders table in the Show Tables dialog box to add it to your new Crosstab query. Click **Close** to close the Show Tables dialog box.

4. Add fields to the Crosstab query by dragging them from the field list box to the query design grid. For this example, you will use the EmployeeID and ShipCity fields from the Orders table.

5. Click the Query Type icon [icon] on the toolbar and select **Crosstab Query,** as shown in Figure 15.4.

FIGURE 15.4

Changing the query to a Crosstab query.

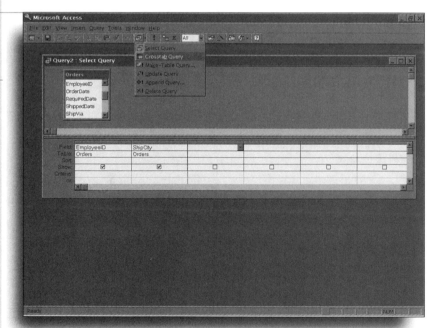

6. This will add a new row to the Query Design Grid called Crosstab. For the fields that you want to appear in the final query as rows of data, click the **Crosstab** row and select **Row Heading**. For this example, let the ShipCity field appear as the rows in your query.

7. Click in the **Crosstab** row of the EmployeeID field and select **Column Heading**. This will set up your query so that the employees' IDs are used for column headings in the resulting datasheet.

8. Because you need to have a value for your datasheet, you need to add the EmployeeID field to your query design grid again so that it shows up twice. Drag the EmployeeID field down to the design grid, click in the **Crosstab** row, and select **Value**.

9. The Crosstab query that you are generating should now look like the one shown in Figure 15.5.

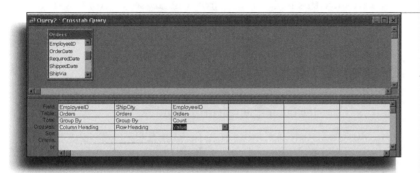

FIGURE 15.5
The final Crosstab query, ready to run.

10. Click the Run icon to run this query. The result set shows the ship cities as rows down the left side of the datasheet, and shows employee IDs as columns across the top. This query shows the total sales that each employee made for each ship city. You can save your query by clicking the Save icon ![save icon] on the toolbar.

Creating a New Table with Selected Data Using a Make-Table Query

In Access 97, there are four types of queries that are collectively known as *action queries*, so named because running them can make changes to many records within your database with just one action. The four types of queries are listed here and covered in the next four sections of this chapter:

- Make-Table query
- Update query
- Append query
- Delete query

Creating a Make-Table Query

You can easily create a new table and populate it with data from one or more existing tables by using a Make-Table query. You can store this table in the current database, or you can specify another database that you want to add the table to.

Follow these steps to create a table using the Make-Table query:

Creating a table with a query

1. Open chap15.mdb or your own sample database. Click the **Queries** tab in the Database window.

2. Click the **New** button. When the dialog box appears, select **Design View** and click **OK**.

3. Double-click the **Customers** table in the Show Table dialog box, and click **Close**.

4. You should now be in the Design view of a new query, with the Customers table showing in the top section of the Query Design Grid.

5. Create a query by dragging the fields that will make up the new table down to the Query Design Grid. For this example, you will build the new table using the CompanyName, Phone, and Fax fields from the Customers table. When your new table is completed, it can be used as a form of phone book for your customers.

6. Click on the Query Type icon 🔲▾ on the toolbar, and select **Make-Table Query** from the pulldown box.

7. The Make-Table query dialog box appears, as shown in Figure 15.6. Enter the name of your new table in the space provided, and click either **Current Database** or

Another Database. If you decide to save the table into another database, you need to indicate the name of that database in the text box titled File Name. If this other database is not located in the same directory as the current database, you will need to enter the full path to the other database. For this example, you will name the table `PhoneDir` and save it to the current database.

FIGURE 15.6
Entering the new table name in your Make-Table query.

8. Now that you are back in the Design view of your query, you can either save the query to your database or click the Run icon on the toolbar to generate your new table right away. When you decide to run the query, and after it is finished processing, you will be prompted with a dialog box like that shown in Figure 15.7. This dialog box will tell you how many rows of data are being pasted into your new table, and asks if you really want to generate a new table. Click the **Yes** button.

FIGURE 15.7
Viewing the creation of a new table with your Make-Table query.

The new table PhoneDir should now be a part of your database. If you have assigned any field properties or primary keys to the data that is used to create your new table in a Make-Table query, you must reconstruct these properties and reassign a primary key. Field properties and primary keys are not transferred with the data in a Make-Table query. Regardless of this, the Make-Table query is a very useful component of Access 97. You can use

Previewing a table before you create it

If you have a Make-Table query open in Design View, you can preview the table that will be created without actually running the Make-Table query. Just click on the View icon and select **Datasheet View** from the pulldown box.

a Make-Table query to archive old records from your current database or to make backups of the data in your database, among other things.

Update Fields within a Table Using an Update Query

Generally, Update queries are used to update a broad range of records that reside in one or more tables. If there are only a few records to update in a single table, most people will simply update those records directly in the datasheet. This becomes much more daunting when you have to change a large amount of data that's spread out over more than one table.

Using an Update query

1. Open chap15.mdb or your own sample database. Click the **Queries** tab in the Database window.

2. Click the **New** button and select **Design View**. Then click **OK**.

   For this example, you will construct an Update query to run against the Orders table. The Orders table has a column called EmployeeID that lists the employee ID of the employee that is responsible for each order. For this example, you will assume that the employee who used employee ID number 1 was promoted to regional sales manager, and that employee 2 is going to assume the first employees' responsibilities. There are 830 records in the Orders table, so clearly it would take too long to reassign all the employee 1 orders to employee 2. This is a perfect case for using an Update query.

3. Double-click the Orders table in the Show Table dialog box, and then click **Close**.

4. Drag the EmployeeID field from the field list box down to the Query Design Grid. Click on the Query Type icon 🔲▾. Select **Update Query** from the pulldown box that appears.

5. A new row has been added to your query design grid called Update To. This is where you will add the value that you want to change the Employee ID to. Click in this field and enter 2.

If you ran this Update query as it is, you would change *all* the employee IDs to "2". You obviously do not want to do this, so you need to add criteria to your query that will tell the Update query which records to update. Right-click in the **Criteria:** row of your Query Design Grid.

6. Select **Build** from the pulldown menu that appears, as shown in Figure 15.8.

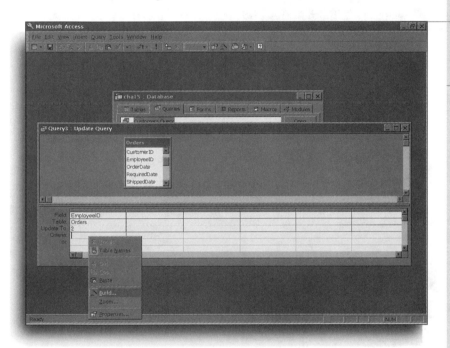

FIGURE 15.8
Beginning to build the criteria for your Update query.

7. The Expression Builder dialog box appears, as shown in Figure 15.9. This is a very complicated-looking dialog box that allows you to create intricate expressions in a visual interface instead of typing in the code by hand. This chapter is only going to scratch the surface of the capabilities of the Expression Builder, however.

8. Double-click the small **+** sign beside the Tables folder. This will open up a listing of all the tables that are currently in your database.

FIGURE 15.9

Using the Expression Builder.

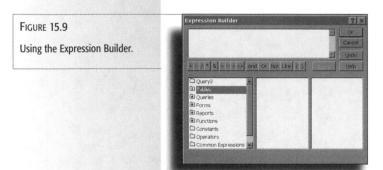

9. Because you are trying to update the Orders table, double-click on this table to open up a listing of all the columns in that table.

10. Select the EmployeeID column out of this listing, and double-click **<Value>** in the next box. This will start writing the code for your criteria in the text box above.

11. Click the **=** button directly underneath the text box and then type in 1. The dialog box should look like the one shown in Figure 15.10.

FIGURE 15.10

The completed criteria for your Update query.

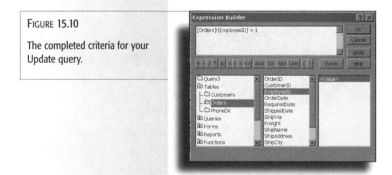

12. Click **OK** to add this newly created criteria to the Query Design Grid.

13. You may now either save this Update query to run at a later time or click on the Run icon to run it right away.

In either case, when you run this Update query, the query will process and then prompt you with a dialog box like that shown in Figure 15.11. This dialog box will tell you how many records are about to be updated and ask if you want to update the records. You cannot undo this command by using the **Edit, Undo** command.

With one simple Update query, you have just updated 123 records and saved yourself a large chunk of editing time. The time savings becomes even more apparent when you are dealing with an update that runs many thousands of records.

Adding Records to an Existing Table Using an Append Query

Another built-in Access 97 query that is a real timesaver is called the Append query. You use this to add records to the end of an existing table or tables in a database. You can use more than one table to generate your Append query. Append queries can be very useful in combining databases without having to retype all the information in the existing tables.

You can also use an Append query to add records to a table when all the fields of the two tables do not match. For example, say you have a table that has 22 fields in it, and another table with only 10 fields that match any of those 22 fields. You can use an Append query to append the records in the table with 10 fields to the table with 22 fields, and have the query ignore the 12 fields that do not match the first table.

Adding records to a table using an Append query

1. Open chap15.mdb or your own sample database. Click the **Queries** tab in the Database window.

2. Click the **New** button and select **Design View** from the dialog box that appears. Click **OK**.

For this example, you are going to use the PhoneDir table that you created in a previous example in this chapter. The PhoneDir table contains the phone and fax numbers of all of your customers, so this Append query you are building would be useful if you drove your competitors out of business and acquired their customers. For the purpose of this example, you are going to append the PhoneDir table to itself, but this query would work just as well if you were appending the contents of your competitor's phone directory to yours. With this in mind, double-click the PhoneDir table in the Show Table dialog box and then click **Close**.

3. Drag all the fields in the field listing down to the Query Design Grid. Click on the Query Type icon 🔲▾ and select **Append Query**, as shown in Figure 15.12.

FIGURE 15.12

Changing your query to an Append query.

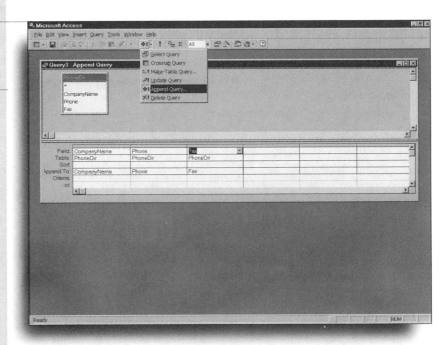

4. A dialog box appears that asks for the name of the table that you want to append to. Select **PhoneDir** from the pulldown box, and make sure that the **Current Database** option is selected.

5. A new row appears in your query design grid called Append To. This row shows the fields in the new table that you will append the fields in the old table to. If there is no field that matches, just delete the field from the Query Design Grid.

6. At this point, you can either save the query to your database or click on the Run icon to execute the query immediately. Whenever you decide to run an Append query, it will process and then you will be prompted by a dialog box such as that shown in Figure 15.13. This dialog box indicates how many records are about to be appended to the end of the table and asks if you want to continue. Click the **Yes** button.

FIGURE 15.13
Viewing the results of your Append query

The Append query that you just ran added duplicate records to your PhoneDir table. Normally that would not happen because you would have a primary key set up on the table not to allow duplicates. Because you built the PhoneDir table using a Make-Table query, your table did not have an unique index.

Deleting Selected Records from a Table Using a Delete Query

You can use the last type of Action query, the Delete query, to delete records from one or more tables. The Delete query can be used to delete old sales records from a table or to update a table that lists inventory items. Remember, though, that when

Ending a query before it is done

You can stop a running query by holding down the Ctrl key and pressing the Break key.

you use a Delete query, it is not possible to delete the contents of only one field in a record. The Delete query always deletes whole records.

The Delete query should be used when you need to delete a large number of records, or when you have to search through a large number of records to find the items to delete. For the purpose of this example, assume that your company has been forbidden by the government of Brazil to continue business in that country. You no longer need the Brazilian entries in your database, so you can use a Delete query to make sure that they are deleted correctly. The Brazilian entries show up in all of your tables, so you need to delete them from all of them.

This also highlights a good reason to use a Delete query. Instead of having to hunt through several records in both tables and cross-reference them yourself, you can use the Delete query to remove all references to your previous customers in Brazil from all of your tables in one transaction.

Ensuring Relationships for a Delete Query

To enable this kind of transaction with the Delete query, you have to make sure that your tables have the right relationship. Your tables need to be able to support a cascading Update and Delete. This is when you delete a record in the primary table and the related records in the secondary tables are also deleted. In this case, it's necessary because you not only need to delete your Brazilian customers' references in the Customers table, but also you need to delete their orders in the Orders table and their phone information in the PhoneDir table.

Follow these steps to ensure that your tables in the chap15.mdb database have the necessary relationships to enable cascading Updates and Deletes:

Checking relationships for a Delete query

1. Open the chap15.mdb or your own sample database. Click the **Tables** tab in the Database window.

2. Click the Relationships icon ⊞. A blank window should appear, unless you have previously defined relationships in your database.

3. Right-click on the blank window, and select **Show Table** from the pulldown box that appears. Click on the first table in the list of tables in your database, and then click on the last table in the list while holding down the Shift key. Click the **Add** button to add all the tables in your database to the Relationships window. Click **Close** to close the Show Table dialog box.

4. Arrange the tables so that you can clearly view them by clicking in the title bar of the table window and dragging it to the location of your choice.

5. Because you know that the CustomerID field is common to both the Customers table and the Orders table, that is the first relationship that you want to construct. Click on the CustomerID field in the Customers table and drag it over to the CustomerID field in the Orders table.

6. A Relationships dialog box appears, as shown in Figure 15.14. This is where you will define the particular relationship between the Customers and the Orders table. Click the box marked **Enforce Referential Integrity** to enable the two boxes marked **Cascade Update Related Fields** and **Cascade Delete Related Fields**. Click both of these boxes to enable cascading Updates and Deletes.

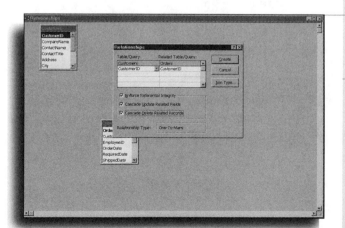

FIGURE 15.14
Defining the relationships of your tables.

7. As you can see in the preceding text boxes, the related fields in both tables are indicated. You can add other related fields or change the fields that you have indicated as related from this box.

8. Click the **Create** button to create the join. This join becomes a one-to-many join and is shown by a line connecting the two fields in their respective tables. The line has a "1" at one end and an infinity sign at the other end to indicate which side of the join is the one side and which side is the many side.

9. To edit this join, right-click on the join line and select **Edit Relationship** from the pulldown box.

10. Now add a join to the Customers and PhoneDir tables by joining the CustomerID fields of those tables. Follow the procedures listed in steps 6–8 to create the join. This join is also a one-to-many relationship.

11. Your Relationship window should now look something like the one shown in Figure 15.15.

FIGURE 15.15

Viewing the completed relationships.

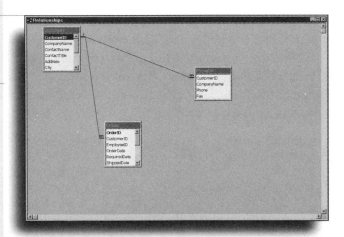

12. Close the Relationship window and click **Yes** when prompted to save its layout.

Deleting Records with a Query

Now that you know your tables can support the effort that you need from your Delete query, you are ready to begin construction of your Delete query.

Using a Delete query to remove records

1. Open chap15.mdb or your own sample database. Click the **Queries** tab in the Database window.

2. Click the **New** button and select **Design View** from the dialog box that appears. Click **OK**.

3. Add the Customers table to the Query Design Grid by double-clicking on it in the Show Table dialog box. Close this dialog box by clicking **Close**.

4. Add all the fields in the Customers table to the Query Design Grid by double-clicking on the asterisk in the field listing for the Customers table. You can also drag the asterisk down to the Query Design Grid.

5. Drag the Country field down to the Query Design Grid because this is the field that you will use to determine which records need to be deleted from your database. If the Country field is not visible in the field listing for the Customers table, scroll down the listing until you can click the **Country** field to add it to the Query Design Grid.

6. Click the Query Type icon 🗔 and select **Delete Query** from the pulldown box that appears.

7. Step 6 added a new row to your Query Design Grid. This row is called Delete and either contains a From or a Where. The From is used to indicate which records you want to delete from, and the Where is used to indicate that the field is being used as a criteria field for the Delete action.

8. Enter Brazil in the Criteria row of the Country field. This tells the Delete query to delete all records whose country matches "Brazil." Your Query Design Grid should now look like the one shown in Figure 15.16.

FIGURE 15.16

Viewing the design grid of your Delete query.

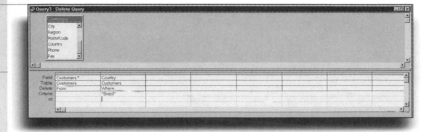

9. You can now either save this Delete query to your database or click the Run icon to activate the query immediately. Regardless of which you choose, after the Delete query processes, a dialog box will be displayed that tells you the number of records that will be deleted from the primary table. The dialog box will ask for confirmation of this action. Click the **Yes** button to continue the Delete action.

Notice that even though the Delete query deleted far more than nine records from your tables, the dialog box that appeared when you ran the Delete query only showed nine records deleted. That is because the Delete query action only shows the number of records that have been deleted from the primary table in the relationships. If you check your database after running the Delete query, you will find no mention of Brazil in any of your tables.

SEE ALSO

➤ *Turn to page 60 if you want to see how to create a Crosstab query with the wizard.*

Using the Query Design Grid

How to Use the Query Design Grid

In the previous chapter you were introduced to the Query Design Grid. By the end of this chapter, you will feel at home with every aspect of the Query Design Grid and you will be able to use it to construct just about any type of Query that you can imagine.

The Query Design Grid, or Design Grid, used to be called the QBE grid. The Design Grid is made up of two parts, as shown in Figure 16.1. The upper pane contains field listings of the tables or queries that you are using to construct your current query. The upper pane also shows the joins that apply to your tables or queries. The lower pane contains columns and rows that apply to the fields of the tables or queries that you are using to construct your current query.

The next three tasks will show you how to add tables, columns, and fields to the Design Grid. Even if you've worked through the exercises in Chapter 15, "Designing and Using Queries," you'll explore the Query Design view in more detail to learn more of its features in detail.

Adding a Table to the Query Design Grid

Examples for this chapter

To work through the examples offered in this chapter, you can work in a test Access 97 database, so that you can save the changes you make here without affecting any other database. If you have already worked through Chapter 15, you constructed a test database in the beginning of that chapter. You can construct a new test database and call it cha16.mdb. If you have not worked through Chapter 15 or you want to apply these concepts in other ways, you can use your own database.

The following steps show you how to add a table to the Design View Grid.

Adding a table to the Design View Grid

1. Open the test database that you have built. Click the **Queries** tab of the Database window.

2. Click the **New** button and then click the **Design View** choice in the dialog box that appears.

3. Your Query will now be open to the Query Design Grid, and a Show Table dialog box like the one shown in Figure 16.2 will be visible.

4. You can add tables or queries to your new query from the Show Table dialog box. The tabs across the top of the dialog box enable you to view tables, queries, or both at the same time.

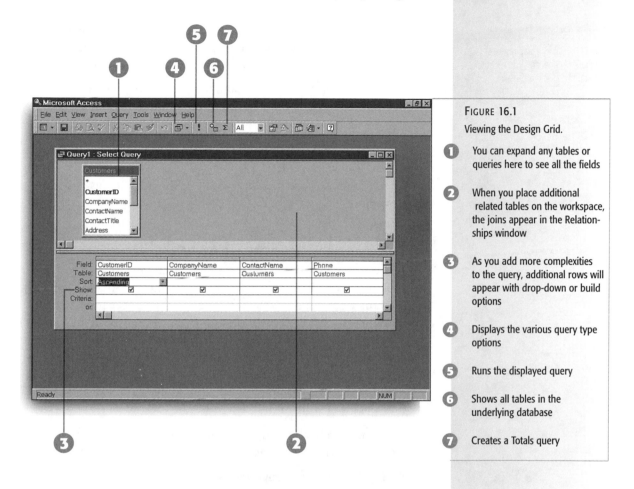

FIGURE 16.1

Viewing the Design Grid.

1 You can expand any tables or queries here to see all the fields

2 When you place additional related tables on the workspace, the joins appear in the Relationships window

3 As you add more complexities to the query, additional rows will appear with drop-down or build options

4 Displays the various query type options

5 Runs the displayed query

6 Shows all tables in the underlying database

7 Creates a Totals query

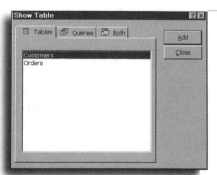

FIGURE 16.2

Adding tables with the Show Table dialog box.

Showing the Show Table dialog

If the Show Table dialog doesn't automatically appear, click the Show Table button [icon].

5. To add a table to a query, double-click the table name in the Show Table dialog box. You can also click the table name and then click the **Add** button.

6. For the purpose of this example, double-click the **Customers** table to add it to your new query. Click the **Close** button to close the Show Table dialog box when you are through.

Now that you have added a table to your query, follow the steps listed in the next two sections to add fields and columns to your new query.

Adding Fields to the Query Design Grid

It is very simple to add fields to a query using the Query Design Grid. One way that you can add fields to your query is to simply drag them from the field listing located in the upper pane of the Design Grid to a column in the lower pane of the Design Grid. If you want to add all the fields that appear in a table or query to your new query, simply drag the asterisk from the top of the field listing in the upper pane of the Design Grid to the lower pane of the Design Grid. You can also double-click a field to add it to the lower pane of the Design Grid.

You can also add all the fields from your queries table or underlying query without adding anything to the Design Grid.

Adding fields with the Properties sheet

1. Open the test database that you have built. Click the **Queries** tab of the Database window.

2. Select the query that you created in the section above and click the **Design** button.

3. Right-click anywhere in the upper pane of the body of the Query Design Grid that is not a field list. Select **Properties** from the pop-up menu that appears or select the Properties [icon] button.

4. A dialog box appears that shows the properties of your query. Click in the text area next to **Output All Fields** and change the default **No** value to **Yes**.

The dialog box should now look like the one shown in Figure 16.3. Close it.

FIGURE 16.3

Adding Fields by changing the Output All Fields Property is useful if you want to copy fields and retain their properties.

The next section shows you how to add a column to your query while you are in the Query Design Grid.

Adding a Column to the Query Design Grid

The columns that appear in the Design Grid in Access 97 are actually repositories of information about the fields that you are including in your query. Even though columns are automatically placed in your Design Grid when you drag and drop a field onto the grid, at times you may want to add a column yourself. You could add a column for formatting reasons, or to arrange the output of your query in a specific way.

Adding a column to your query in the Design Grid

1. Open the test database. Click the **Queries** tab of the Database window.

2. Select the query that you want to add a column to and click on the **Design** button.

3. In the Design Grid, click anywhere in the column that is located to the left of the position where you want to insert a column.

4. Select **Columns** from the **Insert** menu. Click the drop-down button to the left of the first row and a list box with the field names from that table appears. This list box uses the syntax tablename.fieldname to list the fields by table. Select the field name you want.

Specifying criteria and using the Output All Fields option

If you change the **Output All Fields** option to **Yes** and want to set criteria for your query, you must add the fields that will have criteria to the Design Grid. When you do so, make sure that you have unchecked the **Show** check box for that field; otherwise, the column will be listed in your query twice.

Sorting Records Using the Query Design Grid

You can apply a sort order to the records that make up your query by using the Query Design Grid, as long as those columns that you are sorting by are not of the following types of fields:

- Memo
- Hyperlink
- OLE Object

Any sort order that you place on your query is saved with that query. If you later use your query as an underlying query in a form or report, the sort order that you specified for your query will carry over to the form or report. You can sort on more than one field in your query. If you have added the fields to your query by using the asterisk to indicate that all fields shown be returned, you must additionally add the fields that you want to sort by to the Design Grid. Make sure that you uncheck the **Show** check box for this field in the Design Grid to avoid having the column appear twice in your queries resultset. This also applies if you have used the Output All Fields method described in the previous sections to add fields to your query.

Applying a sort order to your query in the Design Grid

Sorting with null values

If you sort a field by ascending order and there are null records in the column, those null records will be listed first.

1. Select a query that you want to apply a sort order to and click on the **Design** button. For the purpose of this example I will use the query that was generated at the beginning of this chapter.

2. Drag the fields into the positions that you want them sorted by. Drag the CustomerID, CompanyName, ContactName, and Phone fields from the field listing of table Customers down to the Design Grid.

3. Access 97 will sort the resultset of this query starting from the leftmost column and going to the rightmost column.

4. For this example you are going to sort your query resultset by the CustomerID field in ascending order. To do so, click in the Sort row under the CustomerID column on the Query Design Grid and select the **Ascending** choice from the drop-down box.

5. Your query should now look like the one shown in Figure 16.4. Click the View icon ~~CustomerID field.~~ Click the View icon again to return to the Design view of your query.

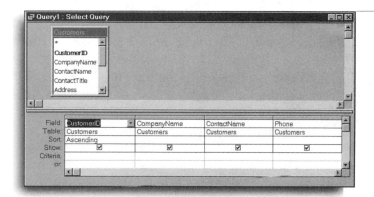

FIGURE 16.4

Finish your query by choosing a sort order for the resultset.

You also could have sorted your query on the CustomerID field without showing that field in the resultset by applying the sort criteria to the CustomerID field as shown in the previous example, and then unchecking the **Show** check box for the CustomerID field.

Selecting Fields to Query

Although you covered how to add fields to your query in the section "Adding Fields to the Query Design Grid," there are some caveats that should be considered when you are adding fields to a query in the Design Grid. If you are going to add all the fields in the underlying table or query to your new query, it is best to use the asterisk as opposed to dragging each field name from the field listing down to the Design Grid. If you use the asterisk, when fields are added to the table or query that the new query is based on, the new query will automatically update to include these fields. In the same manner, if fields are deleted from the underlying table or query, the new query will automatically delete these fields from its resultset.

Numbers stored in text fields

If you have numbers that are stored in text fields within your database, Access 97 will not sort those numbers as actual numbers. Instead Access 97 will view those numbers as characters and sort them accordingly. If you have numbers stored in text fields that you want sorted as numbers, you should either change the data type of the field to the number type, or you can make sure that all the text strings are of the same length by padding the shorter strings with zeros.

It is better to drag the asterisk down from the field listing than to manually enter an asterisk into the Field row of the Design Grid. If you manually enter an asterisk, you must also enter the table name that the fields are to be pulled from.

Remember that if you use the asterisk to indicate that all fields in the table or underlying query are to be used to construct your new query, you must also add any fields for which you want to apply sorting or for which you want to add criteria. You can uncheck the **Show** check box as shown in the next section to avoid having these fields show up twice in your queries resultset. This also applies if you have used the Output All Fields property of your query to indicate that all fields in the underlying tables or queries should be included in your queries resultset.

Setting the Show/Not Show on Output

Even if you have added a field to your query's Design Grid in order to use it for criteria or sorting purposes, you do not have to show the field as a column in your query's final resultset. In fact, in several of the examples used in this chapter already, you have needed to hide a column that you use for criteria purposes.

To hide a column from your queries resultset output, simply uncheck the **Show** box. For example, Figure 16.5 shows a query with four fields sorted in Ascending order. (The resultset is based on the same query as shown in Figure 16.4.)

If you uncheck the **Show** check box in the CustomerID field so that you can hide this column in the final resultset of the query, Access will still consider this field in the sort order.

The new resultset should appear like the one shown in Figure 16.6.

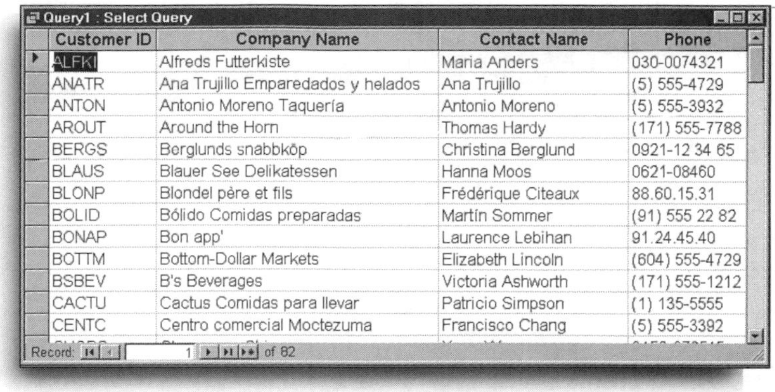

Query1 : Select Query

Customer ID	Company Name	Contact Name	Phone
ALFKI	Alfreds Futterkiste	Maria Anders	030-0074321
ANATR	Ana Trujillo Emparedados y helados	Ana Trujillo	(5) 555-4729
ANTON	Antonio Moreno Taquería	Antonio Moreno	(5) 555-3932
AROUT	Around the Horn	Thomas Hardy	(171) 555-7788
BERGS	Berglunds snabbköp	Christina Berglund	0921-12 34 65
BLAUS	Blauer See Delikatessen	Hanna Moos	0621-08460
BLONP	Blondel père et fils	Frédérique Citeaux	88.60.15.31
BOLID	Bólido Comidas preparadas	Martín Sommer	(91) 555 22 82
BONAP	Bon app'	Laurence Lebihan	91.24.45.40
BOTTM	Bottom-Dollar Markets	Elizabeth Lincoln	(604) 555-4729
BSBEV	B's Beverages	Victoria Ashworth	(171) 555-1212
CACTU	Cactus Comidas para llevar	Patricio Simpson	(1) 135-5555
CENTC	Centro comercial Moctezuma	Francisco Chang	(5) 555-3392

Record: 1 of 82

FIGURE 16.5

The resultset of your query showing all the fields.

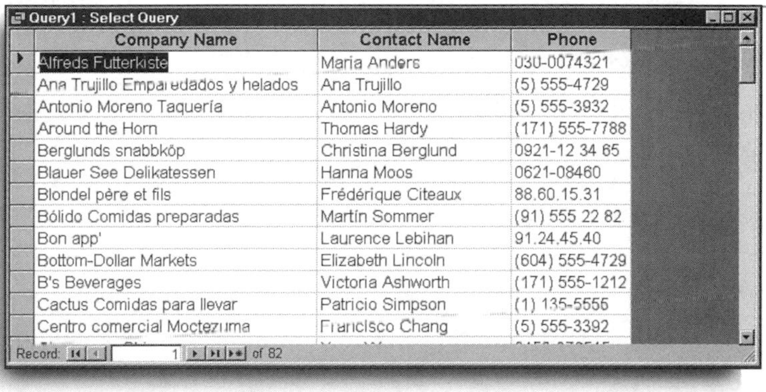

Query1 : Select Query

Company Name	Contact Name	Phone
Alfreds Futterkiste	Maria Anders	030-0074321
Ana Trujillo Emparedados y helados	Ana Trujillo	(5) 555-4729
Antonio Moreno Taquería	Antonio Moreno	(5) 555-3932
Around the Horn	Thomas Hardy	(171) 555-7788
Berglunds snabbköp	Christina Berglund	0921-12 34 65
Blauer See Delikatessen	Hanna Moos	0621-08460
Blondel père et fils	Frédérique Citeaux	88.60.15.31
Bólido Comidas preparadas	Martín Sommer	(91) 555 22 82
Bon app'	Laurence Lebihan	91.24.45.40
Bottom-Dollar Markets	Elizabeth Lincoln	(604) 555-4729
B's Beverages	Victoria Ashworth	(171) 555-1212
Cactus Comidas para llevar	Patricio Simpson	(1) 135-5555
Centro comercial Moctezuma	Francisco Chang	(5) 555-3392

Record: 1 of 82

FIGURE 16.6

The resultset of your query with the sorting field hidden.

Setting Field Criteria

Often when you are constructing a query, you do not want to return all the records in the underlying table or query in your final resultset. For the examples that have been used in this chapter so far, you have always returned all the customers that were listed in the Customers field. This is not a problem if you only have a small number of customers. But after your customer base builds up into the hundreds or thousands of customers, this type of query does not return resultsets that are useful.

For this reason, you need to be able to limit the records that are returned in a resultset and you need a way to tell Access 97 which records out of the resultset you want returned. Access 97

Placement of hidden fields in the grid

If you save this query with the **Show** check box still unchecked, Access 97 will rearrange the appearance of the fields in your Query Design Grid. The next time that you open this query in Design view, the CustomerID field will be located at the far right of the Design Grid. Access 97 relocates all hidden fields to the right every time that you save a query.

includes a way to do this by setting criteria for the field that contains the records you want to use to tell Access 97 which records to return.

For example, if you look at your Customers table, it would be useful to know which customers are located in Germany. To do this you need to add some criteria to the query and tell Access 97 that you only want to view customers from Germany in the final resultset.

The following steps show you how to restrict your query resultset to customers that hail from Germany.

Restricting a query by specifying a field value

1. Select the query that you have used in the preceding examples and open it in Design view.

2. Select the field that contains the value you want to use to limit your data. Because you are going to limit your resultset by indicating which country you want to view, scroll down the field listing of the Customers table until the Country field is visible. Drag this field down to the Design Grid.

3. Click in the Criteria row of the Country column and enter `"Germany"` including the quotation marks. This will limit your resultset to companies that are located in Germany. Your Design Grid should look like the one shown in Figure 16.7.

FIGURE 16.7

Setting criteria for your query.

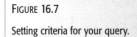 You must type the value by hand and include quotation marks for the value

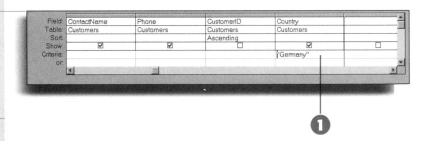

4. Click on the View icon ▦ ▾. Your resultset should look like the one shown in Figure 16.8. Notice that there are fewer companies listed this time and that they are all located in Germany.

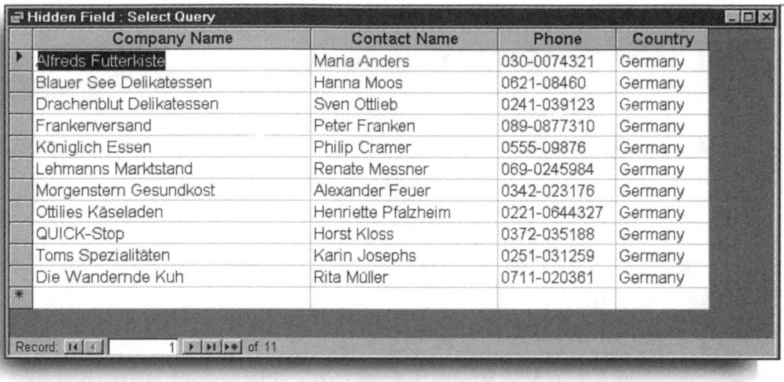

Hidden Field : Select Query

Company Name	Contact Name	Phone	Country
Alfreds Futterkiste	Maria Anders	030-0074321	Germany
Blauer See Delikatessen	Hanna Moos	0621-08460	Germany
Drachenblut Delikatessen	Sven Ottlieb	0241-039123	Germany
Frankenversand	Peter Franken	089-0877310	Germany
Königlich Essen	Philip Cramer	0555-09876	Germany
Lehmanns Marktstand	Renate Messner	069-0245984	Germany
Morgenstern Gesundkost	Alexander Feuer	0342-023176	Germany
Ottilies Käseladen	Henriette Pfalzheim	0221-0644327	Germany
QUICK-Stop	Horst Kloss	0372-035188	Germany
Toms Spezialitäten	Karin Josephs	0251-031259	Germany
Die Wandernde Kuh	Rita Müller	0711-020361	Germany

Record: 1 of 11

FIGURE 16.8
Viewing the resultset of your query with criteria.

You can use much more complicated expressions to indicate criteria for your query to Access 97. In fact, in the sections that close out this chapter you will get the chance to build several involved expressions and further refine your Access 97 database skills.

You can enter more than one criteria for the fields that are listed in your Query Design Grid. If you use more than one criteria, Access 97 will either join the criteria using an AND operator or an OR operator. The next section covers the use of the AND/OR operators in detail.

You can also use the Expression Builder to create the criteria expressions you use in your query. Using the Expression Builder is covered in the last section of this chapter.

AND/OR Criteria

When you use more than one criteria for a field in the Query Design Grid, Access 97 combines those criteria using either the AND operator or the OR operator. If you enter the criteria one after another in the same row in the Design Grid, Access 97 will join those criteria using the AND operator. This means that all of the criteria conditions must be met for a record to be returned.

If you enter the criteria in different rows of the Design Grid for a field, Access 97 will join those criteria using the OR operator. This means that at least one of the criteria listed must be met for a record to be returned.

Using the AND operator on two field values

1. Open the database. Click the **Queries** tab of the Database window.

2. Click the **New** button and select the **Design View** option out of the pop-up box that appears. Click **OK**.

3. Double-click the Orders table to add this table to your query. Click the **Close** button to close the Show Table dialog box.

4. Drag the asterisk from the Field Listing box down to the Design Grid as you want to show all the fields from the Orders table in your resultset.

5. Drag the EmployeeID field and the Freight field down to the Design Grid. (You are going to construct a query that will return all the orders that were processed by Employee number 5 and that had a freight charge of less than $50.00.)

6. Click in the Criteria row of the EmployeeID field and enter 5, excluding the quotation marks. Then click in the Criteria row of the Freight field and enter <50, again excluding the quotation marks. Your query Design Grid should now look like the one shown in Figure 16.9. Remember to uncheck the Show check boxes for the EmployeeID and Freight fields to avoid having them show up twice in the resultset of your query.

FIGURE 16.9

Building a query using the AND operator for your criteria set.

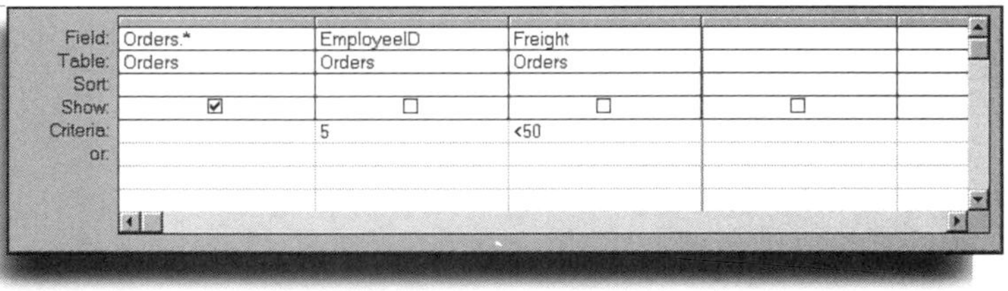

7. The query that you have just created is using the AND operator to indicate to the database engine that you want to see a resultset composed of all the orders processed by Employee number 5 that have a freight charge of less than $50.00. Click the View icon ▦ ▾ If your resultset looks

like the one shown in Figure 16.10, you can see that you were indeed successful.

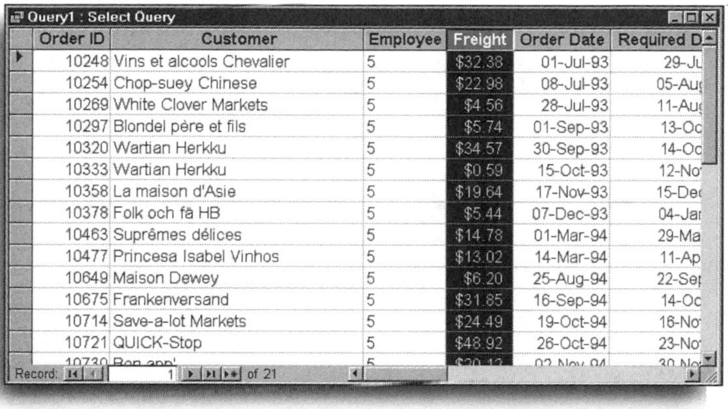
Query1 : Select Query

Order ID	Customer	Employee	Freight	Order Date	Required D
10248	Vins et alcools Chevalier	5	$32.38	01-Jul-93	29-Ju
10254	Chop-suey Chinese	5	$22.98	08-Jul-93	05-Au
10269	White Clover Markets	5	$4.56	28-Jul-93	11-Au
10297	Blondel père et fils	5	$5.74	01-Sep-93	13-Oc
10320	Wartian Herkku	5	$34.57	30-Sep-93	14-Oc
10333	Wartian Herkku	5	$0.59	15-Oct-93	12-No
10358	La maison d'Asie	5	$19.64	17-Nov-93	15-De
10378	Folk och fä HB	5	$5.44	07-Dec-93	04-Ja
10463	Suprêmes délices	5	$14.78	01-Mar-94	29-Ma
10477	Princesa Isabel Vinhos	5	$13.02	14-Mar-94	11-Ap
10649	Maison Dewey	5	$6.20	25-Aug-94	22-Se
10675	Frankenversand	5	$31.85	16-Sep-94	14-Oc
10714	Save-a-lot Markets	5	$24.49	19-Oct-94	16-No
10721	QUICK-Stop	5	$48.92	26-Oct-94	23-No

Record: 1 of 21

FIGURE 16.10
Viewing the results of the AND query.

SQL for the Query

For those among you who have previous database experience, the query that you just constructed was equivalent to the following SQL query:

```
SELECT Orders.*
FROM Orders
WHERE (((Orders.EmployeeID)=5) AND ((Orders.Freight)<50));
```

Viewing the SQL behind a query

Any time you want to see the SQL code that a wizard or query creates, use the **SQL View** command on the **View** menu. You can also right-click the upper pane and select the **SQL View** command.

Using OR

The following steps show you how to build a query with criteria using the OR operator.

Using the OR operator

1. Click the **New** button and select **Design View** from the pop-up menu that appears. Click **OK**.
2. Double-click the Customers table to add it to your query and then click the **Close** button to close the Show Tables dialog box.
3. For this example you will construct a query that retrieves all your customers that are located in France, Germany, and Belgium. Drag the CustomerID, CompanyName, Phone, and Country fields to the Design Grid from the Field Listing box.

4. The only field that you will be putting criteria on is the Country field, so click in the Criteria row of that field and enter "France".

5. Then click in the row directly underneath the one that you just entered France into and enter "Germany". Repeat this process for Belgium. When you are finished, your Design Grid should appear like the one shown in Figure 16.11.

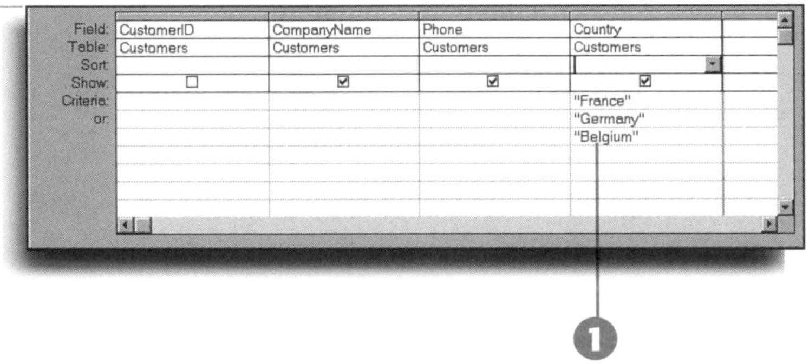

FIGURE 16.11

Building a query using an OR operator.

① An OR query implies that the "or" options will be from a single field

Automatic entry of string indicators

If you do not surround the country names that you have entered with quotation marks, Access 97 will automatically do this for you.

6. Because you do not need to view the CustomerID for this query, uncheck the **Show** check box for the CustomerID field. Click the View icon 🖫▾ to view the result of this OR query.

7. The resultset from your query should appear like the one shown in Figure 16.12. The resultset has returned all the companies that are located in the three countries you indicated in your criteria. But the resultset is confusing because the companies are not sorted by country. Let's add a sort order to the countries field so that your resultset is clearer. Click the View button 🖃▾ to return to your query's Design view.

8. Click in the sort row of the Country field and select **Ascending** from the drop-down box that appears. This time when you run the query, the companies are nicely sorted by the country that they are located in as shown in Figure 16.13.

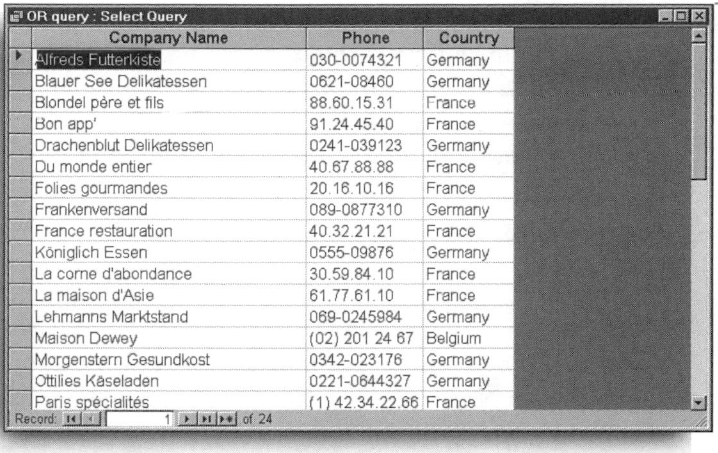

OR query : Select Query

Company Name	Phone	Country
Alfreds Futterkiste	030-0074321	Germany
Blauer See Delikatessen	0621-08460	Germany
Blondel père et fils	88.60.15.31	France
Bon app'	91.24.45.40	France
Drachenblut Delikatessen	0241-039123	Germany
Du monde entier	40.67.88.88	France
Folies gourmandes	20.16.10.16	France
Frankenversand	089-0877310	Germany
France restauration	40.32.21.21	France
Königlich Essen	0555-09876	Germany
La corne d'abondance	30.59.84.10	France
La maison d'Asie	61.77.61.10	France
Lehmanns Marktstand	069-0245984	Germany
Maison Dewey	(02) 201 24 67	Belgium
Morgenstern Gesundkost	0342-023176	Germany
Ottilies Käseladen	0221-0644327	Germany
Paris spécialités	(1) 42.34.22.66	France

Record: 1 of 24

FIGURE 16.12
Viewing the results of your query.

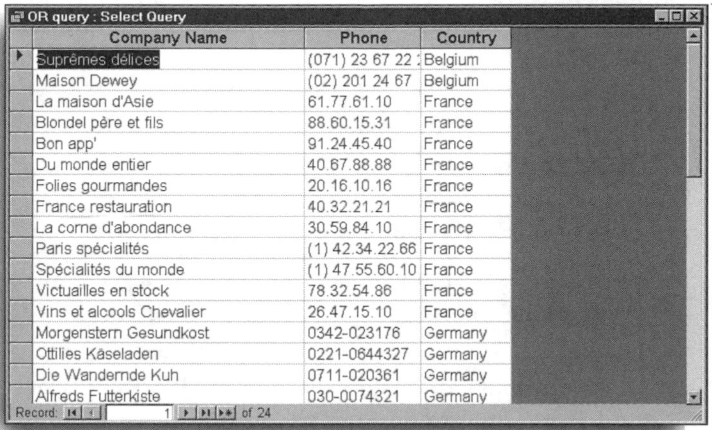

OR query : Select Query

Company Name	Phone	Country
Suprêmes délices	(071) 23 67 22	Belgium
Maison Dewey	(02) 201 24 67	Belgium
La maison d'Asie	61.77.61.10	France
Blondel père et fils	88.60.15.31	France
Bon app'	91.24.45.40	France
Du monde entier	40.67.88.88	France
Folies gourmandes	20.16.10.16	France
France restauration	40.32.21.21	France
La corne d'abondance	30.59.84.10	France
Paris spécialités	(1) 42.34.22.66	France
Spécialités du monde	(1) 47.55.60.10	France
Victuailles en stock	78.32.54.86	France
Vins et alcools Chevalier	26.47.15.10	France
Morgenstern Gesundkost	0342-023176	Germany
Ottilies Käseladen	0221-0644327	Germany
Die Wandernde Kuh	0711-020361	Germany
Alfreds Futterkiste	030-0074321	Germany

Record: 1 of 24

FIGURE 16.13
Viewing the sorted results of your query.

SQL for the OR Query

The query that you just created is equivalent to the following SQL query:

```
SELECT Customers.CompanyName, Customers.Phone,
Customers.Country
FROM Customers
WHERE (((Customers.Country)="France"  _
Or (Customers.Country)="Germany"  _
Or (Customers.Country)="Belgium"))
ORDER BY Customers.Country;
```

As you can see, the queries that you are constructing with the Design Grid are a far cry from the ones that you started out with. In the last section of this chapter, you will get the chance to build some really advanced queries by using an Access 97 tool called the Expression Builder.

Planning for Null Values

A Null value is used in Access 97 to indicate an empty field or a field that is filled with unknown data. Null values can be used to construct expressions for use in queries. A primary key field cannot contain a Null value. A field that contains a null value is known as a Null Field.

Null Fields can affect the results of a query quite strangely. The following listing is a listing of oddities that occur in Access 97 as a result of the Null Field.

The difference between Null and zero

A Null Field is the same thing as an empty field. You do not call a field that contains a zero-length string or a value of zero a Null Field. Those fields are populated even though they appear empty.

- Sorting on a field that contains Null Values will result in all the records that contain Null Values being returned at the top of the resultset if the sort is in ascending order. If the sort is in descending order, the Null Value records will be returned at the bottom of the query resultset.

- You can search for records that contain a Null Value in your query by entering "IsNull" into the Criteria row of the field that you want to examine for Null Values. You can also enter "" (two quotation marks back to back with no space in between them).

- If you are using more than one table or query that is linked by a join for your new query, any records that have a Null Value in the joined fields will not return a record to the resultset.

- If you use an arithmetic operator in an expression that you are using as a criteria and one of the fields in the expression contains a Null Value, the whole expression will evaluate to a Null Value.

Null Values can catch you off guard, but if you pay attention to the points listed above you should be able to use Null Values without a problem in your queries.

Using the Expression Builder for Complex Expressions

This section of the chapter goes into depth about an Access 97 tool called the Expression Builder, which can be used to construct very complicated expressions graphically for use in your queries.

You can use expressions in many places throughout Access 97, but constructing a query is the place where people find the most use for expressions. Expressions are any combination of values, functions, constants, fields, and operators that can be evaluated to a single value.

You can type any expression that you want directly into the Criteria or Field rows of a column in your Design Grid. However, Access 97 comes with a very useful tool called the Expression Builder that you can use to build very complicated expressions for your queries. You can also use the Expression Builder to build a calculated field for your query. This section will take you on a tour of the Expression Builder and you will use it to construct some very handy queries for your database.

Anatomy of the Expression Builder

The Expression Builder is composed of three main parts. You can start the Expression Builder by right-clicking in any criteria or field row of your query that is open in Design view. To follow along with this section of the chapter, open your Expression Builder by following these steps:

Using the Expression Builder

1. Click the **Queries** tab of your database in the Database window.

2. Select a query to view and click on **Design** or start a new query to open that query in Design view.

3. Right-click in the Criteria row of any column and select the **Build** option from the pop-up menu.

4. The Expression Builder dialog box will appear like the one shown in Figure 16.14. The next part of this section will familiarize you with the components of the Expression Builder.

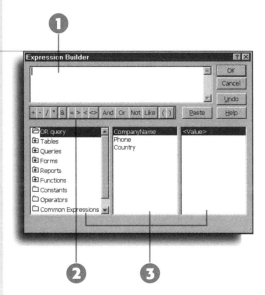

The first thing that you will notice when the Expression Builder dialog box appears is the big empty box at the top. This is where the expression that you are creating will eventually show up. You can use this box to type in any expression that you need, but it is much simpler to build the expression elements that you need graphically by using the components of the Expression Builder that appear underneath the empty box. The empty box is known as the Expression box.

Directly underneath the Expression box is a row of buttons known as the Operator buttons. These buttons are a collection of the most commonly used operators in Access 97. To use an operator from this collection while constructing your expression, merely click on the operator button. The operator will be inserted into the Expression box at the current insertion point.

The bottom half of the Expression Builder is an area containing three boxes that collectively contain all the expression elements available to you in Access 97.

The box on the left contains a series of folders that contain all the database objects that you can use to create expressions with. The folders shown will change depending on the context of the area that you opened the Expression Builder from. The database objects that you can use and that are shown in the Expression Elements section of the Expression Builder are shown in the following list:

- Tables
- Queries
- Forms
- Reports
- Built-in Access 97 functions
- User-defined functions
- Constants
- Operators
- Common expressions

The middle box of the Expression Elements section contains a listing of the contents of the folder that is selected in the left box of the Expression Elements section.

The right box lists the values of the content element that is selected in the middle box of the Expression Elements section. For example, Figure 16.15 shows the Operators folder highlighted in the left-hand box. The listing in the middle box is of the various types of Operators that can be used to build an expression. And because the Logical element is selected in the middle box, the right box shows all the logical operators that can be used to build an expression.

The next to last section of this chapter will walk you through using the Expression Builder to build criteria for a query.

Using the Expression Builder to Build Criteria

You can use the Expression Builder to build quite complicated expressions to use as criteria in your queries. Some of the uses of expressions in criteria could be to calculate a date and use that as a criteria or to use part of a fields value as criteria. For the purpose of the example in this section, you will construct a query that will use the Expression Builder to build an expression for use as a criteria for your queries. The example will be the use of a calculated date.

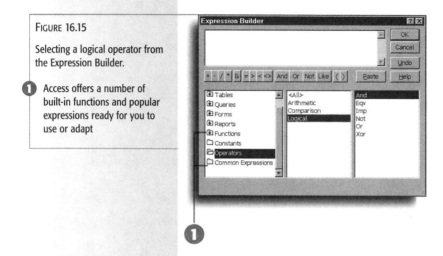

FIGURE 16.15

Selecting a logical operator from the Expression Builder.

❶ Access offers a number of built-in functions and popular expressions ready for you to use or adapt

Join indicators

Using this expression implies a join between the fields you're querying. If you do not have a Join indicator between the two tables in the field listing box, refer to Chapter 14, "Defining and Working with Relationships."

Constructing a query that uses a calculated date as a criteria with Expression Builder

1. In the sample database, start a new query in Design view.

2. Double-click the Orders table and the Customers table to add them to your query. Then click the **Close** button to close the Show Table dialog box.

For this example you will build a query that returns a result-set composed of all the customers that had orders in the year 1995 and whose orders in that year took longer than 15 days to process, from receiving the order to shipping the order. With that in mind, drag the OrderID, OrderDate, and ShippedDate fields down to the Design Grid from the Orders table. Drag the CompanyName field from the Customers table to the Design Grid.

To achieve this query, you will have to assign a criterion to both the OrderDate and the ShippedDate fields. Right-click in the Criteria row of the OrderDate field and select the **Build** option from the pop-up menu that appears.

3. When the Expression Builder dialog box has appeared, double-click the **Functions** folder in the left-hand box of the Expressions Elements section of the dialog box. Click the **Built-In Functions** folder that appears within this same box.

4. Click the **Date/Time** element that appears in the middle box of the Expressions Elements section of the dialog box. Then scroll down the right-hand box until you see an element called **Year**. Double-click **Year** to add this function to your expression. Your Expression Builder dialog box should appear like the one shown in Figure 16.16.

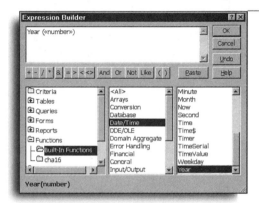

FIGURE 16.16
Building an expression using the Year function.

5. Highlight the << >> objects and the word number and then double-click the Folders folder in the left-hand box of the Expressions Elements section.

6. Click the Order folder that appears in the left-hand box and then click the OrderDate element that is shown in the middle box. Go to the right-hand box and double-click the word <Value> to replace the placeholder in your expression with the Value contained in the OrderDate field of the Orders table used in your query.

7. Your Expression Builder should look like the one shown in Figure 16.17 at this time. Now click at the end of the expression you have built so far in the Expression Box and then click the = button below the Expression Box. Type "1995" into the Expression Box and click **OK**.

Placeholders in expressions

The << >> objects surrounding the word number in the Expression box indicate that you need to replace that placeholder with a real value.

FIGURE 16.17

The Year function with the fields and operators for the expression.

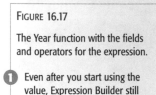 Even after you start using the value, Expression Builder still provides a basic description of the element

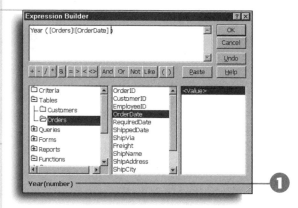

8. You can now go to the Criteria row of the OrderDate column in your Design Grid to view the expression that you just created. If you cannot view the expression in its entirety, right-click the Criteria row and select **Zoom** from the pop-up menu.

9. A window will appear that contains your newly created expression as shown in Figure 16.18. This criteria will limit the resultset to orders that were placed in 1995. Click the **OK** button to return to the Design Grid.

FIGURE 16.18

Using the Zoom window to view the whole expression.

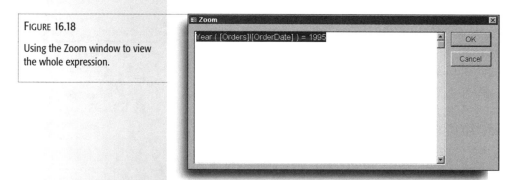

10. Now you need to set the criteria for the ShippedDate field. Right-click in the Criteria row for this field and activate the Expression Builder.

11. Once again you need to double-click the Functions folder in the left-hand box of the Expressions Elements section. Click on the Built-In Functions folder that appears in the left-hand box and click the **Date/Time** element that is shown in the middle box. Double-click the **DateAdd** function that appears in the right-hand box to add this function to your expression.

12. Your Expression Builder should appear like the one shown in Figure 16.19. Again, the placeholders that you need to replace are shown surrounded by the << >> objects.

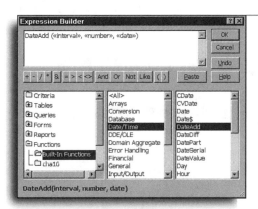

FIGURE 16.19
Building the second part of your query criteria.

13. The DateAdd function enables you to calculate a date by adding a specified time interval to that date. Because you are trying to find all the orders that took over 15 days to process, you need to use days as your time interval. In the DateAdd function, days are represented by the letter d. Replace the <<interval>> placeholder with the letter "d", including the quotes.

14. The next placeholder that you need to replace is the <<number>> placeholder. Because you are looking for orders over 15 days, replace this placeholder with the number "15".

15. And finally, you need to replace the last placeholder with the date that you are adding the time interval to. Because you are calculating the Ship dates that were more than 15 days later than the corresponding Order Dates, you need to use the value contained in the OrderDate field of the Orders table to replace this placeholder. Using the Expression Elements portion of this dialog box, replace the <<date>> placeholder with the OrderDate field value. If you need help with this, refer to step 8.

16. Because you are trying to find all orders that were greater than 15 days in processing, you need to add a greater than sign to the front of your expression. Click in front of your expression to set the insertion point and click the **>** button immediately below the Expression box.

17. Your Expression Builder should now look like the one shown in Figure 16.20. Click **OK**.

FIGURE 16.20

Viewing your second expression.

18. Click the View icon 📊 ▾. The resultset you see should look something like the one shown in Figure 16.21. And as you can see, you had 20 orders placed in 1995 that took longer than 15 days to process.

FIGURE 16.21

Viewing the resultset of your query.

Company Name	Order ID	Order Date	Shipped Date
Berglunds snabbköp	10924	01-Mar-95	05-Apr-95
Berglunds snabbköp	10875	03-Feb-95	28-Feb-95
Blondel père et fils	10826	09-Jan-95	03-Feb-95
Bólido Comidas preparadas	10970	21-Mar-95	21-Apr-95
Bon app'	10932	03-Mar-95	21-Mar-95
Bon app'	10827	09-Jan-95	03-Feb-95
Chop-suey Chinese	10966	17-Mar-95	05-Apr-95
Folk och fä HB	10980	24-Mar-95	14-Apr-95
Folk och fä HB	10824	06-Jan-95	27-Jan-95
Great Lakes Food Market	10816	03-Jan-95	01-Feb-95
HILARIÓN-Abastos	10960	16-Mar-95	05-Apr-95
Hungry Owl All-Night Grocers	10912	23-Feb-95	15-Mar-95
La corne d'abondance	10927	02-Mar-95	05-Apr-95
LINO-Delicateses	10840	16-Jan-95	13-Feb-95
Maison Dewey	10978	23-Mar-95	20-Apr-95
Océano Atlántico Ltda.	10986	27-Mar-95	18-Apr-95
Rancho grande	10828	10-Jan-95	01-Feb-95
Richter Supermarkt	10951	13-Mar-95	04-Apr-95

Criteria : Select Query

Record: 1 of 20

SQL for the Date Function Query

The query that you just created with the aid of the Expression Builder is equivalent to the following SQL query:

```
SELECT Customers.CompanyName, Orders.OrderID,
Orders.OrderDate, _
Orders.ShippedDate
FROM Customers INNER JOIN Orders ON Customers.CustomerID = _
Orders.CustomerID
WHERE
(((Orders.ShippedDate)>DateAdd("d",15,[Orders]![OrderDate]))

_
AND ((Year([Orders]![OrderDate]))=1995));
```

Although this isn't the best way to learn SQL, the automatic creation of SQL from a query can be a good starting point. You can understand the basic logic of how these operators work. For example, the query uses a WHERE clause to continue checking through each record until the condition is met for each criteria. The code also shows the JOIN relationship between the related fields in the two tables.

For related information...

For more information on SQL, try *Sams Teach Yourself SQL in 24 Hours.*

Setting Parameters

Setting parameters in the criteria section of the Query
Design Grid

Creating an input box for user-requested criteria

Setting parameters in the Parameter dialog box

Using wildcards in parameters

Setting Parameters in the Criteria Section of the Query Design Grid

A *parameter query* is not really a query different than those you have seen up to now. Using a parameter for a query merely allows you to prompt the user for information that will help you construct the query interactively.

For instance, you can prompt the user for a range of dates and use that range to build your query against the database. If you use a parameter for your queries, the parameter will prompt the user for the criteria it needs to complete the query every time it is run.

When you build a parameter query via the Query Design Grid, you set up the parameters directly in the criteria row of the column for which you want to set criteria.

Follow these steps to build a parameter query using the Query Design Grid:

Building a parameter query using the Query Design Grid

1. Open the sample database and click the Database window's **Queries** tab.

2. Click the **New** button and select Design View from the pop-up menu. Click **OK**.

3. We use the Orders table for this example. With this in mind, double-click the Orders table to add it to our query; then click the **Close** button to close the Show Table dialog box.

   Let's build a query that we can use to discover the orders that are required by a certain date. We will prompt our query's user to provide this date. To do this, drag the OrderID and RequiredDate fields from the field listing to the Query Design Grid.

4. Now add a parameter to a query: Enclose the parameter in square brackets and enter it in the Criteria row of the column for which you want to set criteria. For this simple example, enter the following line into the Criteria row of the RequiredDate field:

   ```
   [Enter the Required Date]
   ```

Examples in this chapter

You need a database with data already in it for the examples in this chapter. You can use your own database or follow the convention of the previous two chapters by exporting the Customers and the Orders tables out of the Northwind Sample database that comes with your Access 97 installation. Follow the steps listed at the beginning of Chapter 15 to create this database and name the database "cha17.mdb." You will create your example queries using this database.

Once you've mastered these concepts, you can use any variation or combination in your own queries.

Your Query Design Grid should now look like the one shown in Figure 17.1. You can preview the resultset of this query by clicking the View icon .

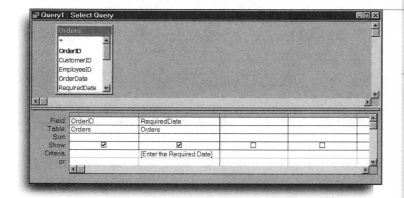

FIGURE 17.1

Creating a parameter for our select query.

When you run this query by clicking the View icon, a dialog box like the one shown in Figure 17.2 appears, prompting the user to enter a required date.

To see a valid resultset, enter 8/13/93 into the dialog box and click on the **OK** button.

FIGURE 17.2

The dialog box that prompts the query users.

The resultset from this query should look like that shown in Figure 17.3.

We used a very simple example to introduce you to parameter queries, but you can set up some advanced queries by prompting the user for one or more criteria to use in your query. The remainder of this chapter familiarizes you with the process of using parameters within your queries.

FIGURE 17.3

Our parameter query's resultset.

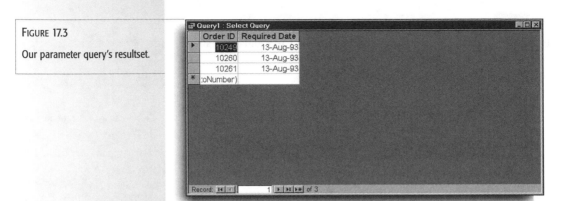

Let's begin by creating a more functional parameter query for our example. We'll prompt the user for a range of dates, which the required date must fall between.

Follow these steps to build a parameter query that prompts your user for a range of dates:

Prompting the user for a range of dates

1. Open the sample database and click the Database window's **Queries** tab.

2. Select the query that we created in the previous section and click the **Design** button to open this query in Design View.

3. Select the Criteria row of the RequiredDate column; press the Delete key to clear the value from the previous example.

4. Enter the following line into the Criteria row of the RequiredDate column:

   ```
   Between [Enter the beginning date:]
   ```

   This line tells Access 97 that we want to set up a range of parameters. The first parameter is used for the beginning date of the range and the second parameter is used for the ending date of the range.

5. Right-click within the Criteria row of the RequiredDate column. Select the **Zoom** option from the pop-up menu to view our query's newly added parameters. Your Query Design Grid should look like the one shown in Figure 17.4.

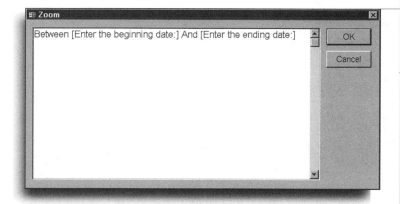

FIGURE 17.4

Add parameters that will prompt for a range of dates from the user.

6. Click the View icon 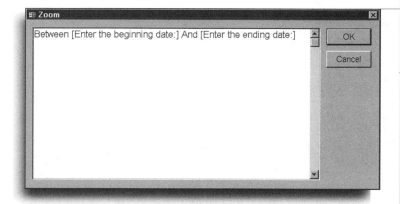 to preview this query; you are prompted by two dialog boxes. The first dialog box asks you to enter a beginning date and the second dialog box asks for an ending date.

When you are setting a parameter for a query, you can also set the data type of that parameter. You must set the data type of the parameters you need if you are building a crosstab query and you are setting parameters for that query.

Follow these steps to set the data types for parameters in your queries:

Setting the data types for parameters

1. Open the sample database and click the Database window's **Queries** tab.

2. Select the query that we created in the previous section and click the **Design** button to open this query in Design view.

3. Click the **Parameters** option on the **Query** menu from the Access 97 menu bar.

4. The dialog box shown in Figure 17.5 appears. There are two columns in the Query Parameters dialog box. The first column holds the parameters you want to set a data type for; the second column is used to set the data type.

5. Enter the parameter that you typed into the RequiredDate field's Criteria row into the Parameters column of the Query Parameters dialog box.

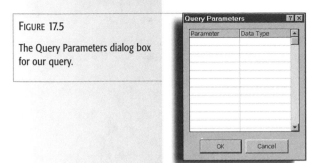

FIGURE 17.5

The Query Parameters dialog box for our query.

6. Click in the **Data Type** column of the Query Parameters dialog box and select the **Date/Time** data type. It's shown in Figure 17.6.

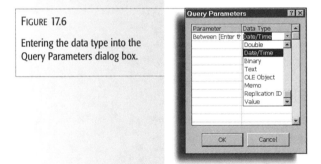

FIGURE 17.6

Entering the data type into the Query Parameters dialog box.

The next section shows you how to create a custom input box for use in your queries.

Creating an Input Box for User-Requested Criteria

If you want to create a custom input box for your parameter query in Access 97, you simply construct a form that is used within your application to gather information from your application's user.

Access 97 allows you to create a *pop-up form*. This means that the form stays on top of the other forms present in your application when it is activated. One of the properties of a pop-up form in Access 97 is called *modal*. If the form's modal property is No, the form is known as a pop-up form; you can access other forms in your application while it is active. If the form's modal property is Yes, the form is known as a *custom dialog box*, and you cannot access other forms in your application until you either close the form or hide it from view.

The next section of this chapter walks you through building both a pop-up form and a custom dialog box, with which you can use to build a parameter query.

Using a Custom Dialog Box or a Pop-Up Form

In this section you build a custom input form in two different ways: by using a pop-up form and with a custom dialog box. We will create the forms in this section and tie them to our query in the following section.

Follow these steps to build a custom input form as a pop-up form:

Building a custom input form as a pop-up form

1. Open the sample database and click the Database window's **Forms** tab.

2. Click the **New** button; the New Form dialog box appears.

3. Select the **Design View** option in the dialog's top input box. Make sure that nothing is showing in this dialog form's second input box. The second input box is used to indicate the table or query from which you are pulling the form's information. Since we are going to build this manually, we do not want to enter anything in this box.

4. Resize the form so that it's an appropriate size for your custom input box. Since the query to which we are attaching needs to return a date range to the query, we need to add the following controls to our form:

   • A label and a text box for the beginning date

   • A label and a text box for the ending date

   • A Run Query command button

   • A Cancel command button

5. Once you have added these controls to your form, click the View button once (on the Access 97 menu bar) to see how your custom input box will appear. Your form should look something like the one shown in Figure 17.7.

FIGURE 17.7

Viewing your custom dialog box as it will appear in the application.

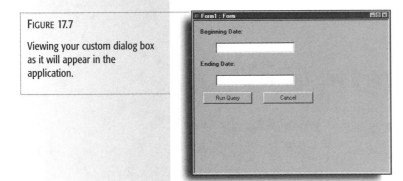

6. Click the View button on the Access 97 menu bar to return your form to the Design view.

7. Double-click the Form Selector to view the property sheet for this form. The Form Selector is the little black square located in the upper-left side of the form when it is in Design view.

8. Click the **Other** tab and change the **Pop Up** property to Yes. This makes your custom dialog box a pop-up form.

You can set other properties for your custom dialog box by following the instructions in the section titled "Setting Properties for the Input Box" later in this chapter. You can also move ahead to "Setting Parameters in the Parameter Dialog Box" if you want to complete building this form for your Access 97 application.

Follow these steps to build a custom input form as a custom dialog box:

Build a custom input form as a custom dialog box

1. Open the sample database and click the Database window's **Forms** tab.

2. Click the **New** button and select the **Design View** option; it's in the top input box of the New Form dialog box. Make sure that nothing is showing in the New Form dialog box's second input box.

3. Resize the form so that it's an appropriate size for your custom input box. Since the query that we are attaching to must return a date range to our query, we need to add the following controls to our form:

   • A label and a text box for the beginning date

   • A label and a text box for the ending date

   • A Run Query command button

   • A Cancel command button

4. Double-click the Form Selector to view the property sheet for this form. The Form Selector is the little black square located in the upper-left side of the form when it is in Design view.

5. Click the **Other** tab and change the **Pop Up** property to Yes. This makes your custom dialog box a pop-up form.

6. Change the **Modal** property to Yes; this makes the form a custom dialog box. The form's property sheet should look like the one shown in Figure 17.8.

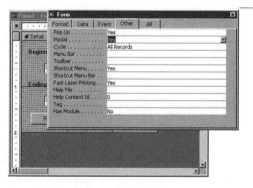

FIGURE 17.8
The property sheet of the custom dialog box.

7. Click the property sheet's **Format** tab and change the **Border Style** property of the form to **Dialog**. This ensures that the form cannot be maximized or minimized.

Just as in the example where you created a pop-up form for your custom input box, you can now adjust some of your form's properties by referring to the next section; you can instead move directly to "Setting Parameters in the Parameter Dialog Box" to tie this form to your parameter query as a custom input box.

Setting Properties for the Input Box

The following properties can be set for any pop-up or custom dialog box that you create. The properties that are listed and the reasons you would set the properties are given in Table 17.1, along with the effect that those properties have.

TABLE 17.1   **Properties for Custom Dialog Boxes**

Property	Description/Reason for Using
AllowEdits	Used to determine whether the user can make edits to the records that are listed on a form. This property is not used when constructing a custom dialog box. The property defaults to **Yes** and can be safely left with that value.
AllowDeletions	Determines whether the user can delete records that are listed on a form. This property is not used when constructing a custom dialog box. The property defaults to **Yes** and can be safely left with that value.
AllowAdditions	Determines whether the user can add records by using the form. This property is not used when constructing a custom dialog box. The property defaults to **Yes** and can be safely left with that value.
AutoCenter	You use this property to indicate whether a form should be centered in the user's application window when the form is activated. The use of this property is a matter of preference. If you are opening several dialog boxes, it makes the application seem smoother if all the dialog boxes open from the same location. This property defaults to **No**.

Property	Description/Reason for Using
BorderStyle	Determines the type of border and border elements to include when displaying the form. This property can be any of the following values: None, Thin, Sizeable, and Dialog. If you recall, we set this property to Dialog when we constructed the custom input box example. If set to Dialog, Access 97 automatically removes the Maximize and Minimize buttons from the form. This property defaults to **Sizeable**.
CloseButton	Indicates whether the user can close the dialog box by using the built-in close button. The built-in close button is the little X that is always present in the dialog box's upper-right corner. This property defaults to **Yes** and can be left that way.
ControlBox	Determines whether the dialog box displays a Control menu. If you change this property from its default value of **Yes**, remember that you must provide a way for the user to close the dialog box—especially if you make the form a Modal form and then take away the Control menu.
DataEntry	Determines whether existing records are shown when the form is opened, or if the form defaults to showing a blank record ready for data entry. This property is not used when constructing a custom dialog box.
DefaultView	This property determines how the data records are displayed on the form and is not used when constructing a custom dialog box.
MinMaxButtons	Indicates whether the Minimize and Maximize buttons are displayed for the user. Remember that if you have set the form's BorderStyle property to **Dialog**, the Minimize and Maximize buttons are automatically removed from the form.
Modal	Determines whether the form takes focus of the application until either closed or hidden. The Modal properties of both forms we constructed were set to **Yes**. That way you can force your application's user to complete the dialog on the custom input box.

continues...

TABLE 17.1 Continued

Property	Description/Reason for Using
NavigationButtons	Indicates whether navigational buttons are shown to the user. This property is not used when constructing a custom input box.
PopUp	Forces the custom input box to remain on top of all other dialog boxes within the application until it is closed or hidden. This property is set to **Yes** when constructing a custom dialog box.
RecordSelectors	Indicates whether the custom dialog box uses record selectors as part of its display. This property is set to **No** when constructing a custom dialog box.
ScrollBars	Indicates whether the custom input box includes scrollbars as part of its display. This property is also set to **No** when constructing a custom input box.
ShortcutMenu	This property is used to determine whether the user can access a shortcut menu by right-clicking the custom input box. This property should be set to **No** when constructing a custom input box.
ViewsAllowed	This property is used to determine whether the user can switch between Form and Datasheet views in your custom input box. This property should be set to **Form** only when constructing a custom input box.

When we constructed the forms that we'll use as custom input boxes for our parameter query, we added two command buttons: Cancel and Run Query. A command button has two properties that are of interest when constructing a custom input box. These properties and their uses are listed in Table 17.2.

TABLE 17.2 Properties for Command Buttons

Property	Description/Reason for Using
Default	Allows you to indicate a command button on your form as the default command button. Only one command button on the form can be marked as the default. The default command button can be

Property	Description/Reason for Using
	activated by pressing Enter, as well as by clicking the command button itself. For this example, set the Run Query command buttons on the forms as the default command buttons.
Cancel	This property allows you to indicate that a command button is used as the cancel button. This means that when a user selects Esc, the marked command button is activated. The user can also either activate this button by selecting the Enter key when the command button is selected, or by clicking the command button itself. For this example, set the Cancel command buttons on our forms as the cancel command buttons for the form.

Now that you have customized your forms' properties, you can follow the directions given in the next section to hook those forms to your parameter query and begin using a custom input box.

Setting Parameters in the Parameter Dialog Box

In this section you integrate one of the forms you just created into the application. That form is integrated as a custom input box for the parameter query that you created at the beginning of the chapter. Follow these steps to integrate a form into a parameter query as a custom input box:

Integrating a form into a parameter query as a custom input box

1. Open the sample database and click the Database window's **Queries** tab.

2. Select the **Parameter** query created earlier and click the **Design** button; this opens the query in Design view.

3. Click the Criteria row of the RequiredDate field; press the Delete key to clear this field after selecting the whole row.

4. While the query is still in Design view, select the **Parameters** option from the Query choice on the Access 97 menu bar.

5. The Query Parameters dialog box appears. Select the query parameter that you inserted earlier in the chapter and press the Delete key to remove this parameter from the query. Click **OK** to close the Query Parameters dialog box.

Using Wildcards in Parameters

You can use wildcards to set your query's parameters. *Wildcards* are typically used in Access 97 as placeholders for unknown values or to cover a range of possible values. Wildcard characters are only to be used with Text data types.

If you are running your parameter query against a data source other than a Microsoft Access 97 table, different criteria rules may apply when using wildcards. You should refer to the documentation that came with the data source you are using to determine the correct usage of wildcards in the context of that data source.

The wildcards shown in Table 17.3 can successfully be used with Access 97. The wildcard itself is given here, along with a brief description of the usage for the wildcard.

TABLE 17.3   Usage of Wildcards in Queries

Wildcard	Description/Reason for Using
Asterisk (*)	This wildcard is used to match any character or any number of any character. You can construct a query that uses the asterisk in the criteria of a field (Name = tr*, for example). This searches for all names that begin with a *tr*. You could also use the asterisk at the beginning of a string if you know the end of the string.
Question mark (?)	This wildcard returns a match to any single alphabetic character. You can use this wildcard to search for words where you know the beginning and end of the word, but the middle characters could be different.
Square brackets ([ ])	You use this wildcard to return any character inside the brackets. This is similar to using the question mark, but with this wildcard you know

Wildcard	Description/Reason for Using
	the range of characters that you are looking for. Using `Name = Jo[he]≠` in a criteria row of a Name field to return `'John or Joey'` is an example.
Exclamation point (!)	You can use the exclamation point (!) to indicate that you are looking for any character that is not in the square brackets by using `Name = Jo[!he][!ne]`. This returns all names that start with *Jo*, but do not contain an *h* or an *e* in the next position or an *n* or an *e* in the last position.
Hyphen (-)	You can use a hyphen (-) to indicate a range of characters. Here's an example: `Name = Jo[a-r][b-o]`.
Pound sign (#)	This wildcard character can be used to match any single numeric character. An often-used example is matching to a range of zip codes, as in the following line of code: `Zip = 36###`. This returns all the zip codes that begin with a *36*.

Advanced Uses of Queries

Querying another query

Using the Query Design Grid to create an SQL statement
for a Macro *RunSQL* action

Using the Query Design Grid to create an SQL statement
for use in VBA

Querying Another Query

For the examples in this chapter, you need an existing database to run your queries. If you need a sample database to test, follow the convention of the previous chapters by exporting the Customers and the Orders tables out of the Northwind Sample database that comes with your Access 97 installation. Follow the steps listed at the beginning of Chapter 15 to create this database, and name it chap18.mdb. You will create your example queries using this database.

One of the interesting things that you can do with Access 97 is generate a query that uses another query as its data source. This can be very useful for such things as building a drilldown query application, which starts with a huge general database. With each iteration the user goes through, the result set's contents narrow until the user is looking at a small subset of the original mass of data. This small subset could be constructed to provide the data that the user was looking for in the first place. You might also create different branches leading from each step, depending on the options or the direction you want to offer your user to narrow the query.

The following example walks you through the construction of such a series of queries. You won't attempt to build the user interface for your drilldown query machine in this chapter, but you should be able to translate the work you do in this section into a useful series of forms for your Access 97 database application.

To begin building the drilldown series of queries, follow these steps:

Building the first in a series of complex queries

1. Open your newly created chap18.mdb database and click the **Queries** tab of the Database Window.

2. Click the **New** button and select **Design View** from the pop-up menu that appears. Click **OK**.

   Because you are going to build a series of queries in this example, you will want to start with one of the base tables.

Double-click the Customers table listed in the Show Table dialog box to add it to the Query Design Grid, and then click **Close**.

3. Double-click on the asterisk at the top of the field listing for the Customers table to add all the fields in this table to the Query Design Grid. This is your first query in the drilldown hierarchy, and you want it to include as much information as possible.

4. Close this query and save it as Drill_1 when prompted. Make sure that the Queries tab of the Database Window is still selected, and click the **New** button. Select **Design View** from the pop-up menu that appears, and click **OK**.

Because you are in the process of building the second query in your drilldown hierarchy, you will not be adding a table to your Query Design Grid as you have in almost every previous example. Instead, select the **Queries** tab of the Show Table dialog box and double-click on the **Drill_1** query that you just created. This adds the query to your new query as a data source. Your application should look like the one shown in Figure 18.1.

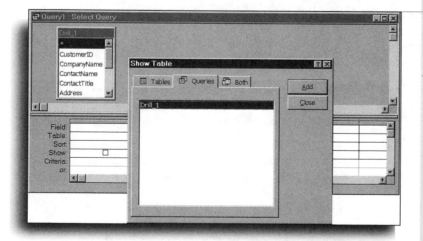

FIGURE 18.1
Creating the first query in your drilldown hierarchy.

What to do with the second step

This query will be step two in your query hierarchy. In step one, the query result set returned every bit of data that was stored in the Customers table of your database. The second query narrowed this data down to the customer names and phone numbers, along with the contact names and the IDs that are stored in the Customers table of your database.

5. Click the **Close** button to close the Show Table dialog box. Drag the CustomerID, CompanyName, ContactName, and Phone fields from the Drill_1 query field listing to the Query Design Grid.

   Close this query and save it as Drill_2 when prompted.

6. Make sure that the Queries tab of the Database Window is still selected, and click the **New** button. Select **Design View** from the pop-up menu that appears and click the **OK** button. This query will be the last query in your example query hierarchy.

7. Because you are using a query as your data source, select the **Queries** tab of the Show Table dialog box and double-click the Drill_2 query that you just created to add it to the Query Design Grid as a data source. Your database application should look like the one shown in Figure 18.2. Click **Close** to close the Show Table dialog box.

FIGURE 18.2

Creating the second query in your drilldown hierarchy.

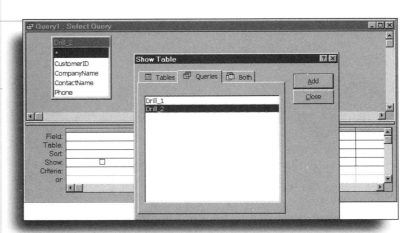

8. Drag the CompanyName field from the Drill_2 query field listing to the Query Design Grid. Click in the Criteria row of the CompanyName field and enter c* as the criteria for the row. Your query should now look like the one shown in Figure 18.3.

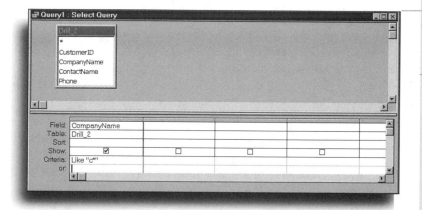

FIGURE 18.3
The third and final table of your drilldown hierarchy.

9. Close this query and save it as Drill_3 when prompted. While the query is still selected, click the **Open** button to view the results of the drilldown query that you just created.

This example was kept very simple so as not to confuse the procedure that you used. You could use this same approach and build a very complex Access 97 application that uses several forms and user prompts to drill up and down through a large data set. If you allow your users to specify which fields they would like to have returned out of each level of the drilldown hierarchy, the chances are good that they will end up with the exact result set they are looking for, even if your original database was made up of several very large tables.

Using the Query Design Grid to Create an SQL Statement for a Macro *RunSQL* Action

You can use a macro in your Access 97 application to run an action query or a data definition query. An action query is one that changes data and includes Append, Delete, Make-table, and Update queries. A data definition query can be used to create tables or indexes on tables, or to delete tables and indexes. You can also edit existing tables' properties. You can use this method of running SQL statements instead of using stored procedures in

Using a transaction for a query

A transaction uses three different statements to ensure that changes to the data in your database are secure. The first statement, `BeginTrans`, is used to mark the beginning of a transaction. Once the query in the transaction has safely run, you can use the second statement, `CommitTrans`, to commit the changes to the data in your database. And if a problem arises, you can cancel all changes to the data in your database by using the third statement, `Rollback`.

your database application. A query in Access 97 is really an SQL statement. You can view the SQL equivalent of any query that you generate using the Query Design Grid by clicking the View icon on the Access 97 toolbar to its **SQL View** position while you are in Query Design mode. To run a SQL statement within a macro in your Access 97 application, you should use the RunSQL action, which has two arguments. The first is the text of the SQL statement that you want to run, and the second is either a Yes or No to indicate if you want to run your SQL statement within the context of a transaction. If you do not run your SQL statement within a transaction, the transaction should run faster. However, the default value for this argument is Yes because it is safer to run a SQL statement within a transaction.

The text of the SQL statement that you use within your macro cannot be longer than 256 characters. If you need to run a longer SQL statement, you should run it from within VBA. The last section of this chapter will show you how to generate a SQL statement and then run it inside VBA.

Table 18.1 shows the Access 97 query type that you should use to accomplish an equivalent SQL action.

TABLE 18.1   SQL Equivalents of Query Types

SQL Action	Access 97 Query Type
SELECT	Select
INSERT INTO	Append
SELECT INTO	Make-table
DELETE	Delete
UPDATE	Update

In the following example you will create a simple query in the Query Design Grid of your Access 97 database application. You will then use that query to build a macro that uses the RunSQL action to execute the query.

To build a macro that uses the RunSQL action to execute a SQL statement using the Query Design Grid, follow these steps:

Building a macro that uses the *RunSQL* action

1. Open a sample database, such as the chap18.mdb database, and click the **Queries** tab of the Database window.

2. Click the **New** button and select **Design View** from the New Query dialog box. Click **OK**.

3. Because you are building a simple example to demonstrate using a macro to run an SQL statement, double-click the Customers table name in the Show Table dialog box that appears. Click **Close** to close the Show Table dialog box.

4. Now that you have a table with which to build a query, drag the CustomerID, CompanyName, ContactName, and Phone fields to the Query Design Grid from the field listing, as shown in Figure 18.4.

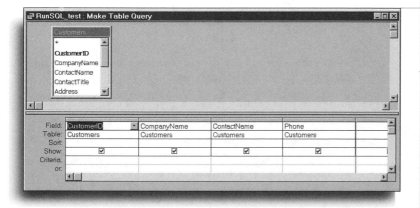

FIGURE 18.4
Creating the query for your RunSQL macro.

5. Select **Query** on the Access 97 menu bar and click the **Make-table** item listed on the menu that appears. Enter CustPhoneBook into the Table Name field of the Make Table dialog box that appears. This will be the name of the new table that is created.

6. Click the View icon on the toolbar to bring the query into SQL View mode, as shown in Figure 18.5.

Using the Make-table option for an action query

Because you need this query to be an action query, you will change the query type to a Make-table query. This will build a table that you can use as a customer phone book.

FIGURE 18.5

Viewing your query in SQL View.

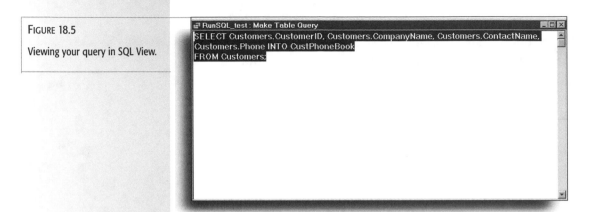

7. The entire query should now be selected. If it isn't, select
the whole query with your mouse. Press Ctrl+C to copy this
query to the clipboard.

8. Close the query design view and save the query as
RunSQL_test when prompted.

9. Select the **Macros** tab of your database window and click
the **New** button. A blank macro sheet should appear.

10. In the Action column of the macro sheet, click the pulldown menu and select the RunSQL action. The arguments for
this type of action will appear at the bottom of the macro
sheet. Click in the **SQL Statement** argument field and press
Ctrl+V to paste the SQL statement that you created in the
Query Design Grid into the argument field. Click the **Use
Transaction** argument field and select either **Yes** or **No**,
depending on your preference. The macro sheet in your
application should look like the one shown in Figure 18.6.

11. Close the macro sheet and save this new macro to your database application as RunSQL_macro when prompted.

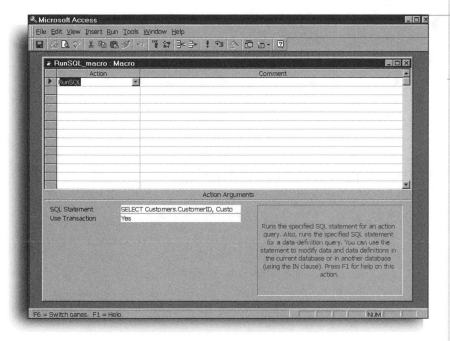

FIGURE 18.6

The finished macro as it appears in your application.

12. With the Macros tab of the database window still selected, click on the macro that you just created and click the **Run** button or the Run Macro icon ![icon]. You should get a message box informing you that you are about to paste 91 records into a new table. Click the **Yes** button, and select the **Tables** tab of the Database window to view the new table that you just created by using the RunSQL action within a macro.

This query example was very simple to give you a feel for the steps involved. You can use this method to run action queries and data definition queries from macros within your Access 97 application. Remember, though, that if the SQL statement that you want to run is longer than 256 characters, you will need to use the RunSQL method of the DoCmd object in VBA, as illustrated in the next section of this chapter.

SEE ALSO

➤ *For more information on using the macro window to create macros, see page 496.*

➤ *For more information on creating macros and the events you can use with macros, see page 516.*

Using the Query Design Grid to Create an SQL Statement for Use in VBA

You can also use the RunSQL method to accomplish the same task that you just completed using the RunSQL action. The difference is that the RunSQL method is called from within Visual Basic or the VBA, and the RunSQL action is used as a macro action in Access 97.

Using the RunSQL method, the VBA allows you to use up to 32,768 characters in your SQL statement, instead of being limited to 256 characters with the RunSQL action.

The RunSQL method is a method of the DoCmd object in Visual Basic. The DoCmd object is used to accomplish Access 97 actions from within the VBA. Prior to Access 95, the DoCmd object was a DoCmd statement, and the arguments for the DoCmd statement have been translated into methods for the DoCmd object. The syntax for using the DoCmd object is

```
[application.]DoCmd.method [arg1, arg2, …]
```

where *application* is the application object itself, which is an optional part of calling the DoCmd object, and *method* is one of the methods that is supported by the DoCmd object. The arguments vary depending on which method you are using.

For this example you are using the DoCmd object with the RunSQL method. The RunSQL method has two arguments: sqlstatement and usetransaction. The syntax for calling the RunSQL method of the DoCmd object is

```
DoCmd.RunSQL sqlstatement[, usetransaction]
```

The *sqlstatement* argument is required, and is a string expression that is the SQL statement that you want to run. The SQL statement must be an action query or a data definition query. And the *usetransaction* argument is used to indicate whether you want to enclose your query in a transaction or not. The default value for this argument is True, so if you leave this argument blank, Access 97 will assume that you want to use a transaction.

SEE ALSO

➤ *VBA coverage begins on page 543.*

➤ *For other examples using the DoCmd, see "Standardizing Forms" and Listing 20.1, beginning on page 349 and "Using Form Events to Open Other Forms" on page 424.*

Creating the User Interface, Input, and Output

Adding Controls to Forms and Reports

Adding, aligning, and modifying controls

Working with the grid

Selecting and working with multiple controls

What's the Toolbox?

As you learned in Chapters 5 and 6, the wizards do a good job of creating forms and reports for us. However, wizards seldom generate the perfect form or report. You can expect to fine-tune a wizard's results. They may need only a simple touch, such as a new label caption, or a new text alignment setting. Or, they may need more heavy duty modifications—such as a calculated control. Fortunately, Access provides easy access to its controls through the Toolbox, shown in Figure 19.1.

FIGURE 19.1

The Toolbox offers the Access native controls.

Displaying the Toolbox

There are several ways to display the Toolbox. You can click the Toolbox button ![toolbox] on the appropriate design toolbar. You can also choose **Toolbox** from the **View** menu. Or, you can choose **Toolbars** from the **View** menu, and then select **Toolbox** from the submenu.

The Toolbox houses all of Access' native controls. By *native*, I mean, all the controls that come with Access. To display other available controls, as shown in Figure 19.2, click the More Controls button ![more controls] on the Toolbox. The controls offered will depend on the foreign software you have installed on your system, so don't worry if your list doesn't match ours. When you open your form or report in Design view, Access generally displays the Toolbox and the form or report's property sheet for you. If the Toolbox isn't available, simply click the Toolbox button ![toolbox] on the Form Design or Report Design toolbar.

SEE ALSO

➤ *For more information on calculated controls, see page 395.*

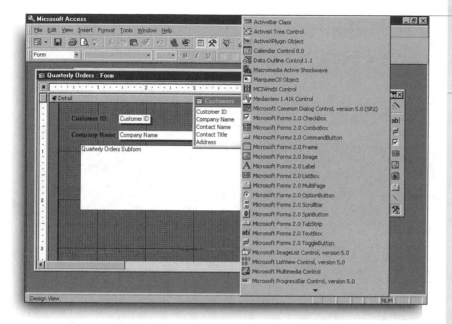

FIGURE 19.2

You can display all the controls by clicking the More Controls button 🛠 on the Toolbox.

Understanding the Grid

You may have noticed that forms and reports in Design view are covered with lines and dots, as shown in Figure 19.3. These lines crisscross to create sections; the dots fill each section. These lines and dots form the *grid*, which will help you position controls more easily. If your form isn't displaying the grid, choose **Grid** from the **View** menu. It's a simple process really: You simply select a control and use the drag-and-drop method to align it to a grid dot or section line.

Altering the Grid

If you find the distance between the grid dots too small or large, you can adjust the distance between them. The default presents 24 dots per inch. To change these defaults you must alter the form's GridX and GridY properties. The lower the setting, the greater the distance between the dots.

FIGURE 19.3

You can use the grid to help position controls.

① Using section lines enables proportional placement across the larger form

② With smaller grid dots you can more accurately and closely place your controls

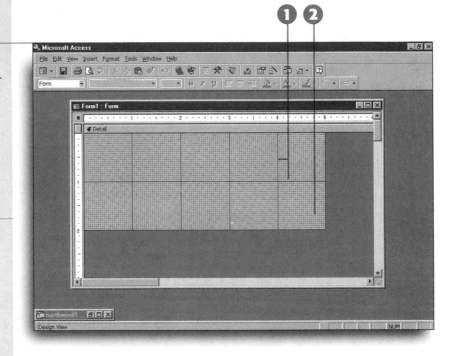

FIGURE 19.3

You can use the grid to help position controls.

① Using section lines enables proportional placement across the larger form

② With smaller grid dots you can more accurately and closely place your controls

The background

You'll see the blank palette you're working on referred to as the *background* of a form or report. It acts something like the desktop in Windows. If you've started to select an icon on the desktop and change your mind, you click a blank space of the desktop. The same thing applies to the background of the form and starting to select or deselect a control—just click the background to deselect a selection.

Altering the distance between the grid dots

1. Open a blank form in Design view by clicking **Forms** and then **New** in the Database window. Then, double-click **Design View** in the New Form dialog box.

2. If Access fails to open the form's property sheet, double-click the **Form Selector** or click the Properties icon 📰 on the Form Design toolbar.

3. Select the GridX property field and change the current setting of 24 to 12. (24 is the default, but yours may be different.)

4. Repeat the previous change with the GridY property. As you can see in Figure 19.4, the dots have twice the space between them as before.

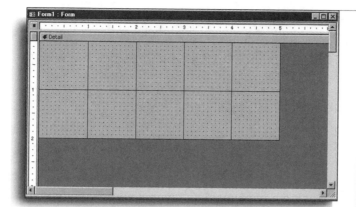

FIGURE 19.4

I doubled the distance between each grid dot; the maximum resolution is 60.

Aligning Controls to the Grid

Access will automatically align controls to the nearest grid dot or line as you create or move them when the Snap to Grid feature is on. (The default is on.) When the feature is off, Access enables you to position or move a control as you like.

Using Snap to Grid to align controls

1. Using your open form, add a command button to the blank form by clicking the Command Button tool ⬜ on the Toolbox and then clicking between two grid dots on the form.

2. Access will automatically align the top-left corner of the new button to the nearest grid mark.

3. Now, try to move the control by positioning the top-left corner of the button in between two grid dots. You'll quickly see that Access won't enable you to do so. Instead, Access always aligns the top-left corner to the nearest intersecting grid points.

4. To turn off the Snap to Grid feature, select **Snap to Grid** from the **Format** menu in Design view.

5. Now, insert a second command button—be sure to click between the dots to get the full effect of the change you just made. This time, Access leaves the control where you place it.

6. Try moving the control. You'll find Access doesn't care a bit where you release the button.

If you find the grid as a whole annoying or you simply don't need it, you can turn it off.

Turning off the grid

1. Open a blank form in Design view by clicking the **Forms** tab and then the **New** button in the Database window. Then, double-click **Design View**, or select **Design View**, and click **OK** in the New Form dialog box.

2. From the **View** menu, deselect **Grid**. The resulting form, shown in Figure 19.5, displays no grid lines or dots.

FIGURE 19.5

You can turn off the grid display.

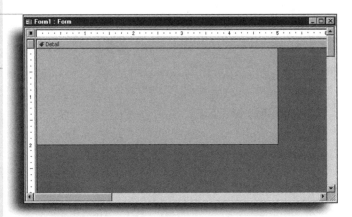

Inserting Controls

The exercises in this section help you practice or review inserting controls. To do so, simply click one of the control tools on the Toolbox and then click inside the form or report. To demonstrate, let's add a few controls to a blank form. (You'll follow the same procedure when adding controls to a report.)

Adding controls to a form

1. Open a blank form by selecting **Forms**, clicking **New** in the Database window, and then double-clicking **Design View** in the New Form dialog box.

Temporarily suspending the Snap to Grid feature

You don't have to turn off the Snap to Grid feature to suspend its behavior. Instead, hold down the Ctrl key while you insert, move, or resize a control. Doing so temporarily turns off the feature. When you release the Ctrl key, Access will turn the feature back on.

2. If Access doesn't launch the Toolbox, click the Toolbox tool ✳ on the Form Design toolbar. Or, choose **T**o**olbox** from the **View** menu. Make sure the Control Wizards control 🔷 is deselected.

3. Click the Text Box tool abl on the Toolbox and then click anywhere inside the blank form. Access will add a text box to the form, as shown in Figure 19.6. By default, Access includes a label control to the left of each text box. Select the label control by clicking it, and then double-clicking it. Then type the text you want for your text box.

4. Now, click the Label tool Aa on the Toolbox and then click inside the blank form to add a label control. Access inserts the control in Edit mode, so you can immediately type your descriptive text. At this point, type the text you want for your label control, as you've done in 19.7. Both label controls are for displaying descriptive text.

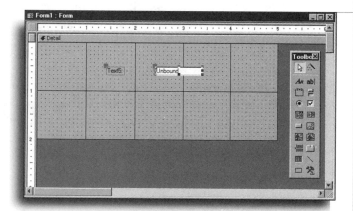

FIGURE 19.6
Adding a text box to this blank form.

Adding or Changing a Control Label

Occasionally, you won't want to use the label that Access includes with each text box. When this is the case, you can easily delete it. To demonstrate this simple procedure, you'll modify a text box like the one in Figure 19.6.

FIGURE 19.7

Adding descriptive text to your label control.

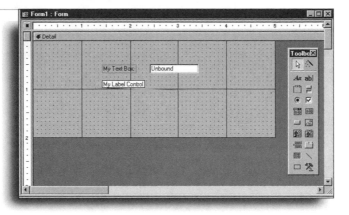

Deleting the text box control's label

1. With the form still in Design view, click the form's background to deselect any controls.

2. Position the mouse pointer over the top-left corner of the label and click it. Access will select the label control and display the hand icon over the top-left handle, as shown in Figure 19.8.

A *handle* is any of the small squares (in contrasting color) that appear in a frame-like box around a control. You'll use these squares to resize the control. If you rest the cursor on one of the lines between the handles, you can click that area and then move the control. The large handle in the upper-left corner selects that control for separate action (such as moving or deleting) from its related label control.

Cursor changes:

- The arrow is for resizing
- The open hand is for moving that control and its label together
- The hand with the finger pointing separates the selection between two related controls. The action you take will affect the single control only.

3. After the mouse-hand icon appears over the top-left handle, press Del, and Access will delete just the label portion of the text box.

Deleting the control

To delete a control, all you have to do is click it and press Del. Or, you can choose **Delete** from the **Edit** menu.

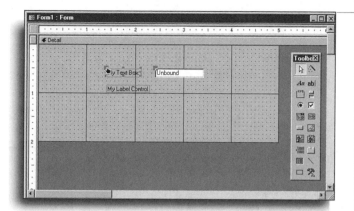

FIGURE 19.8
The hand icon indicates that
you've selected just the label portion of this text box.

SEE ALSO

➤ *To learn more about resizing a control, read page 324.*

Adding Several Controls of the Same Type

If you want to add the same type of control to your form or
report, you have two options: the copy-and-paste method and
the lock option.

Copying Controls

You can add one control, copy it, and then paste as many as you
need. This solution is good when you want the controls to share
similar properties. You create the first control, change the
appropriate properties, copy it, and then paste it as many times
as you need. That way, each of the copied controls will share the
modified property settings of the first control.

The copy and paste method for adding several controls

1. You can open a new blank form by selecting **Forms** and
   then **New** in the Database window. Or, you can continue to
   work with the open form you used in our last example.
   Make sure the Control Wizards button on the Toolbox is
   deselected.

2. Click the Command Button tool 🔲 on the Toolbox and
   then click the form's background. Access will add a command button to the form.

**Shortcut for adding similar
controls**

Adding several controls to the
form in a copy-and-paste
method can save time even if
the properties are not all the
same. If you want the same
type of controls with only minor
differences in the properties,
add several using this method
and then vary the properties
accordingly.

3. With the button still selected, choose **Copy** from the **Edit** menu.

4. Next, choose **Paste** from the **Edit** menu, and Access will add a second command button to the form, as shown in Figure 19.9. Paste a third button by again selecting **Paste** from the **Edit** menu.

FIGURE 19.9

After copying the command button, you pasted a copy of the button to your form.

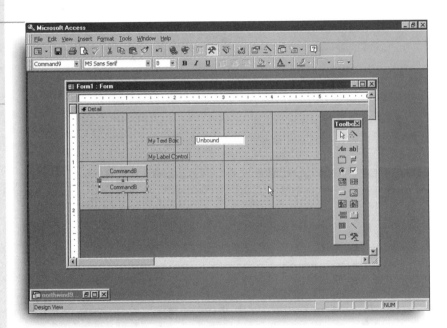

SEE ALSO

➤ *You can learn more about setting properties and the time this shortcut will save for numerous settings on page 346.*

Locking the Toolbox Control

An alternative to the copy and paste method is to lock the control type at the Toolbox. Then, you can select the type of control you want to add and simply click inside the form or report once for each control you want to add. This solution is good when the default properties are adequate, or when you'll be applying different property settings to each control.

Locking the Toolbox to add several of the same control

1. Make sure the Control Wizards control is deselected. Then, double-click the Command Button ▣ tool on the Toolbox.

2. Click inside the form to add a command button.

3. Click inside the form to add a second command button. Continue clicking inside the form to insert as many buttons as you need.

Positioning Controls

Working with controls is easy after you get the hang of it, but adding controls to a form or object is just the beginning. The next step is to position and align your controls. For the most part, you depend on the horizontal and vertical rulers to position the controls you insert.

Positioning a control

1. Open a blank form by clicking **Forms** and then **<u>New</u>** in the Database window. Then, double-click **Design View** in the New Form dialog box.

2. Make sure the Control Wizards button is deselected in the Toolbox.

3. Click the Command Button ▣ tool on the Toolbox and click anywhere inside the blank form.

4. Using the drag-and-drop method, drag the control to the 1 inch horizontal position, as shown in Figure 19.10.

5. Maintaining the new horizontal position, drag the control to the 1 inch vertical position. When you finish, the control should be at the intersection of both 1 inch marks, as shown in Figure 19.11.

How Access names multiple controls

Access will assign a default name to a control, which you're free to change. The default name will consist of the control's type and a number. If the control contains a label, Access will apply consecutive even numbers to the control and consecutive odd numbers to the attached label control. For example, if the first control is a text box, that text box will have the name Text0, the label will have the name Label1. If you add a list box next, the list box will have the name List2 and the label's name will be Label3. When there's no label control, Access will assign consecutive numbers—not consecutive odd or even numbers.

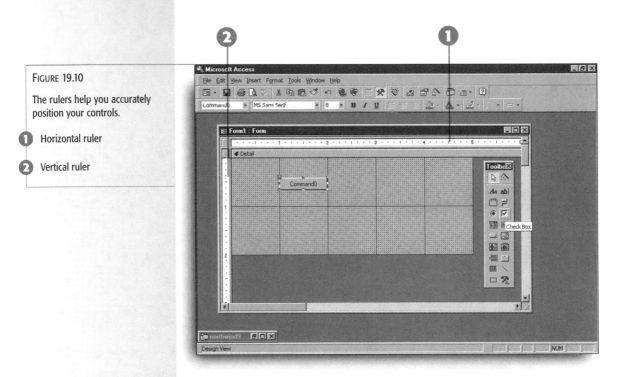

FIGURE 19.10

The rulers help you accurately position your controls.

❶ Horizontal ruler

❷ Vertical ruler

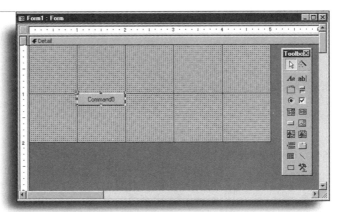

FIGURE 19.11

Now the button is at the intersection of both 1 inch marks.

Sizing Controls

Placing your controls where you want them won't always be enough. Occasionally, you may have to change the size of a control. You may want to make all your controls the same size, or a control may be too small to completely display the contents of a field.

Directly sizing a control

1. Open the an existing form in Design view by selecting that form in the Database window and then clicking **<u>D</u>esign View**.

2. Select a control, especially one where the text runs past the end of a text box, and position the mouse pointer over the center-right sizing handle. When you do, Access will display the double-arrow mouse pointer shown in Figure 19.12. As with other Windows applications, this is an indication that you can change the size of the selected control.

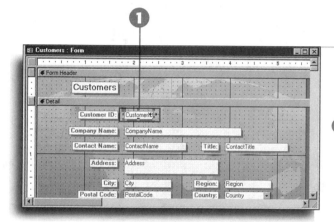

FIGURE 19.12

When the double-arrow mouse pointer appears, you can resize the selected control.

1 Be sure the double-arrow appears or you will slide the control over instead of resizing

3. Now, drag the sizing handle to the right (or away from an adjacent label or control on an empty background) by the length you choose.

You can also resize a control to match that of another control on a form. This works well if you want the size of controls to be even along one edge or if you know the values are of similar lengths.

Matching existing control sizes

1. Select the control you want to resize.

2. Hold down the Shift key and select the control that is the length you want to match. Both the controls are now selected.

Example for this task

The figures in this example use the Customers form of the Northwind database. The same principles apply to any other controls you create.

Sizing by mouse action

The same mouse actions you've used in other Windows applications apply with controls. If you want to expand a control up and to the right, hover the mouse over the upper-right corner handle. The cursor changes to the diagonal, bi-directional arrow. The arrows over each handle show which way the control will expand.

3. Choose **Size** from the **Format** menu.

4. Select **To Widest** from the resulting submenu, shown in Figure 19.13.

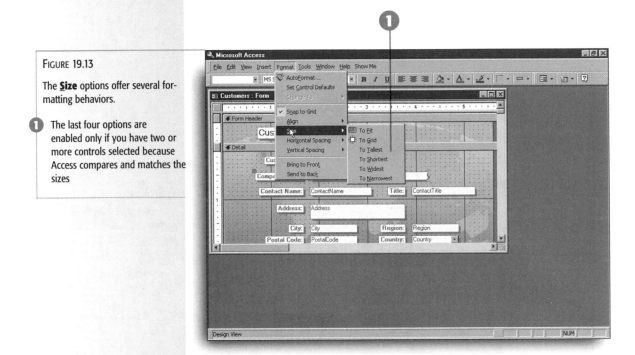

FIGURE 19.13

The **Size** options offer several formatting behaviors.

1 The last four options are enabled only if you have two or more controls selected because Access compares and matches the sizes

Access will increase the size of the smaller control to match the wider control, as shown in Figure 19.14.

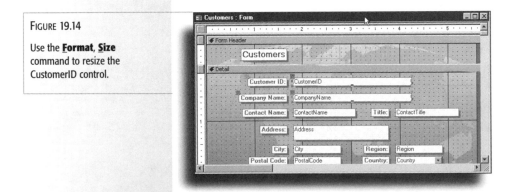

FIGURE 19.14

Use the **Format**, **Size** command to resize the CustomerID control.

SEE ALSO

➤ *You can learn more methods for standardizing the look of your forms on page 349.*

Selecting Multiple Controls

You may find yourself repeating tasks with several controls. Fortunately, Access lets you select more than one control at a time. Then, you can move, resize, or modify the whole group of controls at one time. But before you can make any changes, you must select the controls.

Selecting with the Shift Key

There are several selection methods, but perhaps the simplest is to select a control, press Shift, and then select another while holding down the Shift key. You continue in this manner until you've added all the controls you want to modify in some way. This method enables you to be very specific about which controls you want to select, but it's also a little time consuming. To deselect multiple controls, simply click the form's background.

Using Shift to select multiple controls

1. Open an existing form in Design view by clicking the **Forms** tab, selecting the form, and then clicking **Design View** in the Database window.

2. Select the first of the controls you want. (Be sure not to inadvertently select the control's label instead of the text box control.)

3. Press and hold down the Shift key.

4. Click the remaining controls while holding down the Shift key.

   As you can see in Figure 19.15, Access selects both controls at the same time.

5. Select any additional controls, even if they are not adjacent to the ones you have selected thus far.

Sizing options

As you can see in Figure 19.13, Access offers several formatting options for resizing your controls. For the most part they are self-explanatory. (Access matches the size of all controls you select to the tallest, shortest, widest, or narrowest control in the selection—whichever option you choose.)

The **To Fit** option is especially worth noting. It sets the control size to adjust to the largest data entry in that field.

Standardizing control size

Matching the size of controls is a quick and easy way to standardize the look of your forms. It also helps reduce unused space.

The example for this task

The figures in this section show the Employees form from Northwind.

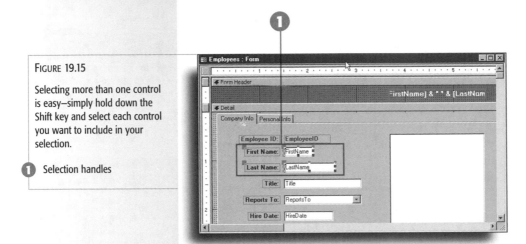

To see the scope of using the Shift key, try selecting the second, third, and sixth controls on your form. Access will add only these controls to your selection without affecting any of the controls in between, as shown in Figure 19.16.

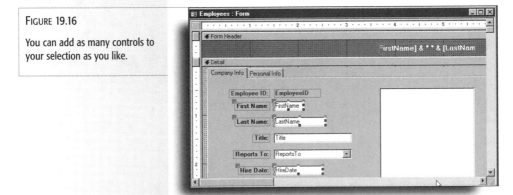

Using Rulers to Select Multiple Controls

You can also use the rulers to select controls. The outcome is a bit different, as you'll select everything below or to the right of the area you select in the ruler. Using the ruler method is less specific than the Shift key method, but it's quicker.

Selecting by simple point-and-click

1. With an existing form open in Design view, click the form's background to clear any previous selection.

2. Then, click a mark on the horizontal or vertical ruler in line with the control(s) you want to select.

Access will select control(s) directly below or across from that inch mark.

Figure 19.17 shows an example of two controls selected by clicking the vertical ruler.

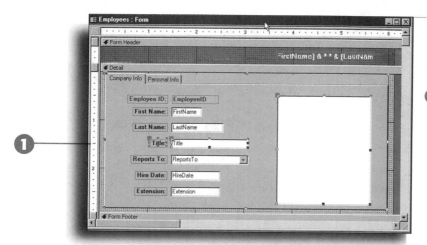

FIGURE 19.17

Access selected both controls to the right of the 1 1/2 inch mark on the vertical ruler.

① 1 1/2 inch mark on the vertical ruler. Both controls are on this line.

When you are selecting by the point-and-click method, you should always note where the guideline falls among your controls. Notice in Figure 19.18 that Access excludes the FirstName control from the selection. That's because the FirstName control is shorter than the others and clicking just to the right missed this control.

Access will respond to more than a simple click on either ruler. You can also drag the mouse pointer along the ruler, and Access will select any control that falls under or to the right of the range that you drag the mouse across.

Proximity guidelines for the ruler

If you click a mark on either ruler a line from the ruler across the form/report appears. If any part of a control falls on that line, the control will be selected.

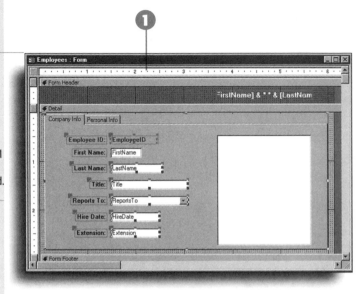

Dragging across the ruler to select multiple controls

1. With a form open in Design view, click the form's background to deselect all controls, if necessary.

2. Gauge the approximate edge of the range of controls you want to select. Click the ruler but don't release the mouse button. This creates the guideline straight from the ruler across the form.

3. Drag the mouse pointer across the ruler to include the controls you want.

Figure 19.19 illustrates this by showing the controls selected in the 3–4 inch range on the horizontal ruler. Access will select the Title and ReportsTo control and the Photo control. That's because only these three controls lie below the fourth inch of the form.

In a similar fashion, Figure 19.20 shows the controls selected in a drag range on the vertical ruler. Access will select the three text box controls to the right of the 1–2 inch range: LastName, Title, and ReportsTo. However, Access will also select the Photo control. Don't forget, it's also to the right of this area.

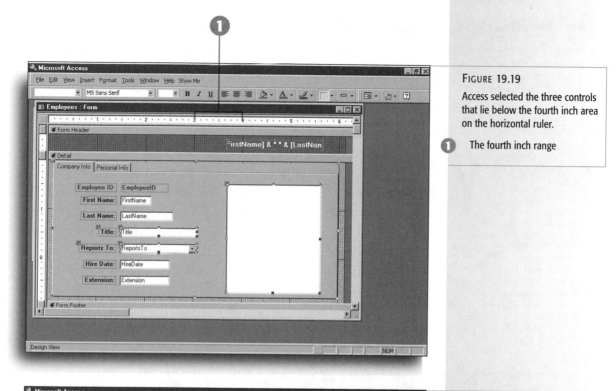

FIGURE 19.19
Access selected the three controls that lie below the fourth inch area on the horizontal ruler.

❶ The fourth inch range

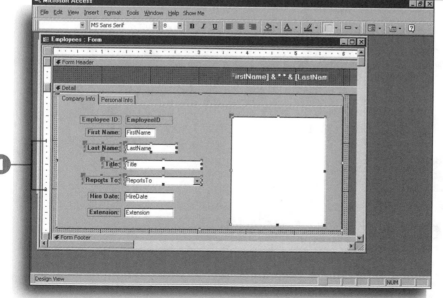

FIGURE 19.20
You selected all four controls that lie to the right of the second inch.

❶ The second inch range

Limitations of this method

If you've used the mouse much to drag across objects or lines of text, you might be familiar with these limitations: You can only select adjacent controls within a loop. You can't "bend" the loop to select or deselect objects that do not form an exact rectangle. You might have trouble controlling the roll of the mouse to get the exact number included if you're selecting a large range.

Selecting Multiple Controls with the Mouse

You might be surprised to learn that there are still two more multiple selection techniques. First, you can select controls by creating an imaginary border around them with the mouse pointer.

Dragging across controls to select them

1. With the form open in Design view, click the form's background to clear any previous selection, if necessary.

2. Place the cursor over the corner of the first control in an adjacent range of control.

3. Click on the corner edge of the first control and drag the mouse across the control in the direction of the range you want to select. (You'll usually drag in a diagonal direction to form the loop.)

   As long as you continue in one fluid motion with the mouse button down, you can drag over any controls to select them.

Figures 19.21 and 19.22 show the beginning and ending points of dragging the mouse to form a border around two text box controls and their respective label controls.

FIGURE 19.21

Start the selection process to the left and just above the leftmost control you want to select.

1 Click here

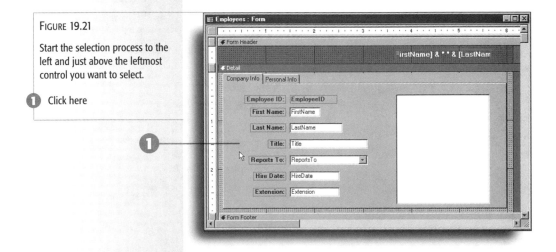

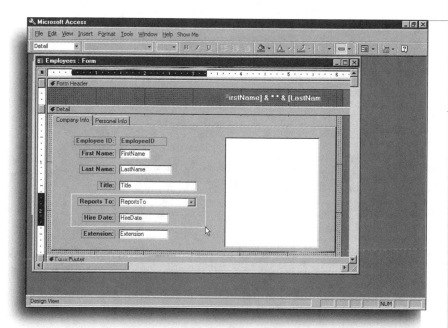

FIGURE 19.22
Drag the mouse pointer to just beyond and below the leftmost control you want to include in your selection.

Selecting Multiple Controls with the Menu

The final selection technique is a simple menu command. To select all the controls in the form, choose **Select All** from the **Edit** menu.

Changing Selection Behavior Defaults

Selecting just the controls you want can sometimes be awkward because, by default, Access will select a control if you enclose any part of it in a selection process. If this presents a problem, you should adjust the way Access selects multiple controls.

Access offers two selection options: Partially Enclosed, the default, and Fully Enclosed. With the default setting, you need enclose only a small portion of a control to include it in the selection. In contrast, the Fully Enclosed option will include a control only if you completely enclose it.

Using the Partially Enclosed default setting

1. With the form open in Design view, click the form's background to clear the selection as necessary. The figures show the Employees form.

Selecting most of your controls

As I've shown, there are several ways to select multiple controls and each has its advantages and drawbacks. To select several controls, but not all, it can sometimes be quicker and easier to select them all and then deselect the few you don't want to include. To select all the controls, choose **Select All** from the **Edit** menu. Then, hold down the Shift key as you click the controls you don't want to include in your selection.

The example for this task

The figures in this section reflect the use of the Employees form from Northwind.

2. Click above and to the left of the control, such as the LastName label box shown in Figure 19.23.

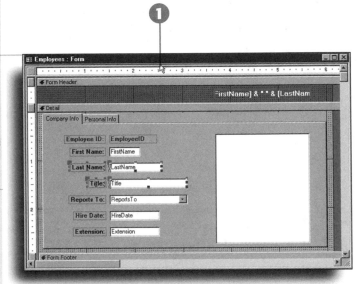

FIGURE 19.23

Access selects both the LastName and the Title controls.

1 Dragging the mouse partially across controls selects all of them with the Partially Enclosed option

3. Without releasing the mouse button, drag the mouse pointer to a point in the middle of the controls you want to select, and release the mouse button.

For example, if you dragged to the 1 1/2 vertical inch mark and 2 1/2 horizontal inch mark on the Employees form, Access will select both the LastName and Title controls, as shown in Figure 19.23, even though you didn't contain them all in your drag loop.

4. If you want to require Access to select only those controls completely enclosed in your drag loop, adjust the selection behavior. To do so, choose the **Options** command from the **Tools** menu, and then select the **Forms/Reports** tab.

5. Next, from the **Selection Behavior** options, choose **Fully Enclosed**. Click **OK** to return to the form.

6. Now, repeat steps 1, 2, and 3. This time, Access selects just the controls that you completely enclose (just the FirstName control, as shown in Figure 19.24).

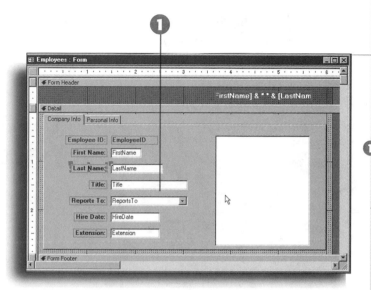

FIGURE 19.24

Access excludes the Title control from the selection because it extends beyond the boundaries of our selection box.

1 The Title control extends beyond the 2 1/2 horizontal inch mark, so you didn't fully enclose it and it isn't selected

Changing the Properties of Multiple Controls

Multiple selection techniques come in handy when you want to make the same modification to several controls at the same time, for example, if you want the text of all your controls to be a certain font or color. Simply create your multiple selection and then make the change to one. Access will apply the same modification to every control in the selection.

Modifying properties in a multiple selection

1. With an existing form, such as the Employees form, open in Design view, click the background to clear any unwanted selections.

2. Use one of the methods described earlier in this chapter to select the controls you want to change. For example, you can click a horizontal rule mark over a stack of controls to select all the text box controls on one side of the form, such as the 2 inch mark for all the controls on the left side of the Employees form.

3. Open a multiselection property sheet by clicking the Properties button 📑 on the Form Design toolbar. Select the tab with the property you want to change, such as the **Format** tab.

Lost toolbar

If you can't find the Form Design toolbar, it may be docked beside the Formatting toolbar. If so, simply drag it down and place it beneath the Formatting toolbar.

If you still can't find it, use the **View** menu's **Toolbars** option to make sure the Form Design toolbar is checked.

4. Change the property, such as the Font Size, from 8 to 10. Access will automatically update the controls in the current selection, as shown in Figure 19.25.

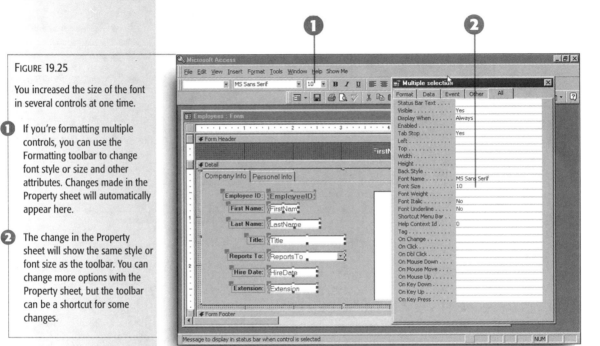

FIGURE 19.25

You increased the size of the font in several controls at one time.

① If you're formatting multiple controls, you can use the Formatting toolbar to change font style or size and other attributes. Changes made in the Property sheet will automatically appear here.

② The change in the Property sheet will show the same style or font size as the toolbar. You can change more options with the Property sheet, but the toolbar can be a shortcut for some changes.

Shortcut for formatting controls

This example changes a property from the formatting list in the property sheet. You can also change several of these properties by clicking the corresponding option on the Formatting toolbar. For example, after you select multiple controls, click the drop-down list box on the toolbar and change the font size.

The change in one location automatically updates the information in the other.

You needn't worry about inadvertently affecting a stray property. When working with a multiple selection, Access will display only those properties that all the controls have in common.

An Introduction to the Control Wizards

Before the exercises in the previous sections, you had to deselect the Control Wizards control [icon] on the Toolbox. That's because you didn't want to launch one of the five control wizards Access offers:

- Option Group Wizard
- Combo Box Wizard
- List Box Wizard
- Command Button Wizard
- Subform/Subreport Wizard

If the Control Wizards button is selected when you click one of these five controls, Access will launch that control's wizard. These wizards are very helpful, but not always necessary. Let's take a quick glimpse at the Command Button Wizard. Similar principles in this exercise apply to the other wizards.

Launching a control wizard

1. Open a new blank form, or use the form from our previous example.

2. Click the Control Wizards button 🔲 on the Toolbox.

3. Select the Command Button tool on the Toolbox and then click inside the form to insert a command button.

4. Access will respond by displaying the Command Button Wizard's first window, shown in Figure 19.26. If you continue, the wizard will display a series of windows—each one prompting you for information about the button's task.

5. You can use the wizard to select the action and the name of the button.

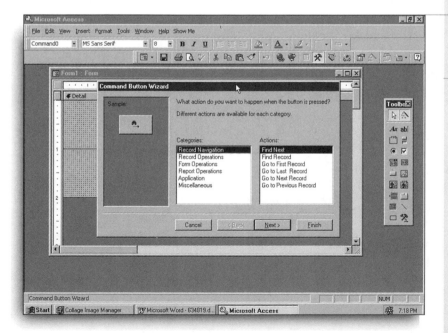

Don't forget the Undo feature

You're probably familiar with the **Undo** feature on the **Edit** menu. This feature enables you to change your mind after making an entry or modification. You can use this feature on a multiple selection as well. After changing a property setting, you have the option to choose **Undo Property Setting** from the **Edit** menu (or press Ctrl+Z).

FIGURE 19.26

Access launched the Command Button Wizard.

Installing wizards

When you install your software, you can exempt the wizards from the process. So, if you attempt to launch one of these controls wizards and receive an error, you probably need to install the wizards.

Table properties that affect your form

If you use a wizard to create a bound form or report, that wizard does a lot of work. Besides creating a control for each field in the underlying table or query, the wizard also assigns a name to each control. Specifically, the wizard assigns the field names to the controls. In addition, the wizard uses the field name as the descriptive text in a text box control's label. You might want to override this default by adding more appropriate text to the underlying table's Caption property. Access will display the Caption property's text instead of the field name in the bound control's label. This is a handy shortcut because efficient field names rarely make good descriptive text.

Other table properties that are carried through to the form are Format, Input Mask, Default Value, and Description. Format and Input Mask are self-explanatory. Access will display the Description property's text in the Status bar for each control, when that control has focus. It's an easy way to display a bit of information about the control to your users.

SEE ALSO

➤ *For more specific instructions for using a Control Wizard, turn to page 141.*

➤ *For a complete look at using the Control Wizards, see page 139.*

What's a Bound Control?

Throughout this chapter, I've referred to bound controls, forms, and reports. A *bound* object is an object that's attached to a data source. That object can be a form, a report, or a control. The underlying record source can be a table or query. For instance, a form bound to a table named tblMyTable will display the data in tblMyTable. In addition, you can use that form to enter new data into tblMyTable. Actually, you can even use the form to modify the existing data in tblMyTable. In contrast, an unbound object has no data source. For instance, a calculated control displays data—the result of its expression—but that control isn't bound to a table or query. In other words, it displays data, but doesn't store it.

A bound form or report's underlying table or query is called the form's *Record Source*. A bound control's underlying field is called the control's *Control Source*. Both the form's Record Source and the control's Control Source are available through the respective object's property sheet.

The Quarterly Orders form in Northwind is bound to the Customers table, as you can see in Figure 19.27. Furthermore, this form contains several bound controls. It also contains a calculated control—the Total control. A *calculated* control uses an expression as its data source instead of a bound field.

SEE ALSO

➤ *For more information on calculated controls, see page 395.*

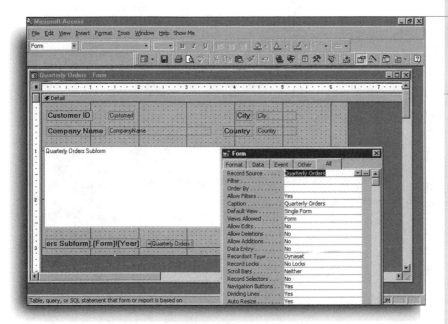

FIGURE 19.27
The Quarterly Orders form is
bound to the Quarterly Orders
query.

Creating a Bound Control

In the previous section I told you what a bound object is, but
didn't show you how to create one. Well, you can use the wizards to create bound fields. However, most likely you will need
to create them yourselves. To demonstrate, the figures in this
example add a bound control to the Quarterly Orders form that's
open in Design view.

Creating a bound control

1. With your form open in Design view, click the Field List
   button [icon] on the Form Design toolbar. Or, choose **Field
   List** from the **View** menu. The Field List will contain all
   the fields in the form's Row Source (bound table or query).

2. Drag the field, such as the CustomerID field, from the Field
   List to the form, as shown in Figure 19.28. As you can see,
   Access has added a bound text box control to your form.

If you're working with an existing form

If you're using a form from
Northwind (or any other) database to practice this exercise,
you can't duplicate a field name
in the same object. So, before
you can add a bound field, you
must delete the ones that are
there. Hold down the Shift key
and select the controls. Then,
press Del.

If you're working with a new form

If you want to create bound
controls on a new form, click
New on the Database window's
Forms tab. Select **Design View**
in the upper list box. Select the
table or query in the drop-down
list box. Click **OK**.

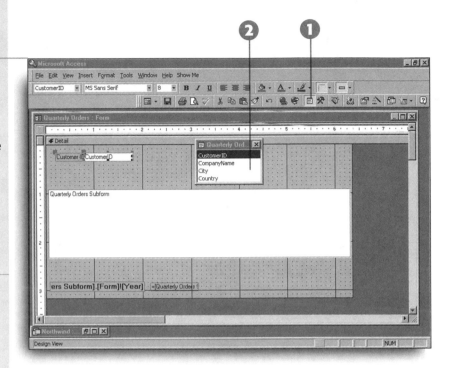

FIGURE 19.28

You added a bound control by dragging the field from the Field List window to the form.

1 The Field List button calls up the fields of the underlying table or query to which your form or report is bound

2 Simply drag the field(s) from the list box to the form. Access creates appropriately sized text boxes for each field.

More about the Field List

If Access opens the Field List in an awkward spot, simply move it. To do so, click the Field List window's title bar, and drag it someplace else. You can also change the window's size. Position the mouse pointer over any of the borders. When Access displays the double-arrow mouse pointer, click and drag the border in the appropriate direction.

Changing the default of a bound control

By default, Access creates a bound text box control when you add a field to a bound control using the Field List window. If you want a bound control of another type beside a text box, you can temporarily change the control default by clicking that other control on the Toolbox *before* you select the field from the Field List.

Adding one bound control at a time might prove time-consuming, so fortunately, Access enables you to select multiple fields in the Field List. To choose a contiguous list of fields, hold down the Shift key and then click the first and last field. Or, hold down the Ctrl key and click each field to create a noncontiguous list. After you've created a multiple-field selection, simply drag the lot of them to the form at the same time. Access will size the controls to fit the data type of the field's property. For example, if you drag a smaller field (such as an ID field), a description, or image field to the form, Access will automatically create a larger display area for the larger fields.

Creating Forms

Examine the form's Design View environment

Become familiar with the form sections

Learn how to change a form's properties

Create form templates

The Form in Design View

The Form Wizards, which were reviewed in Chapter 5, "Form Creation Using a Wizard," can create many useful forms. The wizards are limited, however, and occasionally you may need to enhance or modify a form. Fortunately, doing so is easy. You simply open the form in Design view and go to work.

SEE ALSO

➤ *To review creating a form with a wizard, see page 70.*

Opening a closed form in Design View

1. Open the database you want and select the form in the **Forms** tab of the Database window.

2. Click **Design View**.

Opening an open form in Design View

1. Click the View button on the Form Design toolbar.

Creating a non-wizard form

1. Select the table or query on which you're basing your form in the Database window.

2. Choose **Form** from the **Insert** menu.

3. This brings up the New Form dialog box. The defaults should show **Design View** in the top list box and the table name you selected in the drop-down box. Click **OK**.

   or

1. Select the table or query on which you're basing your form in the Database window.

2. Choose **Form** from the New Object button's drop-down list.

3. In the resulting New Form dialog box, double-click **Design View**.

Essentials for this task

Obviously, to create a form, you need a database to work with. If you haven't created a database yet, open the Northwinds sample database and use one of its many forms.

The changing View button

As you might have noticed, the View button toggles between different icons depending on which mode you are in:

Forms—When you're viewing the design of a form, you'll see the Form view icon on the toolbar. You can also click the drop-down arrow to select the Datasheet view icon.

Reports—A report in Design view will show the Preview icon.

Forms and Reports—A form or report in the Preview or Form view will show the Design view icon to switch you to the Design view of that object.

In all cases where the word "view" is used, assume this means the first button on the toolbar, no matter which icon it displays. Click the drop-down arrow to see the other options in which you can view your object.

The Components of a Form in Design View

Figure 20.1 shows a blank form in Design view. Each form has five components:

- The title bar—The title bar displays the form's name. At the right end of the title bar, you'll find the Windows Minimize ▣, Maximize ▣, and Close ☒ buttons.

- The horizontal and vertical rulers—You'll use the horizontal and vertical rulers to help size and position controls.

SEE ALSO

➤ *Besides sizing and positioning controls, you can use the rulers to select multiple controls, as demonstrated on page 328.*

- The Form Selector—To open the form's property sheet, simply double-click the **Form Selector** tool, which is the gray square at the top-left intersection of the two rulers.

- The blank form—This is the background where you will place the controls.

- The horizontal and vertical scrollbars—The final component, the scrollbars are similar to all other scrollbars. You can use the thumb or the arrows to view areas of your form that stretch beyond the Design view window.

Behind the form are the Access container window and two toolbars: Formatting and Form Design. You're probably familiar with most of the tasks these toolbar buttons offer, so we won't spend any time reviewing them. That brings us to the Toolbox, which houses all the *native* controls you'll add to your forms.

SEE ALSO

➤ *For specific information about the Toolbox, see page 314.*

The New Object button

Be careful with step 2 of this task. You must click on the drop-down arrow to the right of the button to get the drop-down list. If you click on the icon itself, Access might determine that you want an AutoForm or skip straight to the New Form dialog box.

FIGURE 20.1

A blank form in Design View.

1   Title bar

2   Horizontal and vertical rulers

3   Form Selector

4   Blank form

5   Horizontal and vertical scrollbars

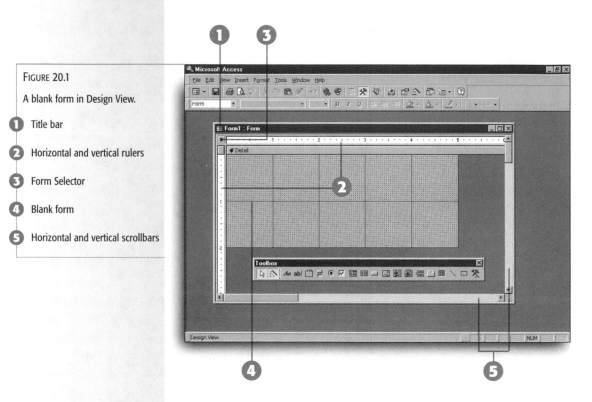

Other windows that open automatically

If you previously had the Fields List icon selected on the toolbar, the Fields List dialog box automatically opens when you open a blank form. If so, click Close to close it.

The Sections of a Form

When you open a blank form, it has only one data section—the Detail section. Most forms only need a Detail section because this is the area that displays the actual record data. You can enhance your form by adding the following sections, which are also shown in Figure 20.2:

- Form Header
- Page Header
- Detail
- Page Footer
- Form Footer

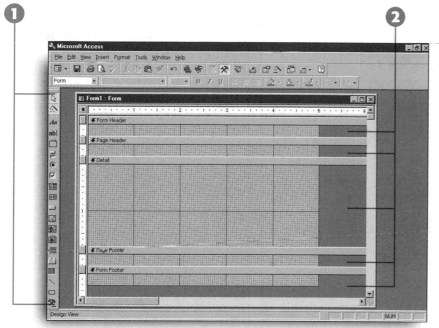

FIGURE 20.2

A pop-up menu appears when you right-click a word marked with a wavy red underline.

1 Move the Toolbox out of your way on any of the four borders

2 Sections of a form appear when checked on the **View** menu

The form's header and footer sections display information, such as a title, for every record. As you might expect, the header appears at the top of the form and the footer appears at the bottom. If you print the form, the header and footer information will appear once, at the top of the first page. Don't hesitate to move task-related command buttons to either the header or footer—command buttons work well in either section. The page header and footer perform similar tasks to the form. The main difference is that the page section prints on each page; the form prints only on the first page.

Every form has a Detail section—it's the basis of every form. You choose whether to add the header and footer sections. To add a form header or footer, choose **Form Header/Footer** from the **View** menu. Similarly, to add a page header or footer, choose **Page Header/Footer** from the **View** menu. Choosing either header/footer option will add both sections to your form. If you need just a header or a footer, you'll need to close the unneeded section yourself by clicking and dragging up the bottom border of that section.

SEE ALSO

➤ *For more information on adding calculated controls to a form's header or footer, see page 395.*

Docking the Toolbox

In Figure 20.2, notice that the Toolbox has been moved to the left side of the Container window to get it out of the way. The Toolbox has no permanent home. You are free to move it using the drag and drop method. You can also *dock* it at any of the four borders of your Container window. Simply drag it to the border as far as it will go. Access will automatically dock the Toolbox for you.

Assigning Form Properties

A form has specific attributes, called properties, that you can use to modify its appearance and task. To access these properties, open the form's property sheet (see Figure 20.3) by double-clicking the Form Selector (refer to Figure 20.1) or the Properties button 🖼 on the Form Design toolbar.

FIGURE 20.3

You can modify a form's attributes by changing its properties in the property sheet.

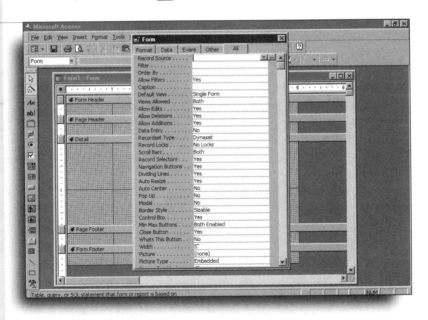

After you open the form's property sheet, making changes is a simple matter. Knowing which properties to change and which settings to use is the trick. Many of them are self-explanatory. Others relate to specific tasks. For that reason, we'll refer to them as we explore form basics and techniques in Chapter 21, "Using Forms to Enter and Review Data," Chapter 22, "Refining Forms: Efficient Data-Entry and Beyond," and Chapter 24, "Advanced Form Techniques." The main thing you'll want to note is that there are properties for the whole form and properties for each individual control you place on the form. The Properties sheet will reflect the properties for the selected object.

SEE ALSO

➤ *To change the properties of the dots on the grid, see page 315.*

➤ *To understand the properties that are carried forward from the underlying table or query to your form properties, see page 338.*

Modifying Form Properties to Create a Dialog Box

To demonstrate the versatility of a form's properties, we'll create a *dialog box*. A dialog box is a specific form style. It displays no navigational toolbars or record selectors, and contains a Close button in the title bar. Also, a dialog box has a unique border. You are constantly interacting with Access via the common dialog box, so you'll want to maintain this format when presenting a custom dialog box.

By modifying a few form properties, you can create a dialog box that looks just like the real thing. For example, the dialog box shown in Figure 20.4 is really a form. You'll learn how to create and save this form as a template. In this context, the term *template* refers to a generic form that you use as a starting point for other forms. Simply open it in Design view, add the appropriate controls and code, give it a new name, and you've got a custom dialog box.

Creating a custom dialog box

1. Open a blank form by clicking the **Forms** tab in the Database window and then clicking the New button.

2. Double-click **Design View** in the New Form dialog box, or select **Design View** and then click **OK**.

FIGURE 20.4

You modified a few form properties to create this custom dialog box.

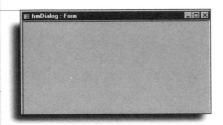

Working in the Properties box

Most of the options in the Properties sheet have hidden drop-down list boxes for each property. Click anywhere on the property's name or in the selection field to make the drop-down arrow appear.

Quick access to a property field's drop-down list

Many properties have fixed settings, and Access displays those settings in a drop-down list. If you're still selecting the property field and then clicking the drop-down arrow to open the list, stop! It's more efficient to click the right edge of the property field, where the drop-down arrow is when it's visible. Access will not only select the field, but it'll open the drop-down list for you. So, what took two clicks before now requires only one.

An even quicker way is to avoid the drop-down list altogether. Click to the left of the property field (in the gray area) to toggle through the property settings. Admittedly, saving one or two clicks here and there doesn't seem like a big deal. However, when you do it over and over again each day, it adds up.

3. If Access doesn't open the form's property sheet, do so now by double-clicking the **Form Selector**, clicking the Properties button 🖻 on the Form Design toolbar, or double-clicking the dark background behind the blank form. (If you double-click the form, you'll open the Detail section's property sheet, which won't apply the properties to the whole form.)

4. Select the **Format** tab and the **Scroll Bars** property field, click the drop-down arrow, and select **Neither** from the resulting drop-down list.

5. Select **No** from the **Record Selectors** property drop-down list.

6. Select **No** from the **Navigation Buttons** property drop-down list.

7. Select **Yes** from the **Modal** property drop-down list. (This setting will retain the focus on the form until you close it.)

8. Resize the form to approximately four inches by two inches (or any size you wish).

9. Click the Save button 🖫 on the Form Design toolbar, enter a name, such as frmDialog, and click **OK**.

You'll reopen this dialog box again and again to customize it and add it to your applications.

SEE ALSO

➤ *If you'd like to learn more about resizing controls and forms, see page 324.*

Standardizing Forms

When you're creating a form, you'll want to consider the form's purpose and the user. The best advice at this point is to standardize your forms. Then apply these standards to all your forms across all your applications. This way you'll maintain continuity in both design and use, thereby reducing both your development time and the user's learning curve with new applications.

You can maintain a library of standardized form types. You'll still have to add controls and code, but the basic form design and properties will already be defined. Instead of starting from scratch each time, you can begin with a basic template.

Now it's time to create a simple form that you might want to store in a library of standardized forms. This library is actually a separate database that you'll create and maintain strictly for archiving standard forms. You can store this database anywhere you like. You'll create the simple display form shown in Figure 20.5. This form won't replace the Form Wizards every time, but it'll come in handy when the wizards aren't adequate.

Once you've built your library, import the necessary form templates into your current project. Then rename them and add the appropriate controls and code.

Whose standards do you use?

Everyone has their own ideas about what looks good and works well. However, we recommend that you stick to the accepted Windows standards as much as possible. Most people are already familiar with these standards, so they'll learn how to use your custom applications more quickly. Besides, Microsoft's already done the hard part. You might as well take advantage of it.

If you don't use the Windows standards, adopt your own and be consistent. Our only recommendation is not to be too creative—simple really is best.

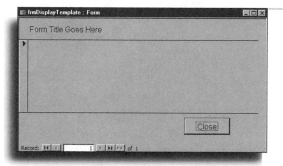

FIGURE 20.5

You can use this or a similar form as your standard display template.

Creating a standard display form

1. Open a blank form by clicking the **Forms** tab, clicking the **New** button, and then double-clicking **Design View** in the **New Form** dialog box.

2. Display the form's header and footer by choosing **Form Header/Footer** from the **View** menu.

3. Increase the size of the header section to approximately half an inch by positioning the mouse over the top border of the **Detail** section title bar. The cursor will switch to the double-arrow cursor. Click and pull down the title bar to expose more of the header.

4. Click the Label tool [Aa] on the Toolbox and then click the left margin of the header section to place a label tool there. Its cursor will begin flashing, signaling for you to type.

5. Enter the text **Form Title Goes Here** and click outside the label when you're finished. Then select the control and apply your standard font and font size to this control. In this example, the Formatting toolbar was used to select **Arial**, size **12**. You may need to add the Formatting toolbar for this step. To do so, choose **Toolbars** from the **View** menu and select **Formatting Form/Report** in the resulting submenu.

6. Now resize and reposition the control as necessary.

7. Open the Label tool's property sheet by double-clicking the label. Select the Name property field and enter a name such as lblTitle.

8. Extend the footer section.

9. Click the Command Button tool [▣] on the Toolbox and then click inside the footer section to place a command button. If Access launches the Command Button Wizard, click the Cancel button in the first window.

10. Open the button's property sheet by double-clicking that control. Select and set these properties:

Property	Setting/Entry
Name	Type cmdClose
Caption	Close
On Click	**[Event Procedure]**

11. After selecting Event Procedure, click Builder.

12. In the resulting module window, enter the code shown in Listing 20.1. This procedure will close the current form without specifically naming it.

LISTING 20.1   **The Code for the *On Click* Property**

```
1   Private Sub cmdClose_Click()
2       Dim strName As String
3       strName = Me.Name
4       DoCmd.Close acForm, strName
5   End Sub
```

SEE ALSO

➤ *If you need more specific instructions for adding an event procedure, go to page 596.*

13. Click the Compile Loaded Modules button 🔄, fix any typos that show up, and then close the module.

14. At this point, apply any further standards you might require.

15. Save the form as frmDisplayTemplate.

Using Form Templates

The following is a timesaving technique for creating form templates that apply your standards. You can also benefit from modifying the Access form template. Keep in mind that this template doesn't affect the wizard defaults.

By default, Access' form template contains standard information that Access applies to each form, such as section size, font characteristics, and color. When you create a form from scratch, Access applies these default standards to it.

However, if you consistently change the same form properties, you should consider creating your own template, like the one shown in Figure 20.6. This form, named **frmStandards**, has a white background and a dialog border style.

FIGURE 20.6

You can make this form your default.

Changing the form template

1. Choose the **Options** command from the **Tools** menu.

2. Click the **Forms/Reports** tab.

3. Access will display the default form template **Normal** in the **Form Template** control, as shown in Figure 20.7.

4. Select the **Form Template** control, and replace **Normal** with the name of the form you created as your template, such as frmStandards.

5. Click **OK**.

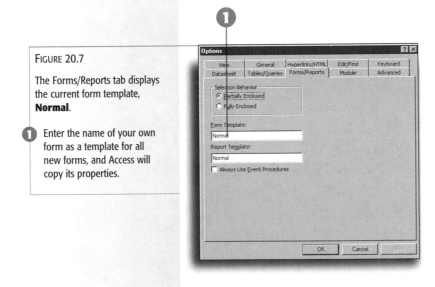

FIGURE 20.7

The Forms/Reports tab displays the current form template, **Normal**.

 Enter the name of your own form as a template for all new forms, and Access will copy its properties.

Using Forms to Enter and Review Data

Become familiar with the different view modes

Learn to navigate your records and controls

Change the tab order

Limit access to the previous and next record

Form View

Most of us use forms like we read a book. We turn the page to see more information, or we turn back to review a previous page. Most forms display one record (page) at a time, but you can't turn the pages. Instead, forms contain several navigational features that you can use to view the records.

Single Form

As mentioned, most forms display one record at a time. This is known as a *Single Form setting*. The Northwind Customers form, shown in Figure 21.1, is a good example of the Single Form setting. There are two other display settings, Continuous Form and Datasheet, which we'll talk about later.

FIGURE 21.1

The Employees form uses the Single Form display setting.

1 First

2 Previous

3 Next

4 Last

5 New

6 Record Number

7 Record Count

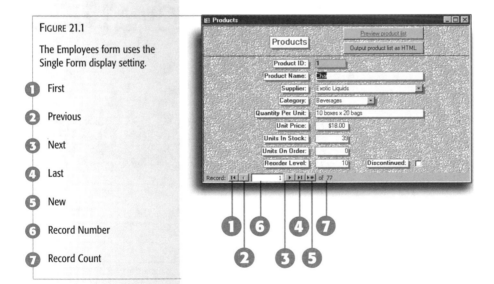

When you open a bound form, Access displays the first record in the form's underlying recordset. A *recordset* is a group of records. As you can see in Figure 21.1, the form hosts several navigational icons at the bottom. Table 21.1 lists these icons and has a brief description of each.

TABLE 21.1   The Navigational Icons on a Single Form

Icon	Name	Description
🔢	First	Select the first record
◀	Previous	Select the previous record
▶	Next	Select the next record
▶❘	Last	Select the last record
▶＊	New Record	Select a new record—creates a blank record for a new entry

At this point, you might want to take a few minutes to familiarize yourself with these five directional icons. Click each one a few times, making note of where that action takes you—pay attention to the updating record count on the navigational toolbar.

When you open the Products form, this toolbar tells you that you are viewing the first record and the total number of records. Access will update the record number as you browse the form's records.

Displaying the record number

1. With an existing form open in Form view at the first record, click the Next ▶ icon.

   Access will select the second record in the recordset and update the Record Number control to reflect that change, as shown in Figure 21.2.

2. Click the Last ▶❘ icon, and Access will display the last record. As you can see in Figure 21.3, the form has 77 records.

3. Click the Previous ◀ icon, and Access will select the record before record 76.

4. Click the First 🔢 icon to return to the first record.

SEE ALSO

➤ *For a definition of* bound, *read page 338.*

Example for this task

This task uses the Products form from Northwind, but the principles apply to any form.

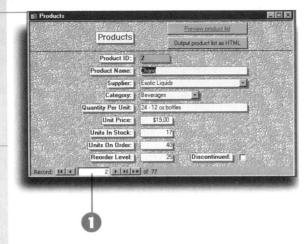

FIGURE 21.2

Access updates the value in the Record Number control to indicate the position of the current record.

1 The record number changes as you navigate to other records

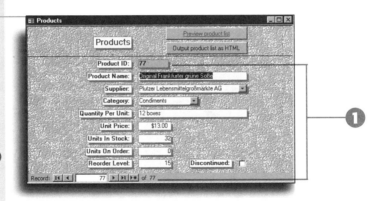

FIGURE 21.3

After you click the Last icon, the Record Number control displays the value 77.

1 The record's Product ID field number and the total record number will match only if you haven't deleted any records (and thus their AutoNumber IDs) and if your table uses an AutoNumber field for the record ID

Continuous Form and Datasheet View

Viewing one record at a time won't always be the best choice for your data, so Access provides Continuous Form and Datasheet view. A few of the wizards will create a continuous form, such as the Customers Phone List form from Northwind, shown in Figure 21.4. Right away you can see a difference—this form displays all the records on one page. If there are too many records to display all of them in the current page, you can use the scrollbar to browse the records that are temporarily out of sight. You can adjust a form's display by resetting its Default View property.

You might have noticed in this form that additional buttons from A–Z appear for easier navigation. Access doesn't provide the alphabetic buttons—those were added and programmed by the developer. This is not an automatic form feature.

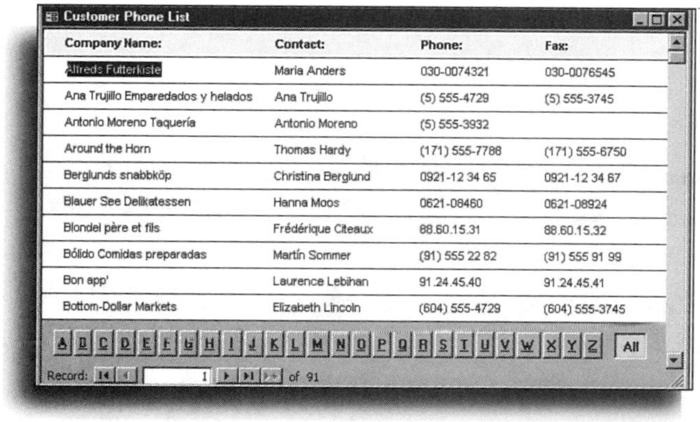

FIGURE 21.4

The Continuous Forms setting displays all the records at the same time.

Changing a form's display

1. With a continuous form, such as the Customers Phone List form, open in Form view and click the Design View icon on the Form View toolbar to open the form in Design view.

2. If Access doesn't launch the form's property sheet, click the Properties icon on the Form Design toolbar.

3. Open the Default View property's drop-down list to display the three possible settings: Single Form, Continuous Form, and Datasheet. The Customers Phone List setting is Continuous Form. Select **Single Form**.

4. To see the result, shown in Figure 21.5, click the View icon on the Form Design toolbar. (Don't save the change.) Access doesn't change the form's layout. However, the form now displays only one record.

5. Return to Design view, and from the Properties sheet, select **Datasheet View**—the last setting. Then, click View on the Form Design toolbar to see the results, shown in Figure 21.6. As you can see, the form now resembles a table.

FIGURE 21.5

You changed the form's Default View property to Continuous Form.

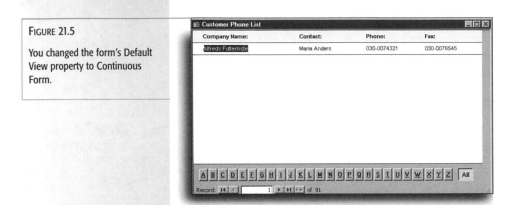

FIGURE 21.6

The Customers Phone List form resembles a table after switching the Default View property to Datasheet view.

Datasheet view without the work

If you want to get a table's-eye view of your form without altering the form's properties, you can choose **Datasheet View** from the Design View icon . When you're done, choose **Form View** to return to the original display mode.

SEE ALSO

➤ *Turn to page 346 for a demonstration of how to set form properties.*
➤ *For more information about limiting a form's display, read page 393.*

Navigating Records

Earlier, you saw the navigational toolbar, which hosts five directional icons: First, Previous, Next, Last, and New. This toolbar and its icons appear on all forms, unless you inhibit them. However, these icons provide just one way to jump from record to record. Another method is to choose **Go To** from the **Edit** menu. Doing so will open a submenu with the following choices: **First**, **Last**, **Next**, **Previous**, and **New Record**. This method is a little tedious, but is useful if your form doesn't have a navigational toolbar. If you know the number of the record you want to display, you can use the F5 key.

Displaying a specific record

1. With the Customers Phone List form in Form view, press F5.

2. Enter a record number and Access will select that number. For instance, if you enter the value 3, Access will select the third record.

3. To select record number 10, press F5, type 10, and press Enter. You can use this shortcut to select any record, as long as you know the record's number.

   Or

1. Select the value in the Record Number control.

2. Enter the value that equals the number you want to view.

3. Press Enter and close the form without saving any changes.

Controlling Navigation in Forms

Now that you know how to get from record to record, let's take a look at a few techniques for moving between the controls on your form. For the most part, you'll press Tab or Enter to select the next control on the current form. When the last control has focus, you can press Enter to select the next record. If the current record is the last record when you press Enter, Access will display a new record. A *new* record contains empty controls so you can enter new data.

SEE ALSO

➤ *If you'd like to learn more about data entry form properties, go to page 393.*

Changing the Tab Order

At this point, you might be wondering how Access knows which control is the next control. That's determined when you create the form by each control's Tab Stop and Tab Index properties.

Properties that affect navigation

Each form has a few data entry properties that can affect navigation. For instance, if the form's Allow Additions property is set to No, Access won't display a new record, regardless of which icons you click.

The Tab Stop property determines whether Access will give focus to a particular control. If the property is set to No, Access won't select it. When the setting is Yes, Access looks to the Tab Index value to determine where that control falls into the selection order. These values are consecutive and begin with the value 0. So, the first control Access will select has a Tab Index value of 0. The second control in the cycle will have a Tab Index value of 1, and so on. Access has three ways to automatically set these properties:

- If you use an AutoForms Wizard to create a form, Access will set the Tab Index values to match the order of the fields in the underlying table or query.

- If you use the Form Wizard, Access will set the properties to follow the order of the fields as you move them from the Available Fields list to the Selected Fields list on the wizard's screen.

- When you create a form, Access assigns the values in the order you add each control. The first control you add has a Tab Index value of 0, the second control has a Tab Index value of 1, and so on.

It's important to note that regardless of the way you initially create your form, the way you eventually arrange the controls has no bearing on the selection order. Access won't update the Tab Index values if you rearrange the controls.

Fortunately, you can easily change the order in which Access selects the controls on a form. You simply change the Tab Stop or the Tab Index property.

Protecting a Field by Using the Tab Stop Property

One of the main reasons you might want to change the Tab Stop property is to protect the data in that field while still enabling the user to view the data. For example, in an Employees table, you might want to view the Social Security number, but not allow the view to change it easily. Setting the Tab Stop property to No means the cursor never enters that field to update or change it.

Removing a control from the selection order

1. Double-click a form in the Database window to open it in Form view.

2. Press Tab enough times to run through the current selection cycle. Access will select each control. If you can reach each field, its Tab Stop property is set to Yes.

3. Press and hold the Shift key and press Tab enough times to return to the first control in the current record.

4. Now, let's change the current selection order. To get started, click Design View [icon] on the Form View toolbar.

5. In Design view, select the control you want. Then, double-click the control to open its property sheet. You can also click the Properties icon [icon] on the Form Design toolbar.

6. From the **Other** or the **All** tab, open the Tab Stop property's drop-down list and change the current setting from Yes to No.

7. Return to Form view by clicking View [icon] on the Form Design toolbar.

8. Cycle through the controls until you select the control just before the one you changed. Then press Enter or Tab one more time. Instead of selecting the next control, Access skips to the following control. That's the result of changing the Tab Stop property.

Changing the Selection Order

After you've created and modified the controls on your form, you won't want to jump back and forth between fields if you've rearranged them. Correcting the selection order helps data entry flow smoothly with the reading order on the form.

Changing the selection order

1. If the selected form is in Form view, click the Design View icon [icon] to open the form in Design view.

2. Select the controls one at a time, beginning with the first one (upper-left, if appropriate).

3. Change each control's Tab Index to match its physical order.

Explaining the change in data entry

If you use the Tab Stop property to prohibit data, you might also consider placing those controls to one side or at the bottom of the screen in a group.

Selection order and control placement

Although Access will accept any selection order you determine, be sure that the order you use follows a logical left-to-right and top-to-bottom order. If you're going to set any Tab Stop properties to No, but might make them available at a later time, include the field in the numbering order as if you were going to use it. This way, when you do enable its selection, the field will be highlighted in a logical order rather than receiving the selection at the end.

Using tab order

The preceding example walked you through the manual process of setting tab order. However, Access has a convenient built-in feature that's much easier to use. Simply select **Tab Order** from the **View** menu to open the Tab Order dialog box. This box lists all the controls and enables you to arrange them in the order you like. As you do, Access automatically updates their selection order. If you really want to save time, you can click the **Auto Order** button. This feature will automatically reset all the tab order values to match each control's relative position. Specifically, Access sets the tab order from left to right and then from the top to the bottom.

Cycling turns the page

In keeping with the book analogy of navigating records, setting the Cycle property to All Records helps you turn the page to the next record as you finish entering or viewing the last control of a record.

4. Next, click View 🔲 to return to Form view.

5. Press Enter or Tab to cycle through the controls as a test.

How the Cycle Property Affects the Selection Order

Forms have another property that affects navigation—the Cycle property. This property controls the selection behavior when the last control on a bound form has the focus. The default is the All Records setting, which selects the first control in the next record when the last control has the focus and you press Enter or Tab.

There are two other settings:

- Current Record—This selects the first control on the current record instead of accessing the next record. If you press Shift+Tab while the focus is on the first control, Access will select the last control for the current record.

- Current Page—The Current Page setting is similar to Current Record. However, this last setting keeps the focus on the current page. (A record can require many pages.)

Unfortunately, you can't depend on this property to inhibit a user's access to other records. The Page Up and Page Down keys and the Previous and Next icons will give focus to the previous or next page, respectively, regardless of the Cycle property's setting.

Limiting Access to the Previous and Next Record

If you must limit access to the previous or next record, you can attach the VBA code shown in Listing 21.1 to your form's Key Down event. Then, set the form's Cycle property to Current Record or Current Page, appropriately.

Using code to prevent paging through records

1. Select the form and then click **Design View** in the Database window to open that form in Design view.

2. Click the Code icon 🔲 on the Form Design toolbar to open the form's module.

3. Select **Form** in the module's Object control.

4. Select **KeyDown** in the module's Procedure control.

5. Enter the code shown in Listing 21.1. (VBA will supply the opening and ending statements.) Then close the module window.

LISTING 21.1 **Limiting Access to the Previous and Next Record**

```
1  Private Sub Form_KeyDown(KeyDown As Integer, Shift As Integer)
2  Select Case KeyDown
3      Case vbKeyPageUp, vbKeyPageDown
4          KeyCode = 0
5      Case Else
6  End Select
7  End Sub
```

6. Select **Current Record** from the Cycle property's drop-down list. (Double-click the Form Selector to select the form's property sheet.)

7. Change the Key Preview property from No to Yes. This setting sends your keystrokes to the Form event before sending it to the control.

8. Click View ⊞ ▾ to display the form in Form view.

9. Press Page Down. Instead of selecting the next record, Access seems to do nothing. Actually, it's executing the form's Key Down event, which checks your keystroke. Because that keystroke equals vbKeyPageDown, Access returns the KeyCode 0, which does nothing. The same thing happens if you press Page Up.

SEE ALSO

➤ *To become oriented with the code entry environment, turn to page 547.*

➤ *For more information about the code you're entering, start on page 567.*

➤ *For more information on attaching code to events, see page 596.*

Saving changes

You can make this alteration to the Customers form. Be sure not to save your modifications when you're done.

Alternate path to the module window

If you prefer, you can go through the properties sheet to open the form's module window. Simply select the appropriate On property, choose **[Event Procedure]** from the property's drop-down list, and then click the Builder icon 🔧 to the right of the property field. Access will respond by opening the form's module and supplying the event's first and last statement (the `Private Sub` and `End Sub` statements).

About the Navigational toolbar

The previous exercise doesn't inhibit the form's Navigational toolbar. If you want to prohibit access to other records, be sure to turn the navigational toolbar off by changing that form's Record Selectors and Navigational Toolbars properties to No.

A shortcut to Design view

To open a closed object in Design view, you probably select that form and then click **Design View** in the Database window. You can also double-click the right mouse button on the form in the Database window.

Sorting in a Form

Access doesn't sort records when it opens a form unless you set a sort order in the underlying bound table or query, or with some event. A form uses the same order as the bound object.

Now, there are several ways to sort records in the form environment. If you don't want a permanent solution, you can select the field you want to sort by and then click one of the two sort icons on the Form view toolbar, Sort Ascending or Sort Descending.

A non-permanent sorting solution

1. Open a form in Form view.

2. Select the field you want to sort your records by.

3. Click the Sort Ascending icon on the Form View toolbar to sort the records in ascending order by the selected field. Sort the product records by the product names, as shown in Figure 21.7, by selecting the Product Name field and then clicking the Sort Ascending icon.

This example

You'll be using the Products form from the Northwind database in this example. However, you can use almost any form.

FIGURE 21.7

The Products form sorts by the Product ID field, but you re-sorted the records by the Product Name field.

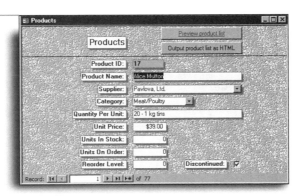

4. For a descending sort, click the appropriate field and click the Sort Descending icon, as shown in Figure 21.8.

If you want a more permanent sorting solution, you have two methods to choose from:

- Set a primary key
- Use the Order By property

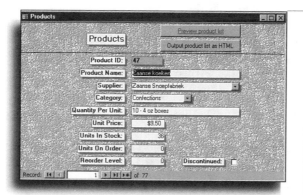

FIGURE 21.8
This time you sorted the records in descending order.

I discuss primary key fields a great deal throughout this book. Basically, a primary key requires a unique entry for each record. However, a primary key also sorts records by the contents of the primary key field. The previous example sorted by the Product ID field, remember? That's because this field is a primary key.

Unfortunately, setting a primary key isn't appropriate for every sort. First, the primary key allows only unique entries, and it doesn't allow empty fields. When a primary key isn't the best solution, consider the form's Order By property.

SEE ALSO

➤ *For more in-depth information on primary keys, read page 199.*

About the Order By Property

The Order By property enables you to specify a sort order for the form. It's a quick solution, but it isn't dynamic. This means Access won't sort records as you enter them. Instead, this property will sort existing records when you open the form. For normal data entry tasks, this is a good arrangement—waiting for your recordset to re-sort each time you enter a new record could be a nuisance.

Using the Order By property to sort

1. Open a form in Form view.
2. The form may already be sorting by a field—look for a good primary key candidate. The Customers form appears to sort by the Customer ID field.

When things don't sort right

A field's data type can affect the resulting sort order because numbers entered into a Text field won't sort in numerical order. They will sort alphanumerically. For instance, the values 1, 2, 8, 10, 11, and 15 sort in that same order numerically. Alphanumerically, they sort as 1, 10, 11, 15, 2, and 8. If this is a problem, use the `Val()` function to return the field's contents as a value instead of text.

The example

We'll work with the Customers form from Northwind. As usual, you can use almost any form you like. Just make sure the form isn't already using the Order By property.

3. Click the Design View icon 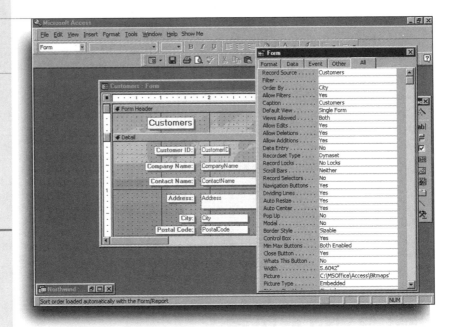 on the Form View toolbar to open the form in Design view.

4. Click the Properties icon 🖺 on the Form Design toolbar to open the form's property sheet.

5. Select the Order By property field and enter the field you want to sort by. Enter City, as shown in Figure 21.9.

FIGURE 21.9

Sorting records by the City field.

A multifield sort

If you'd like to sort by more than one field, simply add the field to the Order By property and separate each field with a semicolon (;). For instance, if you want to sort by the Customers form by the City and then the Contact Name field, you'd use the Order By property setting City;ContactName. In addition, you add the strings **DESC** or **ASC** to specify a descending or ascending sort. For instance, you would use the setting ContactName DESC to produce a descending sort by the Contact Name field. Or, you could use the setting City ASC;ContactName DESC to force a descending sort of the Contact Name field within an ascending sort by the City field. Actually, ascending is the default, so you won't need it for the most part, but including it is helpful for documentation purposes.

6. Return to Form view by clicking the View icon 🖾 on the Form Design toolbar. As you can see in Figure 21.10, Access has sorted the records by the contents of the City field.

Searching in a Form

There are three quick and easy ways to find records that match specific criteria in Form view:

- The Find feature
- Filter By Selection
- Filter By Form

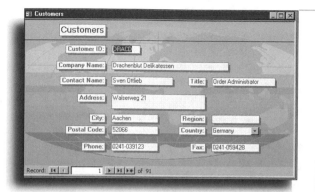

FIGURE 21.10
By specifying an Order By property, you changed the sort order.

The Find Feature

The Find feature is as easy to use as the Sort feature we just discussed. Select **Find** from the **Edit** menu to open the Find in field dialog box, shown in Figure 21.11. If Access finds matching data, it will display the first occurrence. You can then click **Find Next** to find all the subsequent matching entries. If no matching records exist, Access will display the message shown in Figure 21.12. Click **OK** to clear the message box.

FIGURE 21.11
The Find command enables you to search for specific data in Form view.

FIGURE 21.12
Access will let you know if no matching records exist.

Using the Find feature to search for data

1. With the Customers form open in Form view, choose the City field. Then, choose **Find** from the **View** menu.

2. Enter Berlin in the Find What control, and click the **Find First** button.

This example

We'll use Northwind Customers form to demonstrate how to use the Find feature. You can use almost any form you like; just be sure to search for appropriate data.

3. Access will display the first record that contains the entry Berlin, as shown in Figure 21.13.

FIGURE 21.13

Sorting records by the City field.

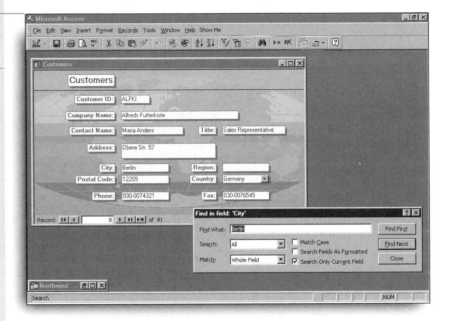

4. Click the **Find Next** button to find the next matching record. Because there are none, Access displays the message shown earlier in Figure 21.12.

The Find feature has several other options:

- **Search**—This option specifies a search order: **Up**, **Down**, and **All**. This enables you to search backward or forward through your records, beginning with the current location (record). For instance, if the current record is record number 14, and you choose **Down**, Access will search records 15 through the last record, but not records 1 through 13. Similarly, if you choose the **Up** option, Access will search only records 1 through 14. **All**, of course, will search all the records.

- **Match**—This option enables you to specify a whole field or parts of a field. **Whole Field** will search the entire field and return a match only when the search criteria matches the

contents of the entire field. The **Any Part of Field** option
will return a match if the search criteria is found anywhere
in the field. The **Start of Field** option will return entries
where the first part of the entry matches the search criteria.

- **Match <u>C</u>ase**—Returns entries that share the same case as
  the search criteria.
- **Search Fields as F<u>o</u>rmatted**—Matches fields that share the
  same display format as the search criteria.
- **Search Only Curr<u>e</u>nt Field**—This option searches only the
  selected field for matching entries.

The Filter By Selection Feature

The Filter By Selection feature combines the sort method covered a few sections ago with the Find feature from the last section. Select a field and click the Filter By Selection icon ⧩, and
Access will create a temporary recordset that consists of all the
records that contain matching data in the current field.

Using Filter By Form

1. With your form open in Form view, select a field that contains the criteria you want to search for.
2. Click the Filter By Selection icon ⧩ on the Form View
   toolbar. As shown in Figure 21.14, search for all the records
   that contain Berlin in the City field. The resulting recordset
   contains only one record. To remove the current filter, click
   the Remove Filter icon ⧩ on the Form View toolbar.

The Filter By Form Feature

This final search feature adds a bit of flexibility to the search
process by enabling you to enter your own text instead of relying
on the current entry.

Using the Filter By Form feature

1. With your form open in Form view, click the Remove Filter
   icon ⧩ on the Form View toolbar to delete any existing
   filters.

This example

Continue to use the Customers
form in these examples.

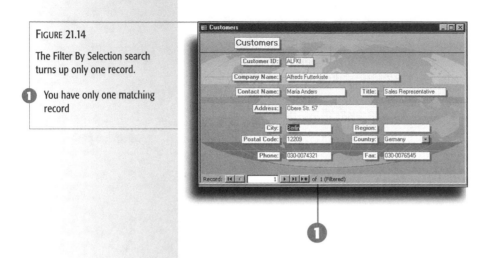

2. Then click the Filter By Form 📇 icon on the Form View toolbar.

3. Access will display a search template similar to the one shown in Figure 21.15. Your previous filter of Berlin is still active; that's why Access displays Berlin in the City field. You see, the Remove Filter icon ▽ simply removes the filter from the current recordset. It doesn't delete it from the form's properties.

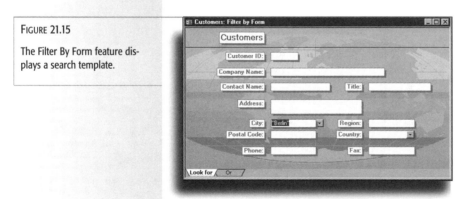

4. At this point you can choose search criteria from one of the combo box controls, or you can enter your own criteria in the appropriate field. Figure 21.16 is the result of choosing London from the City field's drop-down list and then clicking the Apply Filter icon ▽ on the Filter/Sort toolbar.

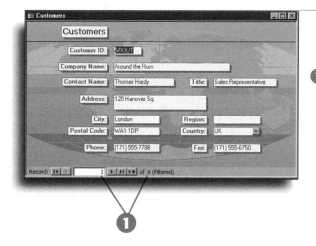

FIGURE 21.16
Your Filter By Selection search turns up only one record.

① This is the first of six records that match the search criteria of London

A Few Other Options

The Filter/Sort toolbar (open during Filter By Form) offers two more options you might want to know about:

- Load From Query 🖼—This feature enables you to load an existing query into Filter By Form instead of creating it.

- Save As Query 💾—This feature is how you'll save a Filter By Form selection to query, so you can reload it at another time.

After you've created a Filter By Form query that you know you may repeat from time to time, click the Save As Query 💾 button on the Filter/Sort toolbar to save it. Then, click the Load From Query 🖼 on the Filter/Sort toolbar when you want to reuse it.

Refining Forms: Efficient Data Entry and Beyond

Learn how to use the Validation Rule, Format, Required, and Input Mask properties to control the type of data your application will accept

Use formats and colors to visually convey information

Control access to your data

Use expressions to display additional information

Learn how to register and insert ActiveX controls

Verifying Data

Let's face it. Getting users to enter data the way your application expects it is an uphill battle. A user's failure to enter the correct data can produce erroneous data or even crash your system. The more work you can get Access to do, the less your users have to remember and the less you'll worry about your application.

If an application requires a lot of data entry, you'll want to take advantage of several built-in features that will make sure your users are entering the type of data your application expects. You'll save your users time and you'll avoid errors.

The best place to start is with data validation. This means that Access will check an entry and reject it when it doesn't match the criteria you've defined for that field. Setting data types is one way to do this. If a field accepts only numbers, and you enter 2e4, you'll want Access to reject that entry. This feature is builtin, and you need only apply the appropriate data type to your fields to get help from Access. When the data type isn't enough, you can set stricter or more complex rules with a field's Validation Rule property.

SEE ALSO

➤ *To learn all the specific data types and their entry criteria, see page 196.*

The Validation Rule Property

You already know that you can limit the type of data a control will accept by assigning a data type to the bound field. However, a data type won't always offer enough control. For instance, you can limit a control to accept only numerals. However, the Number data type won't limit that same entry to a particular range of values. You might want to limit the user to values from 1 to 10. The Number data type will keep your user from entering abc, but it won't keep him or her from entering 12.

Using the Validation Rule Property

To restrict entries to particular requirements, use the Validation Rule property to check an entry *before* your user leaves the field.

More restrictions on using data types

An easy way to restrict an entry is to limit the number of characters a field can accept. Set the field's Field Size property at the table level to the appropriate number of characters. For instance, let's suppose you're storing alphanumeric part numbers that consist of seven characters. If you limit the field's size to 7, Access won't accept more than seven characters in that field. Limiting the size of your field won't guarantee against typos, but it's a start. Besides, you'll save memory.

For the most part, you'll enter simple expressions to limit your entries using this property. An example is your earlier problem—how to limit an entry to the values 1 through 10. In this situation, you'd enter the simple expression >=1 AND <=10 as the field's Validation Rule property setting. After you enter this value, Access would then evaluate the entry to make sure it conformed to the limitations defined by the expression. If the value conformed, Access would accept your entry. If not, Access would display a warning message.

Setting the Validation Rule property

1. Select the table you want to use, and then click **Design View** in the Database window.

2. Select the field in the upper pane of the Design View window by clicking on the far-left button next to that field, as shown in Figure 22.1.

   As you can see in the figure, some fields in the table already have restrictions. The ReorderLevel field already restricts entries to positive values.

About Nulls

If you apply a validation rule to a field, Access won't let you leave the field blank unless you set the field's Required property to No.

The example for this task

To demonstrate this property, you'll see that the figures in this section restrict the ReorderLevel field in the Products table of the Northwind database to the values 0 through 30.

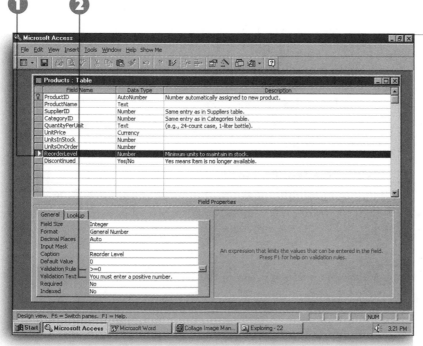

FIGURE 22.1

The existing Validation Rule expression expects a positive value.

1. Click here to select the entire field

2. The **General** tab shows the current validation rules and text

3. Add to the current expression the component for your limitation, such as AND <=30.

4. Enter the warning message you want to display, such as Enter a value between 0 and 30, in the Validation Text property field, as shown in Figure 22.2.

5. Click Datasheet View 📷 on the Datasheet Design toolbar to display the table. Access will warn you about the possible effects of changing the existing Validation Rule property. Don't worry about that right now. Just click **Yes** twice.

6. Now select the first new record and test an entry that breaks your validation rule. Your incorrect entry should trigger a warning message box with the text you entered.

   For the example, try to enter the value 40 in the ReorderLevel field. Because 40 is greater than 30, Access rejects the entry and displays the message shown in Figure 22.3. That message is the string you entered in the Validation Text property field. Press Esc to clear the entry.

   Try entering the value 25. Because 25 falls between 0 and 30, Access accepts this value.

Testing the Related Form

To finish testing the validation rule, you'll need to check any existing forms that are bound to the table whose field you've changed.

Using the Validation Rule in a form

1. Double-click the form in the Database window to open it in Form view.

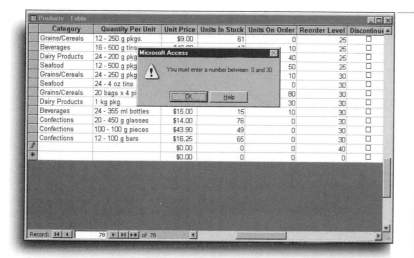

FIGURE 22.3

The value 40 doesn't conform to the new Validation Rule property and triggers an error containing the message defined for the field.

2. Display a new record by clicking the New Record icon 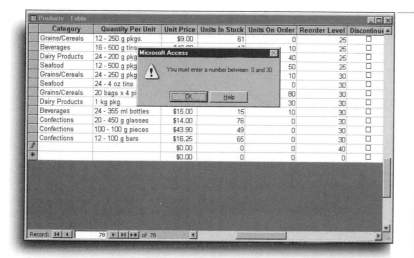 on the navigational toolbar. Or, select **Ne̲w Record** from the **I̲nsert** menu.

3. Enter a value that's outside the restrictions you created into the field you're checking and press Enter or Tab.

   For this example, try 31 in the Reorder Level field. Because 31 is greater than 30, Access rejects the entry, as shown in Figure 22.4.

4. Press Esc to clear the entry. Close the form and save your changes.

The example for this task

The figures show the Products form, which is bound to the Products table.

Changing Northwind

You might want to close the forms and tables from the Northwind examples without changing them. This keeps the database with the same data and restrictions its queries and other design aspects expect.

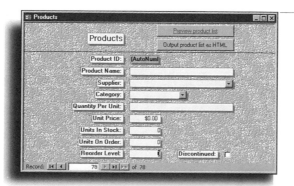

FIGURE 22.4

Access won't accept the value 31 because it's larger than 30.

Where to set the Validation Rule property

For the most part, you'll want to define a Validation Rule at the table level. That's because any bound control will inherit that rule. This behavior saves you time because you only need to set the property once. You're not stuck with this rule, either. You can override the table's property by setting a second Validation Rule property at the form or report level, should the need arise.

SEE ALSO

➤ *To learn more about operators and expressions, read 273.*

➤ *For more information on applying data types, read page 574.*

Forcing an Entry

One of the most important things you can do to protect your application is to force an entry. You won't always need to do this. However, sometimes it's mandatory to protect your application. For instance, if a future calculation depends on a value in a particular field, that field needs to contain something, even if it's 0. The easiest way to force users to make an entry is to enable the field's Required property.

Using the Required Property

The Required property determines whether a field can remain blank. A bound control in a form or a report will inherit the bound table's setting. There are two settings: No, the default, and Yes. No will enable blank fields, and Yes will force you to make an entry before you can continue with your data entry task. If you try to leave the field empty, Access will display a warning message. After this happens, you have two choices:

- Make an entry and continue.
- Delete the incomplete record.

The user must do one or the other; there's no third choice.

Although you'll most often benefit from this setting at the form level, set it at the table level.

Setting the Required property

1. Open the table in Design view by selecting it in the Database window and then clicking **Design View**.

2. Select the field in the upper pane of the Design View window.

The example for this task

This example again uses the Products table from the Northwind database and uses the ReorderLevel field.

3. Locate the Required property in the Field Properties section in the lower pane. Open the Required property's drop-down list and select **Yes**, as shown in Figure 22.5.

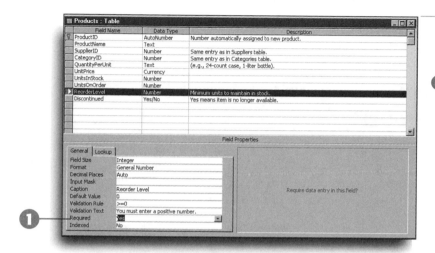

FIGURE 22.5

Setting the ReorderLevel field's Required property to **Yes**.

① Toggle the Required property to require an entry in the field

4. Click the Datasheet View icon ▦▾ on the Table Design toolbar, and then click **Yes** twice to save the change.

5. Now test the enforcement of the new rule. First select a New Record ▶✳. Try to enter data in all fields but the required field and see if Access accepts a blank field.

When you try to leave the field blank, Access will display the warning message shown in Figure 22.6.

6. Click **OK** to clear the message. Press Esc to delete the incomplete record.

7. If you want to save your changes, close and save the table.

FIGURE 22.6

Access will display this message if you try to leave a required field blank.

After you've set a field's Required property to **Yes**, all bound controls in forms and reports will also require an entry. If you try to leave the related control blank, Access will display the same warning message.

SEE ALSO

➤ For more information on event timing, go to page 422.

Formatting Data with the Format Property

Formatting data is a wide-open topic, and you could probably write several chapters on that subject alone. Instead, this section will discuss some basic issues and then show you some techniques you might not have considered.

Like many properties, you can apply the Format property at the table or control (form or report) level. If you apply a Format at the table, a bound control will inherit that format. If you apply a format at the control level in a form or report, Access will override the table format. However, if there's no format defined at the table level, the control format won't affect the data you store in that table. The format you assign to a field or control is dependent upon the field's data type. Actually applying the formats is easy.

Applying formats at the table level

1. Select the table and click **Design View** in the Database window.

2. Select the field you want to format in the upper pane of the Design View window. Notice which data type this field is.

   For example, if the data type is `Number`, open the Data Type drop-down list to display the formats you can apply to the current field, as shown in Figure 22.7.

3. Now select the Format property field in the Field Properties section. Open the Format property's drop-down list to see the format choices available to a `Number` data type, as shown in Figure 22.8.

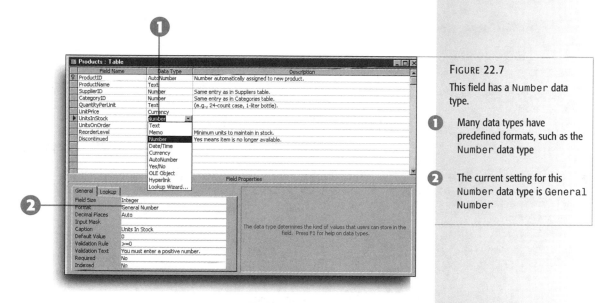

FIGURE 22.7

This field has a Number data type.

1 Many data types have predefined formats, such as the Number data type

2 The current setting for this Number data type is General Number

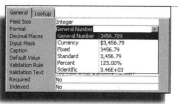

FIGURE 22.8

These are the formats available to a Number field.

You can also change the format at the control level, though this won't affect how data is stored in your table.

Applying formats to controls

1. Open the form or report in Design view.
2. Double-click the control you want to change and open its property sheet.
3. Open the Format property's drop-down list to display the available formats, as shown in Figure 22.9.
4. Select the one you want. Again, the choices in the drop-down field are dependent on the bound control's data type.

FIGURE 22.9

The **Units in Stock** control offers these format options.

1 Double-click any control to open its property sheet

2 The formatting options in the drop-down list correspond to the table setting of the field the control is bound to

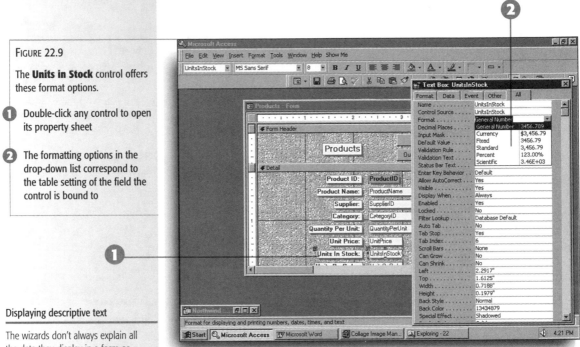

Displaying descriptive text

The wizards don't always explain all the data they display in a form or report. When this happens, you can sometimes use the Format property to display descriptive text. For instance, the Report Wizard displays the current date in the footer. To add descriptive text to the date, choose one of the following two options:

Open the report in Design view and double-click the date's text box (it should contain a **Now( )** function) in the report's footer to open the control's property sheet.

Delete the current format (**Medium Date**) and enter **Printed on "mmm dd", "YYYY"**.

In Print Preview, the modified property will display a text string similar to **Printed on June 1, 1998**. This will alert those reviewing the report that the date is only a print date and not a part of the report's data.

Using the *Format()* Function

The Format property offers many display options, but not every option you might need. When the Format property isn't enough, try the Format( ) function. You won't apply this function via a control's property sheet. Rather, you'll use this function in expression form. You can format the results of a calculated control, or the results of a criteria expression in a query. In addition, you can use this function in a VBA module. This function in the form

```
Format (entry, "format")
```

displays *entry* as defined by *format*. The *format* argument is a set of characters that define the way you want to display *entry*, which you may have seen referred to as *code characters*. This function is very versatile because the value you're formatting can be a value, string, function, or field. To demonstrate this function, let's use it to display some values.

Using *Format()*

1. Open the Debug window by pressing Ctrl+G.

2. Enter the statement ?Format(.10, "percent"). As you can see in Figure 22.10, Access applies the percentage format to the value .10. The *percent* argument is a *named* format. You can use any of the appropriate data type formats in this manner. A named format is an existing format—you'll find them in the Format property's drop-down list. You can spell out any of these within a Format() function. This example uses percent, but you can also use General Number, Currency, Fixed, Standard, Scientific, General Date, Short Date, Medium Date, Long Date, Short Time, Medium Time, or Long Time.

Using Format Painter

The Format property offers only a few formats. Others, such as font face, size, and weight, alignment, and so on, are available on the Formatting toolbar and as properties themselves. If you want to copy a particular control's formats, click that control and then click Format Painter ⟨ ⟩ on the Form Design toolbar. Next, select the control you want to assign those same formats to. The Format Painter will apply all the first control's formats to the second.

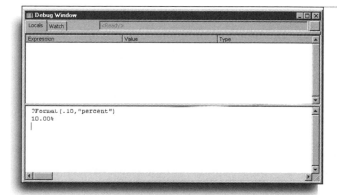

FIGURE 22.10

The Format() function can apply the percentage format to a value.

3. Now enter the statement ?Format(#6/25/98#, "mmm"). This time, Access displays Jun, as shown in Figure 22.11. This is the abbreviated month component for June 25, 1998. The "mmm" argument is a user-defined format, otherwise known as a custom format.

SEE ALSO

➤ *If you'd like more information on calculated controls, read page 395.*

➤ *To learn how to create criteria expressions in queries, go to page 265.*

VBA's Format property

You can use VBA to change an object's format. Add a statement in the form

object.Format = new format property

where *object* is the control, form, or object whose property you're changing. For instance, you could apply the Currency format to a control named **MyControl** on a form named MyForm using the statement

Forms!MyForm!MyControl .Format = "Currency"

Finding more information on code

For a complete list of code characters, refer to the Access Help section.

FIGURE 22.11

This time, a date's month component was returned.

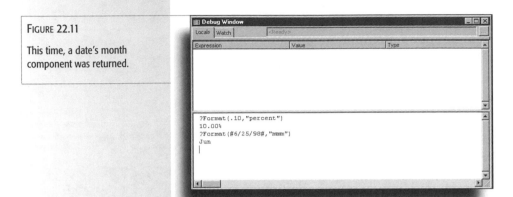

About user-defined codes

The *user-defined* or *custom* codes referred to are predefined codes or symbols you combine to create a unique format. In this example, mmm returns Jun, an abbreviated form of the month June. There are many of these codes, and you can mix and match them to suit your needs. The function `Format(#6/25/98#, "mmm dd yyyy")` would return Jun 25, 1998. If you want to add a literal character, enclose it in quotation marks. The function `Format(#6/25/98#, "mmm dd"," "yyyy")` would return Jun 25, 1998.

Now, what if you didn't want an abbreviated month? You'd use the mmmm code. In this case, the function `Format(#6/25/98#, "mmmm dd"," yyyy")` would return June 25, 1998. For a complete list of these predefined codes, do a search for "Format property" in the Access Help section.

Using *Format()* to Round Values

Access doesn't have a rounding function like Excel's. Instead, several functions have rounding behaviors:

- CInt() returns the rounded integer portion of a value. However, when the decimal portion equals .5, CInt() rounds to the nearest even value.

- Int() truncates a positive value. When the value is negative, Int() returns the first negative integer that's less than or equal to the value.

- Fix() returns an integer that's greater than or equal to a value when that value is negative. When the value is positive, Fix() truncates the integer portion.

As you can see, all these functions have some behavior that keeps them from being an ideal rounding tool. For the most part, you can depend on the Format() function for most of your rounding needs. Use the # or 0 placeholders. The # code displays a blank when no digit exists; 0 displays an 0 when no digit exists. For instance, the function Format(1.5,"##") will return the value 2, as you'd expect. The function Format(1.5,"00") will return the string 02. Both times, Format rounds the value 1.5 to 2. You can also use Format() to round decimal values.

Applying Input Masks

Perhaps one of the most common ways to ensure the integrity of the data you enter is to use an input mask. An *input mask* is a pattern that you define and that Access applies to limit an entry. For instance, a common phone number input mask is (###) ###-####. This encloses the first three digits (the area code) in parentheses and displays a hyphen between the third and fourth digit in the local number. By applying this input mask, you save your data entry operator three keystrokes. The input mask characters and their purposes are listed in Table 22.1.

TABLE 22.1   **Input Mask Code Characters**

Character	Purpose
0	Forces a digit character
9	Allows only a digit, but doesn't require an entry
#	Allows a digit, + or - sign, or space character, but doesn't require an entry
L	Forces an alpha character
?	Allows only an alpha character, but doesn't require an entry
A	Forces an alpha character or digit
a	Allows only an alpha character or digit, but doesn't require an entry
&	Forces an entry, but accepts any character
C	Doesn't force an entry and accepts any character
<	Displays characters to the right as lowercase
>	Displays characters to the right as uppercase
!	Fills the mask from right to left
\	Allows you to include a literal character by displaying the character that follows

The mask character determines which character you can enter and how many. To create a mask, enter mask characters as a field's Input Mask property. To demonstrate, this example adds an input mask to the different fields in the Orders table.

Adding an input mask

1. Open your table in Design view by selecting it in the Database window and then clicking **Design**. The Orders table opens.

2. Select the OrderDate row in the top panel of the Design View window.

3. Now select the Input Mask property field in the lower pane. Doing so will display the Input Mask Wizard's Builder icon to the right. You won't use the wizard for this example.

4. You have many options at this point. For now, let's keep it simple and enter a mask that will accept only digits, because this is a Date/Time field. Specifically, enter the mask 00/00/00;0;_, as shown in Figure 22.12. You know that the 0 code forces a digit entry. That means any entry must consist of six digits—no more, no less. In addition, the mask will display a slash character between each set of digits. The second section, 0, tells Access not to store the slashes in the underlying table with whatever data you enter. The final character, the underscore, is a placeholder—the mask will display this character until you enter each character in the entry.

Literal characters

You may have noticed that your input mask contains literal characters, namely the slashes, but you didn't preface them with the \ code. That's because the backslash character is an acceptable character in a Date/Time field. You only need to preface the character with the \ code when that character is totally alien to the field's data type.

FIGURE 22.12

You entered a date input mask that will force double-digits for each date component.

Quickly selecting a new record

To select a new record, or the first blank row, click the New Record icon on the table's navigational toolbar.

5. Click the Datasheet View icon on the Table Design toolbar, and click **Yes** when Access asks you if you want to save your changes. Select a new record (the first blank row in Datasheet view).

6. Click the OrderDate field and Access will display the input mask shown in Figure 22.13. (You must click the field; if you just press Enter to access this field, it won't display the mask characters until you start to enter data.) As you can see, the

mask includes two slashes and displays an underscore as a placeholder.

FIGURE 22.13

The mask displays two slashes and an underscore placeholder.

❶ The mask displays a slash between each set of digits it expects

❷ Until you enter a character, the mask displays the underscore character as a placeholder

7. At this point, you might try entering some inappropriate entries. For instance, you already know that the 0 code forces a character. So try entering your example date, June 25, 1998, as 62598. The mask will display your entry as 62/59/8, as shown in Figure 22.14. Then, if you press Enter, Access will display an error message telling you the entry isn't appropriate. Click **OK** to clear the message and press Esc to delete your entry.

8. Now enter a date the mask will accept. Remember, the mask wants two digits for each section, so your month component, 6, needs a leading zero. This time, enter 062598 and press Enter. Access will accept the entry, but it won't look like the mm/dd/yy format you might expect. Instead, Access displays your date in Medium Date format, as 25-Jun-98. That's because this field already has a Format property, the Medium Date format. (Refer to Figure 22.12.)

FIGURE 22.14

Your mask displays two slashes and an underscore placeholder.

1 The mask expects two digits in each section

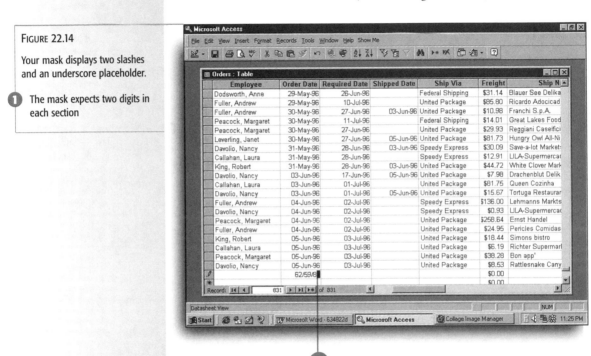

At this point, you've experimented with only one mask. Table 22.2 displays several example masks and their results with sample data.

Property precedence

The Format property and the Input Mask property may seem to conflict with one another, but they don't. Remember, an input mask controls how you enter the data; the Format property controls how Access displays the entry. That means you can enter data in one format and display it in another.

TABLE 22.2   **Input Mask Examples**

Mask	Valid entry	Invalid entry	Explanation
>LLLLL	UPPER or upper	9999	Five alpha characters are required; displays entry in uppercase
(000) 000-0000	5555555555	5555555 or 555ttt5555	Forces ten digits

Mask	Valid entry	Invalid entry	Explanation
(999) 000-0000	5555555555 or 5555555	5555 or 555tttt	The first three digits are optional; the remaining seven are required
#999	L333 or p33	Y33333	Accepts up to four characters; the first can be a digit, space, +, or -; the remaining three or fewer must be digits
>L<???	p or pl or plew	9kkk or 9kk	Accepts up to four alpha characters; at least one is required
\e00?	99e or 99	999 or e99	Displays an e as the first character and requires two digits, followed by an optional alpha character

One last point about input masks: Not all data types lend themselves to masks. Table 22.3 lists all the data types and whether or not they have an Input Mask property.

TABLE 22.3   **Data Types and Masks**

Data Type	Mask
Text	Yes
Memo	No
Number	Yes
Date/Time	Yes
Currency	Yes
AutoNumber	No
Yes/No	No
OLE Object	No
Hyperlink	No

SEE ALSO
➤ *For an introduction to the Input Mask Wizard, see page 134.*

About the Other Input Mask Components

You may have noticed that most input masks have three sections, separated by the semicolon character. The first section consists of the mask characters. The second component is the value 0 (the default) or 1. This value tells Access whether to store any literal characters you've included in your mask with your data in the table. For instance, a date mask might include the slash or hyphen character. If you specify the 0 argument, Access won't store these characters in the underlying table. Thus, the mask will display the date 06/25/98 as 062598 in Datasheet view. On the other hand, if you use the value 1, Access will store that same date as 06/25/98.

The last component denotes a placeholder. You can use almost any character you like, but the type of field may lend itself to certain characters. For instance, if you're entering values and 0 is an acceptable entry, you may choose to use the value 0. On the other hand, in the date examples, you used the underscore character as your placeholder. However, a placeholder character isn't necessary. If you leave that section blank, Access won't display anything.

Formatting for the 21st Century

If you're using Access to enter 21st Century dates, you can use the two-digit year format as long as you're entering dates that fall between January 1, 2000 and December 31, 2029. In other words, if you enter the date 06/25/16, Access will use and store the date June 25, 2016. (This is different from earlier versions, which interpret the two-digit components 00 through 29 as 20th century dates.)

If you're used to using the two-digit format, mm/dd/yy or dd/mm/yy, you can continue doing so as long as you don't need to enter dates that fall between 1900 and 1929 or dates after December 31, 2029. If you can't meet both of these conditions, you should use the four-digit format mm/dd/yyyy or dd/mm/yyyy.

Perhaps the easiest solution is to assign an input mask that requires four digits in the date's year component.

Forcing a four-digit year

1. Open in Design view the table with the date you want to restrict.

2. Double-click the date field and enter the input mask 99/99/0000;0;_ in the Field Properties section.

3. Click the View icon [image] on the Form Design toolbar.

4. To test the field's entry restriction, select a New Record [image] and try to enter the date 06/25/16. As you can see in Figure 22.15, Access won't accept a two-digit year. Click **OK** to clear the message. Press Esc to delete the entry.

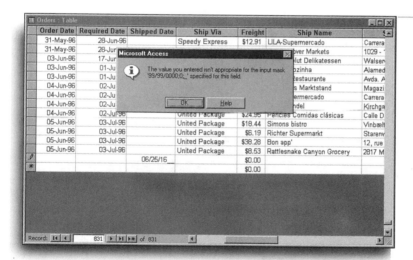

FIGURE 22.15

Your input mask won't accept an entry with less than four digits in the year section.

Working with Multiple Input Masks

If the mask characters aren't adequate, you might need VBA. For instance, let's suppose you want to force your user to enter an area code in the phone number field. You can use the mask \(000\)000\-0000, or you can include a default area code by including the appropriate digits in the mask. For instance, the mask \(502\)000\-0000 will display and store the area code 502 with each phone number entry. A better solution might be to offer both options. That way, your user can accept the default area code or enter a new one when necessary.

The example for this task

You can enter any appropriate VBA code into any form's control when you want to restrict its data entry. This example uses the Customers form from Northwind and restricts phone number entry.

Using VBA to define more than one input mask

1. Open the form that contains a field that requires more than one input mask in Design view.

2. Click the Code icon 🖼 on the Form Design toolbar. In the resulting module, select the phone field from the **Object** control and the procedure from the **Procedure** control. In this case, you'll use the AfterUpdate event to "fix" the entry after checking it. Enter the code for the module. The code shown in Listing 22.1 checks the phone number entry.

LISTING 22.1   Code for Correcting a Phone Number Entry After the Entry Is Made

```
1 Private Sub Phone_AfterUpdate()
2 Dim strPhone As String
3 strPhone = Me!Phone
4 Select Case Len(strPhone)
5   Case 7
6     Me!Phone.InputMask = "(555) 000-0000"
7   Case 10
8     Me!Phone.InputMask = "(000) 000-0000"
9   Case Else
10     MsgBox "Please enter an appropriate phone number"
11 End Select
12 End Sub
```

3. Next, select an additional procedure from the **Procedure** control and enter the code to check its entry. The code shown in Listing 22.2 checks the entry on Got Focus. I chose this event so VBA will reset the input mask for each record.

LISTING 22.2   Resetting the Input Mask

```
1 Private Sub Phone_GotFocus()
2 Me!Phone.InputMask = "(999) 999-9999"
3 End Sub
```

4. To test the entry restrictions, click the View icon 🖼▾ on the Form Design toolbar and select a New Record ▶*.

5. Then, select the field and test the entry with various combinations of data.

SEE ALSO

➤ *To familiarize yourself with the Module Window, turn to page 547 and, in particular, Figure 31.1.*

➤ *You can use the information found on page 567.*

Analyzing the Results of the Code

When you select the field you've modified, Access will execute the code in the Got Focus event. If you followed the example, Access applies the mask (999) 999-9999, from Listing 22.2, to the current field.

If you type a seven-digit phone number, such as 5555555 (don't type the hyphen character), and press Enter, Access launches the After Update event from Listing 22.1. This procedure counts the number of characters in your entry. Because there are seven characters, VBA sets the control's Input Mask property to (502)000-0000.

Press Escape and enter the ten-digit number 5555555555. Because there are ten digits, VBA assigns the mask (000)000-0000, which includes no area code and requires ten digits. (You could use the 9 code and it will work just as well.) This procedure enables you to specify a default area code, which is convenient when one area code dominates your data but isn't the only code you'll need to enter.

If your entry doesn't contain seven or ten digits, VBA will display a warning message prompting you to enter the appropriate number of digits.

Controlling Access

Access will display a bound form's first record when you open the form. Actually, all the records are there and available for review; Access just sets the focus to the first record. This means anyone who can open the form can review, modify, delete, and even add to your data. Most of the time, you won't want to allow such freedom to all your users.

Restoring default values

If you repeatedly enter the same value, you can assign that value as a field's default value using the Default Value property. During data entry, you can easily overwrite the default value if it isn't appropriate for the current record. But what if you then decide the default value was right after all? Do you retype the default value? Fortunately, this isn't necessary. To restore the default value, press Ctrl+Alt+Spacebar.

There are four form properties you can use to limit the access users have to the existing data:

- Allow Edits—If you set this property to Yes (the default) you can modify saved records.

- Allow Deletions—When set to Yes (the default), you can delete saved records.

- Allow Additions—A Yes setting (the default) enables you to add new records.

- Data Entry—When set to Yes (No is the default), this property restricts the form to data entry only. You can't view existing records.

To set these properties, open the form's property sheet and choose the appropriate setting from each property field's drop-down list.

Restricting access to existing records

1. Open the form in Design view.

2. Open the form's property sheet by double-clicking the Form Selector or clicking the Properties icon 🖾 on the Form Design toolbar.

3. Choose **Yes** from the Data Entry property's drop-down list. Make sure the Allow Additions property is set to Yes.

4. To see the result, click the View icon 🖾▾ on the Form Design toolbar. You can use the blank form to enter new customer records, but you can't access the existing ones. The record navigation buttons shouldn't allow you to go backward beyond the new record.

You'll combine the four properties to get the data entry limits you need. Table 22.4 lists the possible combinations and their effects.

OpenForm overrides form properties

There is one thing you should be aware of. The **OpenForm** method or action takes precedence over the form's properties. So be careful when using **OpenForm** to open your forms. Use the data mode argument only when you intend to override the form's current settings.

TABLE 22.4   **Limiting Access with Form Properties**

Action	Data Entry	Allows Edits	Allows Additions	Allows Deletions
Enter new records only	Yes	No	No	No
Enter and modify new records only	Yes	Yes	Yes	No
Enter, modify, and delete new records only	Yes	Yes	Yes	Yes
Enter, modify, and delete all records	No	Yes	Yes	Yes
Enter new records, delete any record, no edits	No	No	Yes	Yes
Delete records only	No	No	No	Yes
View records only	No	No	No	No

Using Expressions in Controls to Display Additional Data

If you think forms are just for data entry, you're in for a surprise. Just think about it. Most applications display a splash screen when you launch the application. A *splash* screen identifies the application and the organization. Most of us use switchboard forms to direct the flow of an application, even though you don't realize you're using a form. You also solicit and display information in forms.

On a more traditional note, calculated controls are a good way to display additional information in any kind of form. A *calculated control* is a control that contains an expression. An *expression* combines other values and operators to produce a result. *Operators* are the mathematical symbols, such as the +, -, *, and / signs, that you use to perform mathematical operations.

You'll use calculated controls to display information that isn't stored in your database. For instance, let's suppose you want to show the total sales for a particular product. Or perhaps you

Operators

In this section, the +, -, *, and / signs are referred to as operators. Actually, they are mathematical operators. Access has several different kinds of operators, not just mathematical:

Mathematical operators perform calculations: +, -, *, /, \, and ^.

Comparison operators allow comparisons: =, <, >, <=, >=, <>, IS, and LIKE.

Concatenation operators enable you to combine strings: & and sometimes +.

Logical operators: OR, AND, and BETWEEN.

Zooming in

If you need more room to type or review your expression, press Shift+F2 to display the expression in the Zoom box.

want to show a discounted amount for certain customers. These are values that you won't normally store in your database, but that you might need to conduct business. Calculated controls are just the right tool to get the job done.

For the most part, you'll use text box controls to display the results of expressions. You can use other controls, but the text box is inherently more suitable to the task. Fortunately, adding a calculated control to a form is easy:

- Add the expression as the control's Control Source property
- Precede the expression with the = operator

Now, let's take a minute to review an existing calculated control. You'll need an existing calculated control, so just open Northwind to explore one.

Reviewing a calculated control

1. Open Quarterly Orders Subform in Design view by choosing that form and then clicking **Design View** in the Database window.

2. Double-click the **TotalQ1** control (that's the first control on the left in the totals section). As you can see in Figure 22.16, the field contains the expression =NZ(Sum([Qtr 1])) instead of a field reference. As a result, that control displays the sum of all the first-quarter amounts when the form is in Form view.

Now let's create a calculated control. This example uses the Quarterly Orders Subform form and adds a text box. The expression you'll enter as the control's Control Source will calculate the average sale for the first quarter.

Creating a calculated control

1. With an existing form (the Quarterly Orders Subform) open in Design view, find or create the space you'll need for the control. You might have to extend the form's footer until there's enough room to insert another text box.

2. Click the Textbox tool abl on the toolbox and then click the location to insert a new text box.

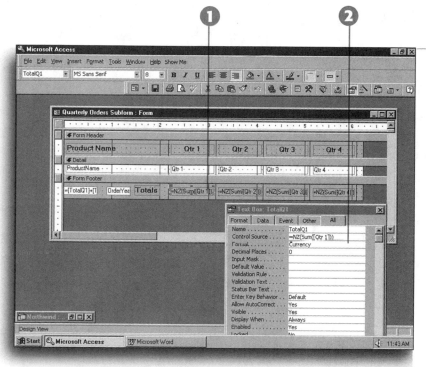

FIGURE 22.16

The unbound text box contains an expression.

1 Select the control for the calculation

2 Enter the expression in the Control Source property

3. There are two ways to add the expression. You can open the new control's property sheet and enter it in the Control Source property field, or you can click inside the control and just enter it there.

4. Click View [icon] on the Form Design toolbar to return to Form view. If you've created your own form for this task, save it.

Figure 22.18 shows the results of your new calculated control—the average of the first quarter's sales. (At this point, you haven't formatted the control.)

One thing you should know: You can't refer to a calculated control in a Sum() or DSum() function. For instance, you can't use the expression =Avg([TotalQ1]), because TotalQ1 is a calculated control. Any attempt to enter data returns an error.

The example for this task

I used the property sheet method, shown in Figure 22.17, to enter the expression =Avg([Qtr 1]). (To open the control's property sheet, double-click the control.) I also deleted the control's label.

FIGURE 22.17

Enter an expression into a text box to create a calculated control.

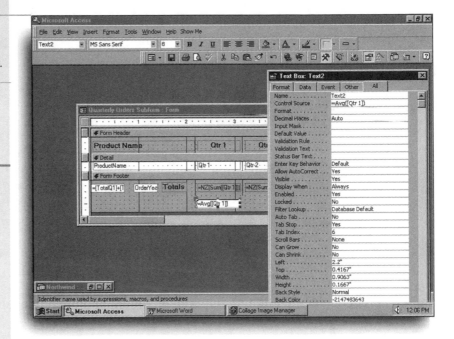

Using the Expression Builder

If you need a little help with your expression, you can launch the Expression Builder. Click the Builder icon to the right of the Control Source property field. In the Expression Builder, identify the elements you want to calculate and the operation you want to perform. After the expression is complete, click **OK** to copy the expression to your control.

FIGURE 22.18

The expression you entered returns the average first-quarter sale.

Product Name	Qtr 1	Qtr 2	Qtr 3	Qtr 4
Alice Mutton			$702	
Alice Mutton	$312			
Alice Mutton	$1,170			
Alice Mutton	$1,123			$296
Alice Mutton		$281		
Alice Mutton	$62			
Totals	$144,981	$145,361	$134,671	$165,912
	606.6164			

SEE ALSO

➤ *To learn more about the AND and OR operators, go to page 267.*

➤ *To learn more about expressions, see page 273.*

Inserting Custom Controls

Access has such a wide variety of controls that you may never need any others. However, you can insert custom controls (ActiveX) when the native controls aren't adequate. A *custom control* is like any other control; it just doesn't come with Access.

The Calendar control shown in Figure 22.19 is an ActiveX control. In earlier versions, ActiveX controls were called OLE controls. You can use the toolbox or the **Insert** menu to add a custom control to a form (or report).

If you'd like to experiment with some ActiveX controls, you can view a comprehensive list of third-party ActiveX controls at www.download.com and check out their development tools. These controls are available for downloading. However, you should be aware that not all ActiveX controls will work properly (or the same) in all Office applications.

FIGURE 22.19

The Calendar control is an ActiveX (custom) control.

Recalculating controls

Most calculated controls update themselves when the form or the control gets focus. If you want to update all the calculated controls in your form at the same time, you can use the `Recalc` method in the form

`form.Recalc`

where *form* is the form object that contains the controls you want to calculate. Or, with the form open and current, you can press the F9 key.

The `Requery` method may be effective in this area too. However, the `Requery` method updates the contents of a control. If you want to calculate the very latest data, you should preface a `Recalc` method with a `Requery` method.

Inserting a custom control

1. With a form open in Design view, click the More Controls tool 🔧 on the toolbox. In response, Access will open the window shown in Figure 22.20. Don't worry if yours is different; Access will display the controls that are available on your system.

   Or...

1. With a form open in Design view, choose the **ActiveX Control** command from the **Insert** menu. Access will display the same list as before in the Insert ActiveX Control dialog box, shown in Figure 22.21.

ActiveX Properties

ActiveX controls have two sets of properties:

- The normal control object properties that all controls have in common.
- A set of properties that are unique to the ActiveX control.

FIGURE 22.20

Access lists the ActiveX controls available on your system.

1 Click the More Controls tool on the toolbox to view the available ActiveX controls

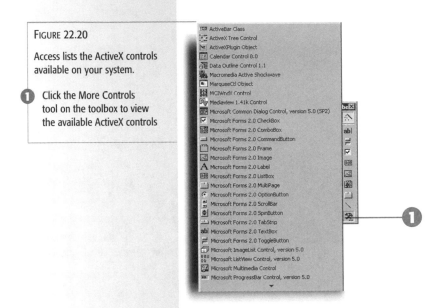

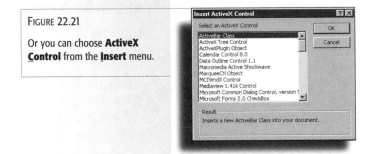

FIGURE 22.21

Or you can choose **ActiveX Control** from the **Insert** menu.

You can access the control properties by selecting the control and clicking the Properties icon on the Form Design toolbar. Or, you can right-click the control and select **Properties** from the resulting submenu. To modify the ActiveX properties, double-click the control in Design view. Most ActiveX controls will launch a set of tabs from which you can select and modify that control's unique properties.

SEE ALSO

➤ *To learn more about ActiveX controls, go to page 677.*

Registering an ActiveX Control

Before you can insert and use an ActiveX control, you must register it. To *register* the control means to tell Access that the control is available and where the files reside. You'll need to register any controls that you purchase, and sometimes you must register controls from other applications.

Registering Active X controls

1. If you've purchased a control, install it as instructed in the documentation that came with the control.

2. In Access, choose **ActiveX Controls** from the **Tools** menu.

3. Select the appropriate control in the ActiveX Control dialog box and click the **Register** button. Likewise, click **Unregister** to unregister a control. Click **Close** when you've finished.

SEE ALSO

➤ *For more information on setting a library reference, read page 557.*

When you can't find the control to register it

If you can't find a control to register it, but you know you've installed the control's native application, check the current references. To set this reference, open a blank module and choose **References** from the **Tools** menu. Next, choose the appropriate library in the References dialog box and then click **OK**. After you've registered the application's library, its controls should also be available to you. Although Access may let you refer to an ActiveX control in a non-referenced library, your application will run faster if you reference the library.

The World of Subforms

Use subforms with ease and confidence

Learn how to reference subforms correctly

A review of a subform alternative—the Tab control

When to Use a Subform

Anytime you base a form on a *one-to-many* relationship, you have the potential for a subform. The main form will display the *one* data and the subform will display all the *many* records that relate to the current record in the main form. For instance, you can use a subform to display open purchase orders for the same customer, or you can display all the items on a particular order. To set up a subform, you follow four simple steps:

- Create a form to represent the one side.
- Create a form to represent the many side.
- Make sure the two forms share a field—the primary key on the one side and the foreign key on the many side.
- Position the many side form in the one side form.

SEE ALSO

➤ *For more information on relationships, see page 13.*

A *subform* is a complete form and can function separately from the main form. Once you place the subform in the main form, Access views the subform as a control of the main form. However, the subform retains its properties and behavior in all but one respect—the purpose of the subform is to support the main form. As a result, the subform will display only those records that relate to the record in the one form. For this arrangement to work properly, the underlying tables or queries must be related, or you must link the two forms.

Linking a Subform to the Main Form

To ensure that the relationship between the two forms has the effect you want, Access provides two properties at the subform level:

- Link Child Fields—Identifies the foreign key in the subform.
- Link Master Fields—Identifies the primary key in the main form.

After properly assigning these two properties, the subform will display only those records where the *child* field equals the *parent* field.

Creating a Subform

The easiest way to create a subform is to simply create the main form—the one side—and the subform—the many side—as you would any other forms. Then, open the main form in Design view and place the subform in the main form.

A perfect example is the Customer Orders form in Northwind, shown in Figure 23.1. Actually, this form contains two subforms. The main form is based on the Customers table. Customer Orders Subform1 is based on the Orders table and identifies the orders for the current customer in the main form. The second subform, Customer Orders Subform2, is bound to the Order Details Extended query, which is based on the Order Details and Products tables.

Figure 23.2 shows the relationship between the underlying data sources. The Customer Orders form is based on the Customers table. Customer Orders Subform1 displays dates from the Orders table where the OrderID value is the same as the Customer form's current record. Customer Orders Subform2 displays product data from the Order Details table, matching the ProductID value in the Customer Orders Subform1 to that in Customer Orders Subform2.

Inserting subforms

There are two ways you can add a subform to a main form. Both ways, you begin by opening the main form in Design view. Then, you can use the Subform/Subreport tool on the Toolbox to insert another existing form as a subform. Or, you can select the form you want to insert as a subform in the Database window and drag it to the main form.

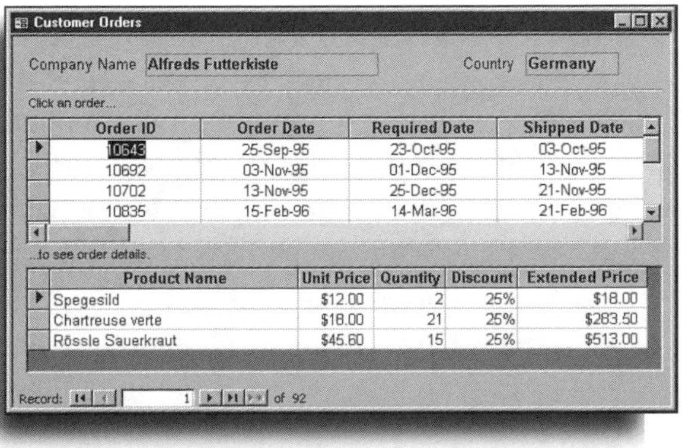

FIGURE 23.1

The Customer Orders form contains two subforms.

FIGURE 23.2

The underlying data sources that complete the Customers form are all related in some way.

1 The Customer Orders form is based on the Customers table

2 This relationship creates Customer Orders Subform1

3 This relationship configuration is Customer Orders Subform2

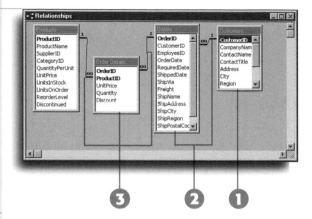

Creating a subform

1. Select the table you want to base your main form on (in this case, the Customers table) in the Database window, choose **Form** from the **New Object** button's drop-down list, and double-click **Form Wizard**.

2. Specify the fields you want to display in your main form (in this case, **CustomerName** and **Country** are added to the **Selected Fields** list box). Then, click **Next** three times. Name the form—this one is named frmMain. Next, choose to **Modify** the form's design option, and then click **Finish**. Chose **Modify** because you want to arrange the controls.

3. In Design view, move the Country field to the right of the CompanyName field. Doing so has nothing to do with the subform or their links—you're just rearranging the controls.

4. Now you're ready to add the subforms. You don't have to create them because they already exist. First, click the Control Wizards tool 🖎 on the Toolbox. Then, click the Subform/Subreport tool 🖽 on the Toolbox and click inside the form below the CompanyName field. Access will launch the Subform/Subreport Wizard.

5. In the wizard's first window, select the **Forms** option and then choose **Customer Orders Subform1** from the **Forms** control drop-down list, as shown in Figure 23.3. Then click **Next**.

FIGURE 23.3

Select the **Customer Orders Subform1** form in the Subform/Subreport Wizard.

6. The second window will attempt to link the subform to the main form. In this example, Access wants to link the two forms by the CustomerID field, so click **Finish**. The relationship between the main form and this subform is based on the CustomerID field. This subform will display only those records that match the CustomerID field in the main form.

7. If you open the subform's property sheet, you can see that Access has already provided the Link Child Fields and Link Master Fields settings—CustomerID—as shown in Figure 23.4.

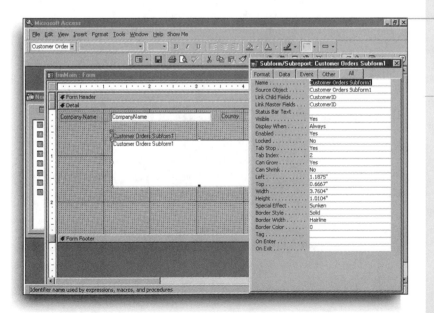

FIGURE 23.4

The Subform/Subreport Wizard sets the Link Child Fields and Link Master Fields properties for you.

8. The second subform is a little more complex. Click the Subform/Subreport tool on the Toolbox and then click inside the form below the first subform. Click the **Forms** option, choose **Customer Orders Subform2**, and click **Finish**. You can't use the wizard to set up your child and parent links because you want the second subform to relate to the first subform, not the main form. The wizard will try to link the new subform to the main form.

9. You'll have to set the links in the second subform yourself. To do so, open the subform's property sheet by clicking the Properties button 🖼 on the Form Design toolbar. Then, enter OrderID as the Link Child Fields property because you want to link the two subforms by the OrderID field.

10. You can't reference the OrderID field on the first subform as easily. You must also tell Access which form or subform you're referencing. To this end, enter the reference [Customer Orders Subform1].Form![OrderID] as the Link Master Fields setting. (There's more about referencing subforms later in this chapter.)

11. To see the completed form, click the View button 🖼▾ on the Form Design toolbar. Your form should resemble the one shown in Figure 23.1. (It isn't critical that all the controls be in the same position.) The first subform displays all the orders for the customer in the main form. The second subform then displays information about the selected order in the first subform.

Working with Both Sets of Subform Properties

When you set the linking properties for the subform in the previous example, you opened the subform's property sheet. If you're unfamiliar with subforms, you may not have recognized those properties and are probably wondering where the subform's form properties are. They're still available. You see, subforms have two sets of properties, form properties and subform properties, which control different behaviors. This chapter won't review each individual property, but will show you how to access both sets.

Throughout this section, we'll refer to the two sets as the *form* and *subform* properties. The form properties control the subform as a form—they're the set of properties you're most familiar with. To access them, simply double-click the subform control in Design view. Access will open the subform as a form. At this point, you have two forms open in Design view—the main form and a subform. With the subform still selected and open in Design view, click the Properties button [icon] on the Form Design toolbar to display a list similar to the one shown in Figure 23.5. These are the properties that all forms share.

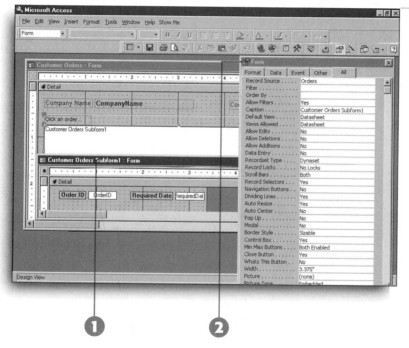

FIGURE 23.5

A subform has form properties, like all forms.

1 Even though you'll use this form as a subform, open it separately in Design view

2 With the future subform open in Design view, you can see its form properties

Now, to display the subform's property sheet, close the Design View window that's displaying the subform as a form. The subform is still the selected object, but now Access views it as a subform (or control). Consequently, Access updates the property sheet, as you can see in Figure 23.6.

FIGURE 23.6

When the subform's not open in Design view, you have access to the subform's properties.

1 After placing the form here, it becomes a subform, which is really a control

2 With the subform selected, you can display its subform properties

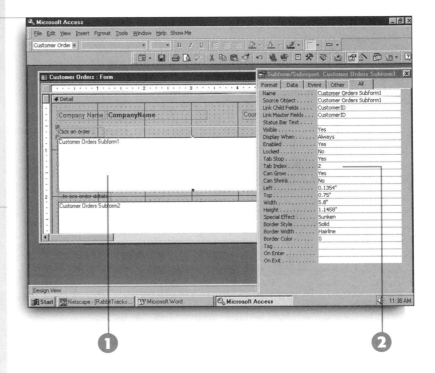

There's really no trick to it. When the subform is open in Design view, you can modify the form properties. When the form isn't in Design view, and you've selected the subform as a control, you can modify the subform's properties. Just remember: a subform has two sets of behaviors, so it requires two sets of properties.

SEE ALSO

➤ To learn more about form wizards, see page 69.

Referring to Subforms and Their Controls

Access views a subform as a control, not a form. Unless you know this, referencing a subform's controls can prove very frustrating. To see why, let's take a step backward. To reference a subform, you use the following syntax:

```
Forms![frmMainForm]![frmSubForm]
```

So it stands to reason that you'd you reference a control on a subform using the following syntax:

```
Forms![frmMainForm]![frmSubForm]![cmdSubFormControl]
```

But it doesn't work that way. Remember, Access sees the subform as a control, and controls don't contain other controls. The proper way to reference a subform's control is to use the Form property in the following form:

```
Forms![frmFormName]![frmSubForm].Form![cmdSubFormControl]
```

To change a subform control's value, you use the following form:

```
Forms![frmFormName]![frmSubForm].Form![cmdSubFormControl] =
 newvalue
```

To change a subform control's property, use the following form:

```
Forms![frmFormName]![frmSubForm].Form![cmdSubFormControl].
property = newpropertyvalue
```

SEE ALSO

➤ *You'll find more information on referencing objects and controls on page 567.*

A Subform Alternative—The Tab Control

There's another way to display one-to-many records, and in some cases it may be more appropriate—the Tab control. A Tab control is an object that allows you to display several controls or multiple pages of data on individual tabs. However, you can also use it to display one-to-many records. Using a Tab control is a good choice when you want to keep one side of the relationship available for quick review, but you don't want it constantly in view.

To demonstrate this subform alternative, you'll rework one of Northwind subform solutions. Specifically, you'll display the relationship shown in the Quarterly Orders form shown in Figure 23.6 in a Tab control. The main form displays customer information; the subform is based on the Quarterly Orders by Product query.

Displaying a one-to-many relationship in a Tab control

1. Select the **Customers** table in the Database window, then choose **Form** from the New Object button's ⬚ ▾ drop-down list. Then double-click **Design View** in the New Form dialog box.

2. Click the Tab control tool ⬚ on the Toolbox and then click inside the blank form.

3. You'll create page 1 first. To begin, display the Field List by choosing **Field List** from the **View** menu or clicking the Field List button ⬚ on the Form Design toolbar.

4. Double-click the Field List box's title bar to select all the fields. Next, drag all the fields at once to the first page of the Tab control. This one is arranged in sections, as you can see in Figure 23.7.

FIGURE 23.7

All the Customer fields have been added to the first page of your Tab control.

❶ Placing extensive information into tabs and sections gives the form a clean appearance, with information available at a glance

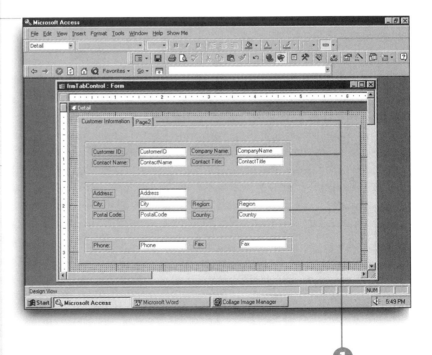

5. Double-click the Page1 tab and enter the caption Customer Information. This page is equivalent to a subform's main form.

6. Now you're ready to create the subform's equivalent on the Tab control's second page. Click **Page2** to select the second page. Make sure the Control Wizard button [icon] is selected and then click the Subform/Subreport tool [icon]. Then click anywhere in **Page2**.

7. When Access launches the Subform/Subreport Wizard, click **Next** without making any changes to the first window.

8. In the second window, choose **Quarterly Orders by Product** from the **Tables and Queries** drop-down list. Then, add all the fields to the **Selected Fields** list box and click **Finish**. Increase the size of the subform control so it can display more records. Then add the page caption Quarterly Products, as shown in Figure 23.8.

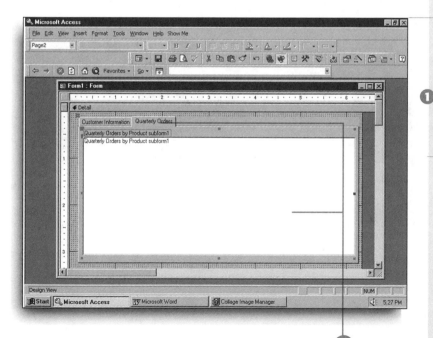

FIGURE 23.8

Quarterly product information has been added to the second tab in the form of a subform.

❶ Placing the subform on a second tab moves the large block of information to its own page for undistracted viewing

9. Click the View button 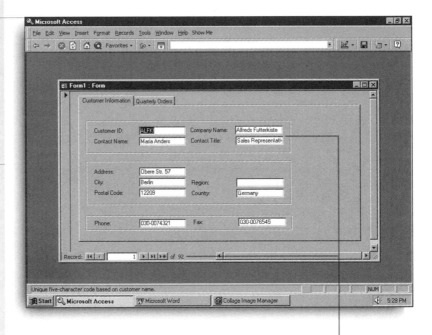 on the Form Design toolbar to see the results, as shown in Figure 23.9. As you can see, the first page of the Tab control displays customer information.

10. To see quarterly order data for the current customer, as shown in Figure 23.10, click the **Quarterly Orders** tab. This page shows only those orders that pertain to the customer in the tab's first page. (You may have to adjust the controls a bit to get the display just the way you want it.)

FIGURE 23.9

The first page of your Tab control form displays customer information.

1 This style of form works well for finding specific records quickly before looking at the extended information

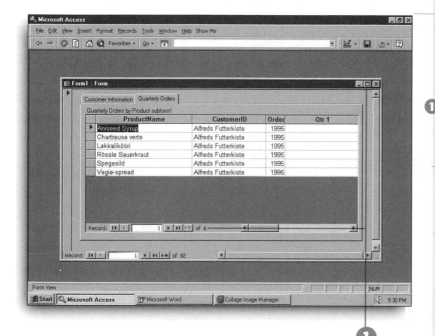

FIGURE 23.10

The second page of your Tab control form displays order information for the customer on the first page.

❶ Expanding the tab with the subform creates an even better view for navigating through the detailed information quickly

Advanced Form Techniques

Learn about form events

Create form event procedures

Open forms from other forms

Link forms with VBA code or a macro

Exploring the Form Module

As you've seen in the last few chapters, forms aren't just for data entry. What you might not realize at this point is that you can use VBA to program your forms (and form controls) to perform specific tasks that aren't inherent to the form object.

If you want to program your form (or form controls) with VBA code, you'll need to open the form's module (a class module), choose the appropriate object and event, and enter the procedure code. (All form modules are class modules; not all class modules are form modules.) In this chapter, we'll take a quick look at the form's module and then show you some code you might want to use with your own forms. (The information in this chapter about class modules also applies to report modules.)

SEE ALSO

➤ *For another look at class modules, see page 547.*

Figure 24.1 shows a typical form module. For the most part, it's just like the standard module reviewed in Chapter 31, "An Introduction to VBA." The form module has a title bar, object and procedure controls, and two view buttons (Procedure view and Full Module view), just as the standard module does. However, the title bar does give you a clue that it's different—it identifies the module as a class module.

The main difference between a standard module and a class module isn't visible onscreen. A form's module is limited in *scope* to the form and its controls. A standard module is available to the entire application. The code you'll enter in a form module will respond to the form and control events. These procedures are known as *event procedures* or *sub procedures*.

SEE ALSO

➤ *You can learn more about scope on page 582.*

➤ *For an explanation of a sub procedure, see page 596.*

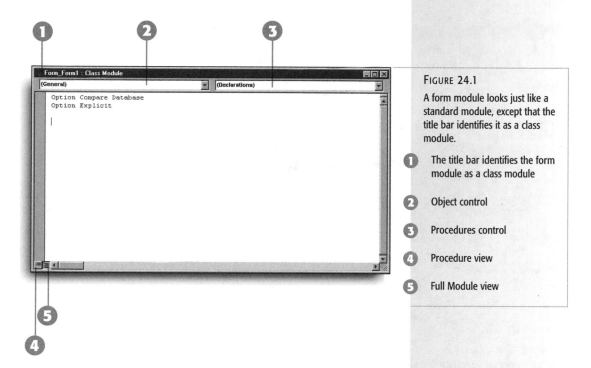

FIGURE 24.1

A form module looks just like a standard module, except that the title bar identifies it as a class module.

1 The title bar identifies the form module as a class module

2 Object control

3 Procedures control

4 Procedure view

5 Full Module view

Creating Event Procedures

There's only one way to create an event procedure—open a class module and enter the appropriate code. However, there are a number of different ways to access a form module.

The different ways to open a form module

1. In the Database window, select the form whose module you want to open and click the Code icon ⬚ on the Database toolbar.

Or

1. Open a form in Design view and click the Code icon ⬚ on the Form Design toolbar.

Or

1. With a form in Design view, open the form's property sheet. Select a form event (event properties begin with the word "On"), and click the Builder icon ⬚ to the right of the property field to display the Choose Builder dialog box, shown in Figure 24.2.

2. Select the **Code Builder** option and click **OK** to open the form's module to the appropriate event. For instance, if you select the form's On Activate property, the Code Builder opens the module to the Activate event, as shown in Figure 24.3. As you can see, the Code Builder has supplied the procedure's first and last statements.

Or

1. With the form in Design view, open the form's property sheet and select the appropriate event property.

2. Open the Property field's drop-down list and choose **Event Procedure**. (This drop-down list will also display macros. If you select one of the macros, Access will execute that macro in response to the event.)

3. After selecting **Event Procedure**, click the Builder button and Access will open the form's module to the appropriate event, bypassing the Choose Builder dialog box.

Once you've opened the form module, you're ready to enter code. If you used one of the methods that opens the module to the appropriate event and supplies the first and last statement, you simply begin by entering your code.

If you've opened the module to the General Declarations section, you'll need to specify the appropriate object and procedure. The Object control will offer a list of all the objects currently in your form, including the form itself. In Figure 24.4, the Suppliers form module (from the Northwind database) has been opened. As you can see, this form offers several objects.

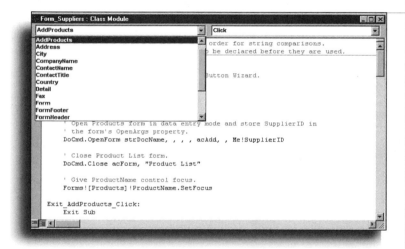

FIGURE 24.4
A form module's Object control lists all the objects in the form.

To attach an event procedure to any of these objects, select the object from the Object control's drop-down list. When you do, the Procedure control (to the right of the Object control) selects the selected object type's most common event, or the object's first attached procedure. For instance, if you select a command button from the Object control's drop-down list, VBA will select that button's Click event in the Procedure control. In addition, VBA will supply the appropriate beginning and ending statement for that button's Click event. Specifically, the first line will name the button and the event in the form

```
Private Sub buttonname_Click()
```

The last statement is a simple End Sub statement. All procedures require both statements. At this point, you simply enter the appropriate code between the first and last statement. If a Click event already exists, VBA will display it.

If the event offered by the Procedure control isn't the one you need, select the appropriate event from the Procedure control's drop-down list. Figure 24.5 shows the many events available to a form. You may have noticed that some of the events appear in bold type. That means these events already have an attached procedure.

FIGURE 24.5

The Procedure control offers events for the selected control in the Object control.

1 Bold typeface means the event already has an attached procedure

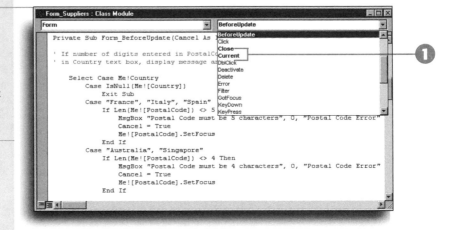

Events and VBA

Event procedures (or sub procedures) are actually VBA code.

SEE ALSO

➤ *You can also use the Insert Procedure command to enter a sub procedure; for more information, see 551.*

➤ *You can also use procedure in reports; for more information, see page 463.*

➤ *If you'd like to learn more about VBA and progress beyond events, see page 543.*

Responding to Form Events

Forms have many events, and knowing the order in which Access executes these events is important. Table 24.1 lists form events, each event's property, and the order in which Access executes these events. The timing can be critical to some tasks. For instance, suppose you want to execute a task when the form displays a record—any record. If you attach the code to any Form event other than the Current event, it just won't work as expected. That's because the Current event is the only one that Access executes every time a record gets the focus. Or suppose you want to set the form's record set when you open the form—on-the-fly style. In this case, you must attach the code to the form's Open event, because it's the only event that Access executes before it loads records.

TABLE 24.1 **Form Events, in Order from *Open* to *Close***

Event	Property	Description
Open	OnOpen	When you open a form from memory and before Access displays the first record
Load	OnLoad	After you open the form and load all its records
Resize	OnResize	Changes the form's size using a macro or event procedure
Activate	OnActivate	When a form becomes the active window but before Access selects a record
Current	OnCurrent	When a record receives the focus (or the form is refreshed or required)
Unload	OnUnload	When a form is closed but before Access removes it from the screen
Deactivate	OnDeactivate	When the form loses focus
Close	OnClose	When Access closes and removes the form from the screen

If your form has a subform, Access will load the subform, its controls, and records before it loads the main form. You'll also want to keep this timing behavior in mind when planning events.

Beware of cascading events

When you're writing sub procedures, be careful to consider all the repercussions of the code. You need to avoid including commands in event procedures that trigger the same event. For instance, if you include a **Maximize**, **Minimize**, or **Restore** command in a **Resize** event, you'll create what's known as a *cascading event*. This either directly or indirectly calls itself and creates a terminal loop or a runtime error. The previous commands cause a cascading event because they execute the **Resize** event, which executes the offending command, which triggers the **Resize** event again.

This example

These examples use the Products and Main Switchboard forms. You can use most any form you like.

Using Form Events to Open Other Forms

You'll often open additional forms to view additional information or allow additional input. There are a number of ways you can trigger a form-opening event from another form—you can use a form event or a control event. A logical form event might be the Close event. For instance, you might open the application's Switchboard when you close a form in order to control the user's choices.

Opening a form from a form event

1. Open the Products form module by selecting that form in the Database window and then clicking the Code icon 🔯 on the Database toolbar.

2. Select **Form** and then **Close** from the Object and Procedure controls, respectively.

3. Enter the code shown in Listing 24.1 between the opening and ending statements provided by VBA.

4. Save the form, and then open it in Form view by closing the module window and clicking the View icon ▣ ▾ on the Form Design toolbar.

5. In Form view, close the form, which will trigger the Products form's Close event. As a result, VBA will execute the OpenForm method and open the Main Switchboard form.

6. Be sure to delete the Close event and resave the form if you used the Products form from the Northwind database.

LISTING 24.1   **Open the Main Switchboard Form**

```
1    Private Sub Form_Close()
2    DoCmd.OpenForm "Main Switchboard"
3    End Sub
```

Similarly, you can use a control event to open another form without closing the current one. For instance, you could attach the same OpenForm command to a command button's Click event. Then, when you clicked it, VBA would open the Main Switchboard form without having to close the Products form. Admittedly, this is a simple event, but one that's used a lot.

Linking Forms with VBA Code

In the last section, you learned how to open a form using a command button event. Specifically, you added an OpenForm method to the form's Close event. In this section you'll learn how to link two forms using a command button. We don't recommend one method over another. You'll have to decide which method works the best in a given situation.

The easiest way to link two forms is to create the forms and then use the Command Button Wizard to link them. This wizard will add all the code you need, and do it quickly. The finished product may need a little tweaking, but the wizard does a very thorough job on its own.

Linking forms

1. You'll need two forms—a main form and a linked form. The main form will be the one that opens the linked form. This example uses Products as your main form and the Main Switchboard as your linked form. To get started, open the main form in Design view.

2. Make sure the Control Wizard icon  is selected, and then add a command button to your form. In response, Access will launch the Command Button Wizard. In the first window, choose **Form Operations** from the **Categories** list and **Open Form** from the **Actions** list, as shown in Figure 24.6. Click **Next** to continue.

This example

You'll continue to work with the Products and Main Switchform forms from Northwind.

FIGURE 24.6
Launching the Command Button Wizard.

3. The next window will ask you to identify the form you want to open. You'll specify your linked form. In this example, that's the Main Switchboard form, as shown in Figure 24.7. Click **Next** to continue.

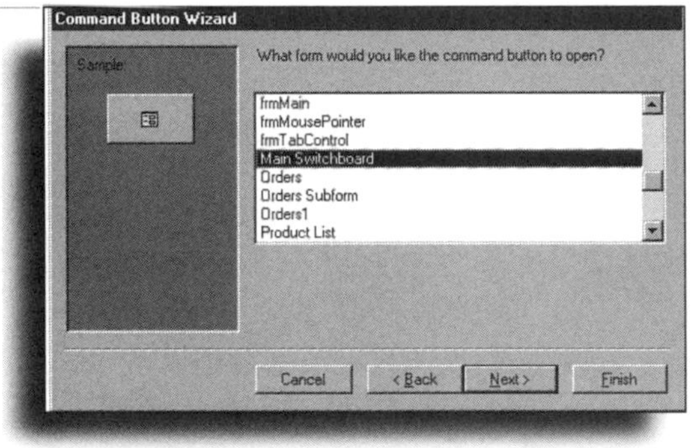

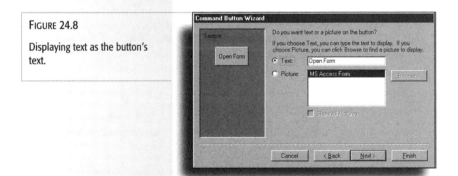

FIGURE 24.7

Identify the form you want to open when you click the command button.

SEE ALSO

➤ *For more information on using the Command Button Wizard, see page 156.*

4. The third window lets you choose between a text caption and a picture. Choose **Text** and retain the default text, as shown in Figure 24.8. Click **Next** to continue.

FIGURE 24.8

Displaying text as the button's text.

5. In the final window, name the button and click **Finish** to return to the main form (which is the Products form if you're following this example). This button is named cmdOpenMain.

6. Click the View icon [⊞ ▾] on the Form Design toolbar and
    click the new **Open Form** button on your main form. This
    executes the code the wizard added to your command but-
    ton. The code opens your linked form (the Main
    Switchboard form in this example), as shown in Figure 24.9.

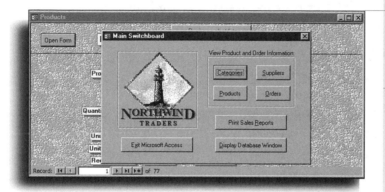

FIGURE 24.9
Clicking the **Open Form** button
will open the Main Switchboard
form.

7. If you'd like to review the code added by the Command
    Button Wizard, open your main form in Design view, select
    the main form, click the Code icon [🕮] on the Form Design
    toolbar, and choose **cmdOpenMain** from the Objects con-
    trol and **Click** from the Procedures control.

SEE ALSO

➤ *For exact instructions on how to add a control to a form, see page 318.*

➤ *The Tab control is a good alternative to linking forms; to find out more information, see*
   page 411.

Linking Forms with a Macro

You don't have to use VBA code to link forms. You can always
use a macro—and a simple one at that. The OpenForm macro
action has one argument that specifies the form you want to
open. Now, let's create the example from the last section using a
macro instead of VBA code.

Using a macro to link forms

1. In the Database window, click the **Macros** tab and then the **New** button to display a blank macro window.

SEE ALSO

➤ *For a more complete look at creating macros, see page 495.*

2. Create the macro shown in Figure 24.10. First, choose **OpenForm** from the Action column's drop-down list. Then, choose the linked form from the Form Name field property's drop-down list. Following this example, that argument is the Main Switchboard form.

FIGURE 24.10

This macro will open the Main Switchboard form.

3. Save the macro as macOpenMain and close the macro window.

4. Open the Products form in Design view. You can use the command button from the previous exercise, or you can create a new one. Either way, open the button's property sheet by clicking the Properties icon 🖼 on the Form Design toolbar or by double-clicking the button. Then, select the On Click property field and select **macOpenMain** from that property's drop-down list. If the field displays [Event Procedure], simply ignore it—choosing **macOpenMain** will overwrite the current entry.

5. Click the View icon 🔳▾ on the Form Design toolbar and click the command button. As in the previous example, doing so will open the Main Switchboard form.

Printing Form Data without the Form

Another frequent form task is printing records. If you choose the **Print** command from the **File** menu, Access gives you several choices—you can print all the records, the current record, or a selection of records. If you click the Print icon on the Form View toolbar, Access will print all the records.

For better or worse, Access prints the record and the form when you execute any print task in Form view. If you want to print the current record without the form, you'll need VBA.

A procedure that prints data without the form

1. Open the form you want to add this printing capability to in Design view and add a command button. This one is added to the Products form's header section. Name the button cmdPrint and enter the caption Print Current Record.

SEE ALSO

➤ *For complete instructions on how to add a control to a form, see page 318.*

2. Click the Code icon 🖻 on the Form Design toolbar to open the form's module. Choose **cmdPrint** and **Click** from the Object and Procedure controls, respectively.

3. Enter the procedure shown in Listing 24.2.

This example

This example continues to work with the Products form from the Northwind database. You can use almost any form you like to demonstrate the following technique. This printing solution works best when the form's bound table or query has a primary key field. If there's no primary key field, use the field that contains the most unique entries.

LISTING 24.2   **Printing a Record without the Form**

```
1    Private Sub cmdPrint_Click()
2    Dim varID As Variant
3    If IsNull(Me![ProductID]) Then
4       MsgBox ("Can't print this record")
5       Exit Sub
6    End If
7    varID = Me![ProductID]
8    DoCmd.OpenReport "rptPrint", , , "[ProductID]= " & varID
9    End Sub
```

4. Close the module window, and then click the View icon 🖾 ▾ on the Form Design toolbar to open the form in Form view.

5. Don't try the new button just yet. First, select the table or query on which your current form is based and create a new report. In this case it's the Products form. Then, choose **Report** from the New Object icon's 🖾 ▾ drop-down list, and then double-click **AutoReport: Tabular** in the New Report dialog box.

6. Save the report as `rptPrint` and then close it.

7. Return to the Products form and click the new command button, which will execute its `Click` event. This event creates a report, using only those records where the table or query's primary key entry matches the current entry in the form. We're relying on the ProductID field. Because the form is currently open to a record whose ProductID field contains the value 1, Access prints only that record in `rptPrint`.

If you don't have a primary key field, this technique will print the current record and any other record that contains a matching entry.

Dealing with Strings

If the field you end up choosing is a text field, you'll need an extra step. Specifically, you must enclose the contents of the text field that you're matching in quotation marks. In these situations, use the code shown in Listing 24.3. This procedure contains an extra line:

```
varID = Chr(34) & varID & Chr(34)
```

This line inserts a double quotation mark around the contents of the text field, so the `OpenReport` method can use the string in its *where* argument. Remember, if the field you're matching doesn't contain unique entries, this technique might print more than the current record.

LISTING 24.3   **When the Matching Entry Is a String**

```
1    Private Sub cmdPrint_Click()
2    Dim varID As Variant
3    If IsNull(Me![ProductID]) Then
4      MsgBox ("Can't print this record")
5      Exit Sub
6    End If
7    varID = Me![ProductID]
8    varID = Chr(34) & varID & Chr(34)
9    DoCmd.OpenReport "rptPrint", , , "[ProductID]= " & varID
10   End Sub
```

Form tasks

Some of the techniques discussed in this section may
seem more control-oriented
than form-oriented. They're
included here because each
one considers the form environment in some way.

Reducing Data Entry Tasks

If you enter a lot of repetitive data, stop and rethink the application's strategy. There might be a way to get Access to enter some
of this data for you. For instance, if you enter ZIP codes, you
can use the following technique to enter a code's respective city
and state.

The technique is relatively simple. Enter the ZIP code first, in
one of two ways. You can choose the ZIP code from a list box, or
you can enter it in the **ZIP code** control. If you choose an entry
in the list box, that control's Dbl Click event will compare the
selected ZIP code to existing ones in your address table. If a
matching code exists, VBA will copy that record's city and state
to the corresponding form controls. If the ZIP code isn't in the
list box, you'll have to make all three entries yourself. Once you
do, VBA will add the new ZIP code to the list box.

Using shortcuts to data entry

1. First, base a Select query, similar to the one shown in Figure
   24.11, on the table that contains your address fields. This
   query will return all the ZIP codes currently in your address
   table.

2. Choose **SQL View** from the SQL View icon 🔲 on the
   Query Design toolbar and add the DISTINCT keyword, creating the statement
   ```
   SELECT DISTINCT Employees.PostalCode, Employees.City,
   Employees.Region
   FROM Employees;
   ```

This example

This example modifies the
Employees form from the
Northwind database. You can
use a form that contains similar
fields—**ZIP code**, **City**, and
State.

Adding the DISTINCT keyword will return a list of unique ZIP code entries.

3. Finally, save your query appropriately—this one is named qryZIP.

FIGURE 24.11

This query will return all the ZIP codes in your address table.

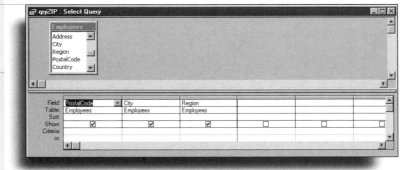

SEE ALSO

➤ *If you need help creating this query, see page 54.*

4. Open your data-entry form in Design view. Remember, you're working with the Employees form, so once you've opened the form, you have to select the **Personal Info** tab to get to the appropriate section.

5. Add a list box to your form and name it lstZIP. This one is added to the right side of the form, as shown in Figure 24.12. Change lstZIP's Row Source property to qryZIP, its Column Count property to **3**, and its Column Width property to 1";0";0". The list box will technically contain all three of **qryZIP**'s fields, but will display only the **PostalCode** field.

SEE ALSO

➤ *For information on inserting controls, see page 318.*

6. Attach the code in Listing 24.4 to lstZIP's Dbl Click event.

LISTING 24.4 lstZIP's *Dbl Click* Event

```
1    Private Sub lstZIP_DblClick(Cancel As Integer)
2    Dim varCity As Variant, varRegion As Variant, strZIP As String
3    strZIP = [lstZIP]
4    [PostalCode] = strZIP
```

```
5    strZIP = "'" & strZIP & "'"
6    varCity = [lstZIP].Column(1)
7    varRegion = [lstZIP].Column(2)
8    Me![City] = varCity
9    Me![Region] = varRegion
10   End Sub
```

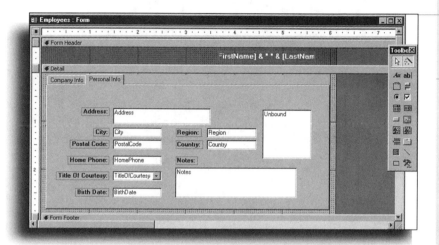

FIGURE 24.12
Adding a list box to your employee
form.

7. In the module window, select **Form** from the Object control
and **Current** from the Procedure control, and enter the
code in Listing 24.5. This procedure will update lstZIP
when you enter new ZIP codes.

LISTING 24.5 **The Current Procedure**

```
1    Private Sub Form_Current()
2    Dim ctrlZIP As Control
3    Set ctrlZIP = Forms!Employees!lstZIP
4    ctrlZIP.Requery
5    End Sub
```

8. Return to the form, select the PostalCode field and set its
Tab Index property to 1. If you need to open its property
sheet, click the Property icon ▦ on the Form Design toolbar.

9. Click the View icon [image] on the Form Design toolbar, and click the **Personal Info** tab. Immediately, you should see that the new list box contains a list of existing ZIP codes, as shown in Figure 24.13.

FIGURE 24.13

The new list contains a list of existing ZIP codes.

❶ The new control, lstZIP, displays existing ZIP codes

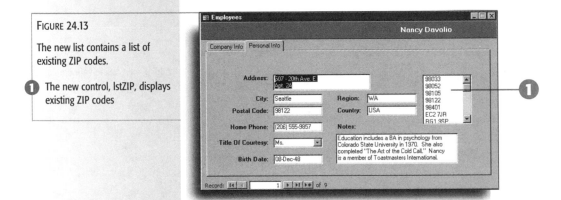

10. Select a new record and press Enter once. You'll notice that instead of selecting the City field, Access skips to the PostalCode control. You now have two choices. If the ZIP code you need is in the list box, you can double-click it. When you do, your VBA code will enter the selected ZIP code in the PostalCode field. In addition, the procedure will enter the ZIP code's city and state in the appropriate controls.

Figure 24.14 shows the result of double-clicking 98033 in lstZIP. When the ZIP code you're entering isn't in lstZIP, enter the code yourself in PostalCode, along with the appropriate city and state. This is where the form's Current event comes in. When you add the new data, the Current event updates lstZIP, and that newly added ZIP is available for the next time.

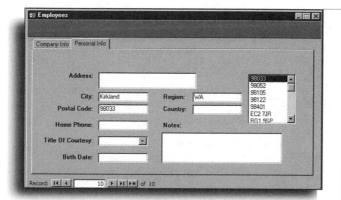

FIGURE 24.14

A ZIP code is selected from lstZIP, and it automatically fills the value in the Postal Code field.

Working with Pop-Up Forms

Occasionally, you may need to display additional information about the current record. Or you may need to prompt the user to take a certain action or provide more information. When this happens, you may want to consider a *pop-up form*, which stays on top of all other open or active forms until you react to it. There are two kinds of pop-up forms:

- Modal—You can't access any other object or menu commands while a modal form is open. Most dialog boxes (even custom ones) are modal. Set the form's Modal property to Yes.

- Modeless—A modeless form will remain on top of the current form, but you can access other objects while the form is open. Set the form's Modal property to No.

SEE ALSO

➤ *You can create custom dialog boxes; for more information, see page 347.*

Most pop-up forms are modeless. That means you can access other objects and menu commands while the form is open. However, you will need to take some action to close the form. The Suppliers form in Northwind has a good example of a modeless pop-up form. As you can see in Figure 24.15, the Suppliers form contains a command button labeled **Add Products**.

FIGURE 24.15

You can open the Products form from the Suppliers form by clicking the **Add Products** button or pressing Alt+A.

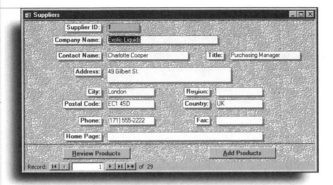

When you click the **Add Products** button, the attached VBA code opens the Products form, shown in Figure 24.16. You may have noticed that the form is empty. That's because the acAdd argument in the attached statement

```
DoCmd.OpenForm strDocName, , , , acAdd, , Me!SupplierID
```

temporarily sets the form's Data Entry property to Yes. That setting won't display or allow access to existing records. You can use the form only for data entry purposes. If you'd like to see the rest of the code, open the Suppliers form in Design view and open the form's module by clicking the Code icon ![icon] on the Form Design toolbar. Then, select **AddProducts** from the Object control's drop-down list. Access will automatically display the button's Click event.

FIGURE 24.16

Open the Products form so you can enter new product information.

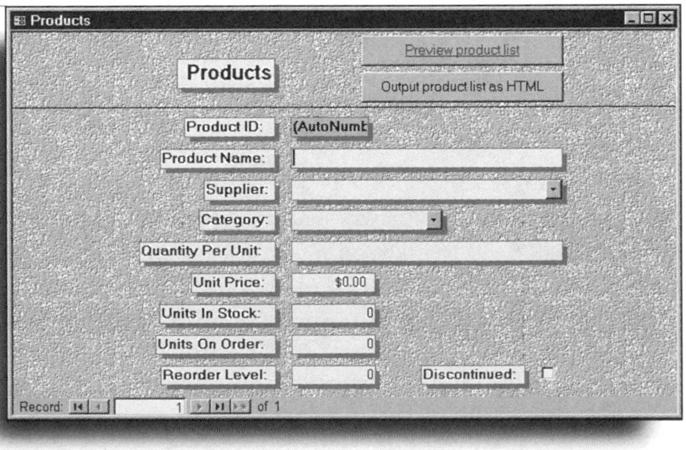

Linking Forms by Fields Using the OpenForm's *where* Argument

In the last example, the Suppliers and the Products forms aren't really related. Simply open the Products form to enter new product data, should the need arise. However, you can use the same technique to open pop-up forms that display more information. For example, the **Review Products** button at the bottom-left corner of the Suppliers form opens the form shown in Figure 24.17. As you can see, this form displays information about the current supplier's products.

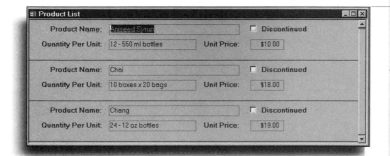

FIGURE 24.17

Clicking the **Review Products** button opens this form.

VBA accomplishes this by specifying a *where* argument in an OpenForm method in the form

```
DoCmd.OpenForm "form", , , "where"
```

The *form* argument specifies the form you want to open; the *where* argument tells Access which records to attach to the form. In this case, the statement

```
DoCmd.OpenForm "Product List", , , "[SupplierID] =
Forms![Suppliers]![SupplierID]"
```

will open the Product List form displaying only those records whose SupplierID field contains the same value as SupplierID on the Suppliers form.

By the way, the Product List pop-up form is another modeless form. All of the Northwind pop-up forms are modeless. The truth is, you may never need a modal pop-up form. However, if you do, there's one important fact you'll need to know. The Modal Yes setting doesn't completely inhibit access to all

The OpenArgs argument

In case you're wondering, the Me!SupplierID reference in the OpenForm method's arguments copies the value in the SupplierID field of the Supplier form to the Product form's OpenArgs property. This is an easy way to keep track of your current position when you open another form. Simply refer to the OpenArgs property in an OpenForm method to return to the exact form and record that had the focus when you opened the Products form.

features. To open a form in true Modal form, use the OpenForm method in the form

```
DoCmd.OpenForm "form", , , , , acDialog
```

The acDialog constant opens the form as a dialog box, which by constraints is a modal form.

Creating Effective Reports

Sooner or later in the life of your database, you will need to create a report that will show off your data. The way you design your report will determine if it's an eye-popping presentation or a jumbled and cluttered mess. The purpose of any report should be to quickly and concisely display its data in a manner that is easily read and understood. The designer of the report needs to take into consideration how this report is going to be used and what the important aspects of the report are going to be.

You can use the Report Wizard that comes with Microsoft Access to design your reports for you. If you want to be a little more creative, or if the wizard's reports don't meet your needs, you can modify and customize the wizard's creation to better suit your needs. Or you can start from scratch and completely design your own report.

As outlined in Chapter 6, "Creating Reports with the Report Wizard," most beginning users will use the Report Wizard to construct their reports. This chapter will help show you how to revise and improve the layout and efficiency of your preexisting report.

One of the first things you will notice after entering Design view is that your report has been broken into sections and that there is no data contained anywhere on the report (see Figure 25.1). The Design view will not contain any data, but only layout, control, and property information. This is nearly identical to the Design view in building your own forms.

The sections normally will consist of a report header, a page header, a detail section, a page footer, and a report footer. If you have a report that is being grouped or sorted, you will have additional sections to your report. Every section tells you which type of data will be placed on your report, and where.

Viewing reports in Design View

Once you have created a report, you can enter Design view (as with forms) to edit its properties and layout to better suit your needs. To enter Design view, you have two options: Right-click on your report name in the Database window and click the Design View option 📝▾, or you can simply highlight the report name and click the **Design** button in the Database window.

Viewing the report with data

To view what your report layout will look like with data, click on the Preview button 🔍 located on the Report Design toolbar.

- A report header will appear only once, at the very beginning of the report.
- A page header will appear at the beginning of every new page.
- Items in the Detail section constitute the "meat" of your report. This is where the data is displayed.

- The page footer will be displayed at the bottom of each page. It is commonly used for page numbering, "privileged and confidential" tags, and the document name, among other things.

- The report footer will appear only once, at the very end of the report.

You will also have your choice of many different toolbars that you can view. The Report Design, Toolbox, and Formatting (Form/Report/Design) toolbars are the most commonly used. By right-clicking on any toolbar, you can see which toolbars are currently open. Add or remove any toolbars by checking this pop-up menu or using **Toolbars** on the **View** menu.

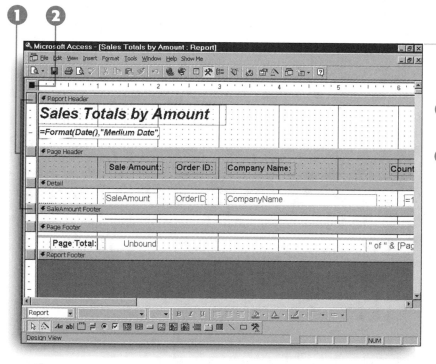

FIGURE 25.1

The Northwind report Sales Totals by Amount in design mode.

❶ Use the **View** menu options to show or hide the header and footer separators

❷ Double-click or right-click the **Report Selector** to view the properties and other items related to the whole report

Assigning Report Properties

Every section in your report, every control, and the entire report itself is made up of properties.

In the Properties sheet, you have several options to choose from that will affect your report. You can change the properties of the entire report, a single section, or a specific entry, as well as create an event, put an image into your report, and many other options.

There are two main ways to select the Property sheet of an item:

- Double-click on that item.
- Use the Object dropdown box on the left end of the Formatting toolbar. This is especially helpful when dealing with hard-to-grab items such as lines, borders, or overlapping fields.

The Properties sheet for reports has the same layout and structure as for other objects you've worked with. Select one of the five tabs, **Format**, **Data**, **Event**, **Other**, and **All**, based on the properties you want to change. The following is a brief description of each tab:

- **Format**—Appearance characteristics such as dimensions, color, graphics, and more. Figure 25.2 shows this tab and its properties.

Getting to the properties you want

When you're having trouble getting the Report Property sheet selected, use the Report Selector square (refer back to Figure 25.1). Double-clicking on this will bring up the Property sheet for the report. If you currently have a Property sheet open, single-clicking on this square will change it to the Property sheet for the report. Otherwise, you can change the item whose properties you are viewing by single-clicking on a different item on the report itself.

FIGURE 25.2

Use the **Format** tab to set properties such as whether to have the header or footer appear on every page.

■ **Data**—Data characteristics such as the control source, any filter information, and order. Figure 25.3 shows the Data tab's properties.

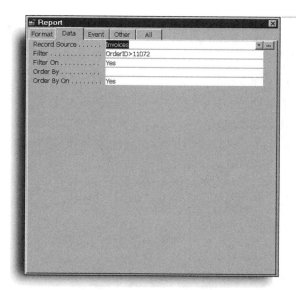

FIGURE 25.3

Use the **Data** tab to set the underlying data sources for your report.

■ **Event**—Characteristics of event procedures and macros. Figure 25.4 shows the events that are associated with a report.

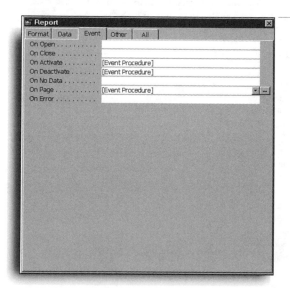

FIGURE 25.4

Use the events here to program your report as a part of the application.

■ **Other**—Report characteristics such as names and date grouping. Figure 25.5 shows the properties that let you control the customization of the report.

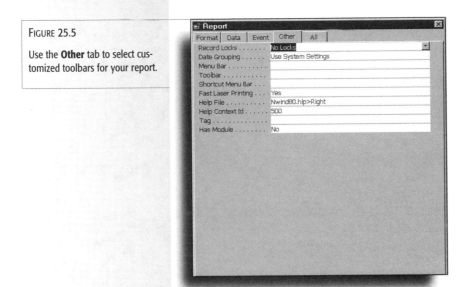

■ **All**—Selecting this tab gives you all the properties available for the item selected, as shown in Figure 25.6.

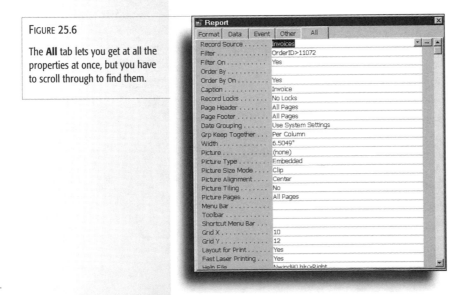

You will also notice that different items have different properties in the Property sheet. A section box will contain different options than a combo box. A text box will be different than a label box. Knowing which properties to change will be a matter of personal preference and experimentation.

The following are a few property items the might be helpful:

- When the data contained in a field is of a random length, such as a description, it is best to change the "can grow" and "can shrink" options to Yes. This will ensure that all the data prints instead of being cut off.

  Select the field that will contain that information, view the Properties sheet, and change "can grow" and "can shrink" to Yes.

- When multiple users are entering data into the same database and running reports, it is best to lock all records to prevent format changes and possible data loss.

  View Report Properties, and select **All Records** under the Record Locks option.

- To print only one record per page, you can select **After Section** under the Force New Page option. This will begin a new page after each item printed in the Detail section.

Planning the Layout and Print Settings for a Report

Trying to get the right look for your report can be a challenge. Ultimately it comes down to two important questions: how will your report be used, and how much data do you want to get onto each page? If your report is to be used in a presentation that will be bindered or bound, a portrait layout with a larger left margin or even a book-style would be appropriate. This would compensate for a three-hole punch, velo-bind, or glue to be used in the spine of the left margin. Likewise, it may be acceptable to spread your data out to occupy the entire sheet, reducing your margins to next to nothing. Be careful to consider your header and footer needs when doing this.

Always preview first

As with documents you've used in other applications such as Word, you should always preview the report before you print it. Use the Preview button 🔍 to check the layout and readability of your report throughout the design process.

Select the layout of your report by going into the **Page Setup** option under **File**, as shown in Figure 25.7. From here you can select your page margins, page orientation, paper size and source, printer designation, and layout settings.

FIGURE 25.7

Use the Page Setup to specify paper styles. Use the **Page** tab to set different page sizes for larger reports, such as the dot-matrix green-and-white-striped mass reports.

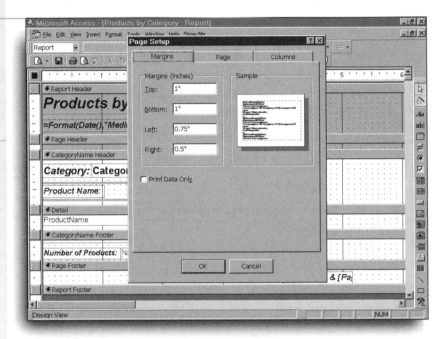

Depending on your margin and header/footer settings within Page Setup, you must be aware of how much space you have available for your report. For example, if you are doing a report in portrait mode and have your left and right margins set at 1", you must be aware that any item hanging over 6.5" on the right edge will be carried over to a new page. This is important to remember when you're resizing lines, borders, and fields.

Shortcut for printing

Ctrl+P performs the same function as selecting **File** and **Print** from the menu bar. This will prompt additional options from the **Print** menu.

You can print your report using a number of methods. Whether you are in Print Preview or the Database window, clicking on the printer icon will print the total report with no further options made available to you. Likewise, from within the Print Preview or the Database window, if you select **File** from the menu bar and then select the **Print** option, you will be prompted for further Print options, as shown in Figure 25.8.

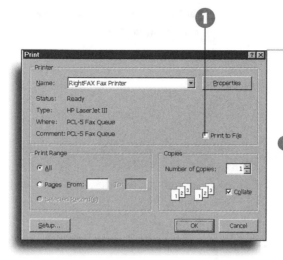

If you created your report using the wizard, you had the option to select a style for your report. Once your report has been created, you can go back and change that style by selecting **AutoFormat** from the **Format** option on the menu bar. From there you can select any one of the standard Access styles, or you can customize your own.

Standardizing Your Reports and Using Report Templates

Have you ever wondered what the paintbrush icon ⬦ on the Standard toolbar does? It's the Format Painter. It copies the *style* of a selection, rather than its content, and applies it to another selection. This is useful in Access because there are many stylistic changes a person will consider before deciding on a final design. The Format Painter is easy to use. Use it as a timesaver when you decide to use the same styles repeatedly in a form or report.

Using the Format Painter to copy styles

1. First, select the area to copy from.

2. Once that area is blocked, click once on the Format Painter ⬦.

3. By holding down the left mouse button, you can now paint across the area that you want to copy the style to.

4. Release when you are finished and *voilà!* Instant format change.

After you've worked in Access a while, you will begin to develop a style that is all your own. If you've used the Report Wizard to create your reports, you've most likely noticed that Access has remembered the last settings you used and recommended them for your next report. Your forms and reports will begin to take on familiar characteristics. You have begun to standardize your Access documents.

Creating a Report Template

If you find yourself using the same types of reports over and over, you should think about making your own templates. Most likely, you've been using the copy-and-paste method. You find a report you like, copy it, paste it, rename it, enter the design of the new report, and revise. This can be a tedious chore. You can have the same layout, font selection, embedded objects, and other report properties saved as a template that you can use to construct your new reports.

Creating a report template

1. Create or select an existing report that has all the ingredients (style, format, structure) you know you'll need on a regular basis.

2. From inside the report, select **Tools**, **Options**, **Forms/Reports**, which brings up the dialog shown in Figure 25.9.

3. In the **Report template** text box, give the template a name you'll recognize later on.

Control options will not be copied, and changing templates will not affect preexisting reports. A template can be used for any report that is being created from scratch, not using a wizard.

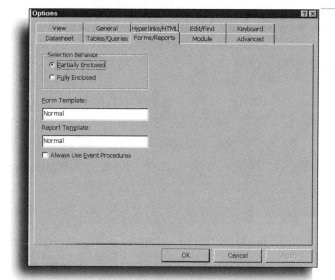

FIGURE 25.9

Saving your report template.

Make sure your template is available

It is important to export the templates that you want to use to the databases you'll be using them in. Otherwise, Microsoft Access will default to the "normal" template.

Making Your Point with Reports

Create a calculated control

Get a grip on graphics

Insert a border

Now it is time to make your reports stand out. In this chapter you will make your reports more attractive and better organized. This chapter will discuss grouping and sorting functions to organize your report. Other topics include how to calculate totals with controls, page numbering, graphics, and adding special effects to spice up your report.

Grouping and Sorting Data

Let's say you work for one of the top coffee distributors in the country. Your boss has asked you to manage a database of all the current wholesale accounts and create a quarterly financial report sorted by the city in which each account is located. This is a piece of cake if you're using Microsoft Access.

If you want to follow along, you can create a temporary table and include the following fields:

Entry number (primary key)

Customer number

Name

Street address

City

State

ZIP

Phone

Year-to-date sales

Save your table.

You will use the Report Wizard to assist you in creating your report. The following is the procedure the wizard will use.

Creating a report using a wizard

1. From the Database window, select the **Report** tab and click the **New** button. Select the **Report Wizard** and the name of the table/query used as the source for your data. (This is the table you created.)

2. Choose the fields you will be including in your report. In this case, select the account name, street address, city, state, ZIP code, and the year-to-date sales amount. You may want to select other information as well, including the phone number, the entry number, the customer number, and whatever else you think is important from your table or query. This is also your last opportunity before your report is designed to change the source for your data.

3. Choose the grouping levels for your report. You want a report sorted by the city in which each account is located, so select the City field. You can have up to four grouping levels.

4. Choose the sorting options for the report. Within each city, you want the accounts listed alphabetically from A to Z. Select the customer name from the field list drop-down box, and then select the proper order (ascending or descending). You can have up to four methods of sorting your data.

5. Select the layout of the report. Because you have selected a number of fields to include in the report (as well as names and addresses), and because some of these fields can be lengthy, you will select Landscape as the orientation to ensure that you have enough room horizontally for your information.

6. Now select the style for your report. The options given include **Bold**, **Casual**, **Compact**, **Corporate**, **Formal**, and **Soft Gray**.

7. Title your report.

You have now created a report that has all of your accounts listed alphabetically by city, and alphabetically within each city. Most likely, you will want to go into the design of the report and modify it to better suit your needs.

Another example you can use, the Sales Totals by Amount report, is contained in the Northwind database. In this report, shown in Figure 26.1, you can see many similarities to what has been discussed so far in this chapter.

SEE ALSO

➤ *For information on creating select queries as the basis of your report, see page 238.*

➤ *For further help on grouping, sorting, and other criteria within queries, see page 258.*

<aside>
Selecting the control source

In gathering its data, your report will look to the control source you have specified. If all of your data is kept in one table, you can select that table as your control source. If your data is kept in multiple tables, you must use a query as your control source.
</aside>

FIGURE 26.1

The Northwind Sales Totals by Amount report in Preview mode shows some samples of grouping and subtotaling.

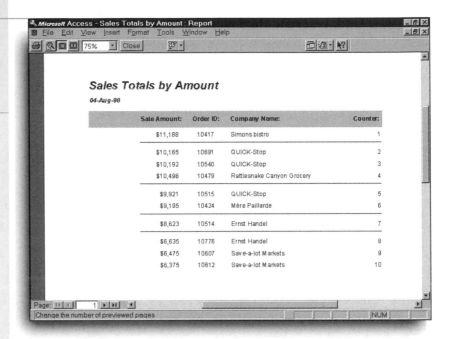

Calculating Totals with Controls

Report controls can be bound, unbound, or calculated. The source of the data that the control displays determines its type. For example, if your control is bound to a table or query field titled Name, anything contained in the Name field will be printed in this area. It is bound to that field. Likewise, in dealing with a label or a text box that does not get its information from a table or query, this control would be unbound. It is simply an item that you have typed.

Practicing with this example

For practice, try to re-create the preceding Northwind report. This report has figures grouped into $10,000 sections. It also uses greater-than criteria and other restrictive values in its queries. This will allow you to test what you have learned.

A calculated control comes from an expression or calculation that you create, not a single field in a table or query. An example would be a mathematical equation that inputs an average based upon year-to-date sales figures divided by the number of months included in the report. This would look like =[YTD]/6 (6 being the number of months included in the year-to-date figure).

Another example would be a control that includes a customer's first name and last name separated by one space, regardless of the length of each name. That expression would look like this: [first name]+" "+[last name]. The name contained in the First

Name field would be printed first. When it was finished, a space would be inserted. Following the space would be the name contained in the Last Name field.

Your toolbox, which you've seen in the chapters on creating forms, contains the items needed to set up controls. These include buttons for creating labels, text boxes, option groups, toggle buttons, option buttons, check boxes, combo boxes, list boxes, command buttons, images, unbound and bound objects, forced page breaks, subreports, and special effects such as lines and rectangles.

Switching the field order

Many times, you want the last name first. If so, you can sort alphabetically according to last name. This would look like `[last name]+", "+[first name]`.

FIGURE 26.2

The toolbox contains the controls and a control wizard for working on reports.

SEE ALSO

➤ *For details on the toolbox, see the techniques on page 314.*

➤ *For more specific information on placing controls onto forms and reports, see the techniques on page 318.*

Creating a calculated control

  1. To begin a calculated control within a text box, you can enter the expression directly into the control. Begin with the = sign.

  2. Enter the field you will be calculating from. For example, `=[Unit Price]`.

  3. Add the calculation. For example, `=[Unit Price]*.15`.

This calculation will give you the dollar amount in the Unit Price field multiplied by .15, or 15 percent. The following is a list of the most commonly used expressions and calculations.

+	Add
-	Subtract
/	Divide
*	Multiply
[ ]	Enter field name between brackets
=	Calculation control, numerical
<	Less than

>	Greater than
<>	Equal to
!	Follows a table selection
" "	Inserts the amount of spaces between the quotes into a calculation
&	Needed to separate calculations

SEE ALSO

➤ *For information on the Expression Builder and how to use it to create calculations, see page 273.*

Use the Expression Builder

The Expression Builder will be a great help when you're attempting to do more complicated formulas.

The Art of Page Numbering

Page numbering is another expression commonly used in most reports. Page numbers help organize your report and are practically a necessity in your finished product. The page number control box will be an unbound control. Why? Because it's not getting its data from a single table or query.

Where you put your page numbering and how it will look is a matter of personal preference. Normally, page numbers are placed in the page header or footer. The format of the page number depends on how you've entered the expression.

Entering =[Page] in the Control Source property will give you only the page number. To include the word "page" before it, you must type that in quotation marks before the [page] expression. It would look like this: ="Page " & [Page].

Another example of commonly used page numbering is the "Page 1 of 3" variety. In order for the page numbering to be shown this way, you must use two fields and include two items of text. It would look like this: ="Page " & [Page] & " of " & [Pages]. Figure 26.3 shows the property sheet with this control source for the page number control.

Starting with a Page Number Other Than 1

Using the Northwind Catalog report as an example, you can see how it makes sense to start your page numbering on a number other than 1. Figures 26.4 and 26.5 show two of the pages and details from this report.

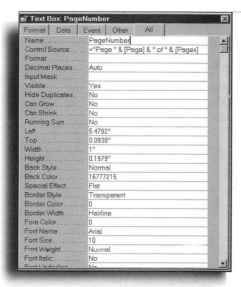

FIGURE 26.3

Viewing the PageNumber property box.

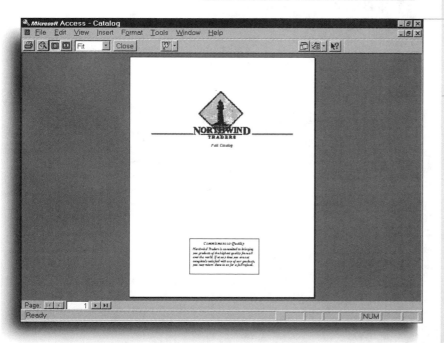

FIGURE 26.4

The cover and the company blurb obviously do not need page numbers.

FIGURE 26.5

Page 3 of the Northwind catalog is the first page that is numbered.

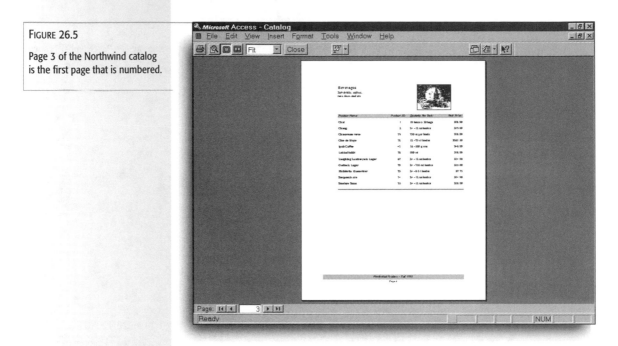

FIGURE 26.5

Page 3 of the Northwind catalog is the first page that is numbered.

Figure 26.6 shows the Design view of the report.

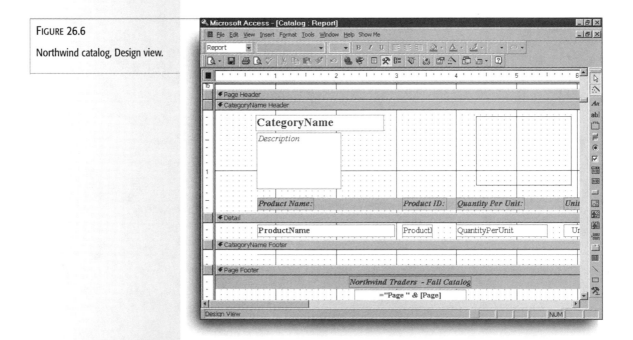

FIGURE 26.6

Northwind catalog, Design view.

The Northwind catalog report has a clever design and should give you an idea of how to creatively achieve very different-looking reports. The cover and the company blurb are kept in the Report Header section. They are separated by using the page break button on the toolbox. There is no page numbering control in the Report Header section. Therefore, the items contained in the header are not subject to having the page number printed.

The page numbering information for this report is kept in the Page Footer section. A header is not technically considered a page, so the page numbering would not print on the header unless it's specifically put into each section of the header.

Inserting Graphics

The use of graphics not only helps your report stand out, but it can serve a valuable purpose as well. For example, let's take another look at the Northwind catalog report, shown in Figure 26.7. In Preview mode, notice how each of the food/beverage sections contains a photograph of what is being described. Without the photographs, it would be just another boring list of products and prices. The photographs add a splash of color and make the catalog look much more attractive.

Another unique way in which graphics can be used is for personalized service. Let's say you take your elephant, Sparky, to your local veterinarian's office for his annual checkup. Back when you took Sparky in for his first visit, his photograph was taken and put into a database. Now, when the vet pulls up Sparky's information on the computer, it not only tells him all of Sparky's past history and vital information, but it also shows the photo. And when you receive your bill, which is just another type of Access report, whose picture is there looking back at you? Sparky, your lovable elephant. A little personalized service goes a long way.

There are two main ways to insert graphics and images into your reports. The first is to pull the graphics from a table, shown in Figure 26.8. The graphic and the item it represents are contained in the same table entry. When the item changes on the report, the graphic will change to represent the new item being displayed. This is a bound OLE object.

Graphics limitations

Keep in mind that graphics can be large and will put a strain on your resources.

FIGURE 26.7

Stand out from the crowd by inserting graphics.

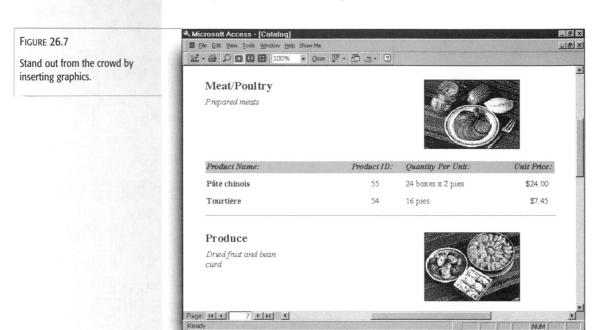

FIGURE 26.8

A table can also contain images.

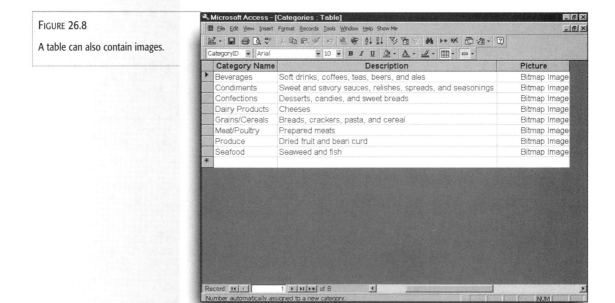

The second way to display a graphic or image is to create a control box for that item. Just as you can display the page number, a text box, or a label, you can just as easily display a graphic or image. Figures 26.9 and 26.10 show the Design view of a report with a graphic and its property sheet.

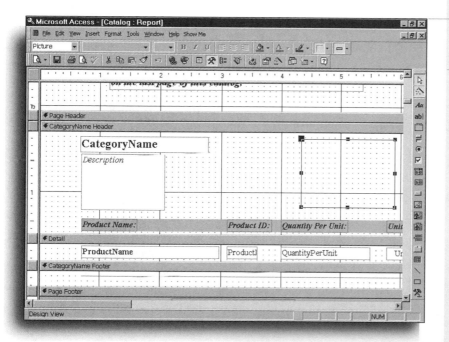

FIGURE 26.9
Create your image frame.

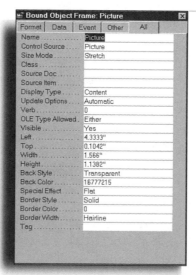

FIGURE 26.10
View your image property sheet.

Check the Size property

If your image does not look right, try changing the size in its property sheet. Selecting **Stretch** will make the image conform to the size of the box you have created for it. Selecting the **Zoom** option will keep the image proportions intact and resize the image automatically. Selecting **Clip** will insert the image at its normal size.

In the Design view of your report, click the Image icon 🖼 on the toolbox. Select where you want the object to go and drag it to approximately the size you would like. As soon as you release the image, the Insert Picture display will pop up. From here, you need to find your image and double-click on its filename.

To Frame or Not to Frame

The choice to frame or not to frame your images will be a matter of personal preference. If the background of your image is the same color as the background of your report, going without a frame would provide a seamless image insertion. This can be useful when you're trying to blend items into a report such as a watermark, logo, or faint background image, or when you want to give your report a very fluid appearance.

Using Transparent

If your back color style is set to Transparent, no special effects or borders will be displayed. If it's set to Normal, your border width will dramatically affect the special effect you have selected. Experiment with the other options, such as the color selections and the border style, to come up with creative combinations.

The benefit of using a frame is that you can produce a contrasting image insertion. You can make your image stand out on the page by using a special effect like Raised or Shadowed. Other options available to you are Flat, Sunken, Etched, and Chiseled special effects. You can also adjust the back color, border color, and border style to further alter the appearance of your frame. Figure 26.11 shows the property sheet and Design view for modifying images.

Working with OLE Graphics

Very simply, *OLE* stands for *Object Linking and Embedding*. One of the options listed in the property sheet for a graphic or image is whether you want the item to be linked, embedded, or either. What's the difference?

When you specify that your graphic is to be linked, you're telling Access that when it prints or views that graphic, it will refer to the graphic and use what is currently available. Let's say you are going to use a graphic that you are designing. You already know the name of the file, but you are constantly making changes to it. By linking the graphic, the most recent edits will appear.

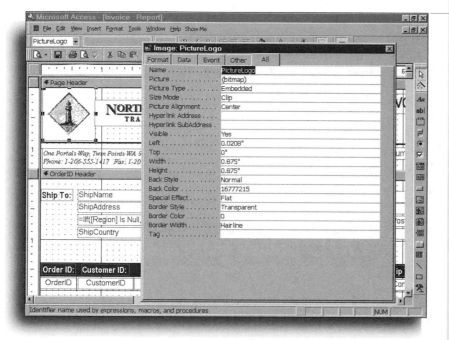

FIGURE **26.11**
Northwind logo property sheet.

When you specify that your graphic is to be embedded, you're telling Access to put the object itself into the database. Access will always refer to that location when displaying the graphic. It has stored the object information into its memory and will always refer to that. An example of this might be a photograph or a logo.

OLE objects don't need to be pictures. They can be a wide variety of objects, including a Microsoft Excel spreadsheet, a chart or graph, a drawing, or any item from a supported extension, such as .tif, .gif, .bmp, .jpg, and so on.

Adding Lines and Circles to a Report

The addition of lines, circles, and other types of artistic design can go a long way toward making your report look professional and pleasing to the eye. Adding lines and circles to your report can assist in separating data fields, highlighting certain areas of your report, and creating borders.

Figures 26.12 through 26.14 are some great examples of how to use lines to separate your data.

FIGURE **26.12**

Invoice report from the Northwind database in Preview mode, page 3.

1 Use the Formatting toolbar to create contrasting colors in the rectangles for heading rows

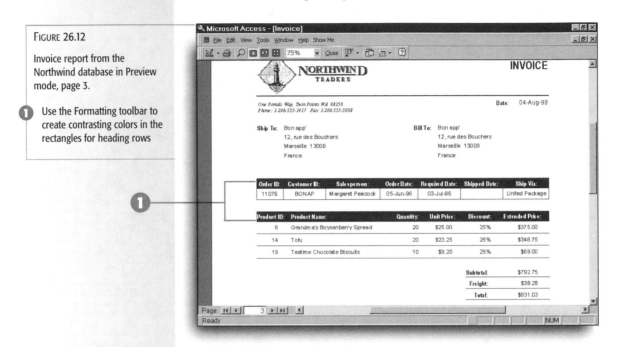

FIGURE **26.13**

Catalog report from the Northwind database in Preview mode, page 9.

1 Use rectangles (cutting and pasting for a series) to leave blanks or a grid in the report

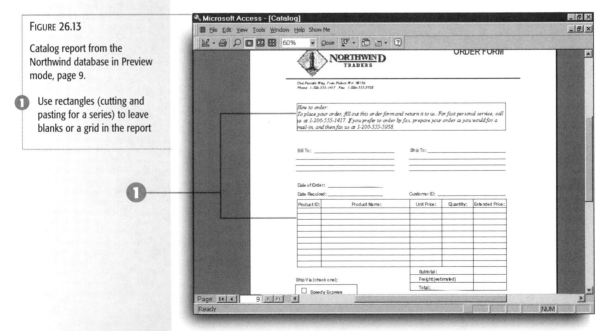

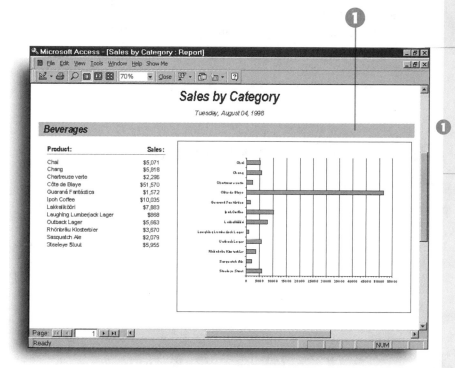

FIGURE 26.14

Sales by Category report from the Northwind database in Preview mode, page 1.

❶ Use a shaded rectangle to catch the reader's eye and set off sections of the report

In the toolbox, you will notice buttons for creating lines and rectangles. You can draw a freehand line or rectangle of any size and at any angle you like. You can put text or an image on top of the rectangle by sending the rectangle to the back of the document.

Drawing a circle or an ellipse is more complicated because you need to create an event procedure or a macro, as specified in the Event property sheet called On Page. The syntax for drawing a circle is as follows:

```
object.Circle [Step](x, y), radius[, [color][, [start][,
[end][, aspect]]]].
```

object determines the report on which the circle will be drawn.

Step determines the keyword around which the circle will be drawn.

x and y are single values that determine the center point for the circle.

radius is a single value that determines the radius of the circle.

Creating depth in the report

Sending an item to the back or bringing it forward determines how deep that item will be on your page. If you have text on top of a rectangle on top of a square and you send the rectangle to the back, the order will become rectangle, square, text on top. Click **Format** on the menu bar for access to this feature.

Tip for drawing lines

Hold down the Shift key to draw a perfectly straight line.

color is a long value indicating the RGB (red, green, blue) color. If left blank, the Forecolor property will be used.

start and end are single values used for partial circles.

aspect is a single value that determines the type of circle to be drawn (a 1.0 equals a perfect circle).

Drawing a Border Around the Report Page

Again referring to the Event properties for the report, a border must be entered into the On Page area, as shown in Figure 26.15. This places the command for adding a border between the time that Access formats the document and when it sends the formatted document to the printer. You can then create an Event procedure for adding a report border in the On Page area, as shown in Figure 26.16.

FIGURE 26.15

Salesletter report from the Solutions database, with Report Properties and the **Event** tab selected.

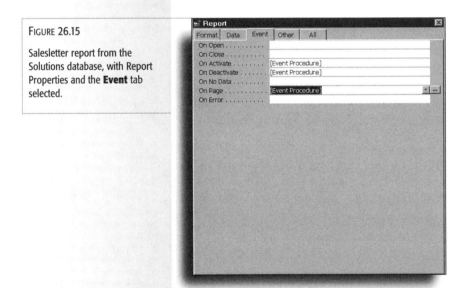

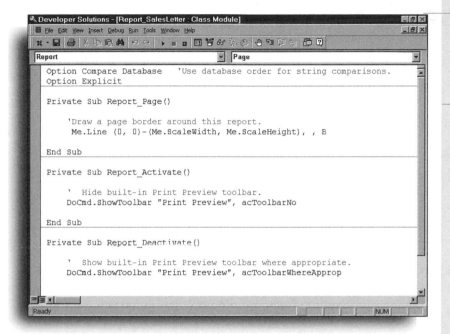

FIGURE 26.16

Salesletter report from the Solutions database, with Report Properties, the **Event** tab, and the On Page module displayed.

SEE ALSO

➤ *For more information on creating event procedures, see page 419.*

Displaying Detailed Data with a Subreport

Learn what a subreport is and when you need one

Link subreports to the data in the main report

Set subreport properties

What's a Subreport and Why Do You Need One?

A *subreport* is a report that you insert within another, or main, report. You'll use subreports to display related, and usually detailed, information about a group or several groups of data in the main report. However, this relationship isn't necessary. You can insert unrelated reports into a main report, which most likely will be unbound. An *unbound* report isn't attached to an underlying table or query.

SEE ALSO

➤ *For more information on subforms, see page 403.*

Many times you'll use subreports to display detailed or summarized data that's related to information in the main report. For instance, you might use a subreport to display quarterly or monthly summaries in a main report that displays specifics about each order. The arrangement could be reversed just as easily.

The Northwind database has two report/subreport configurations you can review. Figure 27.1 shows the Sales by Year report open in Print Preview and maximized. Below the report's title and date is a bordered box with summary sales information. That data is summarized by quarters. However, the records below that display each order in more detail.

Figure 27.2 shows this report in Design view. As you can see, the summarized records at the head of the report are actually a subreport. Both reports are based on the Sales by Year query. The only difference is that the subreport uses the Count() function to return just one record for each quarter, instead of displaying each record. The main report then displays each record.

Lightweight reports and forms

If your report or form is slow in loading and has no event procedures attached to it, remove the object's module by setting the **Has Module** property to **No**. Doing so will reduce the object's size and help it load quicker. Of course, if there's any code attached to the object, you shouldn't change this property. If you delete the object's module and later decide to add a procedure to the object, simply change the **Has Module** property to **Yes**.

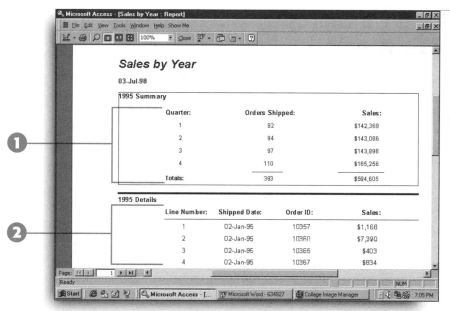

FIGURE 27.1

This report contains a subreport that summarizes sales.

1 This section summarizes the detailed records below

2 This section displays each order in detail

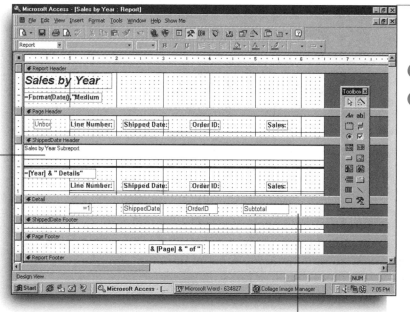

FIGURE 27.2

The summarized data is actually a subreport.

1 The subreport

2 The main report's Detail section, which will display each order

Adding a Subreport to an Unbound Main Report

This example

During this exercise, you'll be working with a number of tables, queries, and reports in Northwind. You can use almost any table with these exercises.

Probably the simplest report/subreport arrangement is a subreport in an unbound report. That means the report is really just a shell and you can add whatever you like to it. Additionally, the subreport records will probably not be related to anything in the main report. You'll probably use this setup when you want to display two or more short but unrelated reports together. This is a simple process. You create all the reports, including the unbound main report, open the main report in Design view, and insert each subreport using the Subform/Subreport tool.

Creating subreports in an unbound main report

1. Start with the main report by clicking the **Reports** tab and then clicking the **New** tab in the Database window. Next, double-click **Design View** in the New Report dialog box.

2. Now you can add text or other controls to your main report. Add a label control to the Page Header section.

3. Save the report (this one is saved as rptMain).

4. Make sure the Control Wizard icon ⬙ is selected, and then click the Subform/Subreport tool ▦ on the Toolbox. Next, click inside the report's **Detail** section to anchor the subreport and launch the Subform/Subreport Wizard.

5. In the wizard's first window, identify the table, query, report, or form that you're adding to the main report as a subreport. If you're adding a table or query, choose the **Table/Query** option and click **Next**.

   If you're adding a report or form, select the **Reports and Forms** options and choose the appropriate form or report from the **Reports and Forms** drop-down box. You're going to add the **Category Sales for 1995** query, so retain the default, **Table/Query**, as shown in Figure 27.3, and click **Next**.

FIGURE 27.3

The wizard's first window asks you to identify the object type you're adding as a subreport.

6. The next window presents a list of tables and queries in the Tables and Queries list box. When you select a table or query from this control, Access updates the field names in the Available Fields list box accordingly.

First select the appropriate table or query from the Tables and Queries list box, and then select the fields you want to include in your subreport from the Available Fields list box. Choose the query **Category Sales for 1995** and choose both fields, as shown in Figure 27.4 When you're satisfied with your choices, click **Next** to continue.

FIGURE 27.4

Choose the table or query and its corresponding fields for your subreport.

7. In the final window, accept or change the default subreport name and click **Finish**. When you accept the default name, Access adds the subreport shown in Figure 27.5 to the report.

FIGURE 27.5

You've added the first subreport.

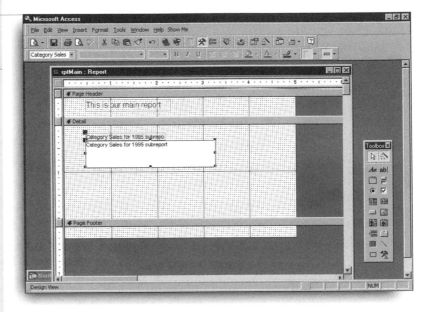

FIGURE 27.5

You've added the first subreport.

8. Now repeat steps 4 through 7 to add a second table or query as a subreport—insert it right below the first. Add the **Sales by Category** query. The completed report/subreport in Design view is shown in 27.6.

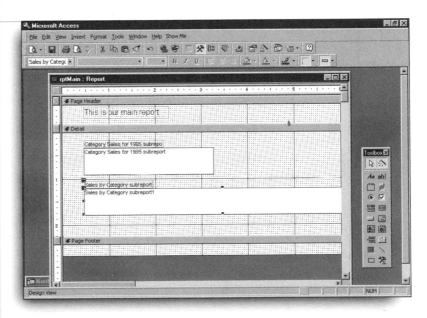

FIGURE 27.6

Adding two queries as subreports to this unbound main report.

9. Click the Print Preview button 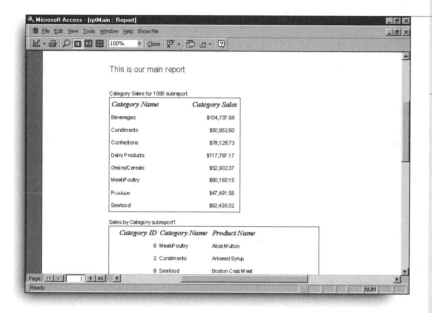. Figure 27.7 shows the report in Print Preview.

FIGURE 27.7
The two subreports are unrelated to one another and to the main report.

At this point, you modify your report or enhance it to suit your needs. You'll probably try several variations before you hit upon just the right one. Frankly, we don't think you'll have much need for this type of reporting.

SEE ALSO

➤ *To learn how to modify reports, see page 439.*

Linking a Subreport's Data to the Main Report

Most of the time you'll probably want the subreport to display more detailed information about some group in your main report (or vice versa). You can do this by linking the two objects together. For instance, the Sales by Year main report, shown in Figure 27.8, summarizes quarterly sales totals. The subreport displays the individual orders for the year.

Deleting the border

The wizard displays a subreport with a border around it. If you don't like this format, delete it by opening the subreport control's **Border Style** property to **Transparent**. To access the **Subform/Subreport** property sheet, right-click the subreport control and choose **Properties** from the resulting shortcut menu.

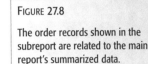

FIGURE 27.8

The order records shown in the subreport are related to the main report's summarized data.

1 The main report

2 The subreport

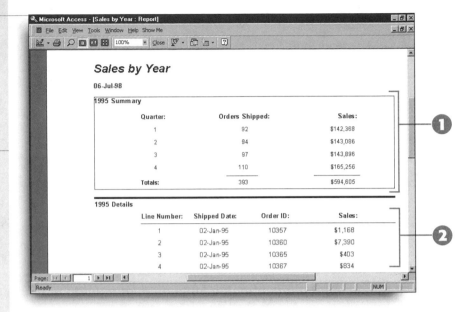

To link the two reports, you'll specify the linking field in both reports. You don't have to display the linking fields in either report, but you must include them in the underlying table or query. If you want to set these links manually, open the subreport's control property sheet and set the following properties:

- Link Child Fields—Identifies the linking field in the subreport.

- Link Master Fields—Identifies the linking field in the main report.

Accessing the Subform/Subreport property sheet

1. "Control" doesn't mean the controls on the subreport. Rather, the subreport is a control in the main report. To access those properties, right-click the subreport control in the main report. Then choose **Properties** from the resulting shortcut menu.

2. Figure 27.9 shows the subreport's property sheet. As you can see, both linking fields are the Year field. That way, the subreport displays all the order records for the same year for which your main report summarizes quarterly data.

Compatible fields

You can link two fields as long as they contain the same kind of data and compatible data type and field size properties. An AutoNumber field is compatible with a Number field if the Field Size property for the Number field is **Long Integer**.

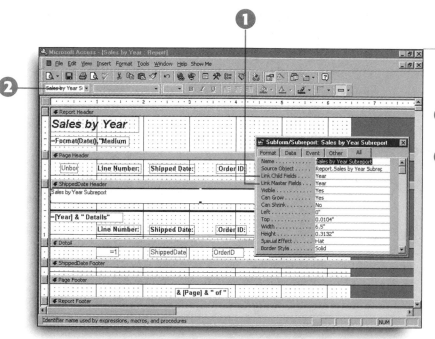

FIGURE 27.9

The subreport's property sheet contains both linking properties.

1 Both linking fields specify the Year field

2 Double-click the Report selector to bring up Properties

Assigning Subreport Properties

You've already learned about the two most crucial subreport properties—Link Master Fields and Link Child Fields. What you might not realize is that a subreport has two sets of properties. First, as a control (subreport), the subreport has a special list of properties, Subform/Subreport, which you saw earlier in 27.9. These properties are consistent with control properties in general. Second, as a report, it has a set of report properties like any other report. Subreports as reports also have report events. However, subreports as a control don't.

You learned how to access a subreport's control properties in the last section. Now let's look at the subreport's report properties.

Accessing a subreport's report property sheets

1. To set a subreport's report properties, open the main report in Design view. Then double-click the subreport control to open the subreport in Design view.

Automatic linking

Access will automatically set the Link Master Fields and Link Child Fields properties for you when conditions are right:

A relationship exists between the tables on which you base the report and subreport.

The main report's table has a primary key, and the subreport's bound table or query contains a field with the same name and a compatible data type and field size.

Using the Database window

In our all these examples, we use the Subform/Subreport wizard to insert subreports in a main report. However, you don't need the wizard. Instead, drag the object you want to add to the main report from the Database window. When you're ready to add the subreport, open the main report in Design view, and then display the Database window by pressing the F11 key or by clicking the Database Window button 🔲. Then select the table, query, form, or report in the Database window and simply drag it to the main report.

2. Now you can double-click the **Report Selector** to open the report's property sheet. Or you can click the Properties button 🖼 on the Report Design toolbar.

3. If you want to open the property sheet for one of the subreport's controls, double-click it or select it and click the **Properties** button.

Other Important Properties

There's probably no way you can estimate the size of the subreport. Therefore, it's a good idea to apply the Can Grow and Can Shrink properties. That way the subreport can grow to accommodate many records, or shrink to save space when there are few or no records to display. You'll find these properties in the Subform/Subreport property sheet. In fact, the Can Grow property's default is **Yes**, meaning it will stretch to display all of its records. The Can Shrink property's default is **No** because reducing the subreport may have an adverse effect on controls that have fixed positions after it.

Creating Mailing Labels

Taking the work out of printing labels

Using custom-sized labels

Using the Label Wizard

You can use Microsoft Word to create mailing labels, but if your data is in Access, you should consider using the Label Wizard instead. You tell the wizard which table or query contains the addresses, the size of the labels you're using, and the information you want to include on each label. The wizard does the rest.

SEE ALSO

➤ *Access offers several report wizards. For more information on them, see page 87.*

Creating mailing labels

1. In the Database window, select the table or query that contains your address data.

2. Select Report [⌸ ▾] from the drop-down list of the New Object button [⌸ ▾], and then double-click **Label Wizard** in the New Report dialog box or select **Label Wizard** and click **OK**.

3. In the wizard's first window, shown in Figure 28.1, you'll specify the label size, the unit of measure, and the label type. If the wizard doesn't offer the label size you're using, you'll need to customize your report by clicking the **Customize** button. (We'll talk more about this option later in this chapter.) For now, let's create a report based on a standard size— Avery number 5096. Be sure to specify the unit of measure and the type labels you're using before clicking **Next** to continue.

4. The wizard gives you the option of modifying several format defaults in the second window, shown in Figure 28.2. You're going to use the defaults, but you should modify these options to suit your needs. When you're done, click **Next** to continue.

5. At this point the wizard asks you to specify the bound fields you want to display on each label, but you're doing much more. You're actually creating the label template. This means you must select each field as you want it to appear on the actual label, as shown in Figure 28.3.

The flexibility of Access labels

The results of using the Label Wizard on the Customers table in Northwind will show one of the more common uses of labels— addresses. You can use these steps with any table or query that contains address data.

However, Access doesn't know or care if you're using addresses for your labels. You can find numerous uses for labels and apply these examples to any table or query with any information. For example, if you're taking a physical inventory count for auditing or moving purposes, you might want to attach a label to each item that displays its ID number, its name, and the location where you want it moved or stored—all based on data in an inventory table. If your inventory records are up to date, you can create as many labels for an item as you think you'll need, as you'll see later in this chapter.

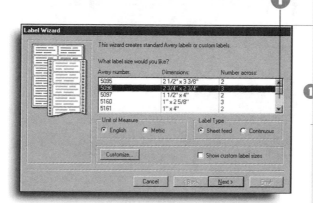

FIGURE 28.1

First you select the label size, unit of measure, and label type.

1 Scroll through to find all the labels supported

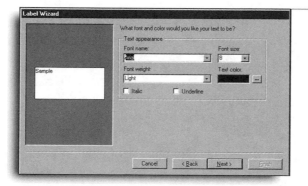

FIGURE 28.2

The second wizard window allows you to specify formats.

You'll select the addressee for the first field; in this case that's the CompanyName field. You can double-click the field selection or click the **>** button to move it to the label template. Press Enter to go to the next line. Then select the address or remaining fields, and press Enter to move to following lines. Be sure to insert a comma and a space where appropriate. (The addressee's country is also included.) Once you've added all the necessary fields, click **Next** to continue.

6. The following window asks you to specify a sort field for your report. This step isn't necessary, but as you can see in Figure 28.4, you're sorting by the PostalCode field (ZIP code). This can speed up sorting if you're following postal regulations to take advantage of reduced postage. Click **Next** to continue.

Finding compatible labels

Access supports several types of Avery labels. You can run this wizard in advance to see which label styles are supported before making your purchase. Use the scrollbars to see all the types, and click **Cancel** after you've gotten the label information.

FIGURE 28.3

You must select the fields you want to appear on each label, in the order they should appear.

1 Access automatically inserts the curly braces {} as field indicators

2 To remove a field, highlight it and press Delete

3 Use commas and spaces to separate multiple fields on a line

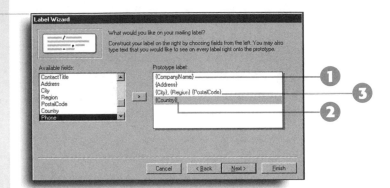

FIGURE 28.4

The wizard will sort your labels by the field you specify.

1 Sort by any field, even if it is not included in the label

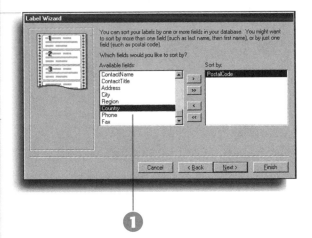

Options for selecting fields

You can include as many fields as you like in your label template—just keep the measurements of the label in mind. Alternatively, if you selected a label type in the dialog shown in Figure 28.1, such as a label that is 4″ x 6″, you can continue adding fields on a single line. The wizard's prototype label viewing area will scroll over as you add additional fields to the right. Access will warn you if you're going too far when you try to click **Next**.

7. The final window, shown in Figure 28.5, prompts you for a report name. You can use the wizard's default or enter a new one. In this example it's rptCustomerLabels. You can also choose whether to view the report in Design view or Print Preview. Choose the **See the Labels as They Will Look Printed** option, which will open the label report in Print Preview. After you've made the appropriate selections, click **Finish** to see the completed report, shown in Figure 28.6. Click the Zoom button 🔍 to get a closer look at the screen, as shown in Figure 28.7.

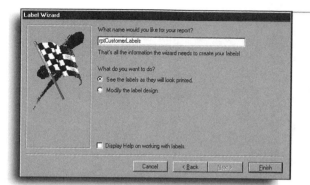

FIGURE 28.5

The last window prompts you for a report name and allows you to specify Design or Print Preview.

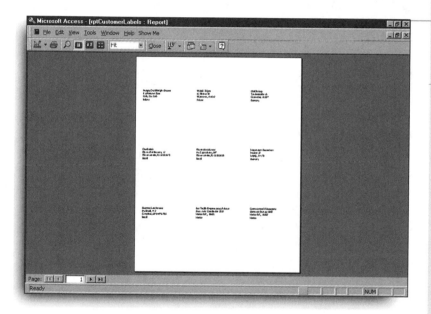

FIGURE 28.6

Here's your completed label report in Print Preview.

8. Once you're satisfied with the report, you can print your labels. Be sure to insert your label sheets in the appropriate printer tray, and then click the Print button 🖨 on the Print Preview toolbar or choose **Print** from the **File** menu.

Sorting labels

Any type of label can also be sorted for your convenience by fields that you don't even include in the label itself. For example, if you don't want to include the Country field in an address label but you still want all the labels grouped by country, you can omit the Country field on the label but select the Country field in the Sort by pane.

Using Custom Labels

Basing a label report is straightforward and simple as long as you're using a standard label size. If this isn't possible, you'll need to customize your report. Although this process takes a little more time, it's easy. You'll need to know some precise measurements before you start:

- Label width
- Label depth
- Top, bottom, left, and right margin
- Space between each label column, sometimes referred to as the gutter or ditch

Using custom labels

1. Select the table in the Database window, select Report 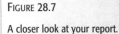 from the drop-down list of the New Object button 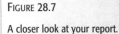, and then double-click **Label Wizard** in the New Reports dialog box.

2. In the first window, click the **Customize** button to display the New Label Size dialog box, shown in Figure 28.8.

Printing tips

If it's too difficult to tell label dimensions from Print Preview, try printing only one page of the report on a set of labels to see if the information fits.

Use the **Print** command from the **File** menu to print by page rather than using the Print icon, which will print all pages.

The example for this task

If you want to follow along, the figures in this task use the Customers table from Northwind.

If you had any custom label reports, which you don't as yet, Access would display them in the list box. When you do have a custom report, you can click **Edit** to modify the report or **Delete** to remove it. You're creating a new report, so do neither. However, be sure to modify the Unit of Measure and Label Type options before continuing, if necessary.

3. Now click **New** to display the New Label dialog box, shown in Figure 28.9. Enter an appropriate name in the Label Name text box. Then choose an Orientation setting and specify the number of columns each sheet has.

4. In the bottom section of this window, you must enter the precise measurements for each of the specified areas. Just highlight the 0.00 setting and enter the appropriate measurement. Figure 28.10 shows your custom measurements.

5. Once you've entered all the measurements, click **OK** to continue. Then click **Close** to return to the wizard's first window, which will display your custom label report in the list box. Click **Next** to continue.

6. At this point, repeat steps 5 through 8 of the previous exercise to complete the label template. The finished label report is shown in Figure 28.11.

If you're not satisfied with the layout

If you don't like the way the labels look in Print Preview, you have two options:

You can click the Design View icon and adjust the fields in the template that appears in the report's design.

You can close Print Preview (eventually delete the report from the Database window) and start the wizard over, making your corrections.

Although the latter seems redundant, it is often easier to let the wizard do the work for you than to try to manipulate or add fields in Design view.

You might print one sheet of incorrect labels onto plain paper and pencil in your changes for reference as you rerun the wizard.

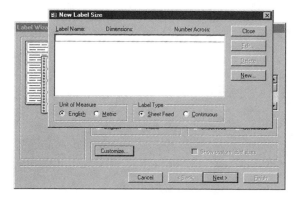

FIGURE 28.8

You're going to base a label report on a custom-sized label.

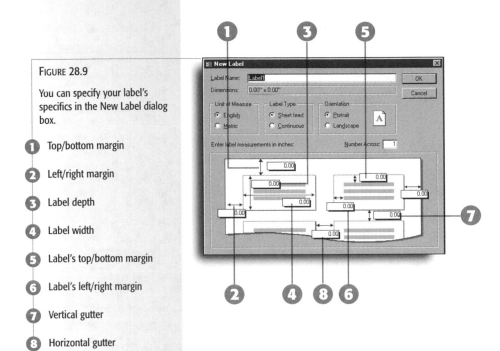

FIGURE 28.9

You can specify your label's specifics in the New Label dialog box.

1 Top/bottom margin

2 Left/right margin

3 Label depth

4 Label width

5 Label's top/bottom margin

6 Label's left/right margin

7 Vertical gutter

8 Horizontal gutter

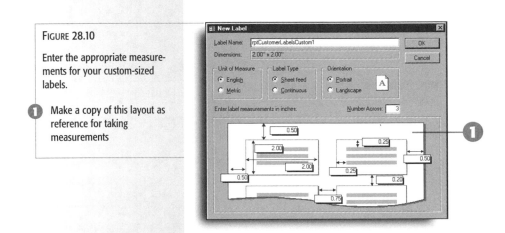

FIGURE 28.10

Enter the appropriate measurements for your custom-sized labels.

1 Make a copy of this layout as reference for taking measurements

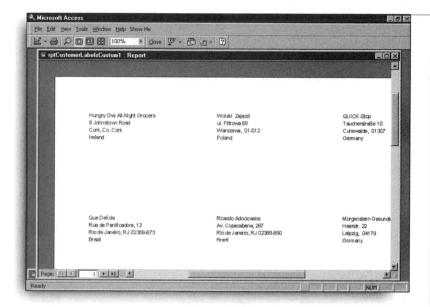

FIGURE 28.11
Custom measurements were used to create this label report.

Printing Multiple Labels

As long as you need to print just one label for each record, the Label Wizard should meet that need. But what if you want to print more than one label for one or more of your records? The solution is a combination of objects: two tables, one query, and your label report. One of the tables will contain your address information and the number of labels you want to print for each addressee (or record). The second table will contain a list of consecutive numbers, from 1 to x, where x equals the maximum number of labels you may ever need to print. Of course, you can change x any time you like by adding to or deleting from this table.

Printing multiple labels

1. Make sure you have a table that contains complete address information. (It can contain additional data as well—simply ignore it.) Open this table in Design view and add a Number field named LabelCount.

Copying the label layout for reference

Because of the number of dimensions used, you might want to print out the layout from this screen (from either Figure 28.9 or 28.10) to use as a reference for all the measurements you need for custom labels. With the wizard open to this screen, press Print Screen on your keyboard. Your computer probably won't print automatically, but pressing Print Screen puts a copy of the screen onto the Windows Clipboard. Open any image program, such as Paintbrush, to a new document. Press Ctrl+V (the Paste key combination), and Windows will paste this screen image into the Paintbrush document. You can print it from there.

This example

In this example, you'll add this label printing utility to the Northwind database. In addition, you'll rely on the Employees table because it already contains address data. You can use any database you like, but just remember that you need a table with address information or any other information for which you want duplicate labels.

2. In Datasheet view, add the appropriate value to each record. In other words, if you want to print two labels for Nancy Davolio, enter the value 2 in the corresponding LabelCount field, as shown in Figure 28.12. You can update this value any time you need more or less labels.

3. Next, create a one-field table named tblLabel. Name the lone Number field Label. In Datasheet view, enter a list of consecutive values.

Create a list from 1 to 5, as shown in Figure 28.13, because in this case you don't anticipate ever needing more than five labels at a time. Your list should reflect your needs—make sure it includes all the values, up to and including the largest value you entered into the address table in the LabelCount field.

FIGURE 28.12

The LabelCount value determines how many labels Access will print for each person in the Employees table.

1 Create multiple labels or no labels by entering the number of labels or the value 0 in this field

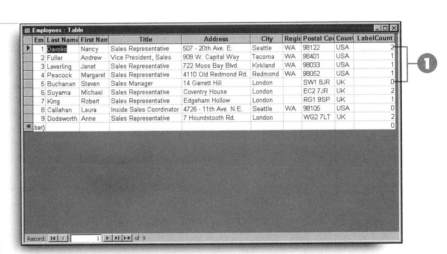

4. Now create a query similar to the one shown in Figure 28.14. Be sure to base this query on your address table—Employees, in this example. Add all of the appropriate address information to the QBE grid. Then add LabelCount from your address table.

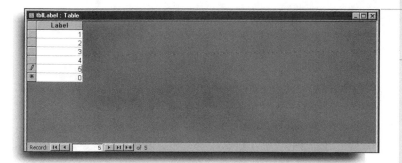

FIGURE 28.13
A list of values from 1 to 5.

5. You'll also need to add tblLabel to the QBE grid. Click the Show Table button on the Query Design toolbar, double-click **tblLabel** in the resulting Show Table dialog box, and then click **Close**.

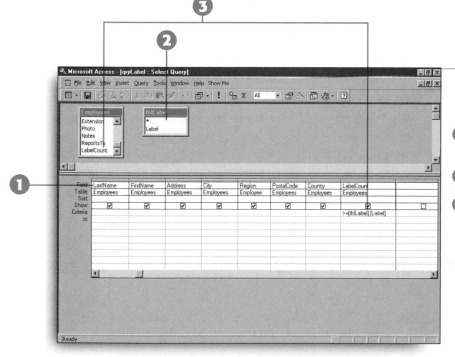

FIGURE 28.14

Your label report will be based on this query.

1. List all the fields you want on the label here

2. Add the Label table

3. One of the consecutive values in tblLabel should match the value you insert in the LabelCount field

6. Next, enter the expression `">=[tblLabel].[Label]"` into the LabelCount field's Criteria cell.

This expression will return one record for each requested label—the corresponding value in your address table. Specifically, the expression will match each record's LabelCount value to the list of consecutive values in tblLabel. When a match is found, the query will display one record for that match. Furthermore, Access will display an additional record for every value in tblLabel that is less than the one you matched.

Be sure to save your query—this one is saved as **qryLabel**.

7. Now let's build the label report. Select the query—**qryLabel**—in the Database window, select Report from the drop-down list of the New Object button, and then double-click **Label Wizard**.

SEE ALSO

➤ *For instructions on using the Label Wizard, check the earlier sections of this chapter.*

8. In the wizard's first window, select the appropriate options and click **Next** to continue. This example uses **5260**, **English**, and **Sheet Feed**.

9. At this point you can change the font formats if you like. Click **Next**.

10. In the third window, add the appropriate fields to the label template in the appropriate order (refer to Figure 28.3). When you're satisfied with the label's structure, click **Next** to continue.

Remember, you don't need to add the LabelCount field to the label itself. Its function should be invisible.

11. In the following window you can choose a sort order for your labels, but not in this example. Click **Next** to continue.

12. In the final window, name your label report rptLabel and click **Finish**. Figure 28.15 shows the resulting report in Print Preview.

FIGURE 28.15
The wizard displays the label report in Print Preview.

As you can see, the number of labels for each employee matches their corresponding value in the LabelCount field of the Employees table. All you have to do is load your label sheets and print the report. Notice also that a few employees don't have any labels—that's because you entered 0 in their respective LabelCount fields.

PART

V

Automating the Database

Creating Macros

When to Use Macros

Because the macros in Access can do just about anything you can do with the mouse or the keyboard, you can use macros just about anytime. The best way to start out designing macros is to find a process that you do in your database over and over, whether it's a daily process or a weekly process. For example, you get a comma-delimited text file from an outside party on a weekly basis, and you have to put the file into your database in a particular table. This is a job for macros.

Let's do a walkthrough of how you would approach this problem. First, lay out and define what you need to do with your macro. It must take a comma-delimited file that is in a directory and append the imported data to the end of a table in your database. In the list of macro actions at the end of this chapter, there's a macro action called TransferText. This macro action allows you to import from a comma-delimited text file and append the data onto the table that you specify. When set up properly, this one macro action completely fulfills your needs.

Another example of actions you can take is renaming database objects. For example, instead of the preceding example appending to the table as specified, say you just wanted the data that was new in your table, but didn't want to lose the current copy. You could rename the table using the Rename action, do a TransferDatabase, copying just the structure of the table, and then do the TransferText action as specified above.

Because so many macro actions mimic VBA functions and subroutines, when you are ready to move on to VBA, you will be that much further ahead than someone who refuses to learn macro actions. VBA can intimidate most people, but if you are familiar with the macro actions in Access, using VBA will not seem that hard when it comes to the point where you haven't found a way to do your programming in macros.

SEE ALSO

➤ *When you're ready to start using VBA, refer to page 544 for the first of several chapters on this subject.*

The Macro Design Window

Once you understand the different areas, the use of the Macro Design window is pretty straightforward. You'll be using the Macro Design window to create and then edit the macros needed to further enhance your application. There are several ways to get to the Macro Design window.

One way is to create a macro, which will take you to the Macro Design window.

Opening the Macro Design Window

1. To create a new macro, click on the **Macros** tab in the Database window and then select **New**, as shown in Figure 29.1.

   or

   Click the dropdown list for the New Object button on the toolbar and select Macro ▨.

FIGURE 29.1
Select the **Macros** tab to see if an existing database, such as Northwind, has any macros. Then select **New** to open a new macro.

The Macro design window will then give you a blank sheet for your new macros. Once you have opened the Macro Design window, you should see a window that is similar to the one shown in Figure 29.2.

If you want to go back later and edit a macro, this also follows the logical steps.

Editing a Macro

1. With the Database Window open, select the macro in the **Macros** tab.

2. Click **Design** to open the Macro Design window with the macro open.

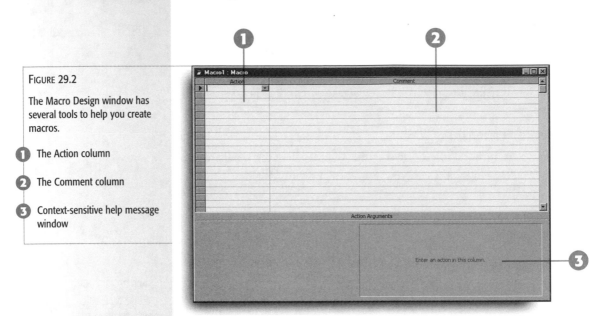

FIGURE 29.2

The Macro Design window has
several tools to help you create
macros.

1 The Action column

2 The Comment column

3 Context-sensitive help message
window

Exploring the Macro Design Window

As shown in Figure 29.2, the Macro Design window in its simplest form shows a screen with a similar look and feel to the other Design view grids. Two other areas not shown here, the Names column and the Conditions column, are for more complex macros that will be discussed later in this chapter.

The first area in the Macro Design window is the Action column. This is where you will tell Access what actions to take in your macros. To add the name of an action that you want to perform as part of your macro, click on the arrow that points down. This is the dropdown list that contains all the actions that are available to use. There are over 50 actions that are available to pick from, with several actions that allow additional sub-actions. For example, the RunCommand action has over 300 additional sub-actions.

The second area in the Macro Design window is the Comment column. This is where you enter the comments for the particular action. You should always use the comment column so that when you come back to edit the macro, you will remember what the macro does. You don't have to put a comment in every line of the macro, unless you are forgetful like me. If you have to edit the macro six months from now, you will thank yourself many times if you have commented it.

Also seen in Figure 29.2, the third area, at the bottom right, is a context-sensitive help message window. This message changes depending on the action picked in the Action column. The help message also gives you hints on the arguments of a particular action. If you need more help than what is provided in the short message, you can press the F1 key and Access will give you a help window that goes into more detail for that particular action and its arguments.

Another area of the Macro Design window is the Arguments area. To see the Arguments area, you need to pick an action in the Action column. To do so, create a simple macro that presents a message box to the user.

Create a message box

1. In the first line of the Action column, click on the dropdown arrow. From the list, select **Msgbox**. See Figure 29.3.

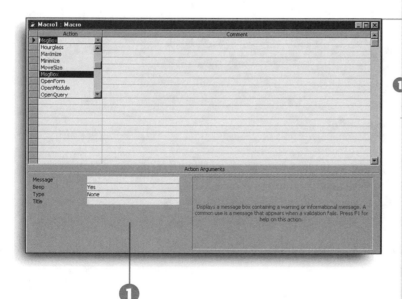

Commenting macros

You're allowed 255 characters in a macro comment. You can extend comments over several lines by indenting subsequent lines. You should include such things as the intent, the affected tables, queries, and so on. You might also include other databases where you also use this macro so that you can change all the macros if needed.

FIGURE 29.3

Select the Macro action from the dropdown list.

1 The Arguments area appears when you select an action

Why so many arguments?

Although the term *argument* has a negative connotation in conversations between humans, it's not a negative term in programming macros. Arguments are descriptive terms you add to an action to tell it specifically what to do, when or where to perform the action, and on which objects. In simple terms, if your action is "to jump," you'd specify arguments such as "the frog," "height," "distance," and "direction."

Arguments also take a certain form, or *syntax*, similar to the way sentences are arranged in a certain order. However, with macros, you enter arguments visually in fields and Access writes the syntax for you.

When you select **Msgbox**, the Arguments area displays four places to put arguments for Msgbox action. The four arguments are Message, Beep, Type, and Title.

2. Place your message in the message argument. You can put any text in this argument, such as "Happy 4th of July!"

3. Turn the annoying beep on or off, according to your preference, by either typing "Yes" or "No" or by selecting from the dropdown list.

4. Select which built-in icon will be displayed next to the message in the Type argument. I usually select **Information** or **Warning?**, and rarely select **Critical**.

5. Place the title of the message box, such as **Reminder,** in the **Title** argument area. This appears in the title bar of the message box.

6. Save your macro by either clicking on the Save icon ![save icon], using the **File** menu's **Save** option, or using the keyboard shortcut, Ctrl+S. See Figure 29.4. Use a logical filename, such as mcrReminder, so you can readily recognize its purpose by name.

FIGURE 29.4

Enter a name to save your macro to.

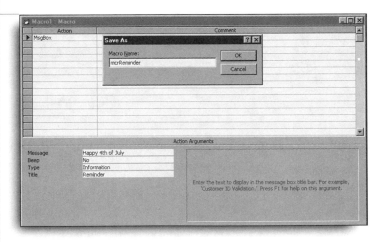

7. Run your macro. This can be accomplished in the Macro Design window by either clicking on the Run icon  or using the **Run** command from the **Run** menu.

If you followed along with the preceding steps, you should see the standard MsgBox form with your options in it. See Figure 29.5.

Generating Multiple Macros

In this simple example, you only are executing one action. What do you need to do if you want to execute multiple actions in a row? In Access you can define multiple actions that execute one right after the other. When you are working with macros in forms and reports, you'll see where being able to specify multiple actions comes in handy.

SEE ALSO

➤ *For information on using macros in forms and reports, go to page 524.*

Now that you are a little more familiar with the basic Macro Design window, let's move on to something a little harder than a "Happy 4th of July!" message box.

Macro Conditions

The Conditions column is an as yet hidden section of the Macro Design window. You can unhide the Conditions column by either clicking the Condition icon ⚟ or using the **View, Conditions** menu.

You will use the Conditions column in the more complex macros that you create. To make your example macro more complex, you need to do a little more work. You want to create a macro that does more than just blindly present a message box when the macro is run. In my example, displaying "Happy 4th of July!" is

Using the selection option in arguments

Similar to options in the Field properties Design view, you can click at the right end of the argument space to reveal a dropdown box that shows options that are available for that field. Also notice that as you fill in the arguments, the help area gives you hints particular to that argument.

okay around July 4th, but doesn't make any sense around December 25th. So what you need to do is limit the time that your message box is shown. The Conditions column allows you to do just that.

Create a condition

1. If you saved your macro that you created previously in this chapter, all you have to do is edit this macro. If you didn't save it, run through steps 1–6 in the previous step-by-step example.

2. Make sure that the Conditions column is displayed. If it is not, you can display it by either clicking the Condition icon 🔁 or using the **View, Conditions** menu.

3. In the Conditions column, on the same line as your Msgbox action, type Date()>#6/30# And Date()<=#7/4#. You do not have to type in the year because Access will do that for you. Refer to Figure 29.6 for placement.

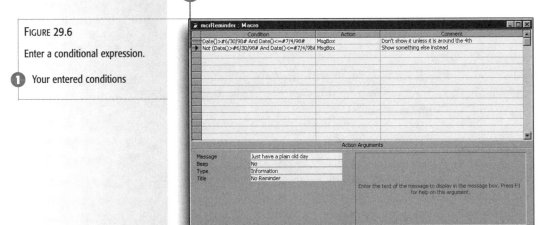

FIGURE 29.6

Enter a conditional expression.

1 Your entered conditions

4. Now run the macro either by clicking on the Run icon 🔲 or using the **Run, Run** menu.

SEE ALSO
➤ *If you're not sure of the meaning of this expression, see page 273 for information and practice with using expressions.*

If you ran your macro and nothing happened, that must mean that the current date is not between June 30th and July 5th. And if nothing happened, how do you know that the macro actually ran? You can turn the condition around and then create another Msgbox action.

Create another condition to test a macro

1. On the row following the condition that you created in the preceding step 3, copy what you typed in that condition, except with the condition in parentheses, and type Not in front of it. Your condition should look like this: Not (Date()>#6/30# And Date()<=#7/4#).

2. In the Actions column, on the second row, select Msgbox.

3. In the Message argument, put a message that will indicate the opposite effect, such as Have a plain old day. Your macro should now look like Figure 29.7.

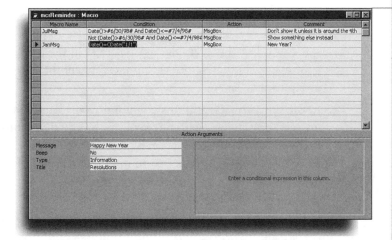

FIGURE 29.7
The completed macro.

4. Save your macro and then run it. You should now see a message box similar to Figure 29.8.

FIGURE 29.8
The result of running your macro.

To help you build complex expressions, you can use the Expression Builder by right-clicking on the Action column or by clicking the Builder icon ⬚ on the toolbar.

Macros Groups

Yet another section of the Macro Design window is the Names column. It's hidden by default, just like the Conditions column, so you will have to unhide it by either clicking the Macro Name icon ⬚ or using the **View, Macro Names** menu. You will need to use the Names column whenever you want to make management of macros easier. By specifying a name in the Names column of the first row, your macro is now considered a macro group. You can now make different groups in the same macro. You could expand the previous example and not only check if it is around the 4th of July, but also what the current date was the first of the year.

Making macro groups

1. In the first row of your macro, in the Names column, enter some text. For this example, use JulMsg. On the third row of your macro, in the Names column, create another macro group named JanMsg.

2. In the third-row Conditions column of your macro, put in my test for the new year. The syntax is a little different in that you want to check for a certain day of the year without worrying about what year it is run in. The syntax is: Date()=CDate("1/1"). This checks for the first day of the year, no matter what year it is.

3. In the third-row Actions column, specify another MsgBox that wishes the user a Happy New Year. When you are done, your macro should look similar to Figure 29.9.

Now when you run your macro, you may not notice it, but the only macro group that is executed is the first one. Well, how do you run the second macro group the same way you ran the first one? The answer is simple: You don't. If you have more than one macro group in a macro, the way to run the other macro groups is to either use a RunMacro action or use the **Run Macro** from the **Tools**, **Macro** menu. Then you can specify which macro group you want to run. You can see how you would execute the other macro groups by selecting the RunMacro action. In the Macro Name argument, you can now see your other macro groups. See Figure 29.9 for example macro groups.

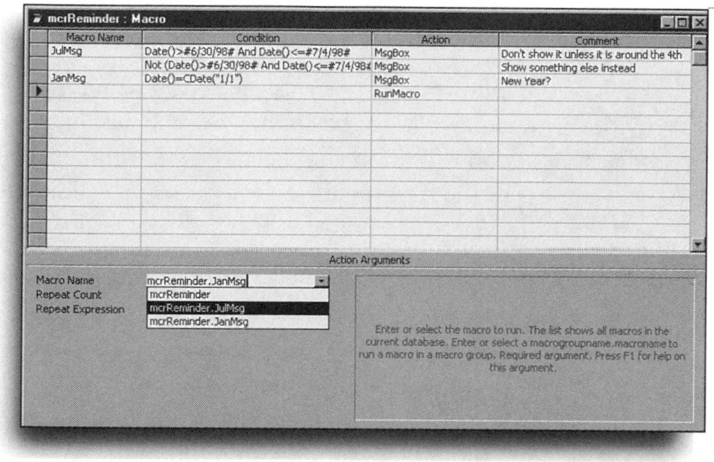

FIGURE 29.9

The completed macro with group names.

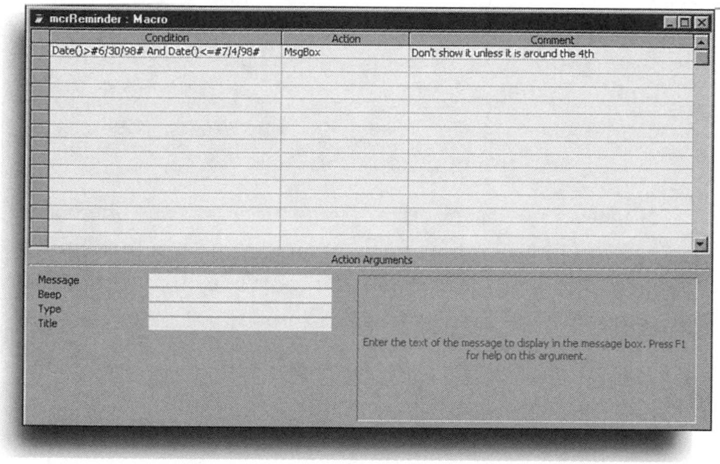

FIGURE 29.10

Use the RunMacro command to run a specific group in a macro.

When you are programming multiple macros for your forms and reports, being able to group macros will help you manage them. If Access didn't have macro groups, you would have to create one macro object for each set of actions that you wanted. With the macro groups, you can have all the actions that relate to a form or a report in one macro.

SEE ALSO

➤ *For information on using macros in forms and reports, go to page 524.*

Macro Actions and Their Arguments

As noted earlier in the chapter, there are over 50 macro actions that you can use. The following section summarizes the categories of these 50 actions.

Each of the following entries lists the action name first, followed by the arguments that can be applied to each action to specify what that action will do to an object. These arguments automatically appear in the Arguments sections as soon as you select the action in the Macro Design window. The rest of the description shows you what each action will do.

SEE ALSO

➤ *The next few pages will come into use on page 524 as you learn to automate more objects with macro actions.*

Opening, Closing, and Printing Database Objects

OpenForm—Form name, View, Filter, Where, Data Mode, Window Mode. The OpenForm action opens a form in Form view, Design view, Print Preview, or Datasheet view. The form's records can be limited by filling in the Filter or Where argument. The Data Mode can be Add, Edit, and Read Only. The Window Mode can be Normal, Hidden, Icon (minimized), or Dialog.

OpenReport—Report name, View, Filter, Where. The OpenReport action opens a report in Print view (prints immediately), Design view, and Print Preview. The report's records can be limited by filling in the Filter or Where argument.

OpenTable, OpenQuery—Table name, View, Data Mode. The OpenTable and OpenQuery actions open a table or query in Datasheet view, Design view and Print Preview. The Data Mode can be Add, Edit, and Read Only.

OpenModule—Module name, Procedure. OpenModule opens a VBA module. If you specify a procedure, the module will be opened at that procedure. The procedure can be the name of a function or a sub.

SEE ALSO

➤ *The VBA module is explained on page 547.*

Close—Object Type, Object Name, Save. The Close action closes the database object specified in the Object Name. The type of database object can be one of the following: Table, Query, Form, Report, Macro, or Module. Notice that while you can close a Macro object, there isn't a corresponding OpenMacro. Depending on what you put in the Save argument, the database object can be saved with Yes, changes can be discarded with No, and you can be prompted whether changes are saved with Prompt.

PrintOut—Print Range, Page From, Page To, Print Quality, Copies, Collate Copies. The PrintOut action sends the active database object to the printer. Only Datasheets, Forms, Reports, or Modules can be sent to the printer. By specifying All, Selection, or Pages in the Print Range argument, you can print all of the object, part of it, or just certain pages. If you specify Pages in the Print Range argument, it will print, starting at the page you specify in the Page From argument and stopping at the page that you specify in the Page To argument. The Page To and Page From arguments are required if you specify Pages in the Print Range argument. The Print Quality argument accepts High, Medium, Low, and Draft. If you want more than one copy, you can specify how many in the Print Copies argument.

Saving, Deleting, Copying, and Renaming Database Objects

SelectObject—Object Type, Object Name, Database Window. The SelectObject action selects (makes active) the database object specified in the Object Name argument. The type of database object can be one of the following: Table, Query, Form, Report, Macro, or Module. The Database Window argument accepts a Yes or No. Specifying Yes indicates that the SelectObject action needs to look in the database window for the object, as opposed to an object that is already opened.

Save—Object Type, Object Name. The Save action saves the database object specified in the Object Name. The type of database object can be one of the following: Table, Query, Form, Report, Macro, or Module. If you leave both arguments blank, the Save action will save the active database object.

DeleteObject—Object Type, Object Name. The DeleteObject action deletes the database object that you specify in the Object Name argument. The type of database object that can be specified in the Object Type can be one of the following: Table, Query, Form, Report, Macro, or Module. If you leave both the Object Type and the Object Name blank, the DeleteObject action will delete the database object that is selected in the database window.

CopyObject—Database Name, New Name, Source Object Type, Source Object Name. The CopyObject action makes a duplicate of the database object that you specify in Source Object Name. If you leave Source Object Name blank, the CopyObject action copies the active object. If you provide a path to another database in the Database Name argument, the CopyObject action will put the copied object in that database. If you leave the Database Name argument blank, the database object is copied to the current database. The new name of the copied object is what you specified in the New Name argument. To keep the same name of the database object when copying it to a different database, you can leave the New Name blank. The Source Type can be one of the following: Table, Query, Form, Report, Macro, or Module. If both the Source Object Type and Source Object Name are left blank, the active database object in the database window is copied when the CopyObject action is executed.

Rename—New Name, Object Type, Old Name. The Rename action renames the database object specified in the Old Name argument to the name specified in the New Name argument. The New Name is required, but if you leave both Object Type and Old Name blank, the active database object is renamed.

Execution and Action Flow

RunCommand—Command. The RunCommand action executes any one of the 300 or more commands available on the standard Access menu. See the Access help file for more information.

RunCode—Function Name. The RunCode action executes any built-in or user-defined functions.

RunMacro—Macro Name, Repeat Count, Repeat Expression. The RunMacro action executes any macro that you specify in the Macro

Name argument. The Repeat Count argument specifies how many times to repeat the execution. If the Repeat Expression argument evaluates to false, the macro is stopped.

StopMacro—No arguments. The StopMacro action stops the currently running macro.

StopAllMacros—No arguments. The StopAllMacros action stops all running macros.

CancelEvent—No arguments. The CancelEvent action cancels the event that called the currently running macro.

Quit—Options. The Quit action quits Access. You can specify whether to save all changed database objects (Save All), prompt the user whether or not to save changed database objects, or just exit without saving.

RunSQL—SQL Statement, Use Transaction. The RunSQL action runs the specified action query in the SQL Statement argument. The SQL Statement argument is limited to 255 characters. If you specify Use Transaction, the whole action query is treated as one transaction.

RunApp—Command line. The RunApp action executes the command given in the Command Line argument. This allows you to run other programs, like Microsoft Word.

Navigation, Exporting, Importing, Modifying of Data

SetValue—Item, Expression. The SetValue action sets a field, control, or property to the expression that is put in the Expression argument.

GoToControl—Control Name. The GoToControl action moves the focus to the control name that you specify in the Control Name arguments.

GoToPage—Page Number, Right, Down. The GotoPage action move the focus to the page number that you specify in the Page Number arguments only if you have entered page breaks for the form or report of note.

FindRecord—Find What, Match, Match Case, Search, Search As Formatted, Only Current Field, Find First. The FindRecord action searches through the current form for the text that you specify in the Find What argument. The Match argument can be the Match Whole Field, Any Part of Field, or Start of Field. The Match Case argument causes the FindRecord action to match the particular case of the text in the Find What argument. The Search argument tells the FindRecord action which way to go when it begins searching. The options for the Search argument are Up, Down, and All. The Search as Formatted argument tells the FindRecord action to search for text that is formatted the same as the text in the Find What argument. The Only Current Field argument tells the FindRecord argument to only search in the field that the focus is currently on. The Find First argument tells the FindRecord action to begin searching at the current record (No), or from the first record (Yes). The FindRecord action mimics the functionality of the Access Find dialog box.

FindNext—No arguments. The FindNext action finds the next record that matches the criteria specified at the last FindRecord action.

GoToRecord—Object Type, Object Name, Record, Offset. The GoToRecord action navigates to a record on the Form, Query, or Table that you specify in Object Name. The Record argument can be one of the following: Next, Previous, New, Go To, First, or Last. The Offset argument specifies how many records to move up or down. The Offset argument affects Next, Previous, and Go To.

ApplyFilter—Filter Name, Where Condition. The ApplyFilter action applies the filter specified in the Filter Name or Where Condition argument.

OutputTo—Object Type, Object Name, Output Format, Output File, Auto Start, Template File. The OutputTo action exports the database object that you specified in the Object Name to the format specified in the Output Format argument. The Auto Start argument tells the OutputTo action whether or not to start up the corresponding application.

SendObject—Object Type, Object Name, Output Format, To, CC, Bcc, Subject, Message Text, Edit Message, Template File. The SendObject action sends the database object, as specified in the

Object Name, to email. The Output Format can be one of the following: *.html, *.xls, *.txt or *.rtf. The To, CC, and Bcc arguments allow you to send the email to whomever it is addressed to. The Subject argument is the subject of the email message. The Edit Message argument, if set to Yes, allows you to edit the message before it is sent to your mail system.

TransferDatabase—Transfer Type, Database Type, Database Name, Object Type, Source, Destination, Structure Only. The TransferDatabase action allows you to import database objects from another database to the current one, export database objects from the current database to another one, or link a table from another database to the current one. The Database Type argument allows you to specify what database you are importing from or exporting to. The databases listed depend on what you installed when Access was installed. The Object Type argument is a database object. The Source argument is name of the database object that is being acted upon by the TransferDatabase action. The Destination argument is the name of the database object that is the result of the action that the TransferDatabse action has taken.

TransferSpreadsheet—Transfer Type, Spreadsheet Type, Table Name, File Name, Has Field Names, Range. The TransferSpreadsheet action allows you to import database objects from a spreadsheet, export database objects to a spreadsheet, or link to a spreadsheet. The Spreadsheet Type argument allows you to specify what spreadsheets you are importing from, exporting to, or linking to. The spreadsheets that are listed depend on what you installed when you installed Access. The Table Name argument is the database object name that is acted upon when you do an import, export, or link to. The File Name argument is the full path of the spreadsheet. The Has Field Names argument tells the TransferSpreadsheet action whether the first row of data is the field names. The Range argument is the spreadsheet range that is being acted upon.

TransferText—Transfer Type, Specification Name, Table Name, File Name, Has Field Names, HTML Table Name. The TransferText action allows you to import data from, export data to, or link to data in delimited or fixed-width text files. Specification Name is the name of a saved specification in the database. The `Table Name` argument allows you to specify the name of the table that you will export to, import from, or link to. The `File Name` argument is the path of the file that you are exporting to, importing from, or linking to. The `Has Field Names` tells the `TransferText` action whether or not the first row of data is the field names.

Controlling Display

`Maximize`—No arguments. The `Maximize` action maximizes the active window.

`Minimize`—No arguments. The `Minimize` action minimizes the active window.

`MoveSize`—`Right`, `Down`, `Width`, `Height`. The `MoveSize` action positions the active window according to the right and down arguments, and sizes the window according to the `Width` and `Height` arguments.

`Restore`—No arguments. The `Restore` action restores a minimized or maximized active window to its previous size.

`RepaintObject`—`Object Type`, `Object Name`. The `RepaintObject` action refreshes the display of the database object specified in the `Object Name`. The type of database object can be one of the following: `Table`, `Query`, `Form`, `Report`, `Macro`, or `Module`. If you leave both arguments blank, the `RepaintObject` action will refresh the display of the active database object.

`Echo`—`Echo On`, `Status Bar Text`. The `Echo` action turns on or off the display of the results until the macro is finished. The `Status Bar Text` argument is the text to display in the status bar while the `Echo` is off.

`Hourglass`—`Hourglass`. The `Hourglass` action turns on or off the display of the hourglass cursor to indicate to a user that an action is running.

`SetWarnings`—`Warnings On`. The `SetWarnings` action turns on or off the display of system messages that would otherwise stop the running of a macro. `Warnings On` if set to Yes, has the same effect as the user pressing Enter to clear the system message boxes.

Beep—No arguments. The Beep action sounds a tone on the computer to alert the user. Everyone should at least try the Beep action one time.

MsgBox—Message, Beep, Type, Title. The Msgbox action presents a message box to alert and inform the user. The Message argument is the text that is displayed to the user. The Beep argument sounds a tone. The Type argument allows the display of built-in icons that can be displayed to the left of the text in the message box. The Title argument is the text of the title bar caption of the message box.

ShowToolBar—ToolBar Name, Show. The ShowToolBar action shows or hides a built-in or custom toolbar specified in the ToolBar Name argument. The Show argument can be set to Yes or No.

ShowAllRecords—No arguments. The ShowAllRecords action removes any filter from a table, query, form, or report, and displays all records in the underlying recordset.

Requery—Control Name. The Requery action forces a requery or recalculation of the control specified in the Control Name argument.

Running Macros

Methods Used to Run Macros

Creating macros is a good way to reduce the number of manual tasks that you have to perform in your database. Knowing where and how to run your newly created macros is even better.

After you've created and saved the macro, there are several ways to run it or execute it. The first three or four ways don't require a lot of detail because those ways entail running the macro using the interfaces that are built in to Access without doing anything extra on your part. The methods used to run macros that require a little extra effort on your part are discussed later in this chapter.

Manually Running Macros

The first method used to run your macro uses the standard interface that Access provides to all macros.

Run a macro from the Database window

1. In the Database window, select the **Macro** tab if it is not already selected.

2. Select the macro that contains the actions that you want to run. Your database window should look similar to Figure 30.1.

FIGURE 30.1

Running a macro from this window is fine for testing, but if you hide the Database window in your application, you'll have to create another means of running the macro.

1 The Database window is the fastest way to run a macro

2 Right-click the macro name for the pop-up menu in Figure 30.2

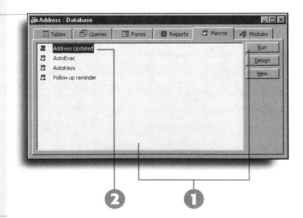

3. Click the **Run** button. Your macro actions will be executed.

This method should probably be used for macros that need to be run infrequently, like a monthly import macro.

Even though it doesn't make sense to run some macros from the Database window, all macros that you create can be run from here. As in the case of macros that contain groups, only the first macro group's actions will be executed. Macro groups other than the first one will be ignored if run from the Database window. Later in this chapter you will create macros that will not make sense to run them from the Database window. These macros most likely will either not run correctly or not run at all because they may rely on a particular database object to be open.

Another way to run macros from the Database window is to use the shortcut menu.

Using a shortcut to run a macro

1. With the Database window open to the **Macro** tab, right-click the macro that contains the actions you want to execute.

A shortcut menu will pop up and should look similar to Figure 30.2.

FIGURE 30.2

Use the pop-up menu to select numerous options for your macro—immediately run it, change its properties, and so on.

3. Select **Run** from the pop-up menu.

The way to execute a particular macro group within a macro is to use the menu.

Running a macro from a macro group

1. Using the **Tools** menu, select **Macro, Run Macro** to bring up the Run Macro dialog box.

You should see a dialog box similar to Figure 30.3.

Differences in running macro groups

As noted before, if you have a macro that contains macro groups and you try to run a macro from the Database window in this manner, only the first macro group's actions will be executed; the other groups will be ignored.

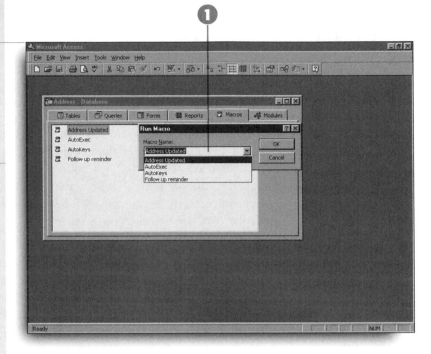

FIGURE 30.3

You need to use the **Tools** menu
to run a macro from a macro
group.

1 Macro name groups require a
different Run dialog box

Finding macro group names

The Run Macro dialog box shows
you all available macros in the
database, with any macro groups
available using the format *macron-
ame.macrogroup*, where *macron-
ame* is the name in the database
window and *macrogroup* is the
particular macro group within that
macro.

2. Select the macro you want to execute by picking from the
drop-down list.

3. After you have selected the macro, click the **OK** button to
execute your macro.

One of the good things about running a macro from the Macro
dialog box is that you don't have to select the macro in the
Database window, nor do you have to navigate to the Macro
window in the database.

Now that you have seen how to execute a macro from Access
standard interfaces, let's move on to methods that automatically
run your macro.

Setting Macros to Run Automatically

Automatically run macros are usually executed in response to
an action that happened in the database. Database actions,
whether user- or application-generated, are called *events*. For

sample purposes, if you click a button, an event (the Click event) is generated. Access enables you to tell the button that you want to execute a certain macro in response to the Click event

You also can tell Access that you want to respond to events that are generated indirectly. These indirect events are usually generated by Access and not directly by the user. An example of this type of event is the Current event.

SEE ALSO

➤ *We'll delve more into events on page 524.*

Command Buttons

As mentioned previously, events are actions generated in the database. The power of Access enables you to tell the database how you want to respond to those events. This is an example of a reaction to a user action. The macro would be executed immediately after the user of the database clicks a command button with the mouse. Using a command button to run a macro is a very powerful way to automate your tasks that you would normally have to do step by step. You can take the steps that you would normally take and translate them into a macro that is run when you click a button on a form.

This macro uses a database generated by the Address Book Wizard.

In our Address Book database, I've noticed that some people aren't being talked to. I really hate it when our staff fails to keep in contact with the contacts in the database. What I've decided is that I need some rules about how long the time interval should be when waiting to contact a person. I have come up with what I think is a good plan to make sure the contacts are contacted. If the contact has not been updated for more than two weeks, the database user will receive a warning message when the macro is run. If he waited for more than 6 months to talk to the contact, I'll give him a notice that he no longer works for the company. First you will set up a macro that does all the work.

You can use events in VBA, too

There are numerous uses for and references to events when you're coding an Access application.

You've probably recognized the use of the Click event from working with forms in Chapter 20. There you started with a control's Property sheet and built code in the Module window.

You can use VBA to respond to events as well.

Creating a notification macro

1. Create a new macro. Show the conditions column by navigating the menu to **View**, **Conditions**.

2. In the first row of the macro design window, at the Conditions column, place the following condition:
```
DateDiff("w",[Forms]![Addresses]![DateLastTalkedTo],
Date())>2 And DateDiff("m",[Forms]![Addresses]!
[DateLastTalkedTo],Date())<6
```

Figuring out the expression

This expression uses a VBA function called `DateDiff`. This function returns the number of intervals between 2 dates. The intervals that are used in your expression are *m* and *w*, which stand for month and weeks respectively.

3. In the Actions column, select Msgbox for the action with arguments similar to the following:
```
Message: This person has not been contacted in over 2
weeks. Please do a follow up.

Beep: No

Type: Warning?

Title: Getting Lazy?
```

4. On the second line of your macro, in the Conditions column, check for a difference of 6 months.
```
DateDiff("m",[Forms]![Addresses]![DateLastTalkedTo],
Date())>=6
```

5. In the Actions column of the second line of your macro, select more Msgbox actions, with the following parameters.
```
Message: Before you go see the boss, clean your desk
out. You're fired! Please tell the boss why you couldn't
talk to this person for more than 6 months.

Beep: No

Type: Warning!

Title: Hasta la vista!
```

6. Save your macro. I named my macro Follow Up Reminder.

If you have previously created the Address Book database using the wizard, you can test your newly created macro. If you have the SwitchBoard form open, click **Create/View Address** to open the Address form. After the Address form is open, navigate to **Tools**, **Run Macro**. Select your newly created macro from the list. Then click the **OK** button. If you used the sample data that the wizard generated for you, you probably have data in the

Date Last Talked To field that is a couple of years old. Because that is more than six months, your macro will display your message box (see Figure 30.4).

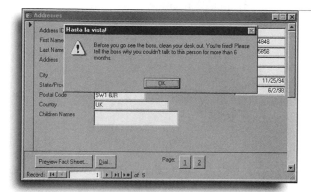

FIGURE 30.4
Because the data in the Northwind database contains older dates, the macro displays the warning box.

If you don't see a message box, there was an error in your conditions. If you don't have the Address form open when you run the macro, you will see a message similar to Figure 30.5.

FIGURE 30.5
You have to have the form you've used open for the macro to run properly. Otherwise, Access generates an error.

If you know that you have the form open and you still have errors, look closely at your conditions. The errors are probably the result of the form name being different than what you put in the conditions columns.

After you know that your macro works, create a command button that uses your macro. When the user clicks the button, your macro will be used to check how long it has been and then take the appropriate action.

Assign your macro to a *Click* event

1. When the form is open, go to Design view by clicking the Design View icon 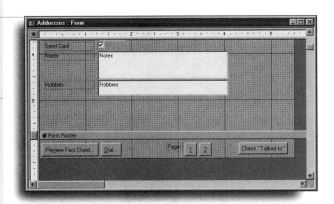, or by navigating the menu to **View, Design View**.

2. On the Toolbox, turn off control wizards by clicking the Control Wizards icon.

3. Again from the Toolbox, select the Command button control.

   If the command button wizard starts because you forgot to turn off the control wizards, you can click the **Cancel** button and you'll be at the correct step.

4. Place the button on the form. See Figure 30.6 for what the form looks like after this step, with the button created in the footer section on the form.

FIGURE 30.6

Place the control on the form first, before attaching a macro to its event.

5. Open the control's Properties sheet. (Select the control and right-click or select the control and then click the Properties icon.)

6. With the Properties window open, you can change any of the command button's properties. Items that you should change right away include the Caption and the Name if you are following any naming convention. For this example, I'll change my caption to Check Talked to and the name to btnTalkedTo.

7. Scroll down in the **All** tab Properties window or select the **Events** tab to reach such properties as On Key Press and On Key Up. These properties are where you can place the name of your macro, to tell Access what to do in case these Events happen.

The one that you are using for this example is the On Click property. Click in the box next to the On Click property. You'll see two buttons to the right of the box:

- One button is a drop-down list of all the macros in the database.

- The other is the Builder button, which leads you to the Expression Builder, the Macro Builder, or the Code Builder window.

Figure 30.7 shows the events and the buttons for entering macros.

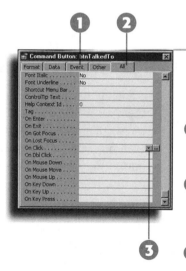

FIGURE 30.7

Add macros to a form or report control by using the property sheet.

1 Use the **Event** tab to cut straight to all the events this control can use

2 Use the **All** tab if you want to change several properties (such as the caption) before scrolling to the events

3 If you've already created and saved a macro, it will appear in the drop-down box for any control in the same database

8. Because you have already created your macro, you can click the down arrow button and find your macro in the list of all available macros to this database.

9. Select the macro that you created in a previous step.

Now when you go back into Form view of your form and click the button that you created, the macro that you assigned to the On Click property will be executed.

If you go back to Design view of your form and select your new button and then go to the properties of the button, you will notice that there are 11 more properties that you can assign macros to. Just by looking at the name, you can notice all the events that an object can have because they start with the prefix On followed by the event name. In this example, you used the On Click property to attach your macro to the Click event of the button. You are telling Access, "If the user clicks that button with the mouse (On Click), perform the action that is attached to that event property."

SEE ALSO

➤ *An explanation of the ! or bang operator as well as other operators and the syntax of code appears in Chapter 32. See page 565.*

➤ *For practice and details on creating complex expressions, see page 273.*

➤ *For information on the controls on the Toolbox, see page 314.*

➤ *For detailed instruction on placing controls on a form, see page 323.*

Form and Report Events

Knowing what events can have macros or VBA code attached to them can be extremely helpful in your design work. Using the events that are available to us, you can automate your application even further. In the last example, you have to push your new button to do the check whenever you navigate to a different record. If you take a couple of minutes to look though all the objects that are on the form, including the form itself, you will notice that there are many possible events that you can attach to.

To make your database more automated, you can identify and attach to several events. First, let's define when you need to run your macro.

One of the problems that you had when the macro was attached to the On Click event of the command button was that whenever you navigated to a different record, you would need to click the button again. Instead of clicking the button every time, it would be even better if Access automatically ran the macro when the user went to a different record. Access allows access to just the form event that you need. One of the events for the form is called On Current. This event property will enable you to attach your macro to it. When this event is generated by Access, your macro will be executed. Following the steps below, your macro will check every record as it is navigated to by the user.

Attaching a macro to the *On Current* event property

1. Go to Design view of the form.

2. Open the Properties window.

3. Scroll the Properties window down to the events. Look for the On Current event property. After you have located the event property in the Property window, click the box next to the text.

4. Click the down arrow of the property box, and select the macro that you want to attach to the On Current event. In your example, select the Follow up reminder macro.

5. Open your form and navigate to different records. Notice that because your macro achieves what you set out to do, you can go back into Design view and delete the command button that was used to run the macro in the first place.

As you put macros to use you will notice tasks in the database that need to be automated. In our Address Book database, I noticed that the Date Updated field has to be manually updated whenever you change the record in any way. What you need to do is write a macro that updates the Date Updated field when you change other fields in that record.

Also in your case you are going to set conditions that keep the macro from changing the Date Updated field if that was the field that triggered the BeforeUpdate event. Use the following steps to create your macro.

When to set updates

When you use a macro that changes the record, be careful of what events you attach your macro to. This example sets the macro to the BeforeUpdate event. If I set the macro to the AfterUpdate event, the macro will keep updating the record.

Updating a record automatically

1. Go to Design view of the Address form.

2. Select the form, and then right-click to bring up the Properties window.

3. Scroll down the Properties window, until you come to the BeforeUpdate event. Click inside the text box next to the BeforeUpdate event.

4. Click the Builder button ![icon]. This will open a Choose Builder dialog box. Select **Macro Builder** from the list.

5. The first thing you'll be asked to do is save the macro. If you want to add your macro to an existing macro as a group, go back to step 4 and click to select your macro.

6. Show the Conditions column by clicking on the Condition icon ![icon] on the toolbar.

7. In the first row of the macro (or on the same row as your name if you are using groups) in the Conditions column, put the following condition:
   ```
   [Forms]![Addresses]![DateUpdated].[OldValue]=[Forms]
   ➥![Addresses]![DateUpdated].[Value]
   ```

8. On the same row that you entered your conditions, select the SetValue action in the Action column. Then, set the following arguments:

   For the Item argument:
   ```
   [Forms]![Addresses]![DateUpdated]
   ```

   For the Expression argument:
   ```
   Date()
   ```

9. Close the Macro Design window and save the macro.

Switch back to Form view and edit the first record. Your macro will not update the field until the record is saved. Notice that if you manually edit the DateUpdated field, your changes will not be overridden by the macro because of the conditions that you set in step 7.

Adding your new macro to an existing macro group

If you want to add to or edit an existing macro, select the macro in the drop-down list, and then click the builder. The Macro Design Window will bring up the existing macro so you can modify it.

To harness the full power of using macros with Access, knowing what events to use and knowing the sequence in which those events occur is important. You should study the events and the sequences given below because this order is the same whether you are using macros or planning to program in VBA at a later date.

Form Events

The events shown below are the events with descriptions that belong to forms. There are some form events that share the same name as control and report events. In those cases you will have to pay attention to the description of each event, depending on the context. For example, the BeforeInsert event is generated in the form and in controls, but they are generated differently. Table 30.1 shows detailed information on a variety of useful form events.

TABLE 30.1 Form Events

Event Property	Event Name	Description
On Current	Current	The Current event is triggered when a record receives the focus. This can happen when the form is opened, refreshed, or required.
Before Insert	BeforeInsert	The BeforeInsert event is triggered when the user types the first keystroke in a new record.
After Insert	AfterInsert	The AfterInsert event is triggered after the new record is added to the database.
Before Update	BeforeUpdate	The BeforeUpdate event for forms is triggered before a record is updated with changed data. This can occur when you save the record or navigate to a new one.

continues…

TABLE 30.1 **Continued**		
Event Property	**Event Name**	**Description**
After Update	AfterUpdate	The AfterUpdate event for forms is triggered after a record has been updated with changed data. This can occur when you save the record or navigate to a new one.
On Delete	Delete	The Delete event is triggered when a record is about to be deleted.
Before Del Confirm	BeforeDelConfirm	The BeforeDelConfirm event is triggered after the Delete event, giving you the opportunity to cancel or confirm the deletion.
After Del Confirm	AfterDelConfirm	The AfterDelConfirm event is triggered after the BeforeDelConfirm event.
On Open	Open	The Open event is triggered when a form is opened and before its records are shown.
On Load	Load	The Load event is triggered after the form is opened and after its records are shown.
On Resize	Resize	The Resize event is triggered when the size of the form is changed.
On Unload	Unload	The Unload event is triggered when a form is closed.
On Close	Close	The Close event is triggered when a form is closed, after the Unload event.
On Activate	Activate	The Activate event is triggered when a form becomes the active window.
On Deactivate	Deactivate	The Deactivate event is triggered before another window in Access becomes active.

Event Property	Event Name	Description
On Got Focus	GotFocus	The GotFocus event is triggered when the form receives focus and only when there aren't any controls on the form that can receive the focus.
On Lost Focus	LostFocus	The LostFocus event is triggered when the form loses focus, and only when there aren't any controls that can receive the focus.
On Click	Click	The Click event is triggered when you click with the mouse in an area of the form that doesn't have a control under it.
On Dbl Click	DblClick	The DblClick event is triggered when you click with the mouse twice in succession, in an area of the form that doesn't have a control under it.
On Mouse Down	MouseDown	The MouseDown event is triggered when clicked with the mouse, in an area of the form that doesn't have a control under it.
On Mouse Move	MouseMove	The MouseMove event is triggered when the mouse is moved over an area of the form that doesn't have a control under it.
On Mouse Up	MouseUp	The MouseUp event is triggered when the mouse button is released, while it is over an area that doesn't have a control under it.
On Key Up	KeyUp	The KeyUp event is triggered when a key is released. The form property KeyPreview affects this event.

continues...

TABLE 30.1   **Continued**

Event Property	Event Name	Description
On Key Press	KeyPress	The KeyPress event is triggered when a key is pressed and released. The form property KeyPreview affects this event.
On Key Down	KeyDown	The KeyDown event is triggered when a key is pressed. The form property KeyPreview affects this event.
On Error	Error	The Error event is triggered when an error is generated in a form.
On Filter	Filter	The Filter event is triggered when the user clicks Filter By Form or Advanced Filter/Sort.
On Apply Filter	ApplyFilter	The ApplyFilter event is triggered when the user clicks Apply Filter, Filter By Selection, or Remove Filter/Sort.
On Timer	Timer	The Timer event is triggered periodically based on the form property, **Timer Interval**.

Control Events

The events show in Table 30.2 are the events with descriptions that belong to controls. There are some control events that share the same name as form events. In those cases you will have to pay attention to the description of each event, depending on the context.

TABLE 30.2   **Control Events**

Event Property	Event Name	Description
Before Update	BeforeUpdate	The BeforeUpdate event for a control is triggered before a field is updated with changed

Event Property	Event Name	Description
		data. This can occur when you save the record or navigate to a new field.
After Update	AfterUpdate	The AfterUpdate event for controls is triggered after a field has been updated with changed data. This can occur when you save the record or navigate to a new field.
On Change	Change	The Change event is triggered when the contents of a text box is changed. This event varies depending on the control it was generated from.
On Enter	Enter	The Enter event is triggered when a control is about to receive the focus.
On Exit	Exit	The Exit event is triggered when a control is about to lose the focus to another control.
On Got Focus	GotFocus	The GotFocus event is triggered when a control receives the focus.
On Lost Focus	LostFocus	The LostFocus event is triggered when a control loses the focus.
On Click	Click	The Click event is triggered when the mouse is clicked on the control.
On Dbl Click	DblClick	The DblClick event is triggered when the mouse is clicked twice in quick succession.
On Mouse Down	MouseDown	The MouseDown event is triggered when a mouse button is clicked.
On Mouse Move	MouseMove	The MouseMove event is triggered when the mouse moves over the control.

continues…

TABLE 30.2   Continued

Event Property	Event Name	Description
On Mouse Up	MouseUp	The MouseUp event is triggered when a pressed mouse button is released over the control that received the MouseDown event.
On Key Up	KeyUp	The KeyUp event is triggered when a key is released while the control has focus.
On Key Press	KeyPress	The KeyPress event is triggered when a key is pressed and released while a control has focus.
On Key Down	KeyDown	The KeyDown event is triggered when a key is pressed while a control has focus.
On Not In List	NotInList	The NotInList event is triggered when a value has been entered in a combo box, even though it is not in the list. The combo box property LimitToList affects this event.

Keep event names straight

Some controls may implement these events differently than the same event name in different controls. To make certain of the desired functionality, be sure to look up each control's events in the Access help file.

Report Events

The events shown in Table 30.3 are the events with descriptions that belong to reports. There are some report events that share the same name as form events. In those cases you will have to pay attention to the description of each event, depending on the context.

TABLE 30.3   Report Events

Event Property	Event Name	Description
On Open	Open	The Open event is triggered when a report is opened and before it is printed.

Event Property	Event Name	Description
On Close	Close	The Close event is triggered when a report is closed.
On Activate	Activate	The Activate event is triggered when a report becomes the active window.
On Deactivate	Deactivate	The Deactivate event is triggered before another window in Access becomes active.
On No Data	NoData	The NoData event is triggered after Access detects that no records will be printed.
On Page	Page	The Page event is triggered after Access has formatted the page for printing, but hasn't actually printed that page yet.
On Print	Print	The Print event is triggered after Access has formatted a section for printing, but hasn't actually printed that section yet.
On Format	Format	The Format event is triggered when Access is determining what data to include in the report for previewing or printing.
On Retreat	Retreat	The Retreat event is triggered when Access must reformat a section.

The *RunMacro* Action

Another way to execute macros is by using the RunMacro action. By using the RunMacro action within another macro, you can tell a macro to run yet another macro.

Debugging Macros

Sometimes unexpected results occur when you run your macros. Actually you can define these unexpected results as *errors*.

Anything that does not produce the intended result is an error. Unintended results can be the result of logic errors, syntax errors, or runtime errors.

Logic errors are probably the most difficult to find or to even understand. These errors are hard to find because they represent a misunderstanding or unawareness on your part of what a macro action does or the side effects of that action. The more difficult logic errors may show no visible manifestation for months. Make sure you understand all the actions and side effects as you go over your macro line by line. Trying to find a logic error can be the most frustrating and time-consuming part of debugging.

Syntax errors are probably the easiest of the three types of errors to find, but they can be just as difficult to fix. Syntax errors usually don't get past Access parser, so you will get immediate feedback in the Macro Design window. See Figure 30.8 for an example of the parse error message.

FIGURE 30.8

Run your macro in the Macro Design window before you finish so you can check for syntax errors.

Some syntax errors will make it past the parser in the Macro Design window, but will show up when you run the macro. These errors are called runtime errors. Runtime errors are a little more difficult to resolve than syntax errors because they don't show up until the macro is run. These errors are easier to find than logic errors, and you shouldn't have too much trouble correcting them. See Figure 30.9 for an example of a runtime error.

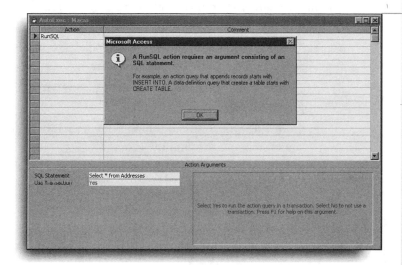

FIGURE **4.8**

The suspected grammar error is marked in green with a description of the error appearing over the box.

Some runtime errors are the result of a misspelled control name or any other database object name. For these kinds of errors, learn how to use the Expression Builder and you will eliminate those errors in the future.

In the more complex macros you will have to resort to stepping through the macro in order to find the row where the error is. The single stepping feature can also be a great learning tool because it will enable you to see how your macro is run. Stepping through a macro is not that complicated after you learn what to do.

Stepping through a macro

1. To step through a macro, select a macro in the Database window that you want to single step through. Click the **Design** button.

2. After you are in the Macro Design window, click the Single Step icon ⌨.

3. Open the form where the macro is generally called from and do whatever triggers the calling of your macro.

Step through a macro to learn

If you are curious to learn more about how macros work, use the Northwind database and study the macros it contains. You can find out where the macro is attached to a control by reading the first comment in the macro's Design view. Then locate the specific control or object, call the macro, and follow the steps to step through the macro. This method will help you understand the function and purpose (along with reading the comments) of how the macro is designed.

4. When your macro is triggered, a Single Step dialog box opens. See Figure 30.10 for the Single Step dialog box.

5. When you single step through your macro, the execution is temporarily halted until you select either **Step**, **Halt**, or **Continue**.

- The **Step** button on the Single Step dialog box lets you execute your macro one line at a time.

- **Halt** will halt the execution of your macro without going further.

- **Continue** will continue running the macro without single stepping through the rest of it.

FIGURE 30.10

You can watch each line's performance to find an error or to learn how an existing macro works.

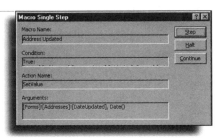

SEE ALSO

➤ *For detailed information on using the Expression Builder, see page 273.*

Special Macros: AutoExec and AutoKeys

There are two special macros that Access handles differently because of their names: AutoExec and AutoKeys.

AutoExec

Any macro that you name AutoExec will be executed automatically when anyone opens the database. This special macro can give you a lot of power because you can set your application up without relying on the end-user. One of the most obvious uses of the AutoExec macro is to display a splash screen. Also, you can set up your AutoExec macro to open a certain form that you want your user to be on after setup.

If you want to call a form when a user clicks on your database filename, perform the following steps. This exercise assumes that you have created the form already with any dialog buttons or graphics that you want to display.

Using AutoExec to call up a form on opening the database

1. In the Action column, select **OpenForm**. Then set the arguments as follows:

For the Form Name: Select the name of the form that you want to display from the drop-down list.

For the View: Form

For the Window Mode: Normal

2. Save your macro with the name AutoExec.

3. To see your macro in action, close the database and reopen it. Your macro will now display this form when you start it up.

You can also trigger certain responses using the Startup options, shown later in this chapter. Access 97 made some uses of the AutoExec macro for previous, obsolete versions. I do use the AutoExec macro to call a VBA routine that sets up my custom security, loads remote data locally, and so on. If you have written some code you want performed when the database opens, you would still name the macro AutoExec, but instead of using the OpenForm action, you would use the RunCode action to execute your VBA code.

SEE ALSO

➤ *You might want to use a template form such as the one created on page 347.*

AutoKeys

The other special Access macro is the AutoKeys macro. Any macro named this will be treated specially by Access. With the AutoKeys macro, you can assign any key combination available to any macro action that you chose. You can even override the default behavior for a certain key combination. For example, one of the uses that I have for the F11 key, which shows the Database window, is to check the security of the user that is logged into a secured database, and if that user belongs to a certain

---

How to bypass AutoExec

If you need to bypass the AutoExec macro, you can do so by holding down the Shift key when you open your database. The AutoExec macro works closely with the startup options.

To try this open the Northwind database and hold down the Shift key. You'll see that the splash screen doesn't appear but you go straight to the Database window.

This example

This set of steps will work with an unsecured database, but to really see this code in action, make a copy of the database and secure it, as shown beginning in Chapter 39, "Applying Security to the Database."

group, I'll display the Unhide Window dialog box so that that user can show the database window.

Setting keyboard combinations

1. Create a new macro (use the New Object drop-down list and the Macro icon 🗗.

2. Show the Condition column 🗗 and the Macro Name column 🗗.

3. In the first row of the AutoKeys macro, in the Macro Names column, place this text: {F11}.

4. In the **Condition** column, place text "CurrentUser()="Admin". Be sure to place yourself in the admin group when you secure your database.

5. In the Actions column, select RunCommand, with WindowUnhide as the argument.

6. Save your macro. Hide any window by selecting **Window, Hide**.

7. Press the F11 key. The Unhide window should open, enabling you to make a choice. If you don't have any windows hidden, you receive an error message.

The key combinations that you can use are in Table 30.4.

TABLE 30.4 **Access Key Combinations**

Text for the Names Column	Key strokes
^A or ^4	Ctrl+Any letter or number key
{F1}	Any function key
^{F1}	Ctrl+Any function key
+{F1}	Shift+Any function key
{INSERT}	Ins
^{INSERT}	Ctrl+Ins
+{INSERT}	Shift+Ins
{DELETE} or {DEL}	Del
^{DELETE} or ^{DEL}	Ctrl+Del
+{DELETE} or +{DEL}	Shift+Del

Notice that the Alt combination is not listed, so you will not be able to reassign any key that has an Alt as part of the combination.

Using the Startup Options as a Shortcut

Even though this chapter is focused on macros, much of what you can do with the AutoExec macro has been automated by Access 97 by using the Startup options. This section gives you a summary of the options you can select here to show a form, hide the Database window, and select menu bars at an application's start up.

Using the Startup options to replace *AutoExec*

1. With a database open, select the **Tools** menu and the **Startup** command.

For this example, you might use the My Address Book database created from the Database wizard. You can have the wizard create the Switchboard menu as the first screen that appears when you click the filename to open the database. Figure 30.11 shows the open Switchboard menu screen and the Startup dialog.

2. Click the **Display Form** drop-down list. This shows all the forms for the database. As long as you saved your form to this database, you can select that form to appear when your database starts up.

3. Select any remaining options. Table 30.5 shows these options. Click **OK**.

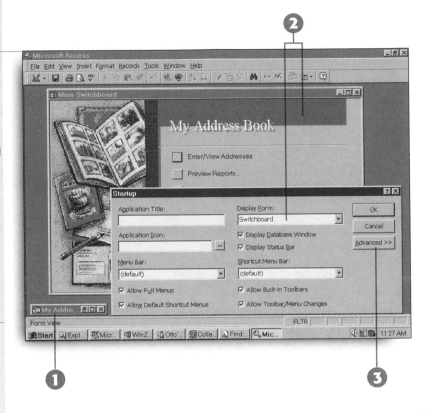

FIGURE 30.11

The Startup dialog box provides some shortcuts for some of the same results as the AutoExec macro.

1 The wizard automatically reduced the Database window to the corner of the screen to show the Switchboard menu instead

2 The Switchboard automatically appears because it is selected in this database's Display Form text box

3 Click the **Advanced** button to reveal more options

TABLE 30.5   Startup Options

Option	Description
Application Title	Instead of saying "Microsoft Access" in the upper left it will display the text that you put here. Also, in VBA if you don't supply a title for your message box function/statement it uses this text for the default. Notice that the Msgbox macro action will still display "Microsoft Access."
Application Icon	This icon replaces the "key" that is displayed to the left of the Application Title, and will be the icon that is displayed for a minimized application in the Status bar.

Option	Description
Menu Bar	The menu that replaces the default menu bar in Access when your application loads. It is global.
Allow Full Menus	Set to False, this takes away the design commands from menus and toolbars, such as Design view. Design commands are still available through the shortcut menus
Allow Default Shortcut Menus	See note above.
Display Form	Opens a form when your database starts.
Display Database Window	Turns off the display of the database window when set to False.
Display Status Bar	Turns off/on the status bar in the lower left and bottom of the Access window.
Shortcut Menu Bar	Replaces the Default shortcut menus, and works in conjunction with **Allow Default Shortcut Menus**.
Allow Built-in Toolbars	Turns on/off the availability of Access default toolbars.
Allow Toolbar/Menu Changes	Can/Can't modify default or custom menus and toolbars.

Advanced Options	Description
Allow Viewing Code	Usually when Access can't handle an error, the code where it erred is displayed so you can edit it. This turns on/off this option.
Use Access Special Keys	Turns on/off allowing users to show Database window and Debug window, even if they know the shortcut key to do so.

An Introduction to VBA

What is Visual Basic for Applications and who needs it?

Familiarize yourself with the VBA coding environment

Learn the easy way to write code

Why you should document your code

Use the Object Browser to find objects, properties, methods, and constants

When to Use VBA

Visual Basic for Applications (VBA) is the language engine that comes with Office 97. If that definition seems a bit daunting, think of VBA this way—it's the standard macro language that supports the larger Office 97 applications: Access, Excel, Word, and PowerPoint. (Outlook uses VBScript, a subset of VBA used to program Web pages.)

A common language across applications means you need to learn only one language to exercise programmatic control over all four Office applications. Furthermore, thanks to OLE Automation (a subset of VBA), you can fully integrate the Office applications to manipulate data across applications or even run one application from another.

All this programmatic control is just part of a bigger picture. You see, VBA is now available to other software developers by special licensing. This means even more compatibility across the application spectrum as non-Microsoft software begins to support VBA in their applications. I won't speculate if VBA will become the standard programming language across the personal computing industry, but you may find it cropping up in more of your applications. In the end, you benefit because you have just one language to learn and grow with.

You may be wondering how VBA applies to you as an Access user. Without VBA, Access is a powerful relational database. When you add VBA to the equation, you've got a versatile development tool for controlling Access, creating custom applications, and integrating other Office applications and even non-Microsoft software.

You may think you don't need VBA, especially if you're proficient with macros. The truth is, anything a macro can do, VBA can do better—and faster. Besides, there are times in an application's life when macros simply aren't enough. When this happens, VBA provides more complex functionality, more protection, and faster performance than macros.

What about Visual Basic and Access Basic?

If you're familiar with Visual Basic (VB) or Access Basic (version 2.0 and earlier), you may find the language and the coding environment similar. The language itself is very similar because VBA is a subset of Visual Basic. In addition, you enter VBA and VB code into a similar module (which is discussed more fully later in this chapter). Unlike Visual Basic, VBA doesn't supply its own interface objects, which are commonly referred to as forms and controls. Instead, VBA uses the hosting application's objects. As a result, a VBA project is always attached, or associated with, an application. You can't write a standalone VBA project.

Increasing Functionality

Suppose you want to add a batch reporting feature to an application. In other words, you want your users to choose all the reports they want to print from a dynamic list of reports, click a Print button, and then go to lunch. A *dynamic* list will update automatically as you add and delete reports from your application. Unfortunately, you just can't accomplish such a task with macros—no matter how many of them you link together. However, VBA can tackle this job with a small amount of code.

Avoiding Errors

You may be a macro-master, but do your macros ever crash your application? If so, you're in good company. A system crash can happen to the best of developers. However, VBA is better equipped to handle errors than macros. In fact, Access macros offer no error protection at all. That means your favorite macros can easily crash your system if everything doesn't go exactly as you planned.

Fortunately, VBA can handle errors with ease. You simply tell VBA which errors to recognize as they occur. Next, you tell VBA how to respond to those errors. There are two ways to handle these errors: You can ignore them or you can redirect them.

SEE ALSO
➤ *For more information on handling errors, see page 624.*

Expanding Control

Handling errors is only a small portion of the control you'll have over your application using VBA. At other times, you'll use VBA to pass variables, prompt users for information, and even direct the application on its way. Macros are too limited for this type of interaction.

SEE ALSO
➤ *For more information on variables, see page 570.*

You may already be using VBA

You're probably using VBA already, and you just don't realize it. Have you written an event procedure? Have you created a user-defined function (UDF)? If you've done either, you did so by using VBA.

Improving Performance

After you have everything under control, speed is an important consideration—no matter how fast your new system runs. Without fail, VBA code is always faster than a comparable macro. However, you won't notice the difference when performing simple tasks. If a simple macro gets the job done, don't hesitate to use it. However, when the task is complicated or manipulates thousands of records, VBA will reduce the time you spend waiting for your application to execute its tasks.

Exploiting Compatibility

Another important consideration when choosing between macros and VBA is compatibility. Because most of the Office applications use VBA, you can share code from one application with another. In addition, you can manipulate Access from the other Office applications. These are features you may never need, but it's nice to know they're available. And as you might suspect, you can't access those features with a macro.

The truth is, VBA is much more than just a macro language. You can use VBA to create custom applications and to extend your application's existing functionality. For instance, using VBA you can

- Present a custom dialog box
- Control the appearance of a report
- Solicit information from your system regarding users or the state of the current application
- Prompt your users for additional information
- Manipulate data in interactive controls
- Manipulate data in other Office applications
- Resolve unique problems with user-defined functions (UDF)
- Customize the menu structure

SEE ALSO

➤ *To learn more about shared components, see page 677.*

➤ *To learn more about appropriate uses for macros, see page 496.*

The Programming Environment

If you've used VBA in Excel or Word, you may already be familiar with the Visual Basic Editor (VB Editor). However, Access doesn't include the VB Editor. Instead, you enter code into a special coding window called a *module*. Technically, a module is an object. However, at this point, you can think of a module as a collection of VBA code tasks, or procedures. A *procedure* is a set of VBA statements that complete a defined task.

Exploring the Module Window

There are two types of VBA modules in Access: *standard* and *class-based* (form or report).

Creating a standard module

1. Click the **Modules** tab.
2. Click the **New** button in the Database window. The result, shown in Figure 31.1, is the VBA coding environment. Any code you enter into a standard module is available to the entire application.

There are two ways to view your code:

- Procedure View—Use the Procedure View icon ▤ if you want to zoom in on just one procedure.
- Full Module View—This setting ▤ is the default and displays all the code in the module.

You'll use the Object and Procedure controls to move from one procedure to the next. The Object control, specifically, will list the different objects attached to the module. In a form or report, this includes the actual form or report, its sections, and any controls you add. The Procedure control will list the different procedures or events that are attached to each object. For instance, Figure 31.2 displays a form module in which you've selected a form's Load event.

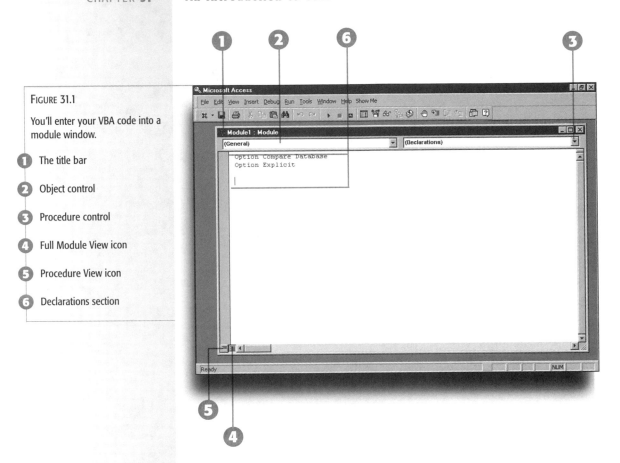

FIGURE 31.1

You'll enter your VBA code into a module window.

1 The title bar

2 Object control

3 Procedure control

4 Full Module View icon

5 Procedure View icon

6 Declarations section

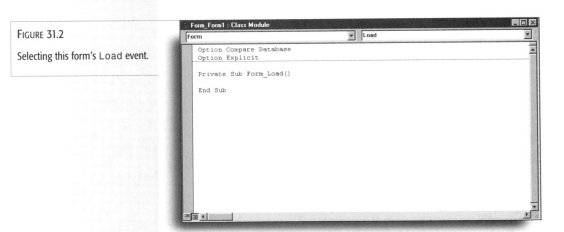

FIGURE 31.2

Selecting this form's Load event.

Each module also contains a *Declarations* section. You'll declare global variables and constants in that area. To *declare* a variable or constant means to make VBA aware that the variable or constant exists by naming it. When you declare a variable or constant in the Declarations section, you make that variable or constant available to all the procedures in the module.

You probably noticed that the Declarations section in Figure 31.1 contains two statements. By default, each module contains these two statements:

```
Option Compare Database 'Use database order for string
comparisons

Option Explicit
```

The first statement, Option Compare, sets the module's sort order. The second, Option Explicit, sets the declaration mode as *explicit*, which means you must declare a variable to use it.

Until now, you've worked with standard modules. As mentioned, forms and reports also have modules called class modules. You'll enter event-related code into class modules. For instance, you might attach code to a command button that opens another form or prints a report. There are three ways to open a class module:

- Select the object's (form or report) module in the Database window that you want to view and click the Code icon [image] on the Database toolbar.

- Open the form or report in Design view and click the Code icon [image] on the Form Design or Report Design toolbar.

- Open the form or report in Design view, select an event from the object's property sheet, and click the Builder icon [image].

SEE ALSO
➤ *To learn how to declare a variable, read page 571.*
➤ *For a more complete look at Option Compare, read page 582.*
➤ *The* Option Explicit *statement is discussed more fully on page 576.*
➤ *Class modules are discussed in more depth on page 596.*

Coding Tips

For the most part, entering code is easy—you simply type the code. When you first open a blank module, you are in the Declarations section. As mentioned earlier, this is where you'll include any variables that your code must share between other procedures and modules. For instance, the code in Listing 31.1 declares a variable named intMyVariable as an Integer data type. However, you won't always enter statements in the Declarations section. (The variable intMyVariable has no connection with the BeepForUs() function.)

LISTING 31.1   Declaring a Variable with its Data Type

```
1  Option Compare Database
2  Option Explicit
3  Dim intMyVariable As Integer
4
5  Function BeepForUs()
6        Beep
7  End Function
```

To enter code, you simply position the cursor below the Declarations section and type. Let's try that now.

Entering code into a standard module

1. Click **Modules** and then **New** in the Database window to open a blank standard module.

2. Position the cursor below the Option Explicit statement, enter the statement Dim intMyVariable As Integer, and press Enter twice.

3. Enter the function's name statement, Function BeepForUs(), and press Enter. After you do, VBA will insert a dividing line between the Declarations section and the function you're entering, as shown in Figure 31.3. Access will also supply an End Function statement.

4. Enter the remaining code and then save the module by clicking the Save icon 🔳 on the Visual Basic toolbar.

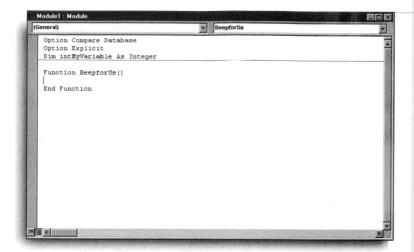

FIGURE 31.3

VBA separates your functions from
the Declarations section.

SEE ALSO

➤ *To learn more about declaring variables, see page 570.*

Entering Code

When you're ready to enter code, you have several methods to
choose from. If you're entering code into a standard module, the
easiest way is to simply type the code. If you're in a form or
report module, you'll want to choose an object and event from
the Object and Procedure controls, respectively. When you do,
VBA will insert the opening and ending statements for your procedure.

Entering code into a class module

1. Click **Forms** and then **New** in the Database window, and
   then double-click **Design View** in the New Form dialog
   box.

2. Add a command button to the blank form. Access will assign
   the default name Command0 to the button.

3. Click the Code icon 🖾 to open the form's module.

4. Select **Command0** from the Object control to select the
   command button. VBA will automatically select the Click
   event in the Procedures control. In addition, VBA will supply the beginning and ending statements for the button's
   Click event, as shown in Figure 31.4.

5. Position the cursor between the two statements and enter the code shown in Listing 31.2.

6. Close the module by clicking the Close icon 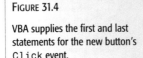 on the module's title bar.

7. Click the View icon on the Form Design toolbar to open the form in Form view.

8. Click the command button to execute its Click event. Your system should beep in response to your click.

LISTING 31.2   Creating a Response (*Beep*) to an Event (*Click*)

```
1 Private Sub Command0_Click()
2        Beep
3 End Sub
```

FIGURE 31.4

VBA supplies the first and last statements for the new button's Click event.

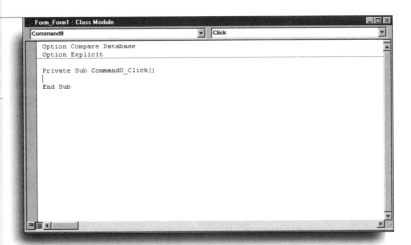

If you'd rather, you can use the **Procedure** command from the **Insert** menu to create your procedure. VBA will enter the beginning and ending statements for you. This feature is especially good at helping you avoid typos.

Using the Insert, Procedure command to create a function in a class module

1. Follow steps 1 through 3 of the previous example.

2. Choose **Procedure** from the **Insert** menu to open the Insert Procedure dialog box.

3. Enter the procedure's name, BeepForUs, into the Name text box.

4. Choose **Sub** from the Type options.

5. Select **Private** from the Scope options. The completed options are shown in Figure 31.5.

6. Click **OK**.

FIGURE 31.5
The Insert Procedure dialog box inserts new procedures.

SEE ALSO

➤ *You can find out how to add command buttons to a form on page 323.*

➤ *For more information on functions and subprocedures, see page 591.*

The Auto List Members List

Perhaps the most difficult coding skill to master is memorizing all the different functions and statements and their appropriate arguments, properties, and methods. Fortunately, Access is loaded with features that remember them for you. These features will make you feel right at home in the module window in no time.

Whether you're a developer or a casual user, the *Auto List Members* list could easily end up being your favorite coding feature because it displays a drop-down list of object types, properties, and methods. As soon as you enter a segment of code that this feature recognizes as an object, the Auto List Members list will display a corresponding list of choices. But this feature doesn't stop there. After you've defined the object's type, the drop-down list will display a list of appropriate properties and methods. If you aren't an accomplished typist, you'll especially appreciate this feature.

Using the Auto List Members list

1. Open a blank module by clicking **Modules** and then clicking **New** in the Database window.

2. Position the cursor below the two Option statements and enter the statement Dim MyReport As Report. As soon as you type the space character that follows the word As, Access will display the drop-down list shown in Figure 31.6.

3. Scroll down the list until you find Report. Or type an *r*, and Access will skip to the first item that begins with the character *r*. Double-click **Report** to add it to the module window.

4. Press Enter to add a new line and then enter MyReport. As soon as you type the period character after MyReport, VBA will display a second list consisting of properties and methods that are specific to the Report object.

5. Double-click **Caption** to add it to the module window.

Auto List and Naming Conventions

Using the Auto List Members list not only saves you time in typing, but it also helps by keeping your naming conventions and case similar and consistent.

FIGURE 31.6

The Auto List Members list box displays appropriate objects, properties, methods, and constants.

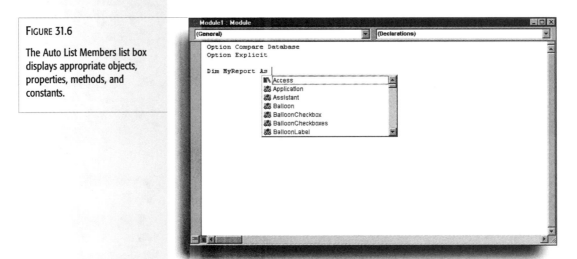

Table 31.1 shows several keyboard combinations you can use to act on the selected item in the Auto List Members list box.

TABLE 31.1 **Copying the Selected Item to the Module Window**	
Shortcut Keys	**Action**
Tab or Ctrl+Enter	Enters the selected item
Spacebar	Enters the selected item and adds a space character
Enter	Enters the selected item and moves the cursor to the following line
Esc	Closes the list

SEE ALSO

➤ *For more information on naming conventions, see page 22.*

Dragging Code

In earlier versions of Access you can copy code, but you can't drag it. Now you can. Simply select the code, drag it, and drop it. If you want to copy it instead of moving it, hold down the Ctrl key while dragging the section of code. You can also use this feature to move code from one module to another.

Documenting Code

Do yourself a favor and get in the habit of documenting your code. You will save yourself, and anyone else that has to modify your application, a lot of time and aggravation. Documenting your code means adding a short explanation to each section. Later, you won't have to spend much time deciphering the code when you return to debug or modify it. Documenting your code is one of the easiest tips you can apply, yet it's the one most often ignored.

To create a comment, you type a single-quote character (') or use the REM statement, followed by your explanation. Most developers rely on the single-quote character. VBA will ignore any line that starts with the quote character when executing the procedure.

The function shown in Listing 31.3 displays a message box with three possible responses—Yes, No, and Cancel. Then, a `Select Case` statement assigns appropriate text to the variable `intResponse`, depending on the user's response to the message box. Reading the comments sure is a lot easier than breaking down the procedure line by line. If you want to be particularly thorough, you can add a comment to each task. Some code needs more explanation—especially code that relies on user input or makes decisions. In those cases, you'll probably want to add more comments than this example.

Comments are a good way to note your application's development history. For instance, if more than one person is working on your application, you should add your name and the date to the functions you add. If you modify the code later, you can add that date as well. It's a good way of documenting your efforts for future reference.

LISTING 31.3

① Using the single-prime at the beginning of a line of comment

LISTING 31.3   **Using Clear Comments Makes Code Much Easier to Understand**

```
1  'GetResponse() solicits a Yes, No, or Cancel response from the user.
2  Function GetResponse()
3      Dim intResponse As Variant
4  'Display a Yes, No, Cancel message box                      ①
5      intResponse = MsgBox("Please choose one:", 3)
6      Select Case intResponse
7      Case 6
8        intResponse = "Yes"
9      Case 7
10       intResponse = "No"
11     Case 2
12       intResponse = "Cancel"
13     End Select
14 End Function
```

You can also append a comment to the end (the right) of a statement, but doing so isn't always convenient. If you want to read it, you'll have to scroll to the right a bit to see the remaining text. This method will quickly become a burden if you use it throughout your code.

Color in the Module Window

VBA distinguishes comments from code by displaying both in different colors. By default, VBA will also display keywords and object references in different colors. A *keyword* is a reserved word with a specific task, such as the If() and Format() functions. Applying different colors to the different components of code makes distinguishing components from one another, and thus understanding your code, a bit easier.

At any time you can modify or turn off these features by opening the **Module** tab in the Options dialog box, shown in Figure 31.7. To display this dialog box, choose the **Options** command from the **Tools** menu. You can customize the module window by selecting those features you want and changing the colors that Access applies to each code component.

FIGURE 31.7

You can customize the module window by modifying the settings in the Options dialog box.

Using the Object Browser

One of the more difficult aspects of VBA coding is remembering which properties and methods pertain to which objects. The Object Browser solves this dilemma by displaying all objects and their respective properties and methods. In addition, the browser will display information about each, as shown in Figure 31.8.

To launch the Object Browser, you can use one of three options:

- Click the Object Browser icon.
- Choose **Object Browser** from the **View** menu.
- Press F2.

However, all three options are available only in a module window.

The Object Browser hosts a varied list of object libraries. A *library* is a set of objects and procedures that are available to an application. (Don't be concerned if your list doesn't match ours.) To see a list of available objects, choose a library from the Project/Library and the Browser will update the Classes list box accordingly. When you want more information about a property, method, or constant, you can select it in the Members Of list box and press F1 to display the appropriate Help screen.

Using the Object Browser to display Access objects

1. Open a blank module and press F2.

2. Choose Access from the Project/Library control. The browser will accommodate your choice by displaying only Access objects in the Classes list box.

3. Choose the Report object from the Classes list box. In response, the Object Browser will update the Members Of list box to display only the properties, methods, and constants (if any) for the Report object, as shown in Figure 31.9.

4. To display additional information on the Report object's Circle method, select **Circle** in the Members Of list box and press F1.

Typically, the bottom section of the Object Browser will display additional information about the item you've selected in the Members Of list box, so you may not need to display a Help screen. For instance, in Figure 31.10, you selected the Report Circle method in the Members Of list box, and the Object Browser displayed pertinent information about that method. Specifically, the browser displayed the method's syntax and arguments. This feature alone can save you many trips to the Help section.

Working between the Help screen and the Object Browser

To save time, you can cut and paste a method or property from the Help screen into your module window for continued reference. Or, you can leave the Help screen up and switch between the Access module and the Help screen by pressing Alt+Tab.

FIGURE 31.8
The Object Browser lists the
available objects and
procedures.

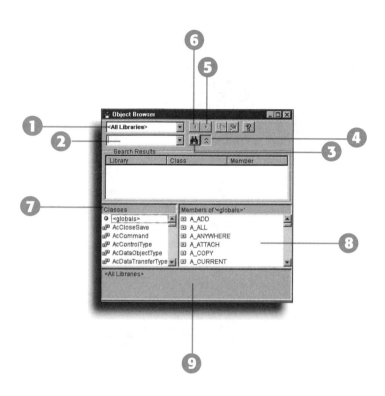

1	Project/Library control	6	Go Back button
2	Search Text control	7	Classes list box
3	Search button	8	Members Of list box
4	Hide/Show button	9	Displays syntax and arguments
5	Go Forward button		

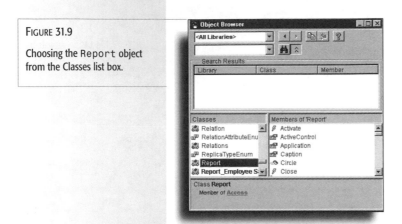

FIGURE 31.9

Choosing the Report object
from the Classes list box.

At this point, you can easily copy the method and its arguments
right into your module. Simply highlight the statement in the
bottom section of the Object Browser and press Ctrl+C. Return
to your module window, position your cursor at the point where
you want to paste the statement, and then press Ctrl+V.

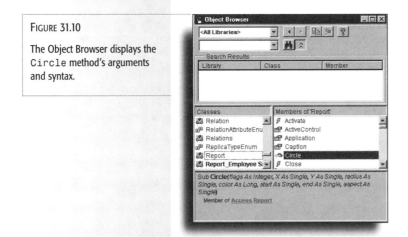

FIGURE 31.10

The Object Browser displays the
Circle method's arguments
and syntax.

As you scroll through the items in the Class and Members Of
list boxes, you'll notice that each is prefaced with a small symbol.
These symbols indicate each item's type: library, object, property, method, event, or constant. Table 31.2 contains an explanation of each symbol.

TABLE 31.2   **Object Symbols and Their Objects**

Symbol	Explanation
📖	Library
🔷	Class (or Object)
📑	Property
🔹	Method
ƒ	Event
🔳	Constant

A Navigational History

As you move from item to item, you can click the **Go Back** or the **Go Forward** button to navigate between your previous and current selections.

Searching

If you don't want to scroll through the list boxes for a particular object, you can search for it instead. To do so, simply enter the object you're searching for into the Search Text control. Then, click the Search icon 🔍. This opens a middle window in the Object Browser that displays the matching object. At this point, you can select any item from the list of items in the middle window to display that item's properties, methods, and constants. If you want to close this middle window, click the Close icon ❎, which is to the right of the Search icon.

Searching for the *Form* object in the Object Browser

1. Enter Form into the Search Text control, and click the Search icon 🔍. As you can see in Figure 31.11, the Object Browser has opened its middle window to display any objects that match the string Form.

2. Select the **A_FORM** Member (the first item) in the middle section of the Object Browser. This displays even more information—its properties, methods, and constants—about that object.

FIGURE 31.11

The Object Browser displays the
result of its search.

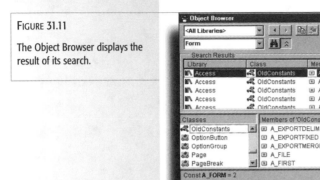

FIGURE 31.11

The Object Browser displays the
result of its search.

The Object Browser remembers your searches. If you need to
repeat a search, you can select it from the Search Text control's
drop-down list, as shown in Figure 31.12. After you select the
item in the drop-down list, press Enter or click the Search icon
.

FIGURE 31.12

You can repeat a search by selecting the search item from the
Search Text control.

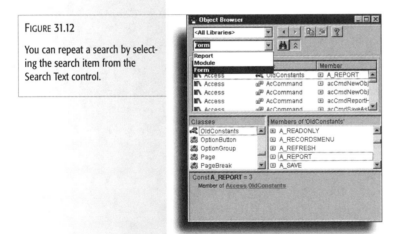

Adding New Libraries

For the most part, you may use the Object Browser to examine
only the Access and VBA libraries. However, the Object
Browser isn't limited to just these two. You can also use it to

display the objects in other libraries that belong to other Office applications. You may never use them in a foreign application, but most Office objects are available to all Office applications. First, check the Project/Library control for the library you're wanting to examine. If it isn't there, you'll need to add it.

Adding a library to the Object Browser

1. To open a new library, choose **References** from the **Tools** library. Doing so will display the References dialog box, shown in Figure 31.13.

2. To expose any of these libraries to the Object Browser, select that library in the Available Reference list box and click **OK**. For instance, you selected the Microsoft Office 8.0 Object Library, as shown in Figure 31.14.

   When you clicked **OK** and returned to the Object Browser to open the Project/Library control's drop-down list, you found that the Office library is now available to the Object Browser, as shown in Figure 31.15.

After you get the hang of using the Object Browser, you may find it quicker and easier to use than the Help section or a reference manual.

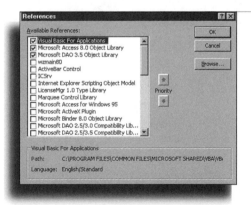

FIGURE 31.13

The References dialog box displays all the available libraries.

FIGURE 31.14

You selected the Microsoft Office 8.0 Object Library.

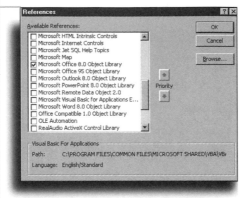

FIGURE 31.15

The Office library is now available to the Object Browser and Access.

Programming Access with VBA

Learn about the Application model's many objects

Speak VBA like a native

Everything you need to know about variables and more

Getting Familiar with the Access Applications Model

When you purchased Access, it may have seemed as though you acquired two products—a relational database and a development package. In fact, you did. With the addition of Visual Basic for Applications in Access 95 (and Office 95), Access has matured into a powerful development tool. The good news is that you don't have to be a professional programmer or developer to use it. Yes, you too can program with VBA!

Perhaps the key to reducing your learning curve is recognizing the key elements that drive Access—objects. Depending on your level of expertise, you'll spend most of your coding time in one of two object models: the *Applications model* or the *Data model*.

- The Access Applications model gives you programmatic control of the many objects Access offers: forms, controls, queries, and reports.
- The Data model gives you access to the actual data using *Data Access Objects* or *DAO*.

About Collections

We won't attempt to teach you everything you need to know about VBA in this book, but we can give you the information you need to get started. First you need a clear understanding of the Access Applications hierarchy, shown in Figure 32.1.

The Application hierarchy contains five objects:

- The Forms collection
- The Reports collection
- The Modules collection
- The Screen object
- The DoCmd object

SEE ALSO

➤ *To review the difference between standard and class modules, see page 547.*

Microsoft, VBA, and VB

Keep in mind that what you learn here can be adapted to apply to any Microsoft Office or Windows application, because with Office 97 they all use VBA.

Learning VBA will also give you a good inroad to learning Visual Basic, which can lead to many opportunities in programming development.

Another way to think of the two models

If you need a cue for how to think of these models, imagine holding a three-dimensional cube. For the most part, the Applications model covers the "flat" horizontal and vertical plane facing you. The DAO model covers all the visible and invisible lines giving the cube depth into your data storage area.

The main thing to consider is that because Access uses industry standards like these, you can eventually scale your applications far beyond the desktop, even beyond Access itself, and into a larger environment.

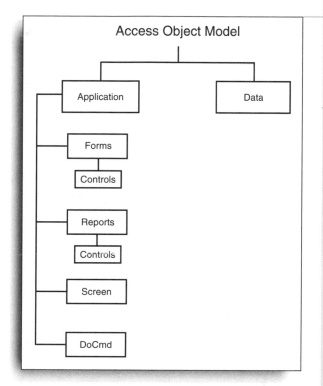

FIGURE 32.1
The Applications hierarchy shows the collections and subordination of objects for use in your VBA code.

Each collection contains like objects. For instance, the Forms contains forms, and so on. The Modules collection stores all of an application's modules, both standard and object. The Screen object controls your application's appearance attributes. Access uses the DoCmd object to execute methods.

Learning to Speak VBA

All languages rely on *syntax* rules for clear communication. In this sense, VBA is also a language. It's the language we use to tell our computers what we want Access do to with our data. Like our spoken language, we must learn how to string words together to form thoughts. In this section, we'll capitalize on this similarity by comparing the basic components of a VBA thought to components of the English language.

All sentences consist of a subject and an action—a noun and a verb. VBA is the same. A VBA sentence, known as a *statement*, generally contains a subject and an action. In VBA language, these components are known as *objects* and *methods*, respectively. The object is the thought's subject; the method is the action.

Some sentences have additional words, called adjectives, that describe the subject's attributes. In VBA, a *property* identifies an object's attributes.

If you're beginning to think VBA isn't so hard to speak, you're right. It really isn't, once you understand a few basic concepts:

- Most objects have methods and/or properties that are specific to that object.
- Almost all VBA code either modifies the physical properties of an object or executes some action specific to an object.

Apply the Syntax Rules

Now you need to think about punctuation. When speaking VBA, it isn't enough to know an object's name and its properties and methods. You have to punctuate the components properly or VBA won't know what you're referring to. Here are a few guidelines:

- Refer to an object by its collection and name.
- Separate the object from its collection with an exclamation point, or *bang*.
- Separate the object from a property or method with a period character, or *dot*.

When to Bang

To properly refer to an object, use the form

```
collection![objectname]
```

Syntax conventions

This book uses the convention that words in italic in a syntax sample are *placeholders*, meaning that you'll fill in your own names without using italic.

where *collection* identifies the object's collection and *objectname* is the name of the object you're referring to. That's why this component is called the *identifier*. Besides the bang, *objectname* is enclosed in brackets. Typically, any object that you have created is enclosed in brackets.

Now, let's suppose you want to refer to a report named rptMyReport. To do so, you'd use the statement

`Reports![rptMyReport]`

`Reports` identifies the report's collection, and `rptMyReport` is the report's name. Notice how the two components are separated with the bang character and the report is enclosed in brackets.

Many Access objects will have two levels of controls. For instance, forms and reports can both contain controls. To reference a control, you simply add a third component in the form

`collection![objectname]![controlname]`

where `controlname` refers to the control on `objectname` that you're referring to.

When to Dot

You learned earlier than most objects have methods and properties; you'll be using VBA to execute methods and modify properties. You'll tack both references to an object reference, but not at the same time. For instance, to reference an object's property, you'll use the form

`collection![objectname].property`

where `property` represents the attribute you're referring to. This time the components are separated with a dot. A similar form is used when referencing methods:

`collection![objectname].method`

Once you've identified an object, you'll most likely want to do something to it. For instance, you might want to change the color of a command button's text to red. To do so, you'd use a statement such as

`Forms![frmMyForm]![cmdMyControl].ForeColor = 255`

SEE ALSO

➤ *To read about referencing a subform, see page 410.*

Elements in the syntax

Using square brackets isn't necessary unless the object contains special characters, such as a space. In the earliest versions, *Access Basics* required these brackets, so many developers continue to use them for the sake of compatibility. Besides, most of the time Access will insert these brackets for you when they aren't required.

All About Variables and Data Types

After awhile, you may find that typing object references is rather tiring. They can grow outrageously long, and most of us aren't ace typists. So the sooner you learn about variables the better, because you can assign an object reference to a variable—a short one—and save yourself time. In fact, you'll also save processing time. You see, VBA has to evaluate each level in every reference. That means Access must evaluate a typical identifier, such as

```
Forms![frmMyForm]![cmdMyControl]
```

for each level—in this case, there are three—before VBA finally finds `cmdMyControl`.

What Is a Variable?

Most likely, you understand the concept of variables. However, if you're not a programmer, you may not know how to apply variables to your code. Generically, a *variable* is a character or symbol that can assume any one of a set of values. In the equation

```
x = 100
```

x is the variable and `100` is the value that x represents.

Now, a variable can equal any one of a set. That means you can change the value of a variable, but only within the confines of a particular set. This concept isn't an absolute, because you could define your variable to equal anything under the sun if that's what you wanted. But even then, you'd have a set—anything under the sun. To define a variable simply means to give it value. Let's continue by applying this idea to VBA.

In programming terms, a variable is a portion of your system's memory where you store a piece of data. Then, sometime during the run of your application, your code will refer to your variable in some way. Generally, you'll use the value in a calculation or you'll update it. There are three advantages to working with a variable:

- You can refer to it as often as you like.
- You can change its value.
- It can represent any type of data.

Fortunately, working with VBA variables is easy. Simply do the following:

- Create and name the variable.
- Identify the variable's data type.
- Define the variable.
- Use the variable.

Naming Variables

VBA is generous with its variable-naming conventions, but there are a few rules you'll want to remember:

1. Begin a variable name with an alphabetic character.

2. Don't use the characters ., %, &, !, #, @, or $ in a variable's name.

3. Variable names must be unique (within the scope of the calling procedure).

4. A variable name can contain up to 255 characters.

At this point you know how to name a variable, but you don't know how to communicate to VBA that you want to use a variable. To introduce a variable to VBA, you *declare* it by entering a statement in the form

```
Dim variable As data type
```

where `variable` is the variable's name and `data type` defines the variable's set type. (We'll talk about data types in the next section.) For instance, the statement

```
Dim strMyVariable As String
```

declares the variable `strMyVariable` as a `String` data type.

What's a Data Type?

Declaring a variable's data type gives you control over the data stored in that variable, which can prevent errors. For instance, let's suppose your code uses a variable named `intMyValue` in a

VBA lingo

We typically use the term *call* when referring to the use of a variable. A procedure calls a variable for use in a function, and so on.

The origins of `Dim`

If you're wondering how you "declare" with the letters `Dim`, this is short for *dimensions*. In effect, you're saying "the dimensions of this variable are defined as...". You'll eventually see other ways to declare a variable.

Don't omit the As argument!

You *can* omit the **As** data type argument, but we don't recommend it. If you omit this component, VBA will assign the **Variant** data type to your variable, and **Variant** consumes more memory than any other data type. Choose a data type that will serve your variable's needs while consuming the least memory.

calculation. Furthermore, you declare this variable using the statement

```
Dim intMyValue
```

which doesn't assign a data type. Instead, VBA defines `intMyValue` as a `Variant`, which will accept any type of data. As a result, VBA will attempt to calculate anything you assign to `intMyValue`—which will result in an error if `intMyValue` equals anything other than a numeric character. A better solution is to declare your variable using the statement

```
Dim intMyValue As Integer
```

Now VBA will only store integer values in `intMyValue`. If you attempt to assign anything other than an integer to `intMyValue`, VBA will return a mismatch error.

SEE ALSO

➤ *For more information on validating entries, see page 374.*

Applying the appropriate data type to your variables takes a little planning, but it's an easy task and well worth the effort. In doing so, you'll conserve memory resources and prevent errors. In addition, your code will run faster. Table 32.1 contains a list of VBA data types, their memory requirements, and their data sets (limitations).

TABLE 32.1   VBA Data Types

Data Type	Memory (in bytes)	Set
Byte	1	0 to 255
Boolean	2	True or False (-1 or 0)
Integer	2	-32,678 to 32,767
Long (long integer)	4	-2,147,483,648 to 2,147,483,647
Single (single-precision floating)	4	-3.402823E38 to -1.401298E45 for negative values; 1.401298E-34 to 3.402823E38 for positive values

Data Type	Memory (in bytes)	Set
Double (double-precision floating point)	8	-1.79769313486232E308 to -4.94065645841247E-324 for negative values; 4.94065645841247E-324 to 1.79769313486232E308 for positive values
Currency	8	-922,337,203,685,477.5808 to 922,337,203,685,477.5807
Date	8	January 1, 100 to December 31 9999
Object	4	any Object reference
String (variable)	10 + string	0 to approximately 2 billion length
String (fixed)	Length of string	1 to approximately 2 billion
Variant (numbers)	16	any number value up to the range of a Double
Variant (characters)	22 + string length	0 to approximately 2 billion

Most of VBA's data types are straightforward and need little extra explanation. We do want to mention a few points that aren't so obvious:

- The Currency data type is a *scaled integer*. VBA will round this value to the fourth decimal place, to conserve memory requirements.

- The Date data type stores both a date and time value as a double-precision floating point number. The integer portion represents the day, the decimal portion represents the time.

SEE ALSO

➤ *If you'd like to know how Access data types handle the year 2000 problem, see page 390.*

- The fixed-length String data type requires less memory, but you must know the actual length of the string you're storing. When the string may vary, or when you don't know the exact length, you should use the variant String data type.

Planning and the Currency data type

The Currency data type is a good example of planning ahead for the data type you want to use. Depending on how accurate your data needs to be, you might want to use another more accurate data type (that rounds to more decimal points) for your calculations. For example calculating averages and percentages often throw off dollar amounts so that your figures don't match "to the penny." You might calculate the averages first on a more accurate data type and then perform a procedure to turn the result into a dollar amount.

■ A Variant data type can store any type of data, except for a fixed-length string.

Why You Should Assign Data Types

Now, suppose you want to declare a simple variable, which you'll use in a simple calculation. You search the data type table and see that Byte handles values from 0 to 255—you think Byte should be adequate. Next, you open a blank module and enter the function shown in Listing 32.1.

Opening the Module and Debug windows

To open a blank module, select the **Module** tab in the Database window and click **New.**

Click the Debug icon ⊞ on the Visual Basic toolbar.

LISTING 32.1   **Testing the Byte Data Type**

```
1 Function ProductTest(x As Byte, y As Byte)
2     Dim bProduct As Byte
3     bProduct = x * y
4     ProductTest = bProduct
5 End Function
```

To test the function, you open the Debug window, and enter the statement

```
? ProductTest(3,5)
```

as shown in Figure 32.2.

At first glance, everything seems to work fine—your function returns the value 15. That's because the Byte data type is adequate for the values 3, 5, and 15. However, let's see how our function handles a negative value. To do so, enter into the Debug window the statement

```
? ProductTest(-3,5)
```

This time, VBA displays the error message shown in Figure 32.3 because we tried to assign a negative value, -3, to a Byte data type. Click **OK** to clear the error.

We have one final test for our function. Enter into the Debug window the statement

```
? ProductTest(30,50)
```

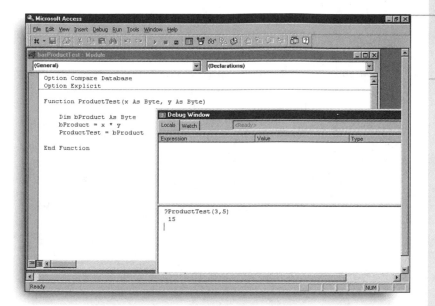

FIGURE 32.2

We tested our function using two one-digit values.

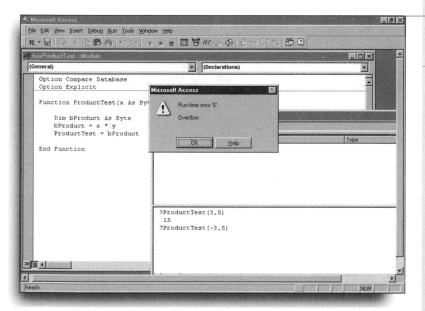

FIGURE 32.3

A negative value causes an error.

Once again, our function fails another test, as shown in Figure 32.4. Click **End** to clear the error. The Byte data type is adequate for both 30 and 50, but not the product of these values. Remember, the Byte data type will accommodate values between 0 and 255, the product of our two values is greater than 255. In the case, the Integer data type is probably the best choice.

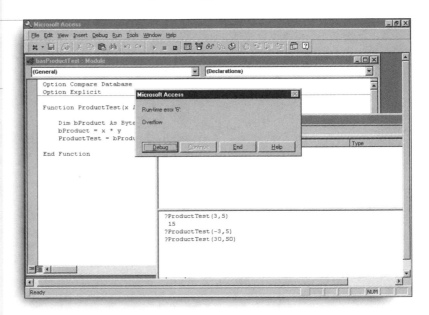

Choosing data types is a balancing act. You need a data type that will adequately handle every possible value, while consuming as little of your memory resources as possible.

Choosing the Option Explicit Option

You've probably noticed that every module contains the statement

```
Option Explicit
```

This statement determines your module's declaration mode—*implicit* or *explicit*. Explicit declaration forces you to declare a variable before you can use it; implicit requires no declarations. We recommend you use the explicit declaration, which is the default setting. With your module set to explicit declaration,

Turning on Option Explicit

The next exercise assumes that you're using the default setting and that your modules include an Option Explicit statement. If this isn't the case, you can enter the statement yourself in the Declarations statement. Or, you can turn the setting on by choosing the **Options** command from the **Tools** menu and then clicking the **Module** tab. In the resulting window, select the **Require Variable Declaration** option in the Coding Options section, and then click **OK**.

you'll catch errors before VBA attempts to run them. Without explicit declaration, you're on your own.

To demonstrate the advantage of using explicit declaration, open a blank Module window and enter some code without it. If your module contains an `Option Explicit` statement, select and delete that statement now. Then, enter the function exactly as we've shown in Listing 32.2.

LISTING 32.2   Testing Implicit Declarations

```
1   Function VariableTest()
2       intVariable = 10
3       intResponse = intVaraible * 10 ————————①
4       VariableTest = intResponse
5   End Function
```

As you can see in Figure 32.5, the function returns an error because we intentionally misspelled our variable in the line 3 of our code. Click **OK** to clear the error. The variable `intVariable` equals 10; the variable `intVaraible` equals nothing. Consequently, `intResponse` equals 0 because 0 * 10 = 0.

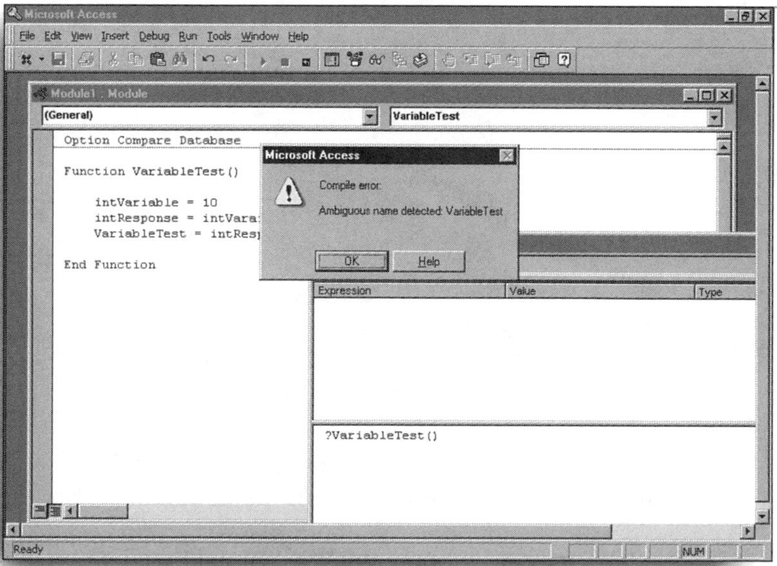

LISTING 32.2

① Access automatically initializes a new variable **intVaraible** with a value of 0 the first time it is used

FIGURE 32.5
We expected our function to return the value 100 (10 * 10), but it returned 0 instead.

When a module contains an Option Explicit statement, you won't encounter this particular coding problem. Let's add one to our sample module and see what happens.

Adding the Option Explicit statement and correcting errant variables

1. Position your cursor behind the Option Compare statement and press Enter.

2. Then, type Option Explicit and press Enter.

3. Now, click the Compile Loaded Modules button 🗊 or choose **Compile Loaded Modules** from the **Debug** menu.

   After doing so, VBA will return a compile error as shown in Figure 32.6.

4. Click **OK** to clear the message and VBA will select the first offending variable—intVariable, as shown in Figure 32.7.

FIGURE 32.6

VBA wants us to declare our variables.

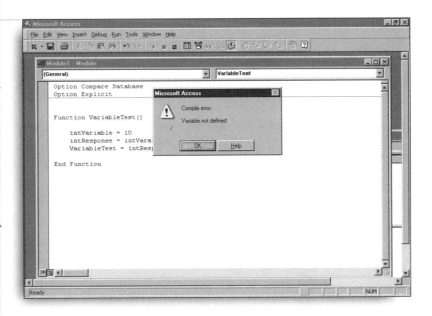

Practice debugging

If you've followed this example, you know that the failure to define a variable has caused a problem in the calculation. If you were looking at Listing 32.2 as a part of your own code, you should notice something else about the variables.

None of the variables have been declared with a data type in the definition. As stated earlier in this chapter, this can cause a number of different errors because Access will default to the Variant data type, which might not suit your purposes.

5. At this point, we need to add a Dim statement, so position the cursor at the beginning of this statement and press Enter to add a new line.

6. Then, enter the statement
   Dim intVariable As Integer

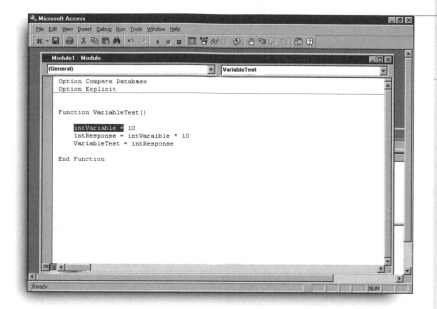

7. Check for any remaining variables. (Listing 32.2 has another variable in the next line, intResponse.) So, as shown in Figure 32.8, add an additional Dim statement.

```
Dim intResponse As Integer
```

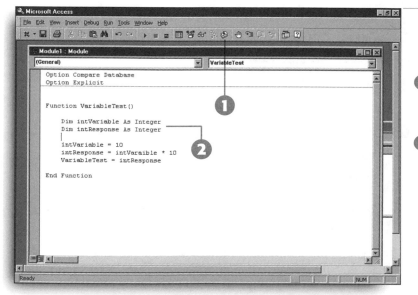

8. Now, click the Compile Loaded Modules button a second time. This time, when you click **OK** to clear the message, VBA selects intVaraible in the second line, which exposes our typo.

We don't need to declare a third variable, we simply need to correct our mistake by replacing intVaraible with intVariable. After doing so, you can click the Compile Loaded Modules button without returning an error.

If you return to the Debug window and execute the function again, it will return 100, as shown in 32.9

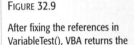

FIGURE 32.9

After fixing the references in VariableTest(), VBA returns the correct product—100.

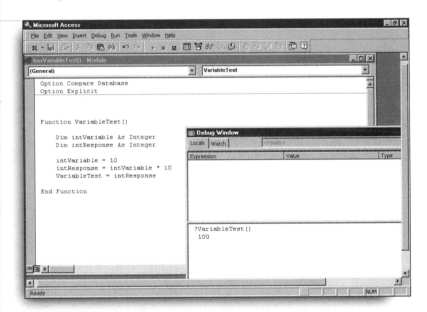

Giving Your Function a Data Type

We've talked a lot about declaring appropriate data types for variables, but we're not done with variables yet. You can also declare a data type for your functions. The reason for doing so is the same one we've discussed throughout this section on variables—to protect the validity of your data.

In all of our examples, we've declared data types for our variables, but not for the function. That means VBA is returning the result of each function as a Variant. That's not inherently wrong, but not limiting the results can let unknown errors slip by. In addition, Variants require more memory.

Let's consider the `VariableTest()` function from the last section. We deliberately left out the declarations and even misspelled a variable to show you how easily mistakes can occur. Once you declared both variables and corrected the misspelling, the function worked just fine, right? Well, not quite. You see, `VariableTest()` returns a Variant, even though we've declared the function's variables as integers. That means, if everything goes as expected, our function will return the results we expect. After all, the logic and code are fine. However, at any time, someone could throw in a line of code similar to

```
VariableTest() = "abc"
```

which would return a string, which we know is incorrect. Why would someone do this? Most likely, they wouldn't on purpose, it's just a possible error that you can and should plan for.

To give a function a data type, simply declare it in the function's name statement in the form

```
Function MyFunction(arguments As data type) As data type
```

For instance, we could declare `VariableTest()` as an Integer using the statement

```
Function VariableTest() As Integer
```

Then, if someone tries to assign an inappropriate value to `VariableTest()`, VBA will return an error instead of accepting the data.

SEE ALSO

➤ *To learn more about preventing errors, read page 624.*

Now, this last topic, declaring a function's data type, is something you may not want to tackle at first. In fact, for most event procedures and simple UDF's, you can get by without declaring a data type for your function. Of course, developers all over will groan at this statement because they sometimes forget that users just need to get their work done. So, don't overwhelm yourself while you're learning. However, declaring a function's data type

---

Two-step process of testing

This process uses two steps in testing code. First, when you click the Compile Loaded Modules button 🔲, VBA catches certain types of errors, including whether you've defined variables and used acceptable syntax.

Even if your code passes the Compiler step, you may still want to test each procedure in the Debug window to make sure it's returning the expected results.

Sometimes your syntax will be fine, but the calculations, data types, or other logic won't work as expected. It's a good idea to always take time for both steps.

is a basic development feature and something you should include as you become more knowledgeable with VBA and the development environment in general.

Using Option Compare

Modules also contain an Option Compare statement in the Declarations section. For the most part, you won't need to change this option, but you can. The Option Compare statement simply sets a module's sort order. By default, Access uses the Option Compare Database setting, which refers to your system's locale settings for more information.

The Option Compare statement has two other settings: Binary and Text.

Binary rules

For the most part, you will never need to consider the options we touch on in this section. We want you to be aware that these options exist, however, you shouldn't worry if you don't grasp the concepts yet. You may never refer to them again after reading this section.

- **Binary** will sort your text according to Binary rules as shown by this examples:

   A, B

   a, b

   Á, É, á, é

- The **Text** setting will sort according to Text rules (this option will sort uppercase first, then lowercase, then special characters):

   A, a

   Á, á

   B, b

   É, é

Understanding Scope

At this point, you know how to declare, define, and assign data types to variables. The next step is to learn about a variable's *scope*. By scope we mean which application's components will have access to a variable. Within Access, VBA has three possible levels, which we discuss in detail in the next few pages:

- Local
- Module
- Public

Local: Keeping It Specific to the Procedure

A *local* variable belongs to its procedure. In other words, only the hosting procedure can refer to it. All of the variables we've used in this chapter, up to this point, have been local variables.

Using a local variable

1. To demonstrate a local variable, open a blank module by opening a database in the Database window, clicking the **Module** tab and **New**.

2. Enter code similar to that shown in Listing 32.3.

3. Then, open the Debug window by pressing Ctrl + G and enter the statement

   ```
   ?ScopeLocal()
   ```

As you can see in Figure 32.10, our procedure returns the string `This is a local variable`.

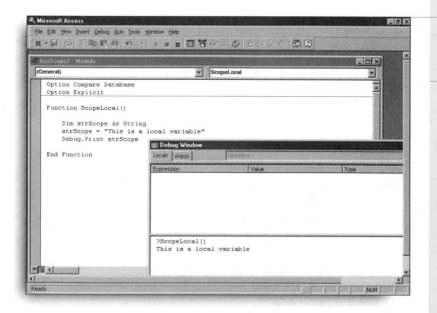

FIGURE 32.10
Our function returns a simple string message.

LISTING 32.3   **Declaring a Local Variable**

```
1  Function ScopeLocal()
2      Dim strScope As String
3      strScope = "This is a local variable"
4      Debug.Print strLocal
5  End Function
```

Now, what do you suppose would happen if we attempt to call this variable from another procedure?

Testing a variable's scope

1. Return to your open module and after Listing 32.2, enter the procedure shown in Listing 32.4.

2. Now, return to the Debug window by selecting it (it might be sitting behind your module). Or, you can choose **Debug Window** from the **Window** menu or press Ctrl + G. In the Debug window, enter the statement

   ?ScopeModule()

Checking the *Dim* statement for scope

You'll notice that this function is similar to Listing 32.3. However, it doesn't contain a **Dim** statement for the **strScope** variable.

LISTING 32.4   **Testing for Variable in a New Procedure**

```
1  Function ScopeModule()
2      strScope = "This is a module variable"
3      Debug.Print strScope
4  End Function
```

In response, VBA will display the compile error shown in Figure 32.11. That's because Listing 32.4 doesn't declare our variable, strScope. At this point, only ScopeLocal() can successfully refer to strScope.

Click **OK** to clear the error message.

Module Variables: Sharing Variables with the Module

Sometimes, it's appropriate to declare a variable once and give all the procedures in your module access to that variable. This is easily accomplished by declaring that variable in the module's Declarations section instead of in a particular procedure. To demonstrate, let's make a variable (strScope from Listing 32.3) available to ScopeModule() (from Listing 32.4).

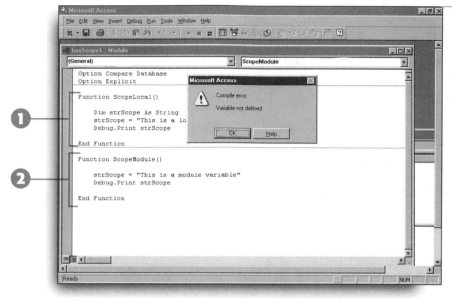

Making a variable available to all procedures in a module

1. First, return to the module from the previous example, and position your cursor at the end of the Option Explicit statement in the Declarations statement, as shown in Figure 32.12.

2. Then, press Enter and type the statement
   `Dim strScope As String`

3. After doing so, return to the Debug window, type again or position the cursor at the end of an existing `?ScopeModule()` statement and press Enter.

This time, VBA responds by displaying the string `This is a module variable`, as shown in Figure 32.13.

Going Public

At this point, a variable declared in the Declarations section (`strScope` from the previous section) is available to every procedure in our current module. It isn't, however, available to any procedure in any other module.

FIGURE 32.12

After declaring strScope in the Declarations section, that variable is available to all the procedures in the module.

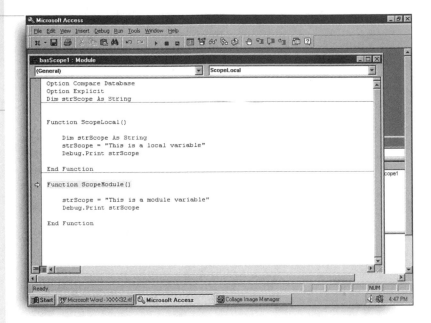

FIGURE 32.13

After declaring strScope in the Declarations statement, ScopeModule() has access to it.

① Add the Dim statement here and the variable becomes a module variable, shared by all procedures in the module

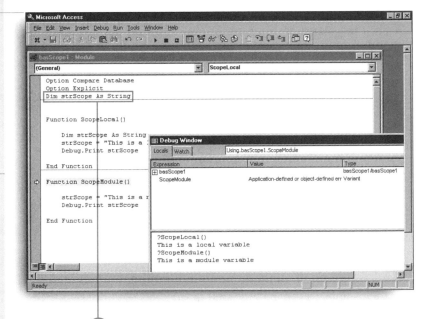

Testing and creating public variables

1. To test this restriction, return to the module from Listings 32.3 and 32.4 or open the one you want to test, save it, using the bas prefix and a descriptive filename, such as basScope1, and then close it.

2. Next, open a blank module and enter the procedure shown in Listing 32.5.

3. Then, open the Debug window and enter the statement
   ```
   ?ScopePublic()
   ```

   The compiler returns an expected error that the variable is not defined. To clear it, click **OK**.

   Fortunately, we have a simple solution—declare strScope as a Public variable.

4. Before declaring a public variable save any new modules (you could use basScope2), and close it.

5. Then, re-open the first module, with the variable you want to make public (basScope1)

6. Replace the Dim statement in that module's Declaration section with the statement
   ```
   Public strScope As String
   ```

7. Next, save the module and close it.

Finding the correct public variable

If there is no variable in the Declarations section of the module you're using, see the preceding section on moving local variables to module variables.

LISTING 32.5 **Public Variables**

```
1 Function ScopePublic()
2     strScope = "This is a public variable"
3     Debug.Print strScope
4 End Function
```

Once you've done so, you can refer to a public variable (strScope) from all procedures, not just those in a module where you have declared that variable as either a local or module variable.

To see the results of this application-sharing declaration, simply return to the Debug window and execute all procedures.

As you can see in Figure 32.14, all the procedures in this example work properly—including `ScopePublic()` which is in a module other than `strScope`'s declaration statement.

FIGURE 32.14

If you declare `strScope` as a Public variable, any procedure in your application can refer to it.

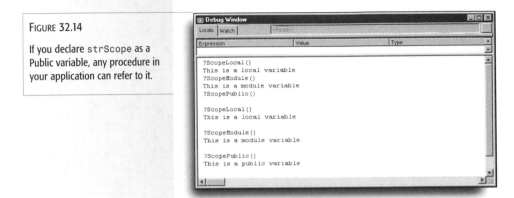

Static Variables

We have one last variable data type we'd like to discuss and that's *Static*. We've waited until now, because a Static variable has a special attribute. A Static variable is a *persistent* variable. That means the variable retains its value beyond the life of the procedure. This concept is similar to scope, but it isn't the same thing. Scope refers to a variable's accessibility; persistence refers to a variable's *lifetime*.

A variable's lifetime depends on where and how you use it. Normally, a variable's lifetime lasts only as long as the procedure is running. Once VBA exits the code, the variable ceases to have value. Let's explore this behavior by running a simple procedure that adds the value 1 to itself.

Testing a variable's persistence

1. Simply open a blank module and enter the procedure shown in Listing 32.6.

2. After you enter the procedure, open the Debug window by pressing Ctrl + G, and entering the statement

    `?Life()`

    which returns the value 1, as shown in Figure 32.15.

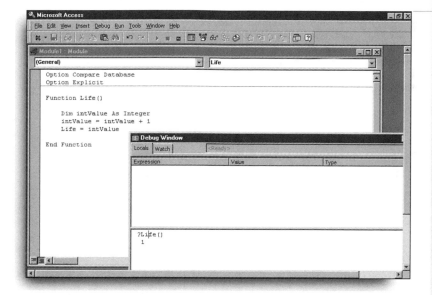

LISTING 32.6   **Testing a Variable's Life Span**

```
1   Function Life()
2       Dim intValue As Integer
3       intValue = intValue + 1
4       Life = intValue
5   End Function
```

The first time we run this procedure intValue = 0. The statement in line 3 then adds the value 1 to 0. As a result, the function returns the value 1.

If we run the procedure again, what will it return? To find out, execute Life() in the Debug window a second time. You can do so in one of two ways, you can enter the ? (print) statement again. Or, you can position your cursor at the end of the existing ?Life() and press Enter.

You may be surprised to find that the function still returns the value 1 as shown in Figure 32.16, and not 2—the result of 1 + 1. That's because the life of intValue ends with the End Function statement. Once VBA executes that statement, intValue no longer remembers its value. When we executed Life() the second time, intValue equaled 0. Therefore intValue + 1 equals 1, just as it did the first time we ran the function.

FIGURE 32.16

The second time we run Life(), it returned the value 1.

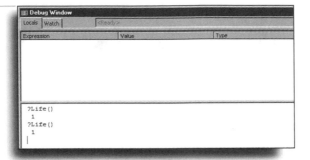

To prolong a variable's life, we use the Static statement instead of the Dim statement. Doing so extends the variable's life beyond its calling function. We can illustrate this behavior by changing intValue's lifetime to Static, as shown in Figure 32.17.

After doing so, return to the Debug window and run the statement twice. The first time, Life() equals the value 1, but the second time, Life() returns the value 2. That's because VBA remembers intValue's value beyond the life of its calling procedure. When we run Life() the second time, VBA recalls intValue's last value.

FIGURE 32.17

Changing the Dim statement to Static prolongs a variable's lifetime.

1 Using Static to declare a variable increases its life beyond the End Function statement.

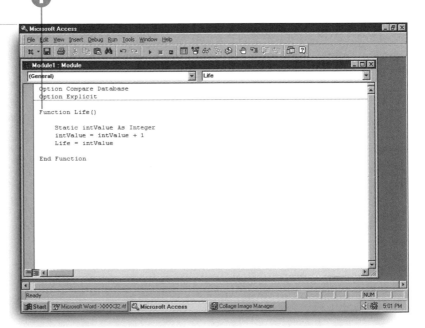

Writing Procedures

Throughout this chapter, we've used the word procedure quite a bit. A *procedure* is any task you execute with code. All procedures have two things in common: their first and last statements. Beyond that, procedures are unique to their task.

Each VBA procedure begins by specifying its name and any arguments its code may need to complete its task. We complete each procedure with an End statement. If you use one of the built-in features Access provides, such as the Insert Procedure dialog box, shown in Figure 32.18, VBA will provide these lines of code for you.

Using Static variables

Static variables are useful in calculations where you will perform a series of actions on a variable and want the value to progress with each procedure or action.

FIGURE 32.18
The Insert Procedure dialog box enters the function's name and End statement for you.

What's a UDF?

What you might not realize at this point is that VBA offers us two types of procedures—sub and function. So far, we've used mostly function procedures in our examples. A *function procedure, or user-defined function (UDF)*, returns a value (as a general rule). You'll execute function procedures by calling them. The proper form is

```
Function name([arguments]) [As type]
```

where *name* identifies the function, *arguments* provide any additional data the procedure may need to complete its task and *As type* defines the data type of the function's result. (For now, we'll use the term function procedure, instead of UDF, to refer to any procedure other than an event procedure.)

Even though we've worked with several function procedures already, let's try one more—this time from the perspective of setting out to create a function procedure.

Let Access do the work

To avoid typos, you should consider letting Access create procedure functions for you. To do so, choose **Procedure** from the **Insert** menu, which brings up the Insert Procedure dialog box shown in Figure 32.18. Next, enter the function name, FP1. Then, choose the function type, which in this case is **Function**. Next, select the **Private** scope option and click **OK**. If required, you can even declare a Static variable by selecting the **All Local Variables as Static** option.

Creating a function procedure

1. To begin, open a blank module and enter the code shown in Listing 32.7. (We haven't declared a data type for the function, but you can easily do so. Refer to the Giving your function a data type section.)

2. To execute FP1(), open the Debug window and enter the statement
   ?FP1()

3. VBA will respond by displaying the input box shown in Figure 32.19. To continue, enter the value 3 and press Enter or click **OK**.

   After you do, VBA will multiply 3 by 10 and return a product of 30, as shown in Figure 32.20.

FIGURE 32.19

Our function procedure prompts us for a value.

The Input box

Listing 32.7 creates an input dialog box for interacting with the user. This is another step toward creating an interactive application.

LISTING 32.7 This Function Will Prompt You for a Value Between 1 and 100 Then display the Product of Your Entry and 10

```
1   Function FP1()
2       Dim intResponse As Integer
3       intResponse = InputBox("Enter any value between 1 and 100")
4       intResponse = intResponse * 10
5       MsgBox (intResponse)
6   End Function
```

SEE ALSO

➤ *You can turn to page 609 to learn more about input boxes.*

As you can see, we've used two built-in functions—InputBox() and MsgBox()—within our function procedure. We can use FP1() to return the product of any value between 1 and 100 by 10. Click **OK** to clear the message box.

FIGURE 32.20
The MsgBox statement displays the product of 3 and 10.

Calling a Function Procedure from Another Procedure

Often, you may need to call one procedure from another. This is especially helpful if you repeat the same task or calculation within the context of several larger but different routines. To demonstrate, let's suppose the previous task, multiplying values between 1 and 100 by 10 is a task you repeat often, but in different areas of your application. In this case, you don't have to repeat your calculating code over and over. Instead, you enter it as a function procedure and then call it when you need it—passing it the appropriate values. Substitute your own functions and procedures into the following example.

What's that function's function?

Don't confuse function procedures with the Access built-in functions as they aren't the same thing. Built-in functions perform a specific task. They can't undertake the many unique tasks required by a custom application. However, you can include a built-in function in a function procedure by assigning the result to a variable.

Calling a procedure from another procedure

1. Open a blank module and enter the procedures shown in Listing 32.8.

2. Be sure to enter the following statement in the Declarations section:
   ```
   Dim intResponse As Integer
   ```

LISTING 32.8   A Sample Procedure for Calling Another Procedure

```
1  Option Compare Database
2  Option Explicit
3  Dim intResponse As Integer
4
5  Function CalProduct(intResponse)                    ①
6      CalProduct = intResponse * 10
7  End Function
8
9  Function NeedProduct100()
10     intResponse = InputBox("Enter a value between 1 and 100")
11     CalProduct (intResponse)                        ②
12     MsgBox CalProduct(intResponse)
13  End Function
14
```

LISTING 32.8

① Creating the CalProduct() function

② Here is the CalProduct() function being called by a subsequent procedure

LISTING 32.8

3 CalProduct() function is called here as well

LISTING 32.8   **Continued**

```
15    Function NeedProduct1000()
16        intResponse = InputBox("Enter a value between 1 and 1000")
17        CalProduct (intResponse)                    3
18        MsgBox CalProduct(intResponse)
19    End Function
```

Task-wise, the procedures in Listing 32.8 are similar to our earlier function, FP1(). However, NeedProduct100() and NeedProduct1000() both solicit the value we want multiplied and then pass it to CalProduct(). Then, CalProduct() actually calculates the product for us and passes that result back to NeedProduct100() or NeedProduct1000(). Finally, the calling procedure accepts the passed result, and displays it.

To see these procedures in action, open the Debug window and enter the statement

?NeedProduct100()

VBA will display the same input box shown earlier in Figure 32.18. Enter the value 3 and press Enter or click **OK**. At this point, Line 11 passes our entry, 3, to CalProduct() (Line 5). Line 6 then multiples 3 by 10. After calculating the product, CalProduct() returns that result to Line 11. Finally, Line 12 displays the result—30, as shown in Figure 32.20. We accomplished the same result, we just went about it a little differently.

You may be wondering how two functions can be more efficient than one but that's where NeedProduct1000() comes in. To demonstrate, enter into the Debug window the statement

?NeedProduct1000()

When prompted, enter 300 into the input box shown in Figure 32.21. Line 17 then passes the value 300 to Line 5 . Next, Line 5 multiples 300 by 10, and passes the result—3000—back to Line 17. At that point, Line 18 displays the result of 3000, as shown in 32.22. The advantage is the availability of the product-producing code to both procedures.

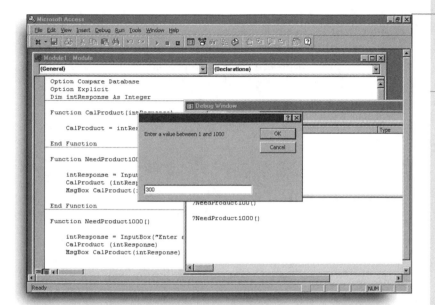

FIGURE 32.21

Our second procedure function prompts you for a value between 1 and 1000.

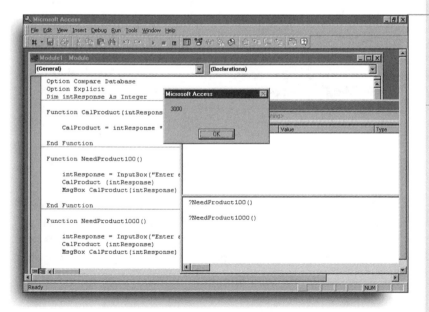

FIGURE 32.22

After CalProduct() returns the product of our entry and 10, NeedProduct1000() displays that result.

What's a Sub Procedure?

Balance is the key to calling functions

Leaving one function to visit another always slows down your code. It may not be worth your time to create extra procedures unless the repetitive code is complex. Our simple example doesn't adequately portray this balance, but it's an important consideration.

The second type of procedure we mentioned earlier is a sub procedure, or *event* procedure. You're probably somewhat familiar with these procedures already. Unlike function procedures, VBA executes a sub function in response to an object event such as a mouse click.

SEE ALSO

➤ *Events are discussed in several places in this book, including page 524 where macros are used in both forms and report events.*

A sub function's programming logic is the same as the logic you use with a function procedure. You just execute the sub procedure differently.

SEE ALSO

➤ *To review opening a form and adding a control button refer to page 318.*

The example for this task

To demonstrate, the examples throughout this section use a new form with a command button to show how to program the button. You can use this illustration on any property of any control on either a form or a report.

Modifying a form objects properties

1. Select the Name property field and enter a name, such as cmdGetProduct.

2. Select the Caption property and enter a descriptive title, such as Get Product.

Opening the Property sheet

(The property sheet should be opened, but if it isn't, click the Properties button 🔲 on the Form Design toolbar or choose **Properties** from the **View** menu.)

Now we're going to program our button to solicit a value and then display the product of that value by 100. The only difference between our earlier example and this one is the way we're executing it. Remember, our earlier examples were function procedures, which we executed by calling their names in the Debug window. In this example, we'll be executing an event procedure—a click event to be precise.

We'll enter our product-displaying code in the form's module. Until now we've been working with *standard* modules, meaning the module isn't attached to any particular object. In contrast, the code we enter into a form module is available only to that form.

Adding the control's sub procedure code

1. To open the form's module, click the Code button 🔲 on the Form Design toolbar.

Access will open a module just like the standard module we studied in Chapter 31. Just like the standard module, the form module will enter the first and last statement of each procedure for us.

2. Select the name of the control you created—we created cmdGetProduct, the command button—from the **Object** control drop-down list box.

Access will automatically update the **Procedure** control with the appropriate events for the control type you're using (a command button). Since we're working with a command button, VBA displays the Click event.

As you can see in Figure 32.23, Access enters the first and last statement for our command button's event procedure. However, VBA uses the identifier Sub in the procedure's name. Similarly, VBA uses the Sub identifier in the End statement.

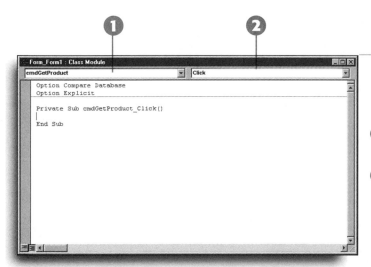

FIGURE 32.23

Access provides the first and last statement of a control's event procedure.

1 Select the name of the object in this control

2 VBA lists the events for that control in the **Procedure** control. Select the one you want to program.

Now enter the code for the procedure. Listing 32.9 shows a procedure for this command button. (Enter the listing minus the first and last statements).

LISTING 32.9 **A Sample Procedure for a Command Button**

```
1 Private Sub cmdGetProduct_Click()
2     Dim intResponse As Integer
3     intResponse = InputBox("Enter any value between 1 and 100")
4     intResponse = intResponse * 10
5     MsgBox (intResponse)
6 End Sub
```

To execute the code, close the module to return to the form, and click the View button  on the From Design toolbar to open the form in Form view and click the button shown in Figure 32.24.

FIGURE 32.24

Simply click the **Get Product** button to execute the button's `Click` event.

In response, VBA will display the input box shown in Figure 32.25. To continue, enter a value (3) and press Enter or click **OK**. Next, our event procedure multiples our entry, the value 3, by 10 and displays that product, as shown in Figure 32.26. Click **OK** to clear the message box.

FIGURE 32.25

First, our event procedure prompts us for a value between 1 and 100.

FIGURE 32.26

Then, our event procedure displays the product of our entry by 100.

As you may recall, we were able to call one function procedure from another. We can do the same with an event procedure, as shown by continuing the preceding example.

Calling a function procedure from a sub procedure

1. Return to Design view by clicking the **view** button ⬓ ▾ on the Form View toolbar.

2. In Design view, click the **code** button 🖳 to open the form's module and alter the code as shown in Listing 32.10.

3. Return to Form view and click the **Get Product** button.

4. Enter 3 in response to the input box, and the event procedure will display the value 30.

LISTING 32.10   **An Example of Calling a Procedure from a Sub Procedure**

```
1  Private Sub cmdGetProduct_Click()
2      Dim intResponse As Integer
3      intResponse = InputBox("Enter any value between 1 and 100")
4      CalProduct (intResponse)
5      MsgBox CalProduct(intResponse)
6  End Sub
```

Our event procedure solicited a value from us. Then, VBA passed that value to `CalProduct`—the function procedure we created during the "Calling a Function Procedure from Another Procedure" section. `CalProduct()` calculated and returned the product to `cmdGetProduct`'s event procedure. The event procedure displayed that product.

Something for the More Advanced VBA User

Learn how to pass data to your procedures at runtime

Display and solicit information with message and input boxes

Use VBA to make decisions

Where to go when your code doesn't work

Passing Arguments to Your Code

The built-in functions and procedures that you provide both begin with the same two elements: the function's keyword or the procedure's name, and a pair of parentheses. For example, the built-in function

```
Sum(expr)
```

has a keyword and one argument. The keyword is Sum, which identifies the built-in function, and *expr* is the argument. You supply this information so the Sum() function knows which field to total. The same is true with procedures. For instance, the Button0_Click() event and the user-defined function MyFunction() both identify the particular procedure and allow for additional arguments if needed. The only difference is that the identifying component in a procedure is known as the procedure's *name*—not a keyword.

You're used to passing additional information to built-in functions such as the Sum() function. You know you must identify the data you're summing in the form

```
Sum([Sales])
```

where [Sales] is the field you're summing. However, you might not realize that you can do the same with procedures.

Why would you want to include additional information? When you write a procedure, you won't always have all the data you need. So you can use the procedure's arguments to pass this information to your procedure in the form

```
Private Sub DoMyWork(morestuff)
```

where *morestuff* is the additional information, or *argument*. Now let's try an example that evaluates a simple mathematical equation.

Passing arguments to a procedure

1. Open a blank module by clicking **Modules** and then **New** in the Database window.

2. Enter the code shown in Listing 33.1.

3. Open the Debug window by pressing Ctrl+G.

4. Enter the statement ?DoMyWork() and press Enter. As you can see in Figure 33.1, Access returns an error message. That's because you defined an argument in your procedure, but you failed to supply one when you tried to execute it. Click **OK** to clear the error message.

5. Try again by entering the statement ?DoMyWork(10). This time, Line 4 displays the results of the calculation in Line 3 (20), as shown in Figure 33.2. Line 3 assigned the value 10 to the variable morestuff, and then VBA evaluated the entire expression:

```
intAnswer = morestuff + morestuff
```

LISTING 33.1 **Passing Arguments to a Procedure**

```
1  Function DoMyWork(morestuff)
2    Dim intAnswer As Integer
3    intAnswer = morestuff + morestuff
4    Debug.Print intAnswer
5  End Function
```

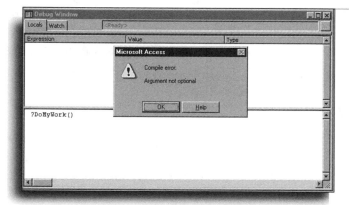

FIGURE 33.1

The procedure returns an error because you failed to include the required argument.

Optional Arguments

It's possible that you won't know how many arguments you'll need when you write a procedure. When this happens, you can declare an argument as optional using the syntax

```
Private Sub DoMyWork(morestuff Optional evenmorestuff)
```

FIGURE 33.2

When you include an argument, VBA returns the result of the procedure's calculation.

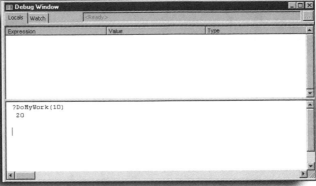

In this example, morestuff is a required argument. As you saw earlier, if you omit morestuff, VBA will return an error. However, evenmorestuff isn't required. You can add a second argument, or omit it without creating an error.

More on Data Types

Whenever possible, you should declare an argument's data type. This will prevent any users from passing incorrect or inappropriate data to the procedure. Let's return to the Debug window and see what happens when you pass an alphabetical character to DoMyWork().

Passing inappropriate data

1. If the Debug window isn't open, press Ctrl+G.

2. Enter the statement ?DoMyWork(abc) and press Enter.

3. As you can see in Figure 33.3, your procedure tries to use abc in its calculation and returns 0 instead of an error.

FIGURE 33.3

Your procedure tries to use the string abc in its calculation.

1 Without declaring the variable, VBA doesn't know this is an error and doesn't warn you

In the preceding example, the procedure returns the value 0 instead of an error. VBA has no way of knowing that the calculation is an error due to inappropriate data, so it can't warn you that the result is wrong. If you don't catch the error, the application will continue to use the wrong result.

To avoid this type of error, you can declare the argument's data type. Then, if you attempt to enter any other type of data, Access will display a warning message. Let's return to the module window and declare morestuff's data type.

Declaring an argument's data type

1. Return to the module by choosing **Module1: Module** from the **Window** menu.

2. Position the cursor after morestuff in the procedure's arguments, and enter the data type definition As Integer, as shown in Figure 33.4.

3. Return to the Debug window, type the statement ?DoMyWork(abc), and press Enter. This time, VBA displays the error shown in Figure 33.5. Click **OK** to clear the message.

FIGURE 33.4

Declaring morestuff as an integer.

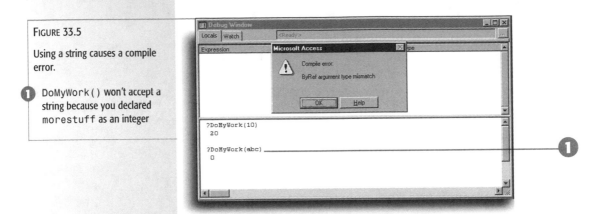

SEE ALSO

➤ *If you'd like to learn more about procedures, see page 591.*

➤ *For more information on assigning data types, see page 574.*

Displaying Information with a Message Box

Almost every application passes information to the user. The most common way of communicating with the user is with a message box using the MsgBox() function. This function displays a message, and the user responds by choosing between the existing options—options you define with arguments.

The MsgBox() function has five arguments:

```
MsgBox(message, type, title, help, context)
```

The *message* argument is the information you want to communicate to your user, *type* defines the choices the message box will offer to the user, and *title* displays a title in the title bar. The *help* and *context* arguments call up help topics. They are optional, but you can't use one without the other. Of the five arguments, only *message* is required. If you omit *type*, Access displays only one choice—OK. Let's take a look at a few message boxes.

The simplest form of *MsgBox()*

1. Open a blank module and enter the code shown in Listing 33.2.

2. Open the Debug window by pressing Ctrl+G, and enter the statement `?MessageBox()`. VBA will display the simple dialog box shown in Figure 33.6. Click the **OK** button to close the box, and VBA will display the value of the **OK** option in the Debug window. You'll use the response value to further direct VBA once your user makes a choice and closes the dialog box. Table 33.1 lists the seven button types and their response values.

LISTING 33.2 Setting Up the Message Box Response

```
1 Function MessageBox()
2   Dim intResponse As Integer
3   intResponse = MsgBox("Shall we continue?")
4   Debug.Print intResponse
5 End Function
```

LISTING 33.2

1 All optional arguments have been omitted here; use quotation marks for your response string

---

FIGURE 33.6

The `MsgBox()` function displays a simple dialog box.

1 Microsoft Access is the default value for the title bar argument

---

TABLE 33.1 Button Types and Their Response Values

Button	Value
OK	1
Cancel	2
Abort	3
Retry	4
Ignore	5
Yes	6
No	7

Adding the *type* Argument

If all you need is an OK option, omitting the *type* argument is fine. When you need a bit more flexibility, you'll want to include the *type* argument, which specifies the number and type of buttons to display, the icon style, the default button, and the modality. The modal value controls whether the message box suspends just the application or your entire system. Table 33.2 displays the different button constants and icon values, and gives more information about the modal choices. You can use the constant or the value when specifying the *type* argument.

TABLE 33.2   **Button Setup, Icons, and Modal Choices**

Constant	Value	Displays
vbOKOnly	0	OK
vbOKCancel	1	OK and Cancel
vbAbortRetryIgnore	2	Abort, Retry, and Ignore
vbYesNoCancel	3	Yes, No, and Cancel
vbYesNo	4	Yes and No
vbRetryCancel	5	Retry and Cancel
vbCritical	16	Critical Message icon
vbQuestion	32	Warning query
vbExclamation	48	Warning message
vbInformation	64	Information message
vbDefaultButton1	0	First button is default
vbDefaultButton2	256	Second button is default
vbDefaultButton3	512	Third button is default
vbDefaultButton4	768	Fourth button is default
vbApplicationModal	0	User must respond to message box before continuing
vbSystemModal	4096	All system applications are suspended until user responds to the message box

Button Defaults

The default response button is generally the button on the left. In the last example, that was the **Yes** button. You can change the default button regardless of the button's relative position to the other buttons. Simply add a specific value to the *type* argument. For instance, if you want the second button to be the default, you add the value 256. If you want the third button to be the default, you add 512. Table 33.3 shows some possible *type* arguments and an explanation of each.

TABLE 33.3 **Determining the Default Button**

Type argument	Explanation
4 + 32	4 displays a Yes/No button combination
	32 displays a question mark icon
	Yes, the first button remains the default
2 + 48 + 292	2 displays an Abort, Retry, and Ignore button
	48 displays an exclamation mark icon
	292 makes the Retry button the default
3 + 32 + 512	3 displays a Yes, No, and Cancel button
	32 displays a Warning query icon
	512 makes the Cancel button the default

Soliciting Information with an Input Box

When you need a user to supply additional information, you'll need an input box—a VBA tool that displays a question and accepts user input from the keyboard. This function takes the form

```
InputBox "question"
```

where *question* represents the information you're soliciting from the user. For instance, let's suppose you need a simple application that solicits loan information from potential borrowers. Specifically, this application will solicit a loan's principal, interest rate, and term, and then display a monthly principal and interest payment.

Soliciting information using an input box

1. Open a blank form and add two text boxes and one command button. Refer to the completed form in Figure 33.7 for placement.

2. Name the text boxes txtPayment and txtPayback. Name the command button cmdCalculate and enter the caption text Calculate Loan.

3. Attach the code in Listing 33.3 to cmdCalculate. Click the Code icon 🖺 on the Form Design toolbar, select cmdCalculate from the **Object** control, and Access will select the Click event for you.

4. Click the View icon 🖾▾ on the Form Design toolbar to view the form in Form view. Then click the **Calculate Loan** button to display the first input box. Enter 150000, as shown in Figure 33.8, and click **OK**. VBA will continue by displaying two more input boxes. Enter 07.5 and 15, respectively. VBA will finish the job by displaying the loan's monthly payment and total payback value in txtPayment and txtPayback, as shown in Figure 33.9. To close the form, click the Close icon ☒ in the title bar. (This simple procedure doesn't allow for tax or insurance costs.)

FIGURE 33.7

You'll use this simple form to calculate loan payments and payback value.

LISTING 33.3   **Code for the *cmdCalculate* Function**

```
1 Private Sub cmdCalculate_Click()
2 Dim dblPrincipal As Double, dblInterest As Integer, _
  intTerm As Double, intResult As Integer
3   dblPrincipal = InputBox("Enter the principal amount.")
4   dblInterest = InputBox("Enter the loan's interest rate.")
5   intTerm = InputBox("Enter the loan's term.")
6   intResult = Pmt(dblInterest / 12, intTerm * 12, -dblPrincipal)
```

```
7    Me!txtPayment = Format(intResult, "Currency")
8    Me!txtPayback = Format(intResult * intTerm * 12, "Currency")
9    End Sub
```

FIGURE 33.8

You entered a principal amount of $150,000.

FIGURE 33.9

After accepting principal, interest, and term information, VBA calculates a payment and payback value.

SEE ALSO

➤ *If you need help creating your example form, see page 318.*

Letting the Code Make Decisions

Until now, your code tasks have been straightforward. But what if you need more flexibility? Sometimes you need code to make decisions based on the available data. Fortunately, VBA provides two powerful decision-making statements:

- If...Then...Else
- Select Case

The *IIf()* Function

There are several forms of the If statement. We'll take a look at them all. First, let's review the built-in IIf() function, which evaluates a conditional expression (you use this function outside of a VBA module). Depending on the true or false result of that evaluation, the function performs an action. Specifically, if the condition is true, the function does one thing. If the condition is false, the function does another. This function takes the form

Evaluating to true or false

In its simplest form, you can use the `Iif()` function to return a simple true or false value, 0 or -1, known as a *Boolean* value. If the statement

`Iif(condition)`

is true, the function returns the value 0. If it's false, the statement returns the value -1.

```
Iif(expression, true action, false action)
```

where *expression* is the condition you're evaluating, *true action* is what you want VBA to do if the condition is met, and *false action* is what VBA will do if the condition isn't met.

The *If…Then…Else* Statement

Now let's take a look at the VBA `If` statement, which has many syntax possibilities. The simplest is the `If…Then` syntax:

```
If condition Then true action
```

In this form, there's no `false` action. VBA continues on to the next statement or quits. Let's look at a quick example of this simplest form of the `If` statement. Even thought it's the simplest, you'll probably use it the least. That's because, for the most part, you'll want to supply a false statement to further direct VBA.

Using VBA's *If* statement

1. Open a blank module by clicking **Modules** and then **New** in the Database window.

2. Enter the code shown in Listing 33.4. This is an example of the `If` statement in its simplest form. If you pass `RunIf()` the value 0 (the Boolean value for false), the `If` statement will be false and VBA won't execute the `Debug.Print` statement. If you pass `RunIf()` any other value or character, the `If` statement will be true and VBA will execute the `Debug.Print` statement.

3. Open the Debug window by pressing Ctrl+G.

4. Enter the statement `?RunIf(1)` and press Enter. Because `checkme` equals 1, the `If` statement equals true. As a result, VBA prints the value of `checkme`, which is 1.

5. Enter the statement `?RunIf(0)` and press Enter. This time `checkme` equals false. There is no false action, so VBA quits without doing anything further.

LISTING 33.4 **The *If* Statement in Simple Form**

```
1   Function RunIf(checkme)
2       If checkme Then Debug.Print checkme
```

LISTING 33.4

1 When checkme is true, VBA prints its value; when checkme is false, VBA prints nothing.

```
End Function
```

An alternate but similar form is

```
If condition Then
    true action
End If
```

In this case, there's still no false action. However, you could follow the *true action* statement with other statements that you want executed if *condition* is true. Let's take a look at the last example, in this second form.

The *If...Then* form

1. Open a blank module and enter the code shown in Listing 33.5.

2. Open the Debug window by pressing Ctrl+G.

3. Enter the statement ?RunIfThen(1) and press Enter. Because checkme equals 1 (which is true), VBA prints checkme and then the string Checkme doesn't equal 0.

4. Next, enter the statement ?RunIfThen(0) and press Enter. Because checkme is 0, which equals a false value, VBA skips the *true action* statement and the following statement and quits.

LISTING 33.5 **Testing the *If...then* Logic with Input**

```
1   Function RunIfThen(checkme)
2       If checkme Then
3           Debug.Print checkme
4           Debug.Print "Checkme doesn't equal 0."
5       End If
6   End Function
```

LISTING 33.5

1 VBA executes lines 3 and 4 when the If condition is true

The If statement's last form is very powerful and versatile because you can have more than one condition and more than one true and false action. When you need this extra flexibility, use the form

```
If condition Then
    true action
[ElseIf condition Then
    [ElseIf true action]]
[Else
    Else action]
End If
```

This form is much like the other two, but it offers more alternatives by checking a second condition when the first condition isn't met instead of executing a false condition. If the second condition is met, VBA executes that condition's true action. If it's false, VBA executes the Else action.

You might be tempted to omit the Else action, and it's legal to do so. However, when an Else action doesn't seem necessary, try adding an Else statement that warns you that neither condition has been met. You may catch some data errors that might otherwise go undetected. Now let's look at an example of this final If statement.

The *If...Then...Else* statement

1. Open a blank module and enter the code in Listing 33.6.

2. Open the Debug window, enter the statement ?RunIfThenElse(-1), and press Enter. Because checkme equals -1, VBA will execute the true action and print the string checkme is true.

3. Enter the statement ?RunIfThenElse(0) and press Enter. This time, VBA executes the ElseIf action, which prints the string checkme isn't true.

4. Enter one last statement, ?RunIfThenElse(2), and press Enter. This time, checkme fails both conditions, so VBA executes the Else action, as shown in Figure 33.10. Remember earlier when we advised you to not exclude the Else action? This is why. The Else action displays an alert that checkme has met neither condition.

LISTING 33.6   **Code for Testing the *Elself* Statement**

```
1 Function RunIfThenElse(checkme)
2   If checkme = -1 Then
3     Debug.Print "checkme is true"
4   ElseIf checkme = 0 Then
5     Debug.Print "checkme isn't true"
6   Else
7     Debug.Print "checkme is neither 0 or -1)    "
8   End If
9 End Function
```

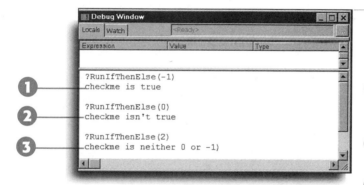

FIGURE 33.10

In this last example, checkme meets neither condition, so VBA displays a warning message.

① Line 3 from Listing 33.6 prints this string when checkme equals -1

② Line 5 prints this string when checkme equals 0

③ Line 7 goes into action when checkme is neither -1 or 0

Select Case

The Select Case statement is similar to the If statement in logic. However, Select Case evaluates just one condition and then reacts with a number of possible responses. You'll use this statement in the form

```
Select Case abcCondition
    Case a Condition
        a action
    Case    b Condition
        b action
    Case c Condition
        c action
    Case Else
        Else action
End Select
```

As with the `If` statement, the `Else` statement isn't required, but we recommend you use it. The `Select Case` statement's *abcCondition* argument is generally an expression that evaluates to several different values. The subsequent `Case` statements then specify individual possibilities and the action you want to be taken when each condition is met. For instance, the statement

```
Select Case 1 To 5, 10 to 15
```

would handle the values 1, 2, 3, 4, and 5, and 10, 11, 12, 13, 14, and 15. You would then have a `Case` statement that directed VBA for each of these possible values.

Using *Select Case*

1. Open a blank module and enter the procedure shown in Listing 33.7.

2. Open the Debug window and enter the statement `?CloseBox()`. Line 3 will display a message box and display a Yes, No, and Cancel button.

3. Click **Yes**, and VBA will execute the `Case vbYes` action in Line 6, which will print the string `Goodbye, and thank you for coming`.

4. Position the cursor at the end of the `CloseBox()` statement and press Enter to run that procedure again. When Access displays the message box, click **No**. This time, VBA executes the `Case vbNo` action, which prints the string `When are you leaving?`.

5. Run the statement again, click **Cancel**, and VBA will execute the `Case vbCancel` action in Line 10. This statement prints the string `Don't go away mad!`, as shown in Figure 33.11.

6. Although it isn't likely, the `Case Else` action in Line 12 is provided for those times when a user closes the box inappropriately.

LISTING 33.7 **Setting Up a *Select Case* Procedure to Test Input**

```
1  Function CloseBox()
2    Dim intClose As Integer
3    intClose = MsgBox("Going out?", vbYesNoCancel)
4    Select Case intClose
5      Case vbYes
6        Debug.Print "Goodbye, and thank you for coming."
7      Case vbNo
8        Debug.Print "When are you leaving?"
9      Case vbCancel
10       Debug.Print "Don't go away mad!"
11     Case Else
12       Debug.Print "You're going the wrong way."
13   End Select
14 End Function
```

LISTING 33.7

1 In a real application, you'd probably use a MsgBox function, not Debug.Print, to display your messages

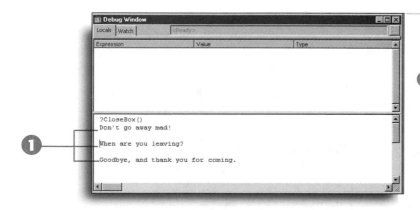

FIGURE 33.11

Clicking **Cancel** results in another message.

1 The Debug window responds to the actions in steps 2 through 6

Looping in VBA

Similar to decision-making is the loop structure. Instead of evaluating a condition and then executing a response based on the result of that evaluation, a loop executes a task as long as a condition is met.

The *For...Next* Loop

VBA's For...Next loop repeats a task a predetermined number of times. You can define the number of cycles, or you can use an expression. This function takes the form

```
For count = start To end [step]
    task statements
Next count
```

The *count* argument tracks the number of times VBA has executed the task statements, *start* is the value *count* begins with, *end* determines the last cycle, and *step* specifies the value range between cycles. For instance, the *step* default is 1, so VBA will add 1 to *count* each time VBA completes a cycle. If you use a *step* value of -1, VBA will subtract 1 from *count*. Let's look at a simple For loop that modifies multiple controls on a form.

Modifying multiple controls with a simple *For* loop

1. Open a blank form by clicking **Forms** and then **New** in the Database window. Then double-click **Design View** in the New Forms dialog box.

2. Add five check box controls to the blank form, and name them chk1, chk2, chk3, chk4, and chk5.

3. Add a command button to the bottom of the form and name it cmdRunFor. Enter the caption Run For Loop.

4. Attach the code in Listing 33.8 to cmdRunFor's Click event. Click the Code icon 🔲 on the Form Design toolbar. In the resulting module, choose cmdRunFor from the Object control. VBA will select the Click event in the Procedure control for you. At that point, simply enter the code. (VBA supplies the first and last statements for you.)

5. Click the View icon 🔲▾ on the Form Design toolbar. In Form view, click the **Run For Loop** button. Doing so executes the button's Click event. During the first loop, int equals 1, so the component Me("chk" & int) evaluates to chk1. As a result, VBA disables chk1. During the second loop, int equals 2, so VBA disables chk2, and so on. During the fifth and final cycle, VBA disables chk5, as shown in Figure 33.12. After executing the cycle five times, VBA quits. If you want to display the controls, simply click the **Run For Loop** button again.

SEE ALSO
➤ *To learn how to add multiple controls, see page 321.*

LISTING 33.8   **Code for *cmdRunFor*'s *Click* Event**

```
1    Private Sub cmdRunFor_Click()
2      Dim i As Integer
3      For i = 1 To 5
4        Me("chk" & i).Enabled = Not (Me("chk" & i).Enabled)
5      Next i
6    End Sub
```

SEE ALSO

➤ *If you don't know how to add controls to a form, see page 318.*

FIGURE 33.12
The For loop disables all the check boxes in your form.

The *For Each...Next* Statement

The drawback to the simple For...Next statement is that you must specify a *start* and *end* argument. You won't always know these values. The For Each...Next statement overcomes this limitation. (This form of For was introduced in Access 95.) This statement takes the form

```
For Each element In group
     task statements
Next
```

where *element* is the type of object in *group*. You don't have to tell VBA where to start or how many items there are, because VBA will keep track of the items for you. That's because the For Each...Next statement executes your code once for each *element* in *group*. For instance, if a form has five controls, this statement would execute its code five times—once for each control. You don't have to know there are five controls because the statement takes care of that for you. The following For Each…Next example displays a dynamic list of objects in a combo box.

Displaying a dynamic list of objects using *For Each…Next*

1. Open a blank form and add a combo box to it.

2. Name the combo box cboReports. Change the **Row Source Type** property to **Value List**.

3. Next, attach the procedure shown in Listing 33.9 to cboReports' Got Focus event by clicking the Code icon 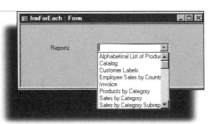 on the Form Design toolbar. Then, choose cboReports and GotFocus from the result module's Object and Procedure controls, respectively.

5. Click the View icon on the Form Design toolbar and open the control's drop-down list. As you can see in Figure 33.13, the combo box offers a list of all the Northwind reports.

LISTING 33.9   **Code for the *Got Focus* Event**

```
1    Private Sub cboReports_BeforeUpdate(Cancel As Integer)
2    Dim db As Database, varItem As Variant, ctlList As ComboBox,
     strName As String
3    Set db = CurrentDb
4    Set ctlList = Me!cboReports
5    For Each varItem In ctlList.ItemsSelected
6      strName = ctlList.ItemData(varItem)
7      DoCmd.OpenReport strName, acNormal
8    Next varItem
9    End Sub
```

FIGURE 33.13

Using a For Each…Next loop to fill this combo box with all the available reports in Northwind.

When the Code Doesn't Work

Few of us are so proficient with VBA that we don't make mistakes. In fact, the best developers depend heavily on VBA's debugging features. During testing, you can count on two types of programming errors you'll need to debug:

- Syntax errors
- Logic errors

Syntax errors are very common, and fortunately, most are caught by VBA when you're entering the code. A syntax error simply means that VBA doesn't understand the code because you've misspelled something or omitted a required argument. If VBA fails to catch the error as you're entering the mistake, it will stop and point to the offending statement when you compile the code. At that point, you simply correct the highlighted statement.

On the other hand, VBA won't point to your logic errors. Instead, it will run but won't respond the way you expect it to. Logic errors can, but usually don't, crash your system. Instead, they return incorrect data or nothing at all. Consequently, logic errors are a bit harder to find and resolve than syntax errors.

Running Code in the Debug Window

Perhaps the easiest way to find logic mistakes is to print the results to the Debug window using the Debug.Print statement. For instance, let's suppose you want to replace all Saturday and Sunday dates with the following Monday. You try the procedure shown in Listing 33.10, but sometimes it works and sometimes it doesn't. Specifically, it works for Sundays not but not Saturdays.

LISTING 33.10   **Using the _Debug.Print_ Statement to Find Logic Errors**

```
1    Function FixDate(today As Variant)
2      Dim intToday As Variant
3      intToday = DatePart("w", today, 2)
4      If intToday = 7 Or intToday = 1 Then intToday = 2
5    End Function
```

The simplest way to debug the procedure is to add a few Debug.Print statements, as shown in Listing 33.11, and then run the procedure in the Debug window.

LISTING 33.11   Using the *Debug.Print* Statement to Find Logic Errors

```
1   Function FixDate(today As Variant)
2     Dim intToday As Variant
3     intToday = DatePart("w", today, 2)
4     Debug.Print intToday
5     If intToday = 7 Or intToday = 1 Then intToday = 2
6     Debug.Print intToday
7   End Function
```

A few strategically placed Dubug.Print statements can help you analyze what's going on, as shown in Figure 33.14. You've passed FixDate() a Saturday, which should equal a 7. However, FixDate thinks it's a 6. The mistake is right in your code. You told VBA to treat Monday as the first day of the week instead of Sunday. Doing so throws off the weekday count by one. To correct the error, simply replace the 2 argument in the DatePart() function with a 1:

```
intToday = DatePart("w", today, 1)
```

(Or omit it, because 1 is the default.) Then run the procedure in the Debug window a second time.

FIGURE 33.14

Debugging the function quickly revealed the error.

❶ VBA thinks Monday, not Sunday, is the first day of the week

❷ After making this slight alteration, the function works as expected

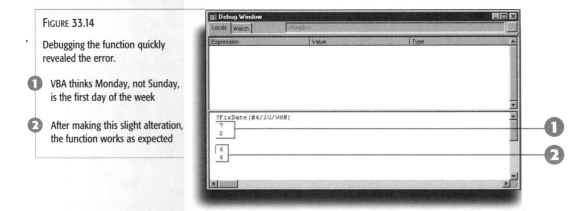

The Debug window doesn't limit you to functions. You can evaluate any expression. For instance, you can enter the expression ?1 + 3, and the Debug window will return the value 4. Just be sure to proceed each expression with the ? character, or *print indicator*.

You can also change the value of an active object or declared variable in the Debug window. Simply enter the change in expression form. For instance, the statement

```
x = 5
```

would set the variable x to the value 5. In addition, the statement

```
Forms![frmMyForm]![txtMyControl] = 5
```

would change the value of txtMyControl to 5.

There are other debugging tools, which are listed in Table 33.4.

Debug window shortcut

You don't have to retype a statement each time you want to execute it in the Debug window. After executing a statement in the Debug window, VBA retains the statement. To reexecute it, simply position the cursor at the end of the statement and press Enter.

TABLE 33.4 Debugging Tools

Tool	Icon	Explanation
Toggle Breakpoint		You can set a breakpoint to temporarily halt the execution of your code at a particular statement.
Call Stack		The call stack will list each active procedure in order as they are called, displaying the current procedure at the top of the list.
Quick Watch		This feature displays information about a variable. Simply position the cursor within the variable name and click the icon to display the calling function and the value of the variable. You can also evaluate an expression.
Step Into		This feature will execute your procedure one statement at a time.
Step Over		This procedure executes only the current procedure one statement at a time. If the current procedure calls another, VBA will execute that entire procedure at once.
Step Out		Returns you to the last line in the calling function.

Preventing Run-Time Errors

When you debug code, you're correcting your mistakes. However, internal errors can stop or even crash your application. Such errors aren't coding mistakes—they're errors that occur when the application doesn't find the conditions it needs to continue. These errors are called *run-time* errors. You can usually anticipate these errors before they occur, so you can direct your application accordingly. Error-handling has three simple steps:

- Executing the On Error statement
- Evaluating and processing the error using the Err statement
- Exiting the error-handling routine

The first step is to enable error-handling by including an On Error statement in your code. You'll want to place this statement *before* the code that may produce an error. Once this feature is on, an internal (or run-time) error won't stop your application and display an error message. Instead, the On Error statement will direct VBA to an error-handling routine, which will evaluate and react to the error.

What Is *On Error*?

The On Error statement's job is to direct VBA to an error handling routine when VBA encounters a run-time error. This statement takes the form

```
On Error GoTo error-handler
```

where *error-handler* identifies the routine that will evaluate and process the error. You can also use the form

```
On Error Resume where
```

which simply ignores the error and continues to execute your code as specified by the *where* argument. There are three possibilities:

- Resume—VBA returns to the line that produces the error and attempts to execute it again.
- Resume Next—VBA continues executing at the line immediately following the line that produced the error.

- Resume *other*—VBA resumes with the procedure specified by *other*.

The error-handler is like any other procedure. However, there are a few differences in the way you enter it:

- Follow the error-handler's name with a colon character.
- Don't indent the error-handler's name.

About *Err* and *Error*

To evaluate run-time errors, you'll use the Err statement, which returns a predefined value. When no error condition exists, Err equals 0. Once an error occurs, Err equals a value that represents the current error. VBA resets the Err value to 0 when you exit the procedure that encountered the error. VBA will also reset Err if VBA encounters another procedure call or a Resume statement. The Error statement returns a text description of the current error.

Now, let's suppose your application attempts to save files to disk. Doing so can cause a run-time error if there's no disk in the drive, or if the disk in the drive is full. If you omit error-handling, such a mishap will stop your application. Instead, you can include a simple error-handling routine to alert the user to the problem, give the user an opportunity to correct the problem, and then continue when the user is ready. The procedure shown in Listing 33.12 handles this situation nicely.

LISTING 33.12   Error-Handling

```
1    Private Function DoMyWork()
2    On Error GoTo ErrHandler
3    .
4    .
5    Exit Function
6    ErrHandler:
7    Select Case Err
8       Case 61
9          MsgBox "Disk is full, please insert a blank disk and try
    again."
10         Resume
```

LISTING 33.12

(1) Insert your code for saving to disk here

continues…

LISTING 33.12 **Continued**

```
11   Case 71
12     MsgBox "Drive isn't ready. Please check and try again."
13     Resume
14   Case Else
15     MsgBox "Undetermined error " & Err & Error(Err)
16     Resume Next
17   End Select
18   End Function
```

This procedure is fairly straightforward. If the run-time error is 61 or 71, the procedure identifies the error and gives simple instructions for correcting it so you can continue. This is where you (or your user) read the message, correct the error, and then click OK to continue. In both cases, VBA will then return to the error-producing line and attempt to execute it again. Everything should be fine as long as you've corrected the error.

If the error is anything other than one of the expected errors, the Case Else statement displays the Err value and the Error description. Then, the Resume Next statement continues at the line immediately following the line that produced the error.

Producing a Table of Error Values and Descriptions

If you frequently look up error codes, you should consider creating a table for them. The Help section provides a UDF for doing so. All you have to do is cut and paste it from the Help section and then run it.

Creating an error table

1. Choose **Contents** and then **Index** from the **Help** menu.
2. Click the **Index** tab, enter error codes, and then click **Display**.
3. Highlight the AccessAndJetErrorsTable() procedure in the resulting Help window, click the **Options** button, and then choose **Copy**.
4. Select the **Modules** tab and then click **New** in the Database window.

5. Press Ctrl+V to paste the copied function to the blank module.

6. Open the Debug window by pressing Ctrl+G. Then enter the statement `?AccessAndJetErrorsTable()` and press Enter. VBA will create a table of error codes and their respective descriptions. VBA will display a message when it's done. Click **OK** to clear the message.

Logging Errors

If people other than yourself use your application, you may want to log errors as they occur. That way you can review the log and make changes to avoid errors that are occurring on a regular basis. You'll need to add an extra table and a UDF to your application. Be sure to add a call to the UDF in your error-handling code. You will also need to pass the following arguments:

- `strProcedure` will equal the name of the error-producing procedure.

- `strModule` will equal the name of the module that contains `strProcedure`.

- `intErr` will equal the result of the `Err` statement.

- `intError` will equal the result of the `Error(Err)` statement.

Refer to Table 33.5 for the suggested table's structure. You can alter it to suit your needs. The procedure code is in Listing 33.13. If you modify the table, be sure to make the appropriate updates to the procedure.

TABLE 33.5   Error Log Table–*tblErrorLog*

Field Name	Data Type
Form	Text
Control	Text
User	Text
Date	Date/Time
Procedure	Text

continues…

TABLE 33.5   **Continued**

Module	Text
Code	Integer
Description	Text

LISTING 33.13   **Error Log Function**

```
1    PrivateFunction ErrorLog(strProcedure As String, _
     strModule As String,
     intErr As Integer, strError As String)
2    Dim db As Database
3    Dim rst As Recordset
4    On Error Resume Next
5    Set db = CurrentDB()
6    set rst - db.OpenRecordset("tblErrorLog")
7    rst.AddNew
8    rst!Form = Screen.ActiveForm.Name
9    rst!Control = Screen.ActiveControl.Name
10   rst!User = GetCurentUser()
11   rst!Date = Now()
12   rst!Procedure = strProcedure
13   rst!Module = strModule
14   rst!Code = intErr
15   rst!Description = strError
16   rst.Update
17   rst.Close
18   db.Close
19   End Function
```

Saving Your Database as an MDE File

What is an MDE file?

Some cautions

Create an MDE file

Benefits

Restrictions

Conversion warning

One of the questions concerning MDE files that are created under Access 97 is whether you can use those files in a later version of Access.

Be aware that if you plan to develop Access databases and distribute them as MDE files, your clients might not be able to upgrade the MDE files themselves unless they also have copies of the original MDB files. In the future, this could cause problems when clients want to upgrade to a newer version of Access. If you don't provide a way for them to upgrade, you could have some very irate clients.

Therefore, it's always a good idea to maintain a backup copy in `.mdb` format.

MDB Files I Know About, But What Is an MDE File?

An MDE file is a special file format that you can save your MDB database file to. This process compiles all your VBA modules and prevents anyone else from viewing, editing, or adding code to the MDE file. Although tables, queries, and macros can be still be edited in an MDE database file, forms, reports, and modules cannot. Your VBA code can't be edited or viewed, but it will continue to run as before (exceptions to this are discussed later in this chapter in the "Restrictions" section).

Saving the file to an MDE format not only removes the code, but it also compacts the resulting MDE database file. Because this step is completed for you, you will not have to worry about whether or not your database was compacted before it was saved as an MDE file.

Saving your MDB database file to an MDE also removes the textual part of the VBA code from your database, after it is compiled. This not only reduces the size of the database, but it also optimizes memory usage because the MDE database will always be in a compiled state.

Contrary to what was reported recently in a popular Visual Basic magazine, classes *can* be used in an MDE file, just as they are in MDB files.

Not So Fast!

With all these benefits, you would think that there wouldn't be any side effects. Well, before you actually save an MDB database to an MDE database file, you'd be wise to read the rest of this chapter. The following sections will discuss some of the caveats to using MDE database files.

Insurance

Before you actually create an MDE file, you need to make a backup copy of the MDB file. Store this backup copy in a safe place in case you need to make a new MDE file.

If you need to make changes to the database application, the original MDB file is the file that you will change. Once you are done with the changes that you want to make to the MDB, you will need to create another MDE file.

Creating an MDE File from an MDB

Once you get past the restrictions, saving your database to an MDE is actually pretty easy. If you run into any problems while you are creating an MDE, you should refer to the "Restrictions" section later in this chapter. The following steps show you how to create an MDE.

Creating an MDE when there isn't a database loaded

1. From the menu, select **T**ools, **D**atabase Utilities, **M**ake MDE File.

2. The Database to Save as MDE dialog box will pop up (see Figure 34.1).

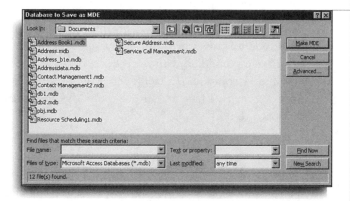

FIGURE 34.1
Save your database to an MDE.

3. Select the MDB or MDA file to save as MDE, and then click the **M**ake MDE button.

4. The Save as MDE dialog will pop up. Enter a name for your MDE.

5. Click the **S**ave button.

Benefits of Creating an MDE File

As mentioned before, there are benefits to creating an MDE file out of your MDB file. If you can find your way through the different scenarios, you can benefit in several ways. These benefits have been mentioned before, but they're shown here in a little more detail.

Protects Your VBA Code

The first benefit that makes MDE files worthwhile is the removal of the textual representation of your VBA source code. On the surface, this may not mean anything to you. But if you dig a little deeper, you'll start realizing the benefit of removing your source code.

When you develop a neat routine using VBA, you want to protect your investment. You don't want to spend four hours carefully coding and debugging a solution, only to have your competition spend five minutes copying it.

Before Access 97 was released, the only way you could protect your code was to secure your database using Access security. If you have ever fiddled with Access security, you know that this is not an easy solution. (In fact, every time that I need to use Access security, I have to get out the books and reread what I'm supposed to do.)

Now, don't take the preceding statement wrong and say, "I'll never use Access security." When done right, Access security will protect your database. But as with all solutions, you should use the right methods to solve your problems. With MDE files, you protect the source code but still have full access to tables, queries, and macros.

For a further discussion on using security with MDE files, see "Restrictions on Access Security" later in this chapter.

Protects the Design of Your Forms and Reports

Another added benefit of MDE files is that Access protects the design of your forms and reports. The benefit of protecting your source code, as mentioned in the previous section, applies to the design of your forms and reports as well. You can immediately tell when you are in a database that has been saved as an MDE. When you navigate to the **Forms** tab in the database window, the **Design** and **New** buttons will be disabled (see Figure 34.2).

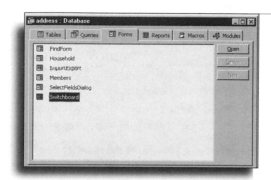

FIGURE 34.2

Notice that the Design and New Buttons are disabled.

It's unclear what happens in the MDE that prevents you from modifying or creating a new form or report. In the case of the VBA source code, you know that it is being compiled. Forms and reports are also compiled, but Access goes one step beyond and disables the Edit commands or creates a new one in an MDE.

If you've done any work with creating a database that is to run on the runtime version of Access, you know that even though end users can't edit or create a form or report, the commands to do so are still available to the developer. In the runtime version of Access, the end user can still click the **Edit** or **New** button, but can't see what they are doing because the screen is not updated. This is not what is happening with the MDE files. In an MDE, these commands are completely off-limits to you as an end user or a developer.

Memory Optimization

Another benefit of MDE is memory optimization. This is really a side effect and not a reason to create MDE database files. Because the textual representation of the forms, reports, and modules is removed, the database is made smaller. Therefore, it uses less memory and fewer resources on the computer that is running the MDE file.

When MDE files were first used officially, beginning with Access 97, Microsoft used to say that MDE databases were faster than MDB databases. This is not true. Their statement should read, "MDE databases are faster than MDB databases *that are not compiled*." When an MDB is compiled, there isn't any difference in speed. Any perceived difference in speed is an illusion because 90% of the time, your database is running in an uncompiled state. You can check whether your database is compiled by performing the following steps.

Checking your MDB database to see if it is compiled

1. Go to the **Modules** tab in the database window.

2. Select any module, and then click the **Design** button.

3. Select **Debug** from the menu.

4. If your database is not in a compiled state, you will see the first three lines completely enabled (see Figure 34.3).

4. The first three menu items will be disabled if the database is completely compiled.

Your MDE database is always in the compiled state.

Restrictions

There are certain features of Access that you can't use with an MDE, and other items that must be done in a certain order. These restrictions will determine whether or not you can use MDE database files.

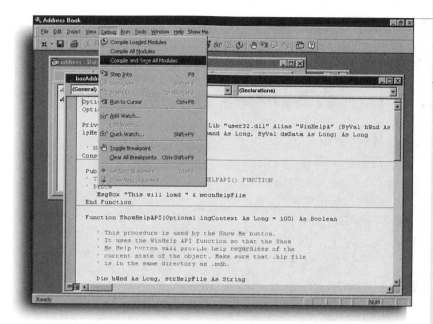

FIGURE 34.3

The code in this database is not compiled.

No Code that Adds or Modifies Forms, Reports, or Modules

One of the restrictions is that you can't create an MDE file containing code that modifies or adds new code, controls, forms, or reports. If you have code that does this, it will refuse to run and indicate that the command can't be used in an MDE database (see Figure 34.4).

Related to the inability to modify or add new code is the inability to import a form, report, or module from another database to an MDE. Nor can you export a form, report, or module from an MDE database.

Can't Reference Another MDB File

MDE cannot reference MDB or MDA files. All referenced databases have to be saved as MDE files. If you have a reference to an MDB, you will get a message similar to the one in Figure 34.5 when you try to create an MDE file.

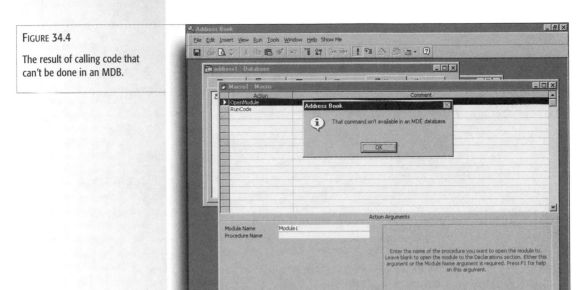

FIGURE 34.4

The result of calling code that can't be done in an MDB.

FIGURE 34.5

Can't reference an MDB file.

Because you can't reference any database that is an MDB, this presents a problem with add-ins. Add-ins usually are saved as an MDE, but if you happen to run across one that is an MDB or MDA, you must first convert it to an MDE before you can save your database to an MDE. If you obtained your add-in from a third party and they have Access security implemented, you will have to contact that third party and see if you can obtain an MDE of the same add-in.

Restrictions on Access Security

Another restriction on creating MDE files is that if Access security is implemented in your MDB and you don't meet the following guidelines, you can't save your database as an MDE. If you don't meet the guidelines, a dialog box will pop up (see Figure 34.6).

FIGURE 34.6
You don't have permissions.

Access lists the following guidelines in the online help for these restrictions:

- You must join the workgroup information file that defines the user accounts used to access the database, or that was in usc when the database was created.

- Your user account must have Open/Run and Open Exclusive permissions for the database.

- Your user account must have Modify Design or Administer permissions for any tables in the database, or you must be the owner of any tables in the database.

- Your user account must have Read Design permissions for all objects in the database.

If your database meets the preceding criteria, you can save your secured database as an MDE. If you don't meet the criteria, you must have the security removed or have someone who has permissions create the MDE for you.

SEE ALSO

➤ *For more information on Access security, see page 733.*

Beyond Desktop Application

Replication

If you have been developing solutions for any length of time, you will run into a situation where you'll need to distribute your application over a network. If some of those users are connecting via a WAN or dial-up connection, you'll probably need to employ Microsoft Jet Replication in one fashion or another.

What Replication Is and When to Use It

Replication enables users at different locations that may not be connected to easily share the changes they are making to a database. Those can be data changes, design changes, or both. Each database is called a *replica*, and the related group of databases is called a *replica set*. Only one member of the set can be considered the master file—the *Design Master*. The Design Master is the only place that structural changes to the database can be made. Each replica can contain its own set of local objects that will not be replicated to the other members of the set. These objects include tables, queries, forms, reports, macros, and modules.

When to use replication? Believe it or not, there is no precise answer to this question. There are a few instances where it does have significant benefits over traditional file-server or client-server systems. Like most solutions you'll design and develop, you'll probably find that a nice mix of techniques will do the best job.

One of the most important things to keep in mind when deciding when to implement replication is update-latency. *Update-latency* is simply the amount of time that it takes to update data between all replicas in a set. If you can live with "real-time-enough" updates of your data, replication might well be the correct choice. Replication also enables you to make updates via LAN, WAN, dial-up, or Internet connections.

Four of the most common scenarios that are well suited for replication are as follows:

- Distributing software—You can add new tables, queries, forms, reports, macros, and modules or make changes to existing objects in the Design Master. The next time the Design Master is synchronized with its replicas, the changes will be dispersed to the replicas.

- Accessing data—If you are a salesperson or other field personnel, you can maintain replicas of a corporate database on your laptop computer. Upon connecting to the corporate network, you can synchronize the changes you made to the replica on your laptop with the changes made in the corporate office replica.

- Load balancing—You can reduce the amount of network traffic by replicating any number of databases to multiple servers across the corporate network. Now each server will share a more evenly distributed load of network traffic.

- Database backups—You can automatically back up a database by keeping a replica on a different computer. Unlike traditional back-up methods that prevent users from gaining access to a database during backup, replication enables you to continue making changes online.

The Tools of the Trade

There are four main tools that enable you to implement replication, distinguish differences between replicas in a set, and initiate synchronization, as well as other Jet management tasks. These tools are:

- Briefcase replication
- Access 97 Menus
- Data Access Objects (DAO)
- Replication Manager

Access 95 refresher

Much of this information on replication began with Access 95. If you're familiar with that version, you'll recognize the menus from the Access 95 ADT.

Briefcase Replication

Briefcase replication uses the Briefcase accessory that is provided with Microsoft Windows 95 or Windows NT 4.0 or later. Briefcase replication is as simple to use as dragging your .mdb file onto the briefcase icon on your desktop.

You normally use the briefcase to keep files synchronized between your desktop PC and a laptop. The Briefcase uses a basic date/time stamp comparison to ensure that the newest version of the file is the only version between the two locations. When Microsoft Access is installed, it adds a CLSID to the Registry, telling the briefcase to use a special Jet replication reconciler whenever an .mdb is dragged into the briefcase. Now when you use the **Update All** or **Update Selection** options in the **Briefcase** menu, Jet will handle all replication chores.

Access 97 Menus

The **Replication** submenu on the **Tools** menu provides a set of four menu selections that will aid in the creation, distribution, and basic upkeep of your replicated database. These commands are as follows:

- Synchronize Now—This option enables you to select an existing replica in the set in which to exchange updates.
- Create Replica—Enables you to make a replica of the database you're working in. If the database isn't already a Design Master, Microsoft Access does the conversion automatically.
- Resolve Conflicts—Enables you to compare two replica set members that have conflicts. Conflicts may occur when members are synchronized. See the section "Resolving Conflicts and Errors" later in this chapter.
- Recover Design Master—Enables you to assign the Design Master to another replica if the current Design Master is damaged.

Data Access Objects (DAO)

DAO through VBA provides a programmatic interface to Jet replication by including a number of extensions to the programming interface. Everything that you can do through Briefcase or the Access menu can be done through DAO. This option obviously is an advanced developer's feature and will not be covered in detail in this chapter.

Replication Manager

The Replication Manager is included with the Microsoft Office 97 Developers Edition (ODE). This tool enables you to better administer your replicated applications via a graphical interface. There are a number of things you can do with the Replication Manager:

- Replicate databases
- Create additional replicas for an established replica set
- Synchronize or schedule synchronization of replicas
- Synchronize via the Internet
- Set LAN/WAN topologies
- Manage various aspects of the replica set

Figure 35.1 shows a managed set and its topology

There is no better way to learn about something than to actually do it. Replication in its basic form is rather simple to do. Planning the how, when, and why you should implement it is the hardest part. There is no substitute for proper planning.

Included on the companion Web site is a series of very simple databases that you can use to run through the examples. The **Tables** tab of Ch36a.mdb is pictured in Figure 35.2. This is what the database looks like prior to replication. The System tables have been shown to help illustrate what actually happens when a normal database has been converted to a Design Master.

FIGURE 35.1

The Replication Manager graphically shows the server and the replicas in relation to one another.

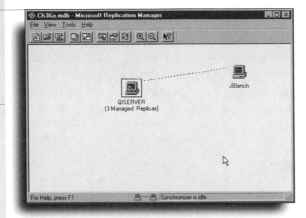

FIGURE 35.2

Sample database table listing with system tables showing.

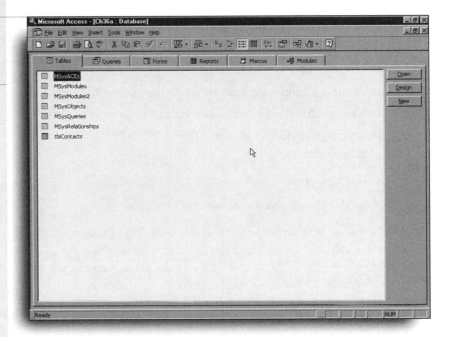

To create a replica from a standard .mdb

1. Navigate to **Tools**, **Replication**, **Create Replica** to begin. First Access will display a message box explaining that the database needs to be closed in order to proceed, as seen in Figure 35.3. Click **Yes**.

FIGURE 35.3

You must close the database before replication or Access will close it for you.

How to show hidden objects

To hide or show the system or hidden objects in the database, navigate through the menu system to **Tools**, **Options**, and the **View** tab. Check the objects you want to show and uncheck the ones you want to hide.

2. Next, a message box asks if you want a backup of your original made prior to converting it to a Design Master (see Figure 35.4). Under most circumstances, you should click **Yes**. It only makes sense to have a backup in case of problems during conversion.

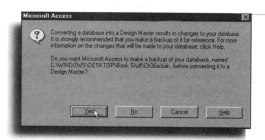

FIGURE 35.4

Back up the database before replication, in case you need a copy if problems arise.

3. Next you're prompted for a name and a location to save the replica of your Design Master in a typical Save dialog box. This is done by default because there is no reason to have a Design Master without a replica to synchronize with.

Figure 35.5 shows the message box telling you that Access has created a Design Master and a replica, and where they are located. It also reminds you that structural changes can be made only at the Design Master, and changes to the data can be made anywhere in the replica set.

FIGURES 35.5

Access repeats the names and paths of your master and replica.

Voilà! Your database has been converted to a Design Master. Wasn't that simple? Now that you have a Design Master, let's take a look at what happened and some of the basic reasons why these changes needed to occur.

What Has Changed and Why

As you saw in Figure 35.2, there is a single table (tblContacts) and a handful of system tables that Microsoft Jet uses to manage the database properly. When you convert your .mdb to a Design Master, it grows. As an example, the Ch36a database prior to conversion was a mere 82KB. After conversion, the database more than doubled in size to 178KB. It isn't a set rule that it will always be x times larger, but it will grow depending on the number of objects and object types in the database. Figure 35.6 shows the changes to the database after the conversion process. These additional tables are required by Microsoft Jet to record the historical changes between replicas in the set, as well as other system information. Table 35.1 shows the system tables that may be of most importance and a brief description of each.

TABLE 35.1   System Table Information for Replication

Table	Where Replicated	Description
MsysErrors	Is Replicated, All members	This table identifies where and why errors occurred during data synchronization. It identifies the table involved, the record that encountered the errors, the replica or replicas where the error was

Table	Where Replicated	Description
		detected, the replica that last changed the record, the type of operation that failed, and the reason it failed.
MsysSidetables	Not Replicated, local to each replica	This table exists only if a conflict has occurred between the user's replica and another replica in the replica set. It's supplied for information only, and its contents may be modified or deleted by custom conflict-resolution routines or by the user. All side tables are named `table_conflict`, where `table` is the original name of the table.
MsysSchemaProb	Not Replicated	This table is present only when an error has occurred while updating the design of a replica. It provides additional details about the cause of the error.
MsysExchangeLog	Not Replicated	This table stores information about replica synchronizations that have taken place.

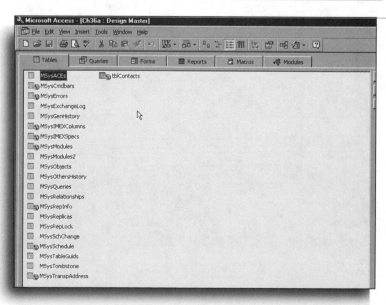

FIGURE 35.6
The database shows numerous changes.

User Tables

In order for Microsoft Jet to properly manage the objects and data in your database, it needs to make a number of structural changes to your tables. For example, each table has three or more fields (columns), s_Generation, s_GUID, and s_Lineage, added to each record (row). Figure 35.7, a Datasheet view of the tblContacts table, shows the fields that were added to the table to make replication a possibility. Each one is explained in the following sections.

GUIDs

The s_GUID field stores the 16-byte Globally Unique Identifier (GUID). The GUID is generated so that no matter where this record resides or when it was created, it will be unique within the replica set. Combine the network node ID, a time value, a clock sequence value, and a version value to create the GUID. An example of a GUID is

42606800-0B4C-11D2-98EA-080009FBC4D3

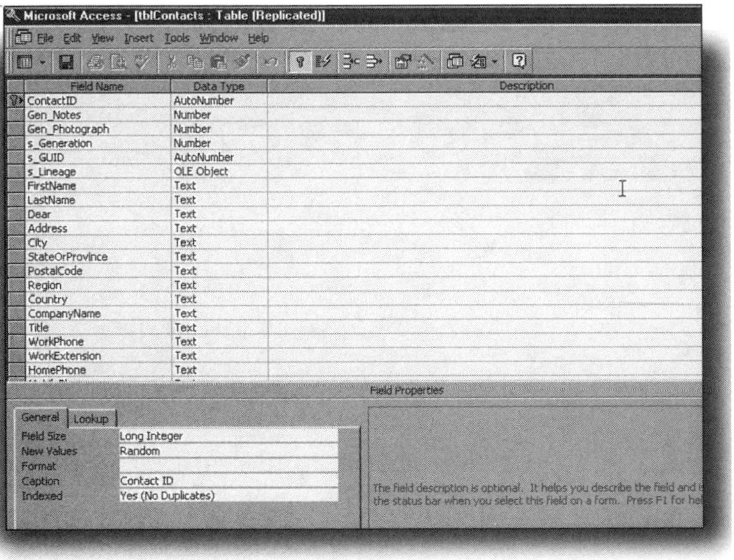

FIGURE 35.7

One of the increases in database size comes from the additional fields for each record for tracking.

Generations

The s_Generation field is added to ensure that only changed data gets exchanged when two replicas are synchronized. When a record is changed, its generation is set to zero (0). The sending replica knows the last generation it sent to a specific replica. Only records that are of a higher generation or a generation of zero will be sent. Microsoft Jet will not exchange records with generation numbers that are out of sequence.

Part of the generation issue is the addition of a field for each occurrence of a Memo or OLE Object field. Your example database has two such fields in it, Picture and Memo. Jet automatically creates a Gen_<Field Name> field so that synchronization can always be optimized. During the synchronization process, each record is checked to see whether it should be sent. Due to the potentially large size of these two field types, Microsoft Jet creates two separate fields to track their individual changes. If the record has changes, but the OLE Object or Memo fields do not, the record is sent without the larger fields. After an OLE Object or Memo field has been changed, its respective Gen_<Field Name> field is updated to zero and sent during the next synchronization.

Lineage

The s_Lineage field is used to determine which replicas have received an update and to determine a winner when a conflict occurs. The lineage consists of a list of entries. These entries are a shortened two-byte version of the replica ID and a two-byte version number. The version number starts at 1 and increments each time the record is modified.

What Is Changing?

In order for Microsoft Jet to exchange data between replicas in a set, it needs to know some basic information, like "What am I changing?" Under normal circumstances, when a change is made to a field in a record, the entire record is marked as changed. The s_Generation field is set to zero, and the version number in

---

Design considerations

There are a few things to consider when replicating a database. Microsoft Access enforces a limit of 2,048 bytes and 255 fields to any record. When planning for a replicated solution, you need to ensure that you have ample space left for growth during the conversion process. At the very least, you are going to add three new fields to each user-defined table (**s_GUID**, **s_Generation**, and **s_Lineage**) that requires 24 bytes per record.

If you use long binary fields (**Memo** and **OLE** type fields), replication will require an additional four bytes per field. This equates at the most to 252 fields and 2,024 bytes of usable space in a given table. Your example database drops those numbers to 250 fields and 2,016 bytes, respectively.

None of this should mean a sacrifice in design strategies, because very few well-written databases ever use the table maximums anyway. This is just a word of warning.

Automatic name changes

If a local object in a replica has the same name as one being replicated to it, its name will be changed to *ObjectName*_Local.

the s_Lineage field is incremented. The exception to this rule is when the OLE Object and Memo fields are part of the table. These two fields have a separate Generation field for each occurrence of that type of field in the table. Only when a change has been made to one of those fields will they be exchanged during synchronization.

When dealing with design changes that need to be updated, you need to ensure that all your changes are made at the Design Master only. Any changes made at replicas will remain local, non-replicable objects. If you need to change a replica to become the Design Master, you can transfer the designation during synchronization.

There may be a time when a developer needs to maintain a set of features locally until they are completed and ready for distribution, or if they are private objects to that individual. You may make them local objects by either unchecking their **Replicable** status in the Properties dialog box of the object (see Figure 35.8) or by leaving the **Make Replicable** check box unchecked when saving a new object to the database (see Figure 35.9).

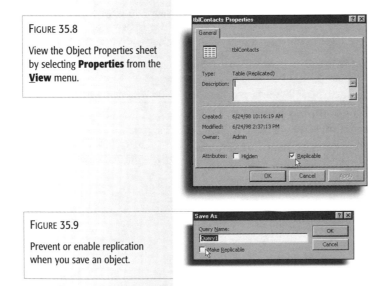

FIGURE 35.8

View the Object Properties sheet by selecting **Properties** from the **View** menu.

FIGURE 35.9

Prevent or enable replication when you save an object.

Synchronization

Synchronization is the process of updating two members of a replica set by exchanging all updated records and objects in each member. Two replica set members are synchronized when the changes in each have been applied to the other. Microsoft Jet implements incremental synchronization, which means that only the modified data is exchanged between replicas.

By default, Jet performs two-way exchanges of data and objects (schema). This means that each replica will send and receive each other's changes. Schema changes will always occur during exchanges between replicas. Using either DAO or the Replication Manager, you can perform one-way exchanges of data, also known as *push* or *pull*.

Using Access menus

1. Open the replica set member you want to synchronize.

2. On the **Tools** menu, point to **Replication**, and then click **Synchronize Now**. (If a Synchronizer on the Internet manages any replica set member, you will see an additional dialog box that prompts you to choose whether you want to synchronize with a member on a local- or wide-area network or on the Internet.)

3. Enter the path and filename of the replica set member you want to synchronize with the current database.

4. If your database is the Design Master and you want to make the other replica the Design Master, select the **Make [insert filename] the Design Master** check box. (This option is unavailable if either of the replicas to be synchronized is a partial replica.) Click OK.

5. When asked if you want to close and reopen the database, click **Yes**. (If you click **No**, you may not see all of the changes.)

Direct and Indirect Synchronization

Direct synchronization is when there is a direct connection between two replicas and both can be open simultaneously. This is the default method Jet uses to propagate changes between two replicas. The upside to this method is that the updates are fast and reliable, making it the best choice for LANs. Because it is the default method of synchronizing two replicas, it doesn't require any additional configuration.

If you have to work with dispersed or remote sites (WANs or dial-ups), this is not the preferred method of synchronizing your data. This is because the networks are potentially unreliable; errors can occur during the exchange that could leave the replica, the Design Master, or both in an unstable state.

Indirect synchronization to the rescue! This is best used to alleviate the problems with direct synchronization. This process is achieved by creating a message file that is written to a predetermined location, known as a drop-box folder. At some later time, the remote replica will look into that drop-box folder to read the message file and apply the necessary changes. The only requirement is that you must have the Microsoft Replication Manager to use indirect synchronization, so you must purchase the Microsoft Office 97 Developers Edition (ODE). The upside to that is that once you purchase it, the licensing agreement allows you to distribute multiple copies of the Replication Manager to each site.

If you have mobile users or are planning on updating via the Internet, indirect synchronization is the way to go. This is because synchronization is performed in two phases, with each phase being controlled by the Jet Synchronizer at each replica, creating a safer and faster synchronization process than can be achieved by a direct remote connection.

Configuring Replication Manager for Indirect Synchronization

Before you can begin using Indirect Synchronization, you must set up the Replication Manager. Figure 35.10 illustrates the Replication Manager Configuration Wizard and the page on which you can choose to enable indirect synchronization (page two).

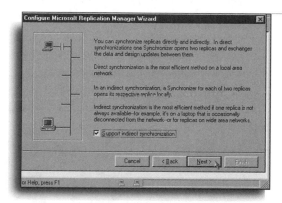

FIGURE 35.10
Performing an indirect synchronization.

As stated earlier, the Replication Manager wants to perform direct synchronization. Normally, you will create your replica using either the Access menus or Replication Manager at the computer or site where the replica will reside. In order to set up indirect synchronization properly, you need to perform the following steps:

Setting up indirect synchronization

On the *local* computer:

1. Ensure that the ODE with Replication Manager is installed.

2. Ensure that a shared folder has been created for the synchronizer drop box.

3. Ensure that the **Support indirect synchronization** check box was selected when the Replication Manager Setup Wizard was run.

4. Run Replication Manager on your local computer, and create or open a managed replica set.

Restarting replica management

If you click **No** or choose to stop managing the replica at some point, you can start replica management by selecting **File**, **Start Managing AnyReplica**, where **AnyReplica** is the name of the replica in question.

On the *remote* computer:

1. Ensure that the preceding steps 1 and 2 have been performed on the remote site.

2. Make a regular Windows version of the replica and move it to the folder on the remote site. Figure 35.11 illustrates the Windows Explorer on the remote computer.

3. Use drag-and-drop to copy from the host machine to the remote machine. Ensure that you place the copy of the file in an unshared folder.

4. Run Replication Manager. Select **File**, **Open Replica Set**. Locate the folder where you just copied the file and select the file. The dialog box shown in Figure 35.12 should appear. Click **Yes** to manage the replica.

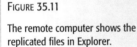

FIGURE 35.11

The remote computer shows the replicated files in Explorer.

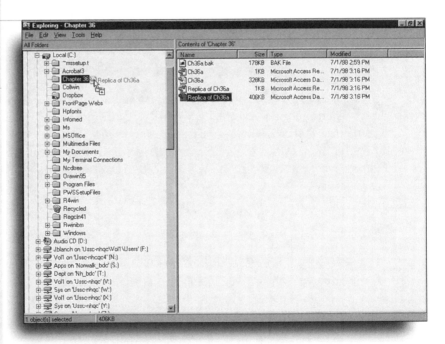

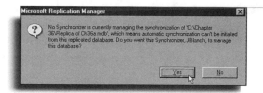

FIGURE 35.12
Click **Yes** to manage replicas.

5. Click **File, Start Managing *Replica*.mdb**, where
   ***Replica*.mdb** is the copied database file. The two sites
   should now appear on the remote Replication Manager's
   site map.

6. Right-click the line connecting the two replicas and select
   Synchronize Now from the shortcut menu (see Figure
   35.13). This lets the local computer know that the copy on
   the remote computer exists.

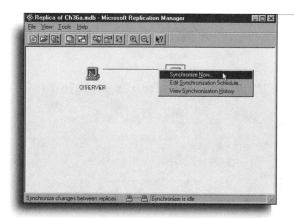

FIGURE 35.13

Use the graphical interface for a
shortcut by clicking the line connecting the images or the systems
you want to modify.

The other two items on the shortcut menu, **Add New
Synchronization Schedule** and **View Synchronization
History**, enable you to add and edit a synchronization schedule,
as well as view the exchanges between the two replicas in the set.

Scheduling

To set up a new schedule, right-click the line connecting the two replicas and select **Add New Synchronization Schedule**. This menu option will change dynamically to **Edit Synchronization Schedule** after a schedule has been established.

Scheduling remote exchanges is as easy as clicking in the day/time matrix for the desired times and clicking **OK**. As shown in Figure 35.14, you've selected to synchronize every weekday at 4:00 a.m. and every weekend at 6:00 a.m.

Now that a schedule has been created, the Synchronizer will attempt to propagate the changes "on time." If the remote computer is offline at the scheduled synchronization time, the local synchronizer will write the information to the designated drop box and routinely check the remote site every fifteen minutes. As soon as the remote site has reconnected, all changes will be transferred to the remote synchronizer, which in turn will update the remote replica.

FIGURE 35.14

Use the Edit Schedule dialog box to select times for synchronization.

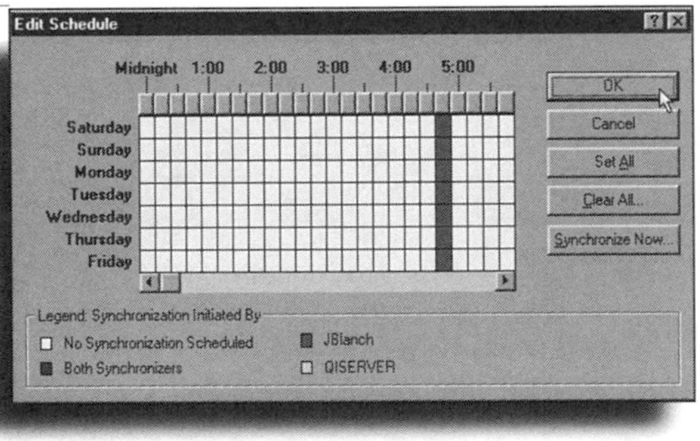

Tip for viewing synchronizer entries

You can also see the synchronization history of the local synchronizer for all the replica set members it manages alone.

To prevent the number of synchronization history entries from growing indefinitely, Microsoft has created an option for controlling the number of entries. To change the number of entries, navigate to the **Keep Design Change History** option on the **Replica Set** tab of the Properties dialog box.

Synchronization History

Replication Manager enables you to review information about past synchronizations for specific replica set members and the local synchronizer. By right-clicking the local machine icon in the Synchronization window, you can see a chronological record of synchronizations that were made between the local synchronizer and another synchronizer that is managing other replica set members. The synchronization history includes the date and time of the synchronization, updates made, problems encountered, and reasons for any failure to update records (see Figure 35.15).

A Brief Look at Internet/Intranet Replication

One of the greatest additions to Office 97 was the set of Internet/intranet features. Access 97 takes advantage of this in many ways, one of which is by enabling synchronization over the Internet or a local company intranet. What is taking place is indirect synchronization, basically, which is optimized for the Internet protocols (HTTP, FTP, and TCP/IP).

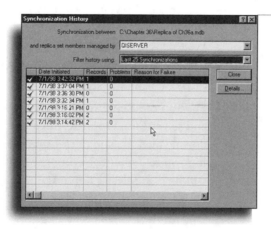

FIGURE 35.15
View the synchronization history to track problems.

In order to use this feature, you must have the following items:

- A server running Windows 95 or Windows NT.
- A copy of Access (retail or runtime) installed on the server.
- The server must be configured for Internet replication.
- Anonymous connections.

Then you must do the following:

- Create a directory where synchronizer can run.
- Create a directory where FTP file transfers are allowed. This directory will be the resting place of the files exchanged during synchronization.

- Make sure a copy of the Replication Manager has been installed on the server.

- Configure Replication Manager for Internet replication.

- Install only Replication Manager from the ODE installation CD. Important: During the installation, you will be asked if you want the synchronizer added to the start-up group. Click **No**. The Internet server will start the synchronizer on demand.

- Run the Configuration Wizard (this starts automatically until the Replication Manager has been successfully set up).

- Set up your replica set for Internet synchronization.

- Start by running the Replication Manager.

- Create or open a managed replica set.

- Create a DOS/Windows copy like you did with indirect synchronization, and paste it in a public FTP directory on the Web server.

- Go to a remote site, log on to the Web server, and download the copy from the server to your local machine.

- Start up the Replication Manager on the remote computer and select **File**, **Open Replica Set**. Navigate to the newly downloaded file and click **Open**. If the dialog box prompting you to begin managing the replica doesn't pop up, you will have to select **File**, **Start Managing** *AnyReplica*.**mdb** (*AnyReplica* being the downloaded database).

- The two sites should now appear on the remote computer's map. (The Web server will appear as the synchronizer, but with a globe denoting that it's Web-based.) Right-click and select **Synchronize Now**, as you did with indirect synchronization.

Run the Configuration Wizard to set up Internet synchronization

1. Click Next.

2. Uncheck the **Indirect Synchronization** option because it isn't necessary to perform Internet synchronization.

3. Answer **Yes** to the question, "Is this computer an Internet server?"

4. When asked if you want to use the Internet server to synchronize replicated databases, answer **Yes**.

5. Page five asks for the server name. For an Internet server, enter the domain name (such as *anydomain*.com). For an intranet server, enter the machine's name (such as *mycomputer*).

6. Path out to the directory that you created previously when you set up your Web server. Also type in an alias for the directory.

7. Again, path out to the previously created FTP subdirectory that you created on your Web server.

8. Finally, you'll be asked to path the log file. Normally, the default will do fine. The last page tells you that you're finished with the Wizard.

Resolving Conflicts and Errors

During synchronization, conflicts and errors can arise. They can come in the form of the following:

- Data Conflicts—Normally occur when two or more users attempt to update the same record.
- Data Errors—Usually arise when one replica tries to add data to a table when:

    A Referential Integrity rule is broken.

    A Table Level Validation rule is broken.

    Duplicate records have been created.

    Another user locks records that are being synchronized.

- Design Errors—Normally occur when changes at the master are in conflict with the design state of a replica.

Resolving Conflicts and Errors Using the Access Menus

Conflicts can occur if data has changed in the same record of two replica set members that have been synchronized.

Figure 35.16 shows your Design Master on top and a directly synchronized replica below it. Each table has the same record in it. The Design Master has added an address of 1 Any Road, and in the replica is an address of 1 Any Way. Next you'll synchronize

Restarting the process

If the wizard doesn't start up automatically, or you chose not to resolve conflicts immediately, you can run the wizard later by selecting the table with the conflicts and then selecting **Tools**, **Replication**, **Resolve Conflicts**.

the Design Master and then the replica. If there are conflicts after the synchronization process is completed, you are asked if you want to resolve them.

Resolving conflicts after synchronization

1. Click **Yes** in the dialog box that announces a conflict. Also notice that Jet has created a new table in the replica named `tblContacts_Conflict`, as shown in Figure 35.17.

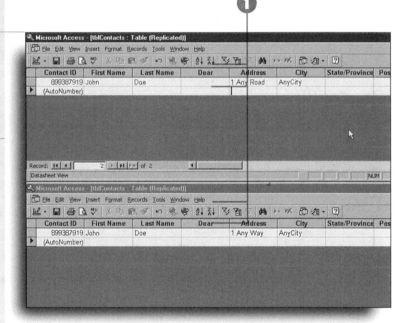

FIGURE 35.16

The two tables have a conflict in the address.

 This conflict needs to be synchronized

Maintaining consistent records

The record of conflicts can be lost if you delete or move a replica. Before deleting or moving a replica, check it for conflicts.

2. Next you're presented with the Resolve Replication Conflicts dialog box, shown in Figure 35.18. This dialog box lists all the known conflicts. Click the **Resolve Conflicts** button.

3. Next a form pops up enabling you to compare the conflicting records (see Figure 35.19). You may either **Keep Existing Record** or **Overwrite with Conflict Record**. Clicking either button will prompt you with a warning dialog box, enabling you to back out of your decision.

    After you have agreed to accept one change or the other, your changes are accepted and the conflicting table is removed.

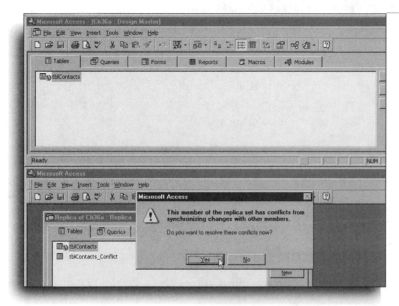

FIGURE 35.17

When you try to synchronize the databases, Access alerts you that there's a conflict between tables.

FIGURES 35.18

Resolve the conflicts one at a time after synchronization.

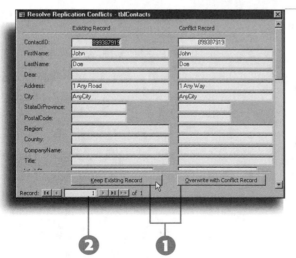

FIGURE 35.19

The conflicting records are displayed in full, side by side, so you can choose which one is correct.

❶ Choose the correct record by clicking the button at the bottom of the record you want

❷ Check here to see if there is more than one problem record for this table

Where to get the Partial Replica Wizard

You can download a copy of the Partial Replica Wizard from the Microsoft Access Developers Forum Web site at www.microsoft.com/ AccessDev/.

Partial replica limitations

You can only synchronize between a full replica and a partial replica. You can't synchronize between two partial replicas. Partial replication is record-level filtering only.

Partial Replication

There may be a time during the life cycle of an application when you want to replicate a portion (or subset) of data to various locations. Microsoft Jet 3.5 and Access 97 have included this functionality in partial replication. You create partial replicas by applying filters and relationships to tables using either DAO or the Partial Replica Wizard.

Let's say you have a customer service database in which field representatives need to view or edit only the information pertaining to their region. This could be a very useful tool for any type of remote operation where dial-up or WAN connections are extremely slow.

Creating Partial Replicas

Using the Partial Replica Wizard is by far the easiest way to create a partial replica. However, you are limited to setting criteria on only one table. If you are looking for more control and are comfortable with your coding skills, DAO is the best way to go.

You first need to ensure that you have downloaded and installed the wizard from the Microsoft Access Developers Forum site.

Partial replication using the wizard

1. Once installed, open any full replica in the set. It doesn't have to be the Design Master.

2. Next select **Tools**, **Add-Ins**, **Partial Replica Wizard**.

   The wizard will now load and display a startup screen asking if you would like to create a new partial replica or modify an existing one. For this example, create a new partial replica.

3. The second page of the wizard prompts you for the location of the new partial replica. Place it wherever it needs to go.

4. Figure 35.20 shows the third page of the wizard, where you create the filter that will be applied to the table. Select the field and operator, click the **Paste** button, and type in the criteria.

5. Repeat this process for each criterion.

6. The last page of the wizard lets you print out a report, giving you a simple record of what you just did. Select **Finish**.

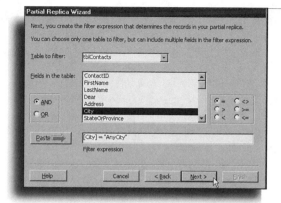

Using DAO

The real power of partial replication relies on the use of VBA and DAO. Listings 35.1 through 35.3 accomplish the same thing. Note the comment lines describing the action.

LISTING 35.1   **Creating a Partial Replica**

```
1  Public Function CreatePartialReplica()
2
3      ' Set the source of the data to the current database
4      Dim dbFull As Database
5      Set dbFull = DBEngine(0)(0)
6      ' Use the MakeReplica method, with the MakePartial
       ' option
7      dbFull.MakeReplica "C:\Ch36 DAO Partial Replica", _
8      "Chapter 36 Partial Replica using DAO",
       dbRepMakePartial
9      'Close the database and free resources
10     dbFull.Close
11     Set dbFull = Nothing
12
13 End Function
```

Using proper notation

You must use proper notation when completing the **where** clause, such as **String** or **#Date#**.

LISTING 35.2   **Setting the Filter on the Table**

```
1  Public Function CreatePartialReplicaFilter()
2
3      Dim dbPartial As Database
4      Dim tdfContacts As TableDef
5      'Set the source of the data to the partial replica
       '(Exclusive)
6      Set dbPartial = OpenDatabase("C:\Ch36 DAO Partial
       Replica", True)
7      'Set a reference to the Contacts table
8      Set tdfContacts = dbPartial.TableDefs("tblContacts")
9      'Set the filter criteria
10     tdfContacts.ReplicaFilter = "[City] = 'AnyCity'"
11     dbPartial.Close
12     'Close the database and free resources
13     Set tdfContacts = Nothing
14     Set dbPartial = Nothing
15
16 End Function
```

LISTING 35.3   **Populating the Partial Replica with the Appropriate Data**

```
1  Public Function PopulatePartialReplica()
2
3      Dim dbPartial As Database
4      Dim strFullReplicaPath As String
5
6      'Set the source of the data to the Full replica
7      strFullReplicaPath = "D:\Chapter 36\Ch36a.mdb"
8      'Set the source of the data to the partial replica
       '(Exclusive)
9      Set dbPartial = OpenDatabase("C:\Ch36 DAO Partial
       Replica", True)
10     With dbPartial
11         .PopulatePartial strFullReplicaPath
12         .Close
13     End With
14
15 End Function
```

Advanced Topics

Continuing the original example earlier in this chapter, you may need to see only the orders for customers in your region. Doing this involves relationships, because the regional identifier would be stored in the customer's table and not the orders table. This is performed by using the PartialReplica property of the Relation object, specifying which relationships, if any, should be used when populating your partial replica.

After you have created a partial replica, it cannot be converted to a full replica. However, you may remove the filter and relationships within the partial—it will contain all the records of a full replica. The downside is that the partial retains the limitations of a partial replica. For example, it cannot synchronize with another partial replica.

Security and Replication

Replicated databases use the same security model as nonreplicated databases. There are two distinct ways to implement a successful security setup, and the choice relies solely with the developer. Because the system database (System.mdw or System.mda (pre 97)) cannot be replicated, you will have to either create a central security file that will be distributed to each location or re-create the settings in the local copy of the System.mdw (usually found in the C:\Windows\System folder).

There is a third option for developers who are replicating only the code half of the application (in the classic split-application design). If you plan to keep a central file server data store and replicate the code, you can also centralize your System.mdw in the same directory as your data.

Good Housekeeping

For your database to continue providing speedy and consistent access to data, you need to maintain it properly. This is also true when you're using replication for your system. The following sections will help you keep a replicated database in good working shape.

Security choices

Deciding which route to take is definitely a personal choice. The former is the easier of the two choices. This is because you would only need to make changes once to the database and then, using the Setup Wizard that comes with the ODE, create a distributable application with only the System.mdw file being distributed.

Furthermore, the database password is completely different from the MDW/user-level security. You can replicate or synchronize a database that has user-level security, but the MDW file (which holds the user and group accounts for the workgroup) will *not* be replicated.

Compacting and Repairing Replicated Databases

When Microsoft Jet converts your database to a Design Master, it adds three new fields and some new system tables. Over time, these additions can grow significantly. To reduce the overall size of your application, you should compact your database frequently. You should also remember to compact your replicas before synchronizing them, thereby reducing the chance of erroneous or lengthy synchronizations.

However, you should not run the repair utility on a replicated database, because it will mark the database as no longer replicable while repairing it. You wouldn't want to propagate the potentially incomplete system information during the next synchronization. The solution is to create a new replica from a known "good" replica and discard the corrupted one.

Cleaning Up Old Replicas

During the life cycle of your application, you may create numerous test replicas or even have sites that no longer need the replicated system. To properly remove them from the replica set, you will have to perform a two-step process.

Removing old replicas

1. Delete the unwanted replica from its original location.
2. Using the Access menus, try synchronizing with the deleted database. Access will tell you that the replica can't be found and ask if you want it deleted from the list. Click **Yes**.

The system will mark that replica as removed, and it will no longer appear in the list.

Recovering a Design Master

There may come a time when your Design Master has been lost, damaged, or moved and needs to be recovered. You can use the final option in the **Replication** menu to recover the Design Master. First, you should always ensure that there is no other Design Master in the set. You should then locate the most recently updated replica in the set. Select **Tools**, **Replication**, **Synchronize Now** for each replica in the set. Next, select **Tools**, **Replication**, **Recover Design Master** to set that replica as the new Design Master.

If you need to transfer control back to the original site of the Design Master, you should make a new replica at the original site. To actually *transfer* control of the Design Master back to the original site, you would use the **Synchronize Now** menu option. When the dialog box pops up, select the newly created replica and check the box labeled **Make *FileName* the Design Master**. Click **OK**. This same transferring process can be useful when you need to transfer control of the Design Master to another member of your team for any length of time.

If there were no replicas in the set when the Design Master went down, or if the last known set of propagated changes were that far removed from the corrupted Design Master, there is a third option. This option is also useful if you decide to get out of the replication game.

Recovering a Design Master

1. Create a new database that will store all the objects needing to be imported, with the exception of tables.

2. Close the new database.

3. Open the old Design Master (if you can't, import the tables into a separate database).

4. Create a new query that will include every field in the table, with the exception of the fields that Jet added during replication (s_Generation, s_GUID, s_Lineage).

5. Choose the **Make Table Query** option. When prompted for the name and location of the query result, select the current table name in the combo box and type in the path to the newly created database, as shown in Figure 35.21.

6. Repeat for each table in the database.

7. Reopen the new database and re-create all relationships, indexes, and properties that existed prior to corruption.

8. Finally, repair and compact the new database.

> **Download the wizard for help**
>
> Microsoft was kind enough to develop a downloadable wizard that will automate this painstaking process; it's called the Replica to Regular Wizard and can be found on the Microsoft Web site.

FIGURE 35.21

Select the current table name in the combo box and type in the path to the newly created database.

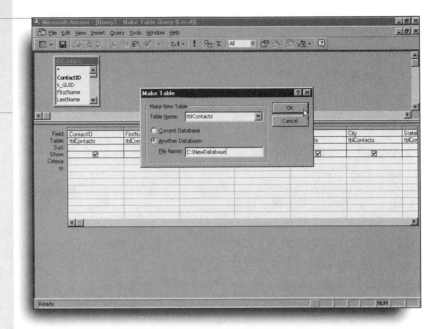

Useful Tools

Using Office Links

Office 97 applications can share data in a variety of ways. This chapter explores many of the common tools that make this data sharing possible. Access 97 provides several tools called Office Links that make using your Access data in other Office applications a smooth process. An Office Link is a wizard that helps you use your Access data in other Office applications.

The following Office Links, all of which are covered in this section, are provided:

- Merge It with MS Word
- Publish It with MS Word
- Analyze It with MS Excel

SEE ALSO

➤ *For more on how to use the Office Links to create mailing labels, see page 163.*

Merging with Word

One of the most useful tools available in the Office suite is Word's mail merge capability, as you saw in Chapter 10, "Using the Mail Merge Wizard." Performing a mail merge involves creating a document that contains special merge fields and then combining this document with a data source, such as an Access table or query. Word uses the data source to replace the merge fields with real data. A separate document is created for each record in the data source.

You can use this feature to enhance normal mail merge purposes, too. Here are some examples of using more complex queries to create the fields you might want to display in a document:

- You could create a query on a sales table that opens the list of all sales employees and how much they have sold in a month's time. Then you could place the employee's name fields and the amount field in a document addressed to that employee to let her know how much she's sold in a month.

- You can incorporate data from employee records in an annual letter announcing individual bonus percentages. This could be calculated from the salary and the employee's

Minimum installation required

You must have Microsoft Word and Excel installed on your system for the Office Links to work.

position in the company, based on underlying records and calculations in a query. Then each letter would reflect data particular to the record for that employee.

- You can even insert several lines of text to vary a mass-mailed letter by inserting a field with a larger data type, such as Memo. Although the formatting on this would be a little more tricky, it's a handy way to tie explanatory text with another field, such as "Your request has been rejected because... [reason field]" or "Congratulations on... [event field]."

Access 97 provides an Office Link called Merge It with MS Word to ease some of difficulties in performing mail merges. Using this Office Link, you can quickly and easily create a merge document and fill it with data from your database. The Merge It with MS Word Office Link can use either tables or queries as the data source, so you'll start out on the **Tables** or **Queries** tab of the Database window.

Using the Merge It with MS Word Office Link

1. Using Access 97, open the database containing the data that will be the source for your mail merge.

2. In the Database window, click **Tables** if your data source is an existing table or **Queries** if you're using a query to provide your data. Select the table or query to be used.

3. Click the **Tools** menu, and then click **Office Links**. Select **Merge It with MS Word** on the pop-up menu. The first dialog box of the Office Link asks whether you're using a new or existing document.

4. If you've already created and saved a merge document using the table or query you selected in step 2, and you want to use that existing document, leave the **Link Your Data to an Existing Microsoft Word Document** option button selected. When you click **OK**, the Office Link will present you with a Select Microsoft Word Document dialog box. This is a standard File Open dialog box where you can select the file to be used as the merge document.

If you're merging this data for the first time or want to create a new merge document, select the **Create a New Document and then Link the Data to It** option button. After you click **OK**, a new instance of Microsoft Word will launch. After Word extracts information about the selected table or query from Access, the application returns to the ready state and enables the Mail Merge toolbar. Figure 36.1 shows the results of clicking the Merge Field toolbar button when the Northwind Traders database's Customers table was selected in step 2.

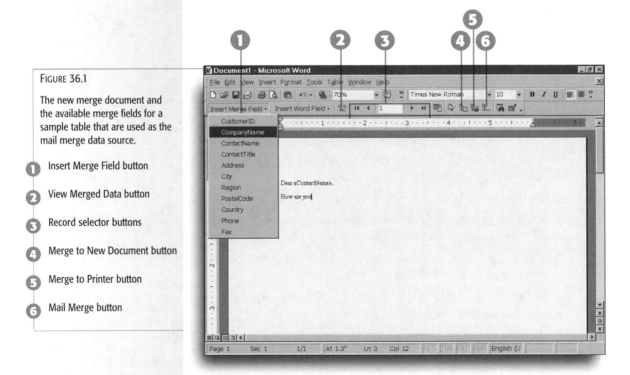

FIGURE 36.1

The new merge document and the available merge fields for a sample table that are used as the mail merge data source.

1. Insert Merge Field button

2. View Merged Data button

3. Record selector buttons

4. Merge to New Document button

5. Merge to Printer button

6. Mail Merge button

5. You use the Insert Merge Field icon Insert Merge Field ▾ to insert placeholders for your data into the document. Click the button to drop down the list of available fields (as shown in Figure 36.1) and click the desired field. A merge field is inserted into the document at the current cursor location. You can type text around the merge fields, of course, to include the data within the actual text of the document.

6. Type the body of your merge document, including the merge fields from your source table or query where appropriate. When you've finished, click the View Merged Data icon ⬚ to see the results of the merge when combined with the source table or query. Check a few records using the record selector buttons and make any necessary changes to your merge document.

7. Click the button appropriate to your desired output. If you want to merge to a new document, click **Merge to New Document**. To merge to a printer, click **Merge to Printer**.

    For other sources, such as email and fax, click the Mail Merge button. The Mail Merge dialog box appears. Here you can choose from other merge destinations and set various options that affect how the data is merged.

8. When you're finished, it's a good idea to save your merge document in case you ever need to reproduce this mail merge in the future. Do so by using the **File**, **Save** menu item.

Publishing Data with Microsoft Word

The Publish It with MS Word Office Link enables you to quickly create a Word document from the Datasheet view of tables, queries, and forms, and also create a document from a report's output. This Office Link creates a file in the Rich Text Format (RTF) and immediately launches Word with this document.

For tables, queries, and forms, the Publish It Office Link will produce a document that uses a table to display the data. You can embed this Word table into another Word document or build a new document around this table. Use this technique whenever you want to export data from a table or query into a report, memo, or other static document that depends on data from your database. For a report, the document will closely resemble the printed report.

Limitation on publishing charts

When you use a report in Word, be aware that charts embedded in the report will not be ported to the Word document.

Publishing a table with Word

1. Open the database containing the data to be published. Select the table, query, form, or report that you want to publish.

2. Click the **T**ools menu, and then select **Office **L**inks,
Publish It with MS Word**.

3. Access will choose the name for the new file based on the
name of the selected object. If the filename already exists,
Access will ask you whether you want to replace the existing
file. If you answer **N**o, a File Save dialog box will appear
that enables you to choose a different name or folder for the
file. If you answer **Y**es, the existing file will be replaced with
the new one.

4. The Office Link launches Word (if necessary) and opens the
newly created document.

Analyzing Data with Excel

The final Office Link is the Analyze It with MS Excel Office
Link. This Office Link enables you to transfer your tables,
queries, forms, and reports to an Excel spreadsheet. Most of the
formatting in the Datasheet views, forms, and reports is pre-
served in the spreadsheet. Forms are saved using their Datasheet
views. If you have grouping levels in your reports, they are saved
as outline levels in the spreadsheet. Using this Office Link is just
as easy as the Publish It Office Link.

Analyzing data with Excel

1. Open the database containing the data to be published.
Select the table, query, form, or report that you want to
publish.

2. Click the **T**ools menu, and then select **Office **L**inks,
Analyze It with MS Excel**.

3. Access will choose the name for the file based on the name
of the report. If the filename already exists, Access will ask
you whether you want to replace the existing file. If you
click **N**o, a File Save dialog box will appear that enables you
to choose a different name or folder for the file. If you click
Yes, the existing file will be replaced with the new one.

4. The Office Link launches Excel (if necessary) and opens the
newly created spreadsheet. Figure 36.2 shows the results of
this with the Northwind Traders Quarterly Orders by
Product query.

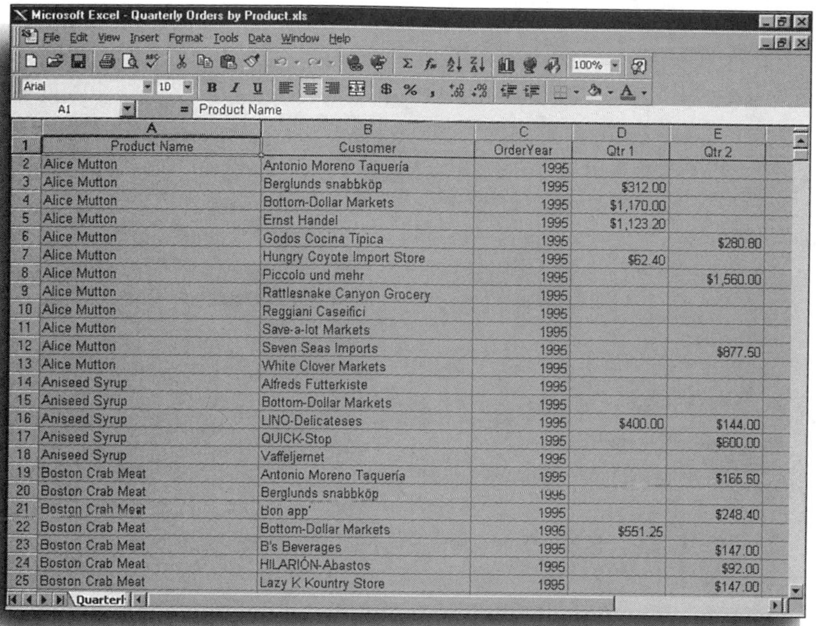

	A	B	C	D	E
1	Product Name	Customer	OrderYear	Qtr 1	Qtr 2
2	Alice Mutton	Antonio Moreno Taquería	1995		
3	Alice Mutton	Berglunds snabbköp	1995	$312.00	
4	Alice Mutton	Bottom-Dollar Markets	1995	$1,170.00	
5	Alice Mutton	Ernst Handel	1995	$1,123.20	
6	Alice Mutton	Godos Cocina Típica	1995		$280.80
7	Alice Mutton	Hungry Coyote Import Store	1995	$62.40	
8	Alice Mutton	Piccolo und mehr	1995		$1,560.00
9	Alice Mutton	Rattlesnake Canyon Grocery	1995		
10	Alice Mutton	Reggiani Caseifici	1995		
11	Alice Mutton	Save-a-lot Markets	1995		
12	Alice Mutton	Seven Seas Imports	1995		$877.50
13	Alice Mutton	White Clover Markets	1995		
14	Aniseed Syrup	Alfreds Futterkiste	1995		
15	Aniseed Syrup	Bottom-Dollar Markets	1995		
16	Aniseed Syrup	LINO-Delicateses	1995	$400.00	$144.00
17	Aniseed Syrup	QUICK-Stop	1995		$600.00
18	Aniseed Syrup	Vaffeljernet	1995		
19	Boston Crab Meat	Antonio Moreno Taquería	1995		$165.60
20	Boston Crab Meat	Berglunds snabbköp	1995		
21	Boston Crab Meat	Bon app'	1995		$248.40
22	Boston Crab Meat	Bottom-Dollar Markets	1995	$551.25	
23	Boston Crab Meat	B's Beverages	1995		$147.00
24	Boston Crab Meat	HILARIÓN-Abastos	1995		$92.00
25	Boston Crab Meat	Lazy K Kountry Store	1995		$147.00

FIGURE 36.2
The results of the Analyze It with MS Excel Office Link.

OLE Automation and ActiveX Controls

OLE Automation is the means by which applications can communicate with one another when running on a Windows-based operating system (Windows 95, Windows 98, and Windows NT). OLE stands for *Object Linking and Embedding* and provides the interfaces necessary for one application to be embedded into or linked to another application's data.

The entire Office 97 suite is OLE-enabled. Most of the applications can function as both an *OLE server*, which provides data to another application, and an *OLE container*, which acts as a host for an instance of an OLE server. For example, you can embed a portion of an Excel spreadsheet into a Word document and operate on the data in that spreadsheet just as if you were in Microsoft Excel.

Access 97 only provides OLE server functionality through its *object model*, which is a way of describing the properties, methods, and events provided by an application. For example, you can create a programmatic instance of Access 97, but you cannot visually embed an Access table into a Word document.

Access 97 can host ActiveX controls and components, of course. ActiveX is not just a pretty new face for an older technology. It's a specification for interoperability between components, applications, the operating system, and the network to which the host computer is attached. Although the push for an object-oriented operating system has taken a back seat to object-oriented application development, ActiveX controls are more important than ever because they serve as the infrastructure upon which future desktop and networked (client/server) applications will likely be built.

OLE, VBX, OCX, and ActiveX

After OLE Automation had been on the scene for a while, a new breed of OLE Automation server came along with a new revision of Microsoft Visual Basic. This OLE server was called a *VBX (Visual Basic eXtension) control*. These were 16-bit OLE servers that could be placed onto Visual Basic forms. They allowed the programmer to easily manipulate their properties and methods and respond to events that they raised. The VBX controls were built with an open architecture, which meant that third-party vendors could create VBX controls to suit their needs. Visual Basic became wildly popular mainly due to its capabilities in the VBX arena.

With the introduction Microsoft Access version 2, Microsoft introduced a new type of VBX, the *OCX* or *OLE custom control*. The OCX was initially a 32-bit version of the VBX standard, but eventually became more than that as Microsoft expanded its vision of the object-oriented operating system. Today, OCXs still exist but are now encompassed by ActiveX controls and components.

Using Third-Party ActiveX Controls

In Access 97, you can place ActiveX controls onto forms or reports. These controls can perform any number of functions, from displaying data graphically to providing a calendar with which users can enter dates. There's a control available for just about every purpose imaginable.

You can purchase third-party controls from many sources. Even computer superstores now carry a wide variety of the more popular ActiveX controls on the market. You can also search on the Web for ActiveX controls. One extremely handy site is ActiveX.COM at `http://www.activex.com`.

Although Microsoft is the instigator of ActiveX and ActiveX controls, they have turned over the standard to an independent body, the Active Group (also known as the ActiveX Working Group). Its Web site is found at `http://www.activex.org` (not to be confused with the aforementioned ActiveX.COM site). This means that ActiveX is and will remain an open standard for developing component-based solutions. For the Access developer, it means a continuing flood of useful ActiveX controls.

Registering an ActiveX Control

Because ActiveX components are actually instantiated by the operating system and can physically exist at any location on the computer, or even on the network to which the computer is attached, you must *register* an ActiveX control before you can use it within Access 97.

The registration process involves placing entries in the system registry, which provides the location and startup properties for the control. Control registration is typically handled by invoking a function that every ActiveX control must expose, `DLLRegisterServer`. When this function is invoked, the control is responsible for placing the required information in the system registry. It is also where many controls perform their "first time up" functions, if necessary. A similar function, `DLLUnregisterServer`, is called when the control will be removed from the system.

There are three primary ways to register a new ActiveX control on your system. In order of preference:

- Run the control's installation application, if available.
- Use Microsoft Access to register the control.
- Register the control manually using a special registration application.

Most commercial ActiveX controls will come with an installation application. This application will create new folders for the control's support files (such as a Windows Help file and sample code), copy the control's OCX file to your system directory, and register the control. If available, you should use this method.

If you've found an ActiveX control in the form of an OCX file on the Web somewhere, or had one developed for you but didn't receive an installation program with it, all is not lost. You can use Access to register the control for you.

Registering a control within Access

1. Start Access 97.

2. Click the **Tools** menu and select **ActiveX Controls**. The ActiveX Controls dialog box appears, as shown in Figure 36.3.

Tip for accessing ActiveX controls

You don't have to have a database open to access the ActiveX Controls dialog box. If you want to register new ActiveX controls for any other application, you can use Access to do so.

FIGURE 36.3

The ActiveX Controls dialog box with a listing of the controls registered on the computer.

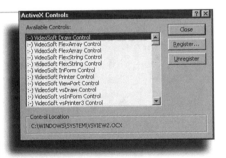

3. The ActiveX Controls dialog box displays a list of all the registered ActiveX controls. Your list will probably look very different because you have different controls installed on your computer. If the control you want isn't among those listed, click the **Register** button. Even if it is in the list and you just didn't see it, there's no harm in registering a control multiple times.

4. An Add ActiveX Control dialog box appears. This is a simple File Open dialog box where you specify the folder for the file, click the file's name, and click **Open**.

5. Access will invoke the control's `DLLRegisterServer` function, refresh the Available Controls list, and return control back to you. The control you just registered will not be the selected item in the Available Controls list, however. You'll have to scroll through the list to verify that it made it. Rest assured that if the registration process fails, you'll be informed of it. If you're finished, click the **Close** button. Otherwise, return to step 3 to register another control.

You can also use the ActiveX Controls dialog box to unregister a control. The only real reason to unregister a control is if you're going to delete its OCX file from your system. The **Unregister** button will unregister the control selected in the Available Controls list. Access does this without a confirmation dialog box, so be sure you've got the correct control selected in the list.

Manual Registration

The third method of registering controls is the manual process. The sole purpose of the tiny application called `REGSVR32.EXE` is to register and unregister ActiveX components. This application does not ship with Windows 95/98 but may be on your system anyway, especially if you've installed any development tools that rely on or create ActiveX components. If you cannot find this application on your system, you can download it from many places on the Web.

`REGSVR32.EXE` is a console application, meaning that it's intended to be run from a DOS box or the Windows **Start** menu's Run dialog box. The command line is

`regsvr32 [/u ]componentfile [/s]`

The /u switch is used when you want to unregister the control, and the /s switch causes the success or failure message box to be suppressed.

Adding a Third-Party Control to a Form

Your forms are not limited to the controls provided natively by Access 97. You can add any third-party ActiveX control to your forms with a few simple steps. When you're finished, that control will behave just like a native control, such as the textbox control.

Getting to the network from here

If you need to get to a network folder that isn't available in the **Drives** list, click the **Network** button and the Map Network Drive dialog box will appear. From here, you can locate the network file share that contains the OCX file.

On some systems it may take a minute or more for the Map Network Drive dialog box to appear. So if Access seems to go blank, give it a minute or two before you panic and press Ctrl+Alt+Del.

Adding a third-party ActiveX control to a form

1. On the Database window's **Forms** tab, select the form to which you want to add the control. Click the **Design** button. To create a new form instead, click the **New** button and select **Design View** on the New Form dialog box.

2. The form opens in the Design View window. If the Toolbox is not visible, use the **View** menu and click **Toolbox** or click the Toolbox icon ⚒.

3. Click the More Controls icon ⚒. If this is the first time you've used this tool since opening the Design View window, Access will churn for a bit, locating the ActiveX controls installed on your system. This tool is really a pop-up menu, as you can see in Figure 36.4. Your menu will most likely look different.

FIGURE 36.4

The **More Controls** menu, displaying an extensive list of registered ActiveX controls.

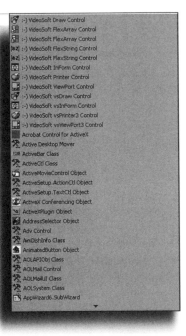

4. Locate the control you're going to add to the form and single-click its entry in the menu. Be careful to single-click and not double-click. Also, do not attempt to drag from this menu. The menu disappears.

5. Move the cursor over the Form Designer window. Notice that the cursor has changed from a pointer to a little hammer with a plus sign. Click the form where you want to insert the control and start dragging. A bounding rectangle will be displayed, showing you the location and shape that the control will have on the form. When you're close to the desired size and shape, release the mouse button.

6. The control will draw any design-time user interface it provides, and will be available for the Properties and Module windows provided by the Design View form. Figure 36.5 shows the Calendar Control 8.0 control added to an otherwise empty form.

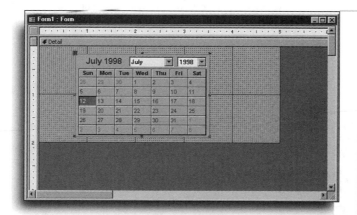

FIGURE 36.5
The Calendar Control 8.0 ActiveX control added to a blank form.

SEE ALSO

➤ *For information on creating forms with a wizard, see page 69.*

➤ *To learn about working with the toolbox, see page 314.*

➤ *For more information on adding controls to a form, see page 323.*

➤ *To learn about working with forms in Design view, see page 342.*

➤ *For more information about responding to control events, see page 419.*

Link or Embed an Office Document

OLE Automation provides the specifications necessary for two applications to share information. For example, you can embed a portion of a spreadsheet within a Word document. Although the uses aren't as exciting in Microsoft Access, you can embed any OLE server's data within an Access field's data, within a form, or within a report.

By far, the most prevalent usage of OLE is to embed or link OLE server data within a field in the database.

Embedding an OLE object

1. Open the table where you want to embed or link an OLE object. Create or change the data type of one field. The field must be defined with a data type of OLE Object.

2. Insert OLE data into the field in Datasheet view. Or, insert it when the field is displayed on a form by right-clicking either the cell in the datasheet or the control on the form and selecting **Insert Object** from the menu that appears.

   This invokes the Insert Object dialog box, shown in Figure 36.6.

FIGURE 36.6

The Insert Object dialog box, for embedding or linking OLE data within Access.

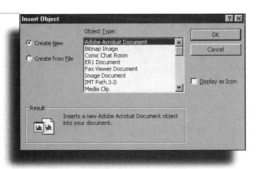

3. In the Insert Object dialog box, you can create a new object or create an object from an existing file. You'll have these options:

   ▪ If you're creating a new piece of data, leave the **Create New** option selected and choose which OLE data type you'll insert from the **Object Type** list box. For example, if you're inserting a new Word document, you would select **Microsoft Word Document**.

- If you already have a file that contains the data to be inserted into the field, select the **Create from File** option button and specify the location of the file.

When you choose **Create from File**, you can also indicate that the data inserted into the field should be linked to the file. This means that when the file is updated, the data in the field will be updated as well. Access accomplishes this by storing the path required to get to the OLE data, not the data itself.

Adding OLE Data Onto Forms or Reports

Using OLE linking and embedding, you can also place data from other applications onto forms and reports, but not in a field in the database. Instead, Access provides a control called the *Unbound Object Frame*, which you can place on forms and reports. This control can hold embedded or linked OLE data, just as an OLE Object table field can. Figure 36.7 shows the Toolbox window icons for both the Unbound Object Frame and Bound Object Frame controls.

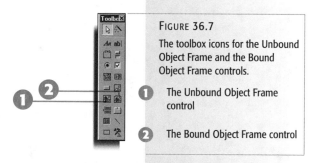

FIGURE 36.7

The toolbox icons for the Unbound Object Frame and the Bound Object Frame controls.

1 The Unbound Object Frame control

2 The Bound Object Frame control

While in the form's or report's Design view, there are several ways you can get OLE data onto forms and reports:

- Place the Unbound Object Frame onto a form or report. After you position the control, the Insert Object dialog box appears.

- Choose **Insert** and then click **Object** to invoke the Insert Object dialog box. After you've created or selected the OLE data to insert, Access will place an Unbound Object Frame control on the form or report. You'll have to size and position appropriately.

- Use the OLE server application's **Edit** menu to **Copy** the selected data to the Windows clipboard. For example, you can copy a paragraph in Word or a range of cells in Excel. Back in Access, use the **Edit** menu and select **Paste Special** to invoke the Paste Special dialog box. This dialog box is similar to the Insert Object dialog box, and enables you to specify how the data from the clipboard should be linked or embedded into the form or report. Again, Access will add an Unbound Object Frame control to your form or report.

SEE ALSO

➤ *To learn about working with reports in Design view, see page 439.*

The Office Assistant

Another tool that is common in the Office suite is the Office Assistant. This is part of Microsoft's effort to create software agents that help users do their work more effectively. The Office Assistant provides not only a gateway to the Office Help system, but also displays (and in some cases extends) the message boxes that Office applications display when they require input or confirmation from the user.

Getting to Know Your Assistant

If you installed Access 97 yourself, you probably saw one of the Assistants the first time you ran the application. If not, just choose **Help** and click **Microsoft Access Help**, or click the Office Assistant icon ⟨?⟩, or press the F1 key, and the Office Assistant will appear.

By default, the Office Assistant will provide you with some context-sensitive Help file choices (see Figure 36.8). Which choices are provided depends on what you happen to be doing at the time. If none of the choices appear to help your particular situation, type a question or phrase describing your current dilemma and click the Assistant's **Search** button. If you enter a question, you don't need to add the question mark. The Assistant will modify the set of Help topics to match your phrase or question.

FIGURE 36.8
The Office Assistant in action.

To access one of the Help topics, click its entry and the Access Help file will launch with the selected topic. If there are more topics than will fit on one screen of the Assistant's dialog box, you'll see an entry labeled **See More**. Click this entry to see the rest of the available topics.

If you still can't find a useful topic among the choices, try to expand your search criteria by removing a word or two.

Setting Office Assistant Options

There are a myriad of options that affect how the Assistant operates. You can choose from these options in the Office Assistant Options dialog box, which you open by clicking the **Options** button on the Office Assistant's main dialog box (see Figure 36.8). Some of the more useful options and their operations are described in Table 36.1.

Common options

Changing one of the Office Assistant's options while using the Assistant in Microsoft Access will also cause the new setting to be in effect when you're using the Assistant in all other Office 97 applications.

TABLE 36.1 Office Assistant Options

Option	Operation
Respond to F1 key	When checked, the Assistant appears when you press the F1 key. When cleared, Windows Help appears.
Help with Wizards	When checked, the Assistant will provide you with help as you work through a Wizard.
Display Alerts	When checked, the Assistant is responsible for displaying any message boxes while it is active. For standard message boxes while the Assistant is active, clear this option.
Move When in the Way	The most useful option of the bunch! This will force the Assistant to get out of your way as you work within the application.
Guess Help Topics	When checked, the Assistant will monitor your actions and display help automatically as you work. This type of assistance is more prevalent in Microsoft Word than in Access.

How to Use AutoCorrect

Another common assistant

The AutoCorrect that you use in Access is the same AutoCorrect that you use in Microsoft Word. So if you're used to the way AutoCorrect works from within Microsoft Word, you shouldn't be too surprised by the ways it works within Access.

Although you wouldn't think a word processing tool would be of much use in a database management system, AutoCorrect actually does fill a great need. When AutoCorrect is active, it can automatically correct common typos and capitalization mistakes, such as typing SMith when you mean Smith. With AutoCorrect, you can prevent many of the typing problems that make reports and mail merges look unprofessional.

Setting Up AutoCorrect

Setting up AutoCorrect is pretty straightforward. After you understand the concept, the options make sense. Figure 36.9 shows the main AutoCorrect options dialog box. Open this dialog box by clicking the **AutoCorrect** item found on the **Tools** menu. Table 36.2 lists the various options available for AutoCorrect.

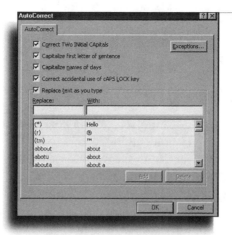

FIGURE 36.9
The AutoCorrect options
dialog box.

TABLE 36.2 **AutoCorrect Options**

Option	Operation
Correct TWo INitial CApitals	When you type a word with the first two letters capitalized (and *only* the first two), AutoCorrect will change the second to lowercase.
Capitalize First Letter of Sentence	AutoCorrect will change the first letter appearing after a period to uppercase.
Capitalize Names of Days	Days of the week, when fully spelled out, will be capitalized (abbreviations will not).
Correct Accidental Use of cAPS LOCK	AutoCorrect will detect/correct if your capitalization is backwards.
Replace Text as You Type	Lists commonly misspelled words and some common symbols. You can use this list as a macro list, enabling you to type a specific abbreviation and have AutoCorrect expand it for you.

In certain cases, you may not want AutoCorrect to perform the corrections for you. Clicking the **Exceptions** button will take you to the AutoCorrect Exceptions dialog box. This dialog box, shown in Figure 36.10, has two tabs, each with a list of exception items. The **First Letter** tab lists most of the abbreviations you may encounter. When you type any of the abbreviations in this list, AutoCorrect will not change the first letter after the abbreviation's period to uppercase. On the **INitial CAps** tab, you specify all the words or acronyms that should not have the SMith-to-Smith correction made. Note, though, that AutoCorrect corrects when only the first two letters are capitalized. If you capitalize three or more letters, as in ASAP, AutoCorrect will leave them alone anyway. So the only exceptions you need to list are ones where the first two letters, but not the third, are supposed to be capitalized.

FIGURE 36.10

The AutoCorrect Exceptions dialog box.

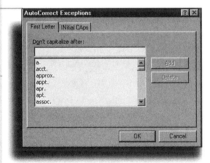

AutoCorrect in Action

The best way to learn how AutoCorrect works is to try it out for yourself.

Working with AutoCorrect

1. Start Access and open any database that has a form you can work in. Use the Northwind Traders sample database if need be.

2. Enable all the AutoCorrect options by launching the AutoCorrect dialog box with the **Tools, AutoCorrect** menu and checking all the check boxes.

3. Enter <ME> in the **Replace** text box, and enter your name in the **With** text box.

Uncommon settings

Although AutoCorrect is a shared tool, changes you make to the AutoCorrect settings within Access will *not* affect other Microsoft applications that use AutoCorrect. This enables you to set different AutoCorrect rules among your various data entry applications. (Yes, typing a Word document does amount to data entry!)

4. Click the **OK** button to save these changes.

5. Open a form that will enable you to insert new records. If you're using the Northwind database, use the Employees form.

6. Click the New Record icon ▶✱. Pick a text box and enter <ME>. Move the focus to another field by pressing the Tab key. Notice that the text you typed is replaced with your name as entered in step 3.

7. In another text box, enter THis is a blast. can i send EMail?. Before you start the first *is*, the double capitalization in THis has been corrected. Then, before you finish the word send, AutoCorrect has capitalized the word can and the pronoun I. But the double capitalization of EMail is left intact because that word is in the INitial Caps exception list.

Programming Command Bars

As you saw in some of the earlier chapters that discussed programming in Access (such as Chapter 31, "An Introduction to VBA," and 32, "Programming Access with VBA"), Access 97 gives you plenty of opportunity to extend the database environment. One of the really handy ways you can make your database unique is by customizing the toolbars and menus to be more specific to your application. Access provides the Office command bar objects to help you do this. This section will cover the basics of creating your own toolbars and menus. There's a lot more capability than will be demonstrated here, but you'll leave this section with more than enough information to get you started.

Programming ahead

This section gets heavy into VBA code. If you haven't read Chapters 31 and 32 yet and are new to Visual Basic programming, you probably want to at least skim these chapters to get some of the basic concepts under your belt.

Common Tool, Common Library

The facilities for creating command bar objects are contained in an ActiveX component that ships with all the Office applications. To use this component within your database's VBA code modules, you must specifically reference (or point Access to) the DLL file that houses this ActiveX component. This provides Access with the information about the objects and classes contained within that ActiveX component, enabling you to instantiate and manipulate instances of said component.

Referencing an ActiveX component

1. On the Database window, switch to the **Modules** tab. Either open an existing code module in Design view by selecting the module and clicking the **Design** button, or create a new module by clicking the **New** button.

2. When the Code Module window opens, click the **Tools** menu and then click **References**. The References dialog box, shown in Figure 36.11, lists all the ActiveX components (libraries) that are installed on your computer. The libraries that the current database already knows about are listed at the top and are checked.

FIGURE 36.11

The References dialog box, listing the available ActiveX component libraries installed on your computer.

3. If you see the entry at the top of this list and it is checked, Access already has a reference to the component. Click **OK** and you're finished. Otherwise, proceed to step 4.

4. Scroll through the list of **Available References** until you find an entry for **Microsoft Office 8.0 Object Library**. Click the check box next to this entry to enable the reference, and then click **OK**.

Creating a New Toolbar

You'll be shocked at how easy it is to add a new toolbar to your database programmatically. The biggest decision you have to make is when to enable this toolbar. You can do it at startup by assigning a user-defined function to the autoexec startup macro, you can do it when the user opens specific forms, or you can do it in response to a click of a button. When you create the toolbar is irrelevant to the discussion at hand and depends on your particular needs. We'll provide you with the snippets of code that will create command bars, but you'll need to put these in code modules that are executed as your needs dictate.

Of course, you can also create a new toolbar or menu using the Customize Toolbars feature (right-click over the toolbar and select **<u>C</u>ustomize** from the shortcut menu). These toolbars and menus cannot be conditionally built, however. They're always going to look and act the same. By applying some VBA code to the situation, you can create a truly dynamic toolbar or menu built for the specific conditions at hand.

The following three lines of code create a new toolbar and make it visible:

```
Dim MyToolbar as CommandBar
Set MyToolbar = Application.CommandBars.Add("Useless
Toolbar")
MyToolbar.Visible = True
```

Figure 36.12 shows the results of this code. Obviously, this is a just a "skeleton" toolbar. You can't even see all of the caption! As you undoubtedly know by now, toolbars need to contain other controls to be truly useful. In the next section, you'll see that it's just as easy to add buttons and drop-down lists to your toolbar as it is to create the toolbar itself.

SEE ALSO

➤ *For more on responding to events on forms, see page 418.*

➤ *For information on creating an* autoexec *startup macro, see page 536.*

FIGURE 36.12

The programmatically created skeleton toolbar.

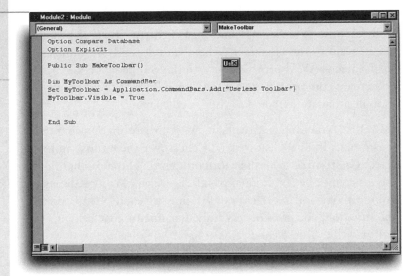

FIGURE 36.12

The programmatically created skeleton toolbar.

Delete thy toolbar

If you run the preceding code a second time, the second line produces an "Invalid procedure call or argument" error message. This happens because you've told Access to add a command bar with the same name as an existing one (Useless Toolbar). Because command bar names must be unique, an error occurs, albeit one lacking a very useful message. To avoid this, delete the new toolbar by right-clicking it, selecting **Customize** from the shortcut menu, selecting the **Useless Toolbar** entry in the **Toolbars** list box, and clicking the **Delete** button.

Adding Tools to Command Bars

In the previous section, you saw how easy it is to programmatically create a new toolbar or menu. But an empty toolbar is about as useful as a table with no fields. To make your new toolbar or menu useful, it needs some tools. This section will cover the basics of adding a tool. In the section that follows, you'll see the various tools that the Office command bars provide to make your toolbars and menus behave as you need them to.

As a review, the following lines of code create a new toolbar:

```
Dim MyToolbar as CommandBar
Set MyToolbar = Application.CommandBars.Add("Useless
Toolbar")
```

After you've created the MyToolbar command bar instance in this fashion, you can use its Controls property to access and manipulate the tools on the command bar. The Controls property is what's called a *collection* property because it contains a collection of another type of object. In this case, the Controls property contains a collection of items of type CommandBarControl. The property itself is of type CommandBarControls, which is a collection data type that encapsulates multiple CommandBarControl objects.

The `CommandBarControls` object contains a method named `Add` that is used to add a new control to the collection. So, to add a control to your new toolbar, you can use

```
MyToolbar.Controls.Add
```

You've just added a blank, generic tool to the command bar. Again, not a very useful task. You won't even see anything on the toolbar but a blank spot. To make a truly useful tool, you need to assign some values to the new control's properties. You can do so in one of two ways: by referencing the new control in the `Controls` collection, or by creating a separate variable to shortcut the reference to the new control. You do the latter by taking advantage of the fact that the `Add` method returns a reference to a variable of type `CommandBarControl` (or, as you'll see in the next section, one of its close cousins). This variable represents the control just added to the command bar.

Listing 36.1 shows some code that creates a slightly more useful button.

LISTING 36.1 **Creating a Button for the Empty Toolbar**

```
1  Dim MyControl as CommandBarControl
2  Set MyControl = MyToolbar.Controls.Add()
3  MyControl.Caption = "Button"
4  MyControl.ToolTipText = "Still blank!"
5  MyControl.OnAction = "=MsgBox(""Clicked!"")"
```

This control is still blank, despite the fact that you assigned it the `Caption` property. But it at least performs some task, albeit a basic one.

The `OnAction` property is where you control what happens when the user clicks the button or selects an item in a drop-down list. You assign a string to the property that represents the action that Access takes when appropriate. This string can be inline, or it can be a reference to a user-defined function that performs some more complicated tasks. You'll see an example of this method in the next section on drop-down list tools.

Available Control Styles

Although you can create a generic tool of type CommandBarControl, as in the previous section, it's really not worth the trouble. Instead, you should create one of the related tools. There are three other data types that are used to create one of the five different control types. The Controls collection's Add method will return one of these three types, depending on the value specified for the method's Type parameter.

The complete syntax of the Add method is

Expression.Add(*Type, Id, Parameter, Before, Temporary*)

All the parameters are optional, as you might have guessed from previous code snippets. The important parameter for our purposes is the *Type* parameter. The value specified here will determine which type of control is added to the command bar. There are built-in constants that you can use for the *Type* parameter. These are defined in the Office object library. Table 36.3 lists the values for the *Type* parameter and the data type of the object returned by the Controls collection's Add method.

TABLE 36.3   The Control Type Constants

Constant	Returned Control Type	Description
msoControlButton	CommandBarButton	A toolbar button or menu item
msoControlEdit	CommandBarComboBox	An edit box
msoControlDropdown	CommandBarComboBox	A drop-down list box
msoControlComboBox	CommandBarComboBox	A drop-down combo box
msoControlPopup	CommandBarPopup	A submenu or drop-down toolbar menu, similar to the View toolbar button available on most objects

So, to create a new control that is a true toolbar button, you'd use the code in Listing 36.2.

LISTING 36.2 **Creating a True Toolbar Button**

```
1 Dim MyButton as CommandBarButton
2 Set MyButton = MyToolbar.Controls.Add(msoControlButton)
3 MyButton.Style = msoButtonIconAndCaption
4 MyButton.Caption = "Click Me"
5 MyButton.FaceId = 321
6 MyButton.TooltipText = "Click here, please!"
7 MyButton.OnAction = "=MsgBox(1) "
```

Let's look at a few of the less obvious properties that were set in this code. First of all, the `Style` property (line 3) defines which kind of toolbar button this represents. The value specified here, `msoButtonIconAndCaption`, indicates that the button will have both an icon (as specified by the `FaceId` property) and some text (specified by the `Caption` property). Other values for this property are `msoButtonAutomatic`, `msoButtonCaption`, and `msoButtonIcon`.

The `FaceId` property (line 5) is definitely unique to Office command bars. There is a huge assortment of icons built into the Office Object Library. Each icon is identified by a `FaceId` value. If you know the `FaceId` value for an icon you'd like to use on your toolbar button, you can specify that value in the `FaceId` property.

The code in Listing 36.3 shows you how to make a toolbar with 100 different icons, each with a different `FaceId` value. Using this routine, you could easily locate the `FaceID` value matching the icon you're looking for.

LISTING 36.3 **Creating a Toolbar Full of Icons**

```
1 Public Sub MakeFaces(FirstFace As Integer, LastFace As
  Integer)
2     Dim FacesToolbar    As CommandBar
3     Dim NewButton       As CommandBarButton
4     Dim i               As Integer
5
6     If FirstFace > LastFace Then Exit Sub
7     If LastFace > (100 + FirstFace) Then Exit Sub
8
9     On Error Resume Next
```

continues…

LISTING 36.3   **Continued**

```
10    Application.CommandBars("Faces Toolbar").Delete
11
12    Set FacesToolbar = _
      Application.CommandBars.Add("Faces Toolbar", , , True)
13    FacesToolbar.Width = 600
14    For i = FirstFace To LastFace
15        Set NewButton = _
          FacesToolbar.Controls.Add(msoControlButton)
16        With NewButton
17            .Caption = "FaceID=" & i
18            .FaceId = i
19        End With
20    Next
21    FacesToolbar.Left = 100
22    FacesToolbar.Height = 300
23    FacesToolbar.Visible = True
24
25 End Sub
```

Figure 36.13 shows a sample toolbar created with
`MakeFaces(0,100)`.

FIGURE 36.13

The Faces toolbar, showing some of the capabilities of the Office command bars.

The world of Office command bars can be quite involved. You can create complicated and extremely useful menus and toolbars with the simple object model provided by Office. You can also transfer the code that you use to create these from one Office application to another, assuming that you don't reference items specific to one application in particular.

Access on the Internet

How Access and the World Wide Web Unite

The original intent of the World Wide Web (commonly referred to simply as "the Web") was to provide scientists with a mechanism for sharing documents across various computer systems. A scientist could publish a *hypertext document* (a document that contains links to other documents or to sections within the document itself, allowing the viewer to quickly move from one document to another) on a server machine connected to a network, and others could then view this document on their own machines. These hypertext documents are written using a format called *hypertext markup language (HTML)*, which is a text-based encoding of documents using tags to specify how the contents should be displayed to the viewer. Anyone who wants to view an HTML page uses a specialized browser application that interprets the HTML and displays a representation of the page on the user's computer screen.

The Web quickly gained acceptance after its public introduction in 1991 and is now an essential element of most businesses. Almost all medium- and large-sized companies today have at least a presence on the Web through a home page, if not a dedicated Web server hosting hundreds of HTML pages. The number of Web pages in place today is astronomical. This is not to say that all of these pages serve a useful purpose; in fact, the vast majority probably do not.

Dual Linking Capability

Companies today are placing a great deal of emphasis on using their Web sites to provide current and useful information to their customers and vendors. Most of this push relies on successfully retrieving and displaying data contained in a company's many (and possibly varied) databases. In some cases this data may be relatively static, such as descriptions from a yearly catalog or prior years' financial statements. In other cases the data may be extremely dynamic, requiring a live connection to the database, such as for inventory or pricing information.

In addition to providing information from a database on the Web, you may also want to provide links within your database to information either on the Web or on an *intranet* (an internal network that operates identically to, but is not necessarily connected to, the global Internet). For example, you may have a product catalog database, with a Web page describing each product. In this case you would want to have a hyperlink from the product's database record to the description page.

Fortunately, Access 97 provides you with both of these capabilities and more. In this chapter you'll walk through all of the steps necessary to create and use hyperlinks within your data, and to publish your data to Web pages. Access provides wizards that will publish your data either *statically* (for data that doesn't change very often) or *dynamically* (for data that requires a live connection to the database).

Hyperlinks within Access

Access 97 allows you to create fields and set up form controls that can provide hyperlinks to documents on your computer, on a machine accessible across your LAN or intranet, or on the Web. The steps required to create a link to a document don't change no matter where the linked document resides (on your machine, on the LAN, or on the Web). The address or path you use to specify the location of the document will change, of course, but the methods used will be the same.

Hyperlinks and Document Addresses

While we're on the subject of document location, let's take a quick look at the various ways you can specify the address (or location) of an object on a networked computer. Table 37.1 describes the three most common methods. Notice that your computer is lumped into the group of networked computers. With Windows 98 or Internet Explorer 4.0, even a detached, standalone computer is considered to be network-addressable by the operating system.

Static versus dynamic

If you've secured your server, dynamic pages allow the most current, interactive information. If you're more concerned about security or do not have a standalone server (that is, you buy space on a service provider), you'll want to supply frequent static pages. These provide a safe, "snapshot" view of your database's information. You can program Access to produce these pages to keep your information as current as possible.

TABLE 37.1   Document Addressing Methods

Location	Method	Example
Your computer	Local Path	`c:\My Documents\sales.doc`
LAN	UNC	`\\FileServer\marketing\sales.doc`
Intranet Web server	URL	`http://FileServer/marketing/sales.htm`
Internet Web server	URL	`http://www.myco.com/marketing/sales.htm`

The acronyms *URL* and *UNC* stand for *Universal Resource Locator* and *Uniform Naming Convention*, respectively. A URL is used to specify the location of an object on the Internet. It typically takes the form `protocol:address`, as shown in Table 37.1. The `//` portion indicates that what follows is the *hostname* (a unique name identifying the computer on a network) for the server on which the object is located. There are forms of URLs that do not specify a hostname, such as `mailto:craig.eddy@cyber-dude.com` or `news:microsoft.public.access.internet`.

A UNC specifies the location of an object (typically a file) on a PC network. The format is typically `\\servername\sharename\document`, where `servername` is the hostname of the network server, `sharename` is the name given to the shared (or networked) directory, and `document` specifies the exact name of the object in question.

Creating Hyperlink Fields

To link records in an Access database to objects on a network, you create hyperlink fields that will hold the addresses of the linked objects. In this section you'll see how to add such fields to existing tables. In the section that follows, you'll learn how to enter and edit the data in these fields.

Adding a hyperlink field to an existing table

1. From the Database window, select the table to which you want to add the hyperlink data and click **Design**. For example, to add a Web address field to the Customers table in the

Northwind Traders database, select the **Customers** table on the **Tables** tab of the Database window and click **Design**.

2. Scroll the Design View window until you come to an empty row, or click the Insert Rows toolbar button 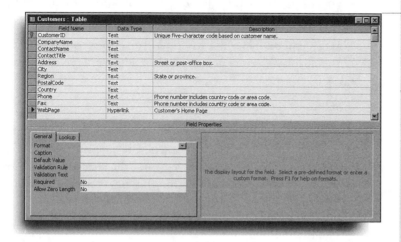 to add an empty row.

3. Enter a name for the field, such as WebPage, in the Field Name column.

4. Click in or tab to the Data Type column. Click on the drop-down arrow to display the list of field data types. Select **Hyperlink** from the list.

5. Press Tab again to move to the Description column. Enter a description if appropriate (and it usually is).

6. On the **General** tab at the bottom, enter a **Caption**, a **Default Value**, any validation rules and message text, and specify the value for **Required** and **Allow Zero Length**.

7. Save the new table design by clicking the **File** menu and selecting **Save**, or by clicking the Save toolbar button.

When you've finished, your screen should resemble Figure 37.1.

<aside>
Setting a default address

Setting a default value for the address is usually not applicable, but in certain cases, such as a product catalog in which all addresses begin the same way, it can reduce the number of keystrokes. At other times, you might want to set a default to a home page so that if no specific address is entered, your user won't click on a dead link, or can at least start from a general beginning point rather than have no link at all.
</aside>

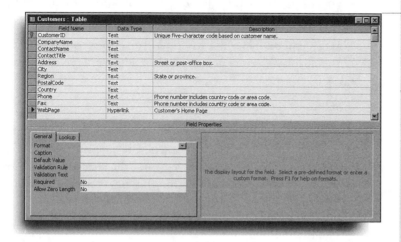

FIGURE 37.1

A hyperlink field added to the Customers table of the Northwind Traders database.

SEE ALSO

➤ *For more information about creating fields, see page 205.*

➤ *For more information about using naming conventions for your fields, see page 22.*

Limitations of the Hyperlink data type

Notice that you cannot index tables using hyperlink fields, and the Lookup tab is blank (meaning that you cannot retrieve the data for a hyperlink field from another table or query).

Editing Hyperlink Data

Now that you have a hyperlink field in a table, let's look at the various ways you can get data into that field. As usual, Access provides several means of accomplishing the same end.

The simplest method for adding the address to a hyperlink field is to just type it into the Datasheet view. As soon as you start typing into a hyperlink field, the data will appear as a hyperlink (usually underlined text with a blue foreground color), as shown in Figure 37.2.

FIGURE 37.2

Entering hyperlink data using the table's Datasheet view.

Fax	WebPage
030-0076545	http://
(5) 555-3745	

Until you save the updated row, the cursor will remain the I-beam (text edit) cursor. If you allow the cursor to hover above a hyperlink after the row is saved, it will change to the hand cursor. Any clicking you do will cause Access to "follow" the hyperlink, loading the referenced object into its default browser or application. To edit the data at that point, you'll need to use the keyboard to set focus to the field and then press F2 to edit the data.

You can enter a hyperlink strictly as an address, or you can enter both a displayed value portion and an address. Hyperlink data takes the form

displaytext#address#subaddress

The *displaytext* portion is the text that you will see when the data is displayed in a field or control, the *address* portion is the address of the document or object, and the *subaddress* portion points to a specific location within the file or page referenced in the *address* portion.

To enter hyperlink data for Microsoft's Home Page, for example, you might enter Microsoft Home Page#http://www.microsoft.com.

Using hyperlink data in VBA and SQL

Access provides a function named HyperlinkPart that will return a specific portion of the hyperlink field's data. You can use this function either in Visual Basic for Applications code or in a SQL query. For example, to work with the displayed value of a hyperlink, you would use HyperlinkPart (Customers.WebPage, acDisplayedValue).

After you enter this data and save the record, the field will display only Microsoft, as shown in Figure 37.3.

FIGURE 37.3

A hyperlink field containing displaytext and address portions.

1. The hand cursor will activate the link rather than let you edit the address

2. Access abbreviates the displaytext portion of the address

To edit the hyperlink shown in Figure 37.3, you could use the keyboard to set focus to the field and click F2, or you could use the following steps.

Editing hyperlink field data

1. Right-click over the hyperlink you want to edit. On the shortcut menu that appears, click on **Hyperlink**. The flyout menu shown in Figure 37.4 appears.

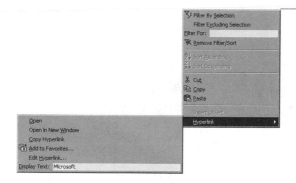

FIGURE 37.4

The **Hyperlink** menu for editing hyperlink field data.

2. To edit the displayed text (Microsoft in Figure 37.4), click in the text box next to **Display Text** and edit the text as you would in any text box. To make the changes stick, click outside the menu or press the Enter key. To revert back to the original text, press the Esc key.

3. To edit the address and subaddress portions, or to remove the hyperlink altogether, click the **Edit Hyperlink** menu item. The Edit Hyperlink dialog appears, as shown in Figure 37.5.

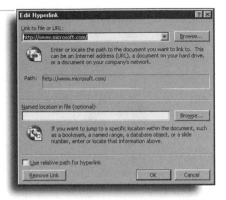

4. Using the topmost text box, you can edit the address portion. The drop-down list contains entries for all of the addresses you've typed into the address box of your Web browser (assuming you use Internet Explorer). If the file exists on your computer or LAN, you can use the **Browse** button to locate it.

5. The **Named Location in File (Optional)** text box allows you to enter or edit the subaddress portion of the hyperlink. Using the subaddress, you can point the hyperlink to a specific location within the file referenced by the address portion. Examples of this include a bookmark in a Microsoft Word document or a named cell in an Excel spreadsheet.

6. The **Remove Link** button is used to empty the field's data completely. Use this to delete the hyperlink, displayed text and all.

The other menu items on the **Hyperlink** menu perform various functions, such as launching the default Web browser with the selected hyperlink, adding the hyperlink to the **Favorites** menu, and copying a shortcut to the hyperlink to the Windows clipboard.

You can also use the Edit Hyperlink dialog to enter hyperlink data into an empty field. Simply use the **Hyperlink** menu and select the **Edit Hyperlink** item. The same dialog will appear, except the caption will change to **Insert Hyperlink** and the **Remove Link** button won't be visible.

Adding Hyperlinks to Forms and Reports

The Datasheet view is not the only place where hyperlink data can be edited and viewed. You can link form controls to hyperlink fields, allowing users of the form to launch their browsers pointing to the address specified in the record. You can also manipulate the Hyperlink Address property available on many controls, allowing you to link those controls to a specific (or programmatically controlled) document. For example, you may link the field caption labels on a form to an HTML document describing the form. (The field caption control that's placed on a form when you add a bound field to it does not support the Hyperlink Address property, though, so you'll have to manually add such a control using the techniques discussed here.)

The following sections illustrate a few of the ways you can use hyperlinks on your forms.

Adding a bound hyperlink field to a form

1. Select the form to which you want to add the hyperlink and open it in Design view. For example, to put the WebPage field added earlier to the Customers table onto the Customers form, select that form in the Database Window and click the **Design** button.

2. Open the Field List window (if it's not already opened) by clicking the **View** menu and selecting **Field List** or its icon
   ⊞ .

3. Drag the hyperlink field from the **Field List** onto the form, dropping it in the appropriate location. Resize and position the form control to match the rest of the form.

Figure 37.6 shows the Design view results of adding the WebPage field to the Customers form. Notice that you can tell it's a hyperlink field because the field name text box is the typical hyperlink text (blue foreground and underlined).

SEE ALSO

➤ *For instructions on how to resize controls, see page 324.*

Browsing for Hyperlink Data

If you're using Internet Explorer, you can browse to the Web page whose address you're interested in storing and insert it directly into your hyperlink field.

Here's how: Go to a record with empty hyperlink data. Click on **Insert**, **Hyperlink** to launch the Edit Hyperlink dialog. Switch to IE, browse to the page whose URL you want to insert into the field, and switch back to Access. The hyperlink data will be filled in for you!

FIGURE 37.6

The Design view of a form with a bound hyperlink field added.

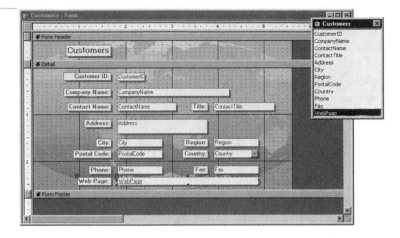

To see the link in action, you'll have to switch to Form view. From there, you can right-click over the hyperlink field and have access to the same **Hyperlink** menu described in the previous section.

The following step-by-step describes how to add unbound hyperlink controls to your forms. The first is a label control that is linked to a specific bookmark in an HTML page describing the form. The second is a button that is linked to that same HTML page, but not to a bookmark on the page.

Adding unbound hyperlink controls to a form

1. Open the form in Design view. In this case, it's the Customers form.

2. If you're going to add the hyperlink to a label for an existing bound control, first delete that label control that was inserted with the bound control. For example, you're going to link the label attached to the CustomerID field to a Web page describing the fields on this form. Delete the Customer ID label control.

3. If necessary, open the Toolbox by clicking the **View** menu and selecting **Toolbox**, or click ![Toolbox icon]. Click the Label control ![Aa] on the Toolbox, click the form where you want to place the label, and drag and drop the label into shape.

4. Type a caption for the label (such as Customer ID:), committing your new caption by pressing the Enter key or clicking elsewhere on the form. Position and size the label appropriately.

5. Click the Properties icon [icon], and select either the **Format** or the **All** tab to edit the hyperlink data for the control. The Hyperlink Address and Hyperlink SubAddress properties are the ones in question (see the section "Editing Hyperlink Data" earlier in the chapter for the format of these properties). You can either type directly into the text boxes or use the **Builder** button to launch the Insert Hyperlink dialog.

6. In the Hyperlink Address property, enter `http://localhost/customers.htm`, replacing the URL with the one appropriate to your situation.

In the Hyperlink SubAddress property, enter the bookmark in the page appropriate for the field to which you're attaching the label. For example, in my Web page I have a bookmark for each field on the form that matches the field name in the Customers table. So for the CustomerID field, I have a bookmark named CustomerID. I'll enter CustomerID into the Hyperlink SubAddress property. Figure 37.7 shows the results so far.

7. Repeat this process for the remainder of the controls you want to provide with this capability. The simplest way to do this is to copy and paste the label control, editing the caption and hyperlink properties. To edit the hyperlink without using the Properties window, simply right-click over the control and use the standard **Hyperlink** flyout menu.

8. Next add a hyperlink command button to the form. This button will launch the Web page without specifying a bookmark. Click the Command Button control [icon] in the Toolbox, and drag and drop the control into place on the form.

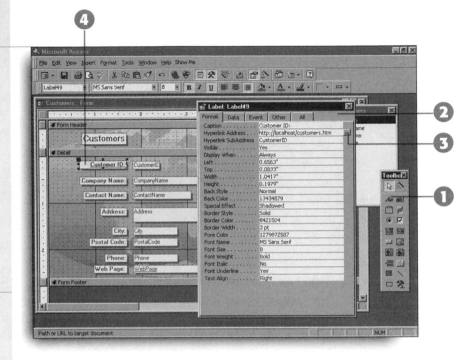

FIGURE 37.7

The Design View of a form with an unbound label control that has its hyperlink properties set.

❶ The **Label** control in the Toolbox

❷ The **hyperlink** properties

❸ The **Builder** button that will launch the Insert/Edit Hyperlink dialog

❹ The label control, sporting its hyperlink look

9. Give the command button an appropriate caption, such as Help, and press Enter. Return to the Properties window and enter the URL for the page in the Hyperlink Address property. Because this is intended to be help for the entire form, don't bother with the Hyperlink SubAddress property. For the Customers form, I entered http://localhost/customers.htm.

10. Save the form.

Figure 37.8 shows the results of the previous step-by-step in Design view. Clicking on one of the hyperlink labels causes the Web page shown in Figure 37.9 to be displayed at thc appropriate bookmark. Clicking the button launches the same page, but the browser will position the display at the top of the page.

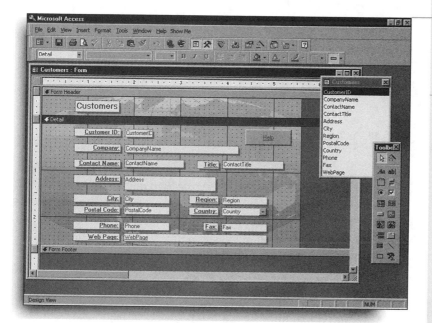

FIGURE 37.8

The Design view of a form with hyperlink label controls and a hyperlink command button.

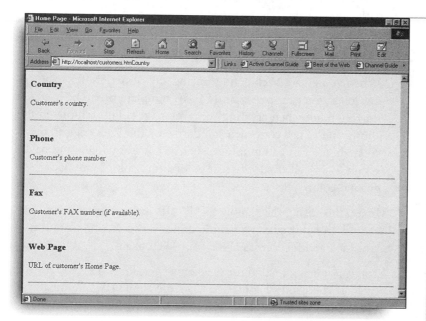

FIGURE 37.9

The Web page launched by clicking on the hyperlink labels.

SEE ALSO

➤ *To learn more about working with the Toolbox, see page 314.*

➤ *To get more information on positioning and sizing controls, see page 323.*

➤ *To learn more about working with forms in Design view, see page 342.*

➤ *For more information on setting properties, see page 346.*

Publishing Basics

Access 97 provides several ways to publish your data to the Web. You can publish either static data or dynamic data. Static pages never change, always displaying the same data. Dynamic pages, however, generate queries against your Access databases and produce Web pages on the fly, using current data from the database. This section discusses both methods.

You can create static Web pages from a single database object using the export method. Using the Publish to the Web wizard, you can create either static or dynamic Web pages. You can also create these pages from more than one database object at a time with the wizard.

Creating an HTML Template File

When you create Web content using any of Access 97's exporting tools, you can specify an HTML template file to be used as a starting point when creating the Web pages. This template file allows you to use your own standards for the Web page to be created. You can add graphics, such as company logos and backgrounds, as well as specify text colors, link colors, and background colors.

If you'll be using the Export to HTML features often, you should probably create a template file or two to provide a consistent look and feel across all of your Web pages.

You can use any text editor or even a specialized HTML editor such as Microsoft's FrontPage to create the HTML template file. Store it in a common directory so that you'll have no trouble locating it when it's time to publish some Web content. A sample template for the Northwind Traders database is installed in the same directory as the MDB file. It's named NWINDTEM.HTM and can be opened using Internet Explorer (see Figure 37.10) or Notepad.

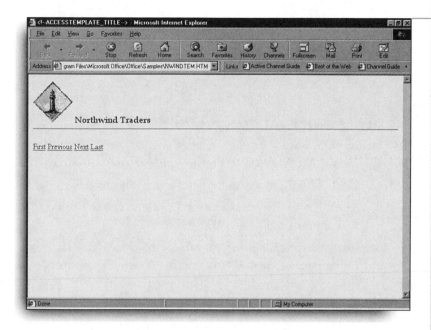

FIGURE 37.10
The Northwind Traders HTML template displayed in Internet Explorer.

In addition to HTML code, template files can also contain tokens that Access replaces with appropriate material, as shown in Table 37.2.

TABLE 37.2 **HTML Template File Tokens**

Token	Replacement
<!--AccessTemplate_Title-->	The object name is placed in the Web browser's title bar
<!--AccessTemplate_Body-->	The exported data
<!--AccessTemplate_FirstPage-->	A link to the first page
<!--AccessTemplate_PreviousPage-->	A link to the previous page
<!--AccessTemplate_NextPage-->	A link to the next page
<!--AccessTemplate_LastPage-->	A link to the last page
<!--AccessTemplate_PageNumber-->	The current page number

Exporting Static Web Pages

The simplest, quickest way to create a static Web page from a database object is to use the Save As/Export method. This will create a Web page based upon a single table, query, form, or report in the current database. You can use a template file here as well, but typically this feature is used as a one-shot quick-and-dirty mechanism for producing an HTML file containing the current contents of the database.

To perform the export to an HTML format, follow these steps.

Exporting a database object to an HTML file

1. In the Database window, select the table, query, form, or report that you want to save in HTML format.

2. Click the **File** menu and select **Save As/Export**.

3. Select **To an External File or Database** from the dialog that appears. Click the **OK** button.

4. On the Save dialog that appears next, select **HTML Documents (*.html;*.htm)** in the **Save as Type** dropdown list.

5. Select the location and name to save the HTML file to. If you want to use an HTML template file, check the box labeled **Save Formatted**. Click the **Export** button.

6. If you elected to use an HTML template file in step 5 (by checking the **Save Formatted** box), a dialog box will appear in which you specify the location of the template file. You can either type the file's name or use the **Browse** button to locate the template using the familiar file dialog.

7. The HTML file is created in the location you specified. You can use Internet Explorer to view its contents.

Figure 37.11 shows the Customers table from the Northwind Traders database exported without using a template file. Figure 37.12 shows the same table, but this time using the NWINDTEM.HTM template file. Notice that the template-created file has a better look and feel than the straight export. The most important difference is the column headings that are displayed when using the template file.

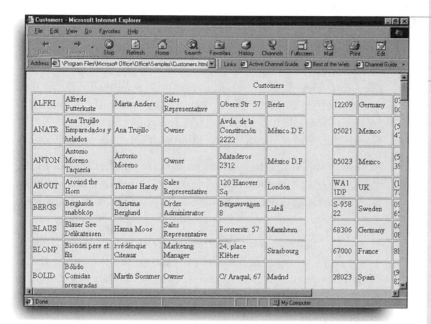

FIGURE 37.11

The Customers table exported to HTML without a template.

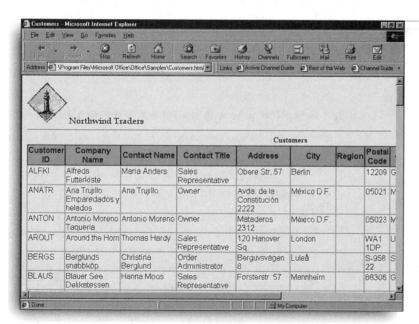

FIGURE 37.12

The Customers table exported to HTML using the Northwind sample template.

The Publish to the Web Wizard

In addition to the manual process of exporting data to HTML, discussed in the previous section, Access 97 sports a Publish to the Web Wizard. This wizard assists you in publishing your data to the Web in a variety of ways: static (as seen in the previous section), dynamic using Microsoft's Internet Database Connector, and dynamic using Microsoft's Active Server Pages.

Although similar to the manual process, using the Publish to the Web Wizard gives you greater flexibility. You can select multiple tables, queries, forms, and reports to export, and you can automatically launch the Web Publishing Wizard to transfer your HTML pages to a Web server.

The following sections describe how to use the Publish to the Web Wizard to create static pages, Internet Database Connector pages, and Active Server Page–based pages to export database objects to.

Static Web Pages

Creating static Web pages with the wizard involves a few more steps, but the results and the added flexibility are worth the trouble.

Creating a static HTML page with the Publish to the Web Wizard

1. To start the Publish to the Web Wizard, click **File** and select the **Save As HTML** item. One of the wizard's dialogs allows you to specify which items of the database to export to HTML, so it doesn't matter what you have selected in the Database window.

2. The first dialog is an introductory dialog that explains what's about to happen. It also allows you to load a previously saved profile. If this is the first time you've used this wizard or you have never saved any profiles, this option will be disabled. The final dialog in the wizard allows you to save the answers from the wizard steps in a profile file, which you can use again by selecting it on this dialog. Click the **Next** button to continue.

3. The next dialog, shown in Figure 37.13, is where you'll specify which database objects to export. You can click the tabs to select which type of object to export, and then select the specific items by clicking the check boxes or by using the **Select** and **Select All** buttons. You can remove items by using the **Deselect All** button or by clearing its check box. After you've selected the item or items you want to save in HTML format, click the **Next** button to continue.

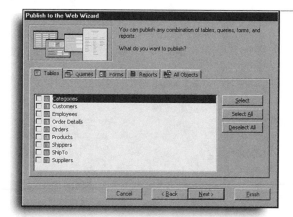

FIGURE 37.13
The Publish to the Web Wizard's database object selection dialog. Use the check boxes and tabs to select multiple tables or queries.

4. In the next dialog, you specify the HTML template file to use if you want to use one. You can type the filename or use the **Browse** button to locate it. If you have multiple selected items in the previous dialog, you can check the **I Want to Select Different Templates for Some of the Selected Objects** check box. If you choose this route, the next dialog will present you with a list box where you can specify different template files for each of the exported objects. Click the **Next** button to continue.

5. This dialog is where you specify how the export file should be created. To create a static Web page, leave the **Static HTML** option button selected. If you want to create different types of exports for the different objects you've selected, there is a check box that allows you to do so in the same manner as specifying different HTML template files for each object. Click the **Next** button to continue.

Using graphics in your template

If you use a template file that contains graphics, make sure that the graphics exist in the folder that you'll specify as the output folder in step 6. Otherwise, the graphics will not be loaded when you open the pages in a browser.

6. The next dialog (shown in Figure 37.14) is where you specify the location to which the Web page(s) should be stored.
The text box is where you enter the name of the folder into
which Access will place the HTML file. You can type the
folder name or use the **Browse** button to locate the folder.
If you were going to move the files to a Web server as well,
you'd select one of the Web Publishing Wizard option buttons in the middle of the dialog. It is best to store all of your
Web content in a single folder or in subfolders of a specific
folder. This will make it easier to manually copy the content
to your Web site or to use the Web Publishing Wizard.
After you've selected the folder to export to, click the **Next**
button to continue.

FIGURE 37.14

The Publish to the Web Wizard's
output location dialog. Remember
that your graphics must be in the
same folder.

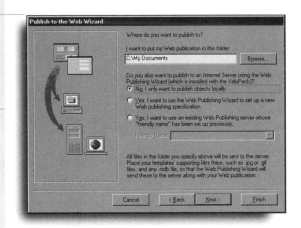

7. This dialog allows you to specify whether a home page is
created for your exported data. If created, the home page
will contain links to the individual pages that are created for
each object you've selected to export. If you choose to create
a home page, you should specify the name for the file in the
text box provided. Make your selection and click **Next** to
continue.

8. In the wizard's final dialog, you can instruct the wizard to
save the answers to the previous dialogs into a publication
profile. You can then use this profile in the future (as
described in step 1) and your current choices will already be

selected for you. It's also a great way to figure out what steps you took to create the Web page if you've forgotten. After you've made your choice on this dialog, click **Finish** to create the HTML files.

Launch Internet Explorer and use the **File**, **Open** menu to locate the HTML file created. It will be placed in the folder you specified in step 6. A page for the Customers table, without specifying a template file, is shown in Figure 37.15.

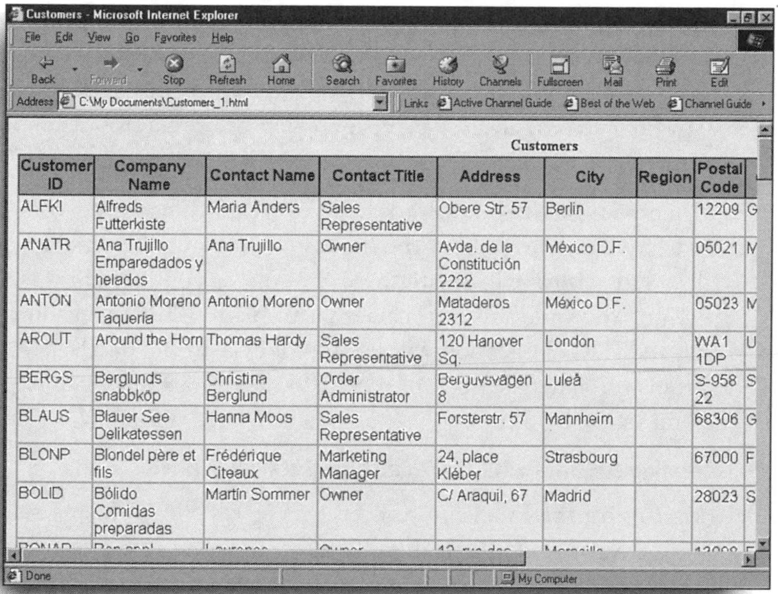

FIGURE 37.15
A Web page produced by the Publish to the Web Wizard. The scrollbars appear automatically as needed.

Notice that even though a template file was not used to create this page, the page looks very similar to the page created with the Northwind template (see Figure 37.12). This is another advantage of using the Publish to the Web Wizard.

Browser Compatibility Warning

Figure 37.15 shows how Microsoft Internet Explorer displays the resulting page. If you're using a different browser, such as Netscape Navigator, your results may be slightly different.

Internet Database Connector Pages

The *Internet Database Connector (IDC)* is a specialized application that can be installed on either the Personal Web Server or the Internet Information Server. Using the IDC, you can produce Web pages that display live data through an ODBC connection to your database. The IDC uses a template file that contains tokens for each database field and a script file that contains the information necessary to retrieve the data from the database. The template files have an extension of .HTX, while the script files have an extension of .IDC. When you create a link to an IDC page, you should link to the IDC file. The Web server (if IDC has been properly installed) knows to provide the requestor with the database-aware Web page when the requestor attempts to retrieve an IDC file.

When you use the Publish to the Web Wizard, however, you don't have to worry about the details of the template or script files. The wizard will create these for you, as you'll see in this section. You will, however, have to set up an ODBC data source that the IDC application will use to connect to the database. Details on how to set up an Access ODBC data source can be found in the help files.

Creating IDC files with the Publish to the Web Wizard

1. To start the Publish to the Web Wizard, click **File** and select the **Save As <u>H</u>TML** item. One of the wizard's dialogs allows you to specify which items of the database to export to HTML, so it doesn't matter what you have selected in the Database window.

2. The first dialog is an introductory dialog that explains what's about to happen. It also allows you to load a previously saved profile. If this is the first time you've used this wizard or you have never saved any profiles, this option will be disabled. The final dialog in the wizard allows you to save the answers from the wizard steps in a profile file, which can be used again by selecting it on this dialog. Click the **<u>N</u>ext** button to continue.

IDC Pointer

For more information on using and creating IDC files, check out Microsoft's IDC support pages at `http://www.microsoft.com/iis/support/iishelp/iis/htm/asp/iiwaidb.htm`.

3. The next dialog, shown in Figure 37.13, is where you'll specify which database objects to export. You can click the tabs to select which type of object to export, and then select the specific items by clicking the check boxes or by using the **S**elect and **S**elect **A**ll buttons. You can remove items by using the **D**eselect **All** button or by clearing its check box. After you've selected the item or items you want to save in HTML format, click the **N**ext button to continue.

4. In the next dialog, you specify the HTML template file to use if you want to use one. You can type the filename or use the **B**rowse button to locate it. If you have multiple selected items on the previous dialog, you can check the **I Want to Select Different Templates for Some of the Selected Objects** check box. If you choose this route, the next dialog will present you with a list box where you can specify different template files for each of the exported objects. Click the **N**ext button to continue.

5. This dialog is where you specify how the export file should be created. To create IDC pages, click the **D**ynamic **HTX/IDC (Microsoft Internet Information Server)** option button. If you want to create different types of exports for the different objects you've selected, there is a check box that allows you to do so in the same manner as specifying different HTML template files for each object. Click the **N**ext button to continue.

6. The next dialog (shown in Figure 37.16) is where you specify the ODBC connection information. This information is used by the IDC to connect to the database. The data source name entered here does not have to exist yet to continue with the wizard, but it will have to exist in order for the IDC pages you're creating to work. If you have secured or encrypted your Access database, you need to enter a user name and password in the appropriate text boxes. If you get really lost, or just want to do some more reading on the topic, click the **H**elp button. After you've entered the necessary details, click the **N**ext button to continue.

FIGURE 37.16

The Publish to the Web Wizard's
ODBC data source and Active
Server Pages information dialog.

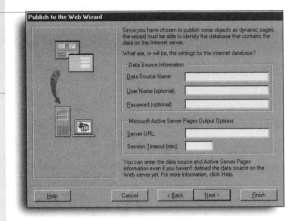

7. The next dialog (shown in Figure 37.14) is where you specify the location to which the IDC/HTX files should be
stored. The text box is where you enter the name of the
folder into which Access will place the output files. You can
type the folder name or use the **B**rowse button to locate the
folder. You must place the output files into a directory accessible by a Web server in order for them to work as expected—the IDC/HTX files only work when interpreted by the
IDC application that runs on IIS. You can select one of
the Web Publishing Wizard option buttons in the middle of
the dialog to assist you in publishing to a Web server.
Otherwise, be sure that the folder specified in the **I Want to
Put My Web Publication in This Folder** text box points
to a server-accessible folder. After you've selected the folder
to export to, click the **N**ext button to continue.

8. This dialog allows you to specify whether a home page is
created for your exported data. If created, the home page
will contain links to the individual pages that are created for
each object you've selected to export. If you choose to create
a home page, you should specify the name for the file in the
text box provided. Make your selection and click **N**ext to
continue.

9. In the wizard's final dialog, you can instruct the wizard to save the answers to the previous dialogs into a publication profile. You can then use this profile in the future (as described in step 1) and your current choices will already be selected for you. It's also a great way to figure out which steps you took to create the Web page if you've forgotten. After you've made your choice on this dialog, click **Finish** to create the IDC/HTX files.

To see the results, launch Internet Explorer (or any browser, for that matter) and type the URL for the IDC file just created. A page for the Customers table, without specifying a template file, looks very similar to the screen in Figure 37.15.

SEE ALSO

➤ *To learn how to encrypt your database, see page 375.*

➤ *For information on securing your Access database, see page 750.*

Active Server Pages

Active Server Pages (ASP) run on Internet Information Server as well as the Personal Web Server. These pages contain some scripting language, typically (but not necessarily) VBScript, which executes on the Web server. After the script executes, it returns a Web page to the requestor but doesn't return any of the script code that has executed. ASP can access any ActiveX/COM component installed on the server machine, including database-aware components and ActiveX controls. You can create an entire Web-based application using ASP, and the details can become quite complicated.

An ASP-based solution has the following advantages over the IDC solution discussed in the previous section:

- No additional components to install.

- No additional components need to be loaded by IIS.

- Pages produced can be readily extended using Active script code to meet needs beyond the simple data export.

Browser Compatibility

IDC is browser-independent by nature and should, in general, display identically on most browsers. You should test your page on several different types and versions of browsers to see if any major problems occur.

Creating ASP files with the Publish to the Web Wizard

1. To start the Publish to the Web Wizard, click **File** and select the **Save As HTML** item. One of the wizard's dialogs allows you to specify which items of the database to export to HTML, so it doesn't matter what you have selected in the Database window.

2. The first dialog is an introductory dialog that explains what's about to happen. It also allows you to load a previously saved profile. If this is the first time you've used this wizard or you have never saved any profiles, this option will be disabled. The final dialog in the wizard allows you to save the answers from the wizard steps in a profile file, which can be used again by selecting it on this dialog. Click the **Next** button to continue.

3. The next dialog, shown in Figure 37.13, is where you'll specify which database objects to export. You can click the tabs to select which type of object to export, and then select the specific items by clicking the check boxes or by using the **Select** and **Select All** buttons. You can remove items by using the **Deselect All** button or by clearing its check box. After you've selected the item or items you want to save in HTML format, click the **Next** button to continue.

4. In the next dialog, you specify the HTML template file to use if you want to use one. You can type the filename or use the **Browse** button to locate it. If you have multiple selected items on the previous dialog, you can check the **I Want to Select Different Templates for Some of the Selected Objects** check box. If you choose this route, the next dialog will present you with a list box where you can specify different template files for each of the exported objects. Click the **Next** button to continue.

5. This dialog is where you specify how the export file should be created. To create Active Server Pages, click the **Dynamic ASP (Microsoft Active Server Pages)** option button. If you want to create different types of exports for the different objects you've selected, there is a check box

that allows you to do so in the same manner as specifying different HTML template files for each object. Click the **Next** button to continue.

6. The next dialog (shown in Figure 37.16) is where you specify the ODBC connection information. This information is used by the ASP to connect to the database. The data source name entered here does not have to exist yet to continue with the wizard, but it will have to exist in order for the ASP pages you're creating to work. If you have secured or encrypted your Access database, you need to enter a user name and password in the appropriate text boxes. If you get really lost, or just want to do some more reading on the topic, click the **Help** button. After you've entered the necessary details, click the **Next** button to continue.

7. The next dialog (shown in Figure 37.14) is where you specify the location to which the ASP page(s) should be stored. The text box is where you enter the name of the folder into which Access will place the output files. You can type the folder name or use the **Browse** button to locate the folder. You must place the output files into a directory accessible by a Web server in order for them to work as expected—ASP files only work when interpreted by IIS. You can select one of the Web Publishing Wizard option buttons in the middle of the dialog to assist you in publishing to a Web server. Otherwise, be sure that the folder specified in the **I Want to Put My Web Publication in This Folder** text box points to a server-accessible folder. After you've selected the folder to export to, click the **Next** button to continue.

8. This dialog allows you to specify whether a home page is created for your exported data. If created, the home page will contain links to the individual pages that are created for each object you've selected to export. If you choose to create a home page, you should specify the name for the file in the text box provided. Make your selection and click **Next** to continue.

9. In the wizard's final dialog, you can instruct the wizard to save the answers to the previous dialogs into a publication profile. You can then use this profile in the future (as described in step 1) and your current choices will already be selected for you. It's also a great way to figure out which steps you took to create the Web page if you've forgotten. After you've made your choice on this dialog, click **Finish** to create the ASP files.

To see the results, launch Internet Explorer (or any browser, for that matter) and type the URL for the ASP file just created. A page for the Customers table, created without specifying a template file, looks very similar to a non-ASP page, such as in Figure 37.15. However, the page is ready to take advantage of the coding benefits that ASP can offer.

Importing and Linking to Data from HTML Tables

Browser Compatibility

As with IDC pages, the Active Server Pages created by the Publish to the Web Wizard are browser-independent and should, in general, display identically across most browsers. Again, you'll want to test these pages in a variety of browsers for maximum compatibility.

The preceding section covered how to export or publish your data so as to be accessible to Web browsers. This section will show you how to go in the opposite direction: importing data from Web pages into an Access database. Although you'll probably use this feature of Access only on rare occasions, it's nice to know that it's available to you. Using the import and link HTML data feature, you can retrieve data from Web pages and store it or link to it, respectively, in an Access database. Figure 37.15 and the raw tables produced for ASP and IDC pages are all wonderful examples of HTML tables and the type of data they may contain. If you ever run across such a Web page and wish you could get the data into an Access database, this section will show you how it can be done.

But what's the difference between importing data and link data? Importing data is a one-shot deal. If the HTML file used as the source of the import is changed after the data is imported, the data in your Access database will not reflect those changes. Performing an import amounts to taking a snapshot of the HTML table data at the point where the import is performed. Linking, on the other hand, will cause the data to be retrieved from the HTML file anytime the linked table that is created in the database is opened. This means that the HTML file you use as the source for the linked data must be available at all times.

In most cases you'll only want to import the data, not link to it. For this reason, the following step-by-step focuses primarily on data import, pointing out where there are differences that are specific to linking to an HTML table.

Importing or linking HTML table data to an Access database

1. Open the database into which you want to import the HTML table.

2. Click **File**, **Get External Data**, and then **Import** to import, or **Link Tables** to link.

3. A file open dialog similar to Figure 37.17 appears. If you choose **Link Tables,** the captions for both the dialog and the default button will read Link instead of Import. In the **Files of type** drop-down list, select **HTML Documents (*.html;*.htm)**.

4. Navigate to the HTML file containing the data you want to import and click the **Import** button.

If the HTML file chosen does not contain an HTML table, you'll receive a message box similar to that shown in Figure 37.18. If it does contain one or more HTML tables, the Import HTML Wizard launches. If the HTML file contains multiple tables, the first dialog that appears will ask you to select one of the available tables. You can only import from a single HTML table at a time, so you must select only one. After you've chosen a table, or if the HTML file contains only a single table, the first real import dialog of this wizard appears (see Figure 37.19).

5. In most cases, the first row of an HTML table contains column headings. If this is the case for the table you're importing, check the box labeled **First Row Contains Column Headings**. The wizard will respond by switching the first row of data in the preview grid to column headings.

FIGURE 37.17

Browse and select the database you want to import.

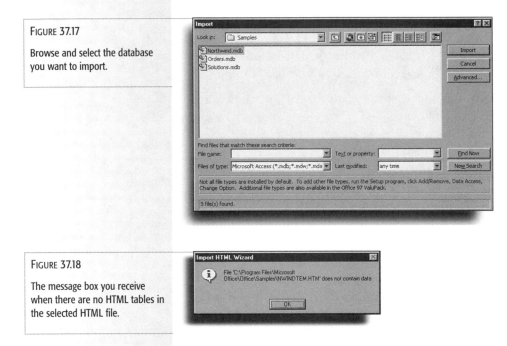

FIGURE 37.18

The message box you receive when there are no HTML tables in the selected HTML file.

FIGURE 37.19

The initial dialog of the Import HTML Wizard.

6. If you want to change or verify the data types that the Wizard is assigning to various columns, or want to check the indexes that will be created, click the **Ad_vanced** button. The Customers Import Specification dialog appears, as shown in Figure 37.20. Here you can alter the field names, data types, and indexing properties of each column found in the HTML table. You can also instruct the wizard to skip a field (not import it) by checking the box in the Skip column for the appropriate field. Note that if you're linking to the HTML file, the Indexed column will not be visible on this dialog. Click **OK** when you're satisfied with the settings. The **Advanced** button is available on all of the wizard's dialogs.

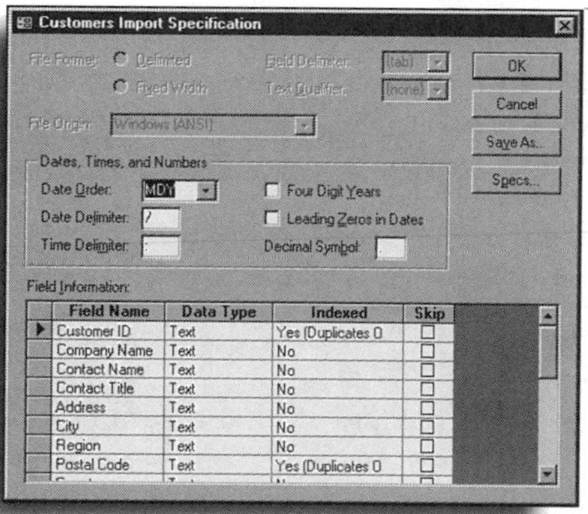

FIGURE 37.20

The Import HTML Wizard's Import Specification dialog. Click the **Four Digit Years** option to reduce Year 2000 confusion.

7. In the Wizard's initial dialog, click **Next** to continue.

8. If you're linking to an HTML file, skip to step 9. If you're performing an import, the dialog that appears is where you instruct the wizard what to do with the data that it will import. You can import the data into a new table (which you'll name in a few steps) or into an existing table (which you'll choose from the drop-down list box). Make your selection and click **Next** to continue. If you choose to import into an existing table, the field definitions of the existing table will be used to perform the import and you will skip to step 11.

9. The dialog that appears next (shown in Figure 37.21) is basically a rehash of the Customers Import Specification dialog you saw in step 6 (see Figure 37.20). The difference here is that you must click a column in the preview grid in order to make it the active field in the Field Options area. Click **Next** to continue.

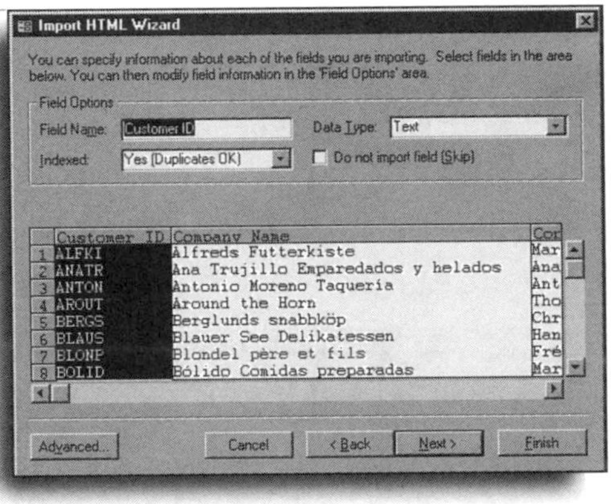

FIGURE 37.21

You must click a column in order to make it the active field.

10. If you're linking to an HTML table, skip to step 11. In this dialog you choose how Access deals with the new table's primary key. The default is to let Access add a primary key field, which the wizard typically will name ID and which, unfortunately, you cannot rename from within the wizard. You can also click **Choose My Own Primary Key**. In this case you'll pick from the list of available fields, or type the field name into the drop-down combo box. You create a new field, however, by typing a new name into this box. You must choose an existing field. Or, you could elect **No Primary Key**. Depending on the table you're importing, make the appropriate selection and click **Next** to continue.

11. Finally you've made it to the wizard's last dialog. Enter a name for the new table. If you choose a name that already exists, the wizard will confirm that you want to overwrite the existing table (chances are you don't). If you're performing an import, you can click on **I Would Like a Wizard to Analyze My Table After Importing the Data** to have the

Table Analyzer Wizard analyze the table when the Import Wizard is finished with it. After you've responded appropriately to this dialog, click **Finish** to create the new table.

If you choose to import to an existing table and the columns in the HTML table do not exactly match the fields in the existing table, you'll receive an error message. This message will inform you of the first offending column found in the HTML table. Clicking **OK** on this dialog will return you to the Import HTML Wizard, where you can use the **Back** button to correct the choices or the **Cancel** button to quit the Wizard altogether.

If a new table was created by the wizard (either by performing a link or an import into a new table), it will now appear on the **Tables** tab of the Database window. A newly imported table will appear no differently than a table you created by any other means. A new table created by linking to an HTML file, however, will have its own special icon, as shown in Figure 37.22.

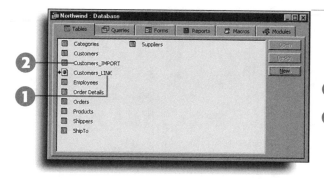

FIGURE 37.22

The Database window's **Tables** tab after an HTML file was successfully linked.

① The linked HTML table icon

② A table imported from an HTML file looks the same as any other table

SEE ALSO

➤ *For information on other import wizards, see page 114.*

➤ *To learn more about indexes and primary keys, see page 199.*

Applying Security to the Database

Why database security is important

How to set a database password

How to create users and groups

How to set permissions for database objects

Using the User-Level Security Wizard

Why Have Security?

In today's business world, corporate espionage is a bigger problem than most people realize. Your competition is always going to snoop around as much as they can in attempts to find out what your latest projects are, who your customers are, and what your potential weaknesses are. For these reasons, among others, corporate IS staffs have started taking desktop data security very seriously. As more and more data is pushed out to mobile employees, salespeople who travel with laptops in particular, there is a greater need for securing corporate data.

Microsoft Access provides several handy methods for securing your databases and their contents. These are listed in order of usefulness:

1. Locking down form, report, and module design through creation of an MDE file

2. Encrypting the database

3. Setting a database password

4. Utilizing workgroup information files and user-level security

I cover the last three in this chapter, with special emphasis on the fourth method; it is the most complicated. In order to utilize user-level security to its fullest, Microsoft has provided the User-Level Security Wizard. This wizard allows you to easily create a fully secured database.

Whenever you're working with database security in Microsoft Access, it's best to have a backup of the original database stored in a safe place. This way, you'll have a fallback position should you ever lose the password information or make your database unreadable.

SEE ALSO

➤ *For more information creating MDE files, see page 629.*

Encrypting and Decrypting the Database

Encrypting your database makes it inaccessible to programs other that Access 97. It's a good idea to encrypt your database after you've applied the user-level security measures discussed later in this chapter. That way someone can't go snooping through the database with a simple hex-dump viewer.

Encrypting alone does not prevent unauthorized access to your data. In fact, if all you do is encrypt your database you haven't really secured it at all—anyone with Microsoft Access can open it. In addition to encrypting the database, you should follow the user-level security procedures outlined later in this chapter.

In addition, you must be logged on as the owner of the database in order to encrypt/decrypt it. If you've enacted user-level security and are not logged in as the database owner, Access fails when you attempt to encrypt or decrypt the database.

Access creates the encrypted database as a copy of the original database. Therefore, you must have enough free disk space available on the target drive you select to support a copy of the database.

Encrypting a database

1. Start Microsoft Access. Do not open the database you're attempting to encrypt.

2. Click the **Tools** menu, select the **Security** flyout menu, and then click **Encrypt/Decrypt Database**.

3. The Encrypt/Decrypt Database dialog box appears. This is a standard File Open dialog box. Locate the database you want to encrypt and click **OK**. Note that the database you select must not have been previously encrypted, or Access attempts to decrypt it as opposed to encrypting it. You might not notice the subtle difference in the dialog box caption.

4. Another File Open dialog box appears. This one is labeled Encrypt Database As and is where you specify the name and location for the encrypted copy of the database. Click **Save** when you're finished.

Caution: You must have all objects closed

Access must be able to open the database in Exclusive mode in order to encrypt or decrypt it. Therefore, you must make sure that no other users have the database opened at the time you attempt to encrypt or decrypt it. This also means that you cannot encrypt the database if you have it opened in Access! The good news, though, is that you don't have to open a database at all in order to get to the encrypt/decrypt menu items. They're available whether a database has been opened or not.

5. Assuming all of the conditions outlined earlier are met, Access encrypts the database and returns to steady state. You won't get a message box—this is one of those "no news is good news" situations—unless something goes wrong in the process.

Decrypting a database

1. Start Microsoft Access. Do not open the database you're attempting to decrypt.

2. Click the **Tools** menu, select the **Security** flyout menu, and then click **Encrypt/Decrypt Database**.

3. The Encrypt/Decrypt Database dialog box appears. This is a standard File Open dialog box. Locate the database you want to decrypt and click **OK**. Note that this must be a previously encrypted database; otherwise Access attempts to encrypt it as opposed to decrypting it.

4. Another File Open dialog box appears. This one is labeled Decrypt Database As and is where you specify the name and location for the decrypted copy of the database. Click **Save** when you're finished.

5. Assuming all of the conditions outlined earlier are met, Access decrypts the database and returns to steady state. You won't get a message box—this also is one of those "no news is good news" situations—unless something goes wrong in the process.

Setting a Database Password

The simplest means of securing a database is to set a database password. This prevents anyone who does not know the password from opening the database with Microsoft Access. However, it does not allow you to prevent anyone from accessing particular objects within the database—that's where user-level security comes into play.

If you apply user-level security to your database properly, setting a database password is unnecessary and annoying; users will have to enter two passwords—one for their user account and one for the database. Likewise, if user-level security has been applied to the database and you do not have administrative privileges on the database, you cannot set or remove the database password.

Once a database password is established, the dialog box shown in Figure 38.1 appears whenever anyone attempts to open the database. The user must enter the correct password or she receives an incorrect password message box. Unlike many password-protected systems, however, there is no maximum number of retries. A user can keep trying passwords until she eventually gets it right. Access will not lock her out after a certain number of failed attempts.

SEE ALSO
➤ *Security and replication are discussed in Chapter 35, "Replication." See page 641.*

FIGURE 38.1

This is the database password prompt that appears after a database password has been established and someone attempts to open the database.

Setting a database password

1. Open the database in Exclusive mode. This is done by opening the File Open dialog and checking the box labeled **Exclusive** before selecting the database you're opening.

2. Click the **Tools** menu, select the **Security** flyout menu, and then click **Set Database Password**.

3. Enter the password in the **Password** box. Enter it again in the **Verify** box.

4. The password has been set when you click OK. (You receive no message indicating this.)

Removing a database password

1. Open the database in Exclusive mode. This is done by opening the File Open dialog box and checking **Exclusive** before selecting the database you're opening.

Caution: passwords and replication

You should not set a database password if the database is being using in a replication scenario. You cannot synchronize a database if it has a password set on it.

   2. Click the **Tools** menu, select the **Security** flyout menu, and then click **Unset Database Password**.

   3. Enter the current password in the **Password** box.

   4. Click OK; the password has been removed. (You receive no message indicating this.)

You can verify that the password has been set or unset by closing the database (use the **File**, **Close** menu items) and opening it again (use **File**, **1** from the menu). You should be prompted for a password if you just set the password, or not prompted if you just removed (*unset*) the password.

Implementing User-Level Security

To truly secure your database, you need to implement user-level security. User-level security provides three main benefits:

- You can limit who can open the database.
- You can restrict user access to specific database objects on a per-user and per-object basis.
- You can create groups of users and restrict access on a per-group basis.

The following steps provide an outline for setting up a secured database. The remaining sections of this chapter explain each step involved in setting up security. Once you know the details, however, the following step-by-step can serve as a quick reference for future work.

The basic steps to securing a database

   1. Create a new, secure workgroup information file. This file contains information about the workgroup represented by the file and needs to be accessible to all of the users who will log on to the secured database.

   2. Open Access 97 and define a password for the Admin user of the new workgroup. This activates the Logon dialog box next time you start Access.

   3. Create a new administrator account for the workgroup. Make sure you put this new user into the Admins group.

4. Exit and restart Access, this time using the new administrator account's logon name. Remove the Admin user (which is created by default in every workgroup information file) from the Admins group. This step is crucial—if you leave the default Admin user as administrator, anyone can use the default system workgroup to gain access to your database.

5. Open the database to be secured and invoke the User-Level Security Wizard. This creates a secured copy of the current database.

6. The new copy is created such that only members of the Admins group will have access to the objects in the database. You should grant permissions to the secured objects to other users or groups as appropriate.

Creating and Using Workgroup Information Files

The first step to creating a secured Access database is the creation of a secure workgroup information file. The *workgroup information file* contains information about the users in a workgroup and the groups of which they are members. The file contains the list users, their passwords, and their group membership. Access reads this file each time it starts in order to determine whether to display the Login dialog box.

The default workgroup information file, system.mdw, is installed when you install Access. It is placed in the windows\system folder on Windows 95/98 systems and in the winnt\system32 folder on Windows NT systems. This file contains one user, Admin, and two groups, Admins and Users. The Admin user does not have a password set for it. Unless you specify otherwise, Access uses system.mdw as the workgroup information file each time it starts.

By default, regardless of which workgroup information file you have active, Access attempts to log on as the user named Admin with no password. Therefore, if you do not change the password for the Admin user (discussed in "Defining User and Group Accounts" later in this chapter), you will never see the Login dialog box; that's because Access' default login attempt will succeed.

Access provides an application, the Workgroup Administrator, which you use to change workgroups and create new workgroup information files.

Joining a different workgroup, using the Workgroup Administrator

1. This application is started by executing `wrkgadm.exe`, which is installed into your `windows\system` (for Windows 95/98) or `winnt\system32` folder (for Windows NT). You can typically run it by clicking the **Start** button, selecting **Run**, and typing `wrkgpadm`. Figure 38.2 shows the Workgroup Administrator's main window.

FIGURE 38.2

This is the Workgroup Administrator program, where you can join different workgroups or create a new workgroup information file.

2. To join a different workgroup, click the **Join** button. The dialog box shown in Figure 38.3 appears.

FIGURE 38.3

The Workgroup Information File dialog box is where you enter the path for the file representing the workgroup you're joining.

3. Here you can type the path to the workgroup information file you want to join. You can also click the **Browse** button to launch a File Open dialog box, which you can use to locate the file. Once you've got the correct path, click **OK**.

4. A message box will appear, informing you that you have successfully joined the workgroup.

If you're simply joining a secured workgroup, this is as far as you need to go.

If you're creating a secured database, you need to create a new workgroup information file. To do so, follow the steps outlined here.

Creating a new workgroup information file

1. Launch the Workgroup Administrator program (wrkgadm.exe).

2. Click the **Create** button. The Workgroup Owner Information dialog box appears; the dialog box is shown in Figure 38.4.

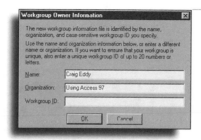

FIGURE 38.4
The Workgroup Owner Information dialog box.

3. Enter the appropriate information in the **Name** and **Organization** fields.

4. Enter a unique workgroup identifier in the **Workgroup ID** field. This can contain up to 20 letters or numbers. Make sure it's unique and known only to you. The workgroup identifier is used to encrypt the workgroup information file. It can also be used to create a new version of the workgroup information file, preventing unauthorized access to your system.

5. Click **OK**. The Workgroup Information File dialog box (see Figure 38.3) appears. Enter the path and name for your new workgroup information file and click **OK**.

6. A confirmation dialog appears, asking you to confirm the information you've entered thus far and encouraging you to write it down. If you need to change any of the information, click the **Change** button. Otherwise, click **OK**. You receive a message box informing you that the new workgroup

Save your information

You should write down the information you enter in all three fields (including all capitalization and punctuation) on this dialog box and keep it in a safe place. Should you ever need to re-create your workgroup information file, you need to enter the exact text (including capitalization, punctuation, and spaces) in order to do so.

information file has been created. Click **OK** here and you are returned to the Workgroup Administrator, which now displays the information for the workgroup you just created.

The new workgroup file contains a single user, Admin, and two groups, Admins and Users. The Users group is a special group in Access 97. All new user accounts you create are placed in this group. Likewise, you cannot remove any user accounts from this group.

Defining User and Group Accounts

Access 97 allows you to create multiple user accounts for your workgroups. You can then further organize the users in a workgroup by assigning them to groups created for the workgroup. This section describes the techniques for performing the following administrative tasks:

- Changing your logon password
- Clearing any user's logon password
- Creating new users
- Creating new groups
- Modifying a group's membership
- Deleting user and group accounts
- Printing the list of user and group accounts

The User and Group Accounts dialog box, shown in Figure 38.5, is where all of the action takes place. If you do not have administrative privileges for the current workgroup (that is, you're not a member of the Admins group), you are only allowed to view the users and the group membership and change your own logon password. All other buttons and the **Groups** tab are unavailable to you.

The **Users** tab is where you do most of the work. The top frame is where you select the user you're working with and it provides buttons for creating a new user, deleting the selected user, and clearing the selected user's password. The bottom frame displays all of the available groups in the **Available Groups** list and the groups to which the selected user belongs in the **Member Of** list.

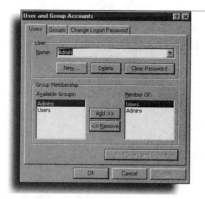

FIGURE 38.5

The User and Group Accounts dialog box is where you define users, groups, and passwords.

Changing a Logon Password

Follow these steps to change your logon password.

Changing your logon password

1. Make sure you've joined the workgroup for which you want to change your logon password. (See the previous section, "Creating and Using Workgroup Information Files," for the details.)

2. Start Access 97 and log on if required. If you have not set a password for the Admin user, the Login dialog box will not appear. Use the steps outlined here to set the Admin user's password.

3. From the **Tools** menu, click the **Security** flyout menu and select **User and Group Accounts**. The User and Group Accounts dialog box, shown in Figure 38.5, appears.

4. Click the Change Logon Password tab. Your screen should appear similar to Figure 38.6.

5. If you currently have a logon password, enter it in the **Old Password** field. Enter your new password twice, first in the **New Password** field and again in the **Verify** field.

6. Click **OK**.

FIGURE 38.6

The User and Group Accounts
dialog box's Change Logon
Password tab.

Clearing Another User's Password

No matter how hard you try, you cannot use the preceding steps to change a different user's logon password. However, if you have administrative privileges in the workgroup, you can use the following steps to clear any user's password. You can then log on as that user (with no password, of course) and use the steps outlined previously to set a new password.

Logging in as the *Admin* user

In all of the step-by-steps outlined from now on in this chapter, you must have previously set a password for the **Admin** user in order for the Login dialog box to appear; you will be logged in as the **Admin** user. If the steps require administrative privileges in the workgroup and the **Admin** user has not been removed from the **Admins** group, this is fine. Otherwise, use the steps outlined in the previous step-by-step to set the **Admin** user's password to something other than a blank password.

Clearing a user's logon password

1. Make sure you've joined the workgroup that contains the user account for which you're going to clear the logon password. (See the previous section, "Creating and Using Workgroup Information Files," for the details.)

2. Start Access 97 and log on as an Admins group member.

3. From the **Tools** menu, click the Security flyout menu and select **User and Group Accounts.** The User and Group Accounts dialog box (see Figure 38.5) appears.

4. The User and Group Accounts dialog box has a **Users** tab; use the tab's **Name** drop-down list to select the user whose password you're clearing.

5. Click the **Clear Password** button. The user's password is cleared without warning or confirmation. Clicking **Cancel** does not undo this operation.

Modifying Lists and Group Memberships

Use this step-by-step to modify the list of users and groups and the membership of those groups.

Creating new user accounts

1. Make sure you've joined the workgroup for which you are creating the new user account. (See "Creating and Using Workgroup Information Files" for the details.)

2. Start Access 97 and log on as a user who's a member of the Admins group.

3. From the **Tools** menu, click the **Security** flyout menu and select **User and Group Accounts**. The User and Group Accounts dialog box appears (see Figure 38.5).

4. The User and Group Accounts dialog box has a **Users** tab; click the tab's **New** button. Although you can type a username that doesn't exist yet as a user into the **Name** drop-down box, you cannot create a new user in this manner.

5. The New User/Group dialog box appears. Enter the username in the **Name** field and a unique, 4–20 alphanumeric personal identifier in the **Personal ID** field. Access combines this with the username to create the user account. You should treat this personal identifier just like the workgroup identifier for new workgroup information files. You cannot re-create an identical user account without both the username and personal identifier (and this information is case-sensitive).

6. Click OK; the new user account is created and appears as the selected user in the **Name** list.

Creating new group accounts

1. Make sure you've joined the workgroup for which you are creating the new group account. (See "Creating and Using Workgroup Information Files" for the details.)

2. Start Access 97 and log on as an Admins group member.

3. From the **Tools** menu, click the **Security** flyout menu and select **User and Group Accounts**. The User and Group Accounts dialog box, which is shown in Figure 38.5, appears.

4. On the **Groups** tab of the User and Group Accounts dialog, click the **New** button. Although you can type the name of a group that doesn't exist into the **Name** drop-down box, you cannot create a new group in this manner.

5. The New User/Group dialog box appears. Enter the group's name in the **N**ame field and a unique, 4–20 alphanumeric personal identifier in the **P**ersonal ID field. Access combines this with the username to create the user account. You should treat this personal identifier just like the workgroup identifier for new workgroup information files. You cannot re-create an identical group account without both the name and personal identifier (and this information is case-sensitive, too).

6. Click OK; the new group account is created and appears as the selected user in the **Name** list.

Modifying the groups to which a user belongs

1. Make sure you've joined the workgroup for which you are modifying group membership.

SEE ALSO

➤ *See the section "Creating and Using Workgroup Information Files" on page 739 for the details.*

2. Start Access 97 and log on as a user who's a member of the Admins group.

3. From the **T**ools menu, click the **Securit**y flyout menu and select **User and Group Accounts**. The User and Group Accounts dialog box (see Figure 38.5) appears.

4. Use the **Name** list that's on the **Users** tab to select the user you'll be modifying.

5. To add the selected user to a group, click the group's name in the **Av**ailable **Groups** list and click the **Ad**d button.

   To remove the selected user from a group, select the group's name in the **Member Of** list and click the **Remove** button.

6. Repeat Step 5 as necessary. To work with a different user account, return to Step 4.

Rules for the *Admins* group

The Admins group must contain at least one user at all times. You cannot remove all users from the Admins group by removing the accounts from the group or by deleting the user accounts.

Deleting Users and Groups

You might need to delete users or groups for various reasons, most commonly if an employee leaves the company or if you're reorganizing groups. Use these following steps to delete users or groups.

Deleting users and groups

1. Make sure you've joined the workgroup that contains the user and or group account(s) you'll be deleting. (See "Creating and Using Workgroup Information Files" for the details.)

2. Start Access 97 and log on as an Admins group member.

3. From the **Tools** menu, click the **Security** flyout menu and select **User and Group Accounts**. The User and Group Accounts dialog box, which is shown in Figure 38.5, appears.

4. To delete a user, stay on the **Users** tab. Use the **Name** list to select the user account you want to delete.

    To delete a group, click the **Groups** tab. Use the **Name** list to select the group account you want to delete.

5. Click the **Delete** button. Access displays a confirmation dialog box; click **Yes** if you're positive you want to delete the user or group. Otherwise, click **No**.

Printing Account Information

It's a good idea to keep a printed list of user groups and accounts in a secure place in case of computer problems, sudden illness, or departure of your administrator.

Printing the list of user and group accounts

1. Make sure you've joined the workgroup whose user/group account list you are going to print.

2. Start Access 97, log on as required, and open any database to which you have access. (You don't need to be a member of the Admins group for this task.)

3. From the **Tools** menu, click the **Security** flyout menu and select **User and Group Accounts**. The User and Group Accounts dialog box appears.

4. Click the **Print Users and Groups** button. This button is disabled if you did not open a database in Step 2.

5. The Print Security dialog box shown in Figure 38.7 appears. Select the option that applies and click **OK**.

6. Access churns for a second or two before printing the selected list(s) to your default printer. If you printed users, the printout also shows which groups each user is a member of. If you printed groups, the printout lists the members of each group.

The User-Level Security Wizard

The User-Level Security Wizard is used to create a secured database accessible only to Admins group members in the currently active workgroup. The wizard makes a copy of the current database, assigning the user account with which you logged into Access as the database's owner. The original database is not modified in any way. You should modify the user and group permissions after running the wizard in order to provide access to the database's objects to other users or groups besides Admins.

Running the User-Level Security Wizard

1. Make sure you've joined the workgroup for which you are creating the secured database. (See the section "Creating and Using Workgroup Information Files" for the details.)

2. Start Access 97 and log on as a user who is a member of the Admins group. Open the database you want to secure.

3. From the **Tools** menu, click the **Security** flyout menu and select **User-Level Security Wizard**. The User-Level Security Wizard dialog, shown in Figure 38.8, appears.

FIGURE 38.8

This is the User-Level Security Wizard's main dialog box.

4. The dialog box displays the currently logged-on user in the Current User frame and the location of the current workgroup information in the Workgroup File frame. If either of these are incorrect—the current user is the owner of the new database, so make sure the user is okay to be the owner—click Cancel and exit Access. If the workgroup is incorrect, use the Workgroup Administrator application to select the correct workgroup and restart Access. If the user is incorrect, restart Access and log on as the correct user.

5. You can decide which types of object to secure after you've verified the current user and workgroup information. The wizard secures all object types by default: tables, forms, macros, queries, reports, and modules. Click OK to continue.

6. The dialog box appears. Use the **Save In** drop-down menu to set the folder in which the new database will be created. Name the database using the **File Name** text box. Click the **Save** button when you're satisfied with the name and location.

7. The wizard does some system-level verifications, exports all of the objects of the types selected on the main dialog, and applies the security information to the new database. If all goes well, a message box similar to that shown in Figure 38.9 appears. Any errors in the process invoke an appropriate message box indicating the cause and possible solutions.

Loosening security

Your situation might not demand such tight security, but it's usually best to allow the wizard to secure all of the objects and then use the user and group permissions to loosen the security as appropriate.

FIGURE 38.9

The message box indicates successful creation of a fully secured
database.

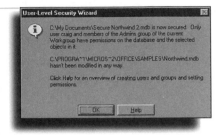

FIGURE 38.9

The message box indicates successful creation of a fully secured
database.

Setting User and Group Permissions

Applying user and group permissions to specific objects is the
final phase of applying user-level security to a database.

If all users will have the same permissions, you only need to use
the Admins group. Add all of your user accounts to this group and
you're finished with this step of the process. If, however, you
want to segregate administrative and user permissions, you need
to add a new group for your users. You could use the built-in
Users group, but guessing the Admin user's password is all it
would take for an unauthorized user to open your database.
Unfortunately, you can't delete the Admin account from any
workgroup.

Implement security in order

Before you assign permissions, you
should have created a secured database and added the appropriate
users and groups to that database.

Permissions are set on a per-object basis. There is a different set
of permissions applicable to each type of object (table, form,
query, report, module, macro, and the database itself). Table 38.1
lists the various permissions, their purposes, and which object
types they apply to.

TABLE 38.1   **User-Level Permissions Available in Access 97**

Permission Type	Allows a User To	Objects Applied To
Open/Run	Open object or run macro	Database, forms, reports and macros
Open Exclusive	Open database exclusively	Database
Read Design	View object in Design view	Tables, queries, forms, reports, macros, and modules

Permission Type	Allows a User To	Objects Applied To
Modify Design	Change design of or delete objects	Tables, queries, forms, reports, macros, and modules
Administer	*For databases:* Set password, replicate and change startup properties *For all other objects:* Full access to objects and data, assign permissions	All objects
Read Data	View the data	Tables and queries
Update Data	View and modify; no INSERT or DELETE	Tables and queries
Insert Data	View and insert; no modifying or deletes	Tables and queries
Delete Data	View and delete; no INSERT or modifying	Tables and queries

You can combine these permissions, as necessary, for an object. For example, you may provide Update Data and Insert Data, but not Delete Data, to a certain group account.

When set, some permissions automatically cause others to be set as well. The opposite condition is also true: You cannot remove certain permissions without also removing permissions that depend upon them. For example, the Modify Design permission requires that the user have Read Design, Read Data, Update Data, and Delete Data permissions. If you select Modify Design, all of these permissions are selected. If you then deselect any one or more of these dependent permissions, the Modify Design permission is also removed. However, this behavior is not consistent across object types.

Apply user-level security permissions

1. Make sure you've joined the workgroup appropriate for the secured database you're working with. (See "Creating and Using Workgroup Information Files" for the details.)

Inconsistency warning!

If a user does not have Open/Run permission on the database and you assign that user administer permission on a table, the user is still unable to open the database. That is, unless you also explicitly assign the Open/Run permission on the database.

2. Start Access 97 and log on as a user who is a member of the Admins group. Open the database you want to set permissions on.

3. From the **Tools** menu, click the **Security** flyout menu, and select **User and Group Permissions**. The User and Group Permissions dialog box, shown in Figure 38.10, appears. Notice that the current logged-on user is displayed in the Current User frame.

FIGURE 38.10

The User and Group Permissions dialog box.

4. The **User/Group Name** list displays the current set of users or groups, depending on the currently selected **List** option button. You can select only one user or group at a time to work with. Select the user or group whose permissions you want to change.

5. The **Object Name** list displays all of the objects of the type selected in the **Object Type** drop-down list, plus an entry for a new object of that type (the **<New Tables/Queries>** entry in Figure 38.10, for example). If you select **Database** in the **Object Type** drop-down list, there is only a single entry in this list: <Current Database>. Select the object type you're interested in from the **Object Type** drop-down list.

6. Using the **Object Name** list, select the object(s) for which you're setting permissions for the selected user/group. You can select multiple objects by using the list box's Ctrl+click and Shift+click extended selection method. You can also click and drag through the list box's entries to select multiple objects.

7. In the Permissions frame, check the boxes next to the appropriate permissions for the selected object(s) and user/group.

8. When you've finished modifying the check boxes, click the **Apply** button to make the changes effective. You can alternatively select another object or user/group; Access asks if you'd like to apply the changed permissions.

9. Repeat Steps 4 through 8 to assign all of the permissions necessary to your situation.

Exporting existing objects

The object's permissions are lost if an object is saved with a new name via the **Save As/Export** command on the **File** menu, or by pasting or importing the object. You are actually creating a new object. This new object is assigned the permissions specified for new objects of that type (see Step 5 in the accompanying step-by-step). If these are not correct, you have to reassign the permissions using the steps outlined in the accompanying step-by-step.

Sample Snippets of Useful and Common VBA

Simulating Green Bar Computer Paper

Attach this event procedure to the Detail section of your report—specifically, attach it to the Print event. This code will print a filled rectangle with a contrasting border behind every other record. First, add the declaration statement

```
Dim intColor As Integer
```

to the report module's Declaration section:

```
Private Sub Detail_Print(Cancel As Integer, PrintCount As
Integer)
If intColor Then
  Me.Line (0, 0)-(Me.Width, Me.Section(0).Height), 65535, BF
  Me.Line (0, 0)-(Me.Width, Me.Section(0).Height), 0, B
End If
intColor = Not intColor
End Sub
```

If you don't want a border, delete the 0 and B arguments in the second Me statement.

Printing a Border Around Your Report

This procedure prints a border around each page of your report. Attach this code to your report's Page event

```
Private Sub Report_Page()
  Me.Line (0, 0)-(Me.ScaleWidth, Me.ScaleHeight), , B
End Sub
```

Open Another Database

You can use this code to open another database. Attach this code to any event, most likely a command button's Click event:

```
Private Sub control_event()
SendKeys "%FOnameofdatabase"
SendKeys "{Enter}"
End Sub
```

Requery Active Control

This code will requery the active object—attach it to the appropriate event:

```
Private Sub control.event()
  Dim strControl
  strControl = Screen.ActiveControl
  strControl.Requery
End Sub
```

Displaying the Record Count

You can use this event procedure to show the number of records in the underlying record set when you've inhibited a form's navigational toolbar. Attach this code to the form's Load event:

```
Private Sub Form_Load()
  Me.RecordsetClone.MoveLast
  Me![displayingcontrol] = Me.RecordsetClone.RecordCount
End Sub
```

Executing Hyperlinks

If you use a combo box or list box to display a list of hyperlinks, Access won't execute the hyperlink when you make a selection. Use this event procedure to do so. Simply attach it to the control's appropriate event:

```
Private Sub combobox_Click()
  Dim ctrl As Control
  Set ctrl = Screen.ActiveControl
  ctrl.hyperlink.Follow
End Sub
```

Flagging Missing Records in a Report

This event procedure will print an asterisk to the left of a set of consecutively numbered records when one of those records is missing.

First, add a control to the far left side of the controls in the Detail section—this control will display the asterisk when necessary. Then, set the control's Control Source property to

```
=SetFlag([consecutivenumberfield])
```

Then, create the following function:

```
Option Explicit
Dim CountFlag As Integer

Function SetFlag (Counter As Integer)
  If CountFlag <> Counter - 1 Then
    SetFlag = "*"
  Else
    SetFlag = ""
  End If
CountFlag = Counter
End Function
```

Flashing Text

You can cause a text message to flash off and on by attaching the following code to a form's Timer event. Don't forget to set the Timer Interval property to the appropriate value:

```
Sub Form_Timer()
  Me![flashingcontrol].Visible =
Not(Me![flashingcontrol].Visible)
End Sub
```

Capturing Keystrokes

You can capture keystrokes and keep Access from responding to them, or you can have Access respond in some particular way other than processing the captured keystroke. Attach the following code to the form or the control's KeyDown event. The KeyCode = 0 statement inhibits the keystroke. If you want to take some other action, reflect that action in this Case action statement:

```
Private Sub controlorform_KeyDown(KeyCode As Integer, Shift
As Integer)
Select Case KeyCode
  Case vb constant that represents keystroke
    KeyCode = 0
  Case Else
    'Exit procedure
End Select
End Sub
```

Suppressing a Report When There Are No Records to Print

If you base your report on a parameter query or some other criteria expression, there may be times when no records meet the condition. When that happens, you can use the following code to suppress the report. If you don't, Access will produce an empty report:

```
Private Sub Report_NoData(Cancel As Integer)
MsgBox "There's no data to print"
Cancel = True
End Sub
```

Returning a List of Objects

This UDF returns a dynamic list of objects, where *ContainerName* specifies the types of objects: databases, tables, relations, forms, modules, reports, or scripts. You can replace the `Debug.Print` `doc.Name` statement with code that produces a list to suit your needs. This statement prints a list in the Debug window:

```
Function ListDocs()
Dim db As Database, cnt As Container, doc As Document
Set db = CurrentDb
Set cnt = db.Containers!ContainerName

For Each doc In cnt.Documents
   Debug.Print doc.Name
Next doc

End Function
```

Launching the Windows Calculator

The following function will launch the Windows Calculator application. You might want to attach the `Shell` statement to a command button's `Click` event instead of calling it from a UDF:

```
Function StartCal()
Shell "Calc.exe"
End Function
```

Assigning a Control's Value to a Variable

Use this generic code to assign the current control's value to a variable. You can attach this to almost any control or event. However, don't try calling this from another form or control. Because you've used the `Screen` object's `Active` method, you must attach this code to the actual control:

```
Private Sub controlname_event()
Dim ctl As Control, varValue As Variant
Set ctl = Screen.ActiveControl
varValue = ctl.Value
End Sub
```

Opening a Recordset

The following code will declare and open a Recordset object. You can execute this from a UDF or an event, where *recordsource* is a table, query, or SQL statement:

```
Dim db As Database, rst As Recordset
Set db = Current Db()
Set rst = db.OpenRecord ("recordsource")
```

Checking if a Particular Object Is Open

When you want to determine whether an object is open, use this code, where *objectconstant* is acTable, acQuery, acForm, acReport, acMacro, or acModule, and *objectname* is the name of the object you're checking:

```
Function TestOpen()
Dim blnOpen As Boolean
blnOpen = SysCmd(acSysCmdGetObjectState, objectconstant, _
   "objectname")
TestOpen = blnOpen
End Function
```

Adding a New Item to the Combo Box List On-the-Fly

If you add this code to a combo box's NotInList event, users can update the control's list. Specifically, if they enter an item that's not in the list, VBA will add it. Be sure that the *boundobjectname* variable equals the combo box's bound table or query's name, and *fieldname* equals the name of the combo box's bound field (Control Source property):

```
Private Sub combobox_NotInList(NewData As String, Response
As Integer)
Dim db As Database, rst As Recordset
Set db = CurrentDb()
Set rst = dbs.OpenRecordset("boundobjectname",
dbOpenDynaset)
```

```
rst.AddNew
rst!fieldname = NewData
rst.Update
Response = acDataErrAdded
End Function
```

Loading a Combo Box

You can use VBA to create a combo box list when you open the
form. To do so, attach this code to the form's Load event. The
recordsource argument is the table that contains the list you
want to copy to the combo box, *fieldname* is the field in recordsource that contains the actual items, and *comboboxname* is the
combo box's name. Be sure to set the combo box Row Source
Type property to Value List:

```
Private Sub Form_Load()
Dim db As Database, rst As Recordset, strList As String
Set db = CurrentDb
Set rst = db.OpenRecordset("recordsource", dbOpenSnapshot,
dbForwardOnly)
Do While Not rst.EOF
   strList = strList & ";" & rst!boundfield
   rst.MoveNext
Loop
Me!comboboxname.RowSource = Mid(strList, 2)
End Sub
```

Using Conditional Colors in Reporting

If you need to emphasize report data, try conditional colors.
Attach this code to the report detail section's Print event. Be
sure to specify *fieldname* as the field you're applying the conditional coloring to, and *colorinteger* as the integer value that represents the color you want *fieldname* to be when *condition* is
met. In most cases, *condition* will be an expression:

```
Private Sub Detail1_Print (Cancel As Integer, PrintCount As
Integer)
Dim intTemp As Integer, strColor As String
intTemp = Me!fieldname
```

```
strColor = "colorinteger"
If intTemp condition Then
   fieldname.ForeColor = strColor
Else
   fieldname.ForeColor = 0
End If
End Sub
```

Opening More Than One Copy of the Same Form

Attach the following code to a command button's Click event to open a second instance of the current form, where *commandbutton* is the name of the command button and *formname* is the name of your form:

```
Private Sub commandbutton_Click()
Set frmX = New Form_formname
frmX.SetFocus
End Sub
```

Also add the following declaration to the form's General Declarations section:

```
Dim frmX As Form
```

Printing an Adjusting Border

You can print a border around a field in a report. If you want to control the border's size, try the following event procedure. The component 1440 / 8 equals approximately 1/8 of an inch. That means Access will print the border approximately 1/8 of an inch from each edge. The variable *fieldname* represents the field you want to print the border around:

```
Private Sub Detail_Print(Cancel As Integer, PrintCount As
Integer)
Dim sngX1 As Single, sngY1 As Single, sngX2 As Single, sngY2
As Single, sngOff As Single
sngOff = 1440 / 8
sngX1 = Me![fieldname].Left - sngOff
sngY1 = Me![fieldname].Top - sngOff
```

```
sngX2 = Me![fieldname].Left + Me![fieldname].Width + sngOff
sngY2 = Me![fieldname].Top + Me![fieldname].Height + sngOff
Me.Line (sngX1, sngY1)-(sngX2, sngY2), , B
End Sub
```

Creating a *Recordset* Object

You can use either of the following pieces of code to create a
recordset object:

Table-type recordset:

```
Dim db As Database
Dim rst As Recordset
Set db = CurrentDb()
Set rst = db.OpenRecordset("recordsource", dbOpenTable)
```

Dynaset-type recordset:

```
Dim db As Database
Dim rst As Recordset
Set db = CurrentDb()
Set rst = db.OpenRecordset("recordsource", dbOpenDynaset)
```

Dynaset-type based on SQL string:

```
Dim db As Database
Dim rst As Recordset
Dim strSQL As String
strSQL = "SELECT [field] FROM recordsource "
Set db = CurrentDb()
Set rst = db.OpenRecordset(strSQL, dbOpenDynaset)
```

Locked table-type:

```
Dim db As Database
Dim rst As Recordset
Set db = CurrentDb()
Set rst = db.OpenRecordset("recordsource", dbOpenTable,
dbDenyRead)
```

Snapshot-type:

```
Dim db As Database
Dim rst As Recordset
Set db = CurrentDb()
Set rst = db.OpenRecordset("recordsource", dbOpenSnapshot)
```

Checking for an Empty Record Set

If you create a record set that happens to be empty, you'll want to skip routines that act on that record set. You can use the following procedure to test for an empty record set:

```
Dim db As Database
Dim rst As Recordset
Set db = CurrentDb()
Set rst = db.OpenRecordset("recordsource")
If NOT rst.BOF AND NOT rst.EOF Then
    routine you want to execute if there are rows
End If
```

Or:

```
Dim db As Database
Dim rst As Recordset
Set db = CurrentDb()
Set rst - db.OpenRecordset("recordsource")
If rst.RecordCount > 0 Then
    routine you want to execute if there are rows
End If
```

Acting on Controls in a Specific Form Section

If you want to execute a routine on just the controls in a specific form section, you can use the following code. The *sectioncon-stant* possibilities are: acDetail, acFooter, acGroupLevel1Footer, acGroupLevel1Header, acGroupLevel2Footer, acGroupLevel2Header, acHeader, acPageHeader, and acPageFooter:

```
Dim ctl As Control
For Each ctl In Me.Sections(sectionconstant).Controls
    routine you want to execute
Next ctl
```

Closing the Current Form

Closing the current form is a common action. You can drop the following code into any form and attach it to a command button's Click event:

```
Private Sub commandbutton_Click()
DoCmd.Close acForm, Me.Name
End Sub
```

Glossary

? A VBA code indicator used to begin each expression when testing so that the result appears in the Debug Window; also an *Input mask* character that calls for a letter from A to Z and is optional; also a *wildcard* character used to indicate a single, unknown character. Refer to Chapter 33.

action query A category of four types of queries that can make changes to records within your database with a single action when the query is run. The four types of queries are *Make-Table*, *Update*, *Append*, and *Delete*. Refer to Chapter 15.

Active Server Pages (ASP) Web pages that contain scripting language, such as VBScript, which executes on the Web server. After the script executes, it returns a Web page to the requesting browser but doesn't return any of the script code that has executed. Refer to Chapter 37.

aggregate function One of two types of functions that returns information about a set of records. Domain aggregates can be used in a VBA module, but not a SQL statement. SQL aggregates are used within a SQL statement, but can't

be called in a VBA module. However, you can use both in a calculated control. Refer to Chapter 13.

Append query An action query that adds records to the end of an existing table. This can be used to combine databases or to combine tables that match only a subset of fields. Refer to Chapter 15.

applications model One of two object models used as a basis for programming in Access. The Access Applications model gives you programmatic control of the many objects Access offers: forms, controls, queries, and reports. The *Data model* is the other of the two methods. Refer to Chapter 32.

argument Descriptive terms used in code. Arguments provide additional information to an action (*function* or *procedure*) to tell it specifically what to do, when or where to perform the action, and on which objects. Refer to Chapter 32.

ASP See *Active Server Pages*.

atomic Term used in *normalization*; data divided into the smallest possible units for separation into fields. Refer to Chapter 1.

Auto List Members list   An intuitive feature of the Modules window that displays a drop-down list of object types, properties, and methods related to the objects you are coding. Use this shortcut to find available options and avoid typing errors. Refer to Chapter 31.

background   The blank palette of a form or report; used in Design view to deselect objects. Refer to Chapter 19.

bang   An exclamation point (!) used to separate the object from its collection in code. Refer to Chapter 32.

bound object or **bound control**   A form, a report, or a control that is attached to a data source. Data sources include tables, queries, or fields, depending on the type of object that is bound. The bound object reflects changes in its data source. Refer to Chapters 9 and 19.

calculated control   A control that uses an expression as its data source instead of a bound field or query. Refer to Chapters 19 and 22.

call   Refers to the use or activation of a variable or procedure. For example, a procedure calls a variable for use in a function. Refer to Chapter 32.

cascading event   A logical flaw in code where a procedure or sub procedure either directly or indirectly calls itself and creates a terminal loop or a run-time error. Refer to Chapter 24.

child   The table or field that contains the *foreign key*; used in association with the related table or field (the *parent*), which holds the *primary key*. More than one table may be the child to a single parent table or child to multiple parent tables. A child to one table may be the parent to another. Refer to Chapters 14 and 23.

Class module   A module that can contain the definition for a new object. Any procedures defined in the module become the properties and methods of the object. Class modules in Microsoft Access exist both independently and in association with forms and reports. See also *scope*.

Class   The definition (or blueprint) of an object, as defined in a *class module*. Once defined, you create a new instance of the object (instantiation).

color matrix   The large rectangle of colored squares used to select or customize colors.

columnar form   A form with all the fields in the underlying table arranged in a single column, one record at a time. Refer to Chapter 5.

constant   Represents a value that doesn't change. Refer to Chapter 9.

control source   The data source in the underlying table or query, usually a field, that provides information to a *bound control*; available through the respective object's property sheet. Refer to Chapter 19.

Crosstab query   A complex query that summarizes data in rows and columns (similar to a spreadsheet). A Crosstab query must contain three elements: a column heading, a summary field, and a row heading. Refer to Chapter 5.

custom codes Predefined codes or symbols you combine to create a unique format. For example, mmm returns an abbreviated form of the month. If you want to add a literal character, simply enclose it in quotation marks. Refer to Chapter 22.

custom control Additional or third-party ActiveX controls, not included with Access. These must loaded and registered before use. Refer to Chapter 22.

custom dialog box or **pop-up form** A customized form for applications whose modal property determines its type and whether it stays on "top" while other forms are active: If the form's modal property is No (or Modeless), the form is known as a pop-up form; you can access other forms in your application while it is active. If the form's modal property is Yes, the form is known as a custom dialog box, and you cannot access other forms in your application until you either close the form or hide it from view. Refer to Chapter 17.

data type Predetermined set of aspects for information kept in a space of memory, such as a variable or field type. These aspects include its allocation of memory space, number and type of characters allowed, and printable format. For example, a Boolean data type for a VBA variable has only two forms: Yes/True and No/False; a Text data type for an Access field has a default size of 50 and can contain numbers and letters, but the field size can be changed. Refer to Chapter 32.

database A software application that stores data, usually in the form of *tables*, *records*, and *fields*. Refer to Chapters 1 and 3.

datasheet A format style for forms, reports, and table information; also a view in Access. The columns and rows look similar to a spreadsheet with fields as cells. Refer to Chapter 5.

Declarations section The section in each module where you *declare* global variables and constants to make VBA aware that the variable or constant exists by naming it. When you declare a variable or constant in the Declarations section, you make that variable or constant available to all the procedures in the module. Refer to Chapter 31.

declare To make VBA aware that the variable or constant exists by naming it. When you declare a variable or constant in the Declarations section, you make that variable or constant available to all the procedures in the module; usually includes setting the data type. Refer to Chapters 31 and 32.

Delete query An action query that deletes records in one or more tables specified by criteria. This can be used on related tables if the relationship supports the cascade delete option. Refer to Chapter 15.

delimited file One of two types of text files, which you may import; uses a defined character to separate fields of data, such as a tab character.

delimiter   A character, such as a tab or comma that separates fields of data; also used in code as a predefined character, such as ' that separates one component or value from another. Refer to Chapters 8 and 13.

design master   Term used in replication; the Design Master is the only place that structural changes to the database can be made in order to affect a *replica's* database structure. However, the replica might have additional objects unaffected by the design master. Refer to Chapter 30.

Design View Grid   The grid-like, Access 97 graphical interface for creating queries; consists of an upper pane where tables are placed and a lower pane, sometimes called the QBE or Query By Example grid. Actions here automatically generate code. Other objects, such as tables and macros also have a grid-like appearance.

dialog box template   Refers to a generic form, which may or may not have some code attached, that you use as a starting point for other forms. Refer to Chapter 20.

domain   In programming, a defined set of records used as the source for a function, such as the DLookUp() function. Refer to Chapter 13.

dot   The period character (.) used to separate the object from a property or method in VBA code syntax. Refer to Chapter 32.

driver   Software that is a set of instructions for a specific task or device. Refer to Chapter 8.

dynamic   A list or output that will update automatically as its source changes. For example, a bound list box on a form adds a new item if its underlying table is changed or a Web site report will change as its underlying data changes and requires a live connection to the database. Some dynamic features are built-in to Access; others must be coded. Refer to Chapters 31 and 37.

encapsulation   The process of wrapping (or tying together) a number of elements into a single process.

event procedure   Code that VBA executes in response to an object event such as a mouse click. Refer to Chapter 32.

events   Database actions, either user- or application-generated, such as clicking a button or opening or closing an object; can also trigger code actions. Refer to Chapter 30.

explicit   A code declaration option that means you must declare a variable before you use it; recommended to help catch errors. Refer to Chapters 31 and 32.

expression   A formula that combines other values and operators to produce a result. Refer to Chapters 15, 16, and 22.

field   A column within a table and the smallest unit of data in the entire database. A field might contain a customer's name, phone number, or ZIP code; one set of fields comprises a record. Refer to Chapters 1 and 3.

fixed-width file   One of two types of text files you may import; the fields are aligned in columns, and space characters—not tabs—are used to arrange the data. Refer to Chapter 8.

foreign key   The result when you relate two normalized tables that have an identical field; specifically it is the field in a related (*child*) table that refers back to a primary key in another (*parent*) table and is used to ensure referential integrity. The table with a foreign key may have another field as its primary key. Refer to Chapters 1 and 14.

form   An Access object that displays information stored in a table in non-table (rows and columns) format; used for data entry and viewing. Refer to Chapter 1.

function procedure or **user-defined function (UDF)**   As a general rule, a procedure that returns a value, as opposed to just performing an action. Refer to Chapter 32.

grid   Lines and dots on a form or report in Design view that help in positioning controls more easily. Refer to Chapter 19.

handle   The small squares (in contrasting color) that appear in a frame-like box around a control or label; used in moving or resizing and indicates the control is selected. Refer to Chapter 19.

hostname   Part of a Web address that follows the // indicators; a unique name identifying the computer's "address." Refer to Chapter 37.

HTML or **hypertext markup language**   The series of tags used for the text-based encoding of documents to specify how the contents should be displayed to a Web browser and to create hypertext links so that the document does not have to be read in a linear fashion. Refer to Chapter 37.

IDC See *Internet Database Connector*.

identifier   A part of VBA syntax that identifies the object's collection and the name of the object, as in `collection![objectname]`. Refer to Chapter 32.

implicit declaration   Refers to options in declaring variables and requires no declarations; not recommended. Refer to Chapter 32.

inner join   A type of join between two tables where only those records from both tables that have a matching value in the related field are selected. In other words, if one table has a value in a related field that doesn't exist in its joined table (and vice versa), that record isn't included in any query results. Refer to Chapter 14.

Input mask   A pattern that you define and Access applies to limit a field's entry; the mask character codes determine which characters you can enter and how many. Refer to Chapters 8 and 22.

instantiation   The creation of a new instance of a class, resulting in a new object.

interface   The application elements that tell Access what you want to do, including dialog boxes, command buttons, menus, and toolbars. Refer to Chapter 5.

Internet Database Connector (IDC)   A specialized application that can be installed on either the Personal Web Server or the Internet Information Server; used to produce Web pages that display live data through an ODBC connection to your database. Refer to Chapter 37.

intranet   An internal network that operates identically to, but is not necessarily connected to, the global Internet. Refer to Chapter 37.

intrinsic constants   Reserved words that ensure compatibility with other VBA-enabled applications; represent a value that doesn't change. VBA intrinsic constants always start with the letters ac. Refer to Chapter 9.

join   Determines how the relationship between two tables affects the result of a query that's bound to those tables. Specifically, the join decides which records are selected or acted on. There are two types of joins: **inner join**—The default join type, which selects only those records from both tables that have a matching value in the related field. **outer join**—Includes all the records from one table and only those records in the second that match the value in the related field. Refer to Chapter 14.

keyword   A reserved word with a specific task, such as the If() and Format() functions. Refer to Chapter 31.

left outer join   A join that includes all the records from the one table and only the matching records from the many table. Refer to Chapter 14.

library   A set of objects and procedures that are available to an application; use the Object Browser to view the contents of a library. Refer to Chapter 31.

limit to list property   A property that can limit the combo box text to only those items in the list; used to restrict data entry. Refer to Chapter 9.

list index value   The value, beginning with 0, used to denote a selected list box item's position; represents its value by storing the integer associated with the selected item rather than the item itself. Refer to Chapter 9.

local variable   A variable that belongs to its procedure; only the hosting procedure can refer to it. Refer to Chapter 32.

lookup task   A task that returns a value or list by referring to coordinates. Those coordinates can be index values or matching criteria. For instance, a combo box with three columns from a table or query would use the Column property to return data from any of the three columns; also used with the DLookUp() function. Refer to Chapter 13.

Make-Table query An action query that generates in a new table from one or more other tables. The new table can be stored in the database. Refer to Chapter 15.

many-to-many relationship A complex relationship that requires a third table. In a many-to-many relationship, one table can contain many records for each record in the other table. Refer to Chapter 14.

methods The "action" part of a VBA statement, which the specified object is to perform. Refer to Chapter 32.

modality or **modal value** A property that controls whether a message or dialog box suspends just the application, or your entire system. See also *custom dialog box* or *pop-up form*. Refer to Chapter 33.

module Window used for entering code; the resulting code module is an object. Refer to Chapter 31.

named ranged A section of the spreadsheet that you've given a specific name to; used for importing partial spreadsheets. Refer to Chapter 8.

native controls All the controls used in the Toolbox, and included with Access. Refer to Chapter 20.

natural primary key A data field (not an AutoNumber) that provides a unique entry for each record, such as a Social Security Number; eases the selection of a primary key. Refer to Chapter 12.

normalization The process of creating and relating tables according to a fixed set of rules; used to design databases where referential integrity can be readily enforced. Refer to Chapters 1 and 3.

object Access components: the database itself, tables, forms, queries, and reports, modules, and so on; in VBA statements, the object is the "actor" that performs the method. Refer to Chapters 1 and 32.

Object Browser An Access interface utility that enables you to view all the objects, classes, modules, methods, properties, and so on, that are available to an application. Refer to Chapter 31.

Object Linking and Embedding (OLE) A technology that provides the interfaces necessary for one application to be embedded into or linked to another application's data; one of the options listed in the Property Sheet for a graphic or image which can be linked or embedded. Refer to Chapters 26 and 36.

object model A way of describing the properties, methods, and events provided by an application. Refer to Chapter 36.

OLE Automation A technology by which applications can communicate with one another when running on a Windows-based operating system (Windows 95, Windows 98, and Windows NT). Most of the applications can function as both an **OLE server**, which provides data to another application, or an **OLE container**, which acts as a host for an instance of an OLE server. Refer to Chapter 36.

OLE container   See *OLE Automation*.

OLE server   See *OLE Automation*.

OLE   See *Object Linking and Embedding*.

one-to-many relationship   The most common relationship between two tables, where the "one" table contains only one record for a given unique value, such as a CompanyID; this relates to any number of records in a related, "many" table, where the unique value can be repeated if necessary, such as the same CompanyID for numerous CompanyProducts. Refer to Chapters 1 and 14.

operators   Usually refers to the mathematical symbols, such as the +, -, *, and / signs, used in expressions for query criteria and calculated controls; may also apply to some code symbols. Refer to Chapter 22.

parameter query   A query that allows you to prompt the user for information to finish providing necessary information interactively. Refer to Chapter 17.

parent   The table holding where the related field is the primary key in a relationship between two or more tables; the *child* table uses the same field as a *foreign key*. Refer to Chapter 23.

pivot table   A resultset that is similar in structure to a *crosstab query*. Refer to Chapter 5.

placeholders   Representative words in code that must be filled in with the actual name or object, such as *variablename*, which might be replaced by intMyValue;

denoted by italic in a syntax sample in this book. Refer to Chapter 32.

pop-up form   See *custom dialog box*.

primary key   A field selected because it contains a unique value for each record, such as a telephone number; AutoNumber is often used as the data type for a generic ID number if the table doesn't have a *natural primary key*. Refer to Chapter 1.

procedure   A set of VBA statements that complete a defined task; all procedures begin and end with the same set of lines. Refer to Chapter 31.

property   In a VBA statement, a property identifies an object's attributes. Refer to Chapter 32.

QBE   See *Query By Example* or *Design View Grid*.

query   An Access object that stores questions about the stored data and returns a resultset or can be used as *record source* for a form or report. Refer to Chapter 1.

Query By Example   A commonly used name for the Design View Grid because the graphic interface of the grid uses graphic example to create the code. Refer to Chapters 15 through 19.

record   One row or one complete set of data, consisting of related fields; for example, one address in a table of contact information. Refer to Chapters 1 and 3.

record source   A bound form or report's underlying table or query; available through the respective object's Property Sheet. Refer to Chapter 19.

recordset The collection of records that's attached to an object at any given time and depends on the underlying table or query and any criteria specified; similar to resultset, which may be partial records also. Refer to Chapters 1, 14 and 21.

referential integrity A set of rules that Access uses to protect the relationships and the data between related tables; controls the ability to add and delete records. Refer to Chapters 1 and 14.

register A process that involves placing entries, such as new ActiveX controls, in the system Registry, which tells an application the location and startup properties for the control; this must be done before using a new control. Refer to Chapters 22 and 36.

relationship An association (link) between two fields (usually with the same data) in different tables. For example, using a related CustomerID in both a Customer information table (as a *primary key*) and in an Orders table (*foreign key*). Relationships help enforce referential integrity. Refer to Chapter 14.

replica In replication, each database that took its structure and original data from the *design master*; a replica can contain its own set of local objects that will not be replicated to the other members of the set. Refer to Chapter 30.

replica set The related group of databases in replication, one of which is the *design master*. Refer to Chapter 30.

replication A configuration of servers, networks, databases, and rules that enables data to be shared and updated among users in different locations. Refer to Chapter 30.

report An Access object that stores the design of a printed report; reports may consist of data from more than one table or query and calculated controls, and may be changed and exported into HTML format. Refer to Chapter 1.

right outer join A join that includes all the records from the many table and only the matching records from the one table. Refer to Chapter 14.

run-time errors Internal errors that occur when the application doesn't find the conditions it needs to continue. Refer to Chapter 33.

scaled integer A data type, such as Currency, where VBA rounds the value to the fourth decimal place to conserve memory requirements. Refer to Chapter 32.

scope Code language rules that determine which application's components will have access to a variable depending on its designation as either Local, Module, or Public; also applies to access of modules depending on whether the module is designated as a Class module (such as for a form) or a standard module (available to all applications). Refer to Chapters 13, 24, and 32.

simple query A query that retrieves data from specific fields and is usually generated either by a wizard or the *Design View grid* without complex criteria or calculations. Refer to Chapter 5.

splash screen   The initial screen used when an application is first launched; identifies the application and the organization and may contain initial user selections. Refer to Chapter 22.

standard modules   A module that isn't attached to any particular object (such as a form or report) and is available to the whole application. See also *scope* and *Class module*. Refer to Chapters 31 and 32.

statement   A VBA "sentence" or set of commands, generally consisting of components such as *objects* and *methods* and follows a set of syntax rules. Refer to Chapter 32.

Static   A variable data type that is a *persistent* variable, meaning the variable retains its value beyond the life of the procedure. *Scope* refers to a variable's accessibility; persistence refers to a variable's *lifetime*. Refer to Chapter 32.

statically or **static data**   Typically used in reference to data on Web pages; data that doesn't change very often or data, such as a report, that doesn't require a live connection to the database. Refer to Chapter 37.

subform or **subreport**   A complete form or report that can function separately from the main form/report on which it is used; after placement in the main form/report, Access views the subform/report as a control of the main form/report. These usually display data related to the data shown on the main object. You can insert unrelated reports into a main report, which most likely

will be unbound. Refer to Chapters 23 and 27.

switchboard   A type of form that ties an application interface together by offering menu options that direct the end user to specific tasks. Refer to Chapter 5.

synchronization   In replication, the process of updating two members of a replica set by exchanging all updated records and objects in each member. Two replica set members are synchronized when the changes in each have been applied to the other. Microsoft Jet implements incremental synchronization, which means that only the modified data is exchanged between replicas. Refer to Chapter 30.

syntax   Coding language rules that specify the order and structure of statements and their various components; with macros and queries, components are entered visually, and Access writes the code syntax. Incorrect syntax results in an error. Refer to Chapter 32.

system-defined constant   A kind of constant with set values such as True, False, and Null. Refer to Chapter 9.

table   An Access object that stores data as a collection of related data in rows (*records*) and columns (*fields*). Refer to Chapters 1 and 3.

table/query list box   A list box (usually on a form) that refers to a table or query (specified in the Row Source property) for its members list; changes in the underlying source update the list box. Refer to Chapter 9.

tabular A type of form or report similar to Datasheet view—displaying all the fields in the same row; works well for displaying multiple records. Refer to Chapters 5 and 6.

template See *dialog box template*.

totals query A query that performs calculations on groups of records. Refer to Chapter 5.

type argument An optional component of the syntax for a message box; specifies the number and type of buttons to display, the icon style, the default button, and the modality; also used as a parameter for some controls and command bars. See also *modality* or *modal value*. Refer to Chapters 33 and 36.

unbound A control or report that isn't attached to an underlying table or query. Refer to Chapter 27.

unbound object frame A control that can hold embedded or linked OLE data for a form or report. Refer to Chapter 36.

UNC See *Uniform Naming Convention*.

Uniform Naming Convention (UNC) A set of conventions for the addressing method that specifies the location of an object (typically a file) on a PC network. Refer to Chapter 37.

Universal Resource Locator (URL) A set of conventions used to specify the location of an object on the Internet, commonly associated with a Web address. Refer to Chapter 37.

update query An action query that uses criteria to update specified records in one or more tables. Refer to Chapter 15.

update-latency In replication, the amount of time it takes to update data between all replicas in a set. Refer to Chapter 30.

URL See *Universal Resource Locator*.

user-defined function (UDF) procedure A type of *function procedure* that, as a general rule, returns a value. Refer to Chapter 32.

user-defined Any value that is selected by either the programmer or end-user, usually from within a set of pre-defined or available options. Refer to Chapter 22.

variable A coding character or symbol that can assume any one of a set of values, usually determined by its *data type* or *declaration*; its value can change within the confines of a particular set. Refer to Chapter 32.

Visual Basic eXtension VBX control A type of *OLE Automation server*; 16-bit OLE servers that could be placed onto Visual Basic forms. Refer to Chapter 36.

wildcards Characters or symbols that are typically used as placeholders for unknown values or to cover a range of possible values. In Access 97, wildcard characters are only to be used with Text data types. Refer to Chapter 17.

wizard A specific program design to rapidly and more easily create an object or perform a task by presenting the user with a series of dialog boxes in a step-by-step manner. Refer to Chapter 2.

workgroup information file A file that contains information about the users in a workgroup and the groups of which they are members. The file contains the list users, their passwords, and their group membership. Access reads this file each time it starts in order to determine whether to display the Login dialog box. Refer to Chapter 38.

zero-length string An actual string that contains no characters—the equivalent of the " " string. A zero-length string isn't the same as a Null value, which indicates there is no entry or result. Refer to Chapter 12.

Index

Symbols

A

Sams Teach Yourself Visual Basic 5 in 21 Days, Fourth Edition

Nathan Gurewich and Ori Gurewich

Using a logical, easy-to-follow approach, this international bestseller teaches readers the fundamentals of developing programs. It starts with the basics of writing a program and then moves on to adding voice, music, sound, and graphics.

Uses shaded syntax boxes, techniques, as well as Q&A, Do/Don't, and Workshop sections to highlight key points and reinforce learning.

Covers Visual Basic 5

$29.99 US / $42.95 CDN   *New–Casual*   *Programming*
0-672-30978-5   *1,000 pp.*

Special Edition Using Access 97, Second Edition

Roger Jennings

Special Edition Using Access 97, Second Edition is a tutorial. Readers will learn to how to build an Access 97 database from scratch and how to work with existing databases. They will learn to build forms, reports, and program more complex applications as they develop their skills.

Special Edition Using Access 97, Second Edition is a reference. After readers have built their database, they will refer back to the text for daily troubleshooting or to install new features.

The one true "must have" Access 97 resource with start to finish coverage. Making the best even better: All new coverage for the #1 Access book on the market. Over 300,000 units of Special Edition Access have been sold within the past 3 years. Expanded coverage of VBA and Office integration.

$49.99 US / $71.95 CDN   *All User Levels*   *Database*
0-7897-1452-3   *1,312 pp.*

Access 97 Unleashed, Second Edition

Dwayne Gifford, Stephen Forte, et al.

POWERFUL RESOURCE: The Unleashed series takes you beyond the average discussions of the technology, giving you practical advice and in-depth coverage. Use the comprehensive index and table of contents to find everything you need. With these extensive guides, you'll obtain the skills, understanding, and breadth of knowledge to unleash the full potential of Access 97.

AUTHORITATIVE ADVICE: Dwayne R. Gifford is a programmer/analyst in several Microsoft products such as Access, Visual Basic, SQL Server, and Visual C++—a hobby that he has enjoyed for the past 7 years. In addition, he is the author and co-author of several books by Sams Publishing on Access, Visual Basic, SQL Server, and Office.

DETAILED INFORMATION ON HOW TO:

- Integrate your Objects with other Microsoft Office products.
- Manipulate your data with DAO.
- Access Data using Queries and SQL.
- Learn how to handle multiuser and client/server issues.
- Optimize applications and improve your database performance.
- Extend abilities of Access with VBA Programming.
- Work with the Windows API.
- Customize Online Help to your Access applications.
- Implement Web publishing.
- Understand how to apply security on the Web.

$39.99 US / $56.95 CDN   Advanced–Expert   Database
0-672-31271-9   936 pp.

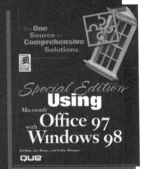

Special Edition Using Microsoft Office 97 with Windows 98

Ed Bott, Jim Boyce, and Faithe Wempen

This book covers the core functionality of the new release of Windows as it relates to its most widely used applications—Microsoft Office 97. With the release of Windows 98, many new computers will begin shipping with Windows 98 and Office 97 (either the Small Business Edition or the Standard Edition) preinstalled. Recent data has shown that the majority of new computer purchases are now being made as replacement computers or as a second computer. So, a large part of this audience will already be familiar with Windows and familiar with Office since it is the most widely used set of applications. So, the user need for this book is to focus on the new features of Windows 98 and the new and intermediate features of Office 97. The focus within the Office coverage will be on Word and Excel as those are the most widely used parts of Office and are included in all versions of Office. There will be some coverage of PowerPoint (from the standard Office suite) and Publisher (from the Small Business Edition of Office which is widely pre-installed on new computers) and Outlook 98. Convenient coverage of the two most widely used pieces of computer software—the operating system in Windows 98 and the core applications of Office 97. Great way for experienced users of Windows to pick up the information and make the most of Office 97 running with Windows 98.

Top-notch author team who are the key authors on *Special Edition Using Windows 98* and *Special Edition Using Office 97, Best Seller Edition.*

$39.99 US / $57.95 CDN   Intermediate   Integrated Software/Suites
0-7897-1661-5   1,168 pp.

Add to Your Sams Library Today with the Best Books for Programming, Operating Systems, and New Technologies

To order, visit our Web site at www.mcp.com or fax us at

1-800-835-3202

ISBN	Quantity	Description of Item	Unit Cost	Total Cost
0-672-30978-5		Sams Teach Yourself Visual Basic 5 in 21 Days, Fourth Edition	$29.99	
0-7897-1452-3		Special Edition Using Access 97, Second Edition	$49.99	
0-672-31271-9		Access 97 Unleashed, Second Edition	$39.99	
0-7897-1661-5		Special Edition Using Microsoft Office 97 with Windows 98	$39.99	
		Shipping and Handling: See information below.		
		TOTAL		

Shipping and Handling

Standard	$5.00
2nd Day	$10.00
Next Day	$17.50
International	$40.00

201 W. 103rd Street, Indianapolis, Indiana 46290   1-800-835-3202 — FAX

Book ISBN 0-7897-1634-8